Introduction to **Early Childhood Education**

4th Edition

Verna Hildebrand

Michigan State University

Introduction to **Early Childhood Education**

MACMILLAN PUBLISHING COMPANY
NEW YORK

Collier Macmillan Publishers
London

Drawings by Berta Lewis

Copyright © 1986, Verna Hildebrand

Printed in the United States of America

Earlier editions copyright © 1971, 1976, and 1981
by Verna Hildebrand

Macmillan Publishing Company
866 Third Avenue, New York, New York 10022

Collier Macmillan Canada, Inc.

Library of Congress Cataloging in Publication Data

Hildebrand, Verna.
    Introduction to early childhood education.

    Includes indexes.
    1. Education, Preschool. I. Title.
LB1140.2.H522 1986   372'.21   85-4957
ISBN 0-02-354520-8

Printing: 8   Year: 9 0 1 2 3 4

ISBN 0-02-354520-8

I wish to dedicate this book to my family—to my husband, John, without whose faith and encouragement this book would never have been written; to my children, Carol and Steve, both of whom weathered the testing of the philosophy presented; and to my parents, Carrel and Florence Butcher, who provided encouragement and an opportunity to study.

Preface

Introduction to Early Childhood Education is a textbook written especially for those who are concerned with teaching young children from infancy through age six. It is an introduction to professional preparation for early childhood teachers. Teachers, psychologists, social workers, and administrators concerned with planning sound programs for fostering children's growth and development will find the book relevant. Parents, nurses, librarians, and people associated with various religious programs for young children will find many useful ideas.

Introduction to Early Childhood Education was written from the experience of many years' teaching in the university classroom and in the kindergarten, nursery school, child care center, and university laboratory school. The additional experience of being a parent of a son and daughter has provided incentive for exploring early childhood education from more than the academic vantage point.

The school for young children is approached through the developmental tasks of early childhood. The work of prominent theorists is cited to help students relate theory and practice. The numerous program ideas contained in this book will help with program planning and thus save time and energy for understanding and helping children as individuals. Photographs and incidents involving real children enliven and illustrate points being made.

University students and Head Start teachers provided the initial stimulus for writing this book. Both wanted help with integrating knowledge about child growth and development into meaningful school programs for young children. In class and after class they questioned the curriculum and the techniques observed in early childhood programs. A continuous search was made for improved ideas to use with young children. This book is designed to help students, teachers, and of course ultimately the children they teach.

Part One gives an overall view of goals, children, schools, techniques, and curriculum. It is a brief survey designed for initial orientation of the student to the field before the numerous details of a program are presented. This survey will be particularly helpful to the student beginning observation and participation in a group of children as the school term gets under way.

Part Two starts with a chapter on how to plan specific learning activities and follows with chapters on all the typical curricular areas, discussing goals and procedures and making suggestions for a wide variety of learning activities. Guidance suggestions, interpersonal relationships, and parental involvement are stressed in each chapter. Planning is emphasized as teachers and assistants are urged to sit down together to think carefully about the why, what, and how of their teaching. Chapter 17, Managing an Early Childhood Group, is designed to teach the student how to integrate the planning, manage the group of children, and evaluate the results.

Part Three discusses the teacher's professional relationship with parents, presents a global view of children's programs, and covers the past, present, and future of early childhood education. Suggestions are made for future professional activities.

Though I was aware of the excellent reception of the first three editions of *Introduction to Early Childhood Education,* I have, during the preparation of this fourth edition, been especially mindful of the need to make improvements. I think no work of this nature is ever really perfected and completed. Unless an author's knowledge and understanding fail to grow, there must be modifications and additions with the passing years. In the fourth edition, besides numerous small changes and inserts, I have tried to capture the current professional enthusiasm as topics such as accreditation of centers, standards for teacher education, and modernized position titles are discussed. The planning of activities was expanded into a new Chapter 6 and separated from total program planning, as some users wished. Within each chapter you will find these new items added in this fourth edition: a listing of chapter objectives, "Talk it Over" discussion items, applications, films, study questions, and new information, and an updated bibliography.

I hope all readers, and especially instructors, student teachers, and teachers of young children, will view this book not as a straitjacket with rigid sequences, answers, and programs but as a flexible aid helping their own creativity and stimulating their minds. Improvements can be made beyond the blueprints frozen into these printed pages. Professionals are expected to modify and improve upon these efforts as experience, reason, and new knowledge guide them—especially if the well-being of our children and of all humankind is to be most effectively served. Without these corrective possibilities I, as an author, would have some trepidation concerning my impact on future generations.

To accompany this fourth edition, I have prepared a fourth edition of *A Laboratory Workbook for Introduction to Early Childhood Education,* which is also published by the Macmillan Publishing Company.

The workbook, covering suggested students' projects and laboratory observations, has been rewritten and expanded to fit the fourth edition of the textbook. Where observation and participation are possible, these workbook learning activities will give realistic and practical aid to students.

I have also authored three related textbooks which may be useful to some readers. *Guiding Young Children* (Macmillan Publishing Company, Third edition, 1985) focuses on interpersonal relations in children's groups. *Management of Child Development Centers* (Macmillan Publishing Company, 1984) presents the managerial principles for managers and administrators. *Parenting and Teaching Young Children* (McGraw-Hill, Second edition, 1985) is directed toward high school and lower division college classes where students are interested in an introduction to parenting, occupational child care, or child development.

VERNA HILDEBRAND

Acknowledgments

To my professors, fellow students, professional colleagues, and graduate and undergraduate students in several universities throughout the country, I am indebted for challenges and stimulation. To the many hundreds of nursery school and kindergarten children and their parents who have given me most of whatever understanding I have of young children, I am especially grateful.

In addition, I wish to renew my thanks to the following educators, who, when they were affiliated with the identified universities, read all or portions of the first edition manuscript: Josephine Stearns of California State Polytechnic; Sam Clark of Iowa State University; Helen Hostetter of Kansas State University; Beverly French of Los Angeles Valley College; Vera Borosage, Jeanne Brown, Mary Fritz, Beatrice Paolucci, and Mary Sanderson of Michigan State University; Jean Dickerscheid of Ohio State University; James Walters of Oklahoma State University; Rebecca Hines of San Jose State College; Henry Draper of Stout State University; Jessie Bateman, Wilma Brown, Bernadine Johnson, Dora Tyer, and Emma Doyle of Texas Woman's University; Catherine Landreth, University of California at Berkeley; Charlotte McCarty, University of Delaware; Phyllis Lueck, University of Guelph; and Lane Butler, University of Ohio.

Recognition is due Michigan State University for a faculty research grant that helped initiate, and Texas Woman's University for an opportunity to complete, the first edition.

For the second edition acknowledgment for specific help is due Sister Marie Hopkins, Marygrove College of Detroit; Lois Mendrygal, Madonna College of Detroit; Judy McKee, Eastern Michigan University; Rebecca Peña Hines, University of Houston; and Vern Seefeldt, John Haubenstricker, Frances Kertesz, and Lillian Phenice of Michigan State University.

For the third edition I wish to acknowledge helpful consultations with the following individuals, many of whom arranged for photographs to be taken of children in their programs: Margaret Browning, San Diego

City College; Bernadette Haschke, Metropolitan State College, Denver; Queenie Mills, University of Illinois; Glenda Strange, Dodge City (Kansas) Community College; Linda Peet, Haslett Child Development Center; Faye Ann Presnal, Kansas State University; Janet Ronk, Marjorie Kostelnik, Carol Austin, and JoAnn Evers, Michigan State University; Janet Allen, University of Minnesota Technical College; Ramona Ware Emmons, Oklahoma State Department of Education; Hilda Segarra, University of Puerto Rico; Jeannie James, Eleanor Duff, and Suzanne Stromen, University of South Carolina; Jean Heggins, South Carolina State College; Betty Larson and Joyce Digby, San Antonio College; Paula Turner, Southwest Texas State University; Vera Gershner and Barbara Jackson, Texas Woman's University; Phyllis Richards and Johanna Hulls, University of Texas-Austin; and Teruko Niwa, Tōyō-Eiwa School, Tokyo, Japan.

For helpful suggestions for the fourth edition I am grateful to Judy Ates, Michigan State University; Joan Raven, Cloud County (Kansas) Community College; and John M. Johnston, University of Wisconsin-Milwaukee. The manuscript was reviewed by Gladys Hildreth, Louisiana State University; Sherrill Richardz, Washington State University; Marjorie Stith, Kansas State University; James Walters, University of Georgia; Jacqueline Paulson, College of Staten Island; and Kathy Thornburg, University of Missouri.

Photo credits are due many photographers, teachers, students, and parents, including Rebecca Peña Hines, University of Houston; Roberta Hay and Ed Breidenbach, University of Idaho; Kathryn Madera, Iowa State University; Ivalee McCord, Kansas State University; Gladys Hildreth and Gayle Mary Clapp, Louisiana State University; Vern Seefeldt, John Haubenstricker, William Mitcham, Connie Lisiecki, Jean and James Page, Vera Borosage, Gayle and Larry Schiamberg, Joe Kertesz, Janet Ronk, Mariella Aikman and Laura Stein, Michigan State University; Mary O'Dell, Southern University; Judith Kuipers, University of Tennessee; Billie Wolfe and Estelle Wallace, Texas Tech University; Jessie Bateman-Barns, Texas Woman's University; Johnnye Goodrich, National Institute of Education Child Study Center; Harriet Wilson, Nazarene Child Care Center; Donna Creasy, *What's New in Home Economics;* Elizabeth Houston, Howard University; Rosalind Stalz, University of Michigan-Dearborn; Mary Gray, University of Missouri-Columbia; Jean Larsen, Brigham Young University; Linda Beveridge, Utah State University; Beverly Rimrodt, Kadena Air Base Child Care Center; Don Arnell, Zukeran Elementary School; Patricia Canning, Mt. Saint Vincents University; Carolyn Rafter and Frank Fortune, Georgia Southern University; Donna Chitwood and Carol Hildebrand, Metropolitan State College; Pauline Turner, University of New Mexico; Ruth Davis, Oakwood College; Beverly Briggs, Kansas State University; Nancy Benham, Marilyn Willis, and Tina Hay, Pennsylvania State University; Jacquelyn Lick-wee, University of Wisconsin-Madison; Dee Dee Jameson, University of Vermont; and Theda Connell, Brenda Golbus, John Naso, and Margot and Gerald Seelhoff.

I would finally like to acknowledge the following members of the Macmillan staff for their work on the fourth edition, Peter Gordon, editor, Berta Lewis, designer, and John Travis, production supervisor.

V.H.

Contents

PART I
Teaching in a School for Young Children Today: An Overview

PART II
The Curriculum of the Early Childhood School

PART III
Professional Considerations

Introduction to **Early Childhood Education**

Teaching in a School for Young Children Today: An Overview

PART I

Introducing Early Childhood Education

- *Identify the qualities needed by an early childhood teacher.*
- *Identify different settings where an early childhood teacher works.*
- *Identify current professional efforts to raise standards in early childhood education.*
- *Recognize current demands for the services of early childhood educators.*

"Let's build an airport," calls Karen to Delbert as they hang up their coats and skip toward the blocks in the early childhood playroom.

"I'm gonna paint," announces Michael while donning a painting apron at the easel.

"My sister lost her tooth," confides Ray to his teacher. He goes on to say, "She bited the apple and it just comed out!"

Each day, these children, like millions of others are starting their day in an early childhood school. Their teacher has planned a curriculum to stimulate their growth and development.

The Curriculum Is What Happens

The curriculum of the early childhood school is the major emphasis in this book. You'll be learning what happens in a school for young children and how to make it happen most effectively. The easels, blocks, and quiet conversations in the above stories are part of the children's curriculum, just as this course is part of your curriculum in early education. Both are stepping-stones to future skills and knowledge.

You are embarking on one of many interesting courses in the profes-

Figure 1-1. The early childhood school is a pleasant place where young friends share new experiences. (Child Development Center, Metropolitan State College)

sional field of early childhood education. Your major tasks will focus on young children's learning activities and learning environments. You will be planning, analyzing, and evaluating materials, equipment, activities, and approaches used in providing learning experiences for groups of children in infant centers through kindergarten.

This course is full of ideas—utilizing your ideas and those of others. You'll enjoy finding out what children like to do, how to present activities, and why certain equipment is recommended for children. You'll be using all you already know about child development and early childhood education and be adding more information as you read, study, observe, plan for, and interact with children. This field is very dynamic. It is action packed. There is always something new to learn about children and early childhood education.

The terms "early childhood education" and "child development center" will be used to replace the terms "preschool" and "nursery school." The terms "preschool" and "nursery school" seem to downplay the importance of the years of early childhood and the vast amount of significant learning that takes place during this early period in children's lives. This change in terminology represents a professional trend that you can begin incorporating in your own vocabulary.

In this course you'll apply what you have already learned about interacting with young children. Interaction techniques of guidance or discipline are based on theories and research in child development and child psychology. These techniques help you when talking to children, moti-

4

vating them, or anticipating their next moves or their next level of competence. You'll build on your present base of guidance information and skill and learn more about interpreting children's levels of development, their needs, and behavior. You'll strive to help children become fully competent individuals.

During this course you'll also apply skills you've learned in cooperating with your class members and the teaching staff of an early childhood center to become a reliable, competent member of the teaching team. The relationships among adults offer opportunities for you to practice job-related skills which are very important to your future success in an early childhood teaching position. For example, in addition to applying knowledge and skills related to children, you'll practice preparing for the teaching role, being on time, shouldering your share of responsibility, assuming increasing levels of responsibility, and being sensitive to the needs, interests, and skills of your co-workers, lead teachers, volunteers, and parents.

*　　*　　*

Talk It Over: No. 1

What are the qualities of a good employee? What is special about being employed to work with young children?

*　　*　　*

Teaching young children is challenging and rewarding, though at times frustrating. It is an awesome responsibility to influence the lives of chil-

Figure 1-2. Early childhood schools are found in the snowy climates of the north. (Child Development Laboratory, Michigan State University)

dren from day to day during their most formative years. This is a profession in the truest sense of the word, and anyone looking for a nine-to-five job should look elsewhere. Your teaching will have long-range implications for the child, the family, the school, the community, and the world. Special preparation is required in order to do well. In fact, you can never stop learning, changing, and updating your knowledge and skill. As in other professions, you must apply ethical procedures in dealing with children, parents, and fellow professionals. You will be on call when needed after hours for a conference or a meeting. Even on vacation you will be a teacher as you see new sights, read new books, or collect objects and ideas that will become learning experiences for your group of children. Teaching young children is one of the helping professions that needs dedicated practitioners.

The foregoing conveys the seriousness of the professional responsibility you are undertaking. Yet there are enjoyment and creativity in it too. An artist takes the elements of a masterpiece—line, color, form, and texture—and puts them together with his or her own perceptions to make a painting. You, as a teacher, will be creative from moment to moment and day to day as you work with a group of young children—each a creative individual in his or her own right. You will create for each child, for each group, for each year, in accordance with needs, goals, plans, and resources of time, money, materials, and help available. No two children will develop in quite the same way. Yes, yours is a creative profession!

Teaching young children will bring enjoyment. If you do not find joy in it, you should look for some other avenue of work, because *work* it surely will be. Young children are spontaneous, loving, curious, and creative. Working with them will keep you young at heart, on your toes, and moving ahead. Children help keep your sense of wonder alive because all things interest them. Little ones express themselves so honestly that it may relieve you to discover a social group so unpretentious.

The early childhood education profession needs happy, intelligent, energetic, and creative teachers to guide it through the years ahead. It is hoped that you will find many satisfactions in the study you have undertaken.

Current Trends in the Profession

The early childhood education profession has matured a great deal during recent decades. An historical perspective of the profession is available in the final chapter of this book. You might like to read it now and then again later when you have become better acquainted with the issues confronting this field.

Parents Demand Education For Young Children

Your chosen field is becoming increasingly important to parents who want their children to have an educational experience in an early child-hood education center before it is time for them to attend elementary school. The U.S. Department of Education predicts an increase from about 4.5 million in 1980 to 6.5 million in 1990.[1] You can see by Figures 1-3 and 1-4 that the more income and education parents have, the more likely they will send their child to an early childhood education center.

There is also an increasing need for full-day child care services be-cause both parents work outside the home or single parents are rearing children alone and need child care services to supplement the care and attention they can give. Child care services are not new, having been started in 1803 by philanthropic groups desiring to assist poor women and children. Child care services are now needed by all classes of fami-lies. In a previous generation most middle-class mothers did not work outside the home, and many parents sent their children to a nursery school for a part-day program. A large percentage of today's parents work full time outside the home and need full-time care for their children. Mid-dle-class parents are generally better educated and less tolerant than poor parents of mediocre child care. Consequently, they are demanding that child care centers provide the same educational opportunities offered in high-quality nursery schools. These parents also expect adequate nur-turing and loving for their child. The 1979 National Day Care Study indicated that children with more professionally educated teachers showed more advancement than children with less well-educated teachers.[2] Therefore, take your education seriously because it will be of great value to children.

* * *

Talk It Over: No. 2

Ask a parent of a young child, "What early childhood services are you using or expecting to use for your child? Why?" Share your findings with your classmates.

* * *

Policymakers Take Action

Policymakers in governmental circles at the local, state, and national levels have taken considerable action regarding early childhood educa-tion programs in recent years. The federal government's program, Proj-

---

[1] See *The Condition of Education,* 1980 ed. (Washington, D.C.: U.S. Department of Education, 1980), p. 197.

[2] Richard Ruopp, *Children at the Center: Final Report of the National Day Care Study* (Cambridge, Mass.: Abt Associates, 1979), p. 98.

ect Head Start, was initiated in 1965 and continues to the present. Head Start has served 9.1 million children, trained hundreds of teachers and aides, mainstreamed handicapped children, and raised program standards to achieve the goals of helping economically poor children get a "head start" on the educational ladder. See Table 1-1 for the numbers of children served by Head Start.

The women's movement of the 1970s and 1980s has pressured policymakers to provide more affordable child care services for mothers who are working on improving themselves by attending school. There are numerous governmental agencies concerned with child care services. The White House Conferences in both 1970 and 1981 cited child care as one of the country's most pressing needs. Recently the plight of "latch-key" children is of increasing concern. These are young elementary-age children who, after school, open their empty house with a key tied to a string around their necks. There is a serious concern about the children's safety and about related fires when children are left unattended. These children need many of the services in a high-quality child care center. A bill for these services was passed in late 1984 by the Congress.

Figure 1-3. Preprimary school enrollment by background characteristics. (*The Condition of Education*, U.S. Department of Education, 1980, p. 209)

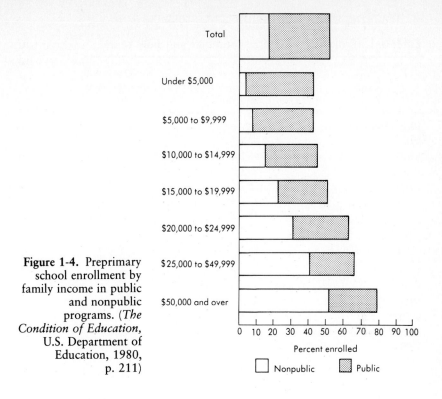

Figure 1-4. Preprimary school enrollment by family income in public and nonpublic programs. (*The Condition of Education,* U.S. Department of Education, 1980, p. 211)

Researchers Show Value of Early Education

Researchers have documented the fact that early childhood education pays off well in that these children find more success in later schooling. Many studies accompanied Project Head Start and other innovative programs. (See references to these studies at the end of this chapter.) One prominent study has been carried on since 1962 by David Weikart and others of the High/Scope Foundation of Ypsilanti, Michigan. The study, called the Perry Preschool Project, followed two matched groups of poor black children in the same community. One group received a high-quality preschool experience plus a visit once each week by a teacher in the child's home with the child's mother. The other group did not receive either a preschool experience or a home visit. Both groups attended the public schools of Ypsilanti, Michigan. By age 19 those children with the Perry preschool experience were found to have—

1. More success in school, with a larger percentage of high school graduates;
2. More success in obtaining and holding a job, with fewer being unemployed;
3. More success in regular classrooms, with fewer assigned to special education; and

9

Table 1-1. Project Head Start* (Summer and Full Year)

Fiscal Year	Enrollment (in 1,000s)	Congressional Appropriation ($ Millions)
1965 (Summer only)	561.0	$ 96.4
1966	733.0	198.9
1967	681.4	349.2
1968	693.9	316.2
1969	663.6	333.9
1970	477.4	325.7
1971	397.5	360.0
1972	379.0	376.3
1973	379.0	400.7
1974	352.8	403.9
1975	349.0	403.9
1976	349.0	441.0
1977	333.0	475.0
1978	391.4	625.0
1979	387.5	680.0
1980	376.3	735.0
1981	387.3	818.7
1982**	395.8	911.7
1983	414.9	912.0
1984	442.1	995.7
1984	452.3***	1,075.0

* *Project Head Start Statistical Fact Sheet,* Washington, D.C., Administration for Children, Youth and Families, Department of Health and Human Services, December 1984, p. 3.
** Since 1982 only full year services have been provided.
*** Projected enrollment for fiscal year 1985.

4. More success in citizen responsibilities, with fewer becoming delinquent or in conflict with the law.

The study concludes that each dollar spent for preschool education returns four dollars to the community—because of the savings in special education and delinquency and because the students can contribute economically through their success in school and in holding a job.[3]

*   *   *

Talk It Over: No. 3

Study the yellow pages of the telephone book under "Day Care Centers" and "Schools—Preschool and Kindergarten," talk to parents and teachers, ask, "What types of early childhood education services are

[3] David P. Weikart et al., *Changed Lives: The Effects of the Perry Preschool Program on Youths Through Age 19* (Ypsilanti, Mich.: High/Scope Foundation, 1984).

available to parents in this community? In nearby smaller or larger communities?" Compare findings with other students.

*   *   *

Types of Early Childhood Schools

There is an interesting variety of settings where you, as a preservice early childhood teacher, may observe and practice during your college program. Students generally like and are advised to gain experience in a variety of types of schools and with a variety of ages of children in order to be better prepared for the positions that await them when they graduate. The variety of early childhood education positions is exciting, especially if, as a graduate, you are free to move about the country or into a foreign country.

Early childhood schools vary as to (1) ages they serve, (2) particular services needed by families and the community, (3) source of funding, and (4) theoretical approach followed.

Ages Served

The particular age or ages served may be a reflection of (1) the legal kindergarten age in the state, (2) parental needs, (3) teachers' or directors' preferences, (4) available facilities or equipment, (5) economic factors, (6) program objectives, and so on. Ages served may range from infants a few weeks old to children around age six. Some centers specialize in certain ages, while others offer a comprehensive program for several or all ages. Some place children in single age groups, all threes, for example, while others place children of various ages, say three-, four- and five-year-olds, together. Either type of grouping is acceptable as long as the teachers individualize the program to meet the special needs of each child.

Ages Birth to Three Years

Care for infants and toddlers has received attention since the late 1970s. There are increasing numbers of single-parent families and couples where both work outside the home who require infant or toddler care. These parents do not have the luxury of staying home to care for their young child. They must work. Career women are returning to their jobs while their babies are still young to keep from giving up needed family income, to keep from losing out on a career already in process, or from fear of being locked out of a job when they are ready to work again. During the peak period of unemployment in the early 1980s many fathers were laid off, and employed mothers feared that they would be unable to find a job if they did not return to work at the end of their allotted maternity leaves. Thus economic factors have stimulated the growth of infant and toddler care centers. According to an economist at the Bureau of Labor Statistics, an important aspect of the increase in the labor force participation of mothers of young children ". . . is the degree to which mothers today do not leave the job market after childbirth. This is clearly demonstrated in the following comparison of married mothers' labor force participation rates:

Age of Youngest Child	March 1970	March 1984
1 year and under	24.0%	46.8%
2 years	30.5	53.5
3 years	34.5	57.6
4 years	39.4	59.2
5 years	36.9	57.0

Nearly half of the mothers with a child age 1 or younger were in the labor force in 1984. By the time the youngest is 3 years old, married mothers' participation rates approach 60 percent, and nursery school attendance or day care in some form becomes increasingly necessary."[4] The report also shows that in 1984, 367,000 children under age six lived in homes maintained by fathers only and over one million children under six had divorced, widowed, or never married mothers who worked full time. These are further indications of the increase in demand for infant and child care.

High-quality infant and toddler care is an expensive enterprise primarily because one person can care for only three infants or five toddlers, according to many state regulations. Both medical and educational attention has been focused on the standards of quality to be specified for infant and toddler care. The physical and mental health of infants and toddlers is considered extremely vulnerable, requiring strict standards of health and personal attention.[5]

Three- and Four-Year-Olds

Educational programs for three- and four-year-old children have been popular over the past decades. You can see by Figure 1-3 that the number enrolled has increased steadily and that at present about 37.5 percent of the three- and four-year-olds, or 2.3 million nursery schoolers, are enrolled. According to the Bureau of the Census, "While over 70

[4] Howard Hayghe, "Working Mothers Reach Record Number in 1984," *Monthly Labor Review*, December 1984, p. 31.
[5] For a detailed discussion see Bettye Caldwell, "Issues in the Quality of Infant-Toddler Care," *Young Children*, 38:5 (July 1983), pp.48–50.

Figure 1-5. Early childhood schools are found on United States military bases. Sukeran Kindergarten, (Kadena Air Base, Okinawa, Japan)

Figure 1-6. Early childhood schools are found in far off China. (Beijing Neighborhood Center)

Figure 1-7. Early childhood schools are found in the warm tropical islands. (Child Development Laboratory, University of Hawaii)

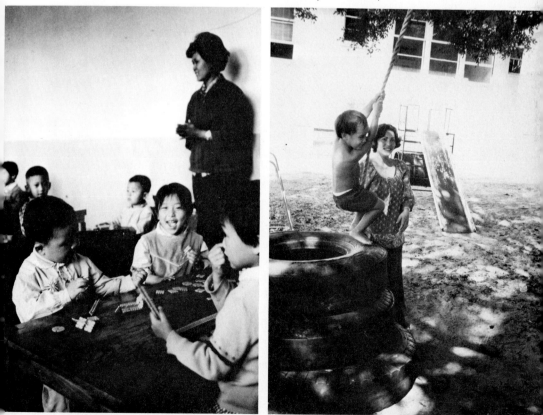

percent of white nursery school students are in private schools, only a third of black nursery schoolers are, indicating that cost and public availability may be serious limiting factors in usage of this still-growing type of schooling."[6]

According to Table 1-1, Project Head Start added large numbers of children to the prekindergarten and kindergarten statistics.

Five-Year-Olds

You may wish to become a kindergarten teacher serving five-year-old children in their first level in what is generally considered to be part of the formal school system. The percentage of children enrolled in kindergarten has been increasing over the years. You can see in Figure 1-8 that 95.4 percent or 3.4 million five-year-olds in the United States are now enrolled. Kindergartens have traditionally been half-day programs, but some states are now experimenting to make them full-day programs equal to the elementary school day. Another current experiment is with "developmental kindergartens." These provide an extra year of kindergarten for children who, on the basis of tests, are not ready for a standard kindergarten program and are predicted to be unable to do first-grade work adequately the following year. There is also a movement in some states to bring the four-year-olds into the public school system. Thus we close a discussion of ages served in early childhood centers and turn to a discussion of the types of schools needed by families or made available due to community decisions.

Community and Family Needs Determine Types of Schools

Families may seek out the early childhood education they need or the community may decide to provide the services and make them available to families. This section will introduce you to a number of typical early childhood education services and give brief information about their funding.

Kindergartens

Kindergartens have become the most universal early childhood service. Public school boards of education make a decision that children who are five years old will benefit from an early childhood education experience. Taxes support public school kindergartens. Kindergarten is typically not compulsory, but most children attend when it is provided. Privately funded kindergartens collect tuition from parents and generally follow the age guidelines of the public schools.

[6] *School Enrollment-Social and Economic Characteristics of Students: October 1983.* (Washington, D.C.: Bureau of the Census) October 1984, p. 1.

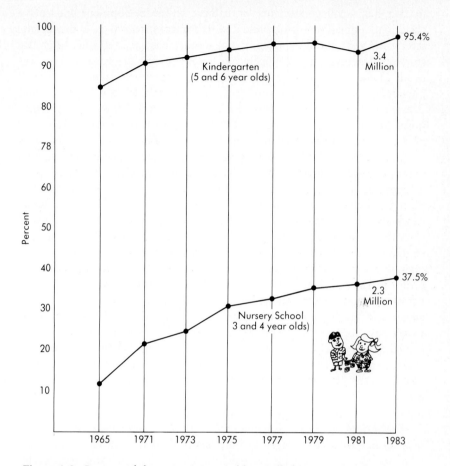

Figure 1-8. Percent of three- to six-year-olds enrolled in nursery school and kindergarten, 1965 and 1971–1983. (*School Enrollment—Social and Economic Characteristics of Students, October 1983*. U.S. Department of Commerce, Bureau of the Census, 1984)

Laboratory Prekindergarten and Kindergarten Programs

The child development laboratory school may be your first experience with an early childhood education program. Laboratory schools are funded and operated by high schools, vocational technical centers, community colleges, and four-year colleges and universities. Laboratory schools may be organized to serve the needs of the college or secondary school curriculum.

PRACTICUM FOR STUDENTS. Laboratory schools are organized to give practicum experiences to students. A well-educated, experienced lead teacher helps college students learn basic child development and early childhood education principles. The laboratory school is a protected setting for your initial experience. The teacher has time set aside to guide students' learning and is expected to focus on your needs as well as the needs of the young children. Serving as a laboratory teacher is a complex role, and sometimes you may have to wait for answers to your questions while the teacher cares for children's needs. However, do make notes of your questions because the laboratory teacher will surely expect to answer them at a later time.

One problem with laboratory schools has been that they may demonstrate a program that is very ideal compared to the community programs. This may occur because the teachers are well educated, are expected to be innovative, and there are several persons like yourself who can help with the many responsibilities, making the total program more elaborate than would be possible for two teachers alone. While you are in this protected environment, it is important that you take full advantage of its offerings. For example, here you can experiment with a small group or even one child, while others take responsibility for the remainder of the group. Out in the real world you'll be responsible for the whole group and find it hard to have time alone with one child because you won't have as many helpers. It is also to your advantage if you record the innovative ideas you see demonstrated by your laboratory teachers and others. Such records are valuable resources for your future teaching roles. See the suggestion for your Resource File at the end of this chapter.

RESEARCH. Research is often connected with laboratory schools, especially in four-year colleges and universities. Such research strengthens educators' knowledge base for teaching about child development, early childhood education, discipline, parent education, and the like. As you study the research documentation in this book you can appreciate more fully the soundness of the ideas presented, knowing they are based on research. Later on you may wish to study at the graduate level and carry on research projects. Or, as a classroom teacher, you might suggest projects to researchers as you analyze your work and evaluate children's and parents' progress. Then, as you get feedback from the research, your group of children, and other children as well, can benefit from improved programs.

EXPERIMENTAL PROGRAMS. Special experimental or innovative early childhood programs are often tried out in laboratory schools before being advocated for wider use. Such programs may focus on a particular researcher's theory or a particular group of children, such as those who have language delays or those from poor families. Others may test a particular part of the curriculum such as science, music, motor skill, or social activities. You can check with your institution to learn whether it has been involved with such experimental programs or research.

Child Care Centers

You may take some of your preservice education in and later work in a child care center. These are centers that provide supplemental care for children from infancy through kindergarten ages during the typical working hours of parents. In some localities the hours are from 6:30 A.M. to 6 P.M. Occasionally centers provide 24-hour service. As part of your education it will be desirable that you become acquainted with the breadth of services offered by a high-quality child care center in order for you to be able to teach in, or eventually direct, such a center after you graduate.

Child care centers are organized by profit and nonprofit groups. Most charge parents a tuition for sending their child to the center, even if they have a subsidy from a governmental agency, church, or the like. Child care centers are regulated by an agency of your state government, typically the department of social services or health services.

CHURCH-SPONSORED CENTERS. Churches are prime sponsors for both part-day and full-day early childhood education programs. These programs are held in the church-school facilities during the week. Large numbers of churches are sponsoring these programs.[7] Church leaders are motivated by a desire to provide a needed public service, to make money to help pay for a church-school building, or as a way to attract members to the faith. Some schools located in churches are completely secular, while others teach various aspects of the religion. Generally, churches must conform to state licensing standards when providing early childhood education services, with the exception of their short-period Sunday schools.

EMPLOYER-SPONSORED CHILD CARE. Employer-sponsored child care is currently experiencing a revival, having been pioneered in the United States during World War II when mothers were needed to work in defense plants. Today child care may be provided on the worksite for employees' children, or an allowance for child care may be part of the employee benefit package, allowing employees to select child care wherever they choose.[8]

Child care on United States military bases both at home and abroad is an example of employer-sponsored child care. These centers may op-

---

[7] For a useful report on the extent of church involvement see Eileen W. Lindner, Mary C. Mattis, and June R. Rogers, *When Churches Mind the Children: A Study of Day Care in Local Parishes* (Ypsilanti, Mich.: The High/Scope Press, 1983).

[8] K. S. Perry, *Employers and Child Care: Establishing Services Through the Workplace* (Washington, D.C.: U. S. Department of Labor Women's Bureau, 1982).

erate nearly around the clock, providing child care during both work and recreational hours for military men's and women's children. Child care on military bases is needed by both men and women in the military and is especially important due to the increased numbers of women and single parents—both men and women—in the military. Efforts are being made to raise the standards of child care in military centers.

FAMILY DAY-CARE HOMES. Providing family day care is a service that graduates of early childhood education programs sometimes organize in their own homes, especially if the graduate is a mother of young children and feels she would prefer staying home with them, yet wants to apply her professional skills. Family day-care homes are regulated by a local or state agency. Some states allow family group care which allows the mother to hire an assistant and enroll more children. Family day care is the service of choice for many families. It often allows care for school-age children who attend after school.

DROP-IN CHILD CARE. Drop-in child care services are another type of center where you may find employment. These centers take young children on an hourly basis, usually for an hourly fee, according to the number they are licensed to accept. For instance, churches and community centers may organize "mother's day out" to relieve mothers of child care for a time so they can shop or get medical treatment. Drop-in centers are also located in places such as shopping centers, amusement parks, or ski areas. Drop-in care is sometimes provided in medical centers giving noncontagious children waiting for tests or their siblings a child-appropriate environment in which to play while waiting.

Some drop-in centers are organized around a child-abuse therapy group to serve parents who may be inclined to abuse their children. Children may be dropped off at the center whenever the parent feels the strain of child care. As a teacher in such a center, you would become an important part of the support team of the mental health agency helping to rehabilitate the abusive parent.

Teaching in a drop-in center requires special preparation. Children are typically strangers with a here-and-now need. The ability to make children feel secure, comfortable, and happy is the primary skill needed. You need to have lots of experience to be most successful in a drop-in center.

Prekindergartens for Three- and Four-Year-Olds

You may gain part of your early childhood education experience in a prekindergarten with a part-day program in either the morning or afternoon. These prekindergartens used to be called preschools or nursery schools, terms which earlier it was indicated were being phased out. The schools may be called early childhood education schools or centers

Figure 1-9. Students prepare to teach by working with groups of children. (Brigham Young University Early Childhood Education Laboratory)

Figure 1-10. Students prepare for teaching by observing others work with children. (Child Development Laboratory, Michigan State University)

Figure 1-11. Students prepare to teach by working with individual children. Children's Center, University of South Carolina)

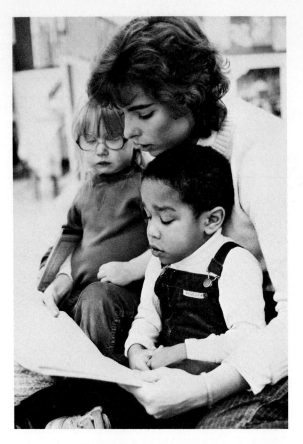

Figure 1-12. Students prepare to teach by working with a few children at a time. (Child Development Laboratory, College of Human Development at Pennsylvania State University)

or child development centers. Prekindergartens were generally credited with being more educational than child care centers. This difference is being eliminated with increased attention to higher quality in child care.

Many excellent prekindergartens are funded by tuition and have high standards of education. Some schools are operated by nonprofit agencies, while others are businesses for profit. The tuition expenses for these schools for some upper-income families can be very high.

PARENT-COOPERATIVE SCHOOLS. Parent-cooperative nursery schools are typically organized by groups of middle-class families in order to provide a high-quality early childhood educational experience for their children at an affordable price. Because of the parents' (usually the mother's) participation as an assistant to the teacher about one-half day each month, the family pays lower tuition rates than they would pay in a typical for-profit school. Parents in cooperatives also contribute labor to build equipment, keep up the facility, and operate the program. One highly valued component of the parent-cooperative is the close link parents feel to their child's education and teacher. Parents learn a great deal about children by helping in their child's group.

20

Parent-cooperative groups are popular today among families where the mother does not hold a full-time job or parents can work out a way to "cooperate." Parent-cooperatives have lost some families in recent years due to mothers taking full-time employment. This model of early childhood education is one you should keep in mind as efforts to involve parents are discussed because parents generally feel involved and satisfied when their children are enrolled in these schools.

There are a few prekindergarten programs for children between eighteen months and three years of age. However, generally speaking, if the mother is not working outside the home, she may prefer to wait a few months before enrolling the child. From a student's viewpoint being able to work with toddlers gives some insight into one of parents' most frustrating periods in the young child's life.

PROJECT HEAD START. Head Start early childhood centers were first organized under the joint sponsorship of the federal government and a local agency in many American communities in 1965. The program was begun as part of President Lyndon Johnson's War on Poverty. The program brought children of the poor together in groups for educational, medical, and nutritional assistance in hopes of reducing the observed handicap that such children experience when they enter elementary school. Some Head Start programs operated only in the summer, and others operated year round. Parent involvement has always been an important part of Head Start programs. For more discussion of Project Head Start see Chapter 20.

HANDICAPPED PREKINDERGARTNERS. The recent trend in education for the handicapped is away from segregated classrooms and toward integrating handicapped children in regular classrooms if their needs can be met there. This trend began in 1975 with the passage of Public Law 94-142. The federal law provides education for children and mandates an individualized program for each child. Head Start, using federal funds, initiated mainstreaming in Head Start groups. States have passed their own legislation and have provided services to young handicapped children in different ways.

HOME START PROGRAMS. Home Start programs are usually arranged by the public schools and have four major objectives: to involve parents directly in the educational development of their children; to help strengthen parents' capacity for stimulating their children's development; and to demonstrate and evaluate methods of delivering services to the parents and children for whom a center-based program is not feasible. The programs are federally funded. A trained visitor helps the parents develop an educational program for their children and helps them learn how to carry out the program.

HOSPITAL SCHOOLS. Hospitals are providing an early childhood school for their young patients. Children are brought to a playroom on the children's floor for as much activity as their illness will permit. There is therapeutic value to being with other children, and the children's education also benefits. The teacher may also provide activities in a child's hospital room if the child cannot be moved to the playroom.

This completes a brief discussion of the types of schools where you may practice or finally teach after graduation. You will learn much more about each type as you progress through your studies.

*   *   *

Talk It Over: No. 4

Make some inquiries about prekindergarten education in your community. Talk over what you learn about the types mentioned in the previous section.

*   *   *

Theoretical Approaches Utilized

The theoretical approach or approaches used by teachers as they plan the goals, activities, modes of interaction, and modes of evaluation in their groups is another possible variation you may encounter in early childhood schools. This book will address those variations in Chapter 2.

Contributions of Professional Associations

A number of professional organizations are helping the early childhood education profession in many ways. You can join one or more of these organizations and become active with other teachers in your chosen profession. One innovative project is being initiated by the National Association for the Education of Young Children (NAEYC). NAEYC is the largest professional organization focusing on the needs of young children. The innovative *Center Accreditation Project* will reward centers with accreditation when they meet standards of high quality. The criteria, agreed upon by a large group of the nation's early childhood educators, parents, and others, are spelled out in *Accreditation Criteria & Procedures of the National Academy of Early Childhood Programs,* published by NAEYC in 1984.[9] The criteria were widely discussed in *Young Children,* the NAEYC journal, during 1983. They were field tested in 1984.

___

[9] Available from NAEYC, 1834 Connecticut Ave., N.W., Washington, D.C. 20009.

The National Association for the Education of Young Children has also succeeded in agreeing on and publishing criteria for accrediting early childhood teacher education programs for students in four-year colleges and universities. The criteria spell out the areas of knowledge and experience required for a capable, competent teacher of young children. The criteria will be used by the National Council for Accreditation of Teacher Education (NCATE) for accrediting and reaccrediting the early childhood teacher education programs of colleges of teacher education. Also, when early childhood education programs require courses in home economics, especially courses focusing on the young child, families, and early childhood education methodology, those courses too will need to meet the accreditation criteria. The criteria are published by NAEYC in *Guidelines for Early Childhood Teacher Education Programs,* a small booklet available for a small fee from the NAEYC.

The Child Development Associate Consortium (CDAC), through grants from the Office of Health and Human Services, has developed the Child Development Associate (CDA) competencies for child care workers. Competencies are published in a booklet, *CDAC Competency Standards,* which is available from the Child Development Associate Consortium, 1341 G Street, N.W., Suite 802, Washington, D.C. 20005. The child care worker can follow the self-paced program which leads to CDA certification. Some CDA programs are available in connection with two-year colleges. Head Start centers usually specify CDA or Early Childhood Education certification for teachers they hire.

In addition to these important credentialing tasks, professional organizations publish readable and helpful journals and books and hold local, state, regional, and national meetings where teachers and others can talk over issues they face in serving young children and their families in early childhood centers. You'll surely want to check with your instructor and join a professional organization at your earliest opportunity. It will make a great contribution to your professionalism when you do. See the list of professional organizations at the end of this chapter.

You as an Adult Educator

The role of being an adult educator often slips up on teachers of young children. They prepare well for teaching young children, but many do not think about the fact that, as an educated professional, they will soon be responsible for giving leadership to the teaching team of adults. In many cases teachers are responsible for teaching adults how to do what needs to be done in early childhood centers.

As you reflect on the chapter so far and read the following bits of

Figure 1-13. Students prepare for teaching by trying out ideas and equipment that are new to them. (Child Development Laboratory, Michigan State University)

advice for starting your work with young children, begin also to think about ways you could teach these steps to others—co-teachers, parents, volunteers, aides, and so on. As you learn from your instructors in this course and in your school with young children, try to become aware of the process for teaching adults. Reflect on those processes that help you the most and those that are less effective. Thus you will begin to prepare for your role as an adult educator in the field of early childhood education. You will feel more skilled when the task presents itself in the future. Some would say that when you teach something is when you really learn it.

Observing in the Early Childhood School

Students in early childhood education usually have regular observations scheduled from the beginning of the term. Thus they can see children in action and relate their observations to the theoretical material they are studying in the classroom. Sometimes students may be asked to seek out children to observe. Children may be observed in laboratory schools, in schools not associated with the university, in informal groups, or in a family. In your preparation to become a teacher of young children, it is most helpful to observe situations similar to those in which you may later teach.

The purposes of observation are to help you to relate theory to practice, to understand what it means to be an infant, toddler, or three, four, or five years old, to become acquainted with methods and materials used in the school, and to sense the complications and satisfactions of being a teacher of young children.

To accomplish these purposes you will want to see a typical group of children behaving in typical ways. The following suggestions will help a new observer learn and be welcome.

1. Determine what you expect to see. Your instructor will indicate the points to look for during each observation. You may be given specific questions to answer as you observe.

2. Study the observation assignments for the entire course, if they are available. This will help you in observing, in understanding, and in collecting meaningful examples for assignments.

3. Be sure to read your text, listen to your instructor, and ask questions so that each assignment will be clear. Children are fascinating, and you may enjoy just watching. However, observation should be done with a purpose if you are to benefit most from it.

4. Take with you an outline of questions you have to answer.

5. Secure or copy a list of names and ages of the children. For easy reference, arrange the list according to chronological age. For some assignments, it is helpful to list the number of months or terms in school and the number and ages of siblings of each child.

6. Generally, it will be necessary to take notes, then write the report of the observation later. A hardbacked notebook is convenient for note taking.

7. An observation booth facilitates observing and makes it easier to watch behavior without affecting it. Safely behind a one-way-vision screen, you can be more objective and will not have to wonder whether you should interact with the child.

8. Be quiet in the booth in order to avoid attracting the children's attention and to avoid disturbing other observers. Sound equipment will, of course, make hearing easier.

9. When it is necessary to observe in the room with children, it is important to be as quiet and unobtrusive as possible. You should sit on a low chair, usually along a wall. Children who are accustomed to observers won't pay much attention to you unless you dress in a startling fashion or talk to them.

10. If a child talks to you, answer briefly and return to your writing. If

he or she continues to seek your company, you can move to a new location and quietly tell the teacher that this child seems to need someone to talk to. Children have been observed going from observer to observer for short chats. Even though each conversation was short, the total effect was that the child made many contacts with adults but few with children. This situation does not help students to observe child-child interaction. Often no contribution is made to the goals the teacher has for the child.

11. Unless your presence will interfere, you should move to areas where you can clearly see what the children are doing.

12. Avoid congregating with other adults. This tends to interfere with children's activity and with students' responsibility.

13. Stand near groups of children, or sit on the benches provided, but not on the children's equipment.

14. Identify each set of observation notes by date, time, group, teacher, activity, names, and a description of the setting so that you can recall it later with ease.

15. Include the child's age in your reports because behavior is much more understandable when related to a specific age. For example, use 3–5 to indicate three years five months.

16. If the assignment calls for an *anecdotal record*, the observer records incidents as the child interacts.

17. If the assignment calls for a *diary record*, the observer writes down a running account of the behavior of a particular child. Because writing is tiring, diary records may be taken for several minutes followed by a period of rest, then repeated.

18. In both anecdotal and diary records use quotation marks and quote the exact words of the children and adults. Exact words are often significant, as we shall discuss in a later chapter.

19. In reporting either type of observation, carefully separate facts from interpretations. Interpretations include what you think the behavior means and what questions arise in your mind about it. Evaluative words, e.g., *good, bad, pretty, ugly, happy, angry,* are part of your interpretation.

20. You may be called on to observe as you work with children. In this case your observation notes will of necessity be briefer. A small notebook and pencil should be carried in your pocket. A short word or phrase can suffice to help you remember a situation to write about in your reports or to discuss with the teacher. Such notes should be expanded immediately after the children leave, or the notes will soon be of little help.

21. Do not ask about or make statements about the children in front of children or parents.

22. Discuss your observations with the teacher after the children leave.

A teacher is usually too busy to give students' questions sufficient thought while attending the children.

23. No one, on the basis of a short observation, is justified in making sweeping statements about what children "always" or "never" do. Remember, even the child's total week in school is only a small part of his or her total experience.

24. Ethical treatment of observation data requires that discussions regarding the material be kept within the classroom. Here observations can be discussed in the light of other observers' experience and the knowledge and experience of the course instructor.

Participating in the Early Childhood School

For most students, participating directly with children is a long-awaited and valuable part of preparation to become a teacher. Through participating, you will begin feeling, thinking, and reacting as a teacher. You will be seeing children live and learn together. Not only will you watch teachers, but you will try your own skill and eventually develop a teaching style of your own.

Because students are often scheduled to participate with children at the beginning of a term, before learning the whys and wherefores of school procedures, the following list of participation hints will help during the first confusing weeks. As the course develops, you will gain an understanding of the reasoning contained in these hints.

Hints for New Student Participators

1. Wear clean, comfortable, colorful, washable clothing during your participation. When you are dressed comfortably in washable clothing you need not worry about your clothing and are free to concentrate on the children around you. A wraparound apron is handy to wear around the finger paints.

2. Wear a badge with your name clearly printed on it. Write "student helper" under your name so visitors or parents will know you.

3. Arrive on time at the designated school and check with the teacher for your particular assignments. Note any posted schedules or directions.

4. Attend any conference the teacher holds prior to the arrival of the children or at the end of the day.

5. Ask for advice in handling teaching material with which you are unfamiliar.

6. Avoid making patterns or models in any media for the children.
7. Write the children's names on pictures, starting in the upper left-hand corner and using manuscript writing in upper- and lower-case letters as shown in Figure 1-14.

Figure 1-14.

8. Sit down to work with the children whenever possible.
9. Talk quietly, using distinct words and short sentences.
10. Sit with the children during group times, for example, storytime, rest, music, and snack.
11. The children will help with cleanup if you make a game of it. Try singing your directions. Try suggesting, "You bring them to me and I'll help you put them on the shelves." Smile and say, "Thank you, John," after each bit of assistance. You'll marvel at how quickly the room or yard gets straightened up.
12. Be an alert observer and you will know when assistance is needed. Move in to help, that's how you learn.
13. Avoid unnecessary conversation with other adults in the room or yard. Save comments for staff meetings.
14. When you have serious doubts about a procedure, say to the children, "Let's ask the teacher."
15. Always keep the children's safety in mind and act to insure safety.

In the Locker Room

1. Sit on a low chair in a central location so that you'll be at the children's level and can see what help they need. Sitting saves the teacher's back, too!
2. Snowpants usually must be put on before boots. Lay the snowpants out in the correct position in front of the child, who sits on the floor. You can arrange several children around your chair like spokes on a wheel. The same circular arrangement works well for helping with boots too. A plastic bag over a shoe helps stubborn boots slip on.
3. Give praise generously as you encourage self-help.
4. Give both verbal directions and demonstrations as you help.
5. Jackets can be laid in open position on a low table. The child turns her or his back to the table and reaches backward, first with one arm and then with the other, to put the arms in the sleeves. Or the jacket can be placed in front of the child with the opening upward and the collar closest to the child. The child slips the hands into the sleeves, raises the arms, and the coat flips over the head into the correct position. Children enjoy this trick. Zippers and buttons require a number of demonstrations. You may have to start them partially to avoid overfrustrating a child trying to help himself or herself. Watch closely and help only when the child needs you.
6. For snowy boot removal, sweep snow off the children's boots and snowpants with a small broom while they are still outdoors. Arrange a number of small chairs around an absorbent rug in the entryway. Preferably, let only a few children enter at a time to avoid conges-

tion. The children sit on the chairs and remove their boots before proceeding to the locker area to remove their other wraps. The rug absorbs moisture and keeps it out of the locker area. An adult can sit in the circle and tug at stubborn boots. Boots may have to be drained and dried before being stored in the lockers. A clothespin with the child's name on it is helpful for clipping pairs of boots together. Boots can be marked with a felt pen.

7. Learn where extra clothes are stored. Three- and four-year-olds need a complete set of extra clothing stored in their lockers for emergency use. Each school needs its own collection of clean "extras" for unusual emergencies. A supply of paper bags should be stored nearby to use for soiled clothes.

8. Kindergarteners usually learn to tie their shoes, but younger children as a rule have difficulty with this skill. If you teach kindergarteners to call the loops "bunny ears" as you demonstrate tying, they will often become interested in learning.

At Storytime or Singing Time

1. You may be asked to read to a small group. You should read the book to yourself before reading to the children.

2. Be sure that the children can see the pictures. When the children sit with their backs to the windows, the light is usually best on a book held up for them to see.

3. Give them opportunities to respond to the story and pictures.

4. If someone else is reading or singing with the group, you should sit with the children. If a child becomes disruptive, quietly suggest appropriate behavior by tapping his or her knee or shoulder. Avoid saying "Shhh" and causing more distraction than the child.

5. Sing along with the children softly so that your voice does not overwhelm their voices.

6. If a child leaves the group, keep an eye on her or him so that the teacher can attend to the total group. If the child does not want to return to the story or singing time, help find a quiet activity that does not disturb the other children who are enjoying the group activity. Such a child might enjoy a story alone, so you could try reading, perhaps with the child sitting on your lap.

7. Should a visitor enter when the teacher is conducting story or singing time, see if you can assist the visitor until the teacher is free. Should the teacher be called out, you should assume responsibility for the group so as to minimize the disruption.

In the Bathroom

1. Certain points in the schedule are usually designated for the toilet routine. However, at other times keep alert for children who are holding their genitals—usually an indication of a need to urinate.

2. Don't offer children a choice when you are virtually certain they need to urinate. Tell them, "Let's go to the bathroom." Take their hands and guide them quickly to the bathroom.

3. When helping in the bathroom, sit on a low chair in order to be comfortable while assisting children with straps, buttons, zippers, and belts. By sitting nearby you avoid pressuring the child.

4. Boys need to learn to raise the seat, aim accurately as they stand to urinate, then lower the seat. These steps usually require many gentle reminders.

5. Children may worry about the noise of the toilet flushing. If the child hesitates when you suggest that he or she trip the lever, then you flush it until the child gains confidence.

6. Since girls and boys use the same bathroom at the same time, be matter-of-fact and factual when answering questions regarding differences in their bodies. Don't be embarrassed when they look at each other. They are learning.

7. Toilet accidents are not unusual in groups of three-year-olds. They are less common in older children but still may happen. Wet pants are more common than accidental bowel movements. If Jimmy has an accident, suggest that he try to use the toilet—sometimes he isn't finished and may only wet again as soon as you get the wet pants changed. Get dry clothing from his locker and dress him. Put the soiled clothing in a sack and label it with his name. Be matter-of-fact when other children ask about what has happened. The teacher will report the accident quietly to the parents so that the child doesn't feel betrayed and the parent doesn't feel inclined to punish the child. The teacher might say, "We'll be able to work out this problem. We'll just remember to encourage Jimmy to go to the bathroom right after snack."

8. Children usually enjoy washing their hands. Watch the temperature of the water. Usually, long sessions at the lavatory indicate that the children would enjoy some water play. Help the children dry their hands well to avoid chapping.

9. Late four-year-olds and fives can usually manage the bathroom routine without much adult help. Sometimes they play. If they spill water, let them mop it up.

10. Avoid having children wait in the bathroom. Keep the number entering in accordance with the number of toilets and lavatories available.

At Snack Time or Mealtime

1. If you are required to serve the meal, ask for advice on procedures.
2. Sit with the children at the small table.
3. Have a quiet conversation with the children. Avoid intertable conversations.
4. Give quiet directions to aid the children in learning the routine.
5. Tipped-over glasses of beverage are probably the most common mealtime accident. Therefore, encourage the children to keep their glasses moved toward the center of the table.
6. Use a sponge to wipe the table as you leave. A child might be encouraged to help you.

During Outdoor Activities

1. Dress for the weather from head to toe. Boots, gloves, scarves, and plenty of warm clothing are a must in winter. Comfortable loose clothing is important when it is hot.
2. Go where the children are. Adults should be spaced throughout the yard.
3. Keep off the children's equipment. Children won't use it if adults are sitting on it.
4. Go to a child and get his or her attention before giving directions.
5. Encourage and assist the children in putting things in the storage areas at the end of the period.

At Rest Time

1. Sit by a child who is having difficulty being quiet.
2. Children may quiet down more quickly if they lie on their stomachs. Some like to have their backs massaged.
3. Sing lullabies or say quiet poems to the children.
4. If children need to go to the toilet, help them leave the group quietly. Assist them in the bathroom.
5. Rest time should be a pleasurable experience free of punishing admonitions.

Student Evaluations

Your instructor will discuss with you and your classmates each of the criteria upon which you will be evaluated during this course. Table 1-2 shows a chart of a list of criteria. Your instructor may wish to add others. Duplicate the chart and on your first day start to rate yourself using 5 = highly satisfactory, 4 = satisfactory, 3 = minimum acceptable, 2 = unsatisfactory, 1 = very unsatisfactory and 0 = not observed or when criteria do not apply. In addition, write a brief diary record of the day's events. See *A Laboratory Workbook for Introduction to Early Childhood Education* by Hildebrand for helpful forms for keeping records of the day's events. Remember that you are expected to be learning—not to be perfect already—so it is important for you to respond positively to your instructor's suggestions and to discuss ways to improve your performance. Always ask for help when you feel uncertain. When you feel good about an interaction or an activity you've carried out, be sure to let the instructor know.

Table 1-2. Student's Self-Evaluation

Ratings

5 = Highly satisfactory	2 = Unsatisfactory
4 = Satisfactory	1 = Very unsatisfactory
3 = Minimum acceptable	0 = No opportunity

Criteria   *Week*
                                                    1 2 3 4 5 6 7 8 9 *etc.*

GENERAL EMPLOYEE BEHAVIOR

1. Arrives on time
2. Calls if ill
3. Makes up excused absences
4. Dresses appropriately
5. Prepares for tasks
6. Attends pre- and postconferences
7. Assumes full share of responsibilities during assigned period
8. Relates to all persons without cultural or sex bias

PLANNED MICROTEACHING PROJECTS

1. Presents several ideas for a project
2. Plans a project in detail and on time
3. Organizes and presents project
4. Uses creative techniques or aids
5. Holds children's interest
6. Relates to individual children
7. Questions and comments to children
8. Sets appropriate limits for children
9. Solves problems quickly and flexibly
10. Evaluates outcomes for children

Table 1-2. Student's Self-Evaluation *(continued)*

Criteria	Week
	1 2 3 4 5 6 7 8 9 *etc.*

APPLICATION OF PROFESSIONAL
KNOWLEDGE

1. Relates child development principles
   to children's behavior
2. Relates goals of early education to
   children's needs and interests
3. Uses approved guidance techniques
4. Is motivated to perform well
5. Demonstrates mature reliable behavior
6. Relates to staff members
7. Relates to parents
8. Evaluates own performance as a
   means of learning

Students:

Rate yourself on all applicable criteria on a five-to-one scale. Rate yourself after each day working with children. To receive feedback, discuss your self-ratings with your supervising teacher from time to time.

You can also gain experience in evaluating the center where you are participating. In Chapter 17 you'll find program evaluation discussed. You can develop a form and rate each item on the 5-to-1 scale, as mentioned earlier. The standards will become clearer as you proceed through the course, but it will be good experience for you to begin evaluating early. A few sentences in a diary record will help you recall the events of the day. When you feel there are omissions in the program, be sure to check with others because those events may occur on the hours or days when you are not present.

Evaluation is an essential task of every professional. Certain standards are expected. It will be up to you as a teacher of young children to know when standards are being met and to make corrections when they are not. The best evaluation is self-evaluation and its related self-correction. The early childhood teacher who does well at self-evaluation will seldom be surprised by what an outside evaluator reports.

Conclusions

Early childhood education is an important support service for families and their young children. Through this chapter you have been introduced to a number of types of services available. Each type has some unique characteristics and some common elements. You will learn more about these as your course progresses. Policymakers, professionals, and parents are currently taking serious interest in making early childhood education a high-quality service.

Applications

1. Do the "Talk It Over" activities placed throughout the chapter. If your instructor divides the topics among the class members, be sure to listen carefully and participate in discussions as others present their findings.
2. Complete Lesson 1 in *A Laboratory Workbook for Introduction to Early Childhood Education.*[10] Hand it in to your instructor as scheduled.
3. Use Table 1-2 to make your personal evaluation chart. Begin immediately to evaluate your participation with children. Continue to rate yourself throughout the term. Talk your ratings over with your instructor.
4. Begin planning a *Resource File* in which you will collect teaching ideas that you can use with young children. You will see some demonstrated and will read about others. Be sure to record complete detail in order to be able to carry out the activity later. To start your file, label manila file folders with the titles of chapters in this book. When you want to add ideas, type them on file cards and place them in the appropriate folder. See *A Laboratory Workbook for Introduction to Early Childhood Education* for forms related to the Resource File project.

Study Questions

1. List and briefly discuss qualities needed in an early childhood teacher.
2. List and briefly discuss settings where an early childhood teacher may be employed.
3. List and briefly discuss factors affecting current demand for early childhood education services.
4. List and briefly discuss current professional efforts to raise standards in early childhood education.
5. Describe a research study which shows the effectiveness of what the researcher called "high-quality preschool education."
6. Cite a study which showed benefits to children of having professionally prepared teachers.

Film

To Teach Young Children   Color   26 minutes   1982

Illustrates the roles a teacher or caregiver assumes when carrying out a short-day early childhood education program. Film designed for preparing teach-

---

[10] Verna Hildebrand (New York: Macmillan Publishing Co., Inc., 1986).

ers. In 16 mm and in film strip-tape with workbook lessons. Brigham Young University Press, Provo, Utah 84602.

Additional Readings

CATALDO, CHRISTINE Z. "Infant-Toddler Education: Blending the Best Approaches," *Young Children*, Vol. 39, No. 2, January 1984, pp. 25–32.

COHEN, D.H., and M. RUDOLPH. *Kindergarten and Early Schooling*. Englewood Cliffs, N.J.: Prentice Hall, Inc., 1977.

FEENEY, S., and D. CHRISTENSEN. *Who Am I in the Lives of Children?* Columbus, Ohio: Charles E Merrill Publishing Co., 1979.

LEEPER, SARAH H., RALPH L. WITHERSPOON, and BARBARA DAY. *Good Schools for Young Children*. New York: Macmillan Publishing Co., Inc., 1984.

Montessori in Perspective. Washington, D.C.: National Association for the Education of Young Children, 1966.

ROTHENBERG, DIANNE (compiler). *Careers with Young Children: Making Your Decision*. Washington, D.C.: National Association for the Education of Young Children, 1979.

SEAVER, JUDITH W., et al. *Careers with Young Children: Making Your Decision,* Washington, D.C., National Association for the Education of Young Children, 1979.

WEISER, MARGARET G. *Group Care and Education of Infants and Toddlers*. St. Louis: The C.V. Mosby Company, 1982.

Note: The following journals will be important resources for further exploration of every topic in this book. Students are urged to become familiar with each journal. The index issue will guide you to particular topics. Many of the associations publishing the journals offer special memberships to students, making it easy to join and become influential in the early childhood education field.

Childhood Education. Published by the Association for Childhood Education International, 3615 Wisconsin Ave., N.W., Washington, D.C. 20016.

Children Today. Published by the Children's Bureau. Department of Health and Human Services, Washington, D.C. 20201.

Dimensions. Published by the Southern Association on Children Under Six, Box 5403, Brady Station, Little Rock, Ark. 72215.

Educating Children. Published by the Department of Elementary, Kindergarten, and Nursery Educators of the National Education Association, 1201 Sixteenth St., N.W., Washington, D.C. 20036.

International Journal of Early Childhood. Published by the *Organisation Mondiale pour l'Education Préscolaire* (O.M.E.P.), 28 Stuart Road, Barnet, Herts, EN4 8XG, United Kingdom.

Journal of Home Economics. Published by The American Home Economics Association, 2010 Massachusetts Ave. N.W., Washington, D.C. 20036.

NAECTE Bulletin. Published by the National Association of Early Childhood Teacher Educators, c/o Dr. Kathryn Castle, Dept. Curriculum, Oklahoma State University, Stillwater, Okla. 74078.

Offspring. Published by Michigan Council of Cooperative Nurseries, 2770 Parkridge Dr., Ann Arbor, Mich. 48103.

Young Children. Published by the National Association for the Education of Young Children, 1834 Connecticut Ave., N.W., Washington, D.C. 20009.

Voice for Children. Published by The Day Care Council of America, 1602 Seventeenth St., N.W., Washington, D.C. 20009.

Goals for Early Childhood Education

- *Identify the bases for goals in early childhood education.*
- *Define a theory and identify ways to judge a theory.*
- *Define and identify developmental tasks and related early childhood education goals.*
- *State the value of play in early childhood education.*

Why are young children being encouraged to throw and catch? Why is a housekeeping corner found in most early childhood schools? Is it important for teachers to read to children every day? Is it alright for a child to play alone? These and countless other questions will come to your mind as you observe and participate in schools for young children.

As you gain experience in different early childhood schools, you'll find many similarities in equipment, supplies, and teaching strategies. However, you'll also find differences, a fact that may at first confuse you. As you gain more knowledge and experience you'll grow to understand that teachers may achieve goals for children through several methods and that some goals may vary according to the teacher's preference and the needs of children in a group. You'll grow to appreciate that being an early childhood teacher requires creativity and professional skills and knowledge and is far from being an assembly-line job where cogs fit perfectly and all the objects come out alike.

Selecting Goals for Early Childhood Education

Selecting goals for an early childhood education center, a classroom, or an individual child will require professional expertise. Dealing with human beings is far different than dealing with mechanical objects. You've

Figure 2-1. Early childhood—a time for learning to give and share affection. (Child Care Center, Haslett, Michigan)

Figure 2-2. Early childhood—a time to grow in independence. (Hoeflin Stone House Child Care Center, Kansas State University)

already learned in your child development classes that children are unique with individual needs, interests, and timetables of development. Dr. Bettye Caldwell, a prominent early childhood educator, put it well in a speech to the assembly of the World Organization for Early Childhood Education. She said, ". . . we can comfortably assert that each child is to some extent like all children, to some extent like some children, and to some extent like no other child."[1] She went on to explain how all children are biological creatures dependent on the same set of conditions to sustain life, that there are similarities among children within certain social and cultural groups, and that each child is unique in temperament, interests, motivation, and so on.

Goals Based on Values

Schools for young children, like all American schools, reflect the values enshrined in the U.S. Constitution. *A value is a concept of the desirable.* When you say, "You should . . ." or "You ought to . . . ," you are stating a value. At this point you can draw on your knowledge of or look up the rights stated in the Constitution.

The Constitution and its Amendments (new values are added by amendments and interpretations) guarantee certain rights to individuals. In early childhood programs these rights apply to children, parents, college students, teachers, and other employees. For example, as a result of interpretations of the Constitution by the Supreme Court, equality of opportunity and treatment should be provided for children of all races.

When you say, "Teachers ought to be fair" (or honest, or patient, or loyal), you are saying that being fair (honest, patient, or loyal) is highly valued. When the teacher says, "All children should be treated as individuals," this indicates that the value of individual uniqueness is held in high regard. Values will be stated throughout this book. You can think about what is written and decide whether you agree or disagree. Values are learned in our homes and schools, in our communities and nation, and through our reading and education. Values are carried into action in homes and schools. Adults teach children values while interacting with them on a daily basis.

* * *

Talk It Over: No. 1

Brainstorm in your class to develop a list of values you hold regarding education—your own and that of young children. Use words like "should" or "ought" to help designate a value. For example, "Chil-

---

[1] Bettye M. Caldwell, "Child Development and Cultural Diversity," paper presented at the OMEP World Assembly, Geneva, Switzerland, August 1983.

Figure 2-3. Early childhood—a time for creative self-expression. (Child Development Laboratory, Michigan State University)

dren should go to school." List the values on the board and talk about the action that flows from the value.

NOTE: to brainstorm, have everyone make contributions to the topic without evaluating. Encourage spontaneity and honor each idea.

*　　*　　*

Goals Based on Parental Needs

The many types of early childhood schools, as discussed in Chapter 1, suggest that there are needs of parents to be met, especially as early childhood educational services are considered part of a support system for the family. *A support system complements, augments, or adds to what the family can do for itself.* The school, for instance, teaches information the parent may not know or may not know how to teach. Also, the school protects the child and furnishes vital nutrition, rest, and nurturing while the parent works. The school provides parenting information or serves as a referral source to other agencies. The early childhood teacher is often the counselor when the family needs an attentive listener. Developing goals for providing services as needed by parents will be very important.

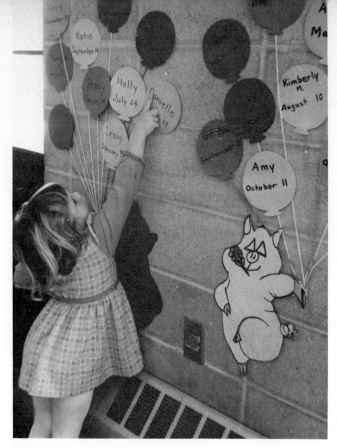

Figure 2-4. Early childhood—a period when self-esteem grows. (Texas Woman's University Nursery School)

Goals Based on Children's Needs

Logically, children's programs should be based on children's needs—physical, social, emotional, and cognitive. Or, you might say the needs are health, nutrition, exercise, education, interpersonal relations, self-esteem, language, and so on. You'll recognize these needs as topics you've studied in your child development course. Historically, research in child development, psychology, and early childhood education has advanced theories to help describe and predict human growth, development, and behavior. *A theory is defined as an organized set of ideas that the theorist formulates about a phenomenon, in this case about children or early childhood education.*

You are probably thinking that you'd rather be practical than theoretical when it comes to teaching young children. You may think of theory as boring, scary, or awesome. You may not like learning theorist's names. These feelings are understandable; however, you'll soon see that the theories help draw your attention to details about children that you might miss otherwise. As a teacher, your goal must be to understand children. It will save you lots of time if you take advantage of the in-

42

sights of other observers of children, including both practitioners and theorists. Knowing the theorist's terms will help you communicate with other professionals. Also, based on your previous experience with children, you may already have a start on formulating your own set of ideas or theories, and you can continue adding new information to your previous information and experience. Before you know it, you'll be handling theoretical ideas with ease.

*   *   *

Talk It Over: No. 2

Discuss with your classmates your feelings about studying child development theory.

*   *   *

Talk It Over: No 3

Discuss with your classmates: "I believe the following influences the development of a child's
   a. personality
   b. ability to learn
   c. social skills."
Summarize your discussion.

*   *   *

Figure 2-5. Early childhood—a time when enjoyment of peers increases. (Child Development Laboratory, College of Human Development at Pennsylvania State University)

Qualities of a Useful Theory

For a theory to be useful, the theorist must

1. Describe the set of ideas as carefully as possible, defining new terminology and clearly stating the definitions of terms used by others;
2. Publish the set of ideas in journals that are accessible to researchers, educators, and the public; and
3. Welcome tests of the theory by other researchers with results published where all can freely evaluate them.

Gradually a theory either gains support or fades out of the current literature. Educators and researchers keep up on both new and old theories in hopes of finding one, or perhaps a combination, that will do a better job of contributing to the understanding and prediction of growth or behavioral outcomes. Because human beings are so unique, and because ethical considerations prevent experimenting with people in any way that might be harmful, theories about people are difficult to prove. The statistical treatment of data usually hides the details of the individual responses, making it difficult to draw conclusions about an individual with a high degree of certainty. You'll notice that researchers usually say, "The data indicate . . ." not "The data prove . . ." If the theory can be proved, it becomes a fact and is no longer a theory. To take a different type of example, you recall that in the pre-Columbus era people held the theory that the world was flat. After the voyage of Columbus and others, the flat-earth theory lost out and the round-earth theory became a fact. Trips into outer space have further supported this fact since 1962.

A number of single-domain or more specific theories are available to help you understand single aspects of child development, such as discipline, language, cognition, or social interaction. Single-domain theories help with problems a child may be having. Occasionally, a single-domain theory has been utilized for research purposes wherein a total early childhood program follows one theory to determine whether careful adherence to one approach to education would be best for outcomes for children. To date, the research has been inconclusive regarding any single theoretical approach. The theory that applies to certain areas of the curriculum will be presented under the most appropriate topic for helping you understand the application of the theory to curriculum. Readings at the end of this chapter will lead you to more depth in theory.

The most prominent theory used in early childhood education program planning today is called *developmental* because the developmental characteristics and maturational timetables of children are considered the most logical basis for decisions about planning and carrying out educational programs for children. A general holistic approach that can be applied to all ages of children and to all areas of the child's development is needed.

The work of Dr. Robert J. Havighurst will be utilized to help formulate the goals for early childhood education schools. Havighurst's use of the concept of developmental tasks for children of various ages is very helpful to teachers. *Developmental tasks are defined as "those common tasks each individual of a given age must master within a given society in order to be happy and to master the tasks of the next age."*[2] Developmental tasks combine biological, psychological, and sociological aspects of development. Teachers find them useful in planning for a child's next level of development. The developmental tasks cover the whole child from head to toe and also cover all ages from birth to old age. Table 2-1 shows the developmental tasks for infants and young children.

Goals for Early Childhood Education

Establishing goals must come before attempting to make plans. Your school may have a goal statement agreed upon by parents, teachers, and administrators. A general goal is to help each child live a happy childhood, reach his or her potential, and become a happy, fully functioning adult.

To define goals in terms more helpful to teachers, the concept of developmental tasks as outlined in the work of Carolyn Tryon and J. W. Lilienthal is useful.[3] The developmental tasks are like rungs on a ladder; they are too far apart for the person to scale the wall of maturity without stepping on each rung. Sufficient experience and skill in each task must be achieved before the next task can be reached successfully. When conditions are right, and if the teacher is prepared, children will likely achieve the tasks.

Ten Major Goals

The developmental tasks serve as a basis for the ten major goals for infants and young children. Parents and teachers will strive to help children—

[2] Robert J. Havighurst, *Developmental Tasks and Education* (New York: David McKay Company, Inc., 1952).

[3] Caroline Tryon and J. W. Lilienthal, "Developmental Tasks: The Concept and Its Importance," *Fostering Mental Health in Our Schools*. Association For Supervision and Curriculum Development (1950 Yearbook), Washington, D.C., pp. 77–128.

See handout from C.D.

Table 2-1. Developmental Tasks for Infancy and Early Childhood

Developmental Tasks	Infancy Birth to 2½	Early Childhood 2½ to 5 yrs. old
① Growing in Independence	A dependent being. Becoming aware.	Needs less private attention. Increase physical independence. Remains emotionally dependent.
② Learning to Give, Share, and Receive Affection	Developing a feeling for affection. Responding to those who love him/her. Bonding and Attachment occur with loved ones.	Developing ability to give affection. Learning to share affection with siblings or others. Responding to acts of affection.
③ Learning to Get Along with Others	Being aware of others. Developing social interaction. Responding to others.	Beginning to develop ability to interact with agemates. Adjusting to family's expectation for child's role. Enjoys peers.
④ Developing Self Control	Beginning to adjust to expectation of others.	Develop ability to take directions. To be obedient to authority. Growing in ability to control own behavior when authority figures are not present.
⑤ Learning nonsexist Human Roles	Socialization begins to influence sex role identification.	Learning to identify with male adult and female adult roles. Differentiates male and female. Believes that sexual identity is based on clothes or hair style.
⑥ Beginning to Understand One's Own Body	Adjusting to adult feeding demand. Adjust to adult cleanliness demand.	Adjusting to expectations resulting from one's improving muscular ability. Developing sex modesty.
⑦ Learning and Practicing Large and Small Motor Skills	Developing physical equilibrium. Developing eye-hand coordination. Establishing satisfactory rhythms of rest and activity.	Developing large muscle control. Learning to coordinate large and small muscles.

Developmental Tasks	Infancy Birth to 2½	Early Childhood 2½ to 5 yrs. old
Beginning to Understand and Control Physical World	Exploring the environment using all five senses.	Meeting adult expectations of restrictive exploration. Manipulate an expanding environment. Satisfying curiosity through exploration.
Learning New Words and Understanding Others	Developing preverbal communication. Developing verbal communication. Beginning concept formation.	Improving one's use of words and understanding of words of others. Improving one's ability to form concepts, reason, describe.
Developing a Positive Feeling About One's Relationship to the World	Developing a sense of trust then a sense of autonomy.	Developing a sense of self as separate from others. Developing a feeling of confidence.

Adapted from Caroline Tryone and J. W. Lilienthal, "Developmental Tasks: The Concept and Its Importance," *Fostering Mental Health in Our Schools.* Association for Supervision and Curriculum Development (1950 Yearbook), Washington, D.C., pp. 77–128.

Grow in Independence

Children will begin to think of themselves as independent, capable individuals. Adults are responsible for helping each child reach an appropriate level of independence. This goal is always in the teacher's mind when planning the program, equipment, materials, and guidance for children and is remembered when deciding whether or not and how much to help with boots or zippers. The objective is to help each child learn to do things for him- or herself, and to make decisions and choices.

Learn to Give and Share, as Well as Receive Affection

From a typical pattern of self-centered affection, children will grow in ability to give and share affection with others their age and with adults both within and outside the family. The teacher helps them to feel secure and loved in their new environment. The teacher makes special plans for working with those children whose home backgrounds have not fostered feelings of love and security, and for working with their parents, in hopes of changing some of the negative aspects of the early experience.

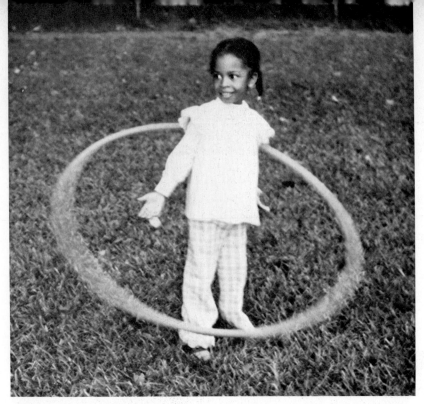

Figure 2-6. Early childhood—a time to learn what one's body can do. (Child Development Laboratory, Louisiana State University)

Figure 2-7. Early childhood—a time when cooperating with friends becomes important. (Child Development Center, Metropolitan State College)

Learn to Get Along with Others

As children move out of the social unit of the family into the social unit of the school, the teacher wants their experiences to be positive and happy. Children are protected until they are ready for social relationships. They are helped to learn techniques of interaction that will bring positive responses from others.

Develop Self-Control

The teacher thinks of discipline as self-control to be developed over time. There are few absolutes. The goal is for each child to become self-disciplined, self-guided or self-directed. This is in contrast with a child who is only adult controlled or directed. It is desirable for children to learn certain behaviors and the reasons for them. The teacher explains how appropriate responses provide protection for each child as well as for the safety and well-being of others. As children gain understanding, they develop a sound basis for appropriate behavior. Fear of an authoritarian figure does not provide an adequate basis for developing self-control. Experience in making judgments and decisions is provided in order that children will become confident that they can make decisions when the adults are not nearby.

Learn Nonsexist Human Roles

Though biological sex roles differ, sex stereotyping is to be avoided. Teachers must be constantly alert to set expectations and use guidance that encourages children of both sexes to develop all aspects of their personalities and talents. Equal treatment and equal career opportunities for either sex are now generally required by state and national laws.

Begin to Understand Their Own Bodies

The teacher plans and carries out a program that helps children understand their bodies and to feed and care for themselves. Health, hygiene, and nutrition are very important.

Learn and Practice Large and Small Motor Skills

A program is designed which challenges each child's small and large muscles. Motor skill practice is encouraged through planning, support, and guidance.

Begin to Understand and Control the Physical World

The teacher develops the child's intelligence by encouraging curiosity, thinking, reasoning, and the gathering and using of information. Every effort is made to help children fit together some of the pieces of their world puzzle through careful planning and selecting of materials, equipment, and experiences. The teacher expects to provide a background of

Figure 2-8. Early childhood—A time for adults to help children find joy in books and in other prereading experiences. (Family Life Center, Georgia Southern College, Statesboro)

experiences and attitudes that will make living and learning more meaningful.

Learn New Words, and Understand Others

Every opportunity is used by the teacher to foster children's use of language and their understanding when others speak.

Develop a Positive Feeling About Their Relationship to the World

The teacher's and parents' roles are to help children feel good about themselves as they gain experience with the world. A positive self-concept can develop during these early years. The early school experiences, being the child's first, should be happy, positive experiences. An environment which is personally exciting and meaningful will add to the child's drive to learn. It is hoped that children will become self-confident in the school situation. It is highly desirable that school, teachers, friends, experiences, books, and learning be positive experiences from the children's view. If children complete early childhood schools with positive views of school, then motivation should be high for accomplishing the developmental tasks of the elementary school years.

Using the foregoing ten developmental tasks for guides, teachers can

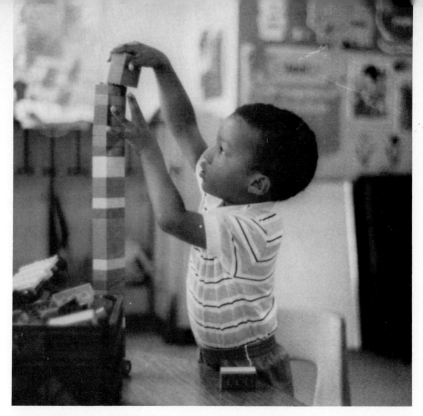

Figure 2-9. Early childhood—A time to practice small-motor coordination and other prewriting activities. (Child Development Center, Metropolitan State College, Denver)

plan early childhood programs that foster all areas of a child's development—physical, mental, emotional, social, and creative. Each of the ten tasks is important for a balanced program. See how they fit into evaluation of programs in Chapter 17.

How Are Goals Achieved?

The first time you visit an early childhood school, you may wonder how the teacher survives the day or how the children ever learn anything. There is usually a free-flowing informality that is far different from the organization adults are likely to remember in their own schooling.

Planning

Despite the apparent informality and lack of regimentation, a great deal of planning and organizing takes place before, after, and even during the school day. The teacher and assistants meet regularly when the children are not at school to map out the days, weeks, and months ahead. Plans are flexible, but a good program for children does not develop haphazardly. The teacher keeps goals for the children firmly in mind.

Goals are considered in terms of individual children. The teacher does not lump all children together and say, "All children must learn to. . . ." There will be a range of skills, behaviors, and competencies in any class. The teacher should expect differences and plan for them.

Learning Centers

The school will generally be arranged in learning centers, or zones. That is, in various parts of the room there will be a place for children to work in art, in science, or in music. They will find zones with blocks, books, and materials for dramatic play. Other zones will display perceptual and number games. In colder climates there may be an indoor zone for vigorous climbing, which substitutes for outdoor activities during bad weather. Though outdoor zones may not be as numerous as those for indoors, the observer will find zones for both quiet and vigorous activity outdoors.

Self-Selected Activity and the Teacher's Role

Finding children talking, laughing, and moving about may be one of the biggest surprises to a new observer. Yet, further observation will reveal that the children are actively learning as they choose their own activities. During the *self-selected activity period* they work individually and in small groups throughout the room or yard. The largest part of the child's day is self-selected.

The informal teaching style may also be a surprise. The teacher's role is to organize the learning centers and see that there is appropriate and sufficient equipment in each for carrying on activities from which the child can choose. Then the teacher relates to each child who is engaged in learning through play. The role is far more than supervisory. The teaching involves moving about, putting in a word here, redirecting there, listening to children's comments and questions.

The assistants and the teacher work as a team. For example, one day the assistant may provide a science experiment in one zone that requires close attention. Another day the assistant may keep an eye on all the zones while the teacher concentrates on teaching language arts at the literature table. Through many one-to-one contacts the teachers contribute to the total growth of each child.

Teacher-Instigated Activities

Routine activities such as cleanup, storytime, and snack time are also part of the child's day. These are teacher instigated, requiring some compliance with the teacher's plan. However, they are loosely organized to leave room for individual differences in response. Group activities contribute to the child's learning and develop an *esprit de corps* in the group.

Figure 2-10. Early childhood—A time when new experiences, such as hearing a cellist, stimulate learning. (Child Development Laboratory, Oakwood College, Alabama)

As a student participator you may be asked to select a zone in which you can begin to develop a relationship with children individually and in small groups. For example, you may sit near the table games or puzzles, observing and helping where needed. The teacher may brief you on procedures, schedules, and the like, or may offer advice when it seems warranted. For the most part, though, you will be left to handle your assignment as well as you can—applying your knowledge from readings and other sources. After you are acquainted with the children, you may move into situations in which you work with larger numbers of children. After the children have gone, you will have an opportunity to question the teacher and seek recommendations for handling special problems.

How Does Organization Facilitate Goals?

Do children really learn anything worthwhile in such a free setting? This may be the student's first reaction and question. Doubt is usually common among teachers who are already experienced in teaching upper elementary and secondary grades.

53

*   *   *
Talk It Over: No. 4

Consider the spatial arrangement of an early childhood classroom. What learning centers did you see? What equipment and supplies were present? How were boundaries defined? What did children do?

*   *   *

Almost inevitably problems arise in groups of small children when an adult tries to get all the children doing the same thing at the same time. A young child is not accustomed to sitting still. The attention span may be short. However, the attention span of many children is longer when they are involved in a self-chosen activity, not an adult-initiated one.

Children have a natural inclination to explore and manipulate. This inclination is to be exploited when the educational environment for the young child is being planned. Put a puzzle on the table so that the child can see it. Usually a child can't resist taking the puzzle apart. And when successful at working it, the child has developed both physically and mentally. The effective school setting provides for numerous learning experiences with a variety of enticing equipment that openly invites the child's use.

The teacher plans learning experiences that permit children to educate themselves. As they make discoveries through their senses—sight, touch, taste, smell, and hearing—they will communicate with other children and teachers, developing language vital to all learning. Also they will concentrate because they are doing something that interests them. They will investigate, manipulate, and create, thereby contributing to their intelligence and storehouse of knowledge.

Through individual, small group, and whole group activities, the teacher structures a flexible, individualized, and academically sound program. To observe or participate in an early childhood school where children are dynamically involved in their own learning is to become convinced that "worthwhile" learning is taking place.

To the casual observer, children who are exercising their free choice during the self-selected activity periods are "just playing." Writers such as Bereiter and Engelmann advocate reducing the amount of self-directed play activity by "focusing upon academic objectives and relegating all nonacademic objectives to a secondary position."[4] However, Lawrence K. Frank, a distinguished scholar of child growth and development, would not consider the self-directed activity previously described as "nonacademic." He wrote, "Hence through play the child continually rehearses, practices, and endlessly explores and manipulates whatever he can manage to transform imaginatively into equivalents of

---

[4] Carl Bereiter and Siegfried Engelmann, *Teaching Disadvantaged Children in the Preschool* (Englewood Cliffs, N.J.: Prentice-Hall, Inc., 1966), p. 10.

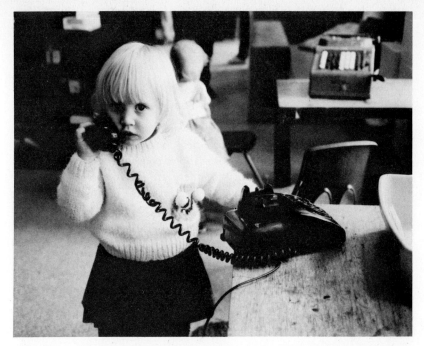

Figure 2-11. Early childhood—A time when talking over the telephone contributes to language development. (Early Child Development Center, University of Vermont)

the adult world. He experiments with and tries to establish the meaning and use of a variety of symbols, especially language, as he tries to cope with this often perplexing grown-up world."[5]

Indeed, play is very valuable. Frank and Theresa Caplan, writing in *The Power of Play*, discuss the following sixteen values of play.[6]

1. Play aids growth.
2. Play is a voluntary activity.
3. Play offers a child freedom of action.
4. Play provides an imaginary world a child can master.
5. Play has elements of adventure in it.
6. Play provides a base for language building.
7. Play has unique power for building interpersonal relations.
8. Play offers opportunities for mastery of the physical self.
9. Play furthers interest and concentration.
10. Play is the way children investigate the material world.
11. Play is a way of learning adult roles.

[5] Lawrence K. Frank, "Play and Child Development," *Play—Children's Business, Guide to Selection of Toys and Games: Infants to Twelve-Year-Olds* (Washington, D.C.: Association for Childhood Education International, 1963), pp. 4–5.

[6] Frank and Theresa Caplan, *The Power of Play* (Garden City N.Y.: Anchor Press, Doubleday, 1973), pp. xii–xvii.

12. Play is always a dynamic way of learning.
13. Play refines a child's judgments.
14. Play can be academically structured.
15. Play is vitalizing.
16. Play is essential to the survival of humans.

The advocates of more academic activities are really suggesting more teacher-instigated or structured activities. Bereiter and Engelmann recommended that drill on teacher-chosen topics consume most of the child's school day.[7] There is no doubt that there are significant problems for teachers who teach disadvantaged youngsters—the youngsters Bereiter and Engelmann had in mind when they proposed their much discussed methods. However, it is doubtful that long-range goals for stimulating the child's love for learning, teachers, and books are accomplished through methods such as they propose.

As a future professional leader and educator of your staff and parents, reflect on ways you might discuss issues of values, goals, and teaching strategies with adults involved in your program.

Conclusion

A developmental philosophy of early childhood education has been described. Teachers establish goals before planning programs. Suggested goals for the young child have been stated in terms of the developmental tasks of early childhood. Goals are achieved through careful planning and through arranging centers in which children can learn as they use the materials and equipment of their choice. Routine activities are organized in a way that leaves room for individual differences.

As you read, observe, participate, and plan for a career in teaching, you must judge the merits of various teaching approaches. In what sort of school atmosphere does a child best learn academically significant concepts? What teaching methods are most appropriate to the philosophy, ideals, and needs of a democratic society?

The teacher is of utmost significance. Perhaps you can sense through your observation and participation what Moustakas calls "the bond" between teacher and child from which "opportunities and resources emerge which enable both child and teacher to realize hidden potentials, to release creative capacities, and to stretch to new horizons of experience, together and alone, where learning has an impact on total being and where life has a passionate, enduring character."[8]

[7] Bereiter and Engelmann, op. cit., p. 10.
[8] Clark Moustakas, *The Authentic Teacher* (Cambridge, Mass.: Howard A. Doyle Publishing Co., 1967), p. 58.

Applications

1. Do the "Talk It Over" activities placed throughout the chapter.
2. List the 10 developmental tasks down one side of a page. After each one write one or more behaviors that you at your present age are doing to prepare yourself for your next level of developmental tasks. What conclusions do you reach about yourself?
3. During your time in an early childhood education school follow Lesson 2 in *A Laboratory Workbook for Introduction to Early Childhood Education*. Complete the exercise after you leave the group of children.
4. Evaluate your participation with children using your chart. (See Application 2, Chapter 1 for details.)

Study Questions

1. Define values
2. Explain how values affect education? Early childhood education?
3. Define a support system. Explain how early childhood education services are part of a family support system.
4. Define a theory.
5. State three qualities of a useful theory. Explain how a theory differs from a fact.
6. How does Dr. Robert J. Havighurst define developmental tasks?
7. List the ten developmental tasks.
8. List one or more behaviors under each developmental task that a young child will do or learn who is working on that task. What difference will the child's age make?
9. List and explain four ways that goals are achieved in early childhood education centers.
10. List the values children derive from playing. Write your answer to a parent who says, "All they do is play."

Films

Setting the Stage for Learning   Black and White   22 minutes

Affirms the importance of play as a valuable and indispensable resource for learning during the early years. Churchill Films, 662 North Robertson Boulevard, Los Angeles, Calif. 90069.

Additional Readings

ANKER, DOROTHY, et al. "Teaching Children as They Play." *Young Children*, Vol. 29, No. 4, May 1974, pp. 203–213.

BEREITER, CARL, and SIEGFRIED ENGELMANN. *Teaching Disadvantaged Children in the Preschool*. Englewood Cliffs, N.J.: Prentice-Hall, Inc., 1966.

Brown, Catherine C. and Allen W. Gottfried, *Play Interactions: The Role of Toys and Parental Involvement in Children's Development*. Skillman, N.J.: Johnson and Johnson Baby Products Co., 1985.

Caldwell, Bettye M. *Project Head Start Program II: A Manual for Teachers*. Washington, D.C.: Office of Economic Opportunity, 1968.

Feelings and Learning. Washington, D.C.: Association for Childhood Education International, 1963.

Havighurst, Robert J. *Developmental Tasks and Education*. New York: David McKay Company, Inc., 1952.

Hymes, James L., Jr. *Teaching the Child Under Six*. Columbus, Ohio: Charles E. Merrill Publishing Co., 1981.

Leeper, Sarah H., et al. *Good Schools for Young Children*. New York: Macmillan Publishing Co., Inc., 1984.

Montessori in Perspective. Washington, D.C.: National Association for the Education of Young Children, 1966.

Murphy, Lois B., and Ethel M. Leeper. *Conditions for Learning*. Washington, D.C.: U.S. Government Printing Office, 1973.

Read, Katherine, and June Patterson. *The Nursery School and Kindergarten*. New York: Holt, Rinehart and Winston, 1980.

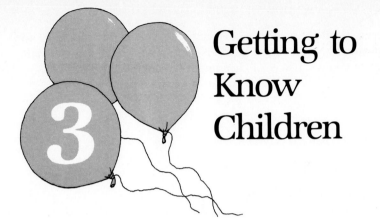

Getting to Know Children

- *Describe characteristics of children of each age from infancy through age five.*
- *Identify factors in decisions regarding group size and age range within early childhood groups.*
- *Identify measures taken to acquaint the child and parents with the staff and facility of a school.*
- *State the obligation to protect the privacy of families.*

"We get to help more with the three-year-olds than we did with the fives." "I feel useless. These fives don't need any help." "Whew! There is never a dull moment in here with the four-year-olds."

Such comments are common when early childhood education students talk about their observing and participating assignments in groups of young children. When given an opportunity to see different age groups, students discover common characteristics of an age. They also note wide differences between children who are the same age.

Teachers and parents can make use of normative-descriptive data derived from research by investigators such as Arnold Gesell (1880–1961).[1] Gesell and others carefully observed large numbers of children and described typical behavior and other characteristics of each age. Although a child may never completely fit the "typical" pattern, it helps to compare individual growth with such norms. Normative data help adults plan new experiences and guidance measures for the child. Comparing the behavior of a child with these data helps adults recognize severe deficiencies and initiate appropriate measures to correct deficiencies.

[1] Arnold Gesell and Frances L. Ilg, *Child Development* (New York: Harper & Row, 1949).

Teachers combine normative-descriptive data and goals in order to plan appropriate programs for children. The following are general characteristics of young children as they might be observed in the school situation.

Characteristics of Children

Infants and Toddlers

You may be assigned to work with infants or toddlers as part of your practical experience in early childhood education courses. Babies will seem to spend a lot of time eating, sleeping, and being changed, but they are learning and there is a great deal for you to learn. They will need lots of cuddling and gentle handling. Some mothers may be able to come to the center to breast- or bottle-feed their infants. Caregivers must welcome the mothers and carefully assist them. Parents and babies are involved in a delicate *bonding and attachment process,* which means they are developing a love affair with each other. They need frequent positive contacts with each other.

Figure 3-1. By listening and talking to children you will learn how children think. (Early Childhood Laboratory, Kansas State University)

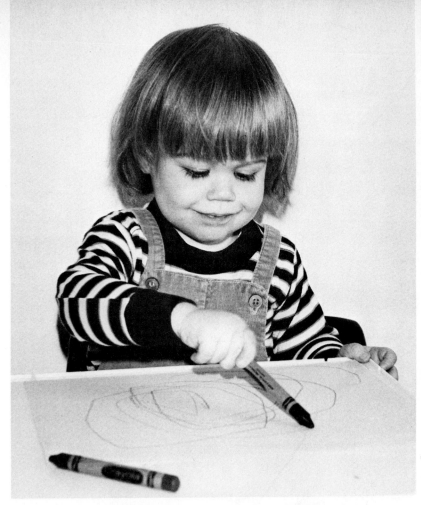

Figure 3-2. A toddler's drawing will give you clues as to why writing is several years away. (Child Development Laboratory, Michigan State University)

Your center will have organized carefully the protective measures for the babies in order to keep them healthy. Washing your hands with soap will become a basic habit before you feed or after you change a baby. Babies cannot protect their own safety; therefore, never take chances with them rolling off a changing or feeding table. Routines should be accompanied by eye contact and a pleasant voice as you talk to, sing to, and in many ways encourage the baby's responses.

According to Harvard pediatrician, Dr. T. Berry Brazelton, responding to the baby's cues, giving verbal stimulation, smiling, and cooing encourage similar behavior in the baby. When the activity gets too intense, the baby will turn away, perhaps resting a bit, then will turn back and smile or continue to suck, if feeding. Parents or caregivers should not get discouraged when the baby turns away, but should wait patiently to pick up the cue from the baby for more action. Brazelton la-

Figure 3-3. The concept of parallel play becomes clear when observing three-year-olds. (Child Development Laboratory, College of Human Development, Pennsylvania State University)

bels such reciprocal interaction *synchrony* which is part of the bonding and attachment process that takes place between parents and the baby. Synchrony must also be a part of supplemental infant care carried on in infant centers and in family day-care homes. Attachment to a caregiver can occur, though not to the same extent as it does with parents. That is one reason for keeping the same caregiver with a given baby. Attachment and its related security and sense of trust are developing in the young babies.[2]

Dr. Erik Erikson is a psychological theorist who suggests that babies during the first year are in the *trust versus mistrust* stage of life. Erikson believes the overall pattern of infant care, rather than a single aspect, is important for the development of trust. The baby's many needs must be met for a sense of trust to develop. The second stage in Erikson's eight stages comes during the toddler stage when toddlers begin to want to make decisions. They say "no" and strive for independence. Erikson labels the stage *autonomy versus shame and doubt*. You'll notice auton-

[2] For a more detailed discussion of Brazelton's ideas about interacting with babies see T. Berry Brazelton, *Mothers and Infants* (New York: Dell Publishing Co., 1969).

omy developing in a toddler's dressing, playing, eating, and so on. It is a period that is frequently frustrating to parents unless they understand that it is perfectly normal and expected of the toddler.[3]

There will be many indications of growth and development as you observe and work with infants and toddlers. Infants begin being toddlers when they start walking. It is important for caregivers to share milestones in development with the baby's parents. High-quality centers develop a means of communicating with parents and try to ease the sense of guilt that many feel for not being with their babies full time.

Toddlers will begin being more sociable with others, but may at times be rough, grabbing a toy or hitting another toddler. This is not malicious hitting, but simply means that they do not yet understand that the other baby has feelings. Infants and toddlers are first in the *solitary* play

[3] Refer to any good text in child development for information on Erikson's work or see Erik H. Erikson, *Childhood and Society* (New York: W. W. Norton, 1963).

Figure 3-4. By watching children closely you'll know when the strategic moment arrives for giving just a little help. (Early Childhood Laboratory, Kansas State University)

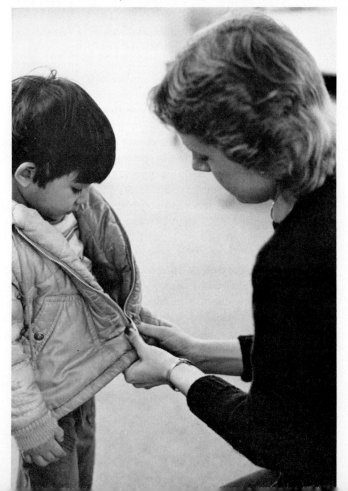

stage, being content to play alone, though you'll notice that they watch as action takes place around them. The second play stage is *parallel,* meaning that two toddlers play alongside of each other. Often they like toys that are alike and may model behavior for each other. In a couple of years they will enter the *cooperative* stage of play.

There are important milestones in language development throughout infancy and toddlerhood. The first communication is cooing and babbling that contains sounds that eventually become words. Long before they can talk, babies like to be talked to and will make inflections in their voice that sound like efforts to talk. During the 18- to 30-month period phrases and two- or three-word sentences will develop. The child can understand your language long before being able to repeat sentences. For example, if you say, "Where's your bottle?" the baby will probably go toward or at least look toward the bottle around nine months of age. You can be helpful by listening to and responding to the toddler's verbalizations, by giving the child a picture book and saying as you turn to a page with a picture of a pair of shoes, "Put your finger on baby's shoe," and continue to other objects pictured. You can consciously label objects for the child such as, "Milk. It's milk. Milk in a cup. Say cup." When the child says milk or cup you can smile and say "Yes, cup. Fine."

Everything is new for infants and toddlers. You'll enjoy your experience of working with them because you'll know that you are seeing fresh learning responses to new perceptions or discoveries every day. You'll learn more about infants and toddlers as the various chapters suggest learning activities to present to them.

*　　*　　*

Talk It Over: No. 1

Discuss experiences you've had playing with and caring for babies. State each baby's age and describe his or her characteristics.

*　　*　　*

Talk It Over: No. 2

Discuss experiences you've had with toddlers. State each toddler's age and describe his or her characteristics.

*　　*　　*

Late Two-Year-Olds and Young Threes

If you observe a group of late twos and young three-year-olds, you may find there is very little conversation. Most children's vocabularies are limited at this age. They get what they want by physical rather than verbal means. Children may be playing quite far apart, yet never seem to feel left out. Even if they are playing close together, each will be playing his or her own game. This is called *parallel play.* You will see little interaction between the children.

Physical skills interest twos and threes. They may seek compliments on how high they are on the slide or jungle gym. They may need encouragement, help, and reassurance the first few times they use a piece of equipment. Twos may prefer to push a kiddie car, but the tricycle usually attracts the threes. Twos look clumsy and precarious to many visitors, who worry that they will fall. However, they generally won't fall if they climb from their own motivation. If they are encouraged by another child or an adult to go beyond what they personally feel is a safe height, then the teacher should be nearby to avoid accidents.

For most twos and young threes, the school is the first group experience away from home. This age group should have a sufficient number of adults ready to provide individualized attention. The ability to play a nurturing role when necessary is a characteristic of a good teacher for this age group. Introduction to group living may be painful for some of the children. It may be difficult for the child's parents, too! Children enter prekindergarten with differing amounts of experience outside the home. One child may readily accept a teacher because of pleasant experiences with baby-sitters, relatives, or church or synagogue school teachers. If previous experience has been unpleasant, however, the teacher may be in for a difficult time. Many young children will have had virtually no experience away from home. When they arrive at school among strange adults and children, they are overcome with fear.

Teachers of twos and young threes must be on the alert for signs indicating a child's need to use the toilet. The child may fidget restlessly, or become unusually quiet, or hold a hand pressing the genitals. As soon as the signs are noticed, the teacher heads straight for the bathroom with the child in hand. Young children can't wait! The teacher talks in a quiet voice while leading the child to the bathroom. Although schools generally prefer to enroll children who are toilet trained, every teacher of two- and three-year-olds knows that bladder control is frequently not well established. The teacher is alert to prevent accidents. The teacher's guidance will vary from child to child as efforts are made to understand each one. Some may need a helping hand, others may need only a reminder. A mature child will go to the toilet when necessary without attention. Some may fear the noise of the flushing water. If this is true, do not require the child to flush the toilet until greater maturity overcomes this fear.

Lunch or snack with twos and young threes is a serious business. They eat well and talk little. Often they spill food and milk. Fingers are the popular eating tool.

Resting time should provide a closeness to the teacher or other adults. In groups that meet only a few hours, children may not be required to lie down to rest. However, in child care centers, where children stay a full day, nap time is essential. These youngsters may get exhausted because of the amount of stimulation they receive in the group and because most arrive at school quite early. Bedtime has many associations for children. They may be weepy because parents are not there. Many hands and much patience are required to get a happy, restful nap time under way.

Comparing the teaching in a group of young children with the teaching in an older group, you will note that the younger child gets more help, more demonstration, more reassurance, and more assistance while trying a new skill. The teacher uses words, gestures, and actions because the young child's verbal understandings are being developed. Action cues help the child to understand.

Late Threes and Fours

Three-and-a-half-, and four-year-olds have many characteristics in common. During their first days in school they may have anxiety periods, just as do the two-year-olds and young threes. Generally, anxiety periods will be of short duration because the child has had more occasions to leave home and enter into groups, knowing parents always return. Being more experienced, this child will be more curious about what the other children are doing and will move in the direction of the action. The parent who remains at school will probably find he or she is not needed.

Children of this age ask many questions. They ask some questions because they really want to know. They ask some simply because they want attention. Others they ask because they wish someone would ask them that question—they know the answer and enjoy a chance to show off. Verbally they have developed by leaps and bounds from the younger age discussed previously. They understand more vocabulary than they are able to use.

At this period there is a rapid increase in reasoning and concept building. They want to know about everything and to experiment with any material provided for them. Interest is maintained over a longer period of time than in younger children.

These children are more active. They run faster, climb more easily, and swing higher. Many can now pump the swing. They ride their tricycles fast, bumping into things and people, and even upsetting the tricycles deliberately.

Socially, late three- and four-year-olds play closer together, sometimes sharing toys. The more mature will make suggestions for the others. This is parallel play, showing the beginning of cooperative play. Increased verbal and motor abilities seem to be facilitating factors.

During the fourth year boys often choose activities traditionally thought of as masculine. For example, they select big blocks and cars. Girls often like the housekeeping area or other more "feminine" activi-

Figure 3-5. By observing children's motor coordination while building you'll learn to judge materials to select for them. (Kadena Preschool, Kadena Air Base, Okinawa, Japan)

ties. However, there is still a great deal of interaction between the sexes as they play in the learning areas. Imaginative themes develop in the group.

Teachers can help avoid sexist orientations by encouraging all children to participate in all activities. For example, with our newer understanding of the impact of socialization and sex role stereotyping, the teacher may not only permit but encourage girls to be more rambunctious, physical, and loud in their play and boys to be more loving, helping, and aesthetic. Societal gains from removing sex role, racial, and ethnic stereotypes can be substantial.

Four-year-olds vacillate between wanting to be big and enjoying being little. One day they can do something for themselves, the next day they would like you to do it for them—or at least give a little help.

The late threes and four-year-olds may be picky eaters. They may indicate their likes and dislikes strongly, thus asserting themselves. Their growth rate has slowed down and they require less food. Therefore, avoid pressuring children to eat.

Toileting is generally quite routine in these groups. A wise teacher is quick to note indications of a child's need and will remind him or her to go. Most four-year-olds prefer to take care of toileting without help.

At this age children usually think they're too old to rest. Rest time is therefore better received if it is called quiet time. However, three- or four-year-olds still need to slow down or they may become exhausted, hyperactive, or grouchy. In child care centers adjustments may have to be made for older children who aren't sleepy. Sometimes they can be given resting and reading privileges in a room away from the sleepers.

Three-year-olds are known for their negativism. Wording questions and requests to avoid that "No" seems to be the key to living harmoniously with threes. Fours, instead of saying "No," typically find other ways (dawdling or talking) to resist what adults want them to do. Almost all have difficulty waiting for their turn.

*   *   *

Talk It Over: No. 3

Discuss experiences you've had with three- and four-year-olds. State each child's age and describe his or her behavior.

*   *   *

Figure 3-6. Joining in a little horseplay helps you learn how much fun young children can be. (Child Development Laboratory, College of Human Development, Pennsylvania State University)

Fives and Young Sixes

The fives and young six-year-olds found in kindergartens are different from the groups we have been discussing. They are much easier to organize into a group because of their increased use and understanding of words. They seem more patient and can wait for their turn—though not indefinitely. They seem to have a genuine interest in pleasing their teachers, their mothers, and anyone else who shows interest in them.

In addition to increased verbal skills, fives and sixes are highly curious about everything they see or hear. They want to know. They like to experiment. They often wonder how something works and will take it apart in an effort to find out. They are highly creative if their previous experience has stimulated their imagination. They will be creative in every aspect of their learning if the atmosphere is conducive to experimentation.

Socially these children enjoy each other. Cooperation on intricate projects may last several days. Each group usually has a number of strong leaders with creative ideas for projects or dramatic play. Boys and girls often play together. However, girls tend to choose a "best friend"—often resulting in easily hurt feelings if the friend finds someone else. Boys are less inclined toward a single friend and usually enjoy activities that incorporate a large group of boys at a time. All activity is not cooperative, however. Because of a longer attention span, a child may work on a project alone while others do something else. This type of independent activity frequently occurs with the more socially secure children.

A charming characteristic of children of this age is their growing sense of humor. At the younger ages children are too literal to appreciate a joke. Now they enjoy jokes, riddles, and nonsense songs and poems. They like to rhyme words and may taunt their friends verbally.

Motor coordination is well developed. Kindergarteners enjoy learning new skills. Chinning, skating, and riding a two-wheel bike are challenges they appreciate. Small motor coordination is also developing, so that a crayon marks where the child wants it to mark. More complicated puzzles and building toys are enjoyed.

With so much growth in all areas of development, the teacher's role is to provide a wide variety of activities. Activities must be constantly new, different, and appealing. When a teacher knows that children have not learned something thoroughly, concepts must be presented in fresh ways; otherwise the group will show that they are bored. Because of the wider variety of interests, the teacher must plan to have many activities going on in a group at once. When kindergarteners have had previous prekindergarten experience or are from advantaged homes, an even wider variety of challenging activities is crucial. There is so much in this world to learn that it is a severe indictment of the teacher if a group of kindergarteners becomes bored.

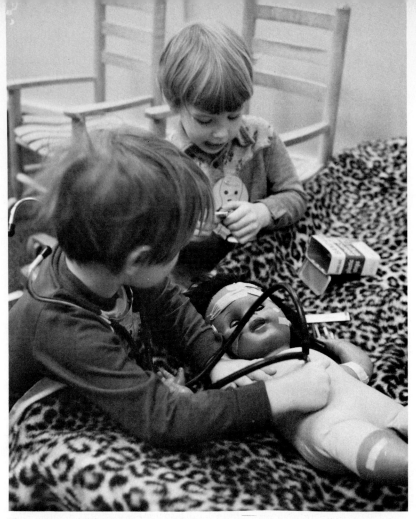

Figure 3-7. Children's imaginative play will give you insight into their knowledge and their concerns. (Southeast Oakland Vocational Technical Center)

Some typical behaviors and other characteristics of children found in early childhood programs have been described. Each child differs regarding these characteristics. When it is said that two-year-olds are typically negative, it means that most, but not necessarily all, two-year-olds are negative. The same is true of the other behaviors described. Normative data only indicate typical characteristics and therefore are not really an evaluation of behavior.

Any plan for learning must take into consideration the ages and stages of the children in the group. To master advanced skills, the child must first succeed in the more elementary ones. This fact is important in all areas of learning and must be taken into account as teachers provide experiences and set expectations for individual children. A three-year-old may advance along the developmental continuum and master some skills that are typical of five-year-olds. A five-year-old may have a slower rate of development and be like three-year-olds in some skills. Both new skills and new knowledge build on past knowledge and skill.

It is important for teachers to become knowledgeable about child growth and development, to learn to assess accurately a child's level of development, and to incorporate this knowledge into planning for children at school.

* * *

Talk It Over: No. 4

Discuss experiences you've had with five-year-olds. Describe their behavior.

* * *

Special Children

Children with special needs or handicapping conditions may be found in early childhood classrooms under a program called *mainstreaming*. States differ as to the age when state funds may be used to help pay for

Figure 3-8. A proud smile lets you know when a child's self-esteem is high. (Early Childhood Laboratory, Kansas State University)

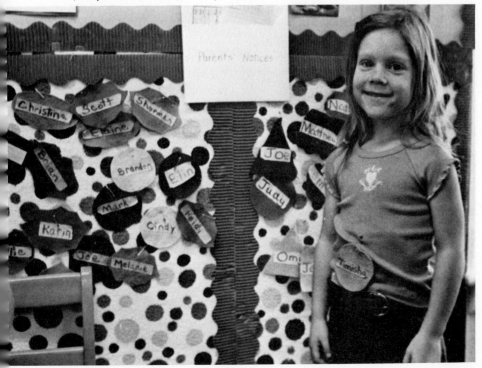

a handicapped child's care and education. Some funds may be available for consultants to help plan and carry out programs for children with special needs. Head Start has pioneered integration of special children in its groups.

Your child development knowledge will serve you well as you learn to plan for young handicapped children. It is important to remember that they are children and that most have a majority of characteristics that are normal and similar to those of other children. Due to their handicapping condition they may go through the normal stages at a slower pace. Thus techniques for working with chronologically younger children may be called for.

Teachers must apply the Developmental Tasks discussed in Chapter 2 to handicapped children's needs and help progress take place little by little—cheering the child and parents as new stages are reached. With a developmental approach one is likely to pace the child properly—knowing that there will be a developmental range in any classroom. Many of the activities suggested for the typical early childhood curriculum will be appropriate at some level for the handicapped child.

Teachers must be willing to read books and articles and attend workshops addressing specific handicaps. For example, learning to do sign language for the deaf is required, while learning to keep the environment clear of hazards is essential for blind children. Teachers should feel free to ask a lot of questions. Consultants should be available at some level to consult with parents and teachers; and both should take full advantage of consultants' expertise.

Students who participate in programs with special children should ask for specific suggestions for dealing with the special child. Sometimes students feel they are the only inexperienced person, when in reality most of the staff may be exploring and learning with the new challenge.

Each child has strengths from which he or she will work to compensate or deal with the handicapping condition. Identifying those strengths may be a first task. For example, a child may enjoy being in the presence of others, or have a sunny disposition that makes others like him or her, or have strong persistence for completing a task. These are strengths that can contribute to overcoming or adjusting to the handicap.

Working with parents is particularly essential with special children. Parents learn techniques for handling the child that can help the school. Parents also can learn from the teachers who may discover a new approach for helping their child. Thus, close communication is essential.

There is a growing demand for early childhood professionals who have had experience and training with special children, thus your initiation to them through your participation could help you decide whether you might like to become specialized in educating handicapped children.

Age for Entering School

Ideally children should enter prekindergarten or kindergarten when their level of development indicates readiness for the expanded environment. However, in practice the teacher may be required to cope with children who are not really ready for school. For example, child care centers sometimes receive children who are not ready for school because their parents must work and they have no other place to send them. Head Start schools enroll children at a young age to begin the compensatory efforts that are needed. Even in the more exclusive schools, children may be sent to school before they are ready because their name is next on a waiting list and the parents know they may have a long wait if they relinquish the place. Public kindergartens set arbitrary chronological age limits without regard for a child's level of development. When situations of this sort occur, the teacher's skill in blending nurturing with teaching may be challenged.

Research points out the immature child's lack of success in school. Immature boys especially have difficulty competing against girls and older boys.[4] When a child will be among the youngest in the class, school officials may urge parents to seek an evaluation of school readiness. Ability to cope with a class of older children and to participate in regular school activities must be considered. Boys appear to be less academically oriented than girls and may have more difficulty than girls with small muscle coordination of the sort required for handwriting.[5] Parents of an immature boy who want to help their boy's first school experiences to be successful may be encouraged to keep him in prekindergarten or kindergarten until he is a year older than most children in his class. These children simply need time to mature and one year may make the difference between school success and difficulty. School counselors support this move. They find their biggest caseload among immature, often hyperactive boys who are not ready for the sitting still that many first grades require.[6] When this type of counseling is taking place in a community, the early childhood education programs may enroll a number of children somewhat older than the typical ages described.

Catherine Landreth summarizes research findings as follows: "In clinics for children with speech and reading problems, there are many more boys than girls. Why? This sex difference could be due to differences in the frequencies with which boys and girls inherit characteristics that lead to speech and reading problems. It could also be due to differ-

[4] Katrina De Hirsch, "Potential Educational Risks," *Childhood Education,* **41:4** (December 1964), pp. 178–183.

[5] See Elizabeth Hurlock, *Child Development* (New York: McGraw-Hill, 1972), p. 141, for a discussion regarding development of handwriting skills.

[6] Katrina De Hirsch, "Potential Educational Risks," *Childhood Education,* **41:4** (December 1964), p. 180.

ences in their rate of development. It may well be that many boys are not ready for the kinds of learning tasks that most girls are ready for at ages 5 and 6."[7]

Grouping Children

Schools vary in their policy of grouping children. A single group may range from ages two to six. In other schools separate homogeneous age groups of threes, fours, and fives exist. Licensing standards are one determinant. Flexible grouping is followed in some programs. For example, a physically skillful late three-year-old may be allowed some time with the four-year-old group. The teacher may even transfer the child if all areas of development justify it.

A case can be made for nearly any age combination. Some teachers like to have older children with the younger. They reason that older children learn to help out the younger ones. In a classroom with a wide

[7] Catherine Landreth, *Preschool Learning and Teaching* (New York: Harper & Row, 1972), p. 3.

Figure 3-9. A student gains more understanding of a child by giving him or her undivided attention. (Early Child Development Center, University of Vermont)

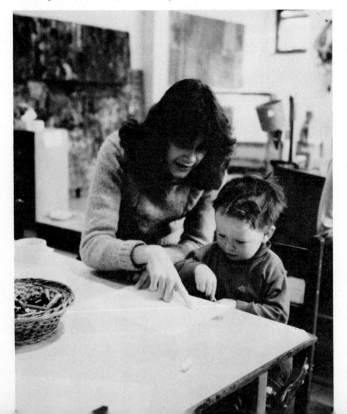

age range an immature older child can find a playmate with similar skills. In a single-age classroom this child may feel inferior. The multiage grouping is more familylike, too, they say.

Some teachers object to a wide-age-range classroom because the wide differences make it difficult to plan activities with sufficient challenge for the most mature children. Frequently a teacher has little to say about the ages of the children in the group. Enrollment lists are often simply handed to the teacher. A public school usually enrolls any child who registers. Sometimes children are recruited with little regard for age. But even if the children were all the same age, teachers would find wide variations in development. With a mixture of ages the range of differences is still greater. Teachers must plan a variety of activities for self-selection— some to challenge the most skillful child and others to encourage the least skillful.

Size of Group

Fewer than eighteen children per group is best from the viewpoint of both the children and the teachers, according to studies. A small group permits the teachers to know the children and the parents better. Children, too, get better acquainted with their teachers and each other if the group is small. Also, it is easier to avoid overstimulation and fatigue. Every group should have a minimum of two adults in order to cope with emergencies. A ratio of one adult per five children is suggested, especially in groups of disadvantaged children, where individualized teaching is of special importance. Research indicates that the larger the group, the more authoritarian the leadership becomes in order to maintain control.

*   *   *

Talk It Over: No. 5

Considering the characteristics of each age child, discuss how being the teacher differs from age group to age group.

*   *   *

Knowing Children as Individuals

Classroom Observation

Teachers begin accumulating information about the children from the first moment they know which children will be in their group. Because each child is unique, understanding each one is a difficult task. The teacher makes a systematic effort to learn about each child by carrying a note-

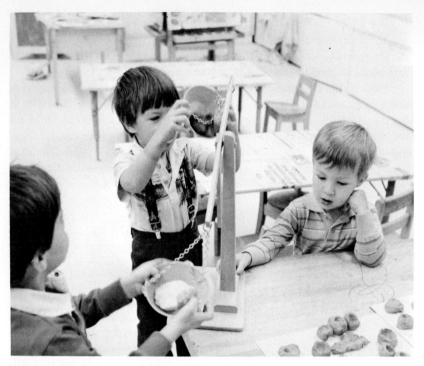

Figure 3-10. Cooperation while weighing the clay is possible when language skills are well developed. (Manzanita Day Care Center, University of New Mexico)

book in which information is recorded. Periodically a progress report is made for each child. An observer may be assigned to take diary records of each child's activity and manner of response. Combining observations and information from various sources, the teacher plans a program to fulfill each child's needs. Students will benefit from the teacher's careful study as they are provided with background information for understanding more about the children. Refer to Chapter 1 for information on being a good observer.

Home Visits

Besides working with the children at school, most teachers make periodic visits to the home in order to get better acquainted with the child and the family. A student may be invited to accompany the teacher on a home visit. Students, and even some teachers, are often hesitant about making home visits. However, once they have made a few visits they realize their value in developing understanding, appreciation, and rapport.

The home visits made prior to the opening of school can be one of the teacher's most important activities of the entire year. Arranging introductions on the family's home premises gives the family a chance to feel more at ease. The focus is on the family and their concerns. If the introduction occurs at school, the focus becomes almost entirely school centered. The goal for the first visit is to learn from the parents about their child and the home environment.

The teacher makes an efficient visiting schedule by grouping children according to their neighborhoods and making telephone calls to arrange a convenient time for a short visit. If the visits are scheduled every half hour, there is a little time to allow for getting mixed up on directions or waiting while the baby's diaper is changed. The home visit can be presented as a routine event and as an opportunity for the child to get to know the teacher before entering school. Cooperation is usually excellent.

For an icebreaker a teacher can show the child a packet of snapshots of former classes of children busily at work at school. Pictures always interest children and help them get over some of their shyness. A toy or a book can substitute for pictures. As the child looks at the pictures or plays with the toy, the parents and the teacher can talk over a few details.

The teacher can provide the parents a school policy statement for later reading, a list of children's names and addresses, a field trip permission blank, health forms, a brief informational questionnaire, and forms for any research data needed. The teacher explains when the forms are to be returned and why they are needed and assures parents that personal documents are confidential.

The teacher discusses with parents their role on the first day of school and seeks their estimate of how much support they feel the child will need. Because the first days are so crucial to the child's attitude toward school, it seems worthwhile to ask the parents to stay with the child if necessary. It is rarely necessary for a five-year-old, especially if the home visit has been thoughtfully done. With younger children it may or may not be necessary for the parent to stay. Sometimes the teacher's role is one of helping the parent permit the child to become independent. Sometimes the parent may be more concerned than the child about the new experience.

One of the values of a short visit early in the year is that, as yet, there are no problems to discuss. The parent or child can't worry that a teacher comes with bad tidings. The parent may welcome the chance to forewarn the teacher of a possible problem area and will be grateful for the opportunity to discuss it. Parents, teacher, and child can visit without feeling that others are waiting for their turn or that others are listening—as they might be at the school or at a parents' meeting. Young children are reassured when they later say to their teacher, "You know where I live." They feel real security in this knowledge and believe that in any emergency the teacher could find their house—and he or she sometimes may have to!

Home visits often give information about family activities, interests, or hobbies. This information may also provide ideas for involving a family in class activities. For example, if Johnny brings out his daddy's banjo, the teacher can remember to ask Mr. Smith to play his banjo at school when the class is studying vibrations or stringed instruments. Questions such as "What did you do this summer?" can help a teacher include the child in future class discussions. For example, a teacher learned that shy Ronnie had flown by jet to visit his grandmother. Ronnie then became the class's jet expert when flying was mentioned.

A classroom storybook featuring the children themselves can begin to take shape during home visits. The teacher carries a camera and uses this opportunity to photograph each child. Looking for siblings, pets, or toys to include in the photo brings about informal visiting that adds further to the rapport among all present. See the chapter on literature for more discussion about this storybook. The pictures may also be placed on lockers to help children identify their personal space.

On parting from the home visit the teacher can tell the parents, "Please call me at school or at home any time a question comes up that concerns the school and your child. We want to work together to make a good year for Johnny." Usually they quickly respond with the counterpart of that statement, "You call us too if anything comes up or if we can help." If they do not so respond, the teacher can add, "And I'll want to feel free to call you if I have any questions." In addition, parents are extended an open invitation to visit during the school year at any time, for a minute or all day.

Parents may have some anxiety concerning their lack of nice furnishings, but a wise teacher does not concentrate on these things or appear to notice. The goal is to build a relationship with people with whom one expects to work at least a year. The human element interests the teacher more than the quality of sofas. After this informative get-acquainted visit, they'll know each other the next time they meet.

Throughout the year the teacher can realize tremendous value from this brief home visit. In the first place, the child's name and face can more easily be remembered after having had some time to talk to the child individually. Calling Sara by name, perhaps asking about a pet or a baby sister, can make her feel more at home those first days at school. Following this procedure, teachers find fewer children who cry on opening day. In addition, during the visit the teacher gains some feeling about the psychological climate of the child's environment. For example, one may sense quite accurately the competition between siblings or the laissez-faire attitudes of parents through first-hand observation. Home visits are as unique as families. Teachers should relax, enjoy these new friends, and not feel any compulsion to teach but only to learn.

When home visits are not feasible before school begins, they should be planned as quickly as possible after the opening of school. On visits later in the year, parents will expect the teacher to tell them about their child. Visits or conferences that are held when there are problems that must be discussed are far more difficult than the initial meeting. They, too, require thoughtful preparation. However, when initial meetings have built a feeling of confidence and respect between teacher and parent, then the relationship can withstand a discussion about a child's problem.

Teachers should write notes on all visits and conferences. These can be written after the session and filed for future reference. Further discussion of the school's partnership with parents in extending the classroom goals to the home follows in the chapter on teacher-parent relations.

Family Visits to the School

During the home visit a time can be agreed upon for the family to see the school facilities. These family visits to the school afford university students who may be assigned to that laboratory an excellent opportunity to get acquainted with children.

As a result of the home visit, the teacher and family now greet each other as old friends. Student helpers can be available to help quietly as the child looks around. The child usually explores quickly, finding the locker with his or her name on it, the bathroom, the various learning centers, and the playground. Sometimes the child meets new classmates because several families (including siblings) may drop in for their visits at the same time. If a child had any worries, they are usually allayed by now. The child is ready for school to begin.

Teacher's Files

Teachers will keep files for each child containing various types of information. Since dealing with a family results in a highly personal relationship, professional standards and adherence to ethical procedure require that personal information revealed by parents be kept strictly confidential. For this reason, teachers are not at liberty to open all files to the students or to tell them all they know about a child's family. Some teachers keep two separate files: one containing objective data, to which the students have access; the other containing more subjective notes and evaluations that are not open to the students.

Students also may have occasion to obtain very personal information about a family. They too must treat the information as confidential. It is sound policy for a school to ask students to discuss the child only with the child's teacher or in the theory class that accompanies the course. Using anecdotal material for dormitory conversation is a sure way to embarrass the student, the teacher, and the parents. In a social situation, information becomes gossip. Parents can quickly lose confidence in the school if they feel their personal lives are not being protected. Imagine the teacher's chagrin when a mother reported that her husband had learned from one of his students that their son was "the holy terror of the nursery school." Even if the story were true, the teacher should be the one to bring the child's conduct to the parents' attention and to discuss the problem in the light of possible remedies.

Health forms, questionnaires, and tests are objective data that may be open to students. When teachers provide parents with health forms they are asking for information, examinations, and immunizations that meet the local and state health codes. For the school to secure all the needed information and examinations, parents may need some help on what is required, where it can be obtained, and what it costs. The teacher may give the parents exact information on days and hours that clinics are open, or names and addresses of physicians who give the examinations. Occasionally arrangements are made for a physician to administer examinations at the school.

Questionnaires should be short and ask only for necessary information. They should be tried out on a few parents before they are used for everyone: a trial run will indicate unclear questions and unnecessary duplications. If research questionnaires are to be used, it is best to include these in the original package to avoid the constant request for information. If questionnaires become a nuisance to parents, they will fill them out haphazardly. Further, a single request facilitates the teacher's checking and filing of questionnaires. Parents should be reassured that personal data will be kept strictly confidential.

Conclusion

Getting to know children is a continuing process. Real understanding requires a depth of perception that comes with training and experience and, of course, may never really be completely achieved. Information regarding children can be obtained from research, from parents, and from previous experience with children. Each child has characteristics that are similar to those of other children of that age. Each child also has unique characteristics. The similarities enable the teacher to work with children in a group. A range of interests and abilities will exist in every age group. The teacher and the student of early childhood education are challenged to learn to gauge the level of a child's development and to plan a program that meets the needs of individual children.

Continuing to grow in your own understanding of human development and behavior and helping all adults involved in your program—parents, aides, principals, or volunteers—also to understand development and behavior will be essential tasks for you as a professional teacher. Think about the educational processes that are effective for this learning. Learning about human development is essential and should be ongoing and dynamic for all concerned.

Applications

1. Do the "Talk It Over" activities suggested in the chapter.
2. During your time in an early childhood education school follow Lesson 3 in *A Laboratory Workbook for Introduction to Early Childhood Education.*
3. Make a chart for identifying characteristics of each child. List the 10 developmental tasks (see Chapter 2) down one side of a page. Across the top make column headings with each age. Fill in characteristic behavior for each task under each age group.
4. Watch a film showing young children of different ages. Make notes on the characteristic behavior of each age child.
5. Test your ability to observe a child, analyze his or her characteristics, make a guess as to the child's age, and check the correctness of your estimate. (This activity could take place in a supermarket or through use of a film.)
6. Add notes to your Resource File on children's characteristics.

Study Questions

1. Describe typical behaviors of each age child from infancy through kindergarten.
2. Explain a. What Dr. T. Berry Brazelton calls *synchrony.*
   b. What Dr. Erik H. Erikson calls *sense of trust* and *sense of autonomy.*
   c. Solitary and parallel play.
   d. Why these concepts are relevant to early childhood teachers.
3. Explain factors affecting a decision on group size and age range within a group in an early childhood center.

Films

In the Beginning: The Process of Infant Development   Color   15 minutes   1980

> Shows the important first two years of life. Dr. Bettye Caldwell traces the stages of development and accents the important role caregivers play in this process. Davidson Films, Inc., 850 O'Neill Avenue, Belmont, Calif. 94002.

A Young Child Is . . .   Color   28 minutes   1973

> A film about seven young children and their families and the interaction between each child and his family. Ages range from eight months to five years with special emphasis on the two- to four-year period. Lawren Productions, Inc., P.O. Box 666, Mendocino, Calif. 95460.

Jenny Is a Good Thing   Color   20 minutes   1969

> A film about Head Start children. The focus is on food and nutrition. Shows warm feeling among staff and children. Available in Spanish and English. Modern Talking Pictures Services, 5000 Park St. N., St. Petersburg, Fla. 33709. Free from any Head Start Office.

Additional Readings

AMBRON, SUEANN R., and NEIL J. SALKIND. *Child Development.* New York: Holt, Rinehart and Winston, 1984.

COHEN, DOROTHY, and VIRGINIA STERN. *Observing and Recording the Behavior of Young Children.* New York: Teachers College Press, Columbia University, 1978.

DUVALL, EVELYN. *Marriage and Family Development.* New York: Harper & Row, 1977.

GESELL, ARNOLD, and FRANCES L. ILG. *Child Development.* New York: Harper & Row, 1949.

HAVIGHURST, ROBERT J. *Developmental Tasks and Education.* New York: David McKay Company, Inc., 1952.

HYMES, JAMES L., JR. *Teaching the Child Under Six.* Columbus, Ohio: Charles E. Merrill Publishing Co., 1981.

JANIS, MARJORIE G. *A Two-Year-Old Goes to Nursery School.* Washington, D.C.: National Association for the Education of Young Children, 1965.

LANDRETH, CATHERINE. *Early Childhood: Behavior and Learning.* New York: Alfred A. Knopf, Inc., 1967.

LANDRETH, CATHERINE. *Preschool Learning and Teaching.* New York: Harper & Row, 1972.

LEFEBVRE, SUE. "Valuing a Curious Child," *Childhood Education,* Vol. 51, No. 5, March 1975, pp. 257–260.

MAIER, HENRY W. *Three Theories of Child Development.* New York: Harper & Row, 1978.

SCHIAMBERG, LAWRENCE B., *Human Development.* New York: Macmillan Publishing Co., Inc., 1985.

SMART, RUSSELL and MOLLIE SMART. *Children: Development and Relationships.* New York: Macmillan Publishing Co., Inc. 1982.

Setting the Stage

- *To define planning and organizing in an early childhood education program.*
- *To identify factors teachers consider in arranging the physical environment of the early childhood classroom and playyard.*
- *To identify factors teachers consider in arranging the schedule of events in the early childhood program.*
- *To identify steps teachers take to prepare for the first days of school.*

"How did you get your group started?" "Was it hard to work with all new children at the beginning of school?" Such questions are often asked by students who watch a smoothly functioning early childhood group during the latter part of a school year. These students are experienced enough to realize that the smooth operation does not happen by accident.

Some early childhood education students have the opportunity to help the teacher make the necessary preparations for the beginning of school. They see exactly what is required for starting a new group.

Planning and Organizing

Setting the stage for a high-quality program for young children requires teachers to perform two activities well. These activities are planning and organizing. *Planning means setting objectives and prearranging the details of the early childhood education program in order to achieve the objectives for individuals and the group.* Planning requires

Figure 4-1. A learning center with a tape recorder and earphones allows children to listen to a story on their own. (Children's Center, University of South Carolina)

time for studious, thoughtful, quiet work. Plans are daily, weekly, and yearly. They focus on individual children and their parents, on the group as a whole, on standards and goals, and on the interests and talents of the teachers. Most plans are written out in detail and are evaluated daily as feedback is received from the children and parents.

* * *

Talk It Over: No. 1

Give examples of how you *plan* your personal routines in order to reach objectives.

* * *

Organizing means putting in readiness the facility, equipment, materials, strategies, and procedures for coherent and cooperative action with the goal of producing a high-quality early childhood program. Organizing requires "getting busy" after the quiet planning sessions. Organizing requires time, energy, and creativity of the staff.

* * *

Talk It Over: No. 2

Give examples of how you *organize* your personal living space, materials, and procedures to reach your objectives.

* * *

Both planning and organizing require that teachers have knowledge of goals for young children (Chapter 2), a philosophical base for the curriculum choices (Chapter 2), knowledge of the particular age being taught (Chapter 3), and information about individual children and their families (Chapter 3). Teachers' experience and ability to evaluate previous planning and organizing, that is, learning from the past, lead to better performance in the future.

The objective of the present chapter is to highlight planning and organizing in order that you will begin to appreciate the time the teacher gives to these responsibilities. By observing closely, questioning the teacher, and assisting wherever you can, you, as a future teacher, can begin to learn to plan and organize. Be particularly observant when the teacher's original plans aren't working out and alterations or substitutions are needed. Often these are the occasions when the teacher's experience shines through.

* * *

Talk It Over: No. 3

Give examples of how planning and organizing reduce stress on children, teachers, and parents. Show how planning and organizing facilitate reaching objectives.

* * *

You can give feedback to the staff that will help in future planning. For example, one student reported that when managing the finger-painting table there had been too many children for each child to work comfortably. The next time they planned finger painting, the staff planned another interesting activity that attracted some children. Thus congestion was reduced. Also the space was arranged with one less chair which suggested the number of children who could use that learning center comfortably. Teachers appreciate such feedback from student helpers.

This chapter is designed to help you begin to appreciate the extent of the teacher's planning and organizing. In Chapter 6 you will be given specific help for planning specific activities, and each subsequent chapter will give you details regarding each type of activity. Finally in Chapter 17 you will be ready to integrate all you've learned into planning a total program. If you have questions along the way, feel free to turn to Chapters 6 or 17 for help in planning and organizing a program. In addition, for a discussion of the manager's role in planning and organizing on a centerwide basis, you may wish to refer to this author's book, *Management of Child Development Centers*, published by the Macmillan Publishing Company in 1984.

Planning for the Opening of School

The week before the children arrive, the teacher should (1) arrange the facility where school is held, (2) plan the daily schedule, and (3) choose the learning experiences for the children. Arranging the facility and or-

Figure 4-2. A learning center with housekeeping equipment allows children to play familiar roles. (Dodge City (Kansas) Community College Child Care Center)

ganizing a workable schedule are covered in this chapter. Learning experiences are referred to only briefly in this chapter but are discussed in detail in Part Two.

Planning the Arrangement of the Facility[1]

Equipping and arranging the schoolroom and yard are similar to furnishing and arranging a house or an apartment. The teacher takes inventory of the functions that must be performed and plans for the most efficient use of the space available. Everyone knows that it is exciting to plan new space before it is built. Using old space may be a greater challenge. More creativity is often required on the part of those planning to operate in old space designed for other purposes.

[1] For a comprehensive analysis of play spaces, floor plans, and recommendations, see Sybil Kritchevsky, Elizabeth Prescott, and Lee Walling, *Planning Environments for Young Children: Physical Space.* (Washington, D.C.: National Association for the Education of Young Children, 1977). Also, for detailed drawings of several children's centers throughout the country, see Fred Lynn Osmon, *Patterns for Designing Children's Centers,* 1971, and Paul Abramson, *Schools for Early Childhood,* 1970, both available from Educational Facilities Laboratories, 477 Madison Avenue, New York, N.Y. 10022.

Careful planning of room arrangement, storage spaces, and equipment can facilitate the teacher's handling of the children. There are many functions the children can perform for themselves. They can help with others if the facilities are carefully arranged. Children learn favorable attitudes toward helping, care of equipment, and cooperation when they are expected to help and are taught to help. For example, older children can wash the easel and the paintbrushes if the cleanup sink is at their height and sponges are provided. When children put away their own toys, the teacher's time and energy can be used for other educational purposes.

A large rectangular playroom containing about 50 square feet per child is usually satisfactory. More space is desirable in colder climates, where longer periods of the day are spent indoors. Where weather permits extensive use of outdoor space, less indoor space might suffice. Space should be allowed for the number of adults in the program. One large room is superior to several small ones in terms of supervising and teaching.

The room is divided into learning centers or zones. *Learning centers are areas of the larger playroom or yard which are partially enclosed, perhaps by low storage shelves, and contain the needed materials and equipment for a certain type of learning activity.* There are centers for (1) art activities, (2) science activities, (3) literature-language activities, (4) music activities, (5) dramatic play, (6) blockbuilding activities, (7) manipulative toys and games, and (8) carpentry or sand activities when space permits. Also, provision must be made for eating, toileting, resting, and storing a child's belongings. Shelves and other storage facilities can serve as dividers between learning centers at the same time that they hold the equipment and materials needed in those centers. Care should be taken to keep the storage facilities low so that the teacher can observe the action in each center. Also, low shelves encourage children to get out and put away materials and thus develop independence. In some climates it is necessary to have a large muscle activity center indoors.

The rooms should have a light, airy, warm look and be friendly and inviting. An artistic use of color—such as subdued walls, with color supplied by equipment and children's art products—is aesthetically pleasing and gives a feeling of happiness without being overstimulating. Soft light and enough electrical outlets with safety features are important. There are many new materials with washable, durable finishes that are useful for decorating and equipping rooms housing young children.

Every effort should be made to reduce the noise level in the rooms by the use of draperies, carpeting, acoustical tile, and other soundproofing. Carpeting is particularly desirable in block, dress-up, and story areas. Flooring that can be readily mopped should be provided for painting, eating, and water-play areas until carpeting proves itself and janitorial services are equipped to cope with carpet cleaning. One corner can be

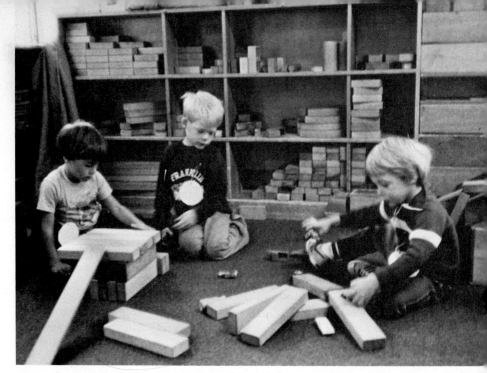

Figure 4-3. An out-of-the-way corner for blocks helps prevent precious buildings from being disturbed. (Child Development Laboratory, Michigan State University)

Figure 4-4. A locker for each child's belongings helps each learn valuable self-help skills. The name and Polaroid photo help the child identify the correct locker. (Child Development Laboratory, Michigan State University)

used for quiet activities, and the opposite corner for active and noisy events.

Traffic Patterns

The teacher visualizes how the children will move thorough the room. Where do they enter and leave the school? Where will they store their wraps? Where do they go to get to the bathroom? Which entrance will they use going to and coming from the outdoors? Where will the snack be served? Where will the children rest? The best arrangement will require a minimum amount of reminding children what to do next. The teacher will study traffic patterns and organize the room to minimize the children's getting in each other's way.

Locker Spaces

Locker spaces should be close to the door where parents will enter and call for their child. If lockers are in out-of-the-way places, reminders will be required to get coats into the lockers. This little space, sometimes just a modest hook, becomes a child's place to call his or her own. Parents, teachers, and child will know where to look for belongings. It is convenient if a cubicle or locker is included where the child's treasures can be placed. Names clearly printed in capital and small letters should be placed above the locker. A symbol or picture is used by some teachers to help children identify their lockers. However, most will quickly learn to locate the locker by its position in the room—or by the name above it.

Bathroom

The toilet often requires rapid entry and should be readily accessible. Toilets and sinks should be at the children's height. A minimum of two toilets and two lavatories for each group of children is recommended. Both sexes use toilets in the same room. Doors are not needed on toilets for children up to five years old. The absence of doors facilitates supervision. Five-year-olds usually are beginning to appreciate privacy, so shutter-type doors that spring closed can be installed. Even for five-year-olds there is no need for separate bathrooms for boys and girls.

Low Sinks

Bathroom lavatories should be about 22 inches high. Faucets that work by the pressing of a lever with the knee or by a foot lever will eliminate running water in an empty bathroom. A low sink in the creative arts center is convenient; here paints can be mixed, paper and sponges moistened, and children and supplies washed without the art cleanup interfering with the bathroom routine. A low drinking fountain both indoors and out permits children to help themselves to a drink—a frequently neglected need.

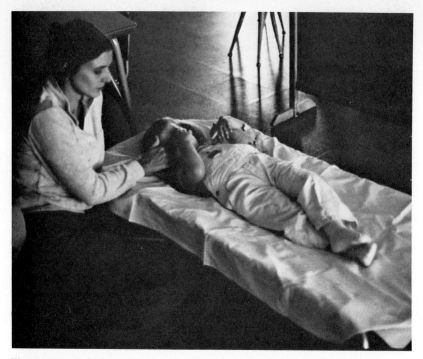

Figure 4-5. A darkened quiet place helps achieve the purposes of naptime. (Child Development Laboratory, University of Illinois)

Resting Space

A quiet time of songs and stories will rest children; hence a space should be designated for quiet-time activity. Ideally this space should be located away from distracting toys. Short rest periods can take place without formal stretching out. If the room is carpeted, the children may stretch out without being told. Where there is no carpeting, a few throw rugs or carpet squares will cushion the lying down or sitting. It should be noted that severe efforts to get everyone lying down often yield negative results and negative attitudes toward sleep.

In full-day groups, where napping is essential, cots with sheets and blankets will be required. Sufficient storage space and space to place the cots will be necessary. When you are putting a number of children together for sleeping, it is urgent that the utmost care be taken that fire exits are accessible.

Eating Space

Snack or lunch is more conveniently served near the kitchen area. Serving carts or trays can be used if food must be carried some distance. Lists of required utensils should be attached to the cart to prevent the forgetting of needed items. Sanitary and aesthetic aspects must be kept in mind. Small tables and chairs are required for serving lunch. Some teachers prefer that all children sit down at the same time for midmorning and midafternoon snack. Others serve snacks in a come-and-go fashion, as the children sit on the floor or the grass, and fewer chairs and tables are needed.

Space for Learning Centers and Storage

Each learning center should have open storage space available for the materials and equipment that the children will use in the center. Closed storage space is best for materials and equipment that are seasonal or that are brought into the room only occasionally. Thought should be given to where the children will use a toy. Toys should be stored close to where they will be used. For example, puzzles are best used on tables, so the storage should be near the tables. Blocks require open building space and should be stored and used in an out-of-the-way area so that other children who are merely passing by will not interfere with block building. Toys, such as cars, that are used with blocks should be on open shelves near the blocks.

The housekeeping corner and dress-up clothes suggesting dramatic play should have sufficient storage space so that the children can constructively select materials for their dramatic games. If possible, the teacher should keep all materials available so that the children can readily get them. When space is limited, the children should know what materials are available and feel free to ask for them to supplement any idea they may have. If props are stored close by, the teacher too will be able to add them quickly to support dramatic play that is developing.

A literature-language arts area should be located in a quiet nook with a low table and with books on an open shelf so that children can use them freely as they are interested. The teacher will also use this learning center for planned language experiences for small groups of children. A collection of science books should be kept as a permanent resource so that the children, assistants, and teachers can develop the habit of looking things up whenever an occasion arises.

A music area can consist of a simple record player for children to operate and a few suitable records in a rack. If it is located adjacent to open space, the children may respond with a dance or organize a band from instruments stored nearby.

The creative arts center needs natural lighting, a close water supply, and materials for artistic endeavors. The following should be easily accessible to the children: drawing paper, crayons, glue, scissors, stapler, string, masking tape, and paper punch. These supplies will be incorporated into many kinds of play if available on a low, open shelf. Art materials that the teachers feel need closer supervision can be stored near the art area sink.

A science center is best located near a window because sunlight is helpful in many experiments. A small table or shelf will encourage chil-

Figure 4-6. Storage bins for small toys help make them accessible yet orderly. (University of Puerto Rico Child Development Laboratory)

dren to display their specimens for others to see and handle. Room should be available to seat several children so that planned discussions can take place in this area.

Arranging learning centers and areas for quiet activity is as important outdoors as indoors. Water available for drinking, for wetting sand, and for mixing and cleaning up paints increases the ease with which the yard functions for the total program. Proper storage is essential for outdoor equipment. Children can be taught proper care of the equipment if storage is designed so that they can easily remove and return equipment.

Planning the Daily Schedule or Sequence of Events

Choosing a schedule is another requirement before the first day of school begins. A schedule becomes the structure within which the teacher and the children work. To an outsider it may appear as if there is no structure at all—the children seem to be doing just what they want to do. Yet it *is* in fact a framework or structure, with flexibility and room for individuality. When you have planned a sequence of events, the children will soon learn to guide themselves. If you implement the plan in a flexible manner, interpreting the needs of individuals in your group, the activity will move with ease. There will be a maximum of learning, a minimum of teacher direction, and a minimum of child tension. The following is an example of a child whose behavior was entirely self-directed because of awareness of the planned sequence of events: Mike noticed the children entering the kindergarten room as he slid down the slide. Finishing the ride, he ran to the door, which was being held open by the teacher. Mike smiled at the teacher, entered, and ran up the stairs. After putting his hat and coat in his locker, Mike went directly to the bathroom. Here he urinated, flushed the toilet, and washed his hands. He went to the snack table and found the place marked with his place card and sat down. He visited with his friends as they too found their places and sat down for a snack.

This short episode occurred without the teacher telling Mike any of the steps he was to take. The routine was the same every day, and Mike was happy knowing and doing what was expected of him. The routine seemed to fit his needs because there was no looking back at the slide or detouring to other areas as he progressed through the routine.

Figure 4-7. A technique for assigning cleanup and snack time duties helps children learn to do their share. (Child Development Laboratory, Michigan State University)

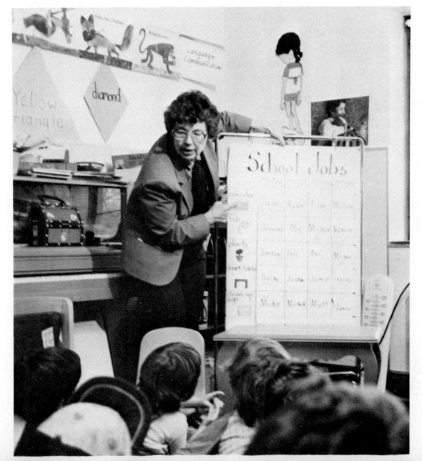

The teacher had planned carefully in the beginning to develop the sequence that fitted the children's needs. The children were reminded of that sequence for a few days. Most learned quickly. Some children reminded those who forgot, until eventually all the children mastered the routine without reminders.

If the routine had not fitted the group, the teacher might have observed resistance, such as children taking one more slide or otherwise not being ready to go indoors. If lockers had been in an out-of-the-way place, Mike might have dropped his coat on a chair and needed a reminder to put it in the locker.

The teacher plans the schedule or the sequence of events by designating big blocks of time that will constitute the framework for fitting in the learning opportunities, which will be discussed in detail in Part Two. The half-day program typically has three large blocks of time; the full-day center, six. See Figures 4-8 and 4-9.

Figure 4-8. Sample of a Daily Schedule.

Daily Schedule

A.M.	P.M.	
9:00–10:00	1:00–2:00	Self-selected activity indoors.
10:00	2:00	Cleanup time (can vary a few minutes either way). As the children finish helping with cleanup, go to the toilet if necessary, and wash their hands.
10:15–10:25	2:15–2:25	Snack. With older children, sharing time* goes on at the same time as snack.
10:25–10:45	2:25–2:45	The children move to a story group or groups. They sit on the floor. They select a book for "reading" as they pass the shelf. They look at the book or just talk quietly. The teacher finishes the period with some songs, a special story, planning, or discussion.
10:45–11:30	2:45–3:30	Outdoor self-selected activity.
11:30–11:40	3:30–3:40	Cleanup time. Preparation to go home.
11:45	3:45	Dismissal.

*Sharing time—A period when children are called on to share some article or news they have brought from home. Discussed in detail in the chapter on language arts.

Time Block Plan*

Time Block I	Self-Selected Activity (Indoors)	
	Art	Music
	Science	Dramatic play
	Table games	Small, wheeled objects
	Blocks	Language arts
	Books	

Time Block II	Teacher-Instigated Activity
	Cleanup
	Toileting, washing hands
	Snack
	Quiet time:
	looking at books
	music
	storytime and discussions

Time Block III	Self-Selected Activity (Outdoors)	
	Climbing	Riding tricycles
	Swinging	Sand play
	Running	Science

Time Block IV	Lunch Period
	Washing hands, toileting
	Resting prior to lunch
	Eating
	Washing hands
	Going home or preparing for nap

Time Block V	Nap Time	
	Dressing for bed	Toileting
	Sleeping	Dressing

Time Block VI	Self-Selected Activity'
	New activities
	Snack
	Outdoor play

*Blocks I, II, and III are typical of half-day programs where lunch is not served. The six blocks are more typical of full-day centers. Blocks I and III may be interchanged for variation and for meeting the needs of the children as discussed elsewhere.

Figure 4-9. Sample of a Time Block Plan.

The major considerations for scheduling activities are (1) goals for the group, (2) special needs of the group, (3) time of day the children arrive, (4) how long the children stay at school, (5) what happens at home before the child goes to school, and (6) season of the year.

Time Block I

A block of about 60 minutes for self-selected activity—either indoors or outdoors—is a good way to start the day. As children arrive, they find an activity that interests them. If they are slow starters, nobody rushes them to socialize; they are free to choose a puzzle and be alone. If they want to socialize, they can approach a friend in the housekeeping corner or one using the slide. Latecomers need not feel unduly uncomfortable, as they may when a group assembly occurs first. Beginning with a self-directed activity period enables teachers to talk to parents and also to give each child a little attention as he or she enters the school. Children should never feel as one little girl put it to her mother after school, "I don't know if my teacher even knew I was there. She never called my name once."

The first large block of time might vary from 30 to 90 minutes, depending on all the factors mentioned above and the number of special learning experiences the teacher may have planned for the day. There should always be provision within each time block for both quiet and vigorous activity to take care of the differing needs and interests of the children.

Time Block II

The second block of time is more teacher-instigated or -directed. It includes a period of cleaning up, washing hands, toileting, serving snack, singing, and listening to a story. It is a slowing down and relaxing time of day. This period could last from 30 to 45 minutes. There is some movement between the various activities. The story and singing groups, especially for younger children, contain, at most, four or five children rather than the entire group.

This quiet group time provides for rest without being called that, since the words *sleep* or *rest* may create strongly negative feelings in children. As the teacher considers the needs of the children, a decision can be made about how much rest the children require. What time do they go to bed? What time do they get up? It is unrealistic to assume that a healthy child who has had 12 hours of sleep and barely gets up in time to reach the early childhood center by 9 A.M. will need to rest on a cot at 10 or 10:30 A.M. As one child said, "I thought we came here to learn stuff. I already know how to sleep!" However, rest routines can provide positive learning experiences. Individual needs should be met. Younger children and those arriving very early may need some real rest.

Time Block III

The third block of time will be another self-selected activity period. If the first one was indoors, then the second one will be outdoors, and vice versa. Again there will be a variety of activities so that children can choose or be guided into quiet or active play as seems to fit their needs. Every school should provide outdoor activities daily.

Time Block IV

If the program calls for lunch, another block of time will be used in preparing for and in eating lunch. Many people feel that a quiet time just prior to lunch rests the children and helps them eat better. Considerable time is required to move the children from their learning activities to toileting, washing, resting, and finally to eating.

The schedule after lunch is also important, and a definite plan for this next step is crucial. Is it time for the children to go home? Or take a nap? Or go outdoors to play? Or begin their school day? Some afternoon groups may begin with lunch as some morning groups may begin with breakfast. Having next steps clearly in mind helps the teacher guide children in the routine. Some children will need to wash again after lunch and frequently will need to use the toilet. In order that all adults are not distracted from attending the children left at the lunch tables, it is usually best to have one adult assigned to supervise the children after they leave the lunch table.

Time Block V

Where naps are given, they usually follow the lunch hour immediately. The sleeping area should be prepared while the children are in the lunchroom or area. After a busy morning that starts early for many, the subdued light, soft music, and comfortable bed should be welcome. Efforts to keep the voices low, the pace slow, and a positive attitude toward the nap period will pay dividends. Because excessively long naps may interfere with the home bedtime schedules, it is well to confer with parents regarding a reasonable length of the nap period for their children.

There may be a few children who won't sleep. Some children get adequate rest at night. Provision can be made to keep nonsleepers from interfering with the sleeping children. Usually the older children do not need sleep. They can rest in an adjacent room while "reading" a book. Some children who seem to need sleep but are alert to all movement can be encouraged to sleep face down. Sometimes if the teacher gently massages the shoulders, the child will relax and go to sleep. Children have varying feelings about bedtime and may become lonesome for their parents. At no time should bedtime become a period for harsh discipline or punishment.

Time Block VI

Following nap time, toileting, and dressing, self-selected activity can again take place. In full-day centers there may be a new shift of personnel because the morning staff comes to work early. For insecure children the new shift may present problems that teachers should be prepared to handle. The new teachers with their different ways will add variety for the children. New materials should be offered that were not available in the morning. Some find this time useful for having children help prepare materials for the next day's activity; for example, filling trays of materials to use for collage, or mixing new paints. Outdoor play is usually enjoyed by children after a nap. Working parents coming home to family responsibilities may not have time to supervise their children outdoors and are happy that the school provides outdoor play. However, every effort should be made to avoid exhausting these children physically. Tired children will be cranky. Cranky children are not pleasant for parents who are tired themselves after a full day's work. For this reason a quiet group for listening to stories and singing songs is popular in late afternoon.

Departure Time

Before it is going-home time, children's belongings, art products, and so forth should be checked to see that all are ready to be sent home. Having everything ready avoids the strain of looking for things that cannot be found and paves the way for a smooth and happy departure of the children with their parents.

Transition Times

Transition points between activities and big blocks of time should be planned carefully. The teacher plans just what the children are to do and then states the directions clearly. If planning is adequate, the children will move with ease through the routines, will not be running into each other, will know what comes next, and will not have to wait. Waiting, to young children, is tedious and probably just as uninteresting as it is for adults, therefore it should be avoided. It may help to have one teacher start an activity while another teacher brings up the stragglers or forms a new group. For more detailed suggestions see Chapters 5 and 12.

Providing for Flexibility

The sample schedule, Figure 4-8, is a flexible guide. Each period of time can be adjusted shorter or longer as needs warrant. If children are just beginning to use something they have spent all hour building, then an additional 10 or 15 minutes will give them a feeling of greater satisfaction. Advising the children a few minutes ahead that there will be a change in activities enables the children to terminate projects to their satisfaction. If presented in a positive manner, cleanup time can be fun for the children—especially if the teacher is assisting. It can also be a learning experience for children and a big help to the teachers.

Providing for Weather Changes

Any plan must be judged against how well it adapts to days of inclement weather. Ideally, the teacher hopes to disturb the routine as little as possible on bad days knowing that changes tend to confuse young children. On a rainy day the first self-selected activity period can be extended about 30 minutes and other routines can occur in sequence until after the story period. Then if, instead of the outdoor activity, the teacher plans some singing games, tumbling activities, or the like, the children will probably move through a rainy day without realizing a difference in schedule until the teacher announces the time to go home. They may then ask, "Well, aren't we going to play outside?" If a rainy-day room or a protected porch or patio is provided, only minor schedule adjustments need to be made on a rainy day. A walk in the rain with boots and umbrellas can provide learning opportunities and can also provide the energy release ordinarily gained in outdoor activities.

The teacher makes the schedule to fit the needs of the particular group of children. A plan is required that takes care of all needs. The plan must be one in which the teacher has confidence and with which he or she feels comfortable working. Morning groups in early fall or late spring or summer may be anxious to have outdoor activities when they arrive. In that case, the teacher may choose a self-selected outdoor activity period as the first large time block.

In cold seasons or wet climates the early morning may be too cold or wet for outdoor activities. The outdoor period would then be postponed until late morning, when the dew is off the grass and the sun has warmed up the atmosphere. In snowsuit climates the schedule may be adjusted to minimize dressing and undressing. For example, in an afternoon group, parents were asked to send the children to school already dressed in snowsuits for outdoor activity. Outdoor self-selected activities were scheduled for the first part of the afternoon at school. This schedule had additional merit because these children were staying indoors during their mornings at home. Their exuberance during the outdoor period, even in very cold weather, indicated that a need was being met.

Children who were not interested in outdoor activity were allowed to enter the indoor play area when they chose. This suggests another alternative a teacher may use. Indoor and outdoor activity may take place at the same time when the spaces are adjacent or when there are enough adults to supervise activities going on in both places.

During warm weather it is possible to provide almost the entire program outside if the teacher moves some activities out that are normally done indoors. Teachers note that when the weather turns warm the children will begin playing outside in their neighborhoods during the

Figure 4-10. An accessible water fountain makes independence possible. (Child Development Laboratory, Louisiana State University)

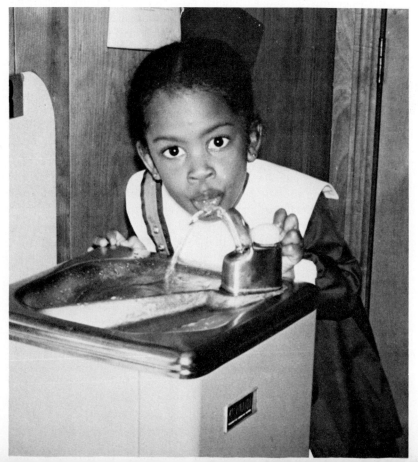

morning. If the children are playing vigorously in the morning, the afternoon program should be restful to avoid excessive fatigue.

Staff Assignments

Staff assignments are important every day, but especially on opening days. Students or other assistants who have accompanied the teacher on the home visits or have helped when the family visited the school will know the children. The staff should get together and pool their guesses regarding individual children's needs. Staff cooperation is important. Team teaching has always been common in prekindergartens and is increasingly common in kindergartens. No one will be able to predict with much accuracy how these first days will go. Brief daily discussion of goals, children, routines, and procedures will give teachers confidence in each other as unpredictable situations arise.

A democratic plan of operation enables all teachers, student teachers, parent assistants, or volunteers to be on an equal plane. The head teacher, who in the final analysis is responsible, must assume the lead. However, more creative teaching will develop within the staff if adults feel that their contributions are significant and that they can follow their own creative teaching ideas without unnecessary interference. Teachers often vary in their teaching styles. Differences need not confuse the children if all adults are working toward common goals.

A head teacher needs at least one assistant, no matter how small the school. If each person is to gain personal satisfaction when working with young children, all responsibilities—the good and bad, the hard and easy, the clean and dirty, and the pleasant and unpleasant—should be shared fairly. The children are the winners when adults work together, the losers when they don't.

Just as each child is unique, so is each adult. Each person has strengths and weaknesses. The individual's strength should be capitalized upon and the weak areas overcome. As one assistant said during a planning session, "I'm not as good as Betty Kay in music, but I'd love to try leading the singing." Another said, "Could I be responsible for the finger painting? I've never supervised that before." The assistants were volunteering to learn. Learning means growing and becoming a better teacher. The stage must be set so that each adult can make a satisfying contribution. Planning and posting of responsibilities help achieve the goals of the center.

Before long in your student teaching course and in your first teaching position you will be in charge of setting the stage not only for a group of children, but also for one or more adult assistants. Therefore, during this course, while you are planning and organizing for children, be sure you give some thought to how adults work together coopera-

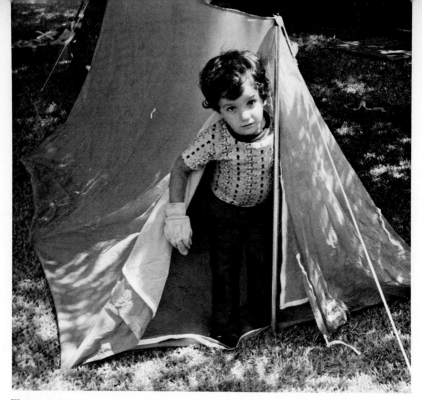

Figure 4-11. A camping tent fosters dramatic play. (Parent–Child Development Center, Houston)

tively. Remember the steps you are learning now are steps you may very soon be helping other adults learn.

*   *   *

Talk It Over: No. 4

Assume you are starting your first teaching position as the head teacher. Give examples of concerns you'll have during the opening of school.

*   *   *

Additional Tips for the First Days of School.

Introducing a Few Children Each Day

When a teacher is starting a new group of children, she or he can assure time to give attention to each child's needs by dividing the group and introducing only a few new children each day. Perhaps by the fifth or sixth day all the children can be attending. If such a plan is not feasible, a number of assistants or volunteers should be available to handle routines while the teacher is kept free to work with children who are uneasy about being at school. First days make a lasting impression on the child. Every effort should be made to ensure that every child has a happy time.

Beginning with Easily Supervised Activities

The activities offered the first day or two should be ones that are very easily supervised. For example, crayons are likely to be familiar to the children and thus require no special help or encouragement for the children to use. Getting involved in finger painting will be fine later on. These first days, the teacher may be needed other places on short notice and would not want to be delayed while washing off finger paints.

Name Tags

The first day of school the teacher should prepare name tags for everyone. Convention badges work fine for adults. For children excellent name tags can be made from two layers of art sponge or felt glued

Figure 4-12. Cooperation and sharing are suggested by a three-place swing. (Children's Center, University of South Carolina)

with a piece of muslin between and trimmed with scalloping shears. Sponge and felt come in pretty colors and might be coordinated into a color scheme or a teaching plan. Tags can be about two inches wide and cut to fit each name. Names are lettered in manuscript printing with a marking pen. Name tags that are made of colored paper and laminated with a plastic film are also satisfactory if laminating equipment is available.

Most teachers prefer to pin the name tag to the front of the child's shirt with a large safety pin. Some prefer pinning the name tags on the child's back to discourage children from pinning their own, thus the name tags will last longer. However, if the tags are pinned in front, the children will feel great satisfaction when they are able to open and close that pin!

Health Measures

Health inspection has been omitted so far. This does not mean that the child's health is not an important concern. Far from it. Parents should be urged to send only healthy children to school. They should be advised to look at their child and say, "If Doug were someone else's child, would I want my child exposed to him?" Parents should know that if a child becomes ill, they will be called. Parents who are working are urged to leave telephone numbers of neighbors or relatives that would care for their sick child. Actually, all children's records should carry a second telephone number because parents often run errands during a child's hours in school and might not be available immediately.

Parents' cooperation on health matters is probably more effective than having an inspection. Persons without training will see very little in the throats of young children. Even registered nurses will miss significant symptoms. Children who attend morning schools may not seem ill at nine o'clock but may be quite ill by eleven. Teachers must always be alert for signs of illness. They should isolate the sick child under proper supervision and call the parents.

In afternoon groups parents are advised that if children have symptoms in the morning, they will be much better off taking a rest at home in the afternoon than going to school, where they might get overtired and might also expose friends to a communicable disease. Attention to vaccinations should be given in admission procedures. With good vaccination programs some communicable diseases can be nearly eliminated.

If a child gets a communicable disease, the parents of children who, according to school records, have not had the disease are notified. Parents may then be on the lookout for symptoms and avoid sending their children to school on days they might expose the entire group to a disease.

When inspections are necessary, the nurse should wear regular street clothes to avoid arousing the anxiety that a uniform often creates.

Conclusion

Setting the stage for the opening of school focuses on the important functions of planning and organizing—especially arranging the facility, planning the daily schedule, choosing the learning experiences for the children, and making staff assignments. The teacher takes an inventory of the functions that must be performed and plans the most efficient use of the space available. Learning centers are arranged along with storage for the needed equipment and supplies. Traffic patterns are a consideration. The schedule or sequence of events is the structure within which the teacher and children work. All planning is of a tentative nature until the teacher becomes acquainted with a particular group of children. Definite planning is required as the teacher sets the stage for the children's behavior and learning.

Applications

1. Discuss the "Talk It Over" activities found in the chapter. Summarize conclusions.
2. Complete Lesson 4 in *A Laboratory Workbook for Introduction to Early Childhood Education.* Hand it in as scheduled.
3. Study the learning centers in your early childhood school.
   a. Label each center using labels found in the chapter.
   b. List the equipment and supplies found in each learning center.
   c. Indicate how many children can comfortably work in each learning center at a time.
   d. Tally the total learning spaces for the classroom and playyard.
   Discuss your findings with your classmates.
4. Evaluate your participation using the evaluation form prepared in Chapter 1. Discuss your progress with your supervising teacher.
5. Add information on room arrangements to your Resource File.

Study Questions

1. Define planning and organizing in an early childhood setting.
2. Give examples of building materials and procedures that will help reduce noise levels in a center.

3. List characteristics of good locker space.
4. List characteristics of good resting space.
5. List characteristics of good eating space.
6. List characteristics of good bathroom space.
7. Define and describe a learning center.
8. Explain the concept of time blocks in planning schedules.
9. List and describe procedures teachers find especially helpful during the first days of school when introducing a new group of young children to the school.

Film

Organized Free Play   Black and white   22 minutes

Depicts the elements of a Head Start center, the equipment, program, and teaching techniques. Zoned areas of activity for group and individual activity are illustrated. Modern Talking Pictures Services, 5000 Park Street N., St. Petersburg, Fla. 33709. Free from any Head Start office.

Additional Readings

CASTLE, KATHRYN. *The Infant & Toddler Handbook: Invitations for Optimum Development.* Atlanta, Ga.: Humanics Limited, 1983.

COHEN, D. H., and M. RUDOLPH. *Kindergarten and Early Schooling.* Englewood Cliffs, N.J.: Prentice Hall, Inc., 1977.

HILDEBRAND, VERNA. *Guiding Young Children.* New York: Macmillan Publishing Co., Inc., 1985.

KRITCHEVSKY, SYBIL, ELIZABETH PRESCOTT, and LEE WALLING. *Planning Environments for Young Children: Physical Space.* Washington, D.C.: National Association for the Education of Young Children, 1977.

LEEPER, SARAH H., RALPH WITHERSPOON, and BARBARA DAY. *Good Schools for Young Children.* New York: Macmillan Publishing Co., Inc., 1984.

LUECK, PHYLLIS. "Planning an Outdoor Learning Environment." *Theory into Practice,* Vol. 12, No. 2, April 1973, pp. 121–127.

READ, KATHERINE, and JUNE PATTERSON. *The Nursery School and Kindergarten.* New York: Holt, Rinehart and Winston, 1980.

ROBISON, HELEN F. *Exploring Teaching in Early Childhood Education.* Boston: Allyn & Bacon, 1977.

SCHICKEDANZ, JUDITH A., MARY E. YORK, IDA SANTOS STEWART, and DORIS A. WHITE. *Strategies for Teaching Young Children.* Englewood Cliffs, N.J.: Prentice-Hall, Inc., 1982.

WEISER, MARGARET G. *Group Care and Education of Infants and Toddlers.* St. Louis: The C. V. Mosby Company, 1982.

Teachers and Techniques Used

- *To define a teaching style.*
- *To define guidance and its goal.*
- *To define and give examples of indirect guidance.*
- *To define and give examples of direct guidance.*

Each teacher is unique, just as each child is unique. Good teachers develop a teaching style all their own. Each teacher's style will be different from all other teaching styles encountered either during your education or in a teaching position.

Developing a Unique Teaching Style

A teaching style is the teacher's manner and method of teaching. The individual's personality is an important factor in determining a teaching style. As each teacher develops a program and builds a relationship with children, conscious and unconscious integration of all she or he knows and feels occurs, and a personal teaching style evolves. The teacher's knowledge of him- or herself, the children, and their families will affect teaching style. One's philosophy of education and political and moral value systems will influence one's personal teaching style.

Teaching styles may be placed on continuums ranging between democratic and authoritarian, organized and haphazard, passive and active, formal and informal, person-centered and subject-matter-centered. Students in training are often frustrated by the differing teaching styles they

Figure 5-1. Answering a child's questions and asking directed questions are techniques that encourage a child to explore. (Parent–Child Development Center, Houston)

observe among demonstration teachers. Universities deliberately assign students to a variety of early childhood groups to give them opportunities to see different teachers in action. This practice should assure students that no one teaching style is the "correct way." For those who still insist on a "right way," this practice may bring confusion. Yet if demonstration teachers can use differing teaching styles while achieving similar goals for young children, students should reason that they too will be free to develop their own style of teaching.

A demonstration teacher worthy of the position is creative, innovative, and inquisitive. She or he experiments and evaluates continuously. Both children and university students are related to differently from class to class. Teaching is looked upon as a creative profession, and the teacher never expects the factors to be enough alike for everything to remain the same. Neither would one expect student teachers to duplicate the teacher's style of teaching.

Students should be encouraged to go forth and develop their own teaching style in the light of their own personality, their own experience, the age they teach, and related research.[1] It is of crucial importance that the professionals in early childhood education keep a ques-

[1] For background research on many concepts in this chapter see Alice Sterling Honig, "Compliance, Control, and Discipline," *Young Children,* 40:2, January 1985, pp. 50–58 and continued in *Young Children,* 40:3, March 1985, pp. 47–52.

tioning attitude and endeavor to make improvements. Each teacher who works with young children should feel this challenge.

*   *   *

Talk It Over: No. 1

Think back over the teachers you remember. What were their teaching styles? What style did you prefer? Why?

*   *   *

Using Methods Appropriate for Young Children

Methods of teaching include lecturing, recitation, discussion, laboratory experiments, demonstrations, field trips, and audiovisual aids. Every teacher uses each of these methods within a personal teaching style. However, because of the way the young child learns, certain methods are more appropriate than others. For example, the teacher rarely lectures to young children. One quickly discovers that lecturing is ineffective. Methods that allow one-to-one contacts with the child are far more in keeping with the needs and interests of young children.

Figure 5-2. A child learns self-help skills while a patient teacher waits. (Hoeflin Stone House Child Care Center, Kansas State University)

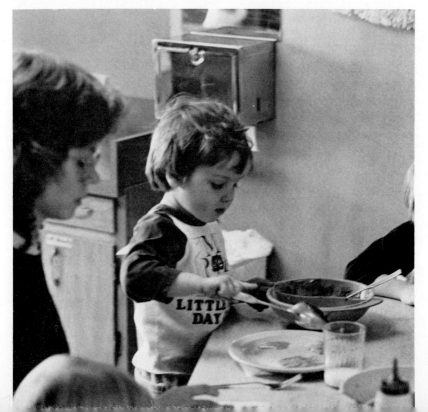

Identification is a process of silent teaching discussed by Hymes. He says that the child feels with the teacher, likes her, and wants to be like her. The teacher is the heroine. Through this intimate relationship teachers have a potent educative force. Identification works only when relationships are close, warm, and friendly.[2]

The student is challenged to observe experienced teachers using various teaching methods with young children. Students should question the use of each method and continue to question as they establish their own groups and incorporate teaching methods into a unique teaching style.

Qualities of a Good Teacher of Young Children

A significant contribution to society is made by a good teacher. The contribution cannot be measured, but it will affect the present generation and, indirectly, the generations to come. The good teacher likes children and is dedicated to instilling in children a desire to learn and to become independent learners. Children are encouraged to express themselves. Their curiosity is aroused, and the teacher gives them understanding, affection, and support when needed; yet they are encouraged to grow up.

The good teacher has self-confidence and is ready to cope with responsibility. She or he believes that the job is important and that teaching will make a significant contribution to the lives of the children. The good teacher feels accepted and liked by children, parents, and colleagues. A good teacher is a happy individual on and off the job. Though serious at times, she or he enjoys life, can laugh and be happy, and can encourage others' sense of humor and laughter. The teacher finds some fulfillment outside of work with children and thus avoids the crippling effect that results when teachers gratify all needs through work.

The teacher has confidence in people, believing that both children and parents are basically good. Recognizing that behavior has meaning, the teacher seeks to discover the meaning. The teacher believes that children *can* learn and that through the efforts of all they *will* learn. She or he is deeply committed to seeking a new and deeper understanding of individuals and families in every walk of life. The good teacher can empathize or feel with the parents and children.

An effective teacher can adapt information to the young child's level. The university curriculum can become the curriculum of the school for

---

[2] James Hymes, Jr., *Teaching the Child Under Six* (Columbus, Ohio: Charles E. Merrill Publishing Co., 1974), pp. 107–109.

Figure 5-3. A child learns to solve the problem of getting the trike out of the sand if the teacher waits before helping. (Child Development Laboratory, Michigan State University)

young children. For example, a university freshman wrote to her younger brother, "I am taking botany. We put a plant in dye to watch the vascular tissue carrying it up through the leaves. You did that in kindergarten with celery, remember?"

The teacher's scholarship should go beyond what she or he expects to teach. An obvious enthusiasm for understanding the political, social, scientific, and aesthetic world will infect the young learner. Beauty has priority in the classroom—in arrangements and relationships. The teacher understands not only the implications of educating a child in a democracy as opposed to education in an authoritarian society but also the applications of scientific method in social as well as physical science.

The teacher is well informed about human growth and development, knowing what to expect and how to plan for and assist growth and maturation.

The teacher of young children works constantly to improve her or his ability to guide children's learning. Parents are helped to learn to contribute effectively to their child's education. The teacher makes a serious effort to discover effective methods of working with children and parents individually and in groups.

A good teacher strives to mold all skills and knowledge into a teaching style that is comfortable and unique. With each new experience the

Figure 5-4. A teacher who is prepared and relates happily to children helps cohesiveness to develop in a group. (Early Childhood Laboratory, Kansas State University)

student who is preparing to teach moves a step forward in developing a personal teaching style.

* * *

Talk It Over: No. 2

Review the qualities of good teachers. Explain how you agree or disagree with the statements.

* * *

Guidance and How the Teacher Can Use It

Many students can accept the philosophy of a democratic, child-centered early childhood education program. They can also accept the rationale for an individualized, self-selected learning environment for the young child. Students are often baffled, however, when confronted with the problem of operating a classroom and relating to children within such a framework.

Most students remember their elementary and secondary classrooms. They may even recall their first grade, when they had 15 minutes of morning news followed by reading circles or seatwork, then 15 minutes of recess followed by science. Teachers who try to organize young children in such a rigid fashion court disaster. Trying to get everyone to do the same thing at one time is virtually impossible. A contest results between the teacher and the children. When silence is highly valued, as it is in some classes, the only way silence can be maintained is through coercion, punishment, and threats.

Order can be maintained within the framework of an individualized, self-directed learning environment. The teacher should feel sure that the activities of individuals and groups of children can be stopped when necessary and that the children will listen and respond. Limits that protect each child, the property, and the learning environment should be set. The teacher should exercise the obligation to set limits (make rules) so that the group can learn together harmoniously. There is no place in early childhood education for a total free-for-all.

Democratic living can begin with very young children. They will learn and respond to rules that keep the group functioning on an even keel. They cannot be expected to learn all the rules overnight. Transgressions are often due to forgetting or misunderstanding and normally occur with only a few children at a time.

*   *   *

Talk It Over: No. 3

What is your definition of discipline? How should discipline be carried out by parents and teachers of young children?

*   *   *

Some people prefer to use the word "discipline" when discussing helping children learn to accept societal standards of behavior. However, the word "discipline" frequently has a connotation of punishment which makes it less desirable in our educational setting. That is, the question, "How do you discipline your child?" usually translates into, "How do you punish your child?" In the educational setting and with a developmental philosophy of early childhood education, the word "guidance" is more accurate.

What Is Guidance?[3]

The term *guidance* is defined as *everything adults deliberately do and say, either directly or indirectly, to influence a child's behavior.* A self-guided or self-disciplined child is the goal. The teacher manages the group of young children through carefully conceived teaching techniques and

---

[3] For a more extensive discussion of guidance in all aspects of an early childhood center see Verna Hildebrand, *Guiding Young Children* (New York: Macmillan Publishing Co., Inc., 1985).

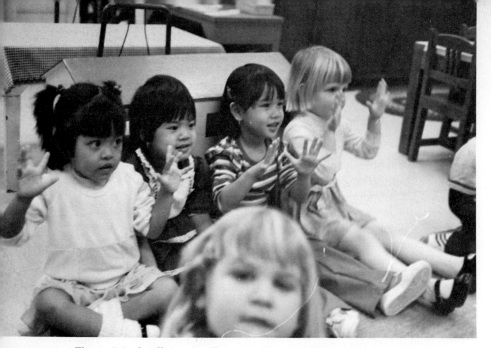

Figure 5-5. Small groups allow a teacher to individualize teaching and to know how each child responds. (Kuwae Preschool, Kadena Air Base, Okinawa)

the special personal relationship being developed with the class. The teacher wants children to assume as much responsibility for conducting themselves as they are ready to assume. The teacher helps children to grow in ability until they can assume the responsibility for conducting themselves when teachers, parents, police, or other authority figures are not present to enforce correct behavior. The teacher does not want the child to be like Janet, who wanted to jump over a bonfire and kept saying, "My mother didn't tell me *not* to!" The teacher knows parents will not always be present to say "No." Each child must learn to make decisions that affect personal safety—perhaps life. One of the developmental tasks for the young child is to develop self-control.

Guidance can be either *indirect* or *direct*. Indirect guidance includes all the teacher's behind-the-scenes work, including that discussed in Chapter 4, that sets the stage for the behavior the teacher expects. Through direct guidance the teacher deals directly with the child.

Indirect Guidance

The teacher guides the child indirectly through the arrangement of learning centers in the room and the yard, through daily schedule, and through work with parents. The type of equipment selected and the richness of the curriculum of learning experiences provided indirectly affect the ease with which children do what is expected. James Hymes,

114

Figure 5-6. One-to-one moments give the teacher a chance to learn what a child thinks. (Early Childhood Laboratory, Kansas State University)

Jr., says in his book *Behavior and Misbehavior:* "Bored children will be bad."[4] Keeping that in mind, the teacher will provide plenty of learning experiences that are neither too hard nor too easy. The youngsters will be so actively involved in learning that they will have little time for misbehavior. Detailed procedures for enriching the curriculum follow in Part Two.

As an example of indirect guidance, the teacher alters the physical environment and thereby influences the behavior of the child. To illustrate: The teacher sees a large group of children having a lively game on top of a large packing box. The teacher is foresighted, knowing from experience that this type of setting often creates difficulty. Falling or pushing may occur. The teacher quietly moves another packing box near and, using a walking plank, makes a bridge between the boxes. The children move to include the second box. The game takes on new dimensions with the additional space. Through quietly changing the physical environment, the teacher averts a possible conflict or danger.

As another example, the teacher may note that a number of children are waiting for a turn to swing. Knowing how hard it is for them to wait, the teacher thinks of an activity that might attract the swingers, or at least give the waiters an interesting activity while they wait. One teacher lines up a few tricycles and gets out the traffic signs. In a moment there is a line of traffic and a police officer directing it. As antici-

[4] James Hymes, Jr., *Behavior and Misbehavior* (Englewood Cliffs, N.J.: Prentice-Hall, Inc., 1955), p. 57.

115

pated, the swingers leave their swings, and no longer is there a line at the swing set. The teacher has not only extended the play of the children but has averted what might have become a difficult problem of sharing the swings.

The teacher can use indirect guidance by taking care of the children's needs for stretching, shifting position, or getting attention during a group activity. For example, during group time the teacher notes that the children are being distracted by a child who is kicking a neighbor's foot. Rather than call further attention to the fidgeting child, a decision is made to teach a new singing game that requires everyone to stand up. The teacher regains the attention of all the children, and the group time proceeds smoothly.

Indirect guidance is a very effective tool for the teacher to use in managing a group of children. If it is used well, many observers will remark that "the children seem to be doing just what they want to do." The teacher can smile, knowing that the stage was set for the behavior being observed. Success is greater than if one were to spend hours lecturing the children on how to behave.

* * *

Talk It Over: No. 4

Record two examples of a teacher altering the environment to improve interaction among the children. Discuss the outcomes with your classmates. Note how your example fits the definition of indirect guidance.

* * *

Direct Guidance

Direct guidance includes all of the *physical, verbal,* and *affective* means the teacher uses to influence the child's behavior. It includes speaking, teaching, demonstrating, helping, leading, loving, approving, disapproving, compelling, restraining, punishing, and even ignoring. The good teacher uses the positive methods in this list far more than the negative. The positive methods contribute more to the goal of the child becoming self-directed. Frequent use of compelling, restraining, or punishing should serve as a warning that the teacher's guidance leaves something to be desired. There is virtually no place in teaching for physical or mental punishment. Punishment produces feelings that may not be conducive to learning, creates negative attitudes toward school and teachers, and does little to help the child develop self-direction.

Verbal Guidance

Verbal guidance is a form of direct guidance. In guiding a child, the teacher gets the child's attention and speaks to him or her in words easily understood. The teacher stoops or sits at the child's level facing the

Figure 5-7. Scuffling releases pent-up energies. Tell children to say "up" when they've had enough. (Hoeflin Stone House Child Care Center, Kansas State University)

child. If the words aren't fully understood, the child can interpret the meaning from facial expressions and gestures. The teacher speaks quietly to individual children, seldom to the whole group. Verbal statements may be accompanied by action such as leading, helping, or demonstrating—whichever seems to be required for fuller understanding. Experience shows that shouting across the room or yard seldom brings forth the desired behavior, and directions given on a to-whom-it-may-concern basis are seldom heeded. Some verbal techniques the teacher will find helpful follow.

USING VOICE EFFECTIVELY. The teacher's tone of voice as well as what is said will guide the children's response. They will know by the firmness in the voice and their previous experience with his or her guidance that they are expected to comply. For example, children generally respond willingly to the teacher calling, "Time to go inside," while standing at the door waiting for them to come. They learn the first day that if they linger, the teacher reinforces the statement by taking their hands and leading them indoors. Through reinforcing the direction, the teacher teaches them to do as asked. Contrast this technique with a parent who makes a similar announcement to the child—that it is time to leave at once—then lingers, visiting with friends and neighbors. Is it understandable why the child doesn't come when called?

SPEAKING SLOWLY AND CALMLY. The teacher generally speaks in a slow, calm, quiet manner with eyes on the listener. On rare occasions she or he might speak with obvious alarm if the situation warrants it and calls for quick compliance; for example, if a serious danger arises. The latter technique will be used sparingly so that the children will not get accustomed to the technique and fail to respond when there is real reason for quick action.

USING FEW DIRECTIONS. The teacher gives a minimum number of directions. However, those directions that are given are reinforced if necessary, and the teacher sees to it that the directions are carried out. Reinforcing or following through simply means that the teacher leads the child to do what is asked. The number of direct commands is limited and appropriate for the children. However, split-second responses are not expected. Children are given some leeway in the time allowed to carry out a direction. For instance, the teacher, before giving direction to children to go indoors, will first remind them that they will be going in soon. This practice helps children bring to a close any activity they have started. When given a little time to terminate their activity, children are likely to comply and are less likely to feel the teacher's decision is unfair.

The teacher should avoid giving several directions at a time. Often teachers forget children's short attention spans and give a long series of unrelated directions which may be confusing to young children. If directions are given one at a time, children are more likely to remember the requests until the tasks are accomplished.

GIVING CLEAR, SHORT, POSITIVE DIRECTIONS. The teacher remembers to be clear in giving directions. Reasons are given for requests. Direct positive statements are best. They tell the child what *to* do instead of only what *not* to do. A "don't" command leaves a child uncertain as to how to proceed. The first part of the statement should contain the action clause. Reasons are then added. For example, "Walk around the blocks, Peter. John isn't ready to have his building knocked down yet." "Mary, hold your glass up straight. The milk will spill." In each example, the child knows immediately what to do and why.

GIVING CHOICES. The teacher guides children by helping them make choices. She or he wants them to have experience in making up their own minds, and deciding things for themselves. The teacher may offer a child a choice between playing indoors or out, between listening to a story now or later, between painting or not painting. When giving a choice, one should leave the choice up to the child. It is easy to use the phrase, "Would you like . . . ," when one really intends the child to do something specific. A teacher uses this phrase only when willing to accept the choice the child makes. The teacher can narrow down choices in order to give the child experience in decision making. Instead of asking a new child, "What would you like to play?" one might say, "You could paint or play with blocks. Which would you like?"

REDIRECTING EFFECTIVELY. Detouring or redirecting children from unsafe or unsociable behavior requires imagination. When children are doing something unacceptable, the teacher's task is to think of an activity that requires behavior of about the same type that is acceptable. For example, if the children holding their fire hoses are climbing on a storage shed that is too steep for safety, the suggestion to move to the packing boxes for their house-on-fire will be acceptable to them.

There are many examples of detouring or redirecting children's behavior. One day three children were piling up locust beans that had fallen from the trees. Two children began pelting the third with the beans. The teacher knew this type of play would not be fun for the third child for long and suggested, "Let's see if we can throw the beans over this packing box." They responded to the suggestion, and a probable crisis was averted. Distraction works well with toddlers but is less effective as the child matures. The teacher simply redirects the child's attention to a new object or situation.

USING WORDS TO MOTIVATE. Motivating the child is a common use of verbal guidance. Self-motivation is by far the most desirable type of motivator. The children should develop plenty of self-confidence. They need to feel competent and important. If the learning environment is set up so that natural curiosity is aroused, then little has to be said to motivate children. As they see others involved in an activity, they usually want to observe and to try it.

Care should be taken to keep competition at a minimum. Avoid motivating by asking who is best, fastest, or tallest. A better method is to motivate according to the child's own record. For example, "You are swinging higher than you did yesterday." It should be remembered that children who are highly competitive are seldom friends. Failing in competition contributes to a lack of self-confidence.

Embarrassing the child is also a poor motivating technique. Calling a child a "baby" or "naughty" or drawing attention to a difficulty such as wet pants in no way contributes to the happy self-confidence for which teachers strive.

Physical Guidance

Physical guidance is the second form of direct guidance. When the teacher uses such techniques as helping, demonstrating, leading, restraining, removing, ignoring, and punishing, this is physical guidance.

Demonstrating is effective with young learners because their language development may be too inadequate for them to learn only through words. Nearly anyone learning a new skill is helped by watching a demonstration. It is even more helpful if the person demonstrating goes slowly enough so that the learner can concurrently copy the motions. An example follows: The four-year-olds were having difficulty opening the door to the school. Telling them to hold down the thumb lever, then push, was ineffective. However, when the teacher took time to show each child how and supervised the practice for a few minutes, many were able to accomplish the task.

The teacher of younger children frequently has to give a supporting hand to encourage them and help them feel safe while trying a new activity. For example, some children were climbing the newly cut log left in their yard. The most skillful children climbed up quickly, walked along the trunk, and jumped off the end. Though more cautious and hesitant, the less agile children still wanted to try. The teacher offered a steadying hand until they had practiced enough to increase their confidence.

The teacher faces many decisions about whether to help children. The goal is for children to grow in independence. Persistence or sticking to a task is also valued. Children vary as to how much frustration they can tolerate. Some children react to frustration by giving up or getting angry. The teacher must decide when and how much to help. Sometimes one helps the child get beyond an obstacle so that he or she can complete the task. For example, Jamie had unzipped his boots. He was struggling to get them off. The teacher watched his effort, reached over, and showed him how to slip the boot an inch or two beyond the heel. Jamie was elated as the boot yielded to his final tug. Soon he could do the task alone.

Teachers may have to restrain children to prevent their hurting others or damaging property. The teacher must protect the entire group. It is much better to stop a child than to allow one to harm others. Efforts should then be made to help the aggressive child reduce angry feelings. Often such activities as hammering nails, pounding clay, or punching the punching bag will help. When restraint is needed frequently with the same child, the teacher must ask, "What does this behavior mean to the child? What are the circumstances that prompt it?" With closer study of the child, the teacher may develop more appropriate guidance.

Removing a child from the group is another way of guiding a child who is having difficulty in a group. Difficulties that arise when a child loses control are often due to overfatigue. For example, when Carlos cannot cope with a situation, the teacher may choose to remove him completely, lead him to a quiet nook, and then talk, read, or sing with him for a while. Or, it is possible to look for the play dough or some favorite toy. By involving Carlos in a way that will relax him, the teacher averts problems. If a firm, loving, nonpunishing attitude is maintained,

Figure 5-8. A comforting arm and a soft voice are affective guidance techniques that convey the teacher's concern for the child. (Nazarene Child Care Center, Lansing, Michigan)

the child will welcome the respite and may even seek help another time when he feels his control slipping.

Affective Guidance

Affective guidance is the third form of direct guidance. Affective, of course, refers to feelings. Affective guidance may simply be a smile across the room. Words may accompany the recognition on the teacher's part that the child feels satisfied, such as, "You feel really good about your building, don't you, Jake?" Sadness or negative feelings may also be recognized by saying, "You feel upset when Penny grabs your mittens, don't you, Sue?" Statements can be somewhat tentative, leaving children opportunity to tell you that you've misunderstood their feeling.

Approval and disapproval or positive and negative feedback are forms of direct guidance. Verbally labeling behavior helps the child learn. In the following example, John knows the teacher will approve if he repeats the behavior. "John, I like the way you shared the cars with Mark," said the teacher. "When you let Mark use your car, you are sharing." Sharing is one of those vague attributes that most adults wish for in children and one that is very difficult to explain to the child. Sharing should be labeled so that children can begin to recognize it and know what the teacher means when saying, "We are learning to share our toys."

The use of praise should be sincere and given for merit—even if small. When a child makes a number of paintings, the teacher need not praise them all. One can say, "You have been working hard. Which painting do you think is the prettiest?" Insincere praise will be suspect even to children. Children should not need praise for all good behavior. That is, in the long run, they should find satisfaction in their behavior and not just the praise received for doing the appropriate act.

Praise and approval should come to children for jobs well done. Likewise, disapproval should focus on the child's act, not the child. "We don't like spitting, Brad. When we need to spit, we spit in the toilet." In this example no accusation is made that Brad is "bad" when he spits.

A silent smile across the room or a pat on the head conveys approval. Privately bestowed verbal praise avoids confusing the other children and discourages competition. For example, Peter heard the teacher exclaiming over David's art project. Peter looked at the praised art product and immediately rearranged his own project to fit the praised model. Peter's self-confidence and creativity were unwittingly undermined by the praise for David's picture. No amount of persuasion would convince Peter that the teacher also liked the way he had first made his picture.

Ignoring some behavior is appropriate, depending on the individual and his or her age. James Hymes, Jr., advises teachers not to make an issue over every little fall from grace and says it is often helpful to be half deaf and nearsighted.[5] Surely the teacher cannot make a Supreme Court case out of every transgression. And transgressions may actually be progress for certain children. For example, Mary never did anything "wrong" and never said "No" to anyone. She was painfully shy and always proper. The teacher's rule was that children stay out of certain pieces of the housekeeping equipment. However, one day when Mary was seen in the dollhouse kitchen climbing up through the opening left for the dishpan "sink," the teacher turned her back and allowed Mary to go ahead without the customary disapproval.

The teacher's interaction with a young child should help keep communication open and help the child feel better about him- or herself. Teachers should be aware that because children are immature and inexperienced they do not see a situation in the same way that teachers do. Before we judge a situation or react strongly or drastically we should try to get the child's view. Thomas Gordon, in his book T.E.T.: Teacher Effectiveness Training,[6] gives teachers a framework for practicing interactional skills with their students that are positive and growth producing. He calls it a "No-Lose Method." Based on humanistic psychology

---

[5] Ibid., p. 29.
[6] Thomas Gordon, T.E.T.: Teacher Effectiveness Training (New York: Peter H. Wyden Publisher, 1974).

Thomas' method allows both children and adults to feel good about the methods used.[7]

*   *   *

Talk It Over: No. 5

Record one example of each type of direct guidance. Discuss the outcomes with your classmates.

*   *   *

Transitions

The schedule is planned in blocks of time. The children gain a sense of security when they begin to know what happens in each time block. It helps them, too, if they know what happens between time blocks. That's where the plans for transitions come in.

How do you move children comfortably from indoors to out-of-doors or vice versa without mass confusion? How do you prevent waiting in lines, pushing, and crowding which may trigger harsh word or harsh fists? The answer is to plan for transitions.

To plan transitions teachers must consider the space and paths available, where children will be congregated, and where they'll need to move for the next activities. Then think about how to get them to the next activity in the space and time available.

Usually a direct path is needed, otherwise you lose some children en route. Having only a few children moving at once helps. Say children's storytime is over and it is time for snacks. Warning, "Don't everyone go at once," won't do. In planning sessions you might color-code name tags; then it is easy to say, "Those with brown tags go to Table No. 1. Those with red tags go to Table No. 2," and so on. If prior arrangements weren't made then say, "All children with red shoes go to Table No. 1," then choose brown, black, and so on. Another day choose other criteria to keep it a surprise. Adapting a song to include the names of different children in each verse can signal them when it is their turn to move. For example, to the tune of "The More We Get Together" the teacher and the children can sing:

> The more we get together,
> Together, together,
> The more we get together
> The happier we'll be.
> We're ready for Becky, and Jimmy,

---

[7] Thomas Gordon's method was used successfully for staff evaluations and is reported by Carol E. Caltron and Earline D. Kendall in "Staff Evaluation that Promotes Growth and Problem Solving," in *Young Children,* 39:6 (September 1984), pp. 61–64.

And Susie, and Milton.
The more we get together
The happier we'll be.

If you are taking a field trip, some prior planning and making of lists are quite essential. Make lists of children who are compatible and give them to the driver. Call out the names and ask them to meet their driver "in the block corner." Then when all are together, that driver can move the group to the car to be buttoned properly in restraint belts.

There are numerous transitions to be planned for every early childhood school. Some specific helps are offered in Chapter 12 for storytime. Your creativity should be operating to think of new ways to make the transitions go smoothly. Staff members all need to know the transition techniques to be most helpful.

You as an Adult Educator

The teaching techniques suggested in this chapter will be among the early lessons you, as lead teacher, will need to teach helpers who are new to work with young children in a center. Adults, like children, take time to get adjusted. Your patience will be required as you help beginners learn the techniques for interacting with young children. Time and again you will give a new person a hint to try out. Then later in staff conferences you will discuss further the reasons for using the suggested technique.

Of course, allowances must be made for individuality; however, as lead teacher—and therefore the responsible adult—you have to require that staff members meet certain standards. If one is punitive or shouts at children, for example, this behavior would be intolerable and the individual would have to change or be dismissed.

Conclusion

The distinct manner and method of teaching make up the teacher's teaching style. The good teacher develops a unique teaching style as guidance is used to influence the behavior of the children. Guidance can be thought of as either indirect or direct. Children are guided indirectly as the teacher arranges the learning centers, plans the daily schedule, and works with parents. Verbal, physical, and affective guidance make up direct guidance techniques.

The teacher relaxes and enjoys the children. Yet he or she is ready to use any of the guidance techniques described above while supervising the group. At times a teacher may appear to have eyes in the back of the head, perhaps giving attention to a single child, and yet responding readily to a difficulty in the far corner of the room or yard. In some ways the teacher is like the cowboys of the Old West who rode with the herd. According to the historian J. Frank Dobie, they "knew how to linger; they had 'ample time'; but their repose was the repose of strength, capable of steel-spring action and not that of constitutional lethargy."[8]

After teaching in an early childhood school, you may feel certain that Frank Dobie was describing you. Teaching young children requires almost instantaneous response to situations. The response that contributes to goals for educating children so that they can reach their highest potential demands insight, knowledge, and empathy from teachers.

Applications

1. Discuss the "Talk It Over" items suggested in the chapter. Summarize your conclusions.
2. Complete Lesson 5 in *A Laboratory Workbook for Introduction to Early Childhood Education*. Hand in as scheduled.
3. Get permission, then rearrange a piece or two of the children's equipment. Record what happens when the children notice the change. Explain how your experience relates to the discussion of indirect guidance.
4. Rate your participation on the evaluation form developed in Chapter 1. Think about how you feel about your learning.
5. Add ideas about guiding children to your Resource File.

Study Questions

1. Define teaching styles. Discuss.
2. Define guidance and state the goal of guidance.
3. Define and give examples of indirect guidance.
4. Define and give examples of direct guidance: (a) physical, (b) verbal, and (c) affective.
5. Write five examples of positive guidance statements you might use with young children.
6. Shorten the following statement to make it follow the rules stated in the chapter. Assume children are playing at the water table. They excitedly splash water. The teacher says, "If you splash water you'll get the floor all wet. People will get their jeans wet and they won't like you if you get them wet." Discuss what you would change and why.

[8] J. Frank Dobie, *The Longhorns* (New York: Bramhall House, 1961), p. xix.

7. Explain how ignoring a child's misbehavior can be appropriate guidance at times.

8. Discuss when giving a choice is appropriate.

9. Discuss punishment as a method of guidance.

Film

Feelings: A Universal Language.   Color   12 minutes   1985

Twenty-five vignettes which portray children ages three to twelve in varying situations. The purpose of the film is to enable students to react to each situation using a variety of communication skills. Instructional Media Center, Michigan State University, East Lansing, Mich. 48824.

Additional Readings

ALGER, HARRIET A. "Transitions: Alternatives to Manipulative Management Techniques," *Young Children*, Vol. 39, No. 6, September 1984, pp. 16–25.

CASTLE, KATHRYN. *The Infant & Toddler Handbook: Invitations for Optimum Development.* Atlanta, Ga.: Humanics Limited, 1983.

COMBS, ARTHUR. *Helping Relationships: Basic Concepts for the Helping Professions.* Boston: Allyn & Bacon, 1981.

DREIKURS, R., and V. SOLTZ. *Children: The Challenge.* New York: Hawthorn, 1976.

GROTBERG, EDITH H., and WILLA CHOPER. *Research: Translating Findings into Action.* Washington, D.C.: U.S. Government Printing Office, 1978.

HILDEBRAND, VERNA. *Guiding Young Children.* New York. Macmillan Publishing Co., Inc., 1985.

HYMES, JAMES L., JR. *Behavior and Misbehavior.* Englewood Cliffs, N.J.: Prentice-Hall, Inc., 1955.

LANDRETH, CATHERINE. *Preschool Learning and Teaching.* New York: Harper & Row, 1972.

MOUSTAKAS, CLARK. *The Authentic Teacher.* New York: Irvington, 1983.

MOYER, JOAN E., and JEAN T. KUNZ, "Trust Is Everything," *Young Children*, Vol. 30, No. 2, January 1975, pp. 107–112.

OSBORN, KEITH, and JANIE D. OSBORN. *Discipline and Classroom Management.* Athens, Ga.: Education Association, 1978.

READ, KATHERINE, and JUNE PATTERSON. *The Nursery School and Kindergarten.* New York: Holt, Rinehart, and Winston, 1980.

ROSENTHAL, ROBERT, and LENORE JACOBSON. *Pygmalion in the Classroom.* New York: Holt, Rinehart and Winston, 1983.

WEISER, MARGARET G. *Group Care and Education of Infants and Toddlers.* St. Louis: The C. V. Mosby Company, 1982.

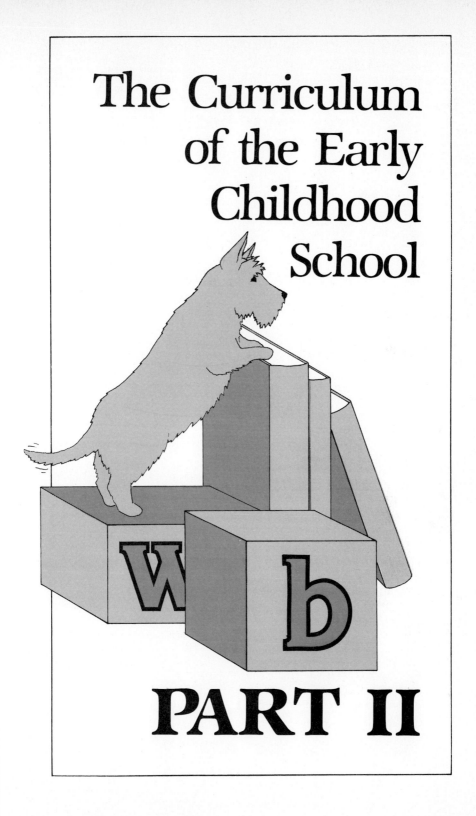

The Curriculum of the Early Childhood School

PART II

Introduction to Activity Planning

- *To know the stages in planning educational objectives as identified in the Bloom Taxonomy of Educational Objectives.*
- *To know the basic components of planning an activity to be carried out in the early childhood school.*

"I just had a super time with the children doing finger painting," reported Roger as he slipped into a chair in the conference room following a session in the early childhood school.

"My! The children were really active in my high-jump activity," reported Mary as she dropped her notebook in a chair and took a glass of juice from the counter.

Mary and Roger are college students who are meeting with the teacher of the children's group where they are doing their practicum for their early childhood education course. The teacher and students will be evaluating where they have been and where they are going. The teacher, in consultation with the instructor of the course, and the students have agreed on some goals and ground rules for the students' participation. The supervising teacher meets with the students to iron out details for their work with the young children. Step by step, Mary and Roger are gaining the experience needed to plan an integrated curriculum which is discussed in Chapter 17.

A Taxonomy of Educational Objectives

A useful guide to activity planning or planning a course for students was devised by Dr. Benjamin Bloom, an educational researcher, with the help of many others. They developed the *Taxonomy of Educational*

Figure 6-1. A food activity requires a plan for teaching children how to handle a knife safely. (Child Development Laboratory, College of Human Development, Pennsylvania State University)

Objectives: The Cognitive Domain which is summarized in Figure 6-2. The classification is often referred to as the "Bloom Taxonomy." Bloom believes that educators must be aware of these levels when planning educational experiences.[1]

By studying Figure 6-2 you can think about yourself and your level of knowledge. On some subjects you may find yourself at the Level 6, ready to do an evaluation and, perhaps, make recommendations to others in this subject area. You may also be at Level 1 (knowledge) on some topic that is new to you when you hear about it on the evening news. Take the subject of early childhood education; where are you, your instructors, and the general population on that subject?

[1] Benjamin S. Bloom (ed.), *Taxonomy of Educational Objectives, Handbook I: The Cognitive Domain* (New York: David McKay Company, Inc., 1956), pp. 62–168.

Figure 6-2. Taxonomy of educational objectives in the cognitive domain. (Adapted from Benjamin S. Bloom, *Taxonomy of Educational Objectives, Handbook I: Cognitive Domain.* New York: David McKay, 1956.)

Children, too, are at different points in their level of information as well as in their level of development. Each child has unique interests and needs. When you plan an activity you'll try to learn where the children are in their knowledge, then start from there to build. You can use the Bloom Taxonomy to help you tailor your objectives and plans to the appropriate level. You'll refer back to the developmental tasks in Chapter 2 as you plan various activities.

*　　*　　*

Talk It Over: No. 1

Using the Bloom Taxonomy, discuss various subjects that you have studied. Decide at which level you fall on the subjects. At which level are you and others you know on the subject of early childhood education?

*　　*　　*

Planning Is the Key

Positive outcomes for children happen by design not by accident. Planning is the key to designing a high-quality early childhood program that fosters the accomplishment of the developmental tasks that were

Figure 6-3. A movement activity requires a plan for appropriate music and space. (Early Childhood Laboratory, Kansas State University)

discussed in Chapter 2. A rich, viable program takes lots of planning, organizing, and coordinating. Teachers, assistants, and students who participate in the classroom should become involved in the planning and evaluating functions. It takes time to sit together to assess children's needs and interests, to evaluate previous plans, and to propose the activities that will meet children's needs and interests. As students, you should avail yourself of every opportunity to participate in planning sessions with experienced teachers.

Writing plans down is essential if high-quality programs are to be assured. The less experience the staff member has, the more the plans must be written in detail. It will save precious minutes if recipes and procedures are written on cards or on lesson plan forms and filed in a convenient book or file enabling future use without additional search.[2] You will find good use for the Resource File suggested in Chapter 1.

Organizing

Organizing the materials and equipment in a manner that will facilitate children's use of them follows decisions in the planning session. You may be designated as the one to set up a certain area. When you plan your special activity, you will be fully in charge of organizing the area where the activity will be presented and of cleaning up the area afterward.

[2] For helpful forms to use in preparing activity plans, daily diaries, and the Resource File, see Verna Hildebrand, *A Laboratory Workbook for Introduction to Early Childhood Education* (New York: The Macmillan Publishing Co., Inc., 1986).

Planning Specific Activities

A typical procedure early in teacher education programs is for students to carry out one activity each week. That activity is selected from each curricular area offered in the school—art, literature, science, and so on. Later, during the practice teaching phase, the student coordinates all the curricular activities and helpers, building on the earlier experience of carrying out one activity at a time. The opportunity to do one activity at a time without being totally in charge gives you a chance to learn in more depth and to get your feet wet gradually. Some students are both excited and a little scared of their new opportunities. If you are well prepared, it will be "a piece of cake," as they say.

Choice of Activity

The selection of a particular activity should be made in consultation with your supervising teacher in the children's school. After you observe the children and read your text for ideas, you can make a list of several activities that you'd like to try out. Confer with the teacher where you both can come to an agreement as to what activity would best fit into the overall plan and when the activity should be carried out within the schedule. Once the written plan is complete, show it to the teacher for approval. Then move ahead getting everything ready. Remember that the materials you prepare can often be used again and again—in student teaching and in future teaching. They can become part of your Resource File. Thus, the time spent on this one activity will have many payoffs for you.

Activity Plan

An *activity plan* could be made for every learning experience offered in the school. It is a challenging exercise to look at each piece of equipment or learning episode in the school and attempt to make an activity plan. Each of the ideas offered in Part 2 of this book will help with this thinking. Figure 6-4 is an example of a completed plan for using one type of equipment. The items entered under each heading on this sample activity plan will vary depending on the activity you select. For many activities, you can refer to the curriculum chapters to help you formulate relevant and rather complete entries fitting the requirements of each heading. It is important to think through each step in the activity plan. Unless you are highly experienced with children and with the activity, you will readily cope with the variety of children's responses and behaviors only if you are super prepared.

*

Sample Activity Plan
(with sample plan)

Name of Activity: *Parquetry blocks*
Developmental Goal:

(Goal

1. Vocabulary development.
2. Perceptual development.

Objectives: Given a set of parquetry blocks with matching forms the child will, each time,

2 object .

1. Match colors.
2. Match shapes.
3. Name colors.
4. Name shapes.

Materials Needed: *3 parquetry sets*

Procedure:
Place parquetry sets in an inviting location in the room.
Sit with children. Observe their use of the sets.
Let them discover and teach each other.
Answer any questions. Note their use of vocabulary.
Encourage naming of shapes and colors.

Guidance Suggestions Including Limits:
Play a game: "Show me the (*red square*)."
Encourage them to make their own designs after they accomplish matching.

Special Objectives:
To see if Amanda is able to name colors.
To see if John can count to four. Encourage his practice.

Evaluation:
Hide shape and/or color—ask child to name it when it is uncovered.
Check chart to see which ones they know.

Suggestions for Future Use:

Figure 6-4. Activity plan.

In planning a finger-painting project, for example, you will find in Chapter 8 all the information for your activity plan. You will find that this medium gives children an opportunity to practice small motor skills and to create their own designs. These could be your *Developmental Goals* for a particular day. Your *Objective* for children on a particular day could be to manipulate the finger paints with fingers, hands, and arms and create a design of their own choosing. Likewise, *Materials*

Needed, Procedures, and *Guidance Suggestions* can be found in each chapter where a particular activity is discussed.

Small Group

It is suggested that you plan your activity for a few children at a time. The major reason for this suggestion is that it will enable you to be more firmly in control and not overwhelmed. Also, you can often repeat an activity several times in a given period and, thus refine your procedure and learn from your mistakes. Children are usually more satisfied, too, because you are less familiar to them than their teacher and it takes more time to get acquainted with you and your ideas. Do try to insist that you work with a few children even if teachers will "let" you work with more. If you do the activity for the whole group, always try it out on a few children first.

*   *   *

Talk It Over: No. 2

Discuss the procedure for overall planning in the school where you participate. Who does it? How much time is allowed for planning? How

Figure 6-5. An art activity requires a plan for assemblying and arranging the needed materials and space. (Child Development Laboratory, University of Missouri–Columbia)

much is written down? How is evaluation done? Make inquiries if you can't answer these questions.

*   *   *

Behavioral Objectives

In planning activities for children suggested in each of the chapters in Part 2, you'll want to think through your goals for children. You may be asked to write *behavioral objectives,* a statement in behavioral terms of what the child will do or say that you can see or hear and thus have an indication the child is learning. Being aware of Bloom's Taxonomy (Figure 6-2), you'll learn to sequence activities by providing simple "knowledge" and "comprehension" opportunities before asking the child to do "application" problems.

An example of a behavioral objective is: "Given two colors of finger paint, Jim will choose one or both colors, put the amount desired on his paper, and then, using fingers, hands, and perhaps arms, will create a design of his own choosing." This objective has the following parts:

1. Audience—Jim.
2. Behavior—*Choose* one or both colors, *put* the amount desired on the paper, and then, *using fingers, hands, and perhaps arms, will create a design* of his own choosing.
3. Condition—Given two colors of finger paint.
4. Degree—Design of his own choosing.

[handwritten margin note: Background Info A, B, C, D]

Arranging the characteristics as *ABCD* helps one recall them. Each objective should be manageable and reachable based on prior assessment of the child or children. Behavioral objectives for an early childhood group require some range of performance.

You may feel frustrated upon being asked to write behavioral objectives so early in your course because you are in a learning phase with young children and may not have had much opportunity to see children behaving with each other and with many materials and learning activities. However, go ahead and make some educated guesses, then watch the children closely to discover what they really do with your activity. Remember that even experienced teachers have difficulty predicting children's behavior. Frequently children's responses are far more interesting than teachers anticipate when writing objectives. Thus, one should be ready to appreciate those responses and learn from watching the children. Until you know children well, you can write open-ended objectives, such as the example given, waiting until you know children and their needs better to make the objectives more specific and detailed.

Figure 6-6. A story activity may require a plan for interesting story aids to use on the flannel board. (Southeast Oakland Vocational Technical Center)

Observing

One of your goals for yourself should be to be constantly alert to all that goes on in your school. This is a big order, especially when you are new.

You will have an assignment. Be sure to do that assignment well. While doing it, observe and make mental or actual notes of which children are in your area and what they do. Eventually you will know such details as which children are left-handed, which ones need reminding to go to the bathroom, or which ones need help putting on their shoes. In addition, keep an eye on the rest of the room or playyard. What activities are the other adults carrying out? How do they handle problems? If you haven't carried out an activity like the one they are doing, ask them later about it. You can learn a great deal from watching others, especially as you have standards for high-quality teaching drawn to your attention in your classes.

Keeping a log or diary of your day in the early childhood school will provide you with a valuable resource for later use when you will be in charge of a group. A special form is suggested in *A Laboratory Workbook for Introduction to Early Childhood Education*[3] which facilitates

[3] Hildebrand, ibid.

Figure 6-7. A music activity plan requires designating a time and place for the activity, selecting songs, preparing aids, and learning to accompany the songs. (Family Life Center, Georgia Southern College, Statesboro)

the writing. With a few personal notes on your reactions you'll be able to recall your day in that school quite vividly. You can also use the diary in an evaluation of the program.

Evaluating

Evaluating must be part of every teaching and every planning session. All staff members can contribute to information on how individual children are progressing and provide ideas for activities suggested by children's interests. Sharing information in a conference should help the staff move toward a professional consultative level where some philosophical ideas about children and early childhood education can be discussed along with the "nuts and bolts" of the operation.

An important characteristic of the best lead teachers is their ability to involve others in planning, preparation, and evaluation. As a student, you can take careful note and learn from the teacher's leadership style because in a very short time you'll be the lead teacher with responsibility for a whole group of children and a number of adult helpers besides.

138

Conclusion

The work of Benjamin Bloom and others has been utilized as a basis for planning a curriculum. The opportunity for students to plan and carry out specific learning activities for the children in an early childhood school is a special learning tool. You are building your expertise little by little. By following the suggestions given, the children, supervising teacher, and college students will all have a pleasant experience in the early childhood school.

Applications

1. Do the "Talk It Over" items in the chapter. Can you draw conclusions about how planning is done in your school?
2. Complete Lesson 6 in *A Laboratory Workbook for Introduction to Early Childhood Education*. Hand it in as scheduled.
3. Discuss with your instructors the desired format of activity plans and evaluations.
4. Evaluate your own participation on your evaluation form.
5. Add sample plans for activities to your Resource File.

Study Questions

1. Identify the six levels of the Bloom Taxonomy of Educational Objectives. Describe each level. Give examples from adult subject matter and from children's subject matter.
2. Identify and give examples of the basic components of an activity plan.

Additional Readings

LEEPER, SARAH H., RALPH L. WITHERSPOON, and BARBARA DAY. *Good Schools for Young Children*. New York: Macmillan Publishing Co., Inc., 1984.

SCHICKEDANZ, JUDITH A., MARY E. YORK, IDA SANTOS STEWART, and DORIS A. WHITE. *Strategies for Teaching Young Children*. Englewood Cliffs, N.J.: Prentice-Hall, Inc., 1983.

SEEFELDT, CAROL. *Teaching Young Children*. Englewood Cliffs, N.J.: Prentice-Hall, Inc., 1980.

Learning Activities in the Outdoors

- To identify motor skill stages discovered by researchers studying the development of young children.
- To explain the rationale for utilizing certain procedures and equipment to foster motor skill development in children.
- To plan and evaluate outdoor activities involving large motor skills and other abilities.
- To identify and evaluate the use of space, equipment, and guidance for developing large motor skills in children.

"Let's go bye-bye," excites the baby at home or in an infant school. Prekindergarten and kindergarten children run for their coats when their teacher says, "Time to go outside." Older children's eyes sparkle and books get shoved into desks when the recess bells ring. Even some elders are happy when friends invite them to go jogging.

Vigorous outdoor activity appeals to the young and to many oldsters as well. Exercise is essential for good health, according to authorities. Attitudes toward exercise are formed in the early years, and competencies are developing that will remain with individuals throughout their lifetimes.

Learning and practicing large and small motor skills are among the important developmental tasks (see Chapter 2). Children make progress on these and other tasks in the outdoor program of a high-quality early childhood education program.

University students are called upon to observe and help in the outdoor program. The first chapter of this section on curriculum is devoted to children's learning activities that typically take place out-of-doors. Students who appreciate these activities will be able to make meaningful contributions when they are outdoors with children during the term.

Figure 7-1. The rope ladder challenges four-year-olds who spend many hours scaling it from both the under and top sides. (Child Development Laboratory, University of Missouri–Columbia)

Motor Skill Development[1]

Motor skills are required to control the body. When skills for moving the body such as running, jumping, or climbing are discussed, they are called *large motor or gross muscular skills*. When skills such as writing, tying, or using scissors, are discussed, they are called *small motor* or *fine muscular skills*. According to developmental studies the pattern of motor development is predictable in its broader aspects with individual differences occurring in the timetable.[2]

Motor skill development is usually the first value of outdoor play activity that comes to mind. Large motor skills are critical to the individual's development and to the enjoyment of life. The long lives that today's children can be expected to live make it even more critical that their physical bodies and motor skills be developed adequately.

In the typical indoor classroom, vigorous activity is not encouraged,

---

[1] The author is indebted to Drs. Vern Seefeldt and John Haubenstricker of Michigan State University for permission to use research results, descriptions of sequential stages of motor skill development, and photographs, and for consultations on the content of this section of this chapter.

[2] Mollie S. Smart and Russell C. Smart, *Children: Development and Relationships* (New York: Macmillan Publishing Co., Inc., 1977), pp. 633–634.

141

Figure 7-2. When executing a Stage 3 punt, the performer steps forward with the supporting limb as the ball is released in a forward, downward direction. The striking leg then swings forward as the ball descends toward the surface.

and children may not be allowed to run, jump, climb, or catch. Although such restrictions might be expected indoors, often these large motor skills are also being curtailed outdoors. Teachers may excuse this lack of large motor skill practice by indicating that they are afraid for the children's safety, that there is little or no equipment, or that they place priority on mental tasks. However, research findings indicate that children need teachers who will plan opportunities for them to practice needed large motor skills.

At Michigan State University Drs. Vern Seefeldt and John Haubenstricker have been engaged in a longitudinal research program designed to examine small children's physical growth, motor maturity, and mo-

Figure 7-3. Striking a ball from a tee, using a Stage 4 pattern. Striking at the Stage 4 developmental level involves a shift of the body weight to the rear or right foot of a right-handed batter. As the bat moves forward the weight is transferred to the forward or left foot. At the point of contact the body weight has rotated so that it is over the left foot, with the right foot in position to provide stability during the follow-through phase.

tor development. The research team observed the same children every month over a period of years. They found that "rudimentary stages of the fundamental motor skills which include walking, running, hopping, jumping, skipping, leaping, throwing, catching, etc., must be established very early in life if a child is to advance to more mature stages."[3]

In addition to this research, Seefeldt and his co-workers have organized remedial groups for children referred to them for the assessment

[3] For a detailed review of the scientific literature and a report of the Michigan State University Motor Performance Study see Crystal Branta, John Haubenstricker, and Vern Seefeldt's chapter, "Age Changes in Motor Skills During Childhood and Adolescence," in *Exercise and Sport Sciences Reviews,* R. L. Terjung (ed.), Vol. 12 (Lexington, Mass.: The Collamore Press, D. C. Heath and Company, 1984), pp. 467–521.

of physical motor skills. Seefeldt says, "The children who come to us at age five with poorly established preliminary stages in fundamental motor skills are unlikely to become highly skilled, even though we provide additional sessions with a one-to-one teacher-pupil ratio."[4] As a result of their work, these researchers have grown increasingly convinced that parents and early childhood teachers must engage children in practicing these skills.

The Seefeldt team has been able to analyze the sequential stages children go through in learning many of the fundamental motor skills. They have grouped the skills as follows:

Locomotor skills—moving from place to place.

walk	jump	hop	stop	fall
run	gallop	skip	start	dodge
leap	slide	roll		

Nonlocomotor skills—moving body parts, with child stationary.

swing	stretch	turn	lift
sway	curl	bend	pull
rock	twist	push	

Projection and reception skills—propelling and catching objects

catch	punt	dribble	trap
throw	strike	kick	bounce

If you have compared the way a toddler and an older sibling throw a ball, you know there are differences in the manner of handling the ball and of managing the body during the throw. Through the use of movies Seefeldt's team has been able to describe in detail the developmental sequence of many of these skills. Seefeldt believes that knowing these stages of development will assist parents and teachers in providing appropriate experiences for individual children. The young child should be helped to the next stage in the hierarchy rather than encouraged or pressed to skip a stage or two. For example, a child should master catching a large ball before being expected to use a baseball and glove.

Seefeldt and Haubenstricker have identified, described, and made available the developmental sequences for catching, kicking, throwing, and the standing long jump. See Table 7-1. They have analyzed additional skills which will be available in their forthcoming publications.

Tables 7-1 to 7-4 give details of the stages for four skills. With practice you can easily recognize each child's level with respect to each skill and can, thus, make plans for activities to stimulate development toward the next stage. Records of children's stages can be kept on forms such as Figure 7-8.

[4] Vern Seefeldt, "The Role of Motor Skills in the Lives of Children with Learning Disabilities," paper presented to the Conference of the Association for Children with Learning Disabilities, Detroit, Michigan, March 1973.

Table 7-1. Developmental Sequence of Catching*

Stage 1   The arms of the performer are directly in front of the body, with the elbows extended and the palms facing upward or inward. As the ball contacts the hands or arms the elbows flex and the arms and hands attempt to secure the ball by holding it against the chest.

Stage 2   The child prepares to receive the object with the arms in front of the body, the elbows extended or slightly flexed. Upon presentation of the ball the arms begin an encircling motion that ends when the ball is secured against the chest. The arm action in Stage 2 begins before the ball contacts the body.

*SOURCE: The sequences of the four motor skills described in Tables 7-1–7-4 were provided by John Haubenstricker and Vern Seefeldt from their Motor Performance Study at Michigan State University.

Figure 7-4. A three-year-old child catching a ball with a Stage 2 pattern. Catching a ball at the second developmental level involves placing the arms in front of the body in preparation to receive the ball. The arms begin moving toward the body while the ball is still airborne. The first point of contact occurs when the ball strikes the chest. At that instant the arms and hands encircle the ball and secure it by pressing it next to the body in a bearhug movement.

Table 7-1. Developmental Sequence of Catching *(Continued)*

Stage 3   The child prepares to receive the ball with arms that are slightly flexed and extended forward at the shoulder.

       Substage 1   The child uses the chest as the first point of contact with the ball and attempts to secure the ball by holding it to the chest with the hands and arms.

       Substage 2   The child attempts to catch the ball with the hands. Failure to hold it securely results in an attempt to guide the ball to the chest, where it is controlled by the hands and arms.

Stage 4   The child prepares to receive the ball by flexing the elbows and presenting the arms toward the approaching ball. Skillful performers may keep the elbows at the sides and flex the arms simultaneously as they bring them forward to meet the ball. The ball is caught with the hands and does not contact any other body part.

Stage 5   The upper body movement is identical to that of Stage 4. In addition, the child is required to change the stationary base in order to receive the ball. Stage 5 is apparently difficult for many children when they are required to move in relation to an approaching ball.

Table 7-2. Developmental Sequence of Throwing

Stage 1   The motion is essentially in a back-to-front or posterior-anterior direction. The feet remain fixed with little or no trunk rotation. The force of movement comes from hip flexion, moving the shoulder forward, and extending the elbow.

Stage 2   The feet generally remain stationary with a wide base of support, but a step with the right or the left foot in the direction of the throw may be taken. The force is directed more toward a direction parallel to the floor, with the hips and trunk moving as one unit. The motion may resemble a "sling" as the body and extended arm rotate as if around a vertical axis.

Stage 3   The primary change from Stage 2 is that the movement of the foot on the same side as the throwing arm strides in the direction of the throw. The trunk rotation may be decreased in relation to Stage 2, but the hip flexion is increased.

Stage 4   The movement is contralateral, with the leg opposite the throwing arm striding forward as the throwing arm moves during the "wind-up" phase. The stride forward with the contralateral leg provides a wide base of support and greater stability during the force production phase of the throw.

Stage 5   The "wind-up" phase begins with the throwing hand moving in a downward arc and then backward as the opposite leg moves forward. This concurrent action rotates the hip and spine into position for forceful derotation. As the contralateral foot strikes the surface, the hips, spine, and shoulders begin derotating in sequence. The contralateral leg begins to extend at the knee, providing an equal and opposite reaction to the throwing arm. The arm opposite the throwing limb also moves forcefully toward the body to assist in the "equal and opposite" reaction.

146

Figure 7-5. Throwing a ball with a Stage 4 pattern. The throw at a Stage 4 developmental level involves opposition of movement between the arms and the feet; as the throwing arm (right) moves backward in the preparatory phase, the left foot moves forward to receive the weight as the arm moves forward to release the ball. The force of the throw is shifted to the left foot as the body "follows through" its motion after the throw.

Figure 7-6. Kicking a ball with a Stage 2 pattern. Kicking involves striking a stationary ball with the foot. Kicking is learned with less difficulty than punting because the former eliminates the need to relate to an approaching object during the performance. The body remains stationary during the contact phase, but the performer generally steps backward after the kick to regain the balance that was lost momentarily during the contact phase. Note that there is cross-body opposition of movement in the arms and feet after the ball is contacted.

Table 7-3. Developmental Sequence of Kicking

Stage 1   The performer is usually stationary and positioned near the ball. Knee joint extension occurs after contacting the ball, resulting in a pushing rather than a striking action. The knee of the kicking leg continues to extend. If the trunk is inclined forward, the performer will step forward to gain balance. If the trunk is leaning backward, the kicking leg will move backward to achieve body balance after the kick.

Stage 2   The performer is stationary. The kicking leg moves forward with the knee joint in a flexed position. Knee joint extension begins just prior to foot contact with the ball. Arm-leg opposition occurs during the kick. Knee extension continues after the ball leaves the foot, but the force is usually not sufficient to move the body forward. Instead, the performer usually steps sideward or backward.

Figure 7-7. Jumping at Stage 1. The preparatory phases of jumping are essentially the same for all developmental levels of jumping. However, the force-production phase—especially those actions that occur immediately before, during, and after the point at which the feet leave the surface— distinguish the various levels of performance. The performer moves his arms backward immediately upon takeoff in an attempt to restrict the forward movement of the trunk. In Stage 1 jumping behavior the arms act as "brakes" to forward momentum.

Table 7-3. Developmental Sequence of Kicking *(Continued)*

Stage 3   The performer takes one or more deliberate steps to approach the ball. The kicking foot stays near the surface as it approaches the ball, resulting in less flexion than in Stage 2. The trunk remains nearly upright, preventing maximum force production. The knee begins to extend prior to contact. The force of the kick may carry the performer past the point of contact if the approach was vigorous.

Stage 4   The approach involves one or more steps with the final "step" being an airborne run or leap providing hyperextension of the hip and flexion of the knee. The shoulders are retracted and the trunk is inclined backward as the supporting leg begins to move forward. The movement of the thigh nearly stops as the knee joint begins to extend rapidly just prior to contact with the ball. In the follow through, if the forward momentum of the kick is sufficient, the performer either hops on the support leg or scissors the legs while airborne in order to land on the kicking foot.

Table 7-4. Developmental Sequence of the Standing Long Jump

Stage 1   The child bends the knees and moves the arms backward in preparation for jumping. The vertical component of force may be greater than the horizontal, resulting in a jump that is upward rather than forward. Arms move backward, acting as brakes to stop the momentum of the trunk as the legs extend in front of the center of mass.

Stage 2   The arms move in a front-to-back direction during the preparatory phase, but move sideward (winging action) during the "in-flight" phase. The knees and hips flex and extend more fully than in Stage 1. The landing is made with the center of gravity above the base of support, with the thighs perpendicular to the floor rather than parallel as in the "reaching" position of Stage 4.

Stage 3   The arms swing backward and then move forward vigorously during the preparatory phase. Upon takeoff the arms extend and move forward to approximately the height of the head. The arms remain in this position during the first half of the jump and then move down and backward in preparation for landing. The knee extension at the takeoff is nearly complete, but the angle of the jump still exceeds 45 degrees.

Stage 4   The arms extend vigorously forward and upward upon takeoff, reaching full extension above the head at "lift-off." The hips and knees are extended fully, with the takeoff angle at 45 degrees or less. In preparation for landing the arms are brought downward and the legs are thrust forward until the thighs are parallel to the surface. The center of gravity is far behind the base of support upon landing, but at the moment of contact the knees are flexed and the arms are thrust forward in order to keep the body from falling backward.

Proper Equipment and Support

Parents and teachers can make an important contribution to children's motor skill development through providing proper equipment, sequencing the tasks to encourage the children to practice comfortably rather than competitively, and giving each some one-to-one attention. For throwing, the child should have a small ball that fits the small hand—usually a tennis ball, sponge ball, or beanbag. A patient adult should play ball with the child because if two unskilled children attempt to play together, they won't be able to make many adjustments necessary for a successful experience for each one.

For catching, a soccer-size ball made of a soft material—rubber, sponge, or polyester filled—is needed. If you notice in Figure 7-4, the child hugs the ball when catching it. Obviously, a tennis ball would fall through the hug. Also, the ball hits the chest and at times bumps the face, hence the ball's softness makes it less of a threat. Children in Stages 1, 2, or 3 need a patient adult to help them practice catching. Their same-stage friends will be unable to accommodate to their needs.

A Floppsy-Doodle, made with a skein of yarn, tied in the middle and cut at the loops, makes a good throwing and catching object. It can be used in a room at school or home, and the yarn ends make catching it easier for some. The Floppsy-Doodle can be carried on the head or shoulder and contribute to games the children find fun.

Skills are not specifically related to chronological age, size, or sex, but are a result of a combination of maturation and experience. Teachers and parents must remember that grouping children by chronological age, body size, or sex will still leave a wide variation in stage of motor skill development. You have heard the derogatory comment, "He throws like a girl." Generally, it means the child is stuck on Stage 2 or 3 of the throwing sequence. That is, he is stepping off on the foot that is on the same side as the throwing arm, thus, is unable to produce adequate velocity or distance on the ball. With only a little attention an adult can

Figure 7-8. Motor skill progress record.

Skill   Throwing

Names	Stage	Date	Stage	Date	Stage	Date
1. Amy	1	9-15	1	11-15		
2. Andy	2	9-20	3	11-15		
3. Angella	1	9-16	2	11-16		
4. Bill	2	9-20	2	11-16		
5. Brad	2	9-20	3	11-16		

help such a child practice stepping off with the foot which is opposite to the throwing arm, turning that side of the body toward the target, and winding up low past the hip and up. (See Stage 4 description under Throwing in Table 7-2, page 146.)

The stereotypic comment, "throws like a girl," would not be true of girls if they were given adequate practice. The study shows that there are no significant differences in the sexes in motor skill stages initially. Differences occur only as socialization and differential practice and training take place.

*   *   *

Talk It Over: No. 1

Discuss some games or techniques you might use that would encourage children to practice fundamental motor skills. Be creative. What are some novel ways?

*   *   *

For some handicapped children gloves with Velcro palms will help them catch a Floppsy-Doodle or a crocheted or knitted ball. They can feel successful in catching this way. For batting practice, a whiffle ball—a lightweight, hollow, molded polyethelene ball—may be tied to an elastic rope and suspended from a tree limb at the right height to allow children to practice batting with a plastic bat. Because the ball is attached, the child can practice alone without having to chase the ball each time after hitting it. A ball may also be placed on a rubber cone (the type used to mark a street) or on a tee to enable the young batter to practice striking a ball that is stationary. See Figure 7-3.

Young "round-ballers" can throw balls into wastebaskets, or hoops can be lowered to encourage their practice. A sponge ball called a Nerf ball, or a crocheted or knitted ball stuffed with polyester is harmless to people or furnishings it might hit while the young child practices throwing, catching, punting, and batting. The child will not fear being hit by such a ball. Proper equipment helps to reach goals for young children, and parents should be encouraged to use such equipment.

Keeping an inflated beach ball, sponge ball, or balloon in the air encourages children to stand on tiptoe and to stretch and leap. Balls and beanbags encourage the practice of projection and reception skills. Children may like to throw the balls against a wall or into a large receptacle, such as a packing box. The smaller the child, the larger the ball required.

An obstacle course may be set up with various pieces of equipment, and the children may be required to climb up on a packing box, jump across a plank held up by sawhorses, climb through the rungs on the jungle gym, and run down an inclined plane attached to the jungle gym. Such a game gives children the opportunity to practice several fundamental skills.

The teacher can encourage jumping by placing one end of a bamboo fishing pole on the ground and the other end on a sawhorse or jungle gym for the children to jump over. The fishing pole should be loosely held, so that if the child hits the pole while jumping, the pole will fall easily and the child will not be hurt. The angle of the pole allows the children to jump where they are ready—high or low. This exercise requires the propelling of the body up and over. The teacher can encourage the long jump by marking a V shape on the grass or tumbling mat and encouraging the children to jump where they can make it across. Children typically fall after a jump, making the softer surface important. Avoidance of failure is important, and competition between children should also be avoided. Games of hopscotch give good hopping and jumping practice. Boys and girls should be equally encouraged to practice all skills.

Nonlocomotor skills can be combined with locomotor skills through music and rhythm activities. A tom-tom, a tambourine, maracas, or recorded music may accompany the activity. The teacher should draw the children's attention to or get them to suggest different ways of using the body. Carrying ribbons or scarves or wearing full skirts encourages using the body to sway, twist, and bend. The hula hoop also encourages body movement.

Other Values of Outdoor Activity

Mental, Social, and Emotional Development

Outdoor activity makes outstanding contributions to young children's lives. The goals for motor skill development are interrelated with goals for mental, social, and emotional development.

The reason outdoor activity is so popular with every age is that it honestly meets the needs of the individuals. Why do elementary children answer, "Recess," when asked, "What do you like best at school?" Recess is popular because it is freer of adult interferences—interferences that must at times be frustrating and stifling to children. A time for outdoor activity provides a release from tensions that build up from prolonged sitting, thinking, creating, being quiet, and trying to be "good."

The outdoor period provides the child additional stimuli to meet friends and talk over mutual interests. Children talk, shout, laugh, and sing outdoors with less restraint than may occur in classrooms. Language flows naturally. Children use their outdoor period to make plans and do things together. Sharing and other social skills develop. Outdoor activity may provide social acceptance and leadership for those children who have difficulty with more formal activities.

Individual motor skills, such as pulling, pushing, lifting, balancing,

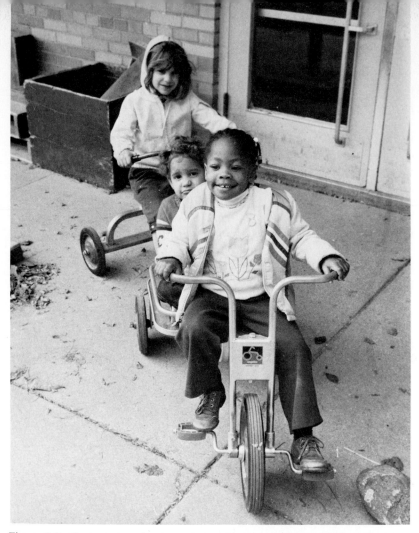

Figure 7-9. Cooperative play is encouraged by the trailer attached to the ever-popular tricycle. (Child Development Laboratory, University of Wisconsin–Madison)

running, climbing, pedaling, steering, riding, jumping, throwing, and swinging, are practiced. These skills contribute to children's self-assurance, making them more confident when facing new experiences. Interaction with people of all ages is facilitated through motor skills. Skill in swimming dramatizes this fact. Once young children swim with confidence, they can swim with adults and teenagers as well as with children their own age. Until they develop swimming skills, they are relegated to the shallow pool and their fellow nonswimmers. Or a five-year-old girl who has graduated to a two-wheel bicycle not only is king in her own crowd, but she also is admitted to the school-age set and is ready for family rides.

Negative and hostile feelings can be drained off through the activities the out-of-doors provides. Throwing balls and beanbags, punching the punching bag, or pounding nails are examples of acceptable outlets for "bad" feelings. Vigorous running and riding also provide release for pent-up feelings.

Of course, the mind continues to develop out-of-doors. In fact, the new environment will stimulate curiosity and exploration in children. They can make many observations on their own. They can test out their ideas and come to many conclusions. Children may seem to be only exercising their legs or vocal chords, but their minds are also developing. Physical and mental development are closely related. For example, such concepts as fast and slow, high and low, long and short, and hard and easy are readily experienced. The child expresses intellectual understanding through motor skills. Adults make inferences about intellectual growth through observing a child involved with activities.

Developing large muscle coordination during vigorous play leads to improved small muscle coordination. Small muscle coordination is required in order to write, draw, cut, tie, or manipulate such things as puzzles and equipment.

The imaginative games and dramatic play observed during children's outdoor activity challenge the child's creativity, concepts, and memory. All are part of the child's mental development.

Vigorous physical activity stimulates all vital processes, such as circulation, respiration, and elimination. Eating habits improve, and rest is more welcome.

Dr. Jean Mayer, professor of nutrition at the Harvard School of Public Health, states that physical activity is the most important environmental variable affecting obesity in children. Obese children exercise less than lean children, yet often eat the same amounts. In diet therapy a long-term regime of increased exercise is needed.[5]

Additional values of the outdoor self-selected activity period are the opportunities it affords children to feel free and to enjoy fresh air and sunshine. Children's happiness in outdoor activities is clearly expressed in laughter, squeals, and shouts.

Requirements of a High-Quality Outdoor Program

A high-quality early childhood education program includes plans for a daily outdoor self-selected activity period. It is possible in some climates to hold virtually the entire school day outdoors. If the outdoor

[5] Myron Winick, "Childhood Obesity," *Nutrition Today*, 9:3 (May/June 1974), p. 9. Also see "Childhood Obesity: Prevention and Treatment," by Phillip M. Wishon, Robert Bower, and Ben Eller. *Young Children*, 39:1 (November 1983), pp. 21–27.

period is to make the maximum contribution to the development of the child, the following are required: (1) careful planning, (2) adequate space, (3) appropriate equipment, (4) sufficient time, and (5) appropriate guidance.[6]

Careful Planning

Teachers should plan outdoor and large motor activities as thoughtfully as they do indoor activities. Too many teachers simply turn children loose in the outdoor playyard with little or no thought about variety, sequencing, or challenging activities. Children should have an opportunity for outdoor activities every day. During severe weather, gymnasium activities may be substituted. Typically, children desire lively action and need little urging to participate.

Referring to the list of fundamental motor skills, the teacher will plan to involve each child in these activities regularly.

The teacher individualizes planning and evaluating of motor skills by (1) observing each child, (2) checking and recording skill mastery, (3) planning and encouraging each child to practice each skill, and (4) encouraging the child to try the next stage in the motor sequence when he or she seems ready.

* * *

Talk It Over: No. 2

Discuss your experience of working in the playyard with young children. What were your concerns? In what way was it enjoyable?

* * *

Locomotor skills can be practiced through such games as follow-the-leader, with a few children at a time following an adult through several skills on the list. For example, the leader could move from running, to jumping, to galloping, to leaping, as the group of children is led around the playyard. Another day several of the other skills can be practiced. Such games are helpful on cold days to get children moving, warmed up, and having a good time. The activities serve similar ends for teachers and help them release the energy and tension that inevitably build up.

Moveable equipment should be regrouped from time to time to stimulate new use of it. Close observation of the children's interests will guide the teacher in planning activities and arranging equipment. Children will gladly give advice and assistance. For example, when cowboy play is popular, the packing boxes are called "barns," and a corral is

[6] For a helpful rating scale for playgrounds see "How Can Playgrounds Be Improved?" by Penny Lovell and Thelma Harms, *Young Children*, 40:3 (March 1985), pp. 3–8.

Figure 7-10. A balance beam and other equipment are useful indoors when weather prevents outdoor play. (Early Childhood Laboratory, Kansas State University)

needed for the cowboy's tricycle "horses." The teacher assists the cowboys in getting the barn in the correct position.

The teacher should make plans to stimulate children's mental development while they are out-of-doors. Many indoor experiments, such as those using inclines or balances, can be repeated outdoors. Spontaneous learning about weather, plants, insects, and animals is natural for the yard. Specimens can be observed, discussed, classified, labeled, imitated, and taken indoors. It is helpful to have science books, specimen jars, butterfly nets, and magnifying glasses available to use in extending the learning. Through close involvement in children's learning, the teacher will be able to ask questions that help children see relationships and make comparisons between their discoveries and the adult world. Planned experiences are initiated for children who don't seem to have questions.

* * *
Talk It Over: No. 3

After observing children, give an example of a child learning a concept while playing outdoors.

* * *

Quiet activities have a definite place outdoors. Children should always be able to choose between active and less active outdoor activity. Music, perhaps with guitar or autoharp, is delightful. Stories told or read to small groups are pleasant. Children enjoy a period of looking at books alone, so books should be available. Even resting takes on positive dimensions when a blanket is spread under a tree.

Plans for social and emotional growth should also be on the outdoor agenda. Planning for small group projects is an excellent time for children to practice sharing, taking turns, persisting toward a goal, and responding to frustration.

The teacher's attitude toward the outdoors is quickly indicated by what is planned and what children are permitted to do outdoors. Teachers who don't particularly enjoy the outdoors should make an effort to learn to enjoy it. They should dress appropriately for the weather. With proper attire from head to toe, the teacher will begin to appreciate the exhilarating freshness of a winter day or the peaceful sunshine of a spring afternoon just as much as the children enjoy the out-of-doors.

Adequate Space[7]

Children probably often feel cooped up. They need the outdoor space that a good school affords. At home their living space may be shared with a number of siblings. Their playground may be the city streets and sidewalks. Even where parks and playgrounds are available, the parent may curtail the child's use of them. When playgrounds are overcrowded, the young child may feel insecure among the many strangers.

Children who live in mansions with plenty of room both indoors and out may also need the outdoor activities offered at school. These children may have few friends their age to share their elaborate home setting or to offer stimulation. They may stay indoors to have the companionship of their mother or the maid.

In the microscopic yards of some hillside slums and suburbs children are unable to use a ball or bike. Even a good run is impossible because the terrain is too steep, and gravity is against them.

Space, then, becomes a cherished item in the modern world. Early

[7] For a comprehensive analysis and recommendations regarding amounts and use of space, see Sybil Kritchevsky, Elizabeth Prescott, and Lee Walling, *Planning Environments for Young Children: Physical Space* (Washington, D.C.: National Association for the Education of Young Children, 1977).

childhood education programs should endeavor to provide 75 to 200 square feet of outdoor space for each child. Careful planning is required to see that all space is used judiciously.

The outdoor space should be safe from traffic so that the children can use it without fear and without constant reminders to protect themselves. The fence should permit children to see the outside world, yet be high enough and designed to discourage climbing. Gates with secure latches are needed. One practical aspect to consider when planning the fence is to provide some way for trucks with sand and equipment to make deliveries.

The space should be large enough for the number of children who may use it at any given time. When space must be shared with other groups, it is well to agree on a time schedule to avoid conflict from overcrowding. In schools housing older children it is wise to take pre-kindergarten children and kindergarteners outdoors when older children are at work in the building. Thus the fear and confusion younger children feel when older children play at the same time may be avoided.

The best outdoor space is adjacent to and on the same level as the indoor room. The toilet must be near the entrance. Time and energy for both teachers and children are used more effectively when indoor and outdoor spaces are adjacent. Materials can be easily moved in and out. Supervision is simpler. Children's needs can best be met if the whole group is not required to be outside or inside at a given time.

Good playground space provides a variety of levels and challenges to the children. There should be knolls and flat surfaces, grassy expanses and hard-surfaced areas. Open space is necessary for exuberant play. A quiet nook for resting and reflecting is just as important. There should be protected areas so that the benefits of the outdoors can be enjoyed when the rains come. Shade is pleasantly cooling when the sunshine is very hot. Protection from prevailing winds makes space usable on wintry days. The space should be located where children can be allowed to be noisy.

Phyllis Lueck designed a creative outdoor learning environment. The tricycle paths had various textures and finishes—pebbly, smooth, gravel, asphalt, and cement ridged like a washboard. A bridge across a little gully required careful driving, for it had narrow tracks that just fit the tricycle tires. In addition, various types of wind chimes gave the children an opportunity to hear variations in sounds when they rang the chimes.[8]

Adequate drainage is important. A sloping yard of slightly sandy soil dries off quickly after a shower. Wood chips, gravel, and other materials can be used to weatherize the surface and keep the children out of

[8] Phyllis Lueck, "Planning an Outdoor Learning Environment," *Theory into Practice,* **12**:2 (April 1973), pp. 121–127.

the mud. When planning a riding lane for wheel toys, one should remember that a ribbon of hard surface encircling the play area simplifies driving rules. Ramps, inclines, or knolls add interest and challenge young riders.

The playyard should be designed to facilitate teaching. Out-of-the-way corners, equipment, and foliage that block the teacher's view prevent good teaching and supervision.

The space should be attractive. A variety of plantings can provide interesting natural science experiences as well as beauty. Special attention to finishes and colors will make the yard more inviting to all.

In some schools there is space to house several animal pets, which provide learning experiences for the children. In other schools the yard might be used for a day to house someone's pet rabbit or a lamb borrowed from a farmer friend. From watching a wriggling worm or a soaring bird the children can be stimulated to observe and learn about living creatures.

Children may not get enough vigorous outdoor exercise in climates that are extremely hot or cold. In such situations protected space for large motor activities—climbing, sliding, running, and riding—should be located elsewhere. For example, a protected patio, a rainy-day room, or a gymnasium can serve this purpose if it is carefully planned and equipped.

Appropriate Equipment

Equipping the schoolyard is a major endeavor. A knowledge of children's needs, interests, and abilities is required for choosing appropriate equipment. Money, planning, and imagination are also required.

There should be equipment for climbing, swinging, balancing, pulling, lifting, chinning, sliding, riding, building, and pounding. Some large boxes or structures are needed that lend themselves to imaginative games for children to develop. Sand, mud, and water are essentials.

There must be enough equipment so that all children using the yard at one time may find a suitable activity. If there is a shortage of equipment, then children direct their energy against each other and toward climbing on gates and fences. Ample equipment is essential if the outdoor program is to make its rightful contribution to the child's overall development.

The equipment should contain a few pieces that the children will find somewhat difficult to master at the beginning of the school year. For example, only one five-year-old was able to use the trapeze in September. However, during the final weeks of school almost every child went hand over hand on that trapeze.

Trees and Garden

Live trees in the yard can provide challenging climbing experiences, refreshing shade, and outstanding opportunities to watch nature's sequences. A fallen tree trimmed down to two or three major forks provides children a gnarled surface for climbing, sitting, and jumping. As the bark loosens the children will enjoy helping to remove it. With years of use the surface will become shiny. The tree trunk will contribute to imaginative play, serving as a spaceship, an airplane, or a train, depending on the idea of the moment.

When an area in the yard is set aside for the spring garden or the fall bulb planting, sturdy short-handled garden tools are useful. Quality tools should be purchased to encourage a young gardener. A corner can be reserved for "just digging."

Water play is delightful outdoors when the weather is warm. Plastic aprons are essential to keep clothes dry. A specially made portable water table with a galvanized lining that makes a 10-inch deep sink is convenient for both indoor and outdoor water play. Children, however, will enjoy even a dishpan or a bucket of water. When children are furnished soap, they will happily wash the doll clothes or tricycles. A wading pool is popular in summer. Of course, for safety, utmost care must be taken to have the water play supervised at all times.

When given a can of water and a small paintbrush, the young child likes to "paint" the side of the storage shed or the jungle gym—painting as carefully as any painter. A paper cup of water with detergent suds and a drinking straw make bubble blowing easy. Both activities are fun on warm sunny days.

Wintertime, with its snow and ice, gives children water in another form. When dressed properly, children enjoy the snow. Children often lie in the snow making snow angels, like Peter in Ezra Jack Keats's *A Snowy Day,* and gaining information about their body shapes and sizes. Sleds are standard equipment in schools in snowy climates. Only a small knoll is necessary to bring joy to young sledders. Pans of snow can be taken indoors for measurement or experimentation.

Imaginative Play

A playhouse structure—which can double as a storage room—stimulates children's dramatic play. When it is designed with a variety of stairs and ladders, the child's climbing skills are developed. A firepole, a rope ladder, or a metal slide can be built into the structure for the child's quick "escape." Doll carriages and dress-up clothes contribute to imaginative outdoor play.

The jungle gym offers a challenge to children's climbing muscles and their imagination. It should be sturdy. Though the steel gym is cold to the touch, it does not become as dangerously deteriorated as a wooden one. A jungle gym is best located on a grassy surface or over tanbark so that falls will be cushioned.

A slide should be low enough for the teacher to reach the child at the top. This is important for a young group. Also, the slide should be flat enough at the bottom so children will not shoot out into the dirt from a fast ride. Popular slides in some schools are those built into tree houses or other structures. Children can then incorporate the slide into imaginary play more readily than when it is a single, isolated piece of equipment.

Old cars, trucks, boats, and even airplanes have been used in school yards to stimulate imaginary games. Usually these are mere skeletons with doors, windows, and all loose gadgets removed. They should be colorfully painted to avoid giving the area a junkyard appearance.

Large packing boxes of varying sizes and colors can become the center for dramatic play. To imaginative children a large box can be a "barn" for tricycle "horses" or the "living room" of the little "house." Several boxes built from sturdy pine lumber ranging down from $54'' \times 54'' \times 54''$ and painted with high-quality outdoor paint will be invaluable in the outdoor program.

Other accessory pieces such as barrels, ladders, sawhorses, and planks have many uses. Planks can become bridges between packing boxes. A jumping board can be made from low blocks or sawhorses placed under each end of a plank. A sliding board can be made from a plank with one end resting on the jungle gym.

A collection of large hollow blocks painted or varnished for use out-of-doors adds to the quality of the play. Corrals, roads, bridges, and houses are designed by young "engineers" when they are provided with an adequate supply of blocks. Out-of-the-weather storage is required for most blocks. Block storage and movement will be facilitated if blocks are stored on a wheeled dollie that is easily rolled in and out.

A sufficient number of sturdy wheel toys should be available to that children can perfect their cycling skills. Wheeled equipment is also useful in dramatic play. In a group of twenty children about ten wheel toys—tricycles of various sizes, wagons, tractors, and the like—should be available.

Rocking-boat-type equipment, either to stand or to sit on, provides pleasant opportunities for developing arm and leg muscle coordination.

Swings

A good choice of swing is the glider type requiring two children to face each other and cooperate in a push-pull motion. With this type of swing, goals for self-help, cooperation, and socialization are fostered in ways not achieved with traditional swings.

For younger children traditional swings should have strap seats. This seat, which resembles a horse saddle cinch, does not harm the child as a hard seat may if the child gets hit with it. The seat curves to fit the child's body so that falling is less likely. Because children cannot stand up easily in strap seats, they will be less popular with older children. For older children the swing should have a rigid seat made of light-weight plastic material.

The tire swing is the favorite swing in many yards. It is a tire hung from a tree limb with a chain. The tire may be suspended in only one place or anchored with three chains that hold the tire parallel to the ground, making room for three children.

Sand

A sandpile provides a quiet, restful area and an inexpensive medium for children. A good-quality sand can be purchased. A wood-frame box with a 10-inch ledge provides a seat for the children when the sand is wet. Children will use the ledge as a "table" as they turn out their "cakes." A lid for the sandbox is essential in neighborhoods where cats might contaminate the sand. The lid can be hinged along the edges in such a way that it becomes a seat when opened.

Sand should be kept moist. Dry sand gets in hair and eyes more readily than damp sand. Moist sand is more easily molded into cakes or tunnels. Numerous containers should be provided. Kitchen castoffs are ex-

Figure 7-11. Children can measure their jumps on this "Jack Rabbit Sign." (Child Development Laboratory, Michigan State University)

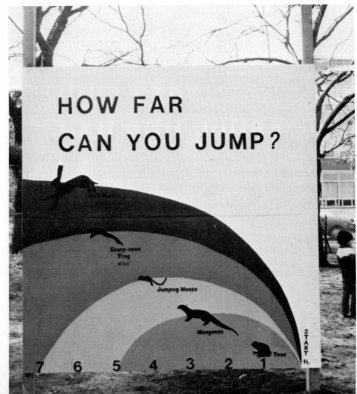

cellent: juice cans, old pots and pans, plastic milk cartons, and funnels made from the tops of plastic bottles are all suitable sand toys. The teacher should examine the collection from time to time and replace broken items. A large number of metal shovels makes sharing less difficult. The sandbox with numerous containers of various sizes gives children opportunities to measure, count, and label the products they are making so carefully. The sandbox affords a place to rest, yet keep busy and in touch with friends.

Carpentry

Young carpenters will enjoy pounding and sawing in the playyard. Carpenter's benches, old worktables, or packing boxes can provide space on which to work. Real tools should be purchased and kept in good working condition. Separate clamps or vises attached to the tables are handy for helping the child hold the wood. Water paints can be made available so that little carpenters can finish up their projects in style. Nuts and bolts make interesting manipulative and sorting experiences and may be used in wood projects. Wrenches may be needed for some projects.

Cabinetmakers will usually give teachers the scraps of wood from their scrap bin. Sometimes the teacher is able to interest the craftsmen in the children's projects, and they will save unusual shapes as they cut them out. Under saws, planes, and drills the teacher will find sawdust and shavings of various sizes that are useful in numerous art projects.

Table Toys and Snacks

Various table toys from inside can be used outside also. Finger painting and clay take on new possibilities when used outdoors. Easels can be set up outside for painting.

Children get thirsty when they are very active. Drinking water should be available, from either a drinking fountain or a pitcher of water brought outside. It is very convenient to have weatherproofed tables so that an outdoor snack or lunch can be served.

Storage and Maintenance

Storage for all outdoor equipment should be designed to encourage the children to help put things away. Proper storage of toys teaches children desirable habits. At the same time children can be very helpful to the teacher. Most equipment deteriorates in wet weather; therefore proper storage is essential.

An adequate budget is needed to keep equipment properly maintained. Equipment with pieces that are loose or missing is often frustrating and unsafe for children's use. Equipment represents a substantial investment in time and money.

Sufficient Time

The time block set aside for outdoor, self-selected activity should be at least 30 minutes long. Thirty minutes or more are needed to encourage the children to go beyond the level of just letting off steam. With a large block of time children will engage in constructive, thoughtful activity. Teachers may observe that the first few minutes outdoors children often seem compulsive in activity. They may grab at the first toy they see, or monopolize the tricycle, or hold a swing with an "I got here first" attitude. After 10 to 15 minutes, when they realize they will have time left over, they begin to plan activities. When children accustom themselves to long outdoor periods, many satisfying learning experiences take place.

In warm climates virtually the entire school day, and most of the school's learning centers, can be carried on out-of-doors. Care should be taken to avoid overtiring those children who use the large muscle equipment extensively in an effort to keep up with a special friend. Routine quiet times are essential in the planning.

Sufficient time outdoors should be considered a must for large motor activities, fresh air, and sunshine. With modern clothing even snowy and rainy days can be enjoyed by children and teachers. Teachers in full-day programs must realize that when children are kept indoors in the center for eight to ten hours, there will be little or no daylight hours left for outdoor activity when the children get home—even assuming they have a productive learning environment in which to play at home. The school's outdoor activities become essential in these cases.

Appropriate Guidance

Applying the principles of guidance learned in Chapter 5, especially indirect and direct guidance, is required. Also the principles learned in Chapter 4 regarding setting the stage will be useful in planning for and interacting with children in activities out-of-doors.

Teachers will enjoy guiding children's learning out-of-doors if they understand the stages of physical and motor development. This understanding will help adults overcome excessive concern that children will hurt themselves, provide clues to when children's safety requires the teacher to stop an activity, and preclude unnecessary labeling of activities as "dangerous."

Many adults are fearful when children climb. A general rule followed by most experienced teachers is that children will climb only as high as they feel safe. If they are overencouraged by adults or other children to go beyond the point where they feel safe, or if they appear to be showing off, then the teacher should stay close by to prevent accidents.

Teachers must be willing to set limits that protect the safety of the children, protect the learning environment, and protect property. The teacher will define and give reasons for the limitations set—"Your sand is for digging. Sand hurts Jane's eyes." Removing a child from the sandbox or other equipment if the child does not abide by the rules may be necessary at times.

When a teacher sees only a single child or two on a piece of high equipment, there may be no need to worry. However, if more than two children are climbing on a slide, a jungle gym, or a packing box, it is a situation to watch. Crowding invites pushing. The teacher can first move closer to the group. If all is peaceful, there may be no need to say anything. The teacher is close enough to know when guidance is needed to ensure safety.

In practice the mere movement of the teacher close to a play group is a reminder to the children to play according to the established rules. Therefore, without saying anything, the teacher will influence the behavior of the children. In addition, if the group is too large for the equipment, the teacher can directly or indirectly extend the play to a larger area. Setting up an enticing new climbing arrangement nearby that will attract some children and thus reduce the size of the first group to a safe number may be desirable.

* * *

Talk It Over: No. 4

Discuss safety measures for children in the playyard.

* * *

Using traditional swings, a child consciously or unconsciously may isolate himself or herself from the group. Guidance may help a child who swings alone all the time to feel confident enough to try other activities. Some will try new things if there is no one to push the swing.

Certain children monopolize a teacher by requesting repeatedly a push in the swing. If the school has a traditional swing, the teacher will want the children to learn to pump themselves. The following is one way to help children learn to pump. When Carla seems eager to learn, the teacher places a plank directly behind the swing, extending from the spot where the child's feet rest. The far end is elevated with a large hollow block or sawhorse, making an inclined plane. Holding the swing chains tight with the seat under her, she then walks backward up the plank. As she sits down on the seat her feet go up in the air and she "takes off." She will be thrilled at the new-found independence in being able to make herself go in the swing, and will practice the feat over and over again. In some schools the incline is built as a ramp under the swings used by the younger children.

Another useful method to encourage pumping is to pull the child forward in the swing, grasping the feet instead of pushing from behind. For example, the teacher warns Tony, then gives both his feet a slight tug. She encourages him as he swings forward, to reach with his feet for her hands, which are held up higher and higher. This reaching gets his feet up, and eventually he feels secure enough to relax and let his shoulders and torso move with the swing. Verbal encouragement and the accompanying words, "bending and stretching," will label the action of his legs and help him get the rhythm. Children enjoy the socializing with the teacher that this technique encourages.

Sharing is one of those elusive qualities that adults would have all children develop. The teacher's guidance is often required in problems of sharing. In addition to social learning, sharing affords children concrete experience with quantity, number, and division—all mathematical concepts. Sharing toys is easier when there is a sufficient quantity, because a child does not like to wait indefinitely for a desired toy. A new toy may have to be rationed so that each child can have a turn. Rationing and sharing are different. With rationing one hopes to ensure equal use of a given supply. With sharing one finds joy and satisfaction in mutual or partial use of a thing.

There is a feeling that goes with sharing that comes from having "enough." Adults may tell Abe that he has had the toy long enough, but only Abe really knows. How would you react if someone told you that you had had "enough to eat"? You'd probably think, "How does she know I've had enough?"

People share voluntarily, willingly, happily, and frequently when they feel that they can decide. Children who feel loved and self-confident are more willing to share. Usually only those who know each other very well share voluntarily. Significant sharing can be observed when two children are having a happy time together. There will be a mutual give-and-take that is the real essence of sharing. Statements like "We share in this school" or "You've got to learn to share" do not really help the child learn. Children interpret these statements to mean you expect them to divide up the goods and will force them to do so if they refuse.

It is helpful to identify activity verbally as "sharing" so that the child will grasp what is meant by the expression. For example, Jack arrived in the kindergarten and observed the children petting some new guinea pigs. He walked up and immediately said, "You've got to share." His behavior indicated that he expected everyone to step aside and give him a guinea pig. When at last he got his turn, he quickly forgot his admonition to the other children. "Sharing," was in Jack's vocabulary but not in his repertoire of behaviors and feelings. The next time the teacher sees Jack share, a helpful statement would be, "There, Jack, you shared with Bill." To promote sharing the teacher provides a sufficient number of toys, then works to establish a climate of mutual love and respect that brings sharing about voluntarily.

A new toy in a school may have to be rationed, but the sooner it can become "yours while you are using it," the better. This "yours while you are using it" policy allows a child to use equipment until there is a feeling of "enough." Then the child will be able to share. The policy also avoids having the teacher become a timekeeper.

Teachers often have difficulty with some children monopolizing certain equipment. Monopolizing may occur because children are unable to think of anything else to do. For example, the boys in one group monopolized the tricycles. The teacher decided to give the girls a chance at the tricycles by dismissing them to the yard first for a few days. Another day everyone wearing red was chosen to go to the yard first. Such procedures gave others a chance to use the tricycles. Guidance in helping the boys find suitable alternatives to tricycle riding was called for. Teachers should be observant and prevent the practice of one child or clique tyrannizing the others in order to get certain equipment.

Toys brought from home handicap the teacher in a "yours while you are using it" policy. Personal toys are usually unsuited for use by a group. Some are so fragile that they may get broken if they are shared. It is well to discourage children from bringing personal toys to school. There are cases in which children need their own toys for personal security. This, of course, will be an exception. In these cases a frank explanation to the other children that "Jill feels better today with her own doll; perhaps tomorrow she will enjoy our dolls" is sufficient.

The teacher's guidance is often required to keep children from getting overheated outdoors or in. Many wraps that are appropriate when the child is moving slowly in the early morning are unnecessary when going full speed in the sunshine later on. A good rule, of course, is to encourage the children to decide for themselves when they need to shed their wraps. The teacher should err on the side of letting the children take off coats if they wish. It is hard for adults to realize how hot children get from their vigorous activity.

In some climates boots are kept in the locker all the time because of the prevailing wet grass in the yard. Extra boots, mittens, and hats stored in the school closet can supply children who do not have their own. Parents often need suggestions as to appropriate clothing to send and even to purchase.

Emergencies

If a child falls while playing, it is better for the teacher to comfort the child on the ground for a few minutes while trying to determine how serious the injury is. For the teacher to jerk the child up to standing or into the arms will certainly be frightening and may do serious damage to a limb if one is broken. In time of emergency a teacher's calmness can relax the hurt child, reassure the other children, and guide the assistants' efforts to be helpful. A coherent report is required by the parents or the doctor if either must be called.

In case of a serious accident a full account should be typed immediately to ensure recall of all details. Reports should be filed with appropriate authorities. If the school is covered by insurance, this report will be required.

Conclusion

A high-quality early childhood program includes adequate motor skill practice and healthful exercise for each child each day. Children's motor development during the early years provides the foundation for their future skill level. Skills can be fostered by adults who analyze the child's level and give the child proper equipment and guidance.

Teachers need to realize the value of offering a rich outdoor program to young children. Adequate plans ensure that goals are achieved for each child. Teachers can make wise use of space and be creative in selection and arrangement of equipment. In addition, appropriate guidance and teaching techniques assure meaningful outdoor learning experiences for all the children.

Applications

1. Discuss the "Talk It Over" items in the chapter.
2. Complete Lesson 7 in *A Laboratory Workbork for Introduction to Early Childhood Education*. Hand in as scheduled.
3. Write an activity plan for a motor skill or outdoor learning activity for a few children using information and the sample (Figure 6-1) in Chapter 6. Secure approval, carry out the plan, and evaluate the results from the children's point of view and from your viewpoint. Prepare a report and hand it in along with your approved activity plan.
4. Evaluate your total participation performance on your evaluation form developed in Chapter 1.
5. Add ideas and plans for motor skill and outdoor activities to your Resource File.

Study Questions

1. Explain the major finding of the Seefeldt/Haubenstricker study of young children's motor skills.
2. Describe the stages of catching. Describe the type of ball to use to play catch with a young child.
3. Describe the stages of throwing. Describe the type of ball to use to practice throwing with a young child.
4. List the advantages for a child's development of adequate outdoor play activity.
5. Discuss the role of planning in the outdoor play program.
6. Discuss the use of space in the outdoor play program.
7. Discuss the allocation of time in the outdoor play program.
8. Discuss guidance measures for outdoor play activities.
9. Discuss safety in the playyard.
10. Classify play activity for the playyard, and list several specific activities for each classification.

Film

Outdoor Play . . . A Motivating Force for Learning   Color   30 minutes   1974

Focuses on the unique physical and intellectual development provided by outdoor play activities and presents the extensive use of improvised materials. Campus Film Distributors Corporation, P.O. Box 206, 14 Madison Avenue, Valhalla, N.Y. 10595.

Additional Readings

BAKER, KATHERINE READ. *Let's Play Outdoors.* Washington, D.C.: National Association for the Education of Young Children, 1966.

CORBIN, CHARLES. *A Textbook of Motor Development.* Dubuque, Iowa: W. C. Brown Company, 1980.

CRATTY, BRYANT J. *Perceptual and Motor Development in Infants and Young Children.* New York: Macmillan Publishing Co., 1979.

D'EUGENIO, TERRY. *Building with Tires.* Cambridge, Mass.: Educational Arts Association, 1971.

ENGSTROM, GEORGIANNA (ed.). *Play: The Child Strives Toward Self Realization.* Washington, D.C.: The National Association for the Education of Young Children, 1971.

ENGSTROM, GEORGIANNA (ed.). *The Significance of the Young Child's Motor Development.* Washington, D.C.: The National Association for the Education of Young Children, 1971.

GERHARDT, LYDIA A. *Moving and Knowing: The Young Child Orients Himself in Space.* Englewood Cliffs, N.J.: Prentice-Hall, Inc., 1973.

HYMES, JAMES L., JR. *Teaching the Child Under Six.* Columbus, Ohio: Charles E. Merrill Publishing Co., 1981.

KRITCHEVSKY, SYBIL, ELIZABETH PRESCOTT, and LEE WALLING. *Planning Environments for Young Children: Physical Space.* Washington, D.C.: National Association for the Education of Young Children, 1977.

LANDRETH, CATHERINE. *Early Childhood: Behavior and Learning.* New York: Alfred A. Knopf, Inc., 1967.

LEEPER, SARAH H., RALPH L. WITHERSPOON, and BARBARA DAY. *Good Schools for Young Children.* New York: Macmillan Publishing Co., Inc., 1984.

LUECK, PHYLLIS, "Planning an Outdoor Learning Environment," *Theory into Practice,* Vol 12, No. 2, April 1973, pp. 121–127.

READ, KATHERINE, and JUNE PATTERSON. *The Nursery School and Kindergarten.* New York: Holt, Rinehart, and Winston, 1980.

SEEFELDT, VERN, and JOHN HAUBENSTRICKER. "Patterns, Phases, Or Stages: An Analytical Model for the Study of Developmental Movement," in J. A. Kelso and J. E. Clark (eds.). *The Development of Movement Control and Coordination.* New York: John Wiley & Sons, 1982, pp. 309–318.

STONE, JEANNETTE GALAMBOS, and NANCY RUDOLPH. *Play and Playgrounds.* Washington, D.C.: The National Association for the Education of Young Children, 1970.

Creative Art Activities

- To *define creativity and identify ways creativity is fostered in the early childhood school.*
- To *explain how children's developmental tasks are fostered through use of art materials.*
- To *identify the developmental stages found by researchers studying children's use of art materials.*
- To *explain how the use of art materials offers children prereading and prewriting experiences.*
- To *describe and evaluate the use of space, supplies, equipment, and guidance for developing children's creativity.*

"I'm gonna paint," said four-year-old Greg, lifting the long-handled brush out of the red paint and stroking it on the easel paper. "You know," he continued, turning to his companion at the adjacent easel, "when we're in kindergarten, we won't ever get to paint. My brother goes to kindergarten and he never gets to do anything that's fun."

Greg's comments regarding kindergarten attracted several listeners. His predictions brought thoughtful, worried expressions to the faces of his young friends. They couldn't imagine a school where they couldn't paint or have fun.

Children enjoy the many and varied art experiences offered in good schools for young children. Through these activities children integrate all areas of their growth—creative, physical, mental, social, and emotional. Greg's forecast of the grim life ahead in kindergarten need not be the reality. Teachers at all levels are accepting the importance of encouraging the inventive, original, self-initiated, and self-motivated behavior that is the creative potential in each child.

Figure 8-1. The easel plus tempera paints provide children an important opportunity for creative expression. (Nazarene Child Care Center, Lansing, Michigan)

What Is Creativity?

Creativity, according to Eisner, is a capacity possessed in some degree by all human beings.[1] Creativity is part of human intellect, which Hofstadter differentiates from intelligence. "Intellect," Hofstadter writes, "is the critical, creative, and contemplative side of the mind. Intelligence is an excellence of mind that is employed in a fairly narrow, immediate, and predictable range."[2]

According to Lowenfeld and Brittain, specialists in creativity and children's art, creativity is exhibited by people who have the motivation, curiosity, and imagination

1. To search for and discover answers,
2. To question existing solutions to problems,
3. To rethink, restructure, and find new relationships,
4. To be open toward the unknown or new,
5. To be flexible, nonconforming, and nondogmatic,

[1] Eliot W. Eisner, "Research in Creativity," *Childhood Education,* **39**:8 (1963), p. 371.
[2] Erhard Hofstadter, *Anti-intellectualism in American Life* (New York: Alfred A. Knopf, Inc., 1966), pp. 24–25.

6. To be self-expressive and original,
7. To use divergent thinking.[3]

Creativity is a state of mind that carries over into all kinds of behavior. Human beings are all creative with language because to speak one must create new sentences each time one makes an utterance. Creativity is demanded in social situations, in physical-motor activities as one adjusts to the environment, and in cognitive activities. Children are all born with creativity.

* * *

Talk It Over: No. 1

Study the definition of creativity. Give examples of children's behaviors in home and school when they fulfill one or more of the characteristics of being creative. Discuss the perils of being a creative child.

* * *

Adults are often confused about creativity. Rigid, stifling, or unsupported early experience may have made them doubt their own creativity. They may think that only artists are creative. It sometimes helps to think of creativity as a personal resource that is part of everyday decision making. Each person has some unique ways of applying knowledge to the tasks of everyday living. That's creativity in operation.

Creative potential gives people the motivation to change, to shift gears in a rapidly changing society. From a very practical point of view, it is extremely important that a person's creativity be fostered to its fullest extent. Village blacksmiths of grandfather's day may have lamented that there were no more horses to be shod, but they turned to repairing the wheels of the tractors that replaced the horse and used many of the same materials and skills. They saw the possibilities and learned new ways of using their resources. They didn't let the need to change throw them into psychological or economic despair.

A walk down any street on any day reveals how someone's creativity has made life easier: the window washer uses a rubber blade on a long stick; the painter uses a roller instead of a brush; the street sweeper now rides a big machine instead of carrying a broom and a pail; the businessman has his computer buttons; office forces have automatic machines; the bus driver serves customers faster because buses have two doors to speed the process of moving people on and off. All are the result of someone's creativity. Industry encourages creative suggestions from employees through incentive payments.

A look in the household section of a historical museum shows how pioneers used their creative ingenuity to lighten household tasks. The pioneer housewife must have said, "I wish there was a better way to

---

[3] Viktor Lowenfeld and W. Lambert Brittain, *Creative and Mental Growth* (New York: Macmillan Publishing Co., Inc., 1982), pp. 69–93.

peel these apples besides sitting here with this knife." Having made the complaint, she set not only her own creative thoughts in operation but perhaps those of others who eventually came up with a gadget for peeling and coring apples.

Modern society needs people who will ask important questions and seek solutions. When people are encouraged to question and are encouraged to engage in creative thought and experimentation, problem solving and progress will come more rapidly. The questioning attitude will contribute to creative thinking whether the question deals with a household task or problems of world peace. Progress can take place only if individuals ask the question, "Couldn't we do this a better way?"

The aesthetic aspects of creativity are available to all. Individuals live more fully when they appreciate beauty, whether in nature, in work, or in human relationships.

Brain Functions and Creative Expression

Supporting Hofstadter's point, mentioned earlier, that "Intellect is the critical, creative, and contemplative side of the mind" is recent research into mapping the various functions of the brain. You may be aware that your brain's left hemisphere controls the motor functions of the right side of your body, while the right hemisphere of the brain controls the left side of your body. According to Dr. David Galin, M.D., "The specialization of the right hemisphere has only recently been widely recognized: it is very good at perceiving and expressing novel and complex visual, spatial, and musical patterns." The right hemisphere is said to function in a *holistic mode,* according to Galin, while the left hemisphere functions in an *"analytic, logical mode,* for which words are an excellent tool." Based on this work it is Galin's conclusion that, "If we want to cultivate creativity, it appears that we must first develop each mode, both the rational-analytic and the intuitive-holistic; second, we must develop the ability to inhibit either one when it is inappropriate to the task at hand; and finally we must be able to operate in both modes in a complementary fashion."[4]

"Integration of the brain's two thinking systems has also been suggested as a model of creativity," according to Languis and others. They write, ". . . creative productivity involves both the intuitive sensing of patterns and the analytic organization of ideas into propositions, thus tapping the high-level cognitive capabilities of both hemispheres. Moreover, access to and communication between the hemispheres may be the key to expanding creative potential. Therefore, an appropriate program

[4] David Galin, M.D., "Educating Both Halves of the Brain," *Childhood Education,* 53:1 (October 1979), p. 18.

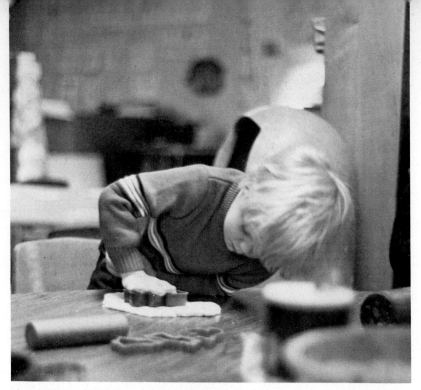

Figure 8-2. Serious concentration is required when cutting out a figure from carefully patted out playdough. (Child Development Center, Metropolitan State College)

goal might be to facilitate in children the ability to shift flexibly between both modes of thinking and to use, value, and trust ideas derived equally from both strategies."[5]

The research in brain hemispheres is giving support to educators who have long advocated lots of hands-on activities and the use of art materials as vital to children's learning. Hands-on activities, pictorial, and three-dimensional figures, called *analog* in the new computer language, are processed in the right side of the brain. Such right brain activities can also aid in the learning of *digital* information such as numbers, letters, and words which are left brain activities. Raising the issue of computers in this context suggests that caution must be taken that the left brain is not the only hemisphere stimulated in the new computer age.

Children have differing learning styles. Some learn the analytic-logical types of information quickly, while others need pictures and function well with objects in space. The first is left-brained, the second is right-brained. What is needed is a combination of learning activities presented in a variety of modes to utilize most fully the marvelous resources of the child's brain. The process of using art materials and tools is extremely important to children's learning.

[5] Marlin Languis, Tobie Sanders, and Steven Tipps, *Brain and Learning: Directions in Early Childhood Education* (Washington, D.C.: National Association for the Education of Young Children, 1980), p. 49.

Developmental Tasks Fostered Through Art Activities

The developmental tasks of each child are fostered through use of art materials. By reviewing those tasks in Chapter 2 and relating them to the discussion that follows, you will be able to see how each task is touched in some way when the child uses art materials and participates in creative activity.

Fostering Creativity Through the Arts

"The goal for art education is to use the creative process to make people more creative regardless of where their creativeness will be applied," wrote Viktor Lowenfeld in *Creative and Mental Growth*.[6] Lowenfeld and Brittain, in a later edition of that book, wrote. "Child art is highly individual. No two children express themselves entirely alike. One of the vital aims of art education is to bring out the individual differences that make up each child's personality. To suppress these individual differences, to emphasize the final product, to reward one youngster over another, goes against the basic premises of creative expression.[7]

In high-quality early childhood programs opportunities abound for children's creativity or divergent thinking to find expression. In every segment of the curiculum there is room for children to "put it together" in new ways. The teacher values the unique, spontaneous, fresh, and imaginative manner with which the child faces the challenge of learning. The child's use of art materials is a regularly offered part of the program.

The end products of the creative process, such as paintings, collages, or other works of art, may have little value in the market, yet the creative process involved is of great value to the developing child. Patterns are not used to get products that look "just so." Coloring-book-type line drawings to fill in are not provided. The teacher has faith in the child and often tells the child so. The teacher refrains from helping the child outright. Confidence in the child is stated time and time again. Bolstering self-confidence, the teacher encourages experimentation, and commends the unique way in which the child solves a problem.

If the teacher loses faith in the child's creative ability or falls victim to pressures to produce products, it will hurt the child and her or his future creativity. Henceforth, the child will wait for the teacher's idea, or "correct" way, before beginning. The child won't enjoy the products or the process.

[6] Viktor Lowenfeld, *Creative and Mental Growth* (New York: Macmillan Publishing Co., Inc., 1957), p. 5.
[7] Lowenfeld and Brittain, op. cit., p. 167.

Max is an example of a child whose creativity suffered when products were emphasized. He was a child who had creative teachers during prekindergarten and kindergarten years. He used new materials with great confidence. In the first grade Max was told that Christmas drawings would be selected for a display in an uptown department store. Max became anxious and practiced diligently so that his drawing might be chosen. It was selected.

Upon seeing the picture, his kindergarten teacher felt something was amiss. She later commented to Max, "Max, I saw your picture in the exhibit uptown." Max responded, "Did you see those angels? My teacher did those and she ruined it." Max had enjoyed neither the process nor the product. He did not enjoy winning with help. The first-grade teacher surely got little satisfaction from displaying her work as child's art.

* * *

Talk It Over: No. 2

Discuss the meaning of the finding that "It is the process not the product that is important to the young child." Tell how you can incorporate this finding in your work with young children.

* * *

Fostering Perceptual-Motor Skills Through the Arts

Creativity should be reason enough for offering children a wide array of art media and for helping them find one that especially allows expression of their feelings, moods, and ideas. However, other important reasons are apparent. The skills developed through the art materials are both prewriting and prereading skills. Clearly, the small motor skills are being developed. One has only to watch in a class of three-year-olds as children draw and cut, then move on to a class of four- or five-year-olds to see how much skill the threes can be expected to develop in the next year or two.

Eye-hand coordination is continually practiced as the hand draws a head in the "right" place or puts a wheel on a "car" in the customary spot. Picking up and placing the collage materials require eye-hand coordination, as does squeezing the glue bottle to drop the glue in the right spot. Using scissors to cut on a line is a complicated coordination task to learn.

Through art activities children learn to concentrate their attention on the figures or designs they place on the page or background, helping them develop figure and ground concepts. Later, in writing, a child must concentrate on the black squiggles, not on the white space surrounding them.

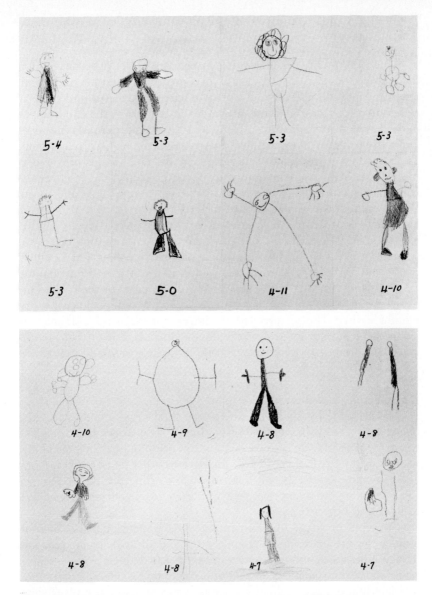

Figure 8-3. Drawings provide information about each child's level of representation. The above array, done in private sessions, is typical of a four-year-old group near the end of the school year. The numbers refer to the child's age in years and months. Drawings range from the scribble stage to the schematic stage including a base line. The teacher directed each one to, "Draw a man, the best man you know how."

Fostering Cognitive Growth Through the Arts

According to Brittain's research in children's art, "The production of art provides one of the best ways for a preschool child to understand, organize, and utilize concepts."[8] Brittain finds that when adults serve as a sounding board for children as they paint and draw, the children put more details in their pictures. Children are constantly translating ideas into various media, showing their awareness of the world around them.

Experience with colors, their various shades and hues, is provided in most of the activities. Children easily learn the names and discover the combinations of primary colors that make secondary colors and so on. Watch them at the finger-painting table, for example, as they combine blue and yellow. "Look! Teacher! Teacher! I made green!" shouts Cindy.

Through art media children also gain experience putting pieces together to make a whole, learning whole-part relationships. For example, when children add eyes, ears, nose, and mouth to a circle to make a face, they are learning with some precision the parts of the body. One five-year-old, Steve looked at a picture he had drawn of himself a few months earlier. The picture had six fingers on the hands. "Hum," he laughed, "I put six fingers on my hand." In only a few brief months Steve had become more discriminating. Now he would add the correct number of parts to his figure.

Early Writing and Reading

The art table is usually the site of the child's first attempts to write his or her name, which must be from left to right in our language. The teacher teaches the child to use manuscript printing (see Chapter 1) and to start in the left-hand corner of the page in order to avoid scrambling and crowding letters, as will happen when starting too far over to the right. Forming those letters is clearly an early reading experience as well as a writing experience.

Concepts of shape are also required in reading and are common among the art materials. Shapes are cut out, drawn, compared, and named. Likenesses and differences in shapes are frequently discussed. "I want some shiny squares like yours," said Jack. "Here," said Todd handing him a piece. "No, I want gold shiny squares, not silver shiny squares," said Jack.

Letters from cereal boxes and other publications can be added to the collage materials. These encourage children to form their name and other words. Carol Seefeldt strongly advocates building curricular activities

[8] W. Lambert Brittain, *Creativity, Art, and the Young Child* (New York: Macmillan Publishing Co., Inc., 1979), p. 18. In this book Brittain reports on recent research conducted with young children using art media. There are many points that will interest early childhood educators.

around the child's name because each has a strong identification with this symbol.[9]

Fostering Social-Emotional Growth Through the Arts

The child's personality often shines through loud and clear when he or she draws or paints, for example, the little red-headed boy who drew red-haired boys in striped T-shirts. No one doubted who the drawings represented. Drawings by young children are typically egocentric. Brittain says that "Art activities not only reflect a child's inner self: they help form it."[10]

Family members are frequently represented in children's drawings. Feelings for others may be reflected in the drawings or through conversations while drawing or painting. However, Brittain cautions against deriving conclusions about a child's emotional state from too little evidence. He says, "It is ridiculous to arrive at conclusions about a child's mental health by diagnosing drawings or paintings we have not seen him creating."[11] Brittain concludes, "Unless the setting is carefully controlled with a good deal of information other than drawings available, interpretations of scribbles and early representations by children provide no insight and are of no clinical value to a teacher in a normal school situation."[12]

Arlie, for example, worried many observers because he painted a solid sheet of black. However, the teacher was not alarmed because Arlie often talked about the fire that burned the garage next door to his home. The teacher knew that the fire had been an alarming event in the neighborhood. Arlie was allowed to paint as he wished. Finally, one day Arlie painted his paper yellow. He reported that the painters had used yellow paint to paint the neighbor's garage. Arlie's opportunity to paint as he chose for all those days perhaps relieved him of tensions associated with the fire.

Pete's mother worried because her five-year-old was drawing armless human figures. In a discussion with the teacher the mother realized that she had seen only a couple of pictures in which he had tried to draw human figures. The teacher also explained to Pete's mother that it was not unusual for Pete to be enticed away from the drawing table by another child or by another activity before his drawing was finished. The

---

[9] Carol Seefeldt, "What's in a Name? Lots to Learn!" *Young Children,* **39**:5 (July 1984), pp. 24–30. Also see Carol Vukelich and Joanne Golden's article "Early Writing: Development and Teaching Strategies," *Young Children,* **39**:2 (January 1984), pp. 3–8.

[10] Brittain, op. cit., p. 184.

[11] Brittain, op. cit., p. 121.

[12] Brittain, op. cit., p. 127.

teacher might discuss the armless drawings with Pete, asking, "What is the man doing?" "What does your man need to throw a ball?" Such questions would help him think of the relationship between activities and body parts.

Considering armless human figures, Jacqueline Goodnow, who has made numerous studies of children's drawing indicates that "Armless humans reflect no strange perception on the part of a child; instead they may often simply reflect the sense of having finished by the time one reaches the bottom." Goodnow reports that children draw from the top of the page to the bottom. Children fall in two groups, those who finish details as they go and those who go back to finish details. The latter are most likely to leave off arms. She said of the 79 children in one study only 40 included arms, and for those 40 children 28 drew the arms on last.[13]

* * *

Talk It Over: No. 3

Observe a child using an art material. Make a five-minute diary record of what you observe the child doing. Share observations among your classmates. What conclusions can you draw?

* * *

[13] Jacqueline Goodnow, *Children Drawing* (Cambridge, Mass.: Harvard University Press, 1977), p. 56.

Figure 8-4. Block printing using an object and thickened tempera interests children. (Kadena Preschool, Kadena Air Force Base, Okinawa)

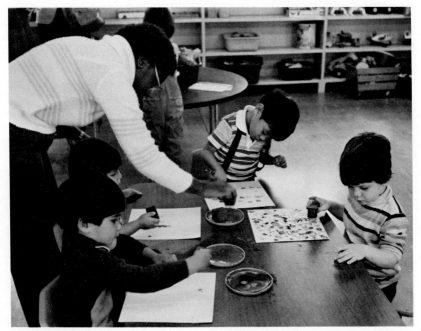

STAGES IN YOUNG CHILDREN'S ART

W. Lambert Brittain

Stage one—Random Scribbling—age one to two or two and a half.

The drawing tool is held tightly and is rarely taken from the paper. It may be held as a hammer at times. Lines are made with simple arm movements, the swing of the arm back and forth determining the direction and length of the lines. The child watches what he or she is doing, watching to follow and enjoy the lines rather than control them.

Stage two—Controlled Scribbling—age two to three or three and a half.

The wrist is more flexible than in stage one. There is a wider range of scribbles and more intricate patterns of loops. The child makes the tool go across the page as desired.

Stage three—Named Scribbling—age three and a half to four or four and a half.

The naming of scribbles illustrates an important step toward the development of abstract thought. Lines become symbols that stand for things.

Stage four—Early Representational—age four years plus.

The child can reproduce a symbol for an object though not a likeness. Representations have little in common with what adults consider the real world. The child does not seem to be attempting a photographic likeness. What adults see as distortions are not distortions to the child.

Stage five—Preschematic Drawing—age five years plus.

Now there is a right-side up and a line for the sky and ground. Relative sizes of objects begin to be portrayed. Objects and people are painted.[14]

Developmental Stages in Children's Art

Creative development, as with other areas of development, has its typical ages and stages. When the teacher and parent understand the various levels, they can help, not hinder, the child's creative growth. Brittain describes several stages of particular importance to teachers of young children. Knowing these developmental stages will help teachers (1) plan art activities at an appropriate level; (2) set an appropriate level of expectations for children; (3) appreciate children's drawings and art projects; and (4) have an appropriate basis for discussing children's art with parents.

According to Harris, the more details children put into their picture, the more intellectual and perceptual growth one can assume is taking

[14] Brittain, op. cit., pp. 28–40.

place.[15] The amount of repetition or exaggeration of a theme can guide the teacher in understanding the child's emotional growth. Social growth is indicated by the themes the child's work takes and how much the themes are related to actual experience.

Children's creative growth can be inferred from the number of independent themes they produce and whether or not they seem to be imitating other children. Physical growth may be indicated by their skill with tools and by exaggeration of some body part and the vigorousness of their participation.

Children may occasionally regress to previous levels of artistic behavior just as they may regress emotionally. When attempting to understand or to explain a child's art products, one should be careful not to draw conclusions from an inadequate sample of a child's work or from scanty knowledge about the child's experience.

General Classroom Procedures

Atmosphere

An atmosphere of freedom is important if the child is to develop creative potential. Children who feel free to try new ways of using materials will be more creative than children who are taught there is only one right way to do everything. From the very first day the teacher must allow children to be experimental. "I know you have ideas. Let's see how many different pictures we can make," says the teacher to the children. If this faith falters or if patterns are given, then the children will wait for the teacher's intervention every day.

An uncritical atmosphere will help the child feel safe, secure, and unthreatened by the teacher, peers, or family. Expectations are kept at a reasonable level so that the child can hope to succeed. Children will set their own pace. In any class there will be a wide range of abilities; therefore materials must be suited to this wide range. For example, in a three- or four-year-old group the stages will range from scribbling to preschematic. Caution should be taken to protect the child's right to "just paint."

Children who feel skillful and self-confident will make the most effort to be creative. Therefore teachers plan to give children opportunities to practice skills. They create an environment in which the child feels safe to practice a new skill. Children receive instruction when they ask or seem mature enough to benefit from it. Such skills as holding a cra-

---

[15] D. B. Harris, *Children's Drawings as Measures of Intellectual Maturity* (A Revision and Extension of Goodenough Draw-a-Man Test) (New York: Harcourt, Brace & World, 1963).

yon, cutting with scissors, using the stapler, tying a bow, or squeezing the glue bottle may profitably be demonstrated to a child who is ready to learn them. Most small motor skills contribute eventually to writing skill. Self-confidence is fostered through the mastery of skills.

The teacher should feel obligated to provide painting aprons that help protect children's clothing. The parents' complaints at home about messy clothing will adversely affect the child's creative expression. The wise teacher will guide parents in choosing appropriate clothing for their children to wear to school in order that they can participate fully in all activities.

In case of an unusual amount of spilling, the teacher can advise parents about helpful laundry procedures. When sending home children's painted or glued products, the teacher should take care that smearing of clothes and cars en route home is avoided. Some products can be sent in paper bags and others rolled together and held by a rubberband. Such measures may sound overprotective of parents; however, some empathy on the teacher's part results in better cooperation from parents.

To say there is freedom does not mean the teacher does not have rules. Logically, messy activity is located where it can be cleaned up readily. Rules are set about splashing paints, dropping clay, and washing hands.

Appropriate Comments

When commenting to a child, it is best to say, "Would you like to tell me about your picture?" rather than to guess what the child is painting. Too many questions may invite casual naming that may not have much relationship to the original ideas. For example, Doug alarmed his father because he always reported having painted a "monster." The father asked the teacher about the paintings, and she recalled quite a different theme during Doug's time at the easel. Apparently Doug was pleased with the increased attention this picture title drew from his father.

The teacher protects the child from the criticism of peers. Verbally the stage is set for acceptance of all children's creations. "You each can paint what you are thinking" and "Each of you sees an object a little differently" are examples of comments one can make to set the stage for individuality. The teacher displays something from everyone. As some children do like to take art products home, it is well for the teacher to ask permission to keep a painting for display. The teacher refrains from choosing only the "best" for exhibit. It is important to avoid arousing competition between children. Hands are kept off children's products no matter how much the teacher might think the picture could be improved.

Parental criticism of a child's art can be devastating. Therefore, the teacher makes efforts to communicate to parents the expected standards and the level of their child's creative development. For example, reassuring parents that scribbling is typical of their Johnny's age group and that other children in the group are scribbling, too, helps the parents become more accepting of Johnny's scribbling. Parents may have to be alerted so that they can curb older siblings' criticisms or efforts to improve a young child's products.

Not infrequently a young child competes with a school-age sibling. One young child, Linda, carelessly splashed paint on many pages to have as many products to show her parents as her school-age sibling brought home. When this happens, parents may then be counseled to lay out the array of paintings and let their child choose a favorite. This technique can help steer the child away from mass production and back onto a track of self-expression. However, the problem of sibling rivalry is also one the parent may need help with. Some young children react to home competition by refusing to create any product the teacher might encourage them to take home. Parents may pressure the child to bring something home. When a child spends the day playing with blocks or

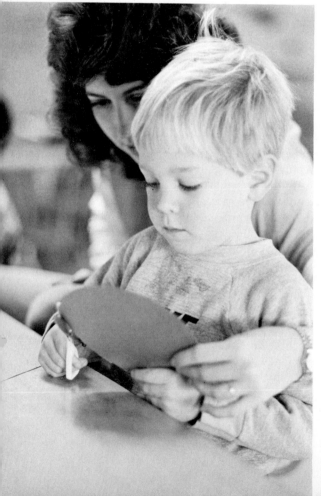

Figure 8-5. Cutting on a line is an advanced achievement in cutting. The teacher gives some physical guidance to help the child get the feel of turning the object while cutting. (Hoeflin Stone House Child Care Center, Kansas State University)

cooperating in the doll house, there is nothing to take home. Parents need this information so that they do not overvalue art products.

Organizing the Art Centers

Most art materials are presented in the early childhood school during the indoor self-selected activity period. In mild climates art materials should be moved outdoors. Having a smorgasbord of art materials available along with other activities enables a child to create when he or she wants to and enables the teacher to work with small groups of children. With a wide variety of materials no one activity attracts all the children at one time. They naturally move to learning centers that attract their attention. After satisfying their need, they move to another center. They may be stimulated by the attractiveness of the center per se or to a valued friend who happens to be interested in that activity. The wise teacher will make the art centers as much self-service from the children's standpoint as possible. Children enjoy independence. When not tied too closely to one center, the teacher is freer to assist in other centers as needed.

The activities of the art center often require using water and washing hands. The logical location of the art center is near the water supply. An ideal situation is to have a low sink in the art center in order to keep the children from running to the bathroom with paint-covered hands and aprons. A dishpan or a bucket of water can substitute for some of the needed water if a sink is not available. Remember to bring along the paper towels.

An area for drying products is required—preferably one that the children can use themselves. Newspapers under drying racks or shelves can eliminate difficult cleanup problems later on.

If supplies are carefully stored and labeled, the teacher can get needed items in a hurry. The stage can be set so that the children can help with cleaning up the art center. They wash easels, brushes, and tables with as much enthusiasm as they paint—sometimes with more enthusiasm.

Children will use art materials spontaneously and incorporate them into other play if they are stored on an open shelf where they can reach them without asking for assistance. Newsprint, colored mimeograph paper, crayons, scissors, bottles of glue, stapler, paper punch, felt pens, masking tape, and string are items children use frequently. Two examples support this idea. The five-year-olds had just returned from a trip to a farm. They were getting their drinks and discussing all they had seen. Sherry quietly walked to the art center, found materials, and created a pig in a basket. Both were made from paper in three dimensions. Sherry used the scissors and stapler. Her spontaneous creation showed clearly what she had liked best about the trip.

Four-year-olds were playing store. A child expressed a need for money in the cash register. One enterprising young man hastened to the art center, cut green mimeograph paper into squares, and returned to set himself up as a banker, giving money to the housewives who were shopping at the store.

Places to display children's art products should be available throughout the room. Art gives the room a personal, colorful appearance. The objects should be changed frequently to keep the interest high. Children lose interest in their own products quickly and may not even want to claim them a day or so after working on them. When children seem to have a special need to take a product home, the teacher can ask if they would like to make something special to put up in the display. If they indicate they would not, then of course it isn't important to them.

Planning so that the art center is efficiently arranged encourages the children's use of the center and facilitates the teacher's supervision.

While the following pages contain suggestions for numerous art activities, the teacher who wants depth of expression to develop in children will give them repeated opportunities to use basic paint, clay, and crayons rather than continuously changing materials. Lowenfeld and Brittain say of schools where materials continuously change, "The danger is that students may begin to feel that art is nothing more than a series of little projects or a series of experimentations with materials, bearing little relationship to expression or creativity."[16]

Painting

Easel Painting

Easel painting is an enjoyable activity for young children and most teachers feel it should be available every day. Such painting helps children develop their motor skills and express concepts and feelings. They learn to judge space size and to fill the space. They learn about colors and lines.

Tempera paints in either liquid or powdered form are available from art shops and school supply houses. A cup of liquid starch mixed in a quart of water used to mix dry tempera will prevent the watery consistency caused by the settling out of the paint. Watery paint is unpopular with children. About a quart of each color should be mixed and stored to be ready when needed. For very young children one primary color at the easel at a time is sufficient. As they gain skill and show interest in more color, then all of the primary colors are added. Older children will enjoy variety in the paint, including brown and black. Pastel colors delight children and are made by the addition of color to white. White

[16]Lowenfeld and Brittain, op. cit., p. 88.

paint is popular when colored paper is available. Jars or disposable plastic or styrofoam cups may be used for paints. Disposables save a tedious washing chore.

Brushes to use at the easel should be a long-handled (12-inch) variety that allows a full shoulder stroke. A stiff bristle is best. A variety of brush sizes is appreciated by older children.

Mixing or stirring paint with brushes breaks off the bristles. To avoid damaging brushes, care should be exercised in the washing and drying of brushes. A useful aid in washing and drying brushes can be made from the bottom half of a plastic milk bottle. Puncture the bottom with holes so that water will run through, then place the brushes in the container and set it under running water for a few minutes. The paint on the brushes will soak loose. Place the brushes to dry, handles down, in a storage container. Washing the easel brushes is a popular activity with children. Perhaps it runs a close second to clapping the erasers!

Several styles of easels are available commercially. Also, excellent ones can be homemade. A board can be hung along a wall to be used for an easel. A 4-inch wedge at the bottom will hold the board out from the wall and give the board an appropriate angle. Or two masonite boards can be hinged and held folded as a triangle with a metal strap. This easel can be used at the table. You can also make easels from large cardboard boxes by cutting through them diagonally. Paper is held with large tack pins. Painting paper can be placed on the wall, the table, the floor, or the sidewalk. The easels used should be the correct height for young children. Easel legs can be sawed off to an appropriate height.

Painting on large sheets of newsprint with the large brushes is suggested for young children. Large materials encourage the use of their large muscles and accommodate their large designs. A minimum of $20'' \times 27''$ is suggested. Paper cut to size is available from school supply houses. Some newspaper shops will cut newsprint for the school. Other publishers may donate roll ends to the school. If donations are common at the school, a paper cutter such as is used for cutting wrapping paper in stores might be a good investment. A cutter speeds the preparation of the paper.

Manila paper $12'' \times 18''$ is appropriate for some painting. Colored paper is available and is especially delightful with white paints on a snowy day. For variety, textured paper such as the back of embossed wallpaper is interesting. Outdated wallpaper sample books can be secured from wallpaper companies. Printed newspaper can be used occasionally. Large shapes like pumpkins or hearts can be cut out and used for painting to add further variety.

Attention must be given to attaching the easel paper to the easel. The common manner of using clamps or clothespins is not satisfactory because young children can't operate the clamps without dropping the paper. Some easels have two smooth-headed nails placed about 24 inches apart at the top of the easel. The newsprint is then punched with a paper punch so that the holes match the nails. A day's supply of paper can be hung on the easel. Children can then easily remove their paper when finished and hang the painting to dry. They become more self-sufficient, taking care of the job themselves. The busy teacher is helped at the same time. Paper supplies should be stored close by the painting area.

Easel painting is very popular and is commonly planned on a daily basis. A stampede of painters results when easel painting is offered infrequently. Regular usage helps avoid complicated problems of sharing. Children who desire to produce a detailed painting or several paintings need not be rushed to finish. Closure or completion is an important aspect to encourage in creative people. Thus allowing children to finish a product to their satisfaction is important if we are to foster a habit of becoming finishers as well as starters. The child who wants to paint and is required to wait can be reassured that paints will be available the next school day.

There is good reason to place easels side by side so that children can socialize as they paint. They may share both paints and ideas. If easels are available daily, two easels are usually sufficient for a group of twenty children. More places to paint will be necessary if painting is planned only occasionally.

Guidance may be required to encourage children to squeeze their brushes against the side of the jar—especially if the teacher notes that the child is disturbed by the drips. Teachers can encourage the use of the same brush for each color by saying, "Keep the red brush in the red paint." Children's names are printed at the top left-hand corner of the painting in manuscript letters to help identify paintings, to stress the importance of the child's name, and to teach recognition of names.

Custodians will appreciate the use of a speckled throw rug under the easels to catch the occasional drips. Throw rugs are easily washed and are more aesthetic than newspapers.

Suitable paint aprons can be made from cotton-backed plastic. (See Figure 8-6.) The edges need no finishing. The neck strap of elastic and ties of cotton tape are quickly attached by sewing machine. Some schools use men's shirts for painting smocks. Big brother's shirts are a better size for children under six than are men's sizes.

It is well to pour only a small amount of paint in the paint jars for a class of young painters. With close observation for a few days teachers can judge the approximate amount of paint needed for a session. Children normally overlay one color on the others when making their paintings. Overlaying is not to be discouraged, because children learn about the mixing of colors this way. They frequently forget, or as yet don't understand, about matching up the brush in hand with the color from which it came, so that further mixing results. Mixing and matching are, of course, two of the important learnings from the painting ex-

Figure 8-6. An easy-to-make painting apron made of cotton-backed plastic with an elastic neck strap and cotton tape ties.

perience. Even though the teacher knows paints will get mixed up, it is best to start with clear colors each day. By starting with a small amount of paint and replenishing as needed, the wasting of paint is avoided and clear colors are more likely.

* * *

Talk It Over: No. 4

Discuss among your classmates the outcomes of your planned art activity with young children. What did you learn that might help others? What did you discover about children? Yourself?

* * *

If children are painting a mural on the floor, the wall, or a table, or if makeshift easels do not have the usual tray for holding paint jars, then some arrangement should be made to prevent paint jars from tipping over. Muffin tins can be used to hold jars containing paint. A cardboard serving tray from the drive-in hamburger stand is just right to hold paint jars. Simply place the paint jars where soft-drink bottles are usually set. A similar holder can be cut from a cardboard box.

String Painting

The same mixture of tempera paint as discussed above is used for string painting. The child holds one end of a 15-inch string, such as twine, yarn, or thread, and drops the string into the paint. Slowly the child pulls out the string and lets the paint drip off. The wet string is moved around on the paper to make various patterns. Several colors can be available, with different strings in each color.

For variation children may pull the string through folded paper. For example, they arrange the paint-covered strings on one half and fold over the paper. Holding the folded paper together, they pull the dry end of the string with their free hand. Interesting variations in designs result. The child observes the shading and blending of colors.

Block Printing

The same mixture of tempera paint is used for block printing. A shallow pan is used to arrange stamp pads of various colors. Pads are cut of several layers of paper towel, cheesecloth, or thin sponge and saturated with color. There should be only enough paint to leave color on the object without dripping. Prints can be made from a variety of objects, such as clothespins, a potato masher, a sponge, vegetables, toys, pieces of wood, and spools. Children enjoy making prints from designs cut in potato halves.

You may make rollers by dipping heavy strings in glue and wrapping them around tubes from paper towels. When the glue is dry, roll the roller on a paint pad, then roll it across paper. Fingers too make interesting designs. In fact, children may see any painting activity as an opportunity for finger painting—a response that teachers should be prepared to accept.

Squeeze-Bottle Painting

Squeeze bottles with small openings are available with everything, from soap to mustard. Teachers save such bottles to fill with tempera paint. Using the bottle tip as a painting tool makes an acceptable substitute for dribbling the white glue that children seem inclined to do. Practice in using the squeeze bottle helps the child control the amount of paint used. Tempera is used with manila or construction paper. The children use the bottle tip to draw their design. They may like to place drips of color on the paper, then fold the paper. Unusual designs are discovered as they unfold the paper. Shoe polish bottles and roll-on deodorant bottles can be used in a similar fashion.

Splatter Painting

Splatter painting is done by the brushing of a paint-filled toothbrush across a wire screen. A kitchen strainer works fine for a screen. You can also make a screen by attaching a square of window screen to a wooden frame of about 6 inches to 8 inches square. The children place their paper on the table. Then they place an object such as a leaf or a key on the paper. Over this goes the screen. The child brushes the paint-filled toothbrush back and forth, getting the splatter effect around the outline of the object. A similar finished product is accomplished when a small sponge dipped in paint is used to stipple around the object.

Blot Painting

Blot painting is the result when paper is folded in half and the child then brushes, squeezes, or strings paint on one side of the fold. The paper is then folded back over the painted side, and the palm of the hand is rubbed across the paper. Children enjoy the surprise of the blending and duplicating effect.

Sand or Sawdust Painting

Sand or sawdust is mixed with moist tempera. A shaker with large holes is used to shake the mixture onto paper covered with glue or paste. Sand painting is best done out-of-doors to avoid difficult cleaning problems.

Object Painting

Using the tempera to paint wood and box collages and carpentry projects is a worthwhile conclusion to three-dimensional projects. Children enjoy painting props for their dramatic play, such as a cardboard train or a valentine mailbox.

Color Absorption

A thin solution of tempera or vegetable coloring is placed in a small dish. Several colors are provided. The child folds paper towels or squares of old sheeting and dips corners into the various colors. Children will be fascinated by the blending and shading of colors. A surface well padded with newspaper is necessary for drying these drippy products.

Finger Painting

Finger painting provides both an outlet for children's creativity and a medium for messing. This latter objective is important because modern children are often under a great deal of parental pressure to stay clean. Designs with finger paint can be made, erased, and made again. Personal problem areas can be expressed, then obliterated with one stroke—a behavior that gives evidence that finger painting has therapeutic value. The medium is highly relaxing for children. Children learn concepts through their experimentation with the mixing and blending of colors. Pictures are rarely a pure color because children can't resist trying to find out what happens if they add a little blue here or a little yellow there. Teachers and parents should not be disturbed that paintings turn out a uniform muddy color. The only way to obtain pictures of pure color is to limit the choice to one color. If the children know there are several colors available, they will certainly feel deprived if not allowed to choose from all of them and mix them together.

The majority of children will enjoy finger painting. The teacher may encourage the children to participate by sitting with them and actually manipulating the paint while talking to them. Seeing the teacher's hands in the paint will reassure the doubters that she or he really means that it is all right to get messy. The teacher may involve a hesitant child by permitting him or her to help mix the paint with a beater or a spoon. However, some children prefer to watch for a long time and may never

Figure 8-7. Fingerpainting gives children an opportunity to mix colors and to use a messy medium. (Early Childhood Laboratory, Kansas State University)

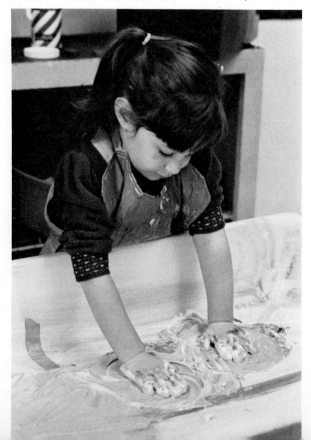

feel comfortable with finger paints. They should, of course, not be forced to finger paint.

If finger paints are provided frequently, there is less necessity for the teacher to permit large numbers of children to finger paint on a given day—which would make supervision difficult. From the practical side it is much easier to have five children painting on four different days then to try to manage finger painting for twenty on one day. It is well to limit the number of painters to a number the teacher can supervise and still keep an eye on the other activities in the room. Actually some teachers store the finger paints where children can help themselves whenever they desire to paint. The less pressure there is to give many people turns, the more satisfying the experience will be for the individual child.

Of course, the only tool needed for finger painting is the child's hands. The child gets full shoulder and arm movement from a standing position. Hands, knuckles, fingernails, and even the whole lower arm produce various effects. Questions like "How does it look if you use the side of your hand?" will encourage the child to experiment.

Music with soothing rhythms is especially appropriate while the children are finger painting. If the teacher plays staccato music, one shouldn't be surprised that the children splash the paint all around.

There are five necessities for finger painting—finger paints, a place to paint, aprons, a place to wash up, and a place to dry paintings.

Finger paints can be obtained commercially or mixed in the school. Two types are available commercially: one is the consistency of a thick paste; the other is a powder that the child shakes onto the wet paper from a shaker-type container. The young child likes lots of paint per picture and enjoys making many pictures. Commercial finger paints are quite expensive when provided in the amount that is necessary in the average class. Therefore a less expensive material is usually essential. Homemade products fulfill all the objectives of the medium. However, the exception is the quality of the finished picture. If a finger painting is desired for a placemat or a book cover, the teacher can use the commercial paint on that occasion.

Finger painting may be done on paper, on trays, or directly on the table. Suitable paper is of a glossy variety available in $20'' \times 24''$ sizes from school supply companies. Shelf paper and pages from glossy magazines can be substituted. Painting directly on wet trays, heavy plastic, oilcloth, or a wet table is practical because young children gain much of their satisfaction from the finger-painting process and little from the resulting picture. Some parents have reported allowing their child to use a soap-base finger paint on the tile wall around the bathtub. The tub and the child are quickly cleaned when the shower is turned on. These latter suggestions do save the cost of the paper and the problems of wetting the paper and drying the paintings. A suggested variation is to let the child paint on the table or tray and then make a print of the final

RECIPES FOR HOMEMADE FINGER PAINT

WHEAT-PASTE OR WALLPAPER-PASTE UNCOOKED METHOD (TIME: THREE MINUTES)

Mix in a large bowl:
1 pint water
1¼ cups dry wallpaper paste

Put the water in the bowl. Using a quick stirring motion with one hand, pour in dry wallpaper paste with the other. Keep stirring and adding paste until the proper thickness is achieved. Pour into jars and stir in tempera paint for color. A drop or two of wintergreen (purchased in a drugstore) will disguise the odor of the mixture if it seems unpleasant. *Caution:* Some wallpaper pastes have a chemical that has a mouse deterrent, so teachers should be sure the materials do not contain chemicals harmful to children.

COOKED-STARCH METHOD (TIME: TEN MINUTES PLUS COOLING TIME)

Mix in a large bowl:
1 cup laundry starch or cornstarch dissolved in a small amount of cold water
5 cups boiling water added slowly to dissolved starch

Cook the mixture until it is thick and glossy. Add 1 cup mild soap flakes. Add color in separate containers. Cool before using.

LIQUID-STARCH METHOD (TIME: NONE)

Give the children a tablespoon of liquid starch. Let them shake tempera on with a salt shaker. (If you feel this is wasteful of the paint supply, then mix the color in the starch before presenting it to the children.)

SOAP-FLAKED METHOD (TIME: TEN MINUTES)

Mix in a small bowl:
Soap flakes
A small amount of water

Beat until stiff with an eggbeater. Use white soap on dark paper, or add color to the soap and use it on light-colored paper. Gives a slight three-dimensional effect.

design by covering the painted surface with a sheet of paper and smoothing the paper with the palm of the hand. As the paper is peeled back, the transferred design is revealed. Printed newspaper gives an interesting effect when used for these prints.

Aprons are essential if the children are to participate freely and not receive criticism at home for soiled clothing. Aprons are discussed in detail in the section on easel painting in this chapter. Teachers can instruct the children to push up their sleeves. When the children wear their paint-splattered aprons as they go to wash the their hands, paint will rub off on the edge of the sink as they reach forward to turn on the water. The teacher can remind the children to use the sponge to wash off the front of the sink so that the next child using it won't get the paint on clothes. Children frequently enjoy the cleanup as much as or more than the painting activity.

Drying space for finger paintings is a problem in nearly every school. A folding wooden rack (a clotheshorse) such as a homemaker uses for drying clothes and household linen may be satisfactory, or a clothesline, a shelf, a table, or the floor can be used. The children will use a great deal of paint if the amount is not limited by the teacher. The paintings will be excessively wet and may have to be laid flat to dry. Drying areas should be protected by a layer of newspaper because the starch material used to make finger paints stick like glue and is therefore difficult to clean up. When the teacher plans ahead, cleaning up after finger painting is not difficult.

If the children paint on trays or on the table, a container to hold the used paint may be necessary. A rubber spatula or a wooden tongue blade from the nurse's station is useful for scraping up paint. Trays and plastic table coverings are readily washed under the faucet.

When the teacher establishes a routine and has everything ready before the children arrive, the finger-paint project will go smoothly. Materials can be organized in an assembly-line fashion. For example, a table should contain a stack of glossy paper stacked upside down so that names can be written on the back, a dark crayon for writing names, a dishpan with enough water for wetting the paper, and sponges and a bucket of water for cleaning up. With guidance from the teacher the children can learn to handle the preparation and drying of their finger-painting paper themselves.

Teachers commonly complain that finger paints are "too messy" or that children or furnishings get paint all over them. Careful organization eliminates some of these complaints. To minimize messy problems, it helps to cover the table with several layers of newspaper; then when one child uses a large amount of paint that oozes over the side of the paper, you can easily prepare the place for the next child by peeling off a layer of newspaper. Also, less mess results if the children stand up to paint. Without thinking, children will handle chairs with paint-covered hands, so chairs should be removed. The teacher may choose to wear a long apron to eliminate concern over getting paint on clothing.

Foot Painting

Foot painting is a variation of finger painting that you might like to try on a warm spring or summer day when the children are wearing light shoes and shorts and you can work outside without shoes. The children will have the unusual experience of seeing their footprints and perhaps creating designs on a paper or on the sidewalks. This project might create real havoc inside a classroom unless many adults are present to help with shoes and other problems that do not occur outdoors on warm days. Outdoors the garden hose can be of great help in cleaning up the painters' feet and the painting area.

Drawing

Drawing offers children a prewriting experience. Using a tool, they gain experience making lines and filling in the spaces, developing small muscle coordination in order to control the tool. The stages discussed earlier also apply to this technique. Drawing is likely to be more familiar than other techniques when children enter school.

Crayons

Crayons are probably the art medium most familiar to children. If a child has any art material at home, surely it will be crayons. Crayons give children a medium that expresses their creativity and permits them to see clearly the results of the movement of the tool. In comparison with other media crayons make it harder for a small child to obtain depth of color without prolonged effort and are therefore somewhat unsatisfactory. By unwrapping the paper from the crayon, the child can use the side as well as the tip of the crayon. Some of the new types of crayons are softer and make it easier for the child to obtain color intensity. Children enjoy the type of crayon that is dipped in water as it is used.

Because crayons are likely to be familiar, the teacher often plans the use of this medium during the first days of school. The teacher wants the children to feel at home and begin participating freely. They are more likely to do so upon seeing materials they know.

Children should be allowed to create their own designs on newsprint, manila paper, or colored mimeograph paper. Coloring-book-type material tends to stifle the child's creativity and is not recommended. A teacher should have confidence in the child's ability to create designs—and to fill in the color within the borders. The teacher can encourage exploration with various types of lines and shapes. Crayon prints can be made if a flat object—a leaf, a penny, or a piece of lace—is placed under the paper, which the child covers with color, using the side of the crayon.

Crayon Resist

Crayon resist is a technique which involves making a drawing in crayon, then painting over the design with a thin wash of water color. Especially effective is a white wash on black or blue paper or a black wash over Halloween pumpkins. This technique works best with fives and sixes, who will be willing to overlay their drawings with several more layers of crayon. Without the thick layer of wax the resist effect doesn't work. The wash is a thinned tempera paint. The teacher should experiment with the materials before presenting them to the children.

Felt Pens

Felt pens come in many colors and some have washable ink, making them appropriate for use with young children. Though these are a more expensive medium, they may well encourage learning activity by some children who are not happy with other media. The colors are intense and come off easily. Teaching children to cap their pens tightly after use will help make the ink last longer.

Chalk

Using chalk on the chalkboard gives the child another drawing medium. It, too, is a worthwhile prewriting experience. A chalkboard can be made from a wall or a piece of plywood or heavy cardboard painted with blackboard paint. (It need not be black.) Chalks in many colors are available. Children will enjoy the large soft chalk called *pastels* because the color comes off readily. Pastels come in bright colors and are about 4 inches long and an inch thick. Blackboard chalk is much harder.

Wet chalk can provide a creative experience wherein the pastel chalks (mentioned above) are used on wet manila construction paper. Wrapping-paper murals are interesting when done with this chalk. The paper is dipped in water; then the child draws with the chalk. A starchy water is sometimes used to moisten the paper and gives a shiny effect when dry. Because of the size of the chalk, the children are able to make large motions and large objects in their drawings. Children like this medium because they get deep color quickly. Pastels also work well for making murals using large paper tacked to the wall or spread on the floor or a table.

The children will need aprons. They occasionally see wet chalk as another finger paint. The table is more easily cleaned up if it is covered with newspaper. A drying area is required. Care should be taken when you are sending chalk drawings home because chalk will rub off on clothing and car upholstery, making parents unhappy. It is sometimes convenient to roll the drawings and secure them with a rubberband.

Gluing, Cutting, and Tearing

A collage is an artistic composition of fragments of paper and other material. The word comes from a French word meaning "gluing." The opportunity to be creative with odds and ends of "junk" is very popular with young children. They develop skills while using the scissors, glue bottles, and paste brushes. They develop eye-hand coordination; a sense of balance, size, color, and proportion; and a sense of the third dimension (depth).

The collage invites creativity even by adults because they acquire a habit of seeing a creative use for many things one might throw away. What can be done with those colorful bags that department stores put your purchases in? Those perfume and makeup boxes? Or the towel and toilet paper rolls? Your roommate or spouse will probably be dismayed as you hoard such "junk" for creative art activities, so plan early to organize the materials and minimize the fire hazard and the clutter. In a time of high costs and pollution, recycling is of increasing importance—and you get fine materials for children's art activities without cost. Art made by using clean, edible food can be costly and wasteful. In one child care center the children who were pasting pieces of breakfast cereal on collages might have been better off if the cereal had been served to them with milk. Far better are scraps waiting to be given a new use, so look for them.

Tearing and Cutting

Tearing and cutting are two methods of preparing material for the collage. Young children simply enjoy an opportunity to tear and cut. Well before children can manipulate the scissors, they are able to tear paper into bits. Every mother remembers a time when her child tore up the unread newspaper or ripped a favorite magazine. Children can be encouraged to tear paper for their art work. Even after they can use the scissors, they may like to use the tearing method to obtain certain effects. Cutting with scissors requires finer eye-hand coordination and more mature motor skills than does tearing. Older children who have not had experience with scissors will pass through a stage of awkwardness in using them. Older children benefit from suggestions as to how to use scissors more than do younger children. Both groups seem to need ample time to experiment with scissors until they discover a satisfactory way to hold and use them.

Blunt-end scissors should be provided. They should be kept free of paste and glue and in good operating condition. Nothing is so frustrating as scissors that do not cut. The teacher should try scissors out occasionally to be sure they are usable.

Left-handed scissors should be purchased for the left-handed children. This fact seems to surprise some people, but a right-handed teacher need only try to use right-handed scissors in the left hand to see why left-handed children have difficulty cutting with them. They can't see the line that they are trying to cut unless they hold their work far to the right so they can see over the blade of the scissors. Some left-handed scissors come with colored handles to aid children in distinguishing them from right-handed ones. If they are not clearly marked, the teacher may tie colored yarn to the handles of the left-handed scissors.

If a child has difficulty learning to cut with a scissors, a teacher may want to try double-ring training scissors. This scissors has an extra set of rings allowing the teacher's hand to fit over the child's hand, helping the child develop the cutting technique.

It is interesting for children to experiment with cutting different lines— jagged, wavy, straight, fringed, or some combination of these. Kinder- garteners will enjoy cutting strips of lightweight paper and curling them with the edge of the scissors' blade. These curls may be used to decorate various objects. Old magazines provide a stimulus to the young cutters. They can choose one type of object to look for—i.e., cars, food for Thanksgiving dinner, toys, animals, or babies. However, adults should not be surprised when children get sidetracked and cut out other inter- esting objects.

The light weight of colored mimeograph paper makes it especially useful for free cutting by young children. Mimeograph paper is easier to fold and cut than construction paper. Also, five sheets of mimeograph paper cost the same as one sheet of construction paper. Scraps of left- over paper can be prepared for collage work. When the teacher plans to let the children practice cutting—say, hearts—squares of paper can be prepared ahead of time to enable the children to get several objects per page. When it is left up to the children, they will cut their object out of the center of the large sheet, leaving the remainder for scrap.

Gluing or Pasting

Gluing or pasting is a skill children learn to help them complete their collages. Children may at first manipulate the paste or glue much as they do finger paint. They use excessive amounts when judged by adult stan- dards. Using the white glue in squeeze bottles is very interesting to chil- dren. They often use this glue as a white paint, making designs on their paper. To curb this use of glue, the teacher can give the children white tempera paint in plastic squeeze bottles to be used for making designs. Occasionally the teacher can demonstrate the amount of glue required by saying, "The white glue is very strong. See, it takes only a tiny spot to hold this big piece of paper." Sometimes such a demonstration helps reduce the amount of glue children use. Because white glue holds more securely than paste, it is better to give children white glue for structures that have considerable weight or strain. When cherished objects fall apart, it is very frustrating to children. White glue can be purchased in gallon bottles, then transferred first to a squeeze bottle with a large opening, such as those used for mustard, and next, transferred to the small bottles that children can handle. For some projects white glue can be diluted with water and brushed with paste brushes. Some white glues wash out of clothing.

Paste can be made with flour and water. It can also be bought in quantity. Since paste dries quickly, it should be kept covered as much as possible. Children may like brushes or sticks to use with paste.

The variety of materials for collage is limited only by the imagination of the teacher and the children. The home, the yard, the workshop, the park, or construction sites are places to look for castoff materials suitable for three-dimensional art projects. The teacher's role is to see that there is an interesting assortment of materials, and the children's creativity will do the rest. Most of the materials can be castoffs—helping ease the strain on the center's budget. Labeled shoe boxes or coffee cans containing collage materials help keep cupboards tidy and materials easily obtainable.

Suggested materials are

1. Acorns.
2. Bird gravel.
3. Boxes, tubes, and egg cartons from the kitchen.
4. Cellophane and tissue paper.
5. Confetti.
6. Corn—start with dry corn on the cob. Let the children shell it.
7. Cotton, cloth, wool, yarn, and fur.
8. Cupcake papers and candy cups from boxed candy.
9. Doilies (paper).
10. Eggshells—colored or white, to cover collages or to be glued to bottles for vases.
11. Excelsior or other packing material.
12. Feathers.
13. Glitter.
14. Grass, twigs, leaves, flowers.
15. Gummed paper, stamps, and holiday stickers.
16. Magazines and catalogs.
17. Match sticks, toothpicks, popsicle sticks, or tongue blades.
18. Paper cups—the cone-shaped cups are especially interesting.
19. Paper scraps, construction paper, wrapping paper, holiday cards, foils, wallpaper, corrugated paper.
20. Nutshells.
21. Precut shapes—hearts, diamonds, squares, triangles, and circles.
22. Sawdust and wood shavings.
23. Salt or sand colored with tempera.
24. Spools and wood pieces.

25. Straws (drinking) or wheat straw.
26. Strips of newspaper or magazines.
27. Styrofoam curls and pieces.
28. Wire and pipe cleaners.

Three-Dimensional Art

Sculptures made with three-dimensional materials form another type of collage. Box art is one form; the children create their structures from an assortment of disposable containers, such as boxes and tubes. Scraps of wood offer another texture and can be glued together to form sculptures. Wood scraps can be obtained from carpentry and cabinet shops. White glue is essential for these structures. After drying, these art objects can be painted.

Modeling

Plastic modeling materials give children another medium for creative self-expression. The form changes as the child uses the material. Material such as ceramic clay, play dough, plasticene, salt ceramic, "silly putty," sawdust with wheat paste, and sand are common materials for

Figure 8-8. Yarn and glue, available at the art table, invite children to make spiderwebs. (Child Development Center, Metropolitan State College, Denver)

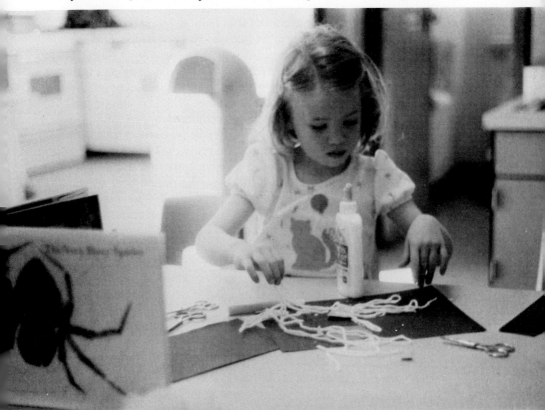

modeling. Children enjoy the opportunity to be messy with these materials. Children can change the material and can add or subtract from the amount. They can experiment with shapes—forming the same piece first into a long worm, then into a flat pancake. There is opportunity to pound and squeeze, which may help a child work out hostile or aggressive feelings. Children imitate and socialize during the activity. While enjoying the "gushy" mixture of clay and water, Kim said, "I'm making chocolate soup."

The products will be quite primitive. The same stages apply in modeling as in drawing. The teacher and the parents will have to be content with simple products. Most teachers of young children make no attempt to save the products. Firing of children's clay products is usually disappointing.

Ceramic Clay

Ceramic clay—sometimes called mud clay—will attract children, especially if the teacher works at the table with them. A visit to an art center to see a potter at work offers an opportunity to observe the relationship of the potter's work to familiar vases, pitchers, and plates. Such a visit will encourage many nonparticipators to use this "messy" medium.

The teacher should provide modeling materials in good condition. It helps for adults to manipulate the clay to be sure that it is soft enough for the children to use. Sitting with the children and manipulating the clay in the manner that they are using it is best. Avoid making models for children, for this invites them to become spectators and does not fulfill goals for individual development.

Ceramic clay may be purchased ready to use or in a powdered form that must be mixed with water. Your local potters' guild may sell you clay or allow you to prepare it in their facilities. The clay can be used and reused. If it becomes dry, the clay is reclaimed by the adding of water. If the clay dries in large lumps, it may be placed in a cloth bag and pounded to a powdery consistency, then moistened again. Children can be taught to leave the clay molded in large balls with a big thumb hole in the side; then water can be added to the thumb hole to help keep the clay a proper consistency. The storage container should be covered tightly. Boards for use on the table where the children will use the clay may be made of masonite and should be about 15 inches square. Covering the table with a cotton-backed plastic with plastic side down makes a good working surface. The covering is simply hung to dry until the next clay experience. The children need no tools. A tongue blade from the nurse's station is useful for scraping clay up from the board. Aprons for the children are important.

Figure 8-9. Pieces of wood to cut, glue, and paint give children a three dimensional creative medium. (Child Development Laboratory, Michigan State University)

Play Dough

Play dough provides many of the same experiences as clay. However, most children do not think of dough as being dirty, as they do clay. Therefore they do not have the inhibitions they may have in working with clay. They are inclined to play at being cooks, saying, "I'm making cookies." If cookies or pancakes have been recent group projects, this experience may be played out with the play dough.

The play dough can be made with little difficulty. The homemade varieties are usually superior to commercial doughs and are, of course, cheaper. Teachers should test the consistency of the doughs they give the children. Play dough should be soft and moist enough so that the child can readily manipulate it. The salt content should be low, so that the dough does not dry out the child's hands. Additional flour may be required if the dough is sticky. Cutters, rolling pins, and plates may add to the child's enjoyment. Parents appreciate play-dough recipes because play dough is a good home activity. Play dough is easily cleaned up and makes a good gift.

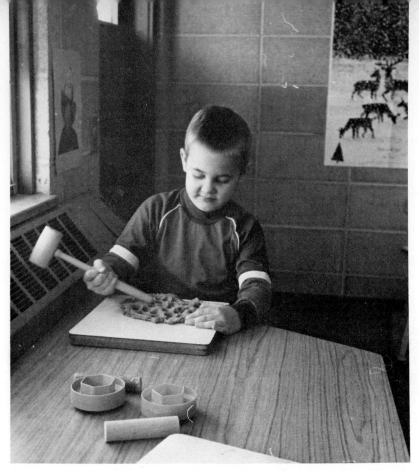

Figure 8-10. Ceramic clay offers endless possibilities for creative expression. (Texas Woman's University Nursery School)

RECIPES FOR PLAY DOUGH

UNCOOKED PLAY DOUGH

Mix in a large bowl:
2 cups flour
1 cup salt
6 teaspoons alum (from grocery store)
2 tablespoons salad oil
1 cup water plus desired color (vegetable color or tempera paint)

This recipe is simple enough so that a group of children can help the teacher make it. Of course, let them use the dough immediately. If stored in a plastic bag, it will keep several weeks.

Cooked Play Dough

1. Mix in a large bowl:
   1 cup flour
   ½ cup cornstarch
   1 cup water
2. Boil in a pan:
   4 cups water
   1 cup salt
3. Slowly pour the boiling water into the bowl mixture until they are mixed thoroughly. The mixture will have a white-sauce appearance. Then put this mixture back in the pan, cook it over low heat, stirring, until it is thickened and stands stiff. Cooking time: 10–15 minutes.
4. Cool.
5. Stir in 4 to 5 cups of flour until a dough consistency is obtained. More flour may have to be added to make the dough workable.
6. Then knead in as much flour as is required to obtain a good, pliable, soft, but not sticky, consistency.
7. Store the dough in a plastic bag. Refrigerate it for best keeping. Allow it to warm before using it. If it becomes sticky, add flour. Children enjoy working in flour. Makes 15–20 medium-sized balls.

"Silly Putty"

Mix in a large bowl:
2 cups white glue
1¾ cups liquid starch or cornstarch
Add desired vegetable coloring

Salt Ceramic

1. Heat in a saucepan until boiling:
   2 cups salt
   ⅔ cup water
2. Add while stirring quickly:
   1 cup cornstarch dissolved in ½ cup cold water
3. Mix with the hands. The mixture may need a few more drops of water to make pliable dough. Use it to make a child's handprint, tree decorations, or beads. Hardens at room temperature in two days. Can be painted.

Sawdust Dough

Mix in a large bowl:
Wallpaper paste with water
Add sawdust until dough consistency is produced
Let figures dry thoroughly for several days. Paint or shellac.

Plasticene

Plasticene is a commercial plastic medium. It is less useful for young children than the materials previously discussed. However, it introduces some variety for the children if offered occasionally. The plasticene must be warm to be malleable for small hands. The teacher may set it near a radiator or work it in his or her own hands before offering it to the children. Variety and art stores sell plasticene.

Sand

Sand can be provided indoors in a sand table or outdoors in the yard. It lends itself to quiet, individual creative play or to creative group interaction. Older children develop themes and carry them out cooperatively. Sand should be of beach quality and clean. It should be kept moist so the children can pack it tightly into molds or tunnels and so it won't fly into hair and eyes. Plenty of shovels should be available. Sifters and containers to fill are popular. Kitchen cast-offs, such as pans and cans, encourage the playing of homemaker roles. Small cars or trucks or chunks of wood to substitute for cars will stimulate road building. When used indoors, sand may damage floor coverings and finishes. The sand table can be located on a cement floor if available. Firm rules (limits) regarding proper conduct around the sand should be established from the beginning. Avoid overcrowding.

Building

Blocks are mentioned here because of the creative opportunities they offer children. They will be discussed in other chapters because of their contribution to outdoor play, to concept building, and to dramatic play—all interrelated. The "whole child" learns when playing with blocks. Gross motor skills and minute small motor coordinations will be challenged by blocks. Some children who are not attracted to other creative media are happy using blocks. Parents may have to be reassured that the child who uses blocks is indeed creative. Because the child's creativity is expressed with the school's blocks, there are no products to take home for parental approval.

Carpentry

Carpentry is a creative medium that offers emotional release and opportunities to develop large and small muscle skills. A table with vises and clamps to hold the wood for sawing or hammering is a big help to young children. Real tools that work well should be purchased. Scrap lumber can usually be obtained from cabinet shops or lumberyards. Bottle caps and spools make wheels for objects.

The safe use of tools is a major item to learn. Rules for using tools must be carefully set by the teacher. Supervising and limiting the number of children at work around the carpentry table are important safety precautions.

The use of glue in place of hammering can satisfy children who like to use wood but don't like to hammer. Paints can be available to paint the products. Of course, outdoors is the best place for this noisy activity. A separate indoor space with acoustical tile can, however, be prepared for young carpenters, and other quiet activities can still be enjoyed in the playroom.

Helping a New Volunteer

When you are the lead teacher, you will frequently be called on to orient new volunteers, assistants, or even parents who assist in the art area. Actually, considerable inservice education should occur before people are assigned with children. Because of the sensitive nature of creative expression, children should have teachers who know and understand them well. However, a new person may need help in setting up the area efficiently to help eliminate problems that often occur with poor arrangements. You will want to state your policy about freedom of expression and creativity and advise specifically against modeling figures or helping the child draw or paint. Help arrange the area so the individual will have only a few children at work in the area at a time.

Conclusion

Creativity is a human potential that integrates physical, mental, social, and emotional growth. Creativity is fostered in good schools for young children by a free, flexible, accepting, and open environment and by teachers who are openly discovering, inventing, and creating. Many activities have been suggested to help start the teacher toward creative teaching. For neither the children nor the teacher are patterns presented—only raw materials have been suggested and the reassurance that "you can do it."

In addition to the opportunity for creative self-expression, the child is practicing many small motor skills, eye-hand coordination, left-to-right progression, and whole-part relationships, all of which are foundations for later reading and writing. The first, opportunity for self-expression should be enough to sell an art program, but the additional benefits further strengthen the reasons for providing art activities.

Applications

1. Do the "Talk It Over" activities suggested in the chapter.
2. Complete Lesson 8 in *A Laboratory Workbook for Introduction to Early Childhood Education.* Hand in as scheduled.
3. Write an activity plan for an art activity for a few children using information and the sample (Figure 6-1) in Chapter 6. Secure approval, carry out the plan, and evaluate the results from the children's point of view and from your viewpoint. Prepare a report and hand it in along with your approved activity plan.
4. Evaluate your total participation performance on your evaluation form developed in Chapter 1.
5. Add ideas and plans for art activities to your Resource File.

Study Questions

1. Define creativity.
2. Identify ways creativity is fostered in early childhood schools.
3. Refer to the developmental tasks in Chapter 2. Make notes on how art activity can contribute to each developmental task for a child.
4. Name and illustrate with a drawing the developmental stages of children's art as described by Brittain.
5. Discuss the findings on right and left brain research and the implications for art education.
6. Explain how writing and reading are fostered by art activities.
7. Consider each category of art activity—painting, drawing, building, modeling, and cutting and gluing—and outline appropriate space recommendations, supplies, equipment, and guidance for each one.

Film

My Art Is Me   Color   25 minutes   1970

A variety of art materials are used by young children in an atmosphere that promotes discovery. The University of California (Berkeley) laboratory school is the scene. University of California Extension Media Center, Berkeley, Calif. 94720.

Additional Readings

BARRY, JAMES C., and CHARLES F. TREADWAY. *Kindergarten Resource Book.* Nashville, Tenn.: Broadman Press, 1965.
BRITTAIN, W. LAMBERT. *Creativity, Art, and the Young Child.* New York: Macmillan Publishing Co., Inc., 1979.

BURNS, SYLVIA F. "Children's Art: A Vehicle for Learning," *Young Children,* Vol. 30, No. 3, March 1975, pp. 193–204.

CHERRY, CLARE. *Creative Art for the Developing Child.* Belmont, Calif.: Lear Siegler, Inc., Fearon Publishers, 1972.

COHEN, ELAINE PEAR. "Does Art Matter in the Education of the Black Ghetto Child?" *Young Children,* Vol. 29, No. 3, March 1974, pp. 170–181.

FUCIGNA, CAROLEE, KATHERINE C. IVES, and WILLIAM IVES. "Art for Toddlers: A Developmental Approach." *Young Children,* Vol. 37, No. 3, March 1982, pp. 45–51.

GETZELS, J. W., and P. W. JACKSON. *Creativity and Intelligence.* New York: John Wiley & Sons, 1962.

GOODNOW, JACQUELINE. *Children Drawing.* Cambridge, Mass.: Harvard University Press, 1977.

HARRIS, D. B. *Children's Drawings as Measures of Intellectual Maturity.* New York: Harcourt, Brace & World, 1963.

KELLOG, RHODA. *Analyzing Children's Art.* Palo Alto, Calif.: National Press, 1969.

LANGUIS, MARLIN, TOBIE SANDERS, and STEVEN TIPPS. *Brain and Learning: Directions in Early Childhood Education.* Washington, D.C.: National Association for the Education of Young Children, 1980.

LOWENFELD, VIKTOR, and W. LAMBERT BRITTAIN. *Creative and Mental Growth.* New York: Macmillan Publishing Co., Inc., 1982.

SPARLING, JOSEPH, and MARILYN SPARLING. "How to Talk to a Scribbler." *Young Children,* Vol. 28, No. 6, August 1973, pp. 333–341.

TAYLOR, BARBARA J. *A Child Goes Forth.* Provo, Utah: Brigham Young University Press, 1980.

TORRANCE, E. PAUL. *Guiding Creative Talent.* Huntington, N.Y.: Robert E. Krieger Publishing Co., 1976.

TORRANCE, E. PAUL. *Encouraging Creativity in the Classroom.* Dubuque, Iowa: Wm. C. Brown Company, 1970.

Science
Activities

- To *identify stages of children's cognitive development according to several research theories.*
- To *define science and the scientific method.*
- To *identify the factors that influence planning of children's science activities.*
- To *identify and give a rationale for a cumulative plan.*
- To *identify and evaluate activities that give children insights into the biological, physical, and social sciences.*

"How do you tell which one is mine if you put them all together?" asked four-year-old Sandra as she helped her teacher arrange the cups of newly planted pumpkin seeds on the window sill.

"If all the people in the state lived in one house it would have to be BIG!" exclaimed four-year-old Josh.

"We have these kinds of flowers in our back yard," said five-year-old Tina. "Snap dragons like to be squeezed and go POP!" she exclaimed, clapping her hands together.

Questions and comments like these flow naturally in high-quality early childhood centers. Sandra is extending her information, Josh is using his ability to reason, and Tina is remembering, relating, and comparing. Each child is functioning cognitively.

Cognitive Functioning: A Definition

The word cognitive comes from the Latin word *cognoscere* which means "to know." Cognitive functioning can be thought of as the act or process of knowing, including awareness and judgment. Some call

212

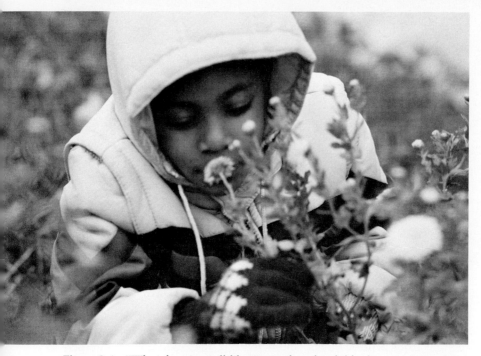

Figure 9-1. "What does it smell like?" wonders the child who examines a late bloom. A sense of wonder is part of scientific education. (Hoeflin Stone House Child Care Center, Kansas State University)

cognitive functioning mental or intellectual functioning. *Cognitive development* refers to the increased depth and breadth of intellectual or mental functioning which occurs as the individual matures. The brain is the center for cognitive functioning—storing and utilizing information gained through the five sensory modes—seeing, hearing, touching, tasting, and smelling. Some researchers describe the brain as functioning like a giant computer; yet, the brain performs feats that computers are not now capable of performing.

Cognitive Development Linked with Other Development

Physiological conditions, including genetic inheritance, affect the development of the brain from the moment of conception. Adequate nutrition, both prenatally and postnatally, restricted or no drug use, and the absence of disease or damage to mother and child set the stage for the healthy child with a well-developed brain.

Figure 9-2. An enthusiastic young scientist shows off the indoor garden to a visitor. (Zukeran Elementary School, Kadena Air Base, Okinawa, Japan)

As the infant matures, learning takes place following sensory stimulation from people, things, and activity in the environment. Interpersonal aspects influence the infant's cognitive functioning. The loving and supporting interaction the child experiences with parents and caregivers influences the child's level of autonomy and developing concept of self. Information is perceived through the senses and is stored in the brain.

The brain is intricately involved with the development of motor skills also. Moving the body involves many levels of knowing and functioning by the brain. The right hemisphere of the brain controls the left side of the body, and the left hemisphere of the brain controls the right side of the body.

During the years before school, "The connection between the two hemispheres of the brain is less complete than it will be after 7 or 8 years of age. In order to develop both sides of the brain fully during the time before much intercommunication occurs, it is recommended that children have abundant music, rhythmic exercises, movement exploration, art materials, and other right-hemisphere-related experiences, as well as those more pertinent to the left hemisphere, such as speaking, reading, and counting." [1]

Other aspects of brain development and functioning are discussed in Chapters 8 and 11. The left-dominant functioning is called *verbal-analytical* because the person operating in the left hemisphere is effective in dealing with the object world, is analytical, rational, and abstract in

[1] Mollie S. Smart and Russell Smart, *Children: Development and Relationships* (New York: Macmillan Publishing Co., Inc., 1977), p. 224.

cognitive style. The cognitive style of the right hemisphere-oriented person is described as *holistic*, meaning that the individual tends to use imagination, creativity, and intuition and is able to see a situation or picture as a whole.[2]

The research into, and suggested applications of brain mapping are still in the formative stage, yet they seem to have implications for parents and teachers of young children. One thing experienced early childhood educators can readily appreciate is the variety of cognitive styles in young children. They've usually called it individuality. Every day a teacher sees children like Tina in our opening anecdote who said, "We have these kinds of flowers in our back yard," and who is operating in a left hemisphere or analytical mode. Teachers also have children like Josh who appears to get the whole picture when he says, "If all the people in the state lived in one house it would have to be BIG!" The challenge is to stimulate both hemispheres of each child's brain and help each one use the style appropriate for each new situation.

Goals for Children's Cognitive Growth

Fostering children's cognitive growth in the early years is very important. By reviewing the developmental tasks in Chapter 2 you will note the cognitive component in each one. Developing and utilizing children's curiosity are prime objectives. Encouraging children to think, reason, infer, and generalize is desirable. Briefly, the children are learning

1. To understand the world around them.
2. To understand people and things.
3. To understand their bodies and feelings, and how to care for themselves.
4. To symbolize—using language and forms to communicate.
5. To make choices and decisions, and grow in independence.
6. To do what is right according to values of the local, national, and global community.

Types of Intellectual Operations

According to psychologist Guilford, children may be capable of five different types of intellectual operations:

1. They may perceive or recognize a problem: *cognition.*
2. They may be able to retain what is recognized and recall it: *memory.*

[2] For an interesting analysis see Thomas Banville, "Brain 'Hemisphericity': A High Voltage Topic," *Early Years*, 10:2 (September 1979), pp. 51–53, and continued in 10:2 (October 1979), pp. 38–41.

3. They may use the information perceived and retained to find the one right answer: *convergent thinking.*
4. They may take off from information already possessed, seeking a novel, a different kind of answer: *divergent thinking.*
5. They may evaluate critically the solution hit upon, perhaps sensing a deficiency in their problem solving and trying to correct it: *evaluative thinking.*[3]

The teacher will plan learning experiences to foster each of these five operations.

If teachers and parents hope to stimulate learning meaningfully they must determine their children's concerns by observing and listening. Adults willingly help the child organize knowledge in meaningful ways. Children are accepted and not ridiculed for their lack of knowledge. They are supported in their need to learn from firsthand experience. Selecting and planning experiences to satisfy children's mental needs are important in both the home and the school.

Piaget's Stages of Mental Growth

In recent years the work of Jean Piaget, the Swiss child psychologist, has received considerable attention from early childhood educators and psychologists. Many of Piaget's observations began as he watched the development of his own three youngsters. His observations and research have been carried on for many years. Piaget has described four stages of cognitive or intellectual development.[4] Two of these stages are of major interest to those who are caring for and teaching young children in homes and in all types of early childhood education programs.

Table 9-1 is a conceptualization of Piaget's stages. It indicates a few important characteristics of each stage and helps you think of each stage as an undergirding support for the next and ensuing stages, an important concept in human development. For progression from infancy upward, read the table from bottom to top.

Sensorimotor

Piaget called the earliest stage *sensorimotor*. This label and stage link movement with stimuli perceived through the senses. The stage includes the months from birth to age two. This period is one in which the child learns to control the body in space. It is a period of reflexes and a period when intelligence exists without language or symbols. During these

---

[3] J. P. Guilford, *Personality* (New York: McGraw-Hill 1959); pp. 359–394.

[4] See Jean Piaget, *The Psychology of Intelligence* (London: Routledge and Kegan Paul, 1950) for additional details of Piaget's theory. For easy-to-understand applications of Piaget's theory see *Cognition in Early Childhood* by Janie Dyson Osborn and D. Keith Osborn (Athens, Ga.: Education Associates, 1983).

Table 9-1. Summary of Piaget's Stages of Cognitive Development

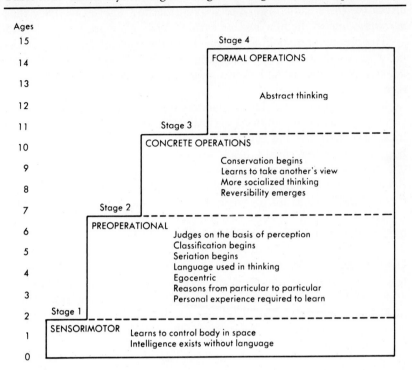

Ages

Age	Stage	
15		Stage 4
14		FORMAL OPERATIONS
13		
12		Abstract thinking
11	Stage 3	
10	CONCRETE OPERATIONS	
9		Conservation begins
8		Learns to take another's view / More socialized thinking / Reversibility emerges
7	Stage 2	
6	PREOPERATIONAL	
5		Judges on the basis of perception / Classification begins / Seriation begins
4		Language used in thinking / Egocentric
3		Reasons from particular to particular / Personal experience required to learn
2	Stage 1	
1	SENSORIMOTOR	Learns to control body in space / Intelligence exists without language
0		

first two years the infant or toddler learns by exploring space bodily and by handling objects and exploring them through touching, tasting, seeing, hearing, and smelling.

Preoperational

The preoperational stage, Piaget's second stage, follows the sensorimotor stage. As the label implies, it is the period prior to logical thinking or operations. The preoperational stage is one of "here and now." It lasts approximately from ages two years to seven years.

The preoperational is a self-centered or ego-centered stage, children viewing their surroundings only in terms of themselves. Their learning requires experiences with real objects and things as opposed to being told about things. The child now begins to think of things that are not present. You can observe examples of this as you watch children play family, pet, or worker roles in dramatic play.

Piaget says a child receives stimuli from the environment and acts on the stimuli with whatever prior experience he or she has in a process called *assimilation*. For example, toddlers flail their spindle toys the same way they learned to shake their rattles. This, of course, creates a problem because it is heavier and more harmful to themselves and others.

Therefore, they must learn some new behavior; for example, putting the discs over the spindle instead of shaking the toy vigorously. They thus *accommodate* to the new toy by learning new behaviors.

The preoperational child reasons from the particular to the particular. Piaget called this type of reasoning *transductive*. The child erroneously puts objects and events together that don't logically go together.

In this stage young children begin to classify objects according to some criterion. After sorting objects according to one criterion, they become focused or *centered* and cannot shift and classify according to another. For example, after sorting beads according to color, they will not be able to cancel that perception and re-sort the beads according to shape. According to this finding, we would only confuse children by presenting them multifaceted problems when they are in this stage of development.

Young children between two and seven think very differently than older children and adults. It will be a challenge for you to listen as children reveal their mode of thinking through their language and behavior. Children have to discover knowledge for themselves. It is of no use to teach them to parrot the right answers before they have any basis for understanding the concepts. Kamii, a researcher studying applications of Piaget's theories writes, "Children can be taught to give correct answers to 2 + 3, but they cannot be taught directly the relationships underlying this addition."[5]

Concrete Operations

The third stage in Piaget's scheme is called *concrete operations*. Now the child can reason logically about things and ideas. This stage occurs from the seventh to the eleventh year. In this stage the school-age child learns to take another's view. He or she learns that substance, weight, length, area, and numbers remain the same regardless of changes in position. Piaget called this process *conservation*. The classic experiment that is simple for anyone to try is to show the child liquid in a tall glass, then pour it into a squat one, and ask the child which glass has the most liquid. During the years from two through six the child says the tall one has the most, while during the period of seven to eleven years the child is said to "conserve" when reasoning that changing the size of the container doesn't change the amount of liquid.

Piaget discusses the aspect of *reversibility* in flexible and controlled thought, which, he says, emerges when the child is from seven to eleven years old. Now the child can think of an act and think it undone. For example, Juanita can stand in the kitchen door in her muddy boots and think of the muddy tracks she'll make if she enters and walks across the

---

[5] Constance Kamii, *Number in Preschool & Kindergarten* (Washington, D.C.: National Association for the Education of Young Children), 1982, p. 15.

floor. She can mentally think of her deed undone (tracks removed). During the early years (0–6) she cannot do this much reasoning. If you ask her after she walks across the floor, "Did you make those tracks on the floor?" she may deny it honestly, being unable to reverse her thoughts or think about the floor when it was clean. By placing reversibility in his older age bracket Piaget helps us understand that our young children are generally unable to do the mental scheming that sometimes is attributed to them. For example, when three-year-old Billy's mother says, "He's flattering me so I'll let him play with his battery car," it is highly improbable that Billy is sophisticated enough to have schemed in that way.

Formal Operations

Piaget's fourth stage is called *formal operations*. This stage begins around the eleventh year and continues through maturity. Now adolescents can think about their own thinking. They can think about what could be as well as what is, something they could not do earlier. They can now think about and deal with concepts in the abstract. At a personal level, for example, they can understand their bank account and the amount of money they have available. They do not have to have their bankbook in their pocket to know when they have funds for a certain need. A young child whose favorite toy or security blanket is left at grandmother's can't reason that it is safe. He or she must have it in hand to be sure.

Clearly stages three and four are far out of the range of early childhood education, but they are presented here because our understanding and designing of programs for the development and education of young children will be aided. The sensorimotor and preoperational stages are of concern to us in our planning. Being familiar with the more advanced stages helps us know what is too complicated for our young children. Piaget's work is helpful to teachers because it serves as a guide in setting expectations for children. Teachers understand that the child is the center of his or her reasoning universe. They realize that they should not be critical of the child for being self-centered; it is simply part of being a young child. Knowing future stages helps adults provide experiences that will help the child move comfortably into advanced stages when he or she is ready.

Piaget, like most researchers, sets age brackets cautiously knowing that many deviations from what appears "normal" in research are still normal for a particular child. Because no child is 100 percent consistent in a behavior, it is unwise to say, "Johnny always does . . ." It is even more unwise to say, "All children do . . ."

Piaget himself has suggested that it is foolish to set out deliberately to "teach" these stages. He thinks they evolve from children's step-by-step development as they use things and socialize in their environment. When he was asked whether teachers should present the same types of tasks to children that he did in his research, Piaget said, "if the aim is to accelerate the development of these operations, it is idiotic."[6]

Kamii, after many experiments and attempts to build a Piaget-type curriculum for nursery school, has said, "I found in Piaget's theory many reasons why dramatic play, painting, block building, paper folding, Jell-O-making, etc., were so relevant to education. The more I studied Piaget's theory, the more I came to respect the intuitive wisdom of the traditional nursery school."[7]

* * *

Talk It Over: No. 1

Study the previous section on brain development, cognitive development, and intellectual operations. What common factors do the three theories contain? Discuss.

* * *

What Is Science for Young Children?

Science can be defined as systematized knowledge. In the adult world, knowledge is grouped into the physical, natural, biological, and social sciences, literature, music, mathematics, and the arts. These are human-made systems. All have important concepts for young children.

It has been said that the university curriculum can become the curriculum for the early childhood school. The teacher needs a liberal education to teach the concepts and to appreciate the meaning of those concepts for the child and the society. No matter how extensive a teacher's education, children will raise questions to which a teacher will answer, "Let's find out," or "Let's go and look that up." There will be surprises. Today's children have amazing bits and pieces of information they are trying to fit into meaningful packages.

Using the *scientific method* requires one to observe, make inquiries, seek reasons, and experiment. Answers today may be inadequate or fallacies tomorrow. Thus, all "truths" are held in a tentative mode. The process of the scientific method is important, especially in early childhood schools. Teachers' efforts should go into keeping children's curiosity alive, rather than teaching specific facts.

Teachers may be surprised at the breadth of information of some children in their groups. Educated parents, television, and travel are all factors contributing to the breadth of a child's knowledge. One boy's

[6] Eleanore Duckworth, "Piaget Takes a Teacher's Look," *Learning*, 2:2 (October 1973), p. 22.

[7] Constance Kamii, "An Application of Piaget's Theory to the Conceptualization of a Preschool Curriculum," *The Preschool in Action*, Ronald K. Parker (ed.) (Boston: Allyn & Bacon, 1972), p. 119.

Figure 9-3. A student can try out one of the Piaget-type tasks to learn about children's reasoning. (Child Development Laboratory, Michigan State University)

"I'm going to be an ichthyologist" sent the teacher scurrying to a dictionary. Many teachers have drawn on concepts from biology class to respond to "Was I in my mommy's stomach before I got borned?" "Today is Hanukkah" need not embarrass a teacher who has studied the world's great religions in humanities classes.

Planning Science Education

If teachers are convinced of the importance of children using the scientific method to gain information about their world, and, if teachers are aware of how children learn cognitive information, what further considerations are relevant in curriculum planning?

Children's Needs and Interests

The teacher begins with the children, assessing continuously what they know and what they want and need to know. Linking new knowledge to prior knowledge is an important psychological principle to follow. At first, plans are based on general knowledge of young children. As the teacher gets to know the group personally, plans are individualized.

A building-block approach is used that lays a firm foundation, then continues building, one block at a time. No chimneys are built before the basement is dug. The children become personally and actively involved in their own education. They are helped to find concrete ways of relating new knowledge to what they already know. Learning takes time and lots of repetition. This is a trying-it-out experimental laboratory approach. Children are more likely to understand and remember information that they discover themselves.

Teachers plan a rich curriculum of science activities to stimulate children's five senses. Spontaneous events are valued and utilized for their scientific teaching whenever they arise. For example, the children find a caterpillar. While other plans wait, this furry creature becomes the focus of learning for several days. The children observe how the caterpillar moves, how it eats, and finally how it spins a cocoon. The teacher tells about the stages of metamorphosis. Good teaching results when a teacher is able to capitalize on a spontaneous interest such as this one. It is also true, however, that children who do not happen to discover a

Figure 9-4. Activities with foods present opportunities for children to learn scientific concepts. (Child Development Laboratory, University of Idaho)

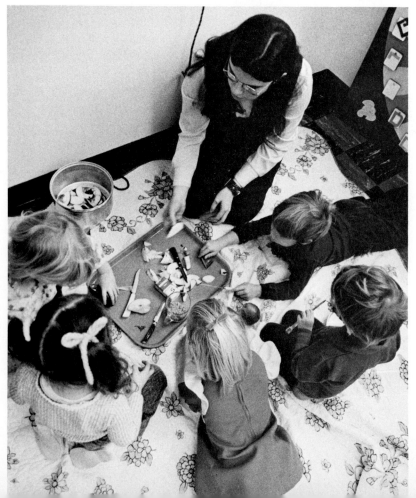

caterpillar may benefit from being introduced to one by the teacher. The motivation may not be as high as when they discover something themselves, but if they are allowed to watch and hold the caterpillar the teacher brings to them, their knowledge will be enhanced. Later, when they find a caterpillar, they may recognize it and learn new facts. Knowledge is seldom a once-over-all-is-learned event. Each time a person confronts a concept his or her previous experience helps add to its meaning, a fact that should be taken into consideration in planning. Concepts worth learning should be introduced numerous times and in a variety of ways. Each time children will add new information to their storehouse of knowledge. It will help you plan educational objectives for science to refer to the Bloom Taxonomy discussed in Chapter 6.

Cumulative Plan

A *cumulative plan* is the name given to this building-block approach just described. This plan is continuous, starting with a simple concept at the beginning of the year and adding experiences throughout the year. As each new experience is added, the children are helped to reflect back to the related experiences they have had. Six broad themes are suggested to run concurrently as cumulative plans. The themes are

1. The child—his or her name, sex, health, safety, and relationship to the family, the school, the community, and the world.
2. The community—its people, workers, institutions, and traditional festivals.
3. The world of plants—especially those the child sees every day and those that provide food.
4. The world of animals—especially those the child sees every day and those that provide food.
5. The world of machines—including vehicles and other large and small machines.
6. The physical forces in the world.

Following is a brief example of a cumulative plan as it develops in relation to plants in the child's world (item 3 above). In September and October the children pick fall crops—corn, apples, and pumpkins. They collect leaves and make a book of them. They plant crocuses and tulip bulbs in the yard and pot geraniums for their classroom. In November and December they make pumpkin custard and pumpkin bread and talk about the leaves in their book as they observe the bare branches of the trees. New plants are brought into the classroom to brighten it up, and they are compared to the geraniums. Apple sauce is made in February, and the children discover crocuses peeking out of the snow and recall having planted them in the fall. They plant seeds in the window box in

March and plan to transplant the seedlings to the playyard or to their homes in the spring. Trees and shrubs are observed as they bloom and get their new leaves. The geraniums are reset in the garden. The children plant lettuce, anticipating a salad later on. They watch a farmer planting corn and recall the corn they picked in the fall. From these activities the children begin to understand the interrelatedness of their learning.

Each of the six themes suggested, and perhaps others, can be developed as a cumulative plan. Teachers in different localities would develop the sequence differently.

Environment

The school environment is the second major consideration when the teacher is planning science education. The total learning environment can stimulate the young child to want to learn. An intriguing array of challenging activities, many displays to look at, and materials available for experimenting will stimulate curiosity. Readily available reference books will promote questions and provide answers. A science table or corner can be arranged where new science projects begin and ongoing projects continue. A special table or shelf can hold treasures children bring from home or yard. They can share and discuss discoveries with friends.

Figure 9-5. A Discovery Shelf allows children to explore scientific items on their own and select books related to the display. (Institute of Child Study, U.S. Department of Education)

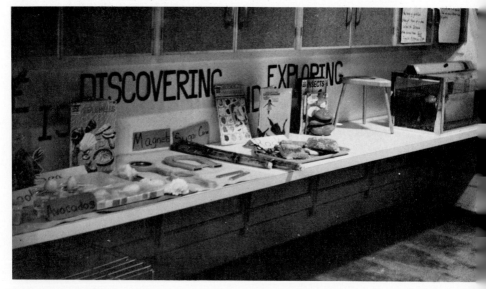

A want-to-know attitude permeates the atmosphere. No shame follows a mistake, as it is safe for a child to admit not knowing. Experimenting is encouraged. If some idea fails to work, there is always something else to try. The teacher encourages exchanging ideas and helping others answer questions. Alert teachers note questions children ask and plan experiences to answer those questions. The self-selection-type organization in the classroom facilitates an individual or small group lesson. Such learning is more meaningful than large group lectures at this age.

Teachers work with parents and encourage their participation in their child's learning. Open communication invites teachers and parents to share the learning experiences that are available to the children. This information better enables both teacher and parent to understand the child and helps parents supplement the school activities. Teachers may need to discuss levels of expectation with parents. The teacher may help one family enrich the child's experience; while encouraging another family to let up on the pressure.

Questioning the Children

Questions have an important place in schools for young children. The children's questions, as well as the teacher's, must be held in high regard. A child's curious questioning must be encouraged. These questions may often be answered by peers, or after the child explores the environment, they may be answered by the child. Often a child's questions require the teacher to encourage further exploration rather than to answer immediately. Normally children are more enthusiastic about seeking answers to questions that they themselves are asking. Therefore, we should encourage children to ask their own questions and seek answers.

Questioning children skillfully is an essential technique for teachers. It is important for the teacher to establish communication with each child and to indicate recognition of each child. Teachers use questioning to stimulate the child's awareness of new information. Questioning signals the child that it is his or her turn to speak and to display knowledge, thoughts, and feelings verbally.

In planning learning activities for children, the teacher must give attention to questioning. Many un-thought-out questions lead only to a "yes" or "no" answer and not at all to the goal the teacher had in mind.

Types of teachers' questions were the subject of a research project by Zimmerman and Bergan.[8] These researchers identified the following

---

[8] Barry J. Zimmerman and John R. Bergan, "Intellectual Operations in Teacher Question-Asking Behavior," *Merrill-Palmer Quarterly,* 17:1 (January 1971), pp. 19–26.

seven categories of questions based on the intellectual operations required by the questions. Note the similarity of these categories with the types of intellectual operations identified by Guilford cited earlier.

1. Perceptual—questions concerning the characteristics of objects; e.g., "What (shape, color, size) is your name tag?"
2. Cognitive—questions about comprehension or knowledge; e.g., "What's wrong with this (picture, wagon, shoe string)?"
3. Memory—questions asking for the recall of information that was received earlier; e.g., "What did the man say he fed the (cows, horses, ducks, pigs)?"
4. Divergent—questions asking for several student ideas regarding the presented stimulus; e.g., "What other ways can you put these (materials, colors, shapes) together?"
5. Convergent—questions asking for a single correct response from the child from a field of alternatives; e.g., "How many (mittens, children, shoes, fingers) do we have?"
6. Evaluative—questions asking for student responses concerning the extent to which information matches criteria; e.g., "Which car went (faster, slower, farther)?"
7. Other—questions that do not fit the above categories; e.g., "Would you like to bring the (book, puzzle, chair)?"

The researchers found that first-grade teachers placed an unusual amount of emphasis on factual knowledge, thereby largely omitting other critical intellectual operations. Teachers who had experience and training in question asking gave more emphasis to teaching those intellectual skills stimulated by divergent and evaluative questions. The researchers said that questions guiding children to perceive and process relevant stimuli would help them become aware of the subtle sensory discriminations they can make in the environment. Increased motivation is an expected result.

Teachers should become aware of the type of intellectual operation they have in mind as a learning goal and develop questioning that helps reveal how the child arrived at the conclusion. Caution is suggested to teachers to avoid overzealous concern for emphasizing every aspect of a learning activity in a single learning episode. Learning is never a one-session experience. We must realize that there will be other days to add new information and learning.

Eric Berne, in the book *Games People Play,* wrote the following about awareness, giving food for thought to questioners, whether parents or teachers.

Awareness means the capacity to see a coffee pot and hear the birds sing in one's own way, and not the way one was taught. It may be assumed on good grounds that seeing and hearing have a different quality for infants than for grownups, and that they are more esthetic and less intellectual in the first years of life. A little boy sees and hears birds with delight. Then the "good father" comes along and feels he should "share" the experience and help his son "develop." He says: "That's a jay, and this is a sparrow." The moment the little boy is concerned with which is a jay and which is a sparrow, he can no longer see the birds or hear them sing. He has to see and hear them the way his father wants him to. Father has good reasons on his side, since few people can afford to go through life listening to the birds sing, and the sooner the little boy starts his "education" the better. Maybe he will be an ornithologist when he grows up. A few people, however, can still see and hear in the old way. But most of the members of the human race have lost the capacity to be painters, poets, or musicians, and are not left the option of seeing and hearing directly even if they can afford to; they must get it second hand. The recovery of this ability is called here "awareness."[9]

Suggested Science Experiences

Understanding Oneself and Others

A number of the developmental tasks (discussed in Chapter 2) which serve as the basis for goals in the early childhood curriculum relate to helping children understand themselves and others.

Developing understanding of oneself and others involves intellectual, social, physical, and emotional learning that must receive prime time in schools. Feelings of self-worth are invariably linked to the individual's success in school and throughout life. The school should seek to build children's feeling of self-importance, their feelings of autonomy, their skill in dealing with the expectations of home and school, and their ability to express themselves through words and deeds. Teachers should think of the child's self-concept as a subject for study throughout the school years.

The total environment of the school should be designed to offer children a maximum of success and a minimum of frustration. Equipment is child-sized and it works. Little is off limits or has to be protected. The teacher-pupil ratio assures each child a teacher who has time for him or her as an individual. The expectations of the school are individually based and developmentally sound.

The Psychological Self

"That means me!" exclaimed five-year-old Anna as she found her name on a list. The answer to the question of "Who am I?" begins when Anna knows her name. The school helps children learn their personal

---

[9] Eric Berne, *Games People Play* (London: Andre Deutch Ltd., 1966), p. 178.

symbol by using names in conversation, by making children name tags, and by writing their names on their products and on their lockers.

Children's self-images are formed largely from how they think others feel toward them. In the free-flowing small groups that are typical in schools for young children the teacher can help each child learn that she or he is a creative, intelligent, important member of the group. "Mary is smiling, she is glad you gave her some clay, Ted." The teacher's comment helps Ted learn that he can make changes in situations—that he can act as well as be acted upon. "Just tell Jack you aren't through" helps a shy child, Sara, defend her rights and moves her a step toward self-confidence in dealing with peers.

Teachers can become effective listeners, and through their responses to children's conversation they can help children understand their own feelings. The teacher frequently hears a child's opinion about how other significant people (parents, siblings, children, teachers) feel toward him. If Leo says, "My daddy hates me," the typical adult wants to say quickly, "Oh, all daddies love their little boys," and change the subject to something more pleasant. The child notes at once that the teacher doesn't want to hear about his feelings. Leo guesses that she is really on his daddy's side. He bottles up his feelings. However, the teacher could respond to "My daddy hates me" with "Tell me about it." If she could use the tone of voice that she would use if Leo had said "My daddy has red hair," then Leo might feel free to discuss his thought and feelings. Through a discussion he would become more able to cope with his situation. When the teacher serves as a sounding board without taking sides or making judgments, she may discover that she needs to work more closely with families or make referrals.

The Physical Self

"How do I look?" is a question regarding the physical self that can best be answered by a look in the mirror. Each classroom should have a high-quality, full-length mirror placed in a strategic spot. Many homes do not have a low mirror and some have no mirrors at all. Children may literally not have seen themselves. With a good mirror children can admire the way they look, see smudges on their faces, straighten the firefighter's hats they're wearing, or adjust dress-up clothes before beginning a dance. Mirrors over lavatories are useful but show only the face.

Photographs, too, make a significant contribution to the child's understanding of physical appearance. A child's picture can be used over his or her locker to identify personal space. Group photos hung at the children's eye level can be used to decorate the room. *Our Very Own Story Book* can be made using individual photos on 10" x 12" tagboard pages put together with notebook rings. Exclamations such as "That's you!" and "That's me!" will continue throughout the year and show

Figure 9-6. A chart placed on a low bulletin board will encourage children to count, to read names, to differentiate between symbols, and to understand the concept of being absent or present. The dolls are made of a double thickness of colored paper. A thumb tack inserted between the layers before the two layers are glued together makes the dolls easy to move on the board. A piece of masking tape under the tack makes the dolls more durable.

the continued satisfaction the children receive from having pictures of themselves continuously available to them.

Attendance charts can become more graphically symbolic and meaningful for the children. Figure 9-6 is an example of a chart that shows the names of the children present. The children learn the concepts of present and absent. They often learn to read the names and count the number of children.

Children talk freely about their ages. They are proud to become four, or five, or six. However, they may worry about their size. One petite five-year-old girl began quizzing her mother at length about midgets. The mother learned through their discussion that her daughter believed she might never grow up because she was the smallest in her class. An observant five-year-old boy was heard to say as he stood beside a three-year-old playmate, "Well, you're taller but I'm older." Occasionally being the tallest or the smallest in a group is cause for deep concern to a child. Teachers should sense whether it bothers a tall child to be chosen frequently to reach something "because you are tallest." Teachers can likewise observe a child's reaction to being chosen to ride in the baby carriage "because you're the smallest." The child's size may be a fact the child would like to discuss but might not enjoy having group attention focused upon. Any comparisons that unnecessarily cause one child to feel inferior to another should be avoided. To help a child build a positive self-image, teachers should avoid comparing children on the basis of tallest-shortest, biggest-smallest, oldest-youngest, fastest-slowest, best-worst, or prettiest-ugliest.

Many opportunities arise to teach about growing. Children get new shoes because their old ones are too small. New teeth replace baby teeth. Hair and fingernails require cutting. Because children seem to want to grow, teachers should use any cue to enlighten or reassure children about growing.

The child's actual motor skills are an important part of the self-concept. Also the way a child compares his or her motor capabilities to those of peers is important. Development of large and small motor skills is fostered in good schools for children under six. For example, Jeff was the oldest and tallest child in a four-year-old group. He was one of several children trying a new rope swing that required standing on the packing box, holding onto the rope, swinging away from the box, and dropping to the ground. Jeff hesitated, obviously afraid but wanting to try it. By explaining the sequential steps and protecting him while practicing, the teacher helped Jeff constructively solve the dilemma. He grew in self-confidence as he practiced the new skill.

Sex Role Identification

Another important aspect of the child's self-concept is sex role identification. Most children are happy with their own sex, and the teacher should help a child to play and understand the concept of maleness and femaleness. Feelings regarding sexuality are laid in the early years. Occasionally teachers need to work with parents who seem to be unaccepting of the child's sex so that parents' negative attitudes will not harm the child's self-concept.

Unisex is common in early childhood schools, with all activities and equipment being used equally by boys and girls. Teachers should evaluate books and activities critically to see whether they arbitrarily assign sex roles. Often teachers themselves must broaden their ideas of male and female roles, both in society and in the family. Modern thinking has merged the roles into more of a single, humanistic one.

Boys and girls under six typically share the same bathroom at school. Such an arrangement provides a healthy environment for learning valuable sex information. Children will look at each other's bodies during the toileting. They will ask questions that can be answered factually. Their concerns over being made differently can be recognized and discussed. Correct terms are used in discussions. Children may seek clarification of information they are receiving at home or elsewhere. It is therefore necessary for the teachers and the parents to compare notes in order that the child is not left more confused than enlightened.

The handling of the genitals, or masturbation, is generally a harmless activity and is often observed among young children. Masturbation may have various meanings, so a child must be observed individually so that the purpose of masturbation for a given child can be discovered. Of course, masturbation can mean that the child is insecure and unhappy. However, it can also mean that the child is bored and needs more active play, that clothing is too tight, that there is a rash on the genitals, or that there is a need to urinate. Teachers must have an enlightened attitude and avoid shaming the child—a technique that would harm the child's positive self-image. Teachers may also need to assist parents in their understanding and handling of this behavior.

Caring for the Self

Caring for the self is an important part of the learning of a child under six. The routines related to eating, eliminating, resting, and bathing will require many reminders before they become comfortable routines. Each routine invites many questions before the child fully understands. School and home supplement each other. Efforts should be made to keep the expectations in line with the child's developmental level and to help the child understand the reasons for learning these routines. Children feel grown-up when taking care of their own needs. It is during routines that children may first show that they have a concept of "self" as a separate entity. They may refuse to eat, to sleep, or to eliminate as prescribed.

The teacher uses the lunch or snack period to help children think about foods and learn how foods make them grow. Cooking projects may serve to interest children in their nutrition. For details on food projects see Chapter 16. Teachers may wish to check their local office of the National Dairy Council and the local Cooperative Extension Expanded Nutrition office for aids for teaching nutrition to children.

Caring for teeth, nails, and hair can be brought to children's attention. Some local dental associations have excellent materials available for teachers to use when teaching dental hygiene. Teachers demonstrate their interest in good grooming by helping children comb their hair after napping or by helping them find a fresh outfit when one gets soiled or damaged. In centers a special holder is made for each child's comb and toothbrush.

The parents' cooperation can be solicited so that they too will encourage and teach the children to help themselves. Figure 9-7 is a visual aid that can be duplicated and sent home with children to encourage and remind them to become more independent. In a note to parents the teacher suggests that the chart be attached to the wall with plastic tape and that parents say to the child. "Have you checked your chart?" Avoid

DUTIES

Wake up Smiling

Wash Face   Wash Hands

Brush My Teeth

Make My Bed

Dress Myself

Put Away Toys

Take My Bath

Clean Finger Nails

Go to Bed Early

Figure 9-7. A reminder chart to help children become independent.

nagging about specifics. This is an effort to get the child to take responsibility for routines. The chart helps some parents realize how capable their child can be.

Safety is an obvious area of study. No one is as vulnerable to accidental death as the child under six. For the first two to three years adults assume total responsibility for a child's safety. After that the child must be relied upon to take more and more responsibility for safety. The teacher's role is to develop an understanding of safety in the home, school, playyard, street, and family car. Some state automobile clubs have had excellent materials prepared for teachers to use on safety in the car and on streets. The use of seatbelts is a good topic to focus on with both children and parents. Developing an understanding of the rules for personal self-preservation is important. The child's conscience must be encouraged to function. Developing inner control with an understanding of rules, not blind adherence to them, can be a major accomplishment of the young child's life.

Young children are at first basically egocentric. They develop into social beings who want to know about and to relate to others in their environment. They will eventually want to know about people far away in time and place. A great number of meaningful learning experiences can stem from a continuing emphasis on helping children to understand themselves and others. Learning experiences, both planned and incidental, must be related personally to the children. The learnings will "take" only if the children are personally involved.

*   *   *

Talk it Over: No. 2

Discuss the appropriateness of including learning about oneself and self-care in a discussion of science education.

*   *   *

The Family—A Part of the Self

The family constellation can be the subject of a great deal of learning. Each teacher of young children hears examples of children's confusion about kinship. "Is that your daddy?" is the usual question when children see the teacher with any man. Youthful aunts or uncles were called "my grandma's kids" by one five-year-old.

Children's literature typically shows a family with one boy and one girl, both about the same age. A discussion can help children talk about their families and begin to understand the variations existing among families. Foster children and grandparents may be part of the family. The teacher may have most uncertainties with those children who have no parents or only one parent. If a recent divorce or death has occurred, the child may need someone who will listen to talk about the event without prying for more information than the child is ready to give.

Teachers should know their children's families well in order to avoid creating unnecessary heartaches for already troubled children. For example, the kindergarten teacher who directed her class to mold ashtrays from ceramic clay for "your father's Christmas present" should have remembered that one child's father had died only days before school started in the fall. Thus, the project was one this child could not do with pleasure and likewise such a specific assignment probably would not be suitable for a child from a nonsmoking family.

When one child's mother has had a new baby, the interest in the event can be used to help the children verbalize questions and seek answers regarding human reproduction, which they may not have had occasion to discuss before. All children enjoy hearing about when they were babies. Teachers can involve children in discussions that will bring out both information and feelings about babyhood. A recognition of family differences and an open discussion of the feelings children have toward their younger siblings or how they, as younger siblings, are treated by their older brothers or sisters can help children work through their jealous or ambivalent feelings.

Fascinating studies about race, language, and culture can be developed from a child's experience in a family. A teacher must first seek to understand and appreciate children and families, including those who differ from him- or herself. Striving for mutual understanding and greater appreciation for all racial and ethnic groups is essential.

Understanding the Community

The local and world community are of interest to children. The study can start with the neighborhood and community, its people, their houses and jobs, community helpers, and institutions. Traditional festivals and holidays can be studied under this theme. Field trips and special visitors are methods often used for this social science education.

A study of the community is relevant to children. Learning about the houses people live in helps to orient children to the world outside their families. Walks can be taken from neighborhood schools to see houses, yards, and pets belonging to members of the class. Occasionally children feel different because they live in a mobile home or an apartment, while others live in single-family dwellings. A suitable study can help each gain some appreciation of his or her own home and more understanding of those of friends.

The whole subject of the world of work can be approached from where "my mother or daddy works." The study takes on added meaning when John's dad is the highway patrolman who shows the class his patrol car. Or they'll look at buses with increased interest after Bettie's dad arranges for the bus to take the class on a tour of the city when he has a day off from his job at the bus station. The police station loses its fearsome aspects when the police officer is Cathy's daddy, whom the children have met at school in his sport shirt. They listen attentively as the police officer tells them how to be safe on city streets. They'll like to look at the officer's badge.

The first and most obvious place to look for learning resources is among the parents of the children in the group. Parents can be encouraged to suggest the names of members of their family and friends who may also be called on to help. There is no particular list of people young children must know, so the enthusiastic cooperation of their families is a worthwhile place to start. Any community helper—firefighter, grocer, filling station operator, or mechanic—could be studied.

The search for people with special talents, hobbies, exhibits, and the like that can be shared with the group of children is well worth the teacher's effort. It may be a father who comes to school to twang his banjo, a retired railroader who displays his electric train hobby, or a mother who has the lead in the civic theater. When a child's parent is a learning resource, the child, of course, gets special recognition through the experience, and other children gain understanding of the diversity among people. The people themselves learn something of the value of educating children under six.

Kindergarten children can begin learning concepts of democracy, government, and voting. Decisions can be arrived at by voting. Leaders can be elected for a day or a special event. Important state or national events can be discussed at school. One inauguration day the teacher said, "Here is a picture of our new President. Tonight when your parents listen to the news, watch to see if you can see our new President." A week later one of the shyest boys in the group led the teacher to the picture on the bulletin board and reported, "I saw him (the President) on TV."

The World—A Part of the Self

Older children are often fascinated by people and customs from faraway countries. This is true especially if they have occasion to know someone from faraway, or if the teacher or a child has had some foreign experience. Parents or grandparents of children may make valuable contributions.

In one group a student from India observed the kindergarten children once each week. They were curious and asked her many questions. She talked with them about school, food, and children in India and showed them pictures and souvenirs. She danced and sang songs from her country. The children were entranced as she demonstrated how her sari was wrapped. The warmth and understanding that developed between the Indian girl and the kindergarten children were heartening to see.

In another instance, some Vietnamese students let kindergarten children try on their rice-straw hats when they came to dance. They invited the children to dance and sing. The next time the Vietnamese girls were to visit, the children suggested that they would like to make hats so that they could dance "better." Before the day of the return visit the children each made a paper Vietnamese hat. Acquaintance with these Vietnamese students occurred during a period when the TV news brought the Vietnamese war raging into nearly every living room. These lovely students represented a striking contrast to the one-sided picture the children had of Vietnam.

A parent's business trip or the teacher's vacation can stimulate interest in travel, maps, and faraway places. Discussion and role playing of travel experiences by the children can follow. A teacher may initiate such study by sending children postcards when away on a trip.

Outer space intrigues young children just as it does their elders. Children can imagine making a trip in a rocket. TV adventures, space museums, and news programs help children learn concepts and vocabulary so they can talk about and play out the roles of space explorers. Teachers will search for ways to answer their questions.

*   *   *

Talk It Over: No. 3

Discuss limitations to the curriculum if holidays are used as the major themes throughout the year.

*   *   *

Understanding the Physical World

Understanding the physical world is a lifelong pursuit that begins in early childhood. The child picks up a piece of ice covering a puddle in the playyard, plucks a dandelion, or buttons a coat against the chilly winds. Each time the child is responding to the physical world. Each response contains some learning experience and motivation that will serve the teacher as the incidents are used to help children understand what is taking place in their world.

Weather and Seasonal Changes

Weather and seasonal changes are worthy subjects for children's science lessons. Weather limits what the children can do and determines their dress; they hear it discussed frequently among adults. There will be numerous opportunities for the teacher to include concepts about the weather, the seasons, and atmospheric changes in the planned experiences for the young children.

A school for young children should use opportunities to observe and discuss all weather conditions—sun, rain, clouds, wind, snow, even hurricanes and tornadoes if the children are interested. Personal experiences reinforce weather concepts. For example, children who take a walk in the rain wearing boots and carrying umbrellas have a chance to see, hear, smell, and feel the effects of the rain. Through questions the teacher can help alert the children to the logic for wearing appropriate clothing. The children eventually learn to choose clothing that is appropriate for the weather. The teacher can ask: "You wore your raincoat today. Can you tell me why?" "If you go outdoors today, what will you need on your hands?" "Why?" "How does it happen we aren't wearing our coats today?"

When studying the seasons, teachers should remember that the child's frame of reference is not well developed. If a child is three years old in the spring of the year, for example, the teacher should remember that a year earlier in the spring this child was only a two-year-old. It is unlikely that anyone spent much time then discussing the seasonal changes that were taking place or that it would be remembered if someone had. Parents, commenting on a child's increased knowledge, often say, "This year the holiday means something to my daughters."

The secrets of nature are awe-inspiring. Yes, nature may be overlooked in our busy, technically oriented world, unless thoughtful teachers keep youngsters tuned in on it. Having a sense of wonder that is alive is surely a prime requisite for teachers of young children. Children will enjoy the tiniest dandelion that "nobody cares if you pick." They will be joyous when they find the crocus they planted in the fall. A spring walk to see, hear, feel, and smell the evidences of spring is surely a delight to all, especially if the children are permitted to bring back a few sprigs of blossoms to decorate the room. A fall walk has equal beauty, with its glorious colors. In fall there are leaves to push into a pile and jump into, and perhaps apples or cotton to pick.

Beauty, too, is morning after a snow. Adults so often ruin such days by complaining about the traffic snarls and the problems with shoveling. Snow is no problem to children. They'll shovel if someone will just let them have a snow shovel. They'll roll in the snow, taste it, and jump into any "mountain" of snow they see.

Some teachers really have to force themselves to enjoy nature. It may take effort to awaken the senses so that one can appreciate how fresh and exciting all nature is for small children. Once awakened, teachers won't be able to pass a fallen hedge apple, a dandelion seed, or a budding shrub without thinking, "Oh, I must let the children see this." Reading Henry David Thoreau's *Walden*, Rachel Carson's *The Sense of Wonder*, or Anne Morrow Lindberg's *Gift from the Sea* may help a teacher appreciate nature after facing the city's gray walls and streets too long.

Growing Plants

WINDOW GARDENS. Classroom projects can involve children in planting, watering, and observing. Plants also add a cheery note to the room. An indoor window box containing a variety of plants with room for adding new ones from time to time is worthwhile. Geraniums, petunias, ivy, philodendrons, tomatoes, and beans are all grown with relative ease.

An attractive indoor plant can be grown from a sweet potato placed in water. Because growers dry sweet potatoes artificially to keep them from sprouting, a teacher may have difficulty finding one with a few purple eyes that will sprout. Sweet potatoes may require several weeks to sprout. It helps to use warm water and to keep the container in a warm place. Tops from carrots, beets, turnips, and pineapples can be planted in water or wet sand. The top should include about one inch of the vegetable or fruit. The children will watch the new shoots grow.

Figure 9-8. A child proudly displays seeds she planted that have come up. Radishes, lettuce, or tomatoes can be planted. (Child Development Laboratory, Louisiana State University)

Figure 9-9. A plant to care for and later take home helps the child carry over science learning into the home. (Texas Woman's University Nursery School)

Onions or garlic can be suspended with toothpicks, about half immersed in water. The children will watch new green shoots and roots grow. Parents can snip the young onion and garlic blades for salads when this project is carried on at home.

Watching the plant "drink" is a favorite experiment. If celery, a white carnation, or an iris is placed in colored water, the leaves and petals will become tinged with color overnight. The children can observe that the vascular tissue carries the water to the leaves.

SEEDS. Study of the seeds of various plants and observation of their travel by wind and water are interesting to children. One group of children who had been alerted to notice tree seeds in the spring called the maple seed the "helicopter blade" and delighted in tossing them up to watch them twirl to the ground. Such labeling is an example of the child's attempt to relate new concepts to those already known.

When seeds are planted in clear plastic cups, the children can see the root systems develop. Learning is also facilitated if some seeds are kept damp on a wet sponge wrapped in a damp cloth. Each day the children can unroll the cloth to see if the seeds are sprouting. They can use the magnifying glass to examine the sprouts. This observation can be related to the seed they have planted under the soil. You can imagine the interest children will have in eating alfalfa sprouts or bean sprouts for lunch or snack during the time of the seed-sprouting experiments. Sometimes the teacher may like each child to have his or her own plant to care for. Beans, pumpkins, and tomatoes can be planted in milk car-

239

tons or styrofoam cups; then when the danger of frost is past, the children can transplant each plant outside, either at home or at school. They can then continue to watch their plant develop. One child's pumpkin vined into the cherry tree. The child thought it was a big joke to tell people that "my cherry tree has pumpkins in it"—and it did!

An outdoor garden is popular in many schools where space permits. Some children planted Kentucky Wonder beans along their kindergarten fence. The vines grew to cover their fence. Imagine the fun they had picking and tasting their own beans!

The plant's need for sunlight, soil, and moisture can be studied. One experimental cup can be kept without light and another can be kept without water, so that the children can learn what happens if the plant does not have these necessities.

BULBS. Tulips, hyacinths, and daffodils can be planted in pots in the fall, stored outdoors during the winter, then brought indoors to force early spring blooms. Pussy willows and forsythia will bloom if cut in the bud stage and brought indoors. Early spring bouquets are especially welcome after long cold winters. In some localities fall is the time to plant bulbs outdoors so that children can discover their blooms in the spring.

PLANTS IN THE FALL. In the fall, Indian corn, pumpkins, and bouquets of dry seeds and beans can add color to the room. A mobile of colored leaves is very effective. Coat leaves with wax by pressing between layers of wax paper with a hot iron before arranging them. The wax helps keep leaves from curling up as they dry.

Tree leaves, buds, cones, fruits, and bark can be collected by the children during various seasons to help increase their awareness of trees. Trees' value for lumber and papermarking should not be overlooked. Leaf collections can be pressed between layers of clear plastic adhesive and kept in a book.

Projects such as picking fruits for eating or making jelly, picking pumpkins for the classroom jack-o'-lantern, or cutting a Christmas tree at the Christmas tree farm add to children's information regarding plants.

A study of local crops that contribute both to the nation's food and fiber and to the livelihood of families in a community can offer numerous learning experiences for young children. Several field trips a year may be possible to follow a crop from planting to harvesting. Even in a farming community where a crop is the mainstay of the economy the teacher will have some children who have no contact with its production. All children will profit from observing and discussing the growing and harvesting process in relation to finished products. The farm children who already know about the crop can be the teacher's outstanding information source. The farm child's own farm and parents may contribute to the learning.

A Texas child, Berta, invited her class to her cotton farm during harvest time. The children ran among the rows of cotton plucking white bolls for a "bouquet." They watched the cotton-picking machine called the cotton stripper pick the bolls and fill huge wagons with them. En route back to school the group stopped at a cotton gin and saw farmers bringing in the wagons piled high with cotton. On the other side of the gin they watched huge trucks being loaded with five-hundred-pound bales of cotton. A few weeks later the children excitedly reported that cotton bales had been placed along the street in the downtown area. (It was cotton promotion week.) They knew where those bales had come from. They felt very knowledgeable. Further discussion and recall of their trip followed. The total experience increased their understanding of cotton as a plant. The study was related to the children personally through the clothing they were wearing and alerted them to the community in which they lived. They appreciated more fully the jobs of their families and friends.

A teacher is encouraged to find resources in the local community that can provide highly relevant learning experiences for children studying the world of growing things. An action program of planting, watering, harvesting, and using plants should be included.

A supply of reference books to supplement discussion and experiments is essential. The more the teacher knows about the subject, the more the children can learn. The children will learn to refer to books for information, a good habit to cultivate.

The Animal World

The world of animals offers almost unlimited opportunities for enriching children's experience. The teacher must search for worthwhile experiences for the group. The teacher seeks accurate information and uses correct terms. While an encyclopedia is helpful, one may wish to call specialists, such as those in the Cooperative Extension service, for localized information. Sufficient time is given the children to observe and to verbalize their findings. The teacher carefully indicates points for observation and tells about relationships that may not have been discovered by the children. Preparations are made to answer such questions as the following:

What is it called?
How and what does it eat?
How does it move?
How does it reproduce?
Where does it live?

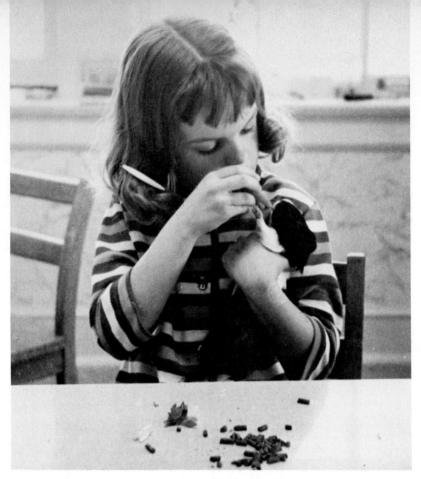

Figure 9-10. "What do you like, guinea pig?" wonders the child trying to feed it bits of various foods. (Texas Tech University Kindergarten)

What sounds does it make?
How does it see, smell, and hear?
How does the animal protect itself?
How do humans use the animal?

IN CLASSROOM. Rabbits, gerbils, guinea pigs, white rats or mice, turtles, and fish are common animals that may be kept for a time in the classroom.

Horny toads are harmless pets. They are common in arid regions, where children frequently bring them to school. They may also be purchased from pet stores. Advice concerning the health, safety, temperature, feeding, watering, and exercising of the animals may be needed from a specialist. The animals must be treated kindly and not overhandled or used as toys. Children can be taught how to care for the animal properly. If adequate care or housing is not available for an animal in the classroom, the teacher should consider keeping the animal for only a few hours so that the children can have some experience with it.

Children learn from sharing their new pups or kittens with their classmates. Pets can be brought to school while they are still young enough to remain in a box or a basket. The teacher can arrange a tour to children's homes to see their mature pets. Pictures of pets and their owners can be taken on a home visit. Children who have pets can tell the non-pet-owners practical pointers on pet care. A visit to a local pet shop can be arranged to increase the children's knowledge of the animals for pets. Here the children will find some of the more unusual pets, too.

Earthworms are favorites of children, but may be far down the list for some teachers. Nonetheless, children learn many things from observing and handling earthworms, and teachers should lay aside their prejudices and learn to tolerate worms. Worms can be collected in dirt and kept in a container for some time. If children have a spot for digging in their yard, they may collect worms for a "fishing trip."

ANIMAL SOURCES OF FOOD AND FIBER Animals as a source of food and fiber will provide valuable learning experiences for children. The sources of familiar foods will interest the children. Teachers should be alert to the specialized nature of modern agriculture. The storybook farmer who owns every kind of animal is a rarity today. To avoid the teaching of misconceptions, up-to-date ideas of farming and farm equipment should be understood by teachers. Watch especially the accuracy of some of the storybooks you choose to use with farm studies.

A visit to a dairy to see a cow being milked is very worthwhile because milk is a familiar food. Visits to farms where pigs, sheep, beef cattle, turkeys, or chickens are raised help children learn about the sources of common foods. The sight, sound, smell, and touch experiences can be related to taste experiences they have at home and school. Farm visits during the spring months show children the mother animals and their young—a subject of high interest to young children. Parents can be encouraged to visit dairies and farms.

ANIMALS AT THE PARK, ZOO, OR MUSEUM. Ducks, geese, and swans may be available for the children to visit and feed in a public pond. Dry bread crumbs offered by the children will encourage the ducks to come close to the child. Children seem to be especially attracted to ducks. Robert McCloskey's book, *Make Way for Ducklings*, is both a delightful story and a help to the teacher who is teaching the ways of the duck world. The children will learn from having a duck visit their classroom and swim in their water table. The teacher should be prepared for the fluttering of wet wings, puddles on the floor or grass, and excited children. This close-up view will help the children see the use the duck makes of its webbed feet.

Studying the familiar animals first is best in a class of young children. Parents who take their children to a zoo consistently report that the favorite exhibits are ducks and other farm animals. These are the animals most frequently seen and most often pictured in children's books. Exotic animals from far away and prehistoric animals are for the older under-six children.

MARINE LIFE. Schools located within travel distance of the sea, lakes, or rivers will give children a special opportunity to learn about animals that make their homes in water. When the families of the children vacation near the water or make their living through fishing or a related industry, marine life is a significant subject for children to study. Some marine animals can be brought into the classroom. Visits can be made to public displays.

Watching tadpoles develop into frogs intrigues nearly everyone. Tadpoles can be secured from ponds. They can be kept in an aquarium until the legs form. The children can use the magnifying glass to observe the leg buds appearing.

The care and feeding of fish make another worthwhile classroom project. A teacher can choose a single bowl with one goldfish or a complicated balanced aquarium with collections of tropical fish. If she or he has the knowledge to build an aquarium or is willing to learn, young children will be eager helpers.

BIRD LIFE. An egg-hatching experience can help children learn answers to some of their questions regarding reproduction. However, incubating the fertile eggs and waiting the twenty-one days required for a chicken to hatch may be too tedious for young children. It may be more feasible to obtain eggs from a hatchery that have been incubated for nineteen or twenty days. A warm box can be arranged with an electric light for heat. If the teacher secures about a dozen eggs, it is probable that a few will hatch during the day. The box should be large enough so that the hatched chicks can move away from the light if they are too warm. Chicks will move closer to the light if they are chilled. Chicks might be kept in the classroom for several days. The teacher should seek advice from a hatchery regarding the proper care and feeding of the chicks. Some hatcheries and museums have exhibits in which the hatching process and day-old chicks can be observed. Teachers can advise parents of the value of taking their children to see such exhibits.

Bird life will interest the children. A small bird such as a parakeet or a canary can be enjoyed in the classroom. The children can learn a great deal from the care and feeding of the bird. Some teachers may prefer having the bird visit school for only a few days or weeks.

Birds in their natural habitat can be observed with interest. Children can learn the names of birds and their housing and eating habits. Children can be encouraged to listen to the birds' songs and may learn to recognize some songs. Children will like to discuss information about reproduction. Birdhouses and feeders can be made from plastic milk bottles or cartons. Ready-cut wooden birdhouses are available in variety stores. Bird feeders can be made to attract birds to the school yard. Advice regarding the appropriate food to attract local species of birds is available from the wildlife service in each state. Drinking water may be provided for birds in cold climates where water sources freeze up. A birdbath will attract birds. A collection of strings, yarn, and bits of cotton or hair for birds to use in building nests will also attract them and give children an incentive to watch birds closely and quietly.

INSECT LIFE. The world of insects offers children opportunities to discover, to observe, to question, to classify, and to relate. A butterfly net and a collecting jar may be enough to encourage an interest in entomology.

Ant farms are easily made. Clean and dry a large glass jar and make a lid of a double layer of nylon net held with a rubberband across the top. Scoop up an anthill—sand, dirt, and ants—filling the jar and covering it with the nylon net. A queen ant (winged) should be included. Wrap a dark paper around the jar for a number of days. The ants will restore order to their empire. The darkness will encourage the ants to redig their tunnels close to the glass. Once the ants feel at home, they will go about their business. The children can provide bits of various foods to see what foods the ants like best and what they do with it. A tablespoon of honey or overripe fruit will be popular. A flashlight and a magnifying glass will help the child follow the ants in the trails. There is a great deal for teachers and children to learn about ants. The children can be taught some safety precautions regarding them. Ant farms are also available through school supply houses.

Butterflies, moths, beetles, and even spiders will be interesting to children. Discovering a spider's web and using a magnifying glass to watch the spider work can be very educational. A class collection of insects can be started. Collections can sometimes be borrowed from libraries or science departments.

CONCEPT OF DEATH. The concept of death frequently comes up during incidental or planned studies of animals. The presence of a pet may encourage children to talk about the death of their own pets. In one five-year-old group the children began telling stories about how their pets had died. The children listened politely to each other and vied for a chance to tell their story. When a lull came in the discussion, the teacher thought it might be time for a pet story with a happy ending, and told one. Again they listened attentively. However, the second the story was over another child had a story of a pet's death. The teacher concluded that the talk of death was meeting a need for these children and took a cue from them as to when to terminate the discussion.

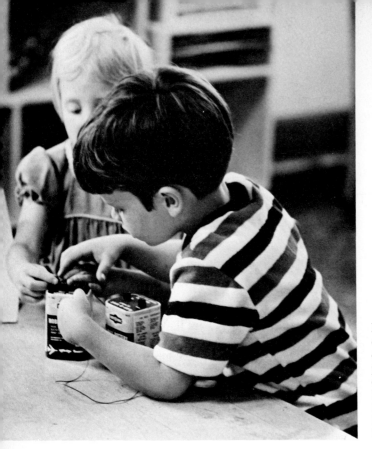

Figure 9-11. Dry cell batteries offer children numerous possibilities for exploration. (Child Development Laboratory, Michigan State University)

*   *   *

Talk It Over: No. 4

Give an example of a planned science activity you've observed in an early childhood school. What happened? What equipment was used? What do you think children learned?

*   *   *

Physical Forces and Their Interaction

The following suggestions will give teachers a few ideas for helping children learn how physical forces interact in their world. Most of the following suggestions are very abstract. Young children may learn a little at Level 1 on the Bloom Taxonomy (See Chapter 6.). That is, they may learn a word for the force and begin to realize that it exists. Remember to plan many hands-on experiences and to relate the concepts to children's interests and questions. For example, if you want to present batteries and circuits to light a bulb or ring a bell, help children to relate the new experience with the batteries they use to run a toy.

Electricity

Electricity is used to produce light, heat, and energy. Dry cell batteries can be used to ring bells and to light bulbs. Children can learn to complete the circuit to make it work. Show the children the electric element on the hot plate or the electric frying pan used for cooking projects. They can learn such words as *battery, circuit, outlets, plugs, bulbs,* and *switches.* Static electricity is produced as children walk across the carpet or rub balloons on slacks. Children enjoy the game of shocking their friends.

Magnetism

Children learn that only certain objects are attracted to magnets. Avoid overgeneralizing that all metals are attracted to a magnet because some metals are not, for example, copper and brass. Make a fishing game using a stick with a magnet on the string and a paper clip on paper fish, numbers, colors, or letters. The children can be encouraged to talk about their catch.

Temperature

Temperature can be related to the children, the room, water, or the outdoors. Temperatures can be compared by the use of two thermometers. A cardboard thermometer can be made so that the child can duplicate the reading of the real thermometer. Children can observe whether the real therometer goes up or down. Teachers can provide experiences with steam, with freezing foods, or with drying clothes. The children can set water outside to freeze on a very cold day or bring ice or snow indoors to melt. Gelatin dessert cooled outdoors helps children conclude that the air outside is as "cold as the refrigerator." Thus children learn about materials that are solid at one temperature and liquid at another.

Air

Provide opportunities to show that air is all around. Make or buy pinwheels to watch in the breeze. Build and fly a kite. Fill balloons with air. Have the children hold their nose and mouth to see how long they can go without breathing. Place a glass over a lighted candle to demonstrate that fire needs air to burn. Have the children learn words like *air, wind, breeze, oxygen,* and *movement.*

Volume

Volume can be studied at the water table as the child pours from one container to another. A number of containers of various sizes should be provided. Funnels, cups, sieves, and a toy water wheel all can provide interesting experiments. Volume is experienced at the snack table as children pour beverages, or during cooking projects as they measure ingredients. You might try out Piaget's experiment on conservation of volume using liquid in a tall and a squat glass and see what happens.

Length and Distance

Length and distance can be learned by comparisons of the length of pencils, nails, pegs, or blocks. The teacher uses "shortest" or "longest" to designate the plank or table being sought. Concepts of length and distance can be experienced in the room or the yard or around the block.

Size, Shape, and Weight

As children use blocks and packing boxes of various sizes, they learn about size, shape, and weight. Concepts such as big-little, large-small, high-low, wide-narrow, and long-short are learned through the motor activities involved in building. Learning names for geometric shapes and relating the concept of shape to toys and materials in the environment are important. Children may use functional labels such as *window* for a square. At that point they are ready to learn to label it a *square*.

Balance

Balancing is needed on teeter-totters, walking planks, and rocking boats and to walk a railing or wall. During block play this concept can be demonstrated if the children fail to grasp it themselves. Use the word "balance" to help children label the concept.

Speed

Opportunities to learn concepts of fast and slow are developed through the use of wheel toys and swings or through rolling objects of different sizes and weights down an inclined plane.

Gravity

Children experience the effects of gravity when rolling down a hill, sliding down the slide, flying paper airplanes, and throwing handker- chief parachutes. The teacher can teach this concept when cautioning children about taking heavy objects into high places.

Machines and Tools

Americans are gadget-minded, and the typical child today has had more experience with large and small machines than many adults of other generations. Machines and tools make work easier. The children help the teacher hammer nails in a favorite packing box. The children use carpenter's tools. The teacher asks them how they would hammer or saw if there were no tools. They help the teacher use pliers to tighten a bolt on a tricycle handlebar. Could they do this with their fingers? When a wheel comes off a toy, there may be an opportunity to examine the axle and perhaps the ball bearing. An inclined plane can help the group move a heavy object up on a packing box. A pulley can be fashioned with a rope and a box to show that through the use of the pulley the child can lift an object impossible to lift outright. It is an interesting game. A collection of bolts and nuts of varying sizes provides a sorting and matching experience related to the world of machines. Small motor skills are practiced as the children screw the nuts on the bolts. Tools and other construction toys give children opportunities to become inventors—discovering new combinations each time.

Large machines are of particular interest to children. They like to get close, even on the machines if safety precautions permit. As various community helpers are studied throughout the year, the children can see a fire truck, police car, cement mixer, road grader, delivery truck, tractor, or wheat combine. During studies of transportation they can visit a plane, train, or bus.

Sounds

Sounds are of interest to children. Most young children learn such parlor tricks as "What does a dog say?" Teachers know that children run to the window or become fearful when a siren is heard near the school. Because children are usually alert to fine differences in sounds, they are good imitators. Their attention may have to be directed so that they learn to identify new sounds. On a walk in the woods they can be encouraged to "listen to the quiet," as one child put it.

A study of sounds can include the sounds of toys; the sounds of household machines, such as a mixer, a sewing machine, the telephone, or a clock; the sounds of people laughing, crying, or scolding; and the sounds of animals. Attention can be drawn to pitch, rhythm, and volume.

Concepts of sound will be better learned if one has real-life experiences with the sounds. Though children learn to answer "Moo" when asked "What does the cow say?" they really understand after a visit to the dairy. "She *does* say moo!" confirmed a five-year-old.

Vibrations produce sounds. Children learn from making, feeling, and hearing vibrations. They discover they can stop vibrations with their hands. Musical instruments of various kinds offer numerous possibilities. Tapping various materials to hear the sound differences allows children to experiment with sound production. Further suggestions will be included in the music and rhythm chapter.

Listening to sound is, of course, one way the child develops language in the first place. Promoting listening as well as talking is important in all communication. Suggestions to help foster language development will be included in the chapter on language experiences.

Many children are concerned by night sounds. Some children have deep fears regarding sounds they hear when they awake at night. Experience identifying sounds can help them realize how the sound is being made so that it will not be frightening. Several stories can help initiate the discussion. They are *Noise in the Night,* by Anne Alexander; *Muffin in the City* and *Muffin in the Country,* both by Margaret Wise Brown; "Hiding in the Dark" and "Nighttime" from *Martin and Judy,* Volume I, by Verna Hills Bayley.

Chemistry in Cooking and Cleaning

The kitchen is one of the best chemistry laboratories. With the teacher's assistance children can stir up food mixtures of various types. The children can discover the effects of heating and cooling. For details related to cooking projects see Chapter 16.

Using solvents to clean up various substances also teaches children the nature of chemicals. For example, waxed crayon stuck to table tops is impossible to clean up with water, yet comes off readily when liquid wax is used. (Teachers should remember this and avoid using harsh cleansers on smooth finishes.) Children can learn that the use of detergent or soap makes the water more effective for removing the dirt from their hands.

Colors

Concepts of color develop during the years before six. Color is closely related to the creative art materials discussed in Chapter 8. Discussion of color should be included in any experience in which it is relevant. The use of the prism to refract the light showing the colors of the rainbow gives children a pleasant way to discover color. Children learn the names for common colors.

Time

Americans, more than people of many other cultures, are time oriented. Children become time conscious early partly due to their TV programs. A phrase like "after *Sesame Street*" is a common time-orienting phrase used by adults. American children learn early that it is important to be on time for an appointment.

Teachers help children's time orientation by developing regular routines; for example, juice is served about 10 A.M. A cardboard clock placed under or beside a real clock can be set with the time for a looked-forward-to event. Children will keep their eye on the real clock to see when it moves to the set time. They are learning to tell time.

The calendar may interest some young children. Little by little they learn the days of the week—that Monday is the first day of school in the week and Friday the last. They will be able to remember some of the names of the months. A class calendar can be marked with special dates—holidays and birthdays. Some teachers like to permit one child to mark the day's weather on the calendar each day. Both calendars and clocks give children experience with numbers. Much of this is very abstract, with depth of understanding to be developed in the children's later years.

As children begin to gain an understanding of time, they are also learning the routine of seasonal changes, the sequence of the sun rising and setting, and their own routine during the day.

Historical time is a difficult concept for young children. When visiting a historical train exhibit, a four-year-old said, "It was an old-old train, and an old-old man showed it to us. He was fifteen or sixteen." The phrases "olden days" and "when you were a little girl" are often used by children to designate times long gone.

Geology

Mike, a five-year-old, showed a favorite rock at "show and tell," saying, "This is a quartz crystal. My brother's Scout leader gave it to me." With Mike's enthusiasm as a starter, the entire class became immersed in a study of rocks that was carried on throughout the school year. The children brought rocks and fossils found along streets and alleys in their neighborhoods. The teacher too brought rocks—pumice that floats, obsidian used by the Indians for scrapers, and lava collected from lava beds in Central America. The lava led naturally to a discussion of volcanoes. The teacher brought slides and set up a viewing area, where some children looked over and over at color photos taken of an erupting volcano. The children pored over the encyclopedia—"the important books," as they called them—looking for pictures of volcanoes. Some volcanoes were pictured with prehistoric animals. This fact led them into a study of dinosaurs. Combining the two interests led naturally to the museum to see minerals under ultraviolet light and to see dinosaur skeletons.

A few rocks and a magnifying glass can start the study of rocks. Purchasing a labeled collection can encourage a beginner, whether teacher or child, to identify, classify, and label. Nearly early locality has its rock hounds (collectors) who are usually eager to share their hobbies with children.

In mining communities and oil-producing areas special emphasis can be placed on the local minerals. Children can learn something of the formations, the method of extracting, and the economic importance of the mines or wells—especially the energy resources used by a family.

Monitoring Science Education

Teachers should spend some time with each child to learn how the science education is being received. During some of the activities the teacher should question the child to learn how he or she reasons out problems. Listen carefully as a child explains an experiment. It helps if the teacher uses an attendance list to be sure of talking to or watching each and every child. If it is discovered that a few are not participating in science, then wondering "why not" is in order. Perhaps activities are wrong, unattractive, or geared at the improper pace. Notes on children's interests can be made and placed in a file for use with parents in conferences.

Conclusion

Stimulating the child's cognitive growth is of foremost importance during the years before six. Brain research and the work by Guilford, Bloom, Piaget, and Kamii suggest how this growth takes place. Children make serious attempts to make sense out of the world they live in. Early education can offer many projects and experiences through which children can discover concepts and build on the concepts they already have. A creative teacher, who has a well-developed sense of wonder and curiosity, will encourage children to discover, think, reason, make inferences, and generalize.

The cumulative plan or building-block approach is suggested; each concept should be firmly based on what the child already knows. Experiences the teacher plans should remain highly relevant to the child's here-and-now experience throughout the early years. Many experiences can be repeated frequently, with children learning each time. The teacher's role is one of being certain that there is a wealth of things to learn throughout the program and that the children feel free to experiment, question, and discover new ideas. The science curriculum for the early childhood school should be planned carefully and concretely. It is well to build on spontaneous experience of the children, but a program that relies wholly on such experiences will be cheating the children. Children want to learn and they can learn. Teachers must have faith in each child's ability. Learning science need not be a grim business but a really satisfying, invigorating experience that brings joy to lips and smiles to faces. Should a child turn away and show no interest, the behavior suggests that the teacher must search elsewhere for a meaningful experience for that particular child. It is a teacher's obligation to do this searching.

Applications

1. Discuss the "Talk It Over" items found in the chapter.
2. Complete Lesson 9 in *A Laboratory Workbook for Introduction to Early Childhood Education*. Hand in as scheduled.

3. Write an activity plan for a science activity for a few children using information and the sample plan (Figure 6-1) in Chapter 6. Secure approval, carry out the plan, and evaluate the results from the children's point-of-view and from your viewpoint. Prepare a report and hand it in along with your approved activity plan.

4. Evaluate your total participation performance on your evaluation form developed in Chapter 1.

5. Add ideas and plans for science activities to your Resource File.

Study Questions

1. Define science, the scientific method, cumulative plan, resource unit.

2. Explain the four stages of cognitive development according to Piaget. Give examples of reasoning at each stage.

3. Identify the intellectual operations as defined by Guilford.

4. Discuss findings in right and left brain research and the implications for early childhood education.

5. List and discuss the factors teachers consider in planning science education.

6. List each category of science activity presented and suggest activities for young children for each category.

7. Describe a high-quality environment in a school that best facilitates children's learning science.

Film

Piaget's Theory: Conservation   Color   26 Minutes

Children from preoperational, concrete operations, and abstract reasoning stages depicted in conservation of volume, distance, and area. Tester questions children to bring out their reasoning. Davidson Films, 3701 Buchanan Street, San Francisco, Calif. 94123.

Additional Readings

ALMY, MILLIE. *Young Children's Thinking: Studies of Some Aspects of Piaget's Theory.* New York: Teachers College Press, Columbia University, 1967.

BIBER, BARBARA, et al. *Promoting Cognitive Growth.* Washington, D.C.: National Association for the Education of Young Children, 1977.

FLEMMING, BONNIE M., et al. *Resources for Creative Teaching in Early Childhood Education.* New York: Harcourt Brace Jovanovich, Inc., 1977.

FORMAN, GEORGE, and DAVID S. KUSCHNER. *The Child's Construction of Knowledge: Piaget for Teaching Children.* Washington, D.C.: National Association for the Education of Young Children, 1984.

HARLAN, JEAN D. *Science Experiences for the Early Childhood Years.* Columbus, Ohio: Charles E. Merrill Publishing Co., 1976.

HOLT, BESS-GENE. *Science with Young Children.* Washington, D.C.: National Association for the Education of Young Children, 1977.

HOPMAN, ANNE B. (ed.). *Helping Children Learn Science.* Washington, D.C.: National Science Teachers Association, 1966.

KAMII, CONSTANCE. *Numbers in Preschool and Kindergarten: Educational Implications of Piaget's Theory.* Washington, D.C.: National Association for the Education of Young Children, 1982.

KAMII, CONSTANCE, and RHETA DEVRIES. *Piaget, Children, and Number.* Washington, D.C.: National Association for the Education of Young children, 1976.

LANDRETH, CATHERINE. *Early Childhood: Behavior and Learning.* New York: Alfred A. Knopf, Inc., 1967.

LEEPER, SARAH H., et al. *Good Schools for Young Children.* New York: Macmillan Publishing Co., Inc., 1984.

NAULT, WM. H. (ed.). *About Me, Childcraft Annual.* Chicago: Field Enterprises Educational Corporation, 1969.

Ranger Rick's Nature Magazine. A children's magazine published by the National Wildlife Federation, 1412 16th St. N.W., Washington, D.C.

SEEFELDT, CAROL. *Social Studies for the Preschool-Primary Child.* Columbus, Ohio: Charles E. Merrill Publishing Co., 1977.

SPRUNG, BARBARA. *Non-Sexist Education for Young Children.* New York: Citation Press, 1975.

SPRUNG, BARBARA (ed.). *Perceptions in Non-Sexist Early Childhood Education.* New York: Teacher's College Press, 1978.

TAYLOR, BARBARA J. *When I Do, I Learn.* Provo, Utah: Brigham Young University Press, 1980.

Perceptual-Motor Activities

- To *relate perceptual-motor materials to stages of cognitive development.*
- To *identify premathematics activities and relate them to Piaget's research in cognitive development.*
- To *identify and evaluate perceptual-motor activities offered in early childhood schools.*
- To *identify factors related to using microcomputers for perceptual-motor learning.*

Maria, standing at a small table, firmly dumped the six-piece wooden puzzle out on the table. She immediately began replacing the pieces in the frame, one at a time. The largest piece went in first. It was the duck's body. Next, in went the head, followed by the bill and the feet. Maria was deeply absorbed in the task and did not notice what others were doing nearby. As the last piece dropped in place, Maria, looking up from her task, clapped her hands joyfully and smiled with self-satisfaction. Something about doing the puzzle must have given Maria some reward, for no one was near who acknowledged her success, yet she flipped the puzzle over and began to work it again.

Puzzles are just one of a number of perceptual-motor materials called *structured* because their form or composition does not change with use. Structured learning materials have size, shape, weight, color, and texture that remain constant.

Figure 10-1. Completing a puzzle gives this child an immediate sense of satisfaction. She knows when it is complete and correct. (National Institute of Education Child Study Center, U.S. Office of Education)

Value of Perceptual-Motor Activities

Young children learn about their world through perceiving stimuli from their five senses and reacting to the stimuli motorically with hands, feet, tongue, and body. They engage in perceptual-motor behavior as a result of things they see, touch, taste, smell, and hear. Many perceptual-motor behaviors are related to routines of home and school, such as eating and dressing. Over time a large number of play materials have been developed to help children learn characteristics and abstractions in the world. These are structured materials such as puzzles, form boards, and various games and manipulatives.

This chapter can be considered an extension of Chapter 9 on Science Activities. The activities and materials to be discussed are designed to help children further understand their world and to discover new relationships.

To help understand the rationale for presenting perceptual-motor activities to children you should review the developmental tasks in Chapter 2, Bloom's Taxonomy of Educational Objectives in Chapter 6, the right-left brain research in Chapters 8 and 9, and Piaget's developmental stages and Guilford's intellectual operations in Chapter 9. These theoretical frameworks will help you think about children's learning as you observe and plan perceptual-motor activities for them.

For example, perceptual-motor materials contribute to all five of Guilford's intellectual operations discussed in Chapter 9. When children recognize the problem or task suggested by the toy, they are using *cognition*. In this case, Maria in Figure 10-1 knew the task required putting the pieces back in the frame. *Memory* was used when Maria recalled other puzzles, recalled the picture, or remembered from previous experience where each of the pieces belonged. It is clear from her speed that she was using little trial and error as she may have during her first use of the puzzle. *Convergent thinking* was being used, for in this type of material there tends to be one right answer or use of the material, as contrasted with art materials, previously discussed, which encourage wide variation in use. However, *divergent thinking* or novel use or response is possible with many structured materials, if the adults will permit novel uses. The puzzle Maria worked, for example, might have been put together on the table without the use of the frame, or upside down without the clues derived from the painted designs on the pieces. Or Maria might have traced around the pieces and made a drawing of a duck, a somewhat unusual use for puzzle pieces. *Evaluation* occurred when Maria put a piece in the wrong place and, realizing her error, retrieved the piece and placed it correctly. Many structured learning materials are self-correcting. That is, they won't work or be complete unless everything is in its correct place.[1]

Sensorimotor experience is derived through structured learning materials. The children use their senses and small muscles to explore the materials. They learn most from having ample time to explore the materials—building, arranging, dismantling, and redoing. Having adults ask questions regarding the characteristics of the material or what they are doing with it is generally considered to be important but is secondary to exploration in the learning process for young children.

Eye-hand coordination is developed with many of the materials because they require seeing the pieces and manipulating them in specific ways. Puzzle pieces are arranged in the frame, beads are strung, pegs are placed perpendicularly in the holes of a pegboard. Many of the materials require small muscle coordination, but large muscles and eyes are also coordinated when planks and packing boxes are manipulated on the playground or in the block corner.

Concepts of many kinds develop through the use of structured learn-

[1] J. P. Guilford, *Personality* (New York: McGraw-Hill, 1959), pp. 359–394.

ing materials. Size, shape, weight, color, and texture are experienced. Spatial concepts—large, small, thick, thin, up, over, around, under, beside, and so on—become clearer as the child uses these toys. The mathematical concepts of number, quantity, and equivalence are experienced as children count, exchange, measure, and balance with these materials.

Perception of whole-part relationships is gained with many of these materials. In Maria's puzzle, for example, she recognized the parts (feet, bill) and their relationship to the rest of the duck. You may observe children who do not recognize the pieces that are eyes or hands, for example, and see them try to fit them into what may appear to you to be illogical places. If so, they may need your help or verbal guidance. Attention can be directed to likenesses and differences. Perhaps in the duck puzzle the two feet are alike and interchangeable, but perhaps not, and the children then learn to note the difference between them. Color is also an important characteristic of many of these toys. Children learn to label and differentiate colors while enjoying puzzles.

Figure-ground perception is experienced through some of the toys. That is, one child, may concentrate on the puzzle frame while another concentrates on the picture design of the pieces. Thus each child would be perceiving the task of the puzzle differently. The child's perception, then, influences how the adult offers help.

Vocabulary is continually growing as children talk about what they are doing, labeling the objects, the parts, and the process they are involved in. Some social conversation arises naturally as children share materials, cooperate on building or putting toys together, or have disputes over prior rights to a toy or a learning space.

Curiosity is developed and satisfied through the use of these structured materials. Motivation is high because children are generally attracted to things that come apart, things that move, and things that they can handle without admonishment. A sense of accomplishment is quickly achieved, and the child can select another toy or repeat the use of the original one. Certain of these materials reward persistence, as children easily note when the puzzle is worked or the lotto board is filled up.

Inventiveness and creativity are fostered by some of these structured learning materials. Structured materials may attract children who shy away from the messy, nonstructured art media. These children are finding an avenue of creative expression that is valid and comfortable for them.

Many premathematics, prereading, and prewriting skills are developed through these materials; for example, handedness, left-to-right progression, symbol correspondence, and observation. Ascertaining likenesses, differences, and whole-part relationships, which are inherent in many of these toys, contributes to these academic skills.

The self-pacing quality and generally individual use of the structured learning materials give children a chance to explore, correct, test, and retest by themselves while remaining freer of competition than they may with some other materials or activities found in the early childhood center.

Premathematics Activities

There are many premathematics activities that children engage in before they are ready for full-blown mathematical problems. Premathematics experiences, like prereading and prewriting, have an important place in the early childhood program.

Recall that in the summary of Piaget's research in Chapter 9 it was indicated that children under seven are in the sensorimotor and preoperational stages of development. This means that children need to act on real objects in real situations for their logical reasoning to develop. Children of these ages do not reason abstractly as do older children and adults.

Constance Kamii, a researcher of Piaget's theories, says that "construction of number" is the principal objective for arithmetic in preschool and kindergarten. She writes, "The construction of number exists in the child's head and is, therefore, unobservable. The quantification

Figure 10-2. Flannel pieces on a flannel board give children one way to explore numbers and counting. (Hoeflin Stone House Child Care Center, Kansas State University)

of objects is partly observable." Kamii goes on to suggest activities of quantification, saying she is ". . . hypothesizing that the thinking involved in the child's attempt to quantify objects must help the child construct number, if he is already at a relatively high level of constructing it."[2] The reader will remember that when a researcher is testing hypotheses about phenomena that information is being sought to confirm or reject the hypotheses. In this case, research so far does not really convince Kamii that quantification of objects (counting) will help children's "construction of number" in their heads. However, she is suggesting that teachers go ahead and help children learn to count because it may help.

To teach number, Kamii advises teachers to remember that the real objective must be an emphasis on the thinking that takes place in the child's head and not on the observable behavior of quantifying objects correctly.[3] In good Piaget fashion, teachers should question the child to discover how the child arrived at the answer. Just getting the right answer is not sufficient. This requires one-to-one teacher-child sessions. Kamii's emphasis on construction of number being unobservable suggests some problems with behavioral objectives (see discussion in Chapter 6.) because behavioral objectives require observable behavior. You should allow for this problem when planning premathematics activities for young children.

The activities that follow are to be offered to young children in an open, free, and comfortable atmosphere with emphasis on the process rather than the product. Some children will be obviously excited about working with numbers in many contexts. Others may show little or no interest and should be given time to become interested. As one teacher says of her plans, "We start early with premathematics and expect mature reasoning to occur late."

Incidental Experiences with Number

"How old are you, little girl?" asks a kindly old lady in the grocery store. Little Mary shyly puts up three fingers. She may say, "Three." Chances are that Mary couldn't do this old parlor trick at two, and after five she'll probably just give a verbal answer. Mathematical learning begins at a young age, especially when concepts are closely related to the child. Mary is beginning to learn mathematics.

Numbers surround us. In fact, with the advent of the computer many people feel that they are being dehumanized by being assigned numbers that can be fed into machines. The child often has a social security number at a young age, a phone number, a house number, a number of

---

[2] Constance Kamii, *Number in Preschool and Kindergarten* (Washington, D.C.: National Association for the Education of Young Children, 1982), p. 24.
[3] Ibid., p. 25.

brothers and sisters, one tricycle, many books, a few dolls, or so many pennies. Children see their mother using money; or a cup of sugar and two eggs in a cake; she divides the candy bar in half; or pours the glass half full of their favorite soft drink. Children hear about a TV program on Channel 2 at eight o'clock. They see mother scurrying around to keep an appointment at a certain hour, or they go for a visit on a given date and hear of plans for next year.

Such incidental happenings as the above may be the children's mathematical experience as they enter school. The teacher's role is one of clarifying present concepts and adding new concepts in a meaningful way. Numbers can continue to be introduced to children in natural ways as they come up incidentally during school activities.

Quantification

Children can count any object from the pegs on the pegboard to the tricycles in the playyard. They won't know at first that every object needs a number. They often skip over some numbers, saying "1, 2, 3, 14, 17." They like to sing counting songs which helps them develop the proper vocabulary when they want to count. It is considerable time before they know that the last number is the total.

One-to-One Correspondence

Matching the number of painters to the number of chairs at the painting table is a problem in one-to-one correspondence. Teachers can involve the children in problem solving by getting them to help with the counting. Many experiences of the school can help with one-to-one correspondence.

Measurements

"How tall are you today, Jeff?" asks the teacher as she proceeds to measure and record the height of each child. She tells Jeff, "You are 44 inches. Last fall you were 43 inches. You've grown 1 inch." She can continue with weights and add both figures to a chart with children's names. She labels the tools used to make the measurements.

In food experiences other tools are used and other measurements are important. The temperature of the oven is a large number. The use of a thermometer in the classroom gives an opportunity for children to see and "read" other numbers. Taking the thermometer outdoors on a cold day will help children become acquainted with the concept of measuring the temperature of the air.

Seriation

Seriation is another perceptual activity described by Piaget. The child looks at at least three objects, determines whether they are the same, and then arranges them in a series, perhaps according to size. Maria

Montessori, a pioneer early childhood educator, also felt that seriation was important. She presented children with numerous graduated cylinders with matching holes in a long bar. This matching game was self correcting; that is, the child knew the correct arrangement by the way the cylinders fitted the spaces.

Nested boxes or cans are examples of seriation toys. Another is the Montessori "pink tower," built from graduated boxes stacked to make a tower. This toy has been replicated by numerous manufacturers since Montessori's day. Teachers can prepare tin cans of various sizes in the same way.

The stacking disc toy, consisting of a single spindle over which the child slips colored discs, is familiar to most. Graduated from the large base to a screw-on top, the toy is a challenge to perceptual, coordination, and seriation skills. When this toy is given to toddlers before the "age of accountability," they frequently use the spindle part for a hammer, much to the dismay of their educationally hopeful parents.

To learn discrimination of relative size, the child may line objects up in order. Many common objects found in the home and school—such as balls, pop bottles, and cold cream jars can be used for this purpose. In guiding the child's participation, be sure that you offer appropriate word pairs—tallest-shortest, biggest-smallest, longest-shortest, and so on.

Children can also practice seriation in arranging chairs or tricycles in the room or yard. "Let's put all the large ones in the back," suggests the teacher. The children may need help with the labels describing these perceptual tasks.

Classification

Classification means grouping items on the basis of some characteristic. Be sure to give children only one variable at a time; that is, if you ask the child to classify according to color, then save classifying according to shape for another day. Piaget's work suggests that children become "centered" on one characteristic and can not "decenter" to classify according to another criterion.

The imaginative teacher can make a classifying experience out of numerous common objects. Helping sort the plastic spoons and forks in the housekeeping corner is a classifying experience. The block corner, with its shelf of squares, triangles, cylinders, and so on, is a classification opportunity. With this perception, teachers realize that putting away the blocks is a valuable learning experience for children. This holds true in most areas of school; that is, the crayons all go together in one basket and the scissors in another, while the tricycles are all grouped in one storage closet.

Cubes, beads, pegs, buttons, bolts and nuts, bottle caps, and other objects can be used for sorting (classifying) experiences. In classifying you simply group things together that are alike in some way. Egg cartons or muffin tins are handy for separating small objects. Boxes can be divided into sections to accommodate larger objects. You might have little cars in several colors. You can work with a child, saying, "Give me one like mine." If the child is learning colors, say, "Give me a red one." After the group has been sorted you can ask, "What color are these cars?" After they are mixed up again you might say, "Put your finger on the red block," helping the child learn the color labels.

Following classification activities, the children can count the various groups of objects. They can lay them out in one-to-one correspondence.

Making Sets

Making sets of items helps develop number skills. "Put your blocks in sets of two." Or, "See how many sets you can make with your pile of blocks." It is important that children be allowed to move their objects around in a spontaneous fashion and discover sets themselves. Making sets can often flow from a classification experience.

Reading Numbers

Being able to read the number is not equivalent to understanding what it means. Reading the clock, the calendar, thermometer, TV dial, prices on items, speed limit signs, and so on is very interesting to some children. They may soon try writing the numbers and should be helped when they desire to learn.

Games

Uncle Wiggily, Candyland, and similar games require the ability to match, count, and take turns with peers. Delbert, Jamie, and the teacher, Sue Smith, were about to begin another game of Candyland. As happens from time to time with some structured learning activities, a dispute developed. Both boys were yelling, "I wanta be first! Let me go first." Sue Smith picked up a red token, placed her hands behind her back, and said, "Whoever picks the hand with the red token goes first." Both boys were satisfied. Sue, like many good teachers, knows and utilizes various successful methods for settling disputes quickly—methods that avoid harsh discipline and that promote good relationships and facilitate a continuation of the desired learning activities.

When using the board games children often devise their own rules. It is interesting to observe a game when they use their own rules. Quietly observe what happens instead of getting upset that they aren't following the rules.

Some children play dominoes—even double nines—and appear to be reading the designs of dots more than they are counting them. Nonetheless dominoes are very good practice with numbers, especially if played simply as a matching game.

Card games such as "concentration" and "fish" can be enjoyed by

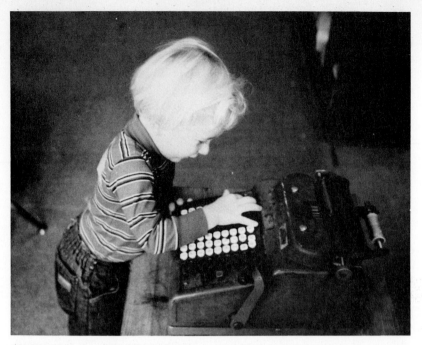

Figure 10-3. An old adding machine contributes to children's number concepts and to practice of perceptual-motor skills. (Early Child Development Center, University of Vermont)

some children in older groups. Some games require the collecting of cards that are alike. A simple way to use the cards with younger children is to let them sort the cards into their various categories.[4]

Attendance Charts

Attendance charts and other records can be posted and will give children some counting and reading experience. See Figure 9-6 for an example of an interesting attendance chart.

Evaluate Children's Number Concepts

The teacher can test an individual child's concepts by using ten cubes or pennies. If the child is momentarily unoccupied or stops for a chat, the teacher initiates a game of hiding the cubes or pennies, brings out a given number and asks, "How many are there?" The teacher can continue the game, arranging items in various sets until getting a clear idea of the child's ability. By keeping a chart the teacher can record concepts

[4] For a helpful discussion and description of numerous games, see Constance Kamii and Rheta DeVries, *Group Games in Early Education: Implications of Piaget's Theory* (Washington, D.C.: National Association for the Education of Young Children, 1980).

264

each child understands. This study can guide the planning of further number experiences.

*   *   *

Talk It Over: No. 1

Discuss the issues involved as children learn mathematics.

*   *   *

Eye-Hand Coordination Materials

Perception materials help the child learn through the senses—touching, seeing, hearing, smelling, or tasting. The perceptual process includes judgment and subtle discrimination.

One group of materials helps the child to learn small motor coordination and to practice these motor skills until they become unconscious and automatic. You, for example, once had to look at and think consciously about tying your shoelace; now you do it automatically.

Small motor coordination plays an important role in reading and writing, which are in their preliminary stages during the early years. Lugo and Hershey suggest four steps in the sequence of mastering a fine mo-

Figure 10-4. Candyland is a game that fours can usually play. It requires matching colors and knowing one and two. (Child Development Laboratory, Michigan State University)

Figure 10-5. A form board challenges matching skills of a toddler who will often work with both hands. (Joe Kertesz, photographer)

tor skill. First, the needed maturation of the visual and hand muscles must be present; second, the child notes the problem or task and is motivated to try to do it; third, the child tries out the task; and fourth, the child practices until mastery is achieved.[5] Children in our early childhood centers may be at any stage of this four-step sequence.

Eye-hand coordination is practiced in many situations in school. The use of writing and drawing tools and scissors, the tearing of paper, and the squeezing of glue bottles are examples. Turning pages of books, placing the needle on the record player, and buttoning and zipping clothing all contribute to coordination practice.

Coordination skills are preliminary to many other motor skills, and teachers can encourage their practice by setting expectations that are individual. Age is not the best criterion, and some three-year-olds excel some fives. A child may be more advanced in some skills than in others. Competitive situations should be avoided, for when a child fails, he or she may grow tense and begin to avoid the practice that is needed. Our task is to present the children with interesting materials and with support while they develop and practice these skills.

[5] James O. Lugo and Gerald L. Hershey, *Human Development* (New York: Macmillan Publishing Co., Inc., 1974), pp. 365–366.

Bead or Ring Stringing

Manipulative skills develop as the child strings beads or rings. Special laces with metal tips are available, making the task easier when the holes are small. In an emergency a piece of masking tape rolled securely around the end of a lace will make the tip firm and enable the child to get it through the bead. At a beginning level the child will mostly be concerned with transferring beads to string. Later the child will become selective, perhaps choosing red beads, or square ones, or even alternating the beads to form a pattern.

Another lacing task is shoelacing. This is a practical task, and parents will be happy if their children learn to do it. There are several shoelacing toys available, but the inventive teacher can merely bring a discarded shoe for children to practice lacing and tying. However, both teachers and parents should remember that tying shoelaces is generally learned when the child is five or six years old. Also in the clothing line are items used to practice buttoning, zipping, and snapping. Though these, too, are available commercially, they can be made by anyone with some time, materials, and elementary sewing skills.

Lacing string or yarn in sewing cards and special lacing cards gives good practice. One drawback is that the teachers generally must unlace

Figure 10-6. A jumbo pegboard holds a fascination for a mainstreamed special child. (Child Development Laboratory, Michigan State University)

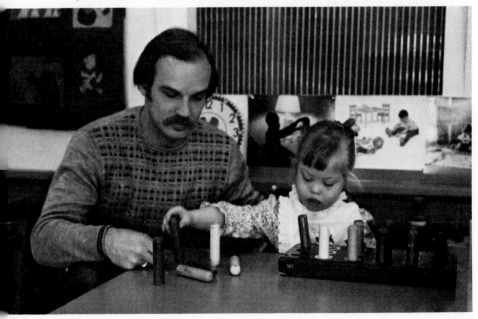

the cards to prepare them for reuse, a task that becomes time-consuming and tedious. Sewing on burlap with yarn in large needles is a similar task, and the child is allowed to keep his or her creation. The teacher will want a needle threader to help with keeping the children's needles threaded. It is wise to start the day with a number of needles already threaded. Tacking burlap to wooden frames helps the children use it more successfully.

Pegboards

Pegboards and a basket of colorful pegs especially intrigue the youngest children. First they select pegs at random and concentrate on fitting them in the holes. Later, children may create designs or follow a friend's pattern or the teacher's. Squares of ceiling celotex with holes can be used for pegboards, thus providing children another sensory experience.

Sorting Shapes

Parquetry blocks require the child to organize basic geometric-shaped blocks according to designs in the bottom of the box. In helping a child new to parquetry, you can say, "Which block looks like this one?" as you point to a geometric shape. Children enjoy sorting the parquetry blocks into piles of "look-alikes" on the table and even like to arrange their own designs without the aid of the printed designs. This is a creative use of the toy that should be encouraged. Various other games encourage children to classify shapes. Teachers should go a step further and call the children's attention to shapes in their classroom and in the playyard. Even snacks come in interesting shapes, from triangle sandwiches to round cookies.

*   *   *

Talk It Over: No. 2

Observe a child using a perceptual-motor material. Exchange information among your classmates about what the children did. What conclusions can you draw, if any?

*   *   *

Construction Materials

Several types of construction materials allow children to build, thus helping them discover balance, weight, height, and depth. Some materials are quite small and can be used most comfortably on a table, whereas others are large and are used on the floor or in the play yard.

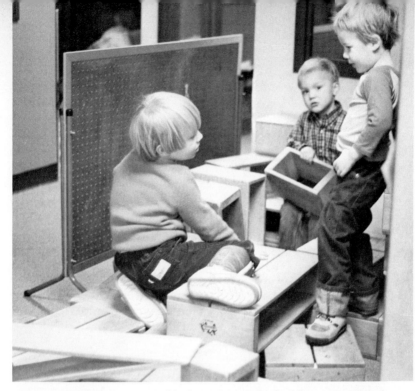

Figure 10-7. Hollow wooden blocks are a popular building material and contribute to cooperative play. (Child Development Center, Metropolitan State College)

Blocks[6]

Blocks are probably one of the most important types of equipment supplied by a high-quality early childhood education center. They give children an opportunity to express their ideas, interpret what they observe, and express their feelings. The shelves of blocks may be the first equipment that impresses a visitor, as blocks are displayed in a prominent place and there are many of them. This arrangement encourages the children to incorporate them into many types of play. Children discover height, balance, and directionality as they use blocks. They learn to judge the amount of space required to enclose themselves or a toy animal or car. They experience distance as they select a block to make a bridge over their road. Ideas, information, and creativity are coordinated as children use blocks. They recall a "house" and build one for a doll family. A "bridge" or "overpass" is recalled and built over a road. Gravity is experienced as blocks topple down or the small toy car runs down the ramps the children build. Note the involvement of the children in the following incident.

[6] For in-depth information on current use as well as the history of using blocks in the nursery school and kindergarten see *The Block Book* by Elizabeth S. Hirsch (ed.) (Washington, D.C.: The National Association for the Education of Young Children, 1984). Chapters are written by early childhood educators who have studied children's use of blocks.

Steve and Eddie were using the large hollow wooden blocks. Using the ramp, they found some excitement in running their cars down the ramp and seeing them shoot rapidly off to one side. They noted other ramps in the corner of the room and brought them to add to their ramp. It didn't work, they discovered, to lay the ramps together on the same level. Steve and Eddie surveyed their problem, then brought a large block to put under one ramp, creating excitement for all when their cars swooshed down the two-ramp run. Now they added two big blocks and a third ramp to make a three-ramp run. "Wow!" exclaimed Eddie, "Everybody stand back. This is really going to be a race now!" The downhill run proved interesting not only to Steve and Eddie but to other children who were attracted by the excitement, until numerous races developed out of the two boys' initial idea. Gravity had been discovered that afternoon, and it was a simple matter for the teacher to give the boys and the others a label for it as the activity came to a close that day.

Large Blocks

Large blocks come in several varieties. The largest are usually about $22'' \times 11'' \times 5\frac{1}{2}''$, with the smaller ones being half or one fourth the large size. Hollow wooden blocks have been available for many years and are extremely popular in early childhood groups. Hollow blocks are large enough for children to use in dramatic play which incorporates them as actors.[7] Though expensive, the large blocks are very durable, making them an almost permanent investment for the school. Large blocks are now being made of polyethylene and other synthetic materials. These latter blocks have the advantage of being weatherproof and not splitting or peeling in moist climates. Auxiliary pieces, such as planks and ramps, greatly increase versatility. A set of sixty large blocks for twenty prekindergarten children and a set of seventy-five for twenty kindergarten children are recommended.

Large packing boxes used in the playyard may contribute the same kind of learning as blocks, having the additional virtue of allowing the child to get inside them. When large wooden boxes are made specifically for school use, they should be made in several sizes. Children will learn that one size may be more useful for one activity than another. Hollow blocks and packing boxes can be combined in interesting and productive play. It is convenient to have a push truck in the playyard to encourage children to take the blocks where they see a use for them. Also, when the play is finished, the blocks are easily loaded on the truck and returned to storage.

Cardboard blocks are an outstanding and less expensive substitute

[7] For an insightful article see "Joining the Block and Housekeeping Areas: Changes in Play and Social Behavior," by Cheryl A. Kinsman and Laura E. Berk, *Young Children,* 35:1 (November 1979), pp. 66–75.

for wooden blocks. These approximately shoe-box-sized blocks are colorful, and they are made with an inside support that reinforces them, making them stronger than they appear at first glance. Surprisingly, even adults won't squash them if they stand on them. Parents who purchased a dozen cardboard blocks when their children were small say these blocks represent their best-spent toy dollar because their children have used them extensively for many years. Five dozen will serve a classroom for a number of years for indoor block play. They are not appropriate for damp play-yards.

Unit Blocks

Unit blocks are all multiples or divisions of the basic unit, which measures $1\frac{3}{8}'' \times 2\frac{3}{4}'' \times 5\frac{1}{2}''$. All are made of hardwoods and are carefully sanded. Besides squares and rectangles there are columns, arches, triangles, quarter circles, and numerous other shapes. All fit together precisely. About five-hundred pieces are needed in a typical early childhood classroom. Storage for unit blocks should include enough shelf space to accommodate each shape and size of block without crowding. These shapes can be marked on the back of the shelves with a drawing to help

Figure 10-8. Children learn equivalency as they build with unit blocks. They also discover architectural forms. (Early Childhood Laboratory, Kansas State University)

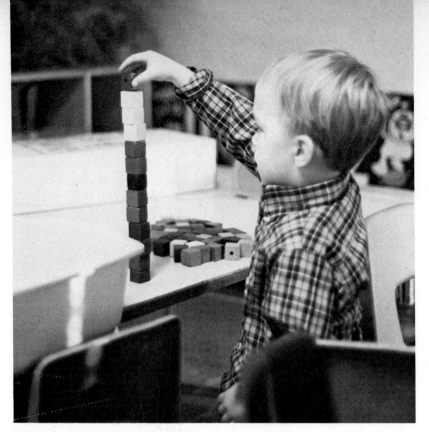

Figure 10-9. Stacking small blocks challenges perceptual-motor skills of the young child. (Child Development Center, Metropolitan State College)

children and adults find where the different blocks go at cleanup time. Obviously sorting and classifying are important opportunities for cognitive learning. Small trucks stored near the blocks encourage children to load and unload blocks as well as to build roads for the vehicles.

Small Blocks

Small blocks are much smaller even than unit blocks and contribute especially to small muscle dexterity. These blocks are made of either wood or plastic. Many are very small, and though interlocking, they make somewhat fragile and unstable buildings; therefore, use at a table is usually preferred. The older four- and five-year-old children generally have the muscle coordination and patience to enjoy these small blocks, whereas younger children find them frustrating. Some sets are profitably kept in the "rainy-day closet" to be brought out only rarely when a new activity is needed to replace "rained-out" activities.

Block Substitutes

Block substitutes are made by some inventive teachers and parents. They stuff one cardboard milk carton with newspaper; then as it stands upright, a second milk carton opened at the top is forced down over the first carton. The edges can be taped with plastic or masking tape.

Guiding Block Play

Guiding block play presents many opportunities for creative teaching. Children will use many blocks and build magnificent structures if the schedule is open enough to allow sufficient time and if adults encourage creativity. With all blocks, the teacher's role is to provide an adequate number for the group of children and to store them where the children have ample building space away from generally used traffic lanes. Auxiliary figures and toys stored nearby make outstanding contributions to block play. Carpeting on the block-playing area will absorb the noise made by falling blocks and the children's exuberant play.

Block structures are often knocked down by the builder. This is quite acceptable when it is the child's own structure, but the teacher can also encourage children to use their creativity in taking down their block structures piece by piece. Sorting and categorizing skills can be learned while the blocks are being placed on the shelves. If the teacher works with the children as they put blocks away, saying, "You bring them to me, and I'll help put them on the shelves," the resulting cooperation may be surprising. With a cooperative air the children will help and others

Figure 10-10. Blocks should be carefully stored on marked shelves, so sorting them for storage will give additional categorizing practice. (National Institute of Education Child Study Center, U.S. Office of Education)

will join in the fun, even though they may not have used the blocks. If the teacher says, "Thank you," or "What a big load!" these rewards will usually be sufficient to get the children's happy cooperation. Singing a song, like "Pickin' up blocks and put 'em on the shelf," to the tune of "Pawpaw Patch," helps, too. By all means avoid having a curse placed on using the blocks by assistants too lazy to help with putting them away. All should avoid the admonition, "*You* got the blocks out, *you* put them away," which is sometimes heard. Such a technique discourages the children's use of this valuable educational resource.

Children should be warned that cleanup time is approaching, so that they can finish their building project and the imaginative play that accompanies it. The teacher may extend the play period to allow the children who have worked diligently to construct something to have a few minutes to use it. In this way the teacher avoids frustrating the children and shows understanding of the children's need to use a building they have constructed.

Sometimes the teacher may permit the children to leave their block structures set up so that they can add to them from day to day. This practice is most feasible when a single group uses the room. With care, it can be allowed when one teacher has two groups using a room or even when two teachers share a room—if good cooperation exists between the teachers.

Other Construction Toys

In addition to blocks there are many other interesting construction toys. Some are plastic and some are wooden. Some pop together over a plastic bubble or knob; some fit together in precut grooves or join with snaps like the grippers on a child's pajamas. Like blocks, these toys give the child an opportunity to build in three dimensions and to use imagination. They also give practice in small muscle coordination. Some can be frustrating to young children who are not coordinated enough to handle them. Some come with patterns to copy, which are generally too difficult for young children and may inhibit creativity. Therefore extensive use of patterns should be avoided. Children should have ample opportunity to create their own designs and structures.

* * *

Talk It Over: No. 3

Discuss the types of guidance you've found effective when children are using perceptual-motor materials. Do you think you should make a child finish a puzzle once it is started?

* * *

Puzzles

Puzzles are popular construction toys as indicated in the opening anecdote of this chapter. Puzzles differ from other construction toys, however, for the task calls for the child to assemble pieces in a specific and preconceived way to make a picture in its original form. This is a clear example of a convergent task—one calling for one right answer.

There are a number of different kinds of puzzles. The most popular for children under six are those made of wood. Recently some have been made in colorful rubber, which adds an interesting textural experience. Puzzles are very durable, withstanding years of use by classes of children if care is taken not to lose pieces. Choices of puzzles include such things as animals, vehicles, and familiar scenes from children's lives and from books they know. Usually each piece is an object, a part, or a body, enabling children to think about replacing a head, a foot, or a wheel. This arrangement helps the child grasp the concepts of whole and part. Another type of puzzle provides inlays of whole objects grouped with related objects—such as five fruits, five vegetables, or five objects to wear when it rains. Some puzzles have knobs for removing the pieces, but although knobs do give the child experience in grasping, they seem unessential to puzzles and are easily broken off. Puzzles can be stored in specially built racks, which aids their care and protection. Knob puzzles require special racks.

Puzzles must be selected according to the number of pieces with which the child is ready to cope. Development and experience are more important than chronological age; however, four to six pieces are usually appropriate for three-year-olds and up to thirty for advanced kindergarteners. Some kindergarteners may even be ready for the United States map puzzle.

Guiding a child's use of puzzles begins with selecting the level of puzzle the child is ready for—not too hard, not too easy. Sometimes a child gains confidence from putting together a simple, familiar puzzle before going on to harder ones. Sometimes suggesting removing one piece, then replacing it, helps a child who is having trouble proceeding. You can offer a little help and encouragement if a child seems ready to give up, though you should avoid compelling a child to complete a puzzle. However, a common situation is for the child to help the adult, for there is nothing so sobering as to be left to work a child's puzzle that you haven't seen whole! Jim, a graduate student, had this happen to him the first day he worked with a four-year-old group. He picked up the jumbled mass in honest embarrassment, asking himself out loud, "Now, how in the world do you do this?" Whereupon a child, Sara, volunteered, "Here, I'll help you." And she did, with the eternal thanks of the young man.

Arranging the puzzle storage adjacent to tables encourages children to use puzzles and other structured learning materials on the tables, helps keep pieces from being mislaid, and helps keep the distractions of other tasks from interfering with the child's work. If a teacher checks the toys after each self-selected activity period, the children can be asked to help look for any missing pieces before the pieces are lost for good. Sometimes children absentmindedly place pieces in their pockets, so simply say, "Children, check your pockets to see if our missing puzzle piece is hiding there." Seek the cooperation of the custodians too, so they won't sweep out your precious pieces. Once a puzzle piece is missing the puzzle should be retired for repair. One method of repairing a puzzle is to line the hole with plastic wrap and fill it with wood filler, letting it set. After it is set, it can be painted, hopefully to match the rest of the puzzle.

Puzzles are a long-range investment. Some puzzles should be stored away to rotate as "new" from time to time. They are an activity that children can usually manage without much help or supervision, leaving teachers free to handle more complicated learning centers.

Children can occasionally make their own puzzles by selecting a magazine picture and gluing it to cardboard—men's shirt boards are good. Put the glued picture flat under books to dry, with a wax paper on top of the picture. Wax paper does not adhere to white glue. After the glue is dry, the pieces can be cut. A paper cutter is helpful in this task. Remember to make the pieces simple at first; then they can be cut further if the child is ready.

* * *

Talk It Over: No. 4

Discuss your experiences with children using computers. In what way is computer use compatible with goals for early childhood education? Incompatible?

* * *

Using Microcomputers

Early childhood schools are beginning to try out computers with young children. In recent years microcomputers have become more affordable to individuals and schools. Elementary and secondary schools have introduced them for instructional purposes. Early childhood teachers are curious as to whether computers will be useful in helping children learn what they want and need to learn at this young age. Mathematics, reading, and perceptual tasks are typical in computer software programs.

Research into using computers with young children is in its infancy stage. Thus, conclusions are unavailable, as yet, on the effectiveness of computers for teaching certain tasks and, perhaps more important, concerning the effect on children who are using computers.

Knowing Piaget's, Kamii's, and others' concern for children needing experiences with real objects in real situations for learning, teachers are wondering if the abstract pictures on the computer screen and the oral instructions (when available) are within young children's level of understanding. As discussed earlier under premathematics activities, research indicates that a child's ability to give a correct answer does not necessarily mean that the child has internalized a "construction of number."

Parental Reaction

Many parents are enthusiastic about their child's learning about and using computers in the early childhood school. Many of today's adults have had to overcome some anxiety in using computers and believe that if children grow up with them, they will not have such discomfort. Many parents in high-technology areas have their own computers at home. Some parents are working at home at a computer which is hooked up to their office and other computers. Children in such homes probably have opportunities to use computers. Some parents interpret the installation of a computer for the children to use in a school as a measure of high quality in the school. Clearly this could be as much of an erroneous criterion of quality as is having a minibus that picks up and delivers children. Computer companies have been using hardsell advertising on parents to get them to buy home computers to "ensure your child's future success." Such tactics are reminiscent of those of the encyclopedia companies in another era. Minority parents are speaking up to their elementary and secondary school administrators because they see the affluent schools being furnished computers and neglecting the schools their children attend. They want their children to have a chance to use this "twenty-first century tool" and don't want the development of new ghettos with inferior schools.

Teachers' Reactions

Early childhood teachers are proceeding cautiously. They want early childhood education to remain a particularly humanistic experience. They worry that sitting at a machine for long periods could dehumanize education. Even though microcomputers are cheaper than previously, they still require a sizable budget to purchase and equip with software (programs). Teachers question allocating such a proportion of the budget to this use. In other words, "What do children have to do without if they have computers?" [8]

Both teachers and parents have questioned the values introduced in some computer programs when the correct answers are shot down with bullets or arrows. These individuals feel that learning should not be associated with tools of violence.

Some teachers who have experimented with teaching reading by computer have felt that the negative feedback from the machine was very harsh. They indicated that early childhood programs had other effective ways of teaching the same thing. Teachers who used the computer to teach *under, over, into,* and *behind* felt the same way. The word-processing component was of interest to some children. As with using the typewriter, children like seeing numbers, letters, and words appear on the screen and then moving them around or making them disappear. Some saw an analogy with playing the piano and experimenting with a melody. The important factor seemed to be allowing the child to explore the machine in his or her own way.

Most of the computer programs require an adult to read and explain the instructions. Thus it is essential for adults to be thoroughly familiar with the computer and the software and take time to work with individual children. Space around the computer is needed for several people. Teachers like to plan for at least three children working together. Some use chairs, while others have experimented with having the computer on a counter at children's height. It is reported that both boys and girls are equally interested in computers. It is important that a sex bias not be introduced into computer usage, that is, making the computer more a boy's machine than a girl's machine.

Practically speaking, packages of software or programs are needed in order for the computer to know what to do when certain keys are pressed. Software has come a long way in a few years, but still has far to go. Companies selling software will allow teachers to check out software packages and try them out in their own schools before buying them. Teachers recommend careful assessment before purchasing the computer as well as after. The type of software available may determine the choice of computer in the first place.

According to Charles Hohmann, who has explored computers with young children, "Good computer-based learning allows children to enter new worlds through images on the screen and to learn educational concepts from the experience. The computer and its programs can be a simple but powerful learning devise that can introduce such concepts as similarity, difference, matching, grouping, space, and time. Many basic

---

[8] For a lively discussion of some pros and cons of computers see, Karen Burg, "The Microcomputer in the Kindergarten: A Magical, Useful Expensive Toy," *Young Children,* 39:3 (March 1984), pp. 28–33.

skills learned in early childhood (learning letters, alphabetical order, basic words, beginning writing, counting, and number skills) can be presented effectively. The computer screen displays information in interesting, colorful, and challenging formats that not only actively engage children but allow them to learn at their own pace and skill level."[9] Teachers must continue to listen, read, and learn as they make decisions regarding the use of computers in the years ahead.

Conclusion

Perceptual-motor activities are called structured because their size, shape, color, and texture do not change as children use them. Children's cognitive, motor, and social development is stimulated through the use of perceptual-motor activities. Premathematics concepts are often part of perceptual-motor activities. According to Kamii's research, the goal for premathematics activities for young children is to help them learn a "construction of number" in their heads, and not to parrot the right answers.

Many perceptual-motor activities are manipulated individually and are self-paced and self-correcting. Inventiveness and creativity are fostered by many of the structured materials and may be an important avenue of expression for those children who do not enjoy nonstructured activities. Prereading and prewriting skills are being developed through the use of structured learning materials, for example, left-to-right progression, handedness, and symbol comparisons.

The pros and cons of the use of microcomputers were discussed. As yet, the research concerning efficient and appropriate use of microcomputers with young children has not been done, nor, do researchers know the effect on young children of using a computer. Use of computers is expected to develop as research and experience give teachers information about what children can appropriately gain by using them.

Applications

1. Discuss the "Talk It Over" items found in the chapter.
2. Complete Lesson 9 in *A Laboratory Workbook for Introduction to Early Childhood Education*. Hand in as scheduled.
3. Write an activity plan for a perceptual-motor activity for a few children using information and the sample plan in Chapter 6. Secure approval, carry

[9] Charles Hohmann, "Computers and 'Active Learning', Are they Compatible?" *High/Scope Resource*, 3:2 (Fall 1984), pp. 2–3.

out the plan, and evaluate the results from the children's point of view and from your viewpoint. Prepare a report and hand it in along with your approved activity plan.

4. Evaluate your total participation performance on your evaluation form developed in Chapter 1.

5. Add ideas and plans for perceptual-motor activities to your Resource File.

Study Questions

1. Define perceptual-motor activities. State their value to children's education.

2. Explain the major objective in premathematics activities.

3. Identify Constance Kamii's research and her conclusions regarding children's "construction of number."

4. Define and explain: quantification, one-to-one correspondence, centered and decentered, classification, seriation, making sets.

5. Describe coordination materials.

6. Describe construction materials.

7. Describe the different types of blocks and the value of each type in early childhood schools.

8. Discuss the pros and cons of computer use in early childhood schools.

Films

Blocks: A Medium of Perceptual Learning   Color   17 minutes   1968

The accompanying narrative focuses on the perceptual learnings that are inherent in block building. The way the young child looks at the blocks and the space in which he or she builds are early learning experiences relevant to intellectual development and academic learning. Campus Film Distributors Corporation, P.O. Box 206, 14 Madison Ave., Valhalla, N.Y. 10595.

Blocks   Color   11 minutes   1974

Set in a classroom, film shows what and how children learn while playing with blocks. The Media Guild, P.O. Box 881, Solana Beach, Calif. 92075.

Additional Readings

ANKER, DOROTHY, et al. "Teaching Children as They Play." *Young Children*, Vol. 29, No. 4, May 1974, pp. 203–213.

CARTWRIGHT, SALLY. "Blocks and Learning." *Young Children*, Vol. 29, No. 3, March 1974, pp. 141–146.

DAY, CAROL M., and R. K. PARKER. *The Preschool in Action: Exploring Early Childhood Programs*. Boston: Allyn & Bacon, 1977.

EARHART, EILEEN. "Classification Training Curriculum." *Child Study Journal,* Vol. 2, No. 4, April 1972, pp. 191–196.

FORMAN, GEORGE E., and DAVID S. KUSCHNER. *The Child's Construction of Knowledge: Piaget for Teaching Children.* Washington, D.C.: National Association for the Education of Young Children, 1983.

HAMMERMAN, ANN, and SUSAN MORSE. "Open Teaching: Piaget in the Classroom." *Young Children,* Vol. 28, No. 1, October 1972, pp. 41–54.

HESS, ROBERT D., and DOREEN J. CROFT. *Teachers of Young Children.* Boston: Houghton Mifflin Company, 1981.

HIRSCH, ELISABETH S. (ed.). *The Block Book.* Washington, D.C.: The National Association for the Education of Young Children, 1984.

KAMII, CONSTANCE. *Number in Preschool and Kindergarten: Educational Implications of Piaget's Theory.* Washington, D.C.: National Association for the Education of Young Children, 1982.

KAMII, CONSTANCE, and RHETA DEVRIES. *Piaget, Children, and Number.* Washington, D.C.: National Association for the Education of Young Children, 1976.

KAMII, CONSTANCE, and RHETA DEVRIES. *Group Games in Early Education.* Washington, D.C.: National Association for the Education of Young Children, 1980.

LANGUIS, MARLIN, TOBIE SANDERS, and STEVEN TIPPS. *Brain and Learning: Directions in Early Childhood Education.* Washington, D.C.: National Association for the Education of Young Children, 1980.

OSBORN, JANIE D., and KEITH OSBORN. *Cognition in Early Childhood.* Athens, Ga.: Education Associates, 1983.

PAPERT, SEYMOUR. *Mindstorms: Children, Computers, and Powerful Ideas.* New York: Basic Books, Inc., 1980.

SIGEL, IRVING E. "The Development of Classificatory Skills in Young Children: A Training Program." *Young Children,* Vol. 26, No. 3, January 1971, pp. 170–184.

SPONSELLER, DORIS (ed.). *Play as a Learning Medium.* Washington, D.C.: The National Association for the Education of Young Children, 1974.

WEIKART, DAVID, et al. *The Cognitively Oriented Curriculum.* Washington, D.C.: The National Association for the Education of Young Children, 1971.

WHIREN, ALICE. "Table Toys: The Underdeveloped Resource." *Young Children,* Vol. 30, No. 6, September 1975, pp. 413–419.

Language Activities

- *To relate developmental tasks and language development.*
- *To identify major goals and state how early childhood teachers foster language development.*
- *To suggest ways to help children learning English as a second language and children with language problems.*
- *To identify and evaluate language activities offered in early childhood schools.*

"I feel like I've had a bath in lollipop suds," said four-year-old Julia, wiping her sweaty brow after running a distance on a hot humid day.

Julia's comment is one of many examples of creative speech you might hear as you listen carefully to children. The out-of-the-mouths-of-babes stories told by proud parents and doting grandparents focus on the unique word combinations children invent. Children enjoy coining new words, rhyming words, and experimenting with words. Unhampered by knowing the "right" way to say something, children's expressions are often colorful and original. Chukovsky, a famous linguist who collects examples of children's creative language, says, "Beginning with the age of two, every child becomes for a short period of time a linguistic genius."[1]

Children's strengths shine through in their early efforts to communicate. They learn first in the family, acquiring their native tongue there. Chukovsky believes they work hard and says, "In truth, the young child is the hardest mental toiler on the planet. Fortunately he does not even

---

[1] Kornei Chukovsky, *From Two to Five* (Berkeley, Calif.: University of California Press, 1968), p. 7.

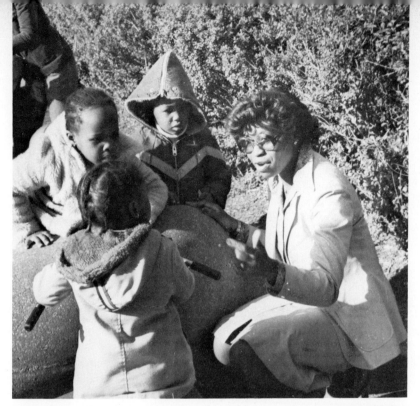

Figure 11-1. When the teacher sits at the children's level they are more likely to hear and understand her language. (Preschool Center, Howard University)

suspect this."[2] However, this uniquely humanizing trait should not be forgotten when later one thinks about helping children who have problems with language.

Relationship of Language Development to Total Development

Language development influences and is influenced by all other areas of development. One look at the developmental tasks discussed in Chapter 2 shows that one task in particular deals directly with language—Learning New Words and Understanding the Language of Others. Other tasks, such as developing independence, giving affection, getting along with others, understanding one's body and the physical world, and developing a positive feeling about one's self, all have language components or, at higher levels, are expressed by language. Understanding the linkages between language development and other areas of development will help parents and teachers plan most effectively for children.

[2] Ibid., p. 10.

Language makes us human and different from all other living organisms. The years from birth to six are crucial for language development. Speaking, listening, reading, and writing are all part of language development. Listening is called *aural* or *receptive* language. Speaking is called *oral* or *productive* language. Both precede reading and writing. The early childhood teacher's purpose is to give children extensive experience in listening and speaking. This is background for later writing and reading. The many concepts learned orally and aurally serve as a frame of reference for reading and writing. Reading and writing can be difficult for children if oral and aural language experiences are inadequate.

Social Development

Of course, the child's first social environment is the family. A child's language is influenced by relationships with family members. If a good verbal relationship exists, children have more advanced language skills than others in their age group. Stimulation from parents, siblings, and playmates is extremely significant. Children want to communicate. Since

Figure 11-2. When children select their activities they frequently choose to go with a friend they enjoy talking to. (Child Development Laboratory, University of Missouri–Columbia)

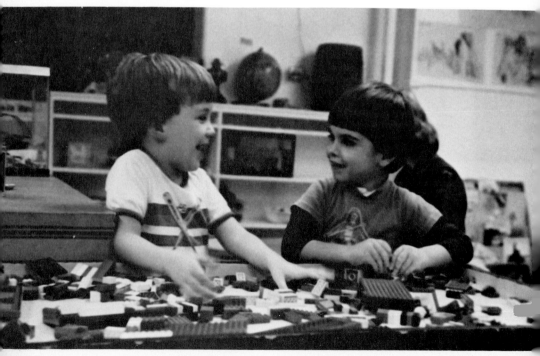

birth they have been learning to interpret the words and actions of family and friends, and in turn, they learn the words and actions that these people will understand. Communication is a two-way street—individuals try to let others know their thoughts and feelings while the recipients try to decode the messages. This is a marvelous human capacity, and we want the child to continue to grow in both the production and the comprehension of language.

Social development is fostered when children have language skills. Language skill encourages a child to make social contacts. The solitary play of a two-year-old develops into cooperative play as the child matures in ability to communicate. Then the child can approach another child verbally as well as physically. Children with the most advanced language skills make the most social contacts, lead others in activities, and organize cooperative play.

Emotional Development

Emotional development is also fostered when the child has language skills. Both good and bad feelings can be expressed verbally. The child is able to protest when things go against his or her wishes. The total emotional climate of the child's environment will affect the child's speech progress. Being very shy or insecure will negatively affect the ability to express oneself. Language skill affects the child's self-concept. Positive feelings accompany successful communication.

Figure 11-3. Snacktime affords opportunities for children to listen and to speak. (Child Development Laboratory, Michigan State University)

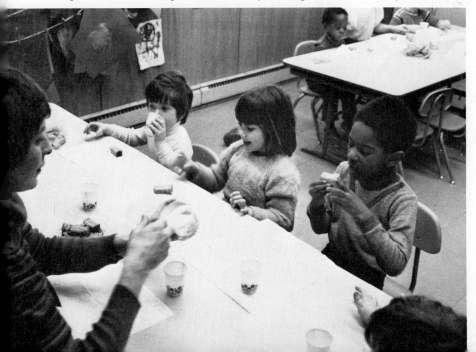

Cognitive Development

The brain is the center of both cognitive and language development. Recent work in mapping the functions of the brain indicates the left hemisphere controls both language and analytical thinking. The right hemisphere is the center for holistic and creative thinking. Healthy people use both sides; however, because of individual differences in dominance, one person may have a cognitive style that is *verbal-analytical* if he or she operates primarily in the left hemisphere and another, a *holistic* style, if operating primarily in the right hemisphere.[3] The first type might be said to see the trees while the second sees the forest. According to Banville, "The kinds of functions involved in recognizing colors and the shapes of letters and words is right-brained; the association of the spoken word with the shapes and colors is left-brained process (occurring in the language areas of the left hemisphere)."[4]

This research helps one to appreciate the complexity of language learning. It may help teachers understand, too, why numerous methods of teaching are required when working with young children. Pictures, which are perceived primarily by the right brain, present an experience different from auditory stimuli. One child may learn better from one than from another.

According to Cazden, a researcher studying children's language,

When we say that a child has learned his native language by the time he enters first grade, what do we mean he has learned? A set of sentences from which he chooses the right one when he wants to say something? The *meaning* of a set of sentences from which he chooses the right interpretation for the sentences he hears? Even if the sets of sentences and interpretations were enormous, the result would still be inadequate. Outside of a small and unimportant list of greetings like *Good morning* and clichés like *My, it's hot today,* few sentences are spoken or heard more than once. Any speaker, child or adult, is continuously saying and comprehending sentences he has never heard before and will never hear or comprehend again in the same way. Creativity in expressing and understanding particular meanings in particular settings to and from particular listeners is the heart of human language ability.

The only adequate explanation for what we call "knowing a language" is that the child learns a limited set of rules. On the basis of these rules he can produce and comprehend an infinite set of sentences. Such a set of rules is called a grammar, and the study of how a child learns the structure of his native language is called the study of the child's acquisition of grammar.

When we say that a child knows a set of rules, of course we don't mean that he knows them in any conscious way. The rules are known nonconsciously, out

[3] David Galin, M.D., "Educating Both Halves of the Brain," *Childhood Education*, 53:1 (1976), p. 18.
[4] Thomas Banville, "Brain Hemisphericity: A High Voltage Topic," *Early Years*, 10:1 (January 1979), p. 53.

of awareness as a kind of tacit knowledge. This way of knowing is true for adults too.[5]

According to some research the necessity of coping with more than one language may, for some children, hamper the development of skill in a single language. It is necessary for them to learn two words for each concept. Other research suggests the opposite. For example, Smart and Smart report, "As international communication grows more and more important, it becomes more and more desirable for children to speak more than one language. In an earlier era, it was thought to be disadvantageous for a preschool child to learn a second language. Current research suggests the very opposite, that the best time to learn is early and the best way to learn is from a person who speaks that language as his mother tongue, that is, a native speaker. Advantages are in terms of ease of learning sounds, flexibility of brain function, and related cognitive development."[6]

Physical and Motor Development

Biological factors may affect the child's speaking and hearing ability. Rubella (German measles) is one serious disease that can infect a woman in the early stages of pregnancy. Such infection may cause abnormalities in the speech and hearing organs of the fetus.[7] Birth injuries may impair the child's ability to speak and hear. Brain damage or injury to the speaking and hearing organs in childhood may be equally disabling.[8] Also, adenoids may grow into a child's ear and nose passages, interfering with hearing and breath control. A child who does not respond to verbal directions or who eats noisily may have a problem with adenoids. Parents should be alerted to the need for a medical checkup.

Physical and motor development affects the organs of hearing and speech. A malfunction in any organ can create language handicaps. Newborn infants are now tested for hearing in maternity wards. Hearing aids are fitted to the infant when a hearing loss is discovered. A hearing aid helps the infant hear all the prelanguage sounds commonly heard by normal infants.[9] A child whose speech and hearing therapy is

[5] Courtney B. Cazden, "Suggestions from Studies of Early Language Acquisition," *Language in Early Childhood Education*, Courtney B. Cazden (ed.) (Washington, D.C.: The National Association for the Education of Young Children, 1972), pp. 3–4.

[6] Mollie S. Smart and Russell C. Smart, *Children: Development and Relationships* (New York: Macmillan Publishing Co., Inc., 1972), p. 267.

[7] Maurice H. Miller and Marcia Rabinowitz, "Audiological Problems Associated with Pre-Natal Rubella," *International Audiology*, 8:1 (1969), pp. 90–98.

[8] L. Fisch, "Causes of Congenital Deafness," *International Audiology*, 8:1 (1969), pp. 85–89.

[9] Marion P. Downs and W. G. Hemenway, "Report of the Hearing Screening of 17,000 Neonates," *International Audiology*, 8:1 (1969), pp. 72–76.

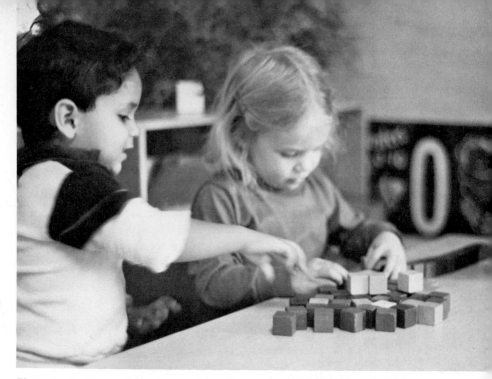

Figure 11-4. Conversation flows comfortably as children talk over activities in which they are involved. (Child Development Center, Metropolitan State College)

left until later childhood may first require training in the infant languages of babbling, lolling, and gibberish. Finally, words are introduced.

The child who can speak and understand is a more lively companion in large motor activities at home and school. The years before six are very important years. A foundation is established for all future development in motor skills and in language skills.

*   *   *

Talk It Over: No. 1

Write down what a child says while speaking. Also write down what another child answers. Share the example with your class, giving the children's ages as you begin. What seems characteristic of the children's language?

*   *   *

Goals for Language Development

The goals for aural or receptive language are closely linked with goals for oral or productive language. *Receptive listening* is combined with the child's ability to hear. Once heard, the verbal sounds must be decoded into meaning for the individual. Newborn infants respond differently to sounds of high and low intensity. Infants especially respond to human voices. A parent who talks to the baby begins to receive positive responses as the baby babbles—often with inflections that parallel those used by the parent. The baby's alert eyes follow the speaking parent's eyes. Long before being able to speak, the toddler can respond accurately to commands such as "Bring me the ball," "Wave bye-bye," or "Give mommy the spoon." Eventually this receptive language is followed by the child's putting sounds together that make words. Language is a two-way street—listening and speaking. Throughout childhood and even in adulthood people can comprehend language which they may not be able to duplicate.

Seven Major Goals

Young children's language achievements should be appreciated. Most children learn sufficient language for communicating with very few problems arising. When problems arise, the teacher should make a careful analysis before intervening. In planning language activities for children and interacting with them, consider the following goals:

Producing Verbal Sounds

The ability to hear and make verbal sounds is essential to speech production. Most babies produce verbal sounds effectively at birth. Verbal sound production is rarely a problem, and hearing difficulty occurs in only a small number of children. If a child is not learning to speak, one of the first things to check is the child's hearing.

Speaking in Distinct Syllables Articulating Clearly

Articulation is an important factor in both speaking and comprehension. There are numerous sounds for the English vowels. Consonants such as s, v, r, t, and l and blends of two or three consonants are frequently not learned completely until children are seven or eight years old. The teacher may have to help interpret a child's comment as in the following: On a trip to a farm four-year-old Michael said excitedly, "The 'ticky 'tepped on it!" Five-year old Angella replied, "Michael, I can't hear you." Michael, raising his voice repeated, "The 'ticky 'tepped on it." Angella raised her voice and shouted, "Michael, I can't hear you." Michael, now quite exasperated, started to shout his statement when the teacher stepped up, "Angella, Michael is telling you that the chicken stepped on the egg." Both children seemed relieved that the teacher had aided their efforts to communicate.

Formulating New Words, New Word Combinations, and Eventually Statements and Questions

Here language, creativity, and the thinking process are combined. Children may often be heard verbalizing as they go about an activity such as climbing, cutting, or dressing. This may serve as a private rehearsal. Even adults sometimes verbalize the directions for an activity that is new or difficult for them. Children work hard, yet enthusiastically, at this task of communicating through language. Every sentence is a fresh new creation.

Learning a Vocabulary

Labels for objects, ideas, actions, and descriptors of many kinds are needed. New experiences enrich the child's vocabulary. In addition, many opportunities to express thoughts out loud, to be talked to, and read to are needed.

Using Standard Rules of Grammar

The child gradually begins to sense the rules of grammar for the language by experimenting with it daily. Each language has specific rules. English has irregular verbs that may cause children considerable difficulty. There is a customary placement of pronouns, articles, prepositions, adjectives, and adverbs for children to learn. The young child will not be able to state grammar rules. Communication can and does take place without perfect grammar.

Developing a Voice of Culturally Appropriate Quality, Pitch, Intensity, and Timbre

Voice, in this context, is culturally approved, being pitched higher in Chinese, for example, than in English. Certain stress, intonation, and pauses are all to be learned.

Developing Fluency of Speech

Fluency refers to the person's ability to choose words quickly and to speak in a smooth effortless manner. Fluency is a long-range goal, as are most of the goals for language development.

*   *   *

Talk It Over: No. 2

Describe the language of a child who you'd say is fluent. Give the child's age and relate prior experiences at home and school to the child's present language level. What conclusions can you draw?

*   *   *

How the Teacher Fosters Language Development

What does the early childhood teacher do to foster language development? A number of suggestions follow.

1. The teacher establishes a comfortably relaxed atmosphere that stimulates the children to talk freely with everyone. Children are encouraged to exchange ideas, share information, and ask questions. Though teachers may make an effort to encourage "indoor voices" in the classroom, they appreciate children who are happy, lively, and talkative. Silence is not a sacred commodity. In fact, the young child's classroom or playyard is almost never quiet. Teachers may at times have to interpret the "noisy classroom" to other teachers, administrators, janitors, cooks, or parents. As Landreth says, "How can a child learn he has views if he is never permitted to express them?"[10]

2. Teachers value each child and find time to let each talk, serving as models for the child's speech, speaking clearly and correctly, and using words, gestures, and examples to help the child understand. They quietly seek out children who are less assured and help them feel at ease when talking with teachers and others. They visit children at home and talk with their parents to learn the personal interests of each child. When teachers know about family events, pets, siblings, or toys, they can engage a child in conversation on personally interesting subjects. A teacher may discover a subject that a child likes to discuss and reserve that topic for their private conversations. One child goes skiing; another goes fishing; another raises rabbits. One teacher learned a few words of Russian to be able to say "Good-bye" to a child who spoke Russian.

3. The teacher capitalizes on every opportunity to extend a child's vocabulary, to increase his or her ability to formulate sentences, and to describe an event in a sequence. Every learning experience is considered for its language possibilities. For example, following a cooking experience, the teacher asks questions to enable the children to practice the new words the experience has introduced. A few days later the children recall the cooking experience and relate it to another project that has been planned for them. The teacher may ask the children to tell what they plan to tell their parents about the activities of their day in school. When children have been personally involved in activities, they can talk more easily. Verbalizing

---

[10] Catherine Landreth, *Early Childhood Behavior and Learning* (New York: Alfred A. Knopf, Inc., 1967), p. 199.

helps them remember. The teacher may send home materials that encourage children to speak. Their products give something to show and to explain to their parents.

4. The teacher gives clear directions. When giving directions, he or she demonstrates as well as talks in order to give the children clues to the meaning of what is said. The teacher also avoids putting too many ideas in a single sentence. She or he gets the children's attention and speaks clearly.

5. The teacher makes plans for the children's language development. Both talking and listening experiences are planned. The teacher assesses the needs of individual children to determine the activities that are most appropriate for each. A variety of activities is planned in order to interest the children and keep them eager to learn. Interesting displays of pictures and objects in the classroom are planned to stimulate conversation.

6. The teacher who hears incorrect pronunciation and grammar allows the child to finish the statement, believing that incorrect speech is preferable to no speech. Having responded to the thoughts in the child's communication, the teacher may then, or later, use the specific words correctly to help the child begin to hear the correct form. All teachers should be aware that though there is considerable uni-

Figure 11-5. Language grows as children are exposed to good books at home and at school. (Southeast Oakland Vocational Technical Center)

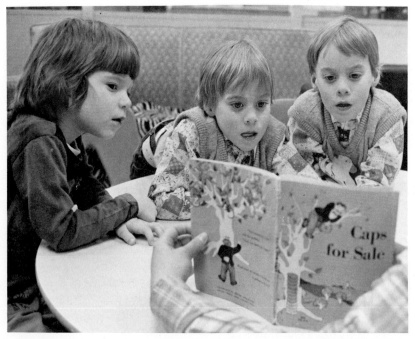

formity in the country in language, there are regional accents and dialects that make it difficult even for educated people to communicate. Teachers must be most sensitive when helping children who are new in the community and children from various ethnic groups. The teacher's language is not "better" than such a child's, just as a New Yorker's language is not "better" than a southerner's. With conscientious effort, they can all communicate.

7. The teacher uses open-ended questions that encourage the children to elaborate on their ideas, information, and feelings—to use their skills in thinking and putting it all together. For example, the teacher says, "What do you think the boy will do now?" instead of, "Did the boy go swimming?" Or, "Tell me about your trip," instead of, "Did you take a trip?" The second question in these two examples can be answered with a yes or a no and does not call for further elaboration. The teacher might say, "Would you tell me about _____?" or, "I'm interested in where you found the _____."

8. The teacher strives to be the kind of person the children want to identify with. Identification is a powerful force in language acquisition. Children try to act and talk like people they identify with.

9. The teacher accepts the children as they are and avoids moralizing. To keep communication channels open, the teacher avoids telling them how they "ought" to act, think, or feel.

10. The teacher pays attention to the children, and reflects their words and body language back to them to let them know their communication is heard and understood. For example, if Ken bites his nails and looks fearful, the teacher recognizes his state—he's scared. She says, "It's scary to get so close to the train, isn't it?" When the teacher is competent at interpreting the meaning beyond the children's words, she or he is really tuned in to children.

11. The teacher picks up on the children's verbal horseplay, chanting as they chant, rhyming as they rhyme, laughing as they laugh, and enjoying their fun with language and all communication.

12. The teacher avoids being fussy about names and titles; such fussiness can stifle the children's conversation. Surely a wise principal would not want to hear the teacher say, "Stop chattering and speak to our principal Mr. Smith correctly and with respect, Jonathan."

13. The teacher watches for the children who don't speak, for those who don't appear to hear, for those who don't respond to directions until after the others start, and for those who talk with a nasal twang or who eat unusually noisily. Such symptoms suggest to the teacher the need for medical referrals, hearing and speech assessment, and possible therapy. It is important to take care of problems before the child develops habits that are difficult to change.

14. The teacher writes down stories, songs, poems, and sayings a child expresses and reads them back to the child, showing that language

is valued and teaching that there is a relationship between spoken language and the written words found in books.

Planning Language Arts Activities

Language is a two-way street—listening and speaking. Listening may be as important as speaking itself. Listening must be done with comprehension. Active thinking should accompany listening. Teachers can't be sure that a child sitting quietly is listening. The entire program, both indoors and out, affords numerous opportunities for involving children with language.

When the teacher starts a new project or a learning experience, techniques are used to quiet the children and gain their attention. A song, a poem, finger play, a puppet, or a new picture can serve this purpose. The teacher will want them to follow the discussion, think critically about what is said, be stimulated to further interest, and react with new behavior or new understanding. All children will not respond to all projects. Therefore other activities are kept available for those with different interests. As each activity is planned, teachers should note new words and phrases that the children can learn. Plenty of time should be allowed for children's comments and questions as an activity progresses.

Games

Games such as "Simon says" can be played with small groups to encourage listening and learning new vocabulary. The common "Simon says, 'Stand up' " can be altered to "Simon says, 'Put your hands *above* your heads' " or " 'Put your hands *below* your chair.' " Such a game can be played at the snack table while the children are waiting for the snack to come, or at the gate when they are waiting for their parents or a bus.

Guessing games can be created by the teacher as the characteristics of familiar objects for children to guess are described. At first, the objects should be near at hand. Later, out-of-sight objects at home and at school can be described. After some experience the children can take turns describing objects.

The teacher can say, "I'm thinking of something that is—HOT. What could it be?" When the children catch on, a child can be invited to choose the object and the adjective, whisper the choice in the teacher's ear, and then tell the others whether they are correct as they guess.

A box or a bag with several objects for children to feel, describe, and name invites conversation. They can learn to use such words as *rough,*

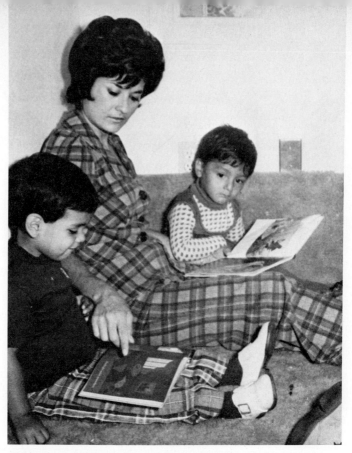

Figure 11-6. Quiet times with books give the teacher an opportunity to label items and encourage the child to respond. (Parent–Child Development Center, Houston)

smooth, large, small, hard, soft as they try to identify the object. The teacher can select familiar items. *Large* and *small* can be learned more readily by using two sizes of the same object—buttons, Jell-O boxes, milk cartons, and so on.

Jokes

Five-year-olds who are beginning to appreciate jokes will enjoy correcting the teacher who says absurd things like "Shall we wait until the street light turns purple?" Children like to play tricks on others, too, once their concepts are well-enough formed so that they can recognize the absurdities.

Records and Tapes

Records and tapes are outstanding aids that encourage listening. A record player that is simple enough for the children to operate will encourage voluntary listening. The collection of records should be changed frequently. A quiet nook that is free of distractions is a good location for the record player.

Tape recordings of the children's conversations, stories, and songs encourage the children to listen for their own voices. Stories the children record can be typed and placed in a book, or they can be sent home. Thus their value is enhanced, and the children begin to see a relationship between spoken and written words.

Headsets for a record player or a tape recorder are valuable additions to equipment. Occasionally a child wants to hear a record that interferes with another child's activity, or a child may want to hear the same record over and over. Using the headset avoids disturbing others. Teachers can record stories for children to use with books, saving many dollars over commercial tape costs.

Music

Teachers can hum or play a tune or a rhythm for the children to guess. Children can learn to lead this listening game too. Children need opportunities both to listen to music and to participate. Songs help children add new words to their vocabularies. Further discussion of music and rhythm follows in Chapter 14.

Literature

The use of good literature contributes to language. Poetry challenges children's listening. Children can help the teacher rhyme words. With only a little experience children will know that the word in a poem to rhyme with *ice* is *slice* or *mice*. Many good poems are available for children, which, when presented enthusiastically, will interest them. Suggestions for books, poems, and finger plays are given in Chapter 12.

Writing

Spoken language precedes written language. However, three- to five-year-olds often have a fascination for people's names and want to write friends' names or their names on their products. They may begin writing phonetically, printing words the best they can while they sound them out orally. They may ask adults to spell names and other words for them. Dictating stories and letters for adults to write down is interesting to some children. A free-flowing oral vocabulary can lead to free-flowing

Figure 11-7. Writing is an advanced level of language development. Writing one's name is frequently a first step. (Child Development Laboratory, Michigan State University)

writing. All of these are early steps in writing and reading that alert early childhood teachers can encourage.

Dramatic Play

Imaginative role-playing, so popular with young children, contributes to their language development. Children need to talk in making their wants known, they have concrete objects to discuss as they play, and they enact roles they have observed. All these conditions contribute to learning. Dramatic play is discussed further in Chapter 13.

Puppets and flannel-board figures are useful aids for encouraging children to speak. Shy children find that speaking through a puppet or a figure is easier. Torrance, who has done notable work in children's creative language expression, gives children a "magic net," under which they imaginatively become whatever they wish. They wear the magic net and stand, walk, talk, or dance like the person, animal, or object they wish to become. Torrance used colored netting 36″ × 72″ and gave about ten children "Magic nets" at one time.[11]

[11] E. Paul Torrance, *Encouraging Creativity in the Classroom* (Dubuque, Iowa: Wm. C. Brown, 1970), pp. 3–5.

Figure 11-8. Telephones contribute to talk, talk, talk. Every school should have several. (Texas Tech University Kindergarten)

Telephones

Telephones are extremely useful in encouraging conversation, and every school should have several. The children will often talk to each other, and the teacher can talk to a child in casual conversation or ask for information such as, "What is your telephone number?" "What is your home address?"

Field Trips

Field trips and other special events will help extend the child's language. From firsthand experiences the child builds a frame of reference with which to compare new information, whether it comes through reading, listening, or experimenting. Details for planning field trips are given in Chapter 15.

Sharing Time

Sharing time, or "show and tell," is a popular activity in the kindergarten. This is an organized time when an individual child shows the group something brought from home or tells about some event. The ac-

Figure 11-9. Grouptime gives a child a chance to speak and others a chance to listen. (Children's Center, University of South Carolina)

tivity gives the child an opportunity to speak before the group. The child is encouraged to develop the discussion in logical sequence. Children learn to listen and then ask the speaker questions. They all learn to take turns.

Parents should be enlisted to help the children select worthwhile things or ideas to share during "show and tell." They can help the children plan what they will tell. Parents can help their children keep track of which day of the week is their sharing day, for once the "show and tell" idea becomes popular in a class, it is seldom feasible to let everyone speak each day. In a class of fifteen or more children the sharing time could take an hour—much too long to expect active listening. Overlong periods rob other meaningful activities of their rightful time in the schedule. A calendar can be arranged designating a certain day for each child to bring or tell something. Exceptions are made, of course, when a child has something very special for "show and tell": a new baby sister or the first flower of spring qualifies.

In some groups sharing time is held during snack time. When only a portion of the group is slated to speak, daily sharing time requires only a few minutes. Table conversation, a valued language experience, is also encouraged.

The key to success is the teacher, who must develop skill in directing sharing time in order to make it a pleasant learning experience for both the speaker and the group. Skill is needed in drawing out the shy speaker and limiting the verbose one. Also, the teacher will preserve the child's dignity and allow for individual differences in ability to participate. Learning can be increased if the teacher judiciously raises questions and directs the children's attention. Occasionally a teacher may designate certain things as being good for "sharing time," such as fall seeds or leaves.

A "sharing table" can be set up for children to display their specimens and treasures. The self-selected activity time can be used for individual discussion of these objects. As many three- and four-year-old children are not ready for an organized "sharing time," a "sharing table" may be substituted.

Teaching Foreign Language

"Why doesn't the school teach a foreign language?" "Are there advantages to teaching a second language to young children living in an English-speaking environment?" These questions are often raised by parents. There is a difference of opinion with regard to the optimum time to introduce a foreign language. Some authorities believe that the training should begin early. Others do not believe that all research supports early foreign language instruction. However, Anita Wagman, a linguist, concludes that studies, especially of Canadian children who enter second-language study in either French or English, ". . . consistently demonstrate that two linguistic perspectives open the child's mind to greater nonverbal, mathematical, and conceptual flexibility."[12]

In some situations the child must learn a second language. Many disadvantaged children are, in effect, learning a second language.[13] The school starts with whatever language skill children have and teaches them English much as a foreign language is taught.[14,15]

A five-year study of the effects of teaching Spanish to kindergarten children was carried on at Texas Tech University. The classes were made up of middle-class five-year-olds in the laboratory kindergarten. During the five years five groups received Spanish lessons. Lessons lasted from 10 to 15 minutes per day and varied from one to two semesters' duration. The study was designed to find:

---

[12] Anita Wagman, "Language Experiences in Bilingualism," *Childhood Education,* 58:1 (October 1981), p. 19.

[13] Joan C. Baratz, "Language in the Economically Disadvantaged Child," *Journal of American Speech and Hearing Research,* 10:4 (1968), pp. 142–145.

[14] Marion Meyerson, "The Bilingual Child," *Childhood Education,* 45:9 (1969), pp. 525–527.

[15] George I. Sanchez, "Significance of Language Handicap," *Learning a New Language,* Margaret Rasmussen (ed.) (Washington, D.C.: Association for Childhood Education International, 1958), pp. 25–32.

1. Whether five-year-olds could be motivated to learn Spanish.
2. What could be taught to them.
3. What methods could be used effectively.

Lessons were carefully outlined with the Spanish staff of the Department of Foreign Languages. Spanish professors and students in language "methods" classes taught three years. The kindergarten teacher and Spanish-speaking child development majors taught the last two. The kindergarten teacher and college students had considerable enthusiasm for the language. Incidental events often became language lessons. For example, during snack time, the teacher would ask,«¿Quien quiere mas leche?» The children learned to hold up their hands and respond, «Mas leche, por favor.» ("Who wants more milk?" "More milk, please.")

The cooperation of the kindergarten teacher and the language instructors was important to the success of the project. The new language was never an isolated experience. Using trained language teachers gave the children good models to imitate. The kindergarten teacher's active participation protected the children from teaching methods that did not consider their individual needs and development. Because of the teacher's participation, the language and related experiences permeated the entire program.

Lessons were planned to focus on familiar objects, expressions, and situations at home and school. A single concept was presented in various interesting ways to keep the interest high. For example, when the children were learning to count, they counted the number of children, the number of girls, and the number of chairs. They also sang "Ten Little Indians" in Spanish and took turns counting individually. Counting was interwoven with other concepts that were being learned. Teaching aids of all kinds were used to present real things and models for the children to talk about. The lessons were short and they were fun.

The outcome seemed positive in most respects. The children leaped the language barrier with grace. Spanish was a natural choice for that community, which had a 20 percent Mexican-American population and a natural relationship to Mexico. The children learned about some of the festivals that are part of Mexican tradition. They were interested in learning the new language. Often they reported having heard Spanish on the radio (not uncommon in that part of Texas), or someone speaking it while they were shopping downtown, or at home where older brothers and sisters were studying Spanish for school.

The games and songs particularly appealed to the children. They liked being called on to participate individually, although they were never forced to respond until they indicated their readiness. Children who had trouble articulating English sounds were actually helped by saying the sound in Spanish. The boy who spoke German was given private help in English during the Spanish lessons. However, he had so much facility with languages that he learned a number of Spanish expressions from the children who were using them in their play.

The staff, the students, and the parents gleaned valuable information during these sessions. It was interesting to all to observe the children learning a subject about which one could assume no prior knowledge or home practice. Many early childhood education students expected to teach Spanish-speaking children in Head Start and felt they had learned teaching methods that would help them.

The importance of planning was clear. Deciding the concepts to teach, planning the sequence for teaching, and preparing the teaching aids took considerable time and thought. Concepts related closely to children were the best choices.

Better pronunciation resulted from individual participation than from group recitation. The teacher's verbal approval was of greatest importance. Approval was given both to the group and to individuals.

Whereas teachers with much teaching experience could keep a large group interested, beginning teachers were more successful with small groups. All planned activities that were fun. Involving children in a variety of songs, games, pictures, toys, stories, and role-playing contributed to the success of the lessons. Teachers frequently shifted from one teaching method to another to maintain high interest.

Learning English as a Second Language

During a teacher's visit to the home of a family with children in prekindergarten, the two daughters, one age three and the other, age four-and-a-half, spoke fluently in English without a hint of accent. These children had spent about two years in United States child care centers. Their teachers and the children spoke only English. Their parents, much shyer, spoke hesitatingly with accents carried over from their Hungarian upbringing. The family speaks Hungarian at home to ensure ability to communicate with relatives when visiting in the "old country." These children are becoming truly bilingual, developing fluency in both languages.

In some sections of the United States numerous language groups are represented among the children found in early childhood schools. The Bilingual Education Act of 1967–68 required teaching children in their native language until their English developed. Unfortunately, the United States has few elementary teachers trained in foreign languages and funding has been minimal for preparing teachers.

In an effort to improve the situation for non-English speaking children, Head Start and many other early childhood education centers have hired aides with the language backgrounds of the children. They help ease the transition for children into the English-speaking world. Developing fluency in English is the primary goal of most groups, rather than parallel development of two languages.

The greatest improvement in the last decade is the increased respect for other languages and cultures among early childhood educators. Many are going beyond teaching respect for the child's home language to teaching all children about customs, dress, foods, and so on from other cultures. Global education has become a popular innovation in the elementary schools' social studies curriculum.

Children's lives are enriched when they associate with children from other countries and cultures. For example, in one group the five-year-olds were especially interested in their new German classmate, Franz. They wanted to know where he had come from, how he had traveled, and if he had gone to school in Germany. The teacher introduced a world map to locate Germany and taught the group a few German words. The new child was delighted. He soon felt at ease and spoke to the children in German. The unfamiliar sounds awed the children and the teacher had to reassure them that it was all right to speak to him in English, explaining that he could tell by their gestures some of the things they wanted him to do. In a short time he learned some English phrases that helped his social relations.

In the case of the German boy the parents were strongly in favor of the child's learning English. Occasionally the families speaking a foreign language do not readily accept their child's learning English. In this case the school must build a bridge of friendship and respect to the other culture to help the family accept and encourage their child's learning the new language.

Teachers who work with young children from ethnic or language groups different from their own sometimes erroneously judge or downgrade the children's language abilities or may fail to have positive expectations for such children. Such judgments are unfair to these children and their parents. Children from such groups are often unusually quiet as new students in a strange school situation, just as vivacious adults often become tongue-tied when they venture into a new country, where the language and the customs are different from their own.

We must remember that the young children entering early childhood schools generally have very few experiences outside their home and neighborhood, regardless of their socioeconomic background. When they are confronted with a school situation in which the setting, adults, language, and ethnic mix are new, different, and perhaps incomprehensible, it is not surprising that these children appear scared, shy, and quiet.

Talk It Over: No. 3

Describe a child you know who has learned or is learning a second language. What is the child's age? What are the child's language characteristics? How do adults help the child?

Working with Spanish-Speaking Children

Mrs. Rebecca Peña Hines is a noted early childhood educator who grew up speaking Spanish at home and learning English at school. She has been associated with the Parent-Child Development Center in Houston, Texas, and she expresses many concerns about the situation facing the Spanish-speaking child.[16]

Mrs. Hines indicated that Mexican-American parents, and especially grandparents, are usually deeply interested in their children's maintaining their Spanish language. Their attitude is, of course, defensible, because it is their language and the language of their ancestors—a beautiful language with a body of great literature. A large portion of the Western Hemisphere speaks Spanish. Some Mexican-American parents who want their child to function in the English-speaking world sometimes go to the extreme of speaking only English at home, creating some raised eyebrows among friends and neighbors who may look upon that family as "putting on airs." However, with the recent Chicano movement, the younger generation of parents and soon-to-be parents has revived an interest and a pride in maintaining the Spanish language, along with the other rich and positive aspects of the Mexican-America culture.

Chicano children (and any non-English-speaking children) may have an uphill language struggle in typical schools. Until recently schools did not teach Spanish in the kindergarten or elementary school, and English is frequently not taught in a manner that builds on a Spanish-speaking child's already-developed language foundation. This makes it difficult for the child to learn either language well. Chicano children are often erroneously considered by observers to be "nonverbal" or "slow" when, in fact, these outsiders are merely observing the child's reaction to strangers and to a largely different environment.

Mrs. Hines finds that young Chicano children are generally friendly, open, and verbal if they have a teacher or an aide who speaks Spanish

---

[16] In making the following suggestions for working with children from Mexican-American homes I have drawn upon discussions with Rebecca Peña Hines and upon materials she presented at the annual meeting workshop of the National Association for the Education of Young Children in 1973, 1979, and 1984.

and who can build warm communication with the children and their parents through appreciation of their unique background and culture. Bilingual-bicultural aides and teachers are needed for young Chicano children. Bilingual adults will teach Spanish to these children, adding to their vocabulary for expressing their needs and concepts. Gradually English is introduced to the children on an individual and small-group basis—thus building a bilingual base for the children. They eventually learn two words for each concept and expression, and at times they integrate the two languages in interesting and unique ways. Reinforcement of the cultural strengths in the children's background, such as Spanish music, literature, and festivals, serves to enhance further the children's feeling of who they are.

Mrs. Hines, whose work has been concentrated in Texas, California, and Washington, believes that English-speaking teachers can learn to communicate with Spanish-speaking children. The teachers can learn some key words and phrases in Spanish in order to understand and to respond, just as a teacher of a deaf child can learn to communicate with a few hand symbols. Spanish songs like those included in this book (Chapter 14) can be learned rather easily and sung with the children. The child's parents might be enlisted to help with pronunciation. Pictures including Chicano children and their families can be displayed and used for learning activities within the classroom. Curriculum plans can introduce cultural objects—piñatas, books, and foods—that are familiar to Mexican-American children, helping them with adjustment and with enhancing their self-concepts.

Even when the class includes only one or two Spanish-speaking children, these steps are important to those individuals and also to the other children, who will learn much from an introduction to different cultures such as the Mexican-American culture.

Teachers are advised to continue talking to the child in English even though they believe the child does not understand. Children frequently can understand much more than they can speak. Eventually the words will take on meaning. The tone of voice and the body language accompanying the words give clues to the child concerning meaning and also communicate warmth and interest. Likewise, English-speaking children in the class should be encouraged to talk with non-English-speaking children in order to develop peer relationships and provide models. Both groups will benefit as the children learn language expressions from each other. Important learning flows in both directions.

All children have a right to expect teachers to respect their culture. If teachers have an attitude of respect and positive expectation, the children and the parents will be responsive to the teachers and the school. The children will then have a firm foundation for climbing up the educational ladder.

*   *   *

Talk It Over: No. 4

Describe a child you know who is or was having speech therapy. What was the problem? How was the child helped? Did the teacher play a role in the speech therapy?

*   *   *

Working with Children with Nonstandard English

Some young black children and others who come with a nonstandard English dialect present certain challenges for teachers. Researchers who have studied the linguistic components of the black dialect find it simply different and not deficient. The dialect is usually well developed and expressive and serves useful purposes in the exchange of ideas, information, and feelings. There are numerous debates as to whether or not children should be taught standard English. A casual survey of black public figures—educators, politicians, artists, writers, and television commentators—generally reveals a high proficiency in standard English.

Researchers Cullinan, Jagger, and Strickland have concluded that it is a defensible objective to expand the language of black children with dialects to include standard English without reducing the proficiency in their native black English.[17] Children who speak black English must be fully accepted as equals, be encouraged to talk using their own language traditions, and be helped to develop new language forms through such opportunities for speaking and comprehending as have been suggested in this chapter and throughout the text.[18]

Dealing with Language Problems

Articulation

It is too much to expect children in early childhood schools to make all sounds correctly. For example, in a study of 308 first-grade children, Roe and Milisen found that 88 percent had trouble with *z*, 69 percent

---

[17] Bernice E. Cullinan, Angela M. Jaggar, and Dorothy Strickland, "Language for Black Children in the Primary Grades: A Research Report," *Young Children,* **29**:2 (January 1974), pp. 98–112.

[18] A helpful discussion of the characteristics of black English is found in Susanna Pflaum, *The Development of Language and Reading in Young Children* (Columbus, Ohio: Charles E. Merrill Publishing Co., 1978), pp. 50–58.

with *g,* 45.7 percent with *t,* and 17.6 percent with *r.* Blends such as *st* and *dr* were easier than either *s* or *d* followed by a vowel for most of the children.[19] Many articulation errors are common and are eliminated without therapy as the child matures.[20] Templin's studies indicate that on the basis of cross-sectional data fewer children than anticipated had achieved adequate articulation at the beginning of the second grade. She found that boys were about one year slower than girls.[21]

How does a teacher help children with obvious language deficiencies? The teacher cannot be a speech therapist. Children with severe problems should be under the care of a trained therapist. The therapist can help the teacher choose activities that will be helpful for a child with problems. Help at this young age includes games that might be played with children with normal speech so that attention need not be focused on the handicapped child.

Only one teacher, and not a whole staff, should focus on a child's speech problems. Excessive pressure may add complications and lead the child to feel that no one is pleased. The teacher who has the best rapport with the child should be the one to intervene actively. Other helpers may correctly restate words misused so that the child can hear them, but they should leave the actual intervention to that one teacher. The total staff, including bus drivers and cooks, should be advised of the procedure because they, too, have an opportunity to help.

One helpful procedure is for adults simply to restate a child's mispronounced words or ungrammatical phrases in a corrected form so that the child may begin to hear the correct pattern. Asking the child to repeat specific words or phrases often produces tension that causes further problems. Van Riper says that it is frequently ear training that is needed rather than mouth training. He suggests that only one sound be worked on at a time.[22] If a child says "wed" for "red," the child may not be hearing the *r.* Speech therapists would not practice with the child on the word *red* but on a completely unfamiliar word, such as *rebel* or *referee.* Therapists use nonsense words to advantage when helping a child relearn a sound.[23] The sounds can be practiced in isolation, in games or singing, or in mimicking animals or machines.

[19] Vivian Roe and R. Milisen, "The Effects of Maturation upon Defective Articulation in Elementary Grades," *Journal of Speech Disorders,* 7:1 (March 1942), p. 42.

[20] Anne S. Morency, Joseph M. Wepman, and Paul S. Weiner, "Studies in Speech: Developmental Articulation Inaccuracy," *Elementary School Journal,* 67 (1967), pp. 329–337.

[21] Mildred C. Templin, "Research on Articulation Development," *The Young Child,* Willard W. Hartrup and Nancy L. Smothergill (eds.) (Washington, D.C.: The National Association for the Education of Young Children, 1967), pp. 109–124.

[22] Charles Van Riper, *Speech Correction Principles and Methods* (Englewood Cliffs, N.J.: Prentice-Hall, Inc., 1963), pp. 248–249.

[23] Ibid., p. 279.

Hearing

Children with hearing difficulties can be mainstreamed into a regular classroom if they wear hearing aids and if they have had enough experience to make their wants known.[24] Sufficient assistance for the teacher is essential. An assistant can work with the handicapped child when the teacher is in charge of activities in which the child cannot or does not want to participate. The teachers can learn many of the signs which deaf children are taught and increase communication greatly. The advice and assistance of a specialist should now be available in all communities. Assistance is provided through Public Law 94-142, the Education for All Handicapped Children Act. Early childhood educators should seek out this assistance for themselves and for the parents of the child.

Conclusion

Language enrichment can permeate the entire early childhood curriculum. A classroom alive with happy conversations is indicative of an environment that is helping children learn language. Seven categories of oral language behaviors are considered to indicate areas of growth expected of the young child. Such goals are helpful when considering problem areas and bilingualism. They can be most helpful in planning formal and informal interaction with young children. Suggestions have been included to help teachers enhance the child's listening and speaking skills. Teachers set the stage for the children to exchange ideas, share information, and ask questions. Teaching a foreign language and English as a second language was discussed.

Applications

1. Discuss the "Talk It Over" items found in the chapter.
2. Complete Lesson 11 in *A Laboratory Workbook for Introduction to Early Childhood Education*. Hand in as scheduled.
3. Write an activity plan for a language activity for a few children using information and the sample plan (Figure 6-1) in Chapter 6. Secure approval, carry out the plan, and evaluate the results from the children's point of view and from your viewpoint. Prepare a report and hand it in along with your approved activity plan.
4. Evaluate your total participation performance on your evaluation form developed in Chapter 1. Discuss your progress with your supervising teacher.
5. Add ideas and plans for language activities to your Resource File.

[24] Vivian W. Stern, "Fingerpaint on the Hearing Aid," *The Volta Review*, 71:3 (1969), pp. 149–154.

Study Questions

1. Discuss how language development relates to social, emotional, cognitive, and physical development. What role does creativity play?
2. State and explain seven major goals for language development.
3. Explain the differences between oral and aural language.
4. List and explain steps teachers can take to foster children's language development.
5. What conclusion does Anita Wagman draw from studies of children learning two languages?
6. State some conclusions regarding working with Spanish-speaking children and those speaking black English.
7. List some conclusions regarding helping children with articulation and hearing problems.
8. Describe a high-quality environment in a school that best facilitates children's language development. What activities can be planned?

Additional Readings

ADAMS, LEAH, and BETTY GARLICK (eds.). *Ideas That Work with Children, Vol. II. Washington, D.C.: National Association for the Education of Young Children, 1979.*

ATKINS, CAMMIE, "Writing: Doing Something Constructive," *Young Children,* Vol. 40, No. 1, November 1984, pp. 3–7.

BROWN, JANET (ed.) *Curriculum Planning for Young Children.* Washington, D.C.; National Association for the Education of Young Children, 1982.

CAZDON, COURTNEY B. *Language in Early Childhood Education.* Washington, D.C.: The National Association for the Education of Young Children, 1981.

CHUKOVSKY, KORNEI. *From Two to Five.* Berkeley, Calif.: University of California Press, 1968.

COCORAN, GERTRUDE B. *Language Experience for Nursery and Kindergarten Years.* Itasca, Ill.: F. E. Peacock Publishers, Inc., 1976.

GARCIA. EUGENE E. "Bilingualism in Early Childhood." *Young Children,* Vol. 35, No. 4, May 1980, pp. 52–66.

HONIG, ALICE S., "Language Environments for Young Children." *Young Children,* Vol. 38, No. 1, November 1982, pp. 56–67.

LANDRETH, CATHERINE. *Early Childhood: Behavior and Learning.* New York: Alfred A. Knopf, Inc., 1967.

MANUEL, HERSCHEL T. *Spanish-Speaking Children of the Southwest, Their Education and the Public Welfare.* Austin, Tex.: University of Texas Press, 1965.

MARTIN, BILL, JR. *Language and Literature: The Human Connection.* Washington, D.C.: Department of Elementary-Kindergarten-Nursery Educators, NEA, 1967.

MOORE, SHIRLEY G., and CATHERINE R. COOPER (eds.). *The Young Child: Re-

views of Research, Vol. 3. Washington, D.C.: National Association for the Education of Young Children, 1982.

SARACHO, OLIVIA N., and BERNARD SPODEK (eds.). *Understanding Multicultural Experience in Early Childhood Education.* Washington, D.C.: National Association for the Education of Young Children, 1983.

SCHICKEDANZ, JUDITH A., et al. *Strategies for Teaching Young Children.* Englewood Cliffs, N.J.: Prentice-Hall, Inc., 1983.

SMITH, GRACE. "On Listening to the Language of Children." *Young Children,* Vol. 29, No. 3, March 1974, pp. 133–140.

VAN RIPER, CHARLES. *Speech Correction Principles and Methods.* Englewood Cliffs, N.J.: Prentice-Hall, Inc., 1978.

VAN RIPER, CHARLES. *Speech Correction: An Introduction to Speech Pathology and Audiology.* Englewood Cliffs, N.J.: Prentice-Hall, Inc., 1984.

Literature Activities

- *To relate literature activities to the developmental tasks and to learning to read.*
- *To identify the opportunities teachers and parents have for introducing young children to literature.*
- *To identify guides for selecting literature for children under six.*
- *To identify reasons for introducing young children to poetry.*
- *To identify and evaluate literature activities offered in early childhood schools.*

"My Mommy got *this* book from the library and I love, love, love it!" exclaimed five-year-old Peter as he turned the pages of a picture book he had selected from the fresh supply neatly arranged in his kindergarten room. The teacher thought, "Being part of the wonderful way children respond to good books is one of teaching's intangible rewards."

Through literature children find the history of the human race, the hopes of the future, and the record of happiness and pathos. Between the covers of a book children find the mechanical, the artistic, the beautiful, and the ugly.

The Major Goal: A Lifelong Love of Books

The teacher and parent who want children to live full lives will help them learn to love books. The teacher is, of course, especially concerned with children's prereading experiences and will, therefore, enrich chil-

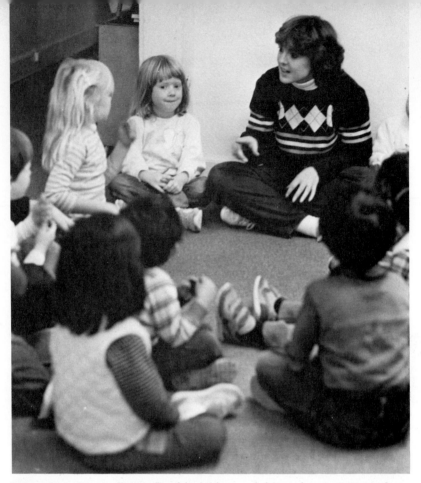

Figure 12-1. Story telling is fun for children and the teacher. It is an art that should be revived in early childhood schools. (Early Childhood Laboratory, Kansas State University)

dren's lives with literature in a variety of ways in order to create in them a strong desire to learn to read. Thus the teacher's main goal when offering literature to young children in the early childhood school is to initiate for each child a romance with books that will continue throughout a lifetime.

Teachers will use five important avenues for achieving a lifelong love of books. These are

1. Providing early prereading experiences which will stimulate children's desire to learn to read.
2. Providing opportunities for children to get acquainted with, handle, and "read" a wide variety of high-quality children's literature.
3. Providing daily opportunities for each child to see, hear, and respond to well-prepared literature experiences.
4. Providing books and other written materials to enhance all components of the young children's program.

5. Providing inspiration and assistance to parents in order to involve them in their children's literature experience.

Literature Supports All Developmental Tasks

It is worthwhile to realize that through literature activities all the developmental tasks are supported. Of course, through literature the oral symbols of the language become the written symbols of the language; and culture can be passed on through written means. Children's vocabularies are increased through exposure to literature.

Other developmental tasks are frequently highlighted through literature, such as achieving independence, giving affection, getting along with others, understanding right and wrong, and being self-confident. Information books help the children grow in understanding, such as books

Figure 12-2. Sharing books spontaneously with friends is a desirable opportunity in an early childhood school. (Nazarene Child Care Center, Lansing, Michigan)

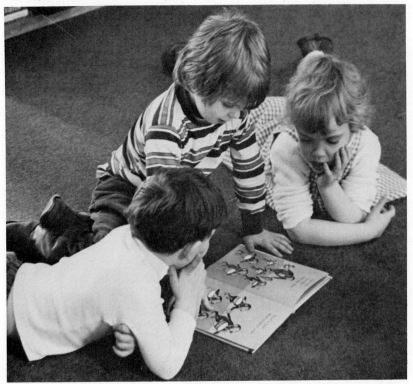

about sex roles, the human body, motor skills, and the world. As children's small muscles develop, they handle books more carefully.

* * *

Talk It Over: No. 1

Explain what you have heard parents say about children learning to read. What are their concerns?

* * *

The Reading Question

"When will my child begin to read?" is a question parents often ask the early childhood teacher. No one skill that children learn receives as much attention as reading. A number of writers have instilled fear and guilt feelings in parents and teachers whose children aren't reading by nursery school age. Of course, all adults want children to learn to read. Reading skills are basic in modern society. However, no one has yet proved that early readers read with more comprehension or, as adults, are more devoted to literature than children who learn later.

What Is Reading?

Reading can be defined as making sense out of letters or symbols. Note the requirement is "making sense . . ."—not merely pronouncing the symbols. To make sense means to comprehend or understand. In reading one must understand the concepts symbolized by the letters.

An example may help clarify this definition. Any adult with reasonable reading skills could probably read a book on nuclear physics—to choose one of the highly technical sciences—could "read" in the sense of pronouncing the words. Yet would the person be able to comprehend the content just because it could be read? Would motivation be high for reading such a book if one did not understand it? The answer is "No" to both questions. Without experiences and background information that provide a frame of reference, the words would be meaningless. Motivation for reading them would be low. Therefore, it seems logical that the young child needs experiences to support the words he or she reads.

Prereading Experiences

What are the experiences that prepare the child to read? Is the school entirely responsible for prereading experiences?

Learning to read has two levels. The first is the desire or motivation to read and having an insatiable curiosity about what a word, page, or volume says. Bright, enthusiastic children often teach themselves to read without lessons. The second level is more mechanical, using methods, procedures, and analytical skills to decipher words or a narrative. This level is laborious, often dull, but worth the effort if the first level of motivation for understanding the printed page is in place.

Reading may be somewhat like driving a car. A driver can drive fluidly, skillfully, park, reverse, and go far without understanding the inner mechanisms of the car or being able to analyze and repair the vehicle. Being interested in driving may precede strong interest in the mechanics of cars, but being interested in mechanics probably does not create the motivation to drive. Thus it is with reading, developing the motivation for reading precedes tackling the mechanics of reading; however, starting with the mechanics of reading may interfere with the motivation to read.

Prereading experiences are those events that occur before the child begins to read. These experiences give the child a background for understanding what is read. Such experiences begin at birth and continue throughout the individual's life. For a child they are the home, the family, the school, the neighborhood, the television, and life's events wherever they occur.

Simply handling lots of books, turning pages, analyzing the drawings, and discussing them with friends as well as having books read aloud provide children with substantial prereading experience. The notion that symbols on the page represent people, places, things, and actions develops in the child's mind as books are used during these early years. The concept of left to right progression begins to be understood as the child turns page after page and notices that the teachers start at the left each time the page turns. The child realizes, too, that the artist's drawings are associated with the printed words, and before long the child begins to sequence the story from memory while looking at the pictures. One frequently notices a child "reading" to friends if an adult is not available.

Vocabulary-building experiences are prereading experiences. In several chapters of this text the opportunity for vocabulary enrichment has been pointed out. The opportunity to practice letter sounds, blend sounds, words, and rhymes are all prereading experiences.

The child who learns to differentiate between largest and smallest, tallest and shortest, and longest and shortest is helped with reading. These concepts help the child to understand when the teacher points out differences in capital letters and small letters. Making lines and forms in art projects, seeing names written from left to right, and learning to write from left to right are all prereading experiences.

One of the first things a child must learn is that little black squiggles (symbols) have meaning. "This label says 'John.' That is your name. Here

Figure 12-3. Children may imitate the teacher and "read" to the other children. (Child Development Laboratory, Louisiana State University)

it is on your locker," says the teacher. She helps him begin to learn that the symbols *J-o-h-n* stand for him. Over and over he sees *John*—on his name tag, on his paintings, on his coat, on his treasures from home. His friend Bill has a different symbol.

Teachers label many objects and write letters and stories, which support the idea that little black marks tell something and convey a message. The child must even learn to concentrate on the black marks—not on the white surrounding them on the page.

Many parents supplement the labeling that teachers are doing. "The red signs says *STOP*," says John's dad. Later, John reminds dad, "But you were supposed to S-T-O-P and you didn't." Thus indicating an understanding of both the symbol and the meaning.

Differentiating puzzle pieces; fitting together the parquetry blocks, with their squares, diamonds, and triangles; choosing pegs and beads; arranging the block-city; aligning toys; and choosing blocks of a correct size and shape are all prereading experiences with structured media.

Games such as Candyland, Merry Milkman, Uncle Wiggily, dominoes, playing cards, and the various lotto games all require prereading skills. Such games contribute to number concepts. These games are especially useful in the kindergarten, where cooperative verbal skills and longer attention spans make sustained interest in games possible.

The children's experience of assuming various roles in spontaneous dramatic play gives them a feeling for the characters in the books they read. The outdoor program, with its opportunities to extend the children's perceptions of nature and with its outlets for energy and imagination, also makes contributions to children's reading background.

The rich curriculum offered by the good early childhood school is full of prereading experiences. These experiences help children develop a frame of reference for relating what is being read and what they will later read.

Will You Teach Reading?

Teachers should anticipate and plan how they will answer parents' questions about teaching reading, if they ask. If you take a positive stance, you'll reassure parents that you've seriously considered the issue. Parents want to know, the community wants to know, and even children want to know. Are you going to teach reading?

An honest answer is probably, "No, not in the same way that you expect the first-grade teacher to teach reading." Then go on to explain, "However, every experience the school offers will be a prereading and prewriting experience. Day after day a rich curriculum in science, language, art, music, and literature will be providing the frame of reference so basic to recognizing symbols and understanding what is read."

Further than this, a policy can be stated that on an individual basis children will be encouraged to learn to read. If Johnny wants to read to the teacher or an assistant, he will find a ready helper. When Jane points to a word and wants to know what the word is, someone will tell her. If a child volunteers to read to the children, she or he will be encouraged—yet the staff will avoid making others feel left out because they haven't learned yet. If a child memorizes a favorite story, it is fine if the child wants to "read" it to some friends. When the child corrects a teacher for omitting or changing a phrase in a favorite story, the teacher can take this in stride, knowing the child's memory for detail is a plus on the reading ledger.

The emphasis on learning to read will be entirely individually focused. For the group as a whole the teaching of reading will be left to the first-grade teacher, who has special visual aids and special techniques that the child will find fresh and exciting if they aren't usurped by the early childhood teacher and labored over prematurely.

Stimulating a Desire to Read

The years before six are important years for developing children's romance with books. This is a period for the adults in children's lives to help them "catch" the enthusiasm for books. The best word is "catch" rather than "teach" because contagion is far more effective than teaching. Attitudes at home and school affect children's attitudes toward books. Loving books makes using them for learning and enjoyment much easier. Many people have lost or never have had a really good feeling associated with books. They may be college students who dread the thought of a library assignment, adults who seldom read, and families who are lost when the television is broken. Or, they may be people who, as children or youths, were accused of being "lazy" when they spent time reading. And to avoid this criticism, they spent time at household chores or other "worthwhile" work instead of reading.

When children have a happy introduction to books, they discover in them fun, laughter, adventure, romance, information, and enlightenment. They want more. They feel that books are their friends. They may want to carry them around or take them to bed. They like the sharing with parent, teacher, friend, grandparent, or sibling that books invite. Children, like adults who love books, will turn to books for solace in lonely moments or for a laugh when in a happy mood. Once a child like Peter in our opening story is "hooked on books," so to speak, she or he will want to learn to read. In fact, motivation is high. Given a rich menu of books in the earliest years, a child will develop ideas, vocabulary, and grammar. The child will discriminate between sounds and begin to differentiate the symbols on the printed page. Reading will come easily.

Some parents and teachers push children into the mechanics of reading before the children have been convinced that books really offer them something. Children have to feel that the task of learning to read is worth the effort.

Neither a teacher nor a parent who lacks enthusiasm can infect a child with enthusiasm for reading. But many parents and teachers have overcome this handicap by working hard to learn about children's books in order to help their own children. In the process they have been inspired to capture the romance with books they missed in their own growing up. Therefore it is never too late. Two books by Annis Duff, *Bequest of Wings*[1] and *Longer Flight*,[2] will help adults who want to get acquainted with children's books. Anne Eaton's *Reading with Children*[3] and Nancy Larrick's *A Parent's Guide to Children's Reading*[4] will offer stimulation.

[1] Annis Duff, *Bequest of Wings* (New York: Viking, 1944).
[2] Annis Duff, *Longer Flight* (New York: Viking, 1955).
[3] Anne Eaton, *Reading with Children* (New York: Viking, 1957).
[4] Nancy Larrick, *A Parent's Guide to Children's Reading* (New York: Bantam, 1975).

Experiencing a Wide Variety of Literature

A well-chosen collection of good books will await all children whose parents and teachers are working to develop in them a love of books. The opportunity to browse for enjoyment and to use books personally and voluntarily helps a child develop a love of books. The school will of necessity budget considerable funds for purchasing the book collection, for keeping it up to date, and for repair and replacement. The collection can be supplemented by the community library collections.

The Book Corner

The book corner should be separated from the other play areas by dividers to provide a quiet, undisturbed atmosphere that encourages concentration. Carpeting will improve the atmosphere. A table will help the children handle books more carefully. Books should be invitingly displayed on a rack that allows the cover of the book to show. Because the book corner is available during the self-selected activity period, the children will browse on their own. Teachers will usually find several eager listeners if they will take time to read a story. A child who wants a story should be able to find someone to read. This area is often popular with new aides, volunteers, or college students who are getting acquainted with the children.

A fresh supply of books should be selected regularly. Certain favorites can remain available for a few weeks. Books can be selected to give information related to concepts being developed or to stimulate questions and observations regarding concepts the teacher anticipates emphasizing in the future. Books "just for fun" should always be available. Here on the shelf can be displayed books that may meet the needs of certain children, such as books on hospitalization, death, or divorce. Such books are used on a one-to-one basis with a child when the teacher feels the child is ready to discuss his or her troubling situation. These books probably would not be selected for a large group storytime.

To ensure a wider selection of books in the book corner and to give children experience in the public library, a kindergarten teacher developed the custom of allowing a committee of three children to accompany an assistant to the library once every two weeks. They chose one book for each child in the class. Often the class made suggestions to the committee about books they'd like. The children became comfortable in the library, chatting with the librarians and looking over the exhibits. The names of the books were recorded and date-due cards removed as precautions against their loss before the books were displayed in the classroom.

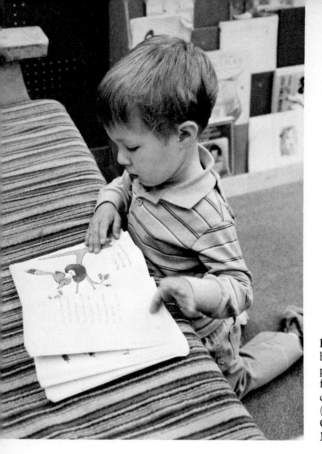

Figure 12-4. "Reading" books alone is an important prereading experience fostered in high-quality early childhood schools. (Manzanita Day Care Center, University of New Mexico)

If children are given opportunity and encouragement to use them, books can be taken outdoors during nice weather for a pleasant small-group story or individual reading. In climates where a major part of the school day is spent outdoors, a book rack can become standard outdoor equipment.

Puppets, flannel board, and flannel-board figures, if stored in the book corner, can readily contribute to literature and language experiences. A place to plug in the record player or tape recorder is also an asset, because these devices are used to advantage here. Recorded stories can be commercial products or recorded by a teacher or parent. The child may look at the book as the record or tape plays.

Illustrations in Books

Teachers should learn to appreciate the art in children's picture books. Much beauty, strength, and feeling are seen in some picture books. Once acquainted with an artist's work, the teacher's enjoyment of picture books will be enhanced. Pictures contribute a great deal to children's enjoyment of books.

320

The Caldecott Medal is given yearly to honor one of the earliest picture book artists, Randolph Caldecott. Caldecott, an Englishman, lived from 1846 to 1886. His children's books were illustrated after 1878.[5] It is interesting to study the evolution of children's books over the years. One method of study is to seek out the Caldecott Medal winners.

As one studies picture books, it is easy to become impressed with the wide variation in technique and medium that is used by artists. An hour-long film highlights a number of outstanding picture book artists, such as Barbara Cooney, Robert McCloskey, Maurice Sendak, and Ezra Keats. The film "The Lively Art of Picture Books"[6] selects artists' representations of lions, trees, and the Notre Dame Cathedral to show the wide variety of ways these objects are seen by artists and represented in children's books. The examples support the concept of creativity discussed in Chapter 8. Both teachers and parents appreciate this film.

Illustrations in books help children understand what is happening in the story even if they don't hear or understand the words. Pictures should leave accurate concepts. Children are less confused if objects appear whole. Some books have small or abstract pictures that are difficult to see from a distance. Teachers should place the books they expect to use for group storytime across the room and judge whether the children will be able to see the pictures. When the children can't see the picture, they can be expected to lose interest and perhaps to misbehave. Books with pictures that are difficult to see can be used for individual reading. If the story is especially strong, the teacher can tell it, using other visual aids such as puppets or flannel-board figures.

One of the teacher's difficulties in choosing books will come when trying to find books that tell stories of peoples of various races, colors, and creeds in this country and the world. For example, the total list of books with black children that are suitable in content and illustration to read to three-year-olds is quite limited. For four- and five-year-olds the list doesn't grow by many items. The list is just as meager for the Mexican-American, native-American, or Asian-American child.

Not only do children need books picturing faces the same color as theirs for identification purposes, but all children at some point will benefit from books with faces, homes, families, and customs different from their own; such books expand their knowledge of the world's peoples. Global or multicultural education is now a popular part of the curriculum.

What, then, can teachers do to remedy the lack of multicultural picture books? First, they should keep asking bookstores, librarians, publishers, and writers for such books. Second, they may have to make their

---

[5] "Randolph Caldecott," Vol. 4, *Encyclopedia Britannica* (London: Wm. Benton, Publisher, 1969), p. 565.

[6] *The Lively Art of Picture Books*, 16 mm, sound, color, 57 min. (Weston, Conn.: Weston Woods Studio, 1964).

own. Teachers have always been self-reliant. If they need something they can't buy, they make a substitute. By taking photographs; finding paper dolls, magazine, newspaper, or catalog pictures; or using some of the interracial teaching aids on the market, teachers can illustrate home-made books or provide visual aids for storytime. Homemade books will be discussed in a later section. Of course, it is worthwhile for children to watch puppets and flannel-board figures that represent minority children even when no children from that group are in the class.

Responding Daily to Literature Experiences

Stories and poetry presented in a regular storytime attract and hold children's attention when presentations are well prepared by teachers. Storytime is one of the times in the early childhood school when the children come together in either a large group or several small groups for stories. Small groups with four to five children are recommended for three-year-olds and young fours. Planning a storytime for an individual child may be needed for a child who is not ready for a group experience. The children will sense that storytime is an important time of day if the teacher (1) chooses a good story and prepares it well, (2) sets the stage for quiet listening-responding behavior, (3) plans some soothing activities, and (4) plans a smooth transition so that the children know what to expect. If, on the other hand, the teacher haphazardly plucks a book from the shelf and sandwiches storytime between snack time and going outdoors, or if the assistants are running around cleaning up the room while the story is in progress, the children can be expected to feel that storytime is rather unimportant.

Choosing a Story

Choosing an appropriate story and deciding on a technique for its presentation are two of the most important aspects of the teacher's planning. Teachers should choose literature that they themselves like. It is not likely they will put their best effort into a story they don't enjoy. The story must be right for the children. They should be able to understand it. The story should be chosen with the children's ages, interests, and previous experience in mind. Teachers must look hard and long to find suitable stories for the youngest children. It is far better to present two short stories that will hold the children's attention than to select a longer story and lose their interest before it ends. However, when the teacher misjudges the children's interest and selects a story that fails to appeal, it is wise to skip hastily through the pages, telling salient parts, and conclude the storytime with something that does appeal to the group.

The following are general guides for selecting children's literature. Stories and books should

1. Be about young children and familiar people, animals, and activities.
2. Contain about one sentence per page for three-year-olds or up to three sentences for five-year-olds.
3. Have a vocabulary the child can be expected to understand or to learn.
4. Be illustrated with clear, whole pictures that depict the action taking place.
5. Be selected both "for fun" and for information.
6. If "for fun," be fantasies that do not harm children.
7. If for information, be accurate information about the real world.

Teachers should become familiar with their school library and with a selected group of outstanding books in order to be able to find a story that will appeal to their children even on a moment's notice. It often happens that emergencies arise—schedules don't work out, special performers are late, or rain pours just when an outdoor activity is planned. If the teacher can reach for a book with knowledge of its special appeal, holding the group together and avoiding the disruptive behavior that emergencies often trigger in children will not be difficult.

Listed below are books that are predictable winners for each age listed. These books incorporate the characteristics of content, illustrations, length of sentences, and number of pages typically enjoyed by children of each age. Of course many other books could have been listed. However, it is each teacher's responsibility to learn to choose the right books for the children in a particular group. New students should study these suggested books, compare other books to them, and try out various books with children in order to learn to select books wisely.

For three-year-olds:
Flack, Marjorie, *Ask Mr. Bear.*
Gipson, Morrell, *Hello Peter.*
Jackson, Kathryn, *Busy Timmy.*
Keats, Ezra Jack, *The Snowy Day.*
Lenski, Lois, *Big Little Davy.*

For four-year-olds:
Brown, Margaret W., *The Noisy Book.*
Flack, Marjorie, *Tim Tadpole and the Great Bullfrog.*
McCloskey, Robert, *Blueberries for Sal.*
McCloskey, Robert, *Make Way for Ducklings.*
Rey, H. A., *Curious George.*

For five-year-olds:
  Burton, Virginia Lee, *Mike Mulligan and His Steam Shovel*
  Daugherty, James, *Andy and the Lion.*
  Gag, Wanda, *Millions of Cats.*
  McCloskey, Robert, *One Morning in Maine.*
  Petersham, Maud and Miska, *The Circus Baby.*
  Zion, Gene, *Harry the Dirty Dog.*

Late in the kindergarten year, when the teacher is sure of the so-phistication of the group, more fanciful stories and those with some distance in time and place might be selected.

Choosing Poetry[7]

Poetry, like good books and music, offers children an avenue of feeling, of expressing, and of learning. Poetry is artistic. It is creative. Poetry can be polite, pompous, pitiful, pretty, and witty. It is, as Josephine Jacobsen, a recent consultant to the Library of Congress says, "Those certain words in a certain cadence that makes poetry different from other literature forms." There are many reasons why poetry can make a valuable contribution to the early childhood curriculum.

Enjoyment
Enjoyment is the number-one reason for using poetry with young children. They have a natural affinity for poetry for they dearly love playing with words, with funny sounds, with repeats and rhymes. Using a wide selection of poems in order to tap the children's many interests is important. Also, do not belabor or dissect poems—as you may have had to do in high school; this will help keep enjoyment in poetry. If children do not immediately enjoy a poem, then save it for a time when you may find them ready to like it.

Listening
Listening is a second reason for using poetry. To get the meaning from spoken communication, a child must listen to what the other person is saying and then decode it. Poetry helps sharpen listening skills. Poems such as "I Want a Rabbit" and "Missing" by A. A. Milne[8] are readily listened to by children. A wintertime favorite is

[7] The author is indebted to Rebecca Peña Hines, who helped formulate the section on children's poetry which was given as a joint workshop at the National Association for the Education of Young Children. Originally illustrations of Spanish poetry were also included. An article, "The Pied Pipers of Poetry" was published in *Young Children*, **36:**2 (January 1981), pp. 12–17.

[8] A. A. Milne, *When We Were Very Young* (New York: E. P. Dutton & Co., 1924).

Figure 12-5. The pockets on the apron hide a toy or picture that illustrates a poem, song, or finger play. Children enjoy the suspense of making their choices. (Family Life Center, Georgia Southern College, Statesboro)

ONCE THERE WAS A SNOWMAN

Once there was a snowman
Stood outside the door
Thought he'd like to come inside
And dance around the floor.

Thought he'd like to warm himself
By the firelight red,
Thought he'd like to climb
Upon the big white bed.

So he called the North Wind,
"Help me now I pray.
I'm completely frozen,
Standing here all day."

So the North Wind came along
And blew him in the door,
And now there's nothing left of him
But a puddle on the floor.

—author unknown

Attention

A perfect attention-getter is the poem "I'm Hiding," by Dorothy Aldis from her collection *All Together*.[9] Every child stops what he or she is doing to find out where the child in the poem is hiding. It works like magic every time. *This Little Boy* is another poem that catches children's attention.

THIS LITTLE BOY

This little boy is ready for bed
Low on his pillow he lays his head
Pulls up the covers so warm and tight
And there he sleeps all through the night.

Morning comes! His eyes open wide!
Quickly he throws the covers aside!
Jumps out of bed, puts on his clothes,
And off to nursery school he goes.

—author unknown

Creative Language Expression

Another reason for including poetry in children's programs is the development of creative language expression. Good poets are masters at the art of using language creatively and expressively. Poets may use few

---

[9] Dorothy Aldis, *All Together* (Putnam, 1952), pp. 71–72.

words, and cause your mind and heart to know and to feel what they have known and felt. They write of ordinary things like Polly Chase Boyden's poem, *Mud,* which starts "Mud is very nice to feel" and children gain a new perception of something they know.

Children, too, are often poetic. Consider the poetry in this exchange between two four-year-olds.

> My name is Michael
> I love to recycle.
>
> My name is Sandy
> I love candy.

Another little boy sang as he swung in a blooming mimosa tree and watched the bees flitting among the flowers—

> I love to sing, sing, sing.
> A bee likes to sting, sting, sting.
> Ping-a-ty Ping!

Special recognition can be given to a child's original poem by writing it down and letting the child take the poem home. Or, the poem could be posted or placed in a class book. Care must be taken to avoid competition.

Teachers and parents, too, can also be creative poets. Here is a poem a teacher wrote for a child on her birthday.

GLENDA'S BIRTHDAY

> Today is Glenda's birthday
> She is four-years-old you see,
> She'll paint with paints,
> Play with clay,
> And maybe climb a tree.
>
> Today is Glenda's birthday
> Now we are here to say
> "Happy birthday, Glenda"
> In a very special way.
>
> "Happy Birthday!"
>
> —*V. Hildebrand*

Guidance

Another use of poems is to help guide a child into desired behavior. You may be familiar with using the fingerplay "Grandma's Glasses" when you want to get little hands to relax for storytime. "The Mitten Song" by Mary Louise Allen[10] is useful for helping children to remember to put their "thumbs in the thumb-place and fingers all together" when putting on their winter mittens.

Concepts

Concepts can be introduced, explained, and expanded through poetry. To learn a concept well, a child must meet it numerous times in numerous ways, and poetry can be very helpful. Here's one about a squirrel

THE SQUIRREL

Whiskey, frisky
Hippity hop,
Up he goes
To the tree top;

Whirly, twirly,
Round and round,
Down he scampers
To the ground.

Furly, curly,
What a tail;
Tall as a feather
Broad as a sail!

Where's his supper?
In the shell.
Snappity, crakity,
Out it fell!

—*author unknown*

Concepts of cultural heritage, holidays, peace, love, numbers and the like all can be found in poetry. Many are in books that are illustrated with delightful drawings. Aileen Fisher is an author-artist who has many beautiful poetry-stories about nature, such as *Cricket in a Thicket*,[11] *Feathered Ones and Furry*,[12] and *Listen Rabbit*.[13]

Vocabulary

Gradual building of vocabulary also comes with the use of poetry. New concepts call for new words. Poetry helps children practice these words. When we show young children pussy willows in the spring, for

[10] Mary Louise Allen, *A Pocket Full of Poems* (New York: Harper & Row, 1957).

[11] Aileen Fisher, *Cricket in a Thicket* (New York: Charles Scribner's Sons, 1963).

[12] Aileen Fisher, *Feathered Ones and Furry* (New York: Thomas Y. Crowell Company, 1971).

[13] Aileen Fisher, *Listen Rabbit* (New York: Thomas Y. Crowell Company, 1964).

example, they are usually new to them—or they don't remember them from last spring. They probably know the word "pussy" from another context. The poem, called "Catkin" is chanted going up the scale, with the "Meow meows" going quickly down the scale.

CATKIN

I have a little pussy,
Her coat is warm and grey,
She lives out in the meadow,
Not very far away.

Now she's a little pussy,
She'll never be a cat,
For she's a pussy willow,
Now what do you think of that?

Meow, meow, meow, meow
SCAT!

—author unknown

Reading Readiness

The use of poetry enhances reading readiness. A careful reading of only a few poems makes this quality of poetry clear. For example, rhyming and listening to rhyming are good phonics practice. Try Maurice Sendak's *Chicken Soup with Rice*.[14] The greatest contribution to reading readiness however, is the love of fine literature that is taught and caught.

Memory

Memory is an important intellectual operation that is enhanced through use of poetry. The little poems and songs give children something to remember. Parents and teachers can evaluate the child's learning as they notice how well he or she recalls poems.

*　　*　　*
Talk It Over: No. 2

Recall a poem or nursery rhyme you learned early in your life. In what circumstances was it taught? Share with your classmates.
*　　*　　*

Humor

Humor often is appreciated in poems, the punch line or pun tickling the funny bones of the late four- and five-year-olds. Try "Eletelephony"

[14] Maurice Sendak, *Chicken Soup with Rice* (New York: Harper & Row, 1962).

by Laura E. Richards[15] for a humorous play on words, or "I Know an Old Lady," by Rose Bonne and Allan Mills.[16]

Teachers and parents should practice reading poetry aloud so that the cadence, rhyme, and message are heard clearly by the children. Puppets and flannel boards may be helpful. Collections of poetry may have few or only small illustrations. You can reproduce these using an overhead projector or simply show the tiny picture so the children will realize that listening is needed to get the message. if you transcribe the poem on a card, children won't demand to "see the picture" as they may when you hold a book. Be sure to use your voice well. Separating conversations in the poem from the narrative aids the hearer in getting the message.

In addition to books of poems mentioned in the footnotes a few important poetry books are listed here.

1. Ciardi, John. *Fast and Slow* (Boston: Houghton Mifflin Co., 1975).
2. Holman, Felice. *I Hear You Smiling and Other Poems* (New York: Charles Scribner's Sons, 1973).
3. Keats, Ezra Jack. *Over in the Meadow* (New York: Four Winds Press, 1971).
4. Lee, Dennis. *Alligator Pie* (Boston: Houghton Mifflin Co., 1975).
5. Mizumura, Kazue. *If I Were A Cricket . . .* (New York: Thomas Y. Crowell Company, 1973).
6. Ness, Evaline. *Amelia Mixed the Mustard and Other Poems* (New York: Charles Scribner's Sons, 1975).
7. Talbot, Toby. *Coplas—Folkpoems in Spanish and English* (New York: Four Winds Press, 1972).
8. Whiteside, Karen. *Lullaby of the Wind* (New York: Harper & Row, 1984).
9. Zolotow, Charlotte. *Summer Is . . .* (New York: Thomas Y. Crowell Company, 1983).
10. Zolotow, Charlotte. *Some Things Go Together* (New York: Thomas Y. Crowell Company, 1983).

Choosing a Storytime Technique

Every effort should be made to make storytime a vibrant, interesting, and unique experience for children. Storytime should never become the same old thing. The teacher can develop a number of techniques that will make it an event that is looked forward to. What are some of these techniques?

---

[15] Laura E. Richards, in *Poems Children Will Sit Still for,* Beatrice S. de Regniers et al. (eds.) (New York: Scholastic Book Services, 1969), p. 92.

[16] Rose Bonne and Allan Mills, *I Know an Old Lady* (New York: Rand McNally & Co. 1961).

Reading Directly from a Book

This technique is best when you have outstanding poetry or prose with outstanding illustrations. Certainly when the author and the artist provide a well-integrated piece of literature, it is well to let it carry the children along.

Using the Illustrations of a Book While Paraphrasing the Story

This technique works well with informational material that is too long and detailed for the children, yet has illustrations related to their interests.

Telling the Story

Storytelling is one of the oldest arts. It certainly should not become a lost art in the early childhood school just because publishers have given us many good books. Listening to a story without the aid of pictures requires more attention from children than listening to stories from picture books. A good storyteller needs preparation and practice.

The storyteller can use various props to invite attention and set the mood for the story, such as wearing an apron when reading *Apron On, Apron Off* by Helen Kay,[17] or an old straw hat during *Who Took the Farmer's Hat?* by Joan Nodset,[18] or a pretty rose for *No Roses for Harry* by Gene Zion.[19] A collection of hats can illustrate *Caps for Sale* by Esphyr Slobodkina.[20] A plush bunny or doggy can sit beside the teacher during a pet story and tell the teacher "when everyone is ready to listen."

The teacher chooses a good story and learns to tell it. For a new story it helps to make notes on index cards until one becomes familiar with the story. It is important to do the story well. The teacher should use vocal inflections to create the various characters and help the children differentiate between them. Eye contact with each listener will help hold attention and help the teacher feel the impact the story is making. The teacher may move the head, body, or arms to help dramatize the story. However, teachers are cautioned not to select frightening stories or to build up unnecessary suspense or fear through their dramatizations.

The teacher can help children realize that they too are storytellers. Type, write, or tape-record a child as he or she tells an exciting event. Read this back to the child to help him or her realize the words really did tell a story.

---

[17] Helen Kay, *Apron On, Apron Off* (Englewood Cliffs, N.J.: Scholastic Book Services, 1968).
[18] Joan Nodset, *Who Took the Farmer's Hat?* (New York: Harper & Row, 1963).
[19] Gene Zion, *No Roses for Harry* (New York: Harper & Row, 1958).
[20] Esphyr Slobodkina, *Caps for Sale* (New York: Scott, 1947).

Telling a Story with Flannel Board

You can make a flannel board by covering a large piece of cardboard with a piece of outing flannel. A neutral gray is a satisfactory color. An easel or some other stand for holding the board will be convenient. You can make another type of flannel board by covering the bottom of a large cardboard box; then cut the sides diagonally to support the flannel board at a 45-degree angle.

Figures that represent the characters in the story are cut out of felt, pelon, flannel, or paper. A small piece of sandpaper or masking tape attached to the back of the figure makes it adhere to the flannel. Figures are available commercially that represent community helpers, family members, and some traditional stories. Such items can be used in many stories. All the characters in a story need not be made. Sometimes a single figure or picture will provide the children a focus for their attention as they listen.

Children will enjoy and learn from using the flannel-board figures. They will not only tell the story the teacher tells but will create their own stories. Such use can take place durng the self-selected activity period. However, during the storytime the teacher may or may not let the children handle the figures. The decision will depend on goals. If the teacher wants the children to hear a meaningful story in sequence, then handling the figures personally may be best, keeping them out of sight until time for them to appear. However, if encouraging individual participation is more important than story sequence, the teacher may give each child a figure to place on the board when it is called for. This technique does detract from the story and may be hard on the figures. It is true that teachers may spend a great deal of time making these figures and often prefer that they remain "special" to add spice at storytime.

The true-to-life stories of Martin and Judy in *Martin and Judy*, volumes I, II, and III, by Verna Hills Bayley[21] lend themselves to adaptation for the flannel board. The series has the advantage of featuring the same little boy and girl, with whom children readily identify. *Ask Mr. Bear* by Marjorie Flack,[22] *The City Noisy Book*, by Margaret Wise Brown,[23] and *I Can Count* by Carl Memling[24] are examples of stories that are readily illustrated on the flannel board.

Telling a Story with Puppets

Puppets often inspire quiet children to talk. Children may appear tense during a story until they have an opportunity to be one of the characters through a puppet. Depending on the objective, the teacher will vary

[21] Verna Hills Bayley, *Martin and Judy*, Vols. I, II, and III (Boston: Beacon Press, 1959).

[22] Marjorie Flack, *Ask Mr. Bear* (New York: Macmillan Publishing Co., Inc., 1932).

[23] Margaret Wise Brown, *The City Noisy Book* (New York: Harper & Row, 1939).

[24] Carl Memling, *I Can Count* (New York: Western Publishing, 1963).

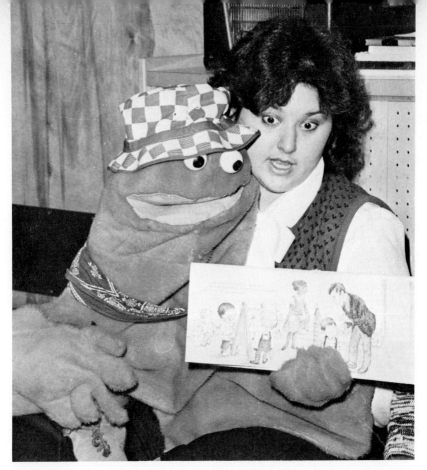

Figure 12-6. "Big Red," a lap puppet, helps children focus their attention and even helps with fingerplays. (Family Life Center, Georgia Southern College, Statesboro)

the decision as to who will speak for the puppets. The choice of stories and the use of puppets will depend on the age and experience of the children.

Homemade hand puppets can be made of paper sacks, socks, vegetables, or cutouts on a stick. Finger puppets can be made of decorated styrofoam balls or of construction paper attached to the finger by a paper ring. Many commercial puppets are available. A worthwhile addition to the school is a set of family puppets made of molded plastic. The puppets come in both black and white families. By purchasing several sets, the teacher can enlarge the family. Extra adults can be grandparents or other relatives. Delightful for animal stories are plush bunny, dog, and lion puppets.

To encourage puppetry during the self-selected activity period, a cardboard box can be cut to resemble a television set, or a table can be turned on its side to make a stage. The children will conceal themselves behind the "TV" or "stage," holding up the puppets for manipulation or speaking. If a few chairs are arranged for the "audience," the listeners will come and go as interested.

Role-Playing a Story

Children can become involved in a story through creative dramatics. The teacher may tell or read a story, then let the children present their version. Care should be taken to avoid indicating that there are certain words that must be said. The children may be encouraged to play various roles without attaching them to a story. The teacher might say, "Who would like to be the mother calling the children to come to breakfast?" Who will be the father? Or the children? A drama suitable for Broadway may result.

Magazine Picture Story

The teacher selects a number of pictures saved from magazines and stacks the pictures in an order that might suggest a story sequence. For example, picture number one is a girl, number two is a dog, number three is a girl and a dog running, and number four is a dog doing tricks or eating. The teacher may start with the phrase, "Once upon a time there was a . . ."—then let the children take it from there. The first few sessions may produce very short stories, so teachers should prepare several sets. However, once the idea catches on, the children will enjoy elaborating on the details in the pictures and the action they can imagine.

This same storytelling technique is used to tell the stories with the pictures in *My Weekly Surprise,* a newspaper published for kindergarteners but usable with many fours.[25] The cover picture invariably is a good story starter. The children's imaginations do the rest.

Filmstrip Stories

Some filmstrip stories have been made from outstanding picture books. To see the enlargement of the drawings from such books as Robert McCloskey's *Make Way for Ducklings*[26] is to appreciate anew the great care he took in illustrating the book. One drawback of filmstrip stories is that they are used frequently on television and may not be new to the children. This, of course, may not lessen the enjoyment of them, but teachers should realize this fact and not be too disappointed if the children say, "We've seen that."

Story Recordings

Story recordings are popular with children. Stories usually include some music and sound effects that would be difficult for the teacher to add. Therefore the recording offers the child a variation. Outstanding

---

[25] *My Weekly Surprise* (American Education Publications, Education Center, Columbus, Ohio 43216).

[26] Robert McCloskey, *Make Way for Ducklings* (New York: Viking, 1941).

stories should be used for group time. The record jacket or a picture related to the story can be attached to the flannel board for a focus of attention.

Recordings of published books are now available, so the book can be held for viewing while the record plays. Some recordings have both book and filmstrip available. Recorded stories will provide important listening opportunities for individual children during the self-selected activity period. Using home recording equipment, many teachers now make their own story tapes for children to use independently.

The following recorded stories are particularly popular with children. The asterisk (*) indicates that a picture book is available for that story.

"Sleepy Family"	* "Andy and the Lion"
* "Muffin in the City"	* "Blueberries for Sal"
* "Muffin in the Country"	* "Madeline's Rescue"
* "The Little Firemen"	* "Make Way for Ducklings"
"Little Indian Drum"	* "Georgie the Friendly Ghost"
* "The Carrot Seed"	* "Story About Ping"

Figure 12-7. Books can be recorded, then children can listen to them on earphones without distracting others. (Zukeran Kindergarten, Kadena Air Base, Okinawa, Japan)

A Story Song

A number of children's songs are complete with plot, suspense, and climax. Teachers will find eager listeners if they occasionally sing a story to the group. They may accompany themselves on an instrument—guitar, autoharp, or piano. Also, they may illustrate the song at the flannel board while singing. "Mary Had a Little Lamb," "John Henry," "Eency Weency Spider," or "Hush, Little Baby"—all familiar songs for young children—can be thought of as stories the first time they are introduced. "I Know an Old Lady," a humorous, fanciful story by Rose Bonne and Allan Mills, is delightful to sing in kindergarten.[27] Younger children, however, take the song too literally. Of course, the children will want to sing along, so let them!

Size of Story Groups

Small groups of four or five children make more effective story groups, particularly for younger children. The youngest children like to feel close to the teacher and to be able to respond to the book individually—verbally and physically—which is sometimes difficult to permit in a large

[27] Rose Bonne and Allan Mills, *I Know an Old Lady* (Englewood Cliffs, N.J.: Scholastic Book Services, 1961).

Figure 12-8. Organizing small groups for stories assures that children can see and hear, that the story may be more appropriate for the specific children, and that they can ask questions if they feel like it. (Butler Child Care Center, Kadena Air Base, Okinawa, Japan)

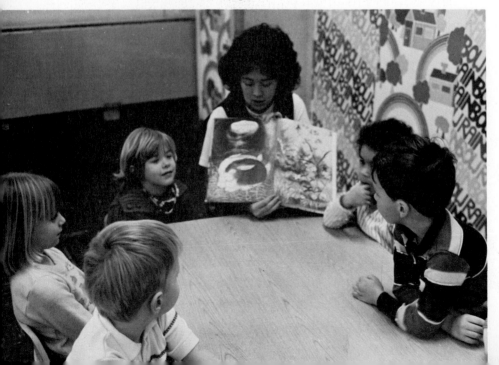

group. Gradually, as children mature, the groups can be combined. When there are a number of assistants in a group—aides, volunteers, cooperating parents, or students—it is especially sensible to use their help in order to divide the group for storytime. Even when the group remains together, the assistants should join the storytime. Their interest will encourage children's interest, and the assistants will become familiar with a situation they may be called on to take over in the future.

When the teacher really believes that there are books for every child, she or he will seek to interest every child in books. For one or two in the group it may mean an almost private story session.

Patty and Martha were examples of three-year-olds who could not tolerate a group storytime even in groups of four or five children. Patty was easily distracted. Martha wanted to sit directly in front of the book, which blocked others' view. These two found joy in books, however, when read to together. Sometimes they asked to hear several books that they had selected. Finally, at age four, they decided they would like to hear the story with the other children.

Patty and Martha could easily have become storytime distractors in the playhouse or at the puzzle shelf. But the teacher felt storytime too important to give up and sought a combination that would interest them. The tiny group was the solution. In thinking of Patty and Martha, one must note that they were three-year-olds. Their experience with storytime before coming to school had been of a warm sitting-on-the-lap variety with their parents. Teachers may have to carry some of this practice into the school. Even in understaffed schools, a nonteaching staff member might have been enlisted to read to Patty and Martha or to supervise as they listened to a story record. Community or student volunteers could provide valuable assistance with such children. When children cannot be enticed to storytime, their activity should not be distracting to the children who do want to take part. Time during the self-selected activity period can be used to encourage children like Patty and Martha to become interested in books.

Chairs or Floor for Storytime?

The choice between having children sit on chairs or the floor will be a personal one of the teacher's. Some like chairs because each child has a place and one does not block the view of another so easily. Others say chairs can become a distracting element—rocking back and forth—or that children on the ends of the circle may be slighted because they can't see the book and therefore lose interest.

Some teachers like to group the children on the floor, especially if it is carpeted. They feel this arrangement promotes a cozier, restful atmosphere. Rug sample "sit-upons" can provide individual places. Children should be able to relax and not be unduly cramped together.

The book or flannel board should be in good light so that the children can see the pictures. Pictures must be large enough to be seen by those in the back of the group. Some books are inappropriate for groups because the illustrations aren't clear from a distance. Children will readily become disinterested if they cannot see the pictures. Teachers should arrange the group so that the children don't face the glare of the windows. The teacher can sit on the floor or on a low chair, whichever makes it easier for all the children to see. It takes practice to hold a book so children can see and you can still read at the same time. That's only one reason why prior planning and careful reading of the book prior to storytime are so essential.

Transition to Storytime

Transitions or changes in activity can be made smoothly and with a minimum of fuss. When the children are expected to make such shifts in their routine, the teacher must first decide what behavior is desirable and plan accordingly. Where do the children go first? Which path do they use? Is the path clear of obstructions? Will the children have room or will they run into each other? Are there distracting elements on the way? Having studied the plan through, the teacher explains it to the children and helps them learn to follow it. A regular routine should be worked out so that the children can predict what will take place and what their role is. Given a general routine with room for individual differences, children will behave in appropriate ways with only a little practice. Other transition suggestions are presented in Chapter 5.

Each teacher will work out the transition to fit the group and room. To shift from snack to storytime, for example, it is common in some groups to have the children deposit snack dishes on a tray, then walk past a book rack and select books. They take the books to the corner of the room reserved for storytime. They relax and "read" their books to themselves, share them with a child sitting nearby, exchange them with others, or visit quietly until most of the group has arrived.

The teacher, too, relaxes while talking with children informally, commenting on pictures they are enjoying in their books, encouraging a child to find a picture of special interest, or just listening attentively.

When it appears that most children are through looking at their books, the teacher sings a song, which is the cue to pass the books to an assistant. The teacher immediately begins a series of finger plays, poems and songs. These activities are valuable for their literary and musical qualities and because they encourage children's attention and participation and help develop cohesiveness within the group. A discussion related to experiences that took place earlier in the day or about tomorrow's projects may be worked in around a wide selection of songs, poems, and finger plays. A finger play will quiet a group of fidgeting children quicker than nearly any technique, especially if the verse is begun in a quiet voice that makes children wonder what is taking place. Teachers can often use finger plays in place of saying "Shh!"

Finger plays are short poems with actions for the child to do while saying the words. The actions seem to help hold the child's attention. Teachers can encourage children to use finger plays creatively by adding new verses and motions. Hundreds of finger plays have been published in a variety of books, so the teacher has only to select those preferred and to memorize and use them frequently. *Let's Do Fingerplays* by Grayson[28] and *Wee Sing: Children's Songs and Fingerplays* by Beall and Nipp[29] are examples of books of finger plays available. A few finger plays with suggested actions are given at the end of this chapter.

Finger plays can be soothing or they can be rollicking. The teacher learns to sense which type is needed to set the mood. For example, if the children are getting ready to listen to a story, the choice would be a quiet finger play—not one that would cause the children to get up and clap. Clapping behavior would dispel the mood the teacher is trying to establish for the story. On the other hand, if the children have been listening quietly to a story, the teacher might choose a lively finger play to give them the cue that it is time for them to get up and become active again.

It is helpful to type new finger plays on index cards and carry them in a pocket in order to have them handy for these moments. Finger plays are simple enough so that children can be encouraged to "Remember to say this to your mommy tonight." Parents enjoy such samples of their child's learning.

Additional Tips for Storytime

The teacher who chooses a good story, perfects a technique, and plans a smooth transition between other activities and storytime still has some steps to take before completing a satisfactory group literature experience.

Once the group is ready, the teacher should proceed directly to the first sentence of the story. To tell young children about an author or discuss why the story is appropriate that day invites disruption of the listening mood the teacher has worked to establish. After a few pages it is sometimes possible to ask children why they think this story was cho-

[28] Marion F. Grayson, *Let's Do Fingerplays* (Washington, D.C.: Robert B. Luce, 1962).
[29] Pamela Conn Beall and Susan Hagen Nipp, *Wee Sing: Children's Songs and Fingerplays* (Los Angeles: Price/Stern/Sloan Publishers, Inc., 1984).

sen today. As for the author, after the book becomes a favorite—after many readings—the group might be interested in some interesting fact about the author.

Children will not automatically know the behavior that is expected at storytime unless the teacher teaches them gently and firmly. A good story experience will be sufficient reward. Eye contact with each child throughout the story helps each feel that the teacher is talking directly to her or him. The teacher's eyes keep moving from child to child. If a child appears to become distracted, the teacher's eyes resting on the child for a moment often is enough to draw attention back to the story. If a child seems about to become disruptive one can say, for example, "John, do you know what the old man said?" The child who is easily distracted can be invited to "Sit up here close to me, and I'll help you remember to be a good listener." Then touching a knee or shoulder can be a gentle reminder. Care should be taken to be sure the children understand that the place by the teacher is not a punishing seat—the offer is to "help," not punish. Also, a second adult who sits with the children is a great help in handling special problems that may arise. The teacher who is reading may then concentrate on holding the attention of the group.

Teachers develop skill in acknowledging a child's verbal contribution during storytime. One of the teacher's reasons for the choice of story is that it will have special meaning for the children. When this goal is successful, the children will be bubbling over with personal references stimulated by the story. This is good—just what the teacher wants. Yet only a limited number of children can be listened to before the group becomes impatient. They are egocentric. If they can't talk, too, and can't have the story, then they take things into their own hands. They may talk or even poke their neighbors. Sometimes the teacher's nod or smile will be sufficient recognition of a child's comment. Sometimes the teacher may pause to listen, then grasp the lead when the child pauses. Using a "secret sign" such as a nod, a wink, or a wave of the index finger that means, "Let's wait until we finish the story," will help quiet children. Of course, when the story is complete, the teacher must then hold a discussion, permitting the children to talk about the ideas in the story. Discussions, besides being excellent for language development, help the teacher correct misconceptions. Discussions help the teacher gain more understanding of individual children.

The Martin and Judy stories [30] are examples of stories that encourage personal identification. In such stories the teacher may read or tell awhile, then let the children talk about their experiences, and finally say, "Let's see how Martin and Judy worked it out." This statement helps regain their attention and the storytime can go on.

[30] Bayley, op. cit.

An old farmer said of the movies, "You gotta go to know if you shoulda gone." And so it is with storytime. The teacher's role is to lead children into an avenue of enjoyment. Then they will be happy to go to storytime each day.

Enhancing the Total Program Through Literature

Providing books to help answer questions children ask is an important way of fulfilling our major goal of helping children learn to love books. Information from books can be used to support a new concept in music as well as in science, sports, or geography. Some of the materials may have to be adapted by the teacher if they are prepared for adults or older children. "Let's look it up," can become an important attitude for young children to develop.

Reference books such as *The Golden Book Encyclopedia*,[31] *Illustrated Golden Dictionary for Young Readers*,[32] and others will help answer some of the children's questions. They should have a permanent place in the room. One group called such a collection "the important books."

Children's books may become obsolete, depicting technical or social concepts that are outdated. For examples, unless specifically designed to depict the historical, books about transportation and farming should be relatively new. Also, books indicating roles of boys and girls, and men and women, need careful scrutiny for sex-role stereotyping. Recent research indicates that many picture books and other books used in early elementary schools depict girls as weak characters in observer, nonaggressive roles, and boys are pictured as leaders and as characters having the most fun and curiosity.[33] Similarly, books showing children of ethnic groups other than white have been quite rare until recently. Also, a variety of family forms is beginning to appear in children's literature—divorced families, multiracial families, and extended families. Such books help children understand aspects of life that may at times be puzzling to them.

Teachers must put extra effort into selecting books with new information. In the interim they can develop some homemade books for their groups. For example, with the aid of magazine pictures and photo-

---

[31] *The Golden Book Encyclopedia*, 16 vols. (New York: Golden Press, 1959).

[32] Stuart Courtis and Gainette Walters, *Illustrated Golden Dictionary for Young Readers* (New York: Golden Press, 1965).

[33] For advice on choosing nonsexist literature, see *A Guide to Non-Sexist Children's Books* written by Judith Adell and Hilary Dole Klein (Chicago, Ill.: Academy Press Limited, 1976).

graphs, books can be made from heavy tagboard and notebook rings. Books with children from various ethnic groups can be made. There are several magazines devoted to black culture, and magazines from Mexico might be a source of pictures of persons of Latin heritage. Ethnic stereotypes should be avoided, such as the depicting of native Americans only in headdresses. It is important for a child of an ethnic group to have some literature depicting his or her group, and it is also important that the children of each group learn about children who have different cultural and ethnic backgrounds.[34]

Children's Own Stories

Children can learn that their own words make stories and even books. A trip or an interesting discovery can prompt a story. The children dictate, the teacher writes. Dictation can be done individually during the self-selected activity period or with the group during storytime. Sometimes the class can be divided into groups to write several stories.

Young children won't have patience enough for the teacher to print carefully as they dictate their story, so the teacher might take the dictation on a lined tablet and transcribe it later. Some version of shorthand to keep up with the flow of ideas may be needed. If two adults can work together, one can write while the other keeps the ideas coming and helps a child hold on to a thought until the writer gets it down. A tape recorder is very useful in these instances. When a lull comes in the contributions, the transcriber can read "the story so far." Then the children can be asked if they had other thoughts as they listened to their story. The story can be typed, posted on the bulletin board, and read at storytime the next day. A copy can be sent home to parents in a special booklet. The children will relive the event each time they hear the story.

Four-year-olds dictated the following story after a trip to see the train engine that is on exhibit on the Michigan State campus.

The five-year-olds dictated "The Turkey Farm" after a Thanksgiving trip to a local turkey farm. The story was duplicated and placed in their class booklet and later shared with their parents.

A picture book can be made of the story. Pages can be cut of cardboard and fastened with notebook rings. A few lines from the story can be lettered on each page. It can be illustrated with drawings, with magazine pictures, with pictures copied from books on a Xerox copier, or

---

[34] See *Cultural Awareness: A Resource Bibliography* by Velma E. Schmidt and Earldene McNeill (Washington, D.C.: The National Association for the Education of Young Children, 1978), and also see *Understanding the Multicultural Experience* by Olivia Saracho and Bernard Spodek (Washington, D.C.: National Association for the Education of Young Children, 1983) for suggestions for increasing the cultural richness of your curriculum.

THE TRAIN

Monday we went to explore the M.S.U. train.

It was as high as the ceiling. No! It was high like a house. There were big, big wheels. Everything was black.

We climbed tall stairs to get to the top.

We got to pull the train whistle rope. It was an old, old train and there was an old, old man. He helped us ring the bell. He was sixteen or seventeen.

It had a dark scary coal car behind it. It was a coal engine. I think it was a steam engine.

We sat in the driver's chair. We found where the brakes were.

We pulled the track switch thing. It was broke. The train was on tracks—that's how it goes.

It was fun to visit that train!

with photographs if available. Because the children are the authors, the book will be one of the most popular in the school.

Sometimes in place of a story the group dictates a thank-you letter to someone who has made a special event possible. An example follows. Mr. Caldwell was a police officer, and Prince was his trained police dog.

Dictating a letter or a story is a creative literature and language experience. Each child derives satisfaction from his or her contribution and will remember that contribution as the story is read and reread.

By recording children's expressions, one is readily impressed with the effects children achieve with language. When dictation is taken from children, care should be used to preserve their original and often charming phrases.

THE TURKEY FARM

At the turkey farm there were 5,000 turkeys. They were white turkeys and black turkeys. The girl turkeys were white and the boy turkeys were black. All the sick turkeys were in the back pens. Mary found a feather that was both black and white.

They fed the turkeys grain—it was maize.

The turkeys make loud noises—it was gobble gobble.

One was following me. Some got out. One of them flied! The teachers caught a turkey and let us pet him. It didn't scare me.

It smelled awful. It smelled like bacon. It smelled like chicken do-do-do—ugh!

It was fun to go to the turkey farm.

Dear Mr. Caldwell,

We liked your dog, Prince. Thank you for bringing him. We liked to see him climb up the slide and slide down it and climb over the boxes. We liked the commands you gave the dog. We liked to see him jump through the swing. His name sounds like "Prince Charming." We liked him to do everything. We liked to see you slide down the big slide. We liked to see him go up and down on the seesaw. We didn't know policemen and dogs went around at night playing on our seesaw!

Love,

The Kindergarten Children

The Library

The school's book collection should be given continuous attention. A sizable budget for new books should be available yearly to add new issues and replace worn-out books. Teachers should keep abreast of the new books coming out by reading reviews in *The Horn Book Magazine*,[35] *Childhood Education*,[36] *Young Children*,[37] and *Parents' Magazine*.[38] Booklets such as *Recommended Children's Books*, published by the *School Library Journal*,[39] and *Bibliography of Books for Children*, published by the Association for Childhood Education International,[40] provide information on both new and old recommended books.

Filing

A system of filing books in the school library should be developed. Some teachers like to color-code the binding of each book with colored plastic tape to designate the subject matter of the book. Books might be grouped according to interests, such as children, animals, transportation, and plants. Books also can be filed according to author. This method encourages the staff to become aware of the names of authors. In either case a cross-listing in an up-to-date card file will help new users find the

[35] *The Horn Book Magazine* (The Horn Book, Inc., 585 Boylston St., Boston, Mass.).

[36] *Childhood Education* (journal of The Association for Childhood Education International, 3615 Wisconsin Ave. N.W., Washington, D.C. 20016).

[37] *Young Children* (journal of the National Association for Education of Young Children, 1834 Connecticut Ave. N.W., Washington, D.C. 20009).

[38] *Parents' Magazine* (Parents' Magazine Enterprises, 52 Vanderbilt, New York, N.Y. 10017).

[39] *School Library Journal* (R. R. Bowker Co., 1180 Avenue of Americas, New York, N.Y. 10036).

[40] Association for Childhood Education International, 3615 Wisconsin Ave. N.W., Washington, D.C. 20016.

books they seek. The microcomputer greatly facilitates keeping the booklist up-to-date.

Books should be removed when they become unrepairable. Out-of-date books should be filed in a separate section to be referred to when they are needed for studies of "the olden days." Many picture books related to farming, housing, and transportation fall into this category now.

Repair

Books should be kept in good repair. If pages are torn, they encourage children's misuse. If pages are missing, the book should be replaced or discarded. Pictures from old books can be salvaged to make illustrations for flannel-board stories or homemade books. For the best book-mending materials, check with your local bookstore or librarian.

Inspiring and Assisting Parents' Participation in Literature Experiences

It is important for teachers to encourage parents to make contributions to children's literature experiences. The school cannot assume the total responsibility if maximum learning is desired. Even highly educated parents often need guidance in helping their children.

Teachers can help parents become enthusiastic about children's books. The reading attitudes of the adults in children's lives—whether parents, teachers, grandparents, baby-sitters, or librarians—will influence children's literature experiences and the pleasure they derive from them.

Whenever an opportunity arises, teachers can promptly suggest titles and authors of books on subjects of interest to parents. Suggestions on how books can be secured at the library or borrowed from the school's collection will be welcomed. Some parents need to know where the library is and how to get there, how many books they can check out, and how much the service costs.

* * *

Talk It Over: No. 3

Describe your earliest experience with using the library. What do you recall about the librarian? Were you encouraged to read by the librarian, parents, or others?

* * *

Figure 12-9. A check out stand for library books emphasizes the opportunity each child has to take books home. (Child Development Laboratory, Michigan State University)

Get Books into the Home

Without books at home the child cannot look at books as desired and, of course, parents cannot read to a child. The school can operate a lending library if it has the resources. For example, in one school paperback picture books were secured, covered with clear plastic adhesive to increase durability, and loaned to the children. A large mailing envelope was labeled with each child's name to provide a safe place for carrying and storing the book. A 5" x 7" card was made for each child and carried the name of the books checked out. At a glance the teacher had an indication of a child's interest in books. Each time the child returned a book, another was chosen. The staff felt that because paperback books were relatively inexpensive, the cost of lost books would not be formidable. In practice, no books were lost.

The teacher plans ways to encourage parents to use the public library with their children. The library habit is a good family habit even

346

for families who buy books. Of course, no family can buy the wealth of books available there. The library should become an enjoyable place to go. Then research assignments in later years won't hold so much dread for children.

If the school can introduce children to the library, they in turn can encourage reluctant parents to take them. Many public libraries have a story hour to which young children are invited. The teacher can give this information to parents, along with a personal endorsement. Parents can be encouraged to use the story hour as an opportunity to check out books for home use.

Both parents and children will find the children's librarians very hospitable. Their goal is to make people feel at home in the library and to make every effort to bring children and books together. One may notice that librarians often know children's names and their reading interests. The librarian will help search for whatever subject the child wants to read about.

* * *

Talk It Over: No. 4

Display, if available, and discuss books designed to help children understand topics such as divorce, adoption, new family styles, and so on. Identify characteristics and evaluate.

* * *

Buying Books

Buying books is another way for children to have them at home. Parents can be reassured that picture books can be enjoyed over and over and will eventually serve as practice reading material. Therefore the money used for books is well spent. Some schools purchase paperback books in quantity and maintain a bookstore where children can spend their allowance. Buying books is, of course, a good way for the child to spend his or her money.

Teachers can help parents buy books by ordering them through the school. Of course, handling money is not one of the teachers' favorite tasks, but the responsibility is sometimes assumed when it means getting books into the homes of children.

There are a number of book clubs that parents may ask about. Parents also seek advice when buying an encyclopedia. Teachers can help children by helping parents make the best decision regarding books to purchase.

Encourage Parents to Read to Children

It is enjoyable for the child if several family members take an interest in his or her picture books. Grandparents and siblings, as well as parents, can read to the child. Choices of books should include old favorites as well as new books that extend the child's knowledge.

Whoever reads should encourage the child to talk about the book. They can ask: "What was the dog's name? Who took the farmer's hat? How was Martin feeling? Why did the father say, that?" Such conversation helps the child think about what is heard and gives language practice. It strengthens the child's understanding and helps remembering, too. However, questions should not be carried on to the point that pure enjoyment of the story is lost.

During the latter months of kindergarten, parents may express the feeling that picture books are "old hat." This may be their impatience over wanting the child to begin reading. The teacher can suggest series books such as *"B" Is for Betsy* by Carolyn Haywood[41] or *Henry Huggins* by Beverly Cleary,[42] to be read on a chapter-a-night basis. Such books carry children into the school age and extend their experience with books.

Parents can be advised to continue to read to their child even after he or she starts reading. The mechanics of learning to read are laborious and often discouraging even to children who have enjoyed a rich background of literature and are highly motivated to learn to read. Of course, the beginning reader needs time to practice reading at home, but the parents can continue a diet of stimulating, exciting books until the laborious read-aloud stage is passed. Hearing books that are advanced beyond those the child can read will motivate the child laboring over those first primers. The parent can let the child gradually assume the reading role—perhaps at first on pages containing pictures. Or, the parent may read the narrative parts while the child reads the conversation. Such reading is also good practice for vocal inflections. Any method that gives the child reading practice, yet keeps the story moving, will help keep reading motivation high.

Conclusion

The most important goal for parents and teachers of young children is to start children on the road to a lifelong love of books. Teachers will use five important avenues for achieving this goal by providing

1. Early prereading experiences which will stimulate children's desire to learn to read,

---

[41] Carolyn Haywood, *"B" Is for Betsy* (New York: Harcourt, Brace & World, 1939).
[42] Beverly Cleary, *Henry Huggins* (New York: Morrow, 1953).

FINGER PLAYS AND BODY ACTION POEMS

Quiet Finger Plays

BUNNY
FINGER ACTIONS

There's nothing as soft as a
  bunny,
A wee little, soft little bunny.
He can hop on his toes,
And wiggle his nose,
And his powder puff tail
Is quite funny.

(One hand is an imaginary bunny
  being petted by the other
  hand.)
(Fingers hop).
(Hand on nose, wiggle it.)
(Move hand to rear to indicate
  tail.)

GRANDMA'S GLASSES

Here are grandma's glasses.
Here is grandma's hat.

Here's the way she folds her
  hands
And lays them in her lap.

(Fingers make glasses over eyes.)
(Two index fingers make pointed
  hat.)
(Fold hands and lay in lap.)

GRANDPA'S GLASSES

Grandpa lost his glasses,
Before he went to bed.
Guess where grandma found
  them?
Right on top of grandpa's head!

(Fingers make glasses over eyes.)

(Move glasses on top of head.)

THREE BALLS

Here's a ball

Here's a ball

Here's a great big ball.
Let's count them.
One, two, three.

(Make round shape with thumb
  and index finger.)
(Make round shape with two
  thumbs and two index fingers.)
(Make third ball with both arms.)
(Repeat for the count.)

TEN FINGERS

I have ten little fingers,
And they all belong to me.
I can make them do things.
Would you like to see?

I can shut them up tight
And open them wide.

(Extend fingers of both hands.)
(Point to self.)

(Make fists.)
(Spread fingers open.)

| I can put them together | (Clasp hands together.) |
| Or make them hide. | (Put hands behind back.) |

I can make them jump high.	(Raise hands high.)
I can make them jump low.	(Reach low.)
I can fold them quietly.	(Fold and lay hands in lap.)
And hold them just so.	

MY TURTLE

This is my turtle.	(Make fist and extend thumb.)
He lives in a shell.	(Indicate fist as shell.)
He likes his home very well.	
He pokes his head out when he wants to eat,	(Extend thumb and wiggle.)
And pulls it back in when he wants to sleep.	(Hide thumb in fist.)

MY EYE AND EAR

This is my eye.	(Cover one eye.)
This is my ear.	(Cover one ear.)
This is to see.	(Look around.)
And this is to hear.	(Cup hand around ear.)

BOISTEROUS FINGER PLAYS

MR. BULLFROG

Mr. Bullfrog sat on a big old rock.	(Fist with thumb up.)
Along came a little boy.	(Left hand walk.)
Mr. Bullfrog KERPLOP!	(Both hands slap knee.)

PIG

I had a little pig	(Fist with thumb up.)
And I fed it in a trough.	(Make cup of left hand.)
He got so big and fat,	(Make circle of arms.)
That his tail popped off!	(Clap both hands and knees.)
So, I got me a hammer	(One hand is hammer.)
And I got me a nail	(Hammer on thumb of other hand.)
And I made that pig	(Continue to hammer.)
A wooden tail!	

FIVE LITTLE ASTRONAUTS

| Five little astronauts | (Hold up fingers of one hand.) |
| Ready for outer-space. | |

The first one said,	(Hold up one finger.)
"Let's have a race."	
The second one said,	(Hold up two fingers.)
"The weather's too rough."	
The third one said,	(Hold up three fingers.)
"Oh don't be gruff."	
The fourth one said,	(Hold up four fingers.)
"I'm ready enough."	
The fifth one said,	(Hold up five fingers.)
"Let's Blast Off!"	
10, 9, 8, 7, 6, 5, 4, 3, 2, 1.	(Start with ten fingers and put one down with each number.)
BLAST OFF!!!	(Clap loudly with "Blast Off!")

FIREFIGHTERS

Ten little firefighters	(Lay all fingers out straight on knees or floor.)
Sleeping in a row.	
Ding-dong goes the bell	(Pretend to ring bell.)
Down the pole they go.	(Pretend to be sliding down pole.)
Jumping on the engine	
EE—RR—OOO	(Make siren noise.)
Putting out the fire.	(Pretend to use fire hoses.)
Then home so slow	
And back to bed again	(Lay all fingers in a row again.)
All in a row.	

LITTLE BUNNY

There was a little bunny	(Make ears over head with fingers.)
Who lived in the wood.	
He wiggled his ears.	(Wiggle fingers.)
As a good bunny should.	
He hopped by a squirrel,	(Fingers hop along arm or on floor.)
He hopped by a tree,	
He stared at the squirrel,	(Cock head and look.)
He stared at the tree,	
But he made faces at me!	(Wiggle nose.)

COUNTING

One, two, three, four,	(Extend fingers one at a time.)
Mary at the cottage door.	
Five, six, seven, eight,	(Change to say "cookies," "celery," or whatever the child is eating.)
Eating (cherries) off her plate.	

FIVE LITTLE BIRDS

Five little birds, high in a tree,	(Extend five fingers.)
The first one says, "What do I see?"	(Extend one finger.)
The second one says, "I see a street."	(Extend two fingers.)
The third one says, "I see seeds to eat."	(Extend three fingers.)
The fourth one says, "The seeds are wheat."	(Extend four fingers.)
The fifth one says, "Tweet, tweet, tweet."	(Extend five fingers.)

FIVE LITTLE HOT DOGS

Five little hot dogs frying in a pan.	(Extend five fingers.)
The grease got hot and one went BAM.	(Clap.)
Four little hot dogs frying in a pan.	(Extend four fingers.)
The grease got hot and another went Bam.	(Clap.)
Three little hot dogs frying in a pan.	(Extend three fingers.)
The grease got hot and another went Bam.	(Clap.)
Two little hot dogs frying in a pan.	(Extend two fingers.)
The grease got hot and another went Bam!	(Clap.)
One little hot dog frying in a pan.	(Extend one finger.)
The grease got hot and another went Bam!	(Clap.)
No little hot dogs frying in the pan.	(Make fist.)
The grease got hot and the pan went BAM!	(Clap loudly.)

I'M THE LITTLE HOT DOG

My father owns the butcher shop.	
My mother cuts the meat,	
And I'm the little Hot Dog	(Clap on "Hot Dog.")
That runs around the street.	

BABY BUMBLEBEE

I'm bringing home a baby bumblebee.	(Cup hand pretending to hold bee.)

Oh, won't my mommy be so
  proud of me?
I'm bringing home a baby
  bumblee.
Oops! He stung me!   (Toss hand excitedly.)

Moderately Active Finger Plays

FIVE LITTLE RABBITS

Five little rabbits	(Show five fingers.)
Under a log,	(Cover with other hand.)
One says, "Hark, I hear a dog!"	(Show one finger. Hand behind ear.)
One says, "Look, I see a man!"	(Point indicating eye.)
One says, "Run, as fast as you can."	(Make fingers run.)
One says, "Pooh, I'm not afraid."	(Thumbs in armpits.)
One says, "Shh, keep in the shade."	(Finger to lips.)
So they all lay still	(Five fingers under hand.)
Under a log,	
And the man passed by	
And so did the dog.	

FIVE LITTLE PUMPKINS

Five little pumpkins,	(Show five fingers.)
Sitting on a gate.	
The first one said,	(Show one finger.)
"It's getting late."	
The second one said,	(Show two fingers.)
"There are witches in the air."	
The third one said, "We don't care."	(Show three fingers.)
The fourth one said,	(Show four fingers.)
"Let's run, run, run."	
The fifth one said,	(Show five fingers.)
"Isn't Halloween fun?"	
"OOOOOOW" went the wind,	
And OUT went the light.	(Clap on "OUT.")
Those five little pumpkins	(Five fingers roll behind child.)
Rolled fast out of sight.	

HERE IS A BUNNY

Here is a bunny	(Fist with two fingers extended.)
With ears so funny,	
And here is his hole in the ground.	(Thumb and index finger.)

When a noise he hears,
He pricks up his ears   (Extend fingers quickly.)
And jumps in his hole in the   (Pretend to put bunny in hole.)
  ground.

TOUCH GAME

Touch your nose.   (Finger on nose.)
Touch your chin.   (Finger on chin.)
That's the way this game begins.
Touch your eyes.   (Fingers on eyes.)
Touch your knees.   (Fingers on knees.)
Now pretend you're going to   (Cover mouth with hand.)
  sneeze.
Touch one ear.   (Finger on ear.)
Touch two lips right here.   (Finger on lips.)
Touch your elbows where they   (Fingers on elbows—cross
  bend.   hands.)
That's the way this touch game
  ends.

ROBIN REDBREAST

Little Robin Redbreast   (Thumb and little finger
                                           extended.)

Sat upon a rail.
Niddle, noddle went his head   (Move thumb.)
And wiggle, waggle went his tail.   (Move little finger.)

Body Action Poems

DRESSING WARMLY

Let's put on our mittens   (Pretend to pull on mittens.)
And button up our coat.   (Pretend to button coat.)
Wrap a scarf snugly   (Pretend to tie scarf around
Around our throat.   neck.)

Pull on our boots,   (Pretend to pull up boots.)
Fasten the straps,   (Pretend to tighten straps on
And tie on tightly   boots.)
Our warm winter caps.   (Pretend to tie bow under chin.)

Then open the door   (Pretend to turn knob on door.)
And out we go   (Make fingers walk on floor if
Into the soft and feathery snow.   sitting or walk out door if
                                           standing.)

KEEPING DRY

Put up your umbrella   (Pretend to extend umbrella.)
To keep yourself dry;
Put up your umbrella,
There's rain in the sky.

Pitter, patter, pitter, patter,   (Make fingers tap on floor.)
Softly it falls.
Hurry home quickly
Before Mother calls.

WHIRLING TOP

I am a top, all wound up tight.   (Loop arms around knees while
                                   sitting.)
I whirl and whirl with all my   (Whirl around fast.)
  might.
And now the whirls are out of   (Whirl slowly.)
  me,
So I will rest as still can be.   (Come to rest.)

BOUNCE LIKE BALL

I'm bouncing, bouncing   (Children standing.)
  everywhere.
I bounce and bounce into the   (Jump up and down with
  air.   rhythm.)
I'm bouncing like a great big ball.
I bounce and bounce, then down   (Fall down in place.)
  I fall.

THE ELEPHANT

The elephant is so big and fat.   (Circle arms.)
He walks like this, he walks like (Walk.)
  that.
He has no fingers, he has no toes, (Point.)
But, oh my goodness, what a   (Swing arm low for trunk.)
  nose!

GARDENING

This is the way I plant my   (Bend down and dig.)
  garden—
Digging, digging in the ground.
The sun shines warm and bright   (Make circle with arms
  above it;   overhead.)
Gently the rain comes falling   (Tap like rain on hard surface.)
  down.

This is the way the small seeds open.	(Open hands slowly.)
Slowly the shoots begin to grow.	(Bending down, put up arm.)
These are my pretty garden flowers,	
Standing, standing in a row.	(Stand proudly and smiling.)

MY GARDEN

I dig, dig, dig,	(Pretend to dig in standing position.)
And I plant some seeds.	(Pretend to drop seeds in row.)
I rake, rake, rake.	(Pretend to rake.)
I pull some weeds.	(Pretend to pull weeds.)
I wait and watch,	(Look at ground.)
And soon I know	
I'll be here to watch	
My garden grow.	

MY RABBIT

My rabbit has two big ears	(Extend two fingers for bunny ears.)
And a funny little nose.	(Pat nose.)
He likes to nibble carrots	(Pretend to nibble.)
And he hops where'er he goes.	(Move hand, making fingers "hop," or if standing, hops on tiptoes.)

HAMMERING

Johnny pounds with one hammer,	(Pound palm with fist of other hands.)
One hammer, one hammer,	(Have one finger extended.)
Johnny pounds with one hammer,	
But Jimmy pounds with two.	(Have two fingers extended.)
Jimmy pounds with two hammers,	(Continue pounding palm.)
Two hammers, two hammers,	
Jimmy pounds with two hammers,	
But Betty pounds with three.	(Have three fingers extended.)

(Use children's names and continue up to five hammers.)

Note: All these finger plays and poems are by unknown authors.

2. Opportunities for children to get acquainted with, handle, and "read" a wide variety of high-quality children's literature;

3. Daily opportunities for each child to see, hear, and respond to well-prepared literature experiences;

4. Books and other written materials to enhance all components of the program, and

5. Inspiration and assistance to parents in order to involve them in their children's literature experiences.

Applications

1. Discuss the "Talk It Over" items found in the chapter.

2. Complete Lesson 12 in *A Laboratory Workbook for Introduction to Early Childhood Education*. Hand in as scheduled.

3. Write an activity plan for a literature activity for a few children using the sample plan in Chapter 6. Develop special aids for your story. (Be sure to try the plan out with only a few children before using it for a larger group.) Secure approval, carry out the plan, and evaluate the results from the children's point of view and from yours. Prepare a report and hand it in along with your approved activity plan.

4. Evaluate your total participation on your evaluation form developed in Chapter 1.

5. Add ideas and plans for literature activities to your Resource File.

Study Questions

1. Discuss literature activities and the developmental tasks.

2. Assume you are the lead teacher in a group of three- to six-year-olds, write a two-page statement for the children's parents stating your school's philosophy about teaching reading. Discuss your statement with other classmates.

3. State and explain the general guides for selecting literature for young children.

4. State and explain the value of using poetry with young children.

5. Describe storytime techniques and the purpose of using a number of different techniques.

6. Discuss the pros and cons of group size for storytime, seating arrangement, placement of lighting, requiring each child to have a storytime experience, and using the library.

7. Suggest several ways to encourage library use by families in your group.

8. Suggest several ways to encourage parental involvement with children and literature.

Films

The Lively Art of Picture Books   Color   57 minutes   1964

Depicts several classic children's books showing their illustrators and authors, especially Maurice Sendak, Robert McCloskey, and Barbara Cooney. Ezra Jack Keats' *Snowy Day* and McCloskey's *Time of Wonder* are shown in their entirety. Weston Woods Studio, Weston, Conn. 06883.

William's Doll   Color   18 minutes   1983

A film about sexism based on the classic book by the same name. Phoenix Films, Inc., 468 Park Avenue S., New York, N.Y. 10016.

What's a Good Book? Selecting Books for Children   Color   27 minutes   1983

The film can help teachers select literature for young children based on literary merit, children's interests, and personal judgment. Weston Woods Studio, Weston, Conn. 06883.

Additional Readings

ADELL, JUDITH, and HILARY DOLE KLEIN. *A Guide to Non-Sexist Children's Books.* Chicago: Academy Press Limited, 1976.

ARBUTHNOT, MAY HILL, and others (eds.). *Children's Books Too Good to Miss.* Cleveland, Ohio: Case Western Reserve, 1971.

BEALL, PAMELA CONN, and SUSAN HAGEN NIPP. *Wee Sing: Children's Songs and Fingerplays.* Los Angeles: Price/Stern/Sloan Publishers, Inc., 1984.

BROWN, JANET F. (ed.). *Curriculum Planning for Young Children.* Washington, D.C.: National Association for the Education of Young Children, 1982.

CIANCIOLO, PATRICIA JEAN (ed.). *Picture Books for Children.* Chicago: American Library Association, 1981.

DE REGNIERS, BEATRICE, and others (eds.). *Poems Children Will Sit Still for.* New York: Scholastic Book Services, 1969.

ELLIS, MARY JACKSON. *Finger Playtime.* Minneapolis: T. S. Denison and Co., Inc., 1960.

GRAYSON, MARION F. *Let's Do Fingerplays.* Washington, D.C.: Robert B. Luce, Inc., 1962.

GRIFFIN, LOUISE (ed.). *Multi-Ethnic Books for Young Children.* Washington, D.C.: The National Association for the Education of Young Children, 1970.

LARRICK, NANCY. *A Parent's Guide to Children's Reading.* Philadelphia: Westminster, 1983.

MARTIN, BILL, JR. *Language and Literature: The Human Connection.* Washington, D.C.: Department of Elementary-Kindergarten-Nursery Educators, NEA, 1967.

MEIGS, CORNELIA, ANN T. EATON, ELIZABETH NESBITT and RUTH HILL VIGUERS, *A Critical History of Children's Literature.* New York: Macmillan Publishing, Inc., 1969.

SCHMIDT, VELMA E., and EARLDENE MCNEILL, *Cultural Awareness: A Re-*

source Bibliography. Washington, D.C.: The National Association for the Education of Young Children, 1978.

TRESSELT, ALVIN, "Books and Beyond." *Childhood Education,* Vol. 51, No. 5, March 1975, pp. 261–266.

WATT, LOIS, "Children's Literature," *200 Years of Children,* Edith H. Grotberg (ed.). Washington, D.C.: U.S. Department of Health, Education, and Welfare, 1977, pp. 323–388.

WEISER, MARGARET. *Group Care and Education of Infants and Toddlers.* St. Louis: The C. V. Mosby Company, 1982.

Dramatic Play Activities

- *To relate developmental tasks to dramatic play activities.*
- *To explain why children like dramatic play activities.*
- *To explain how careful observation of dramatic play helps teachers understand children.*
- *To identify, describe, and evaluate dramatic play activities for early childhood schools.*

Jim busily arranged the empty food boxes and egg trays on the shelves in the four-year-old's "store." He turned all the cash registers away except one. He stood behind it expectantly.

Nancy walked into the "store." "How much are the eggs?" she asked.

"Two dollars," replied Jim. Nancy started away with the egg container. "No, you didn't pay me." Jim said. He altered his voice slightly and continued, "Pretend to pay me." Nancy complied.

"You know why I have to use this big register all alone? Because my helpers aren't here today," explained Jim.

He tried to talk Nancy into buying more items. He said, "These are my secret sauce. These are my secret peaches." Nancy chose an assortment and paid him. "Thank you," said Jim giving her the change. He wanted to do some more business, but Nancy left the store.

"Let's pretend it's ten more days from now," Jim called over the divider that separated "store" from "house." It worked. Nancy returned and took some more groceries.

"Hey, you didn't give me any money and I didn't give you any money." Nancy was leaving and made no move to come back. Jim put his hand out in front of him and pretended to get the money. Then he closed up shop and went to the housekeeping area to join Nancy.

Figure 13-1. "Are you ready to ride?" asks the cowboy. A donated saddle on a wooden horse offers many hours of dramatic play. (Family Life Center, Georgia Southern University, Statesboro)

Figure 13-2. "We're goin' fishin'," sing the children. Fishing is a popular activity in a boat that really rocks and is large enough for several children and even the teacher. The boat is suspended by chains attached to poles anchored in cement. (Family Life Center, Georgia Southern College, Statesboro)

Nancy started out for the "store." Hating to see her go, Jim said, "No, the store closes at four o'clock and it's four o'clock now."

Nancy said, "But, I'm going to the other store," and left.

"Oh," said Jim, "I wonder where wife has gone now."

Dramatic Play: Defined

Scenes like the one played by Jim and Nancy are common among young children. From their front-row seats teachers and parents are privileged to attend children's first performances as they step out on life's stage. No written lines are needed. Few props are called for. The child can be alone or with others when feelings and ideas—real and imagined—spill out in *spontaneous role-playing* called *dramatic play.*

Dramatic play is the champagne of the under-six set. It gives the sparkle to home, school, or wherever children gather. Children are actors without stage fright. They perform as expertly to an empty barn as to a full house. They say what they feel and feel what they say. They unashamedly use erroneous conceptions and unintentional puns. Creativity abounds. Children ride a plank "horse," eat sand "cakes," and drink water "beer" without apology for their realism. If adults have sensitive ears, eyes, and hearts, they may be moved from deepest anguish to poetic ecstasy or be entertained by rollicking slapstick.

Values of Dramatic Play

Contributing to All Developmental Tasks

All areas of a child's growth can be stimulated by dramatic play. Briefly, dramatic play contributes to development of the cognitive, physical, creative, social, and emotional components of the child's being.

Cognitive Development

Children's dramatic roles expand as their world broadens. They integrate concepts from every area into the imaginative play that develops. They wonder, question, and experiment. This active role helps develop the depth needed to make concepts their own. While selecting roles and props, children learn to make choices. They make decisions beginning with whether or not to join an activity. Language skills, so crucial to concept formation, are called for and practiced in dramatic play. The example in the introduction to this chapter illustrates this fact.

Physical Development

It is a rare child who needs encouragement to exercise. Given space, equipment, and a friend or two, activity involving exercise naturally occurs. Many dramatic roles require fast, rugged action. Good health and physical stamina are fostered.

Creative Development

Original thoughts, words, and deeds spill out effortlessly in dramatic play. "Pretend to pay me," said Jim. "Pretend I'm a gorilla," says a petite blond, and for a while she is a gorilla. Children on these untrod paths find new (to them) ways to do things, new things to do, and new uses for old objects—all creative discoveries.

Social Development

In dramatic play the child develops a concept of his or her own sex role. Numerous social roles are tried out and increase the depth of understanding of many other roles. The child begins integrating the rules of society. Often one hears a child admonish friends who forget the rules. A conscience is developing.

In Chapter 3 the stages of social play were discussed in relation to children of different ages. During dramatic play you may observe a toddler pretending to give the doll a bottle while playing alone. That is *solitary play*. Later as a three-year-old the child may feed the doll while playing side by side with another child in an episode of *parallel play*. The children do the same thing with the same equipment at about the same time. Finally, at ages four and five the plot will thicken as *cooperative play* is used to integrate fathers, siblings, and others in a network of baby care, housework, and, perhaps, even a fire with a fire truck arriving with full siren to add excitement. The latter play is possible when children have extensive language or symbolic thinking skills. They become increasingly creative and spontaneous in their dramatic play. You will see examples of these stages of dramatic play as you move from one age group to another. There will be some overlap because the divisions are not sharp.

Emotional Development

The full range of feelings is expressed and experienced as the child plays with others in dramatic play. The child knows joy and sorrow, affection and rejection, anger and pleasure, satisfaction and dissatisfaction. The child learns to know what it means to have feelings.

"If we want to get closer to the truth we must look deeper into the reasons for our behavior," said Virginia Axline, a child psychologist.[1]

---

[1] Virginia M. Axline, *Dibs: In Search of Self* (Boston: Houghton Mifflin, 1964), p. 8. Dibs was first observed by nursery school teachers who after a period of concern called in the psychologist for consultation. This is a report of the author's work with Dibs in play therapy. It is such a moving account that teachers everywhere should read it.

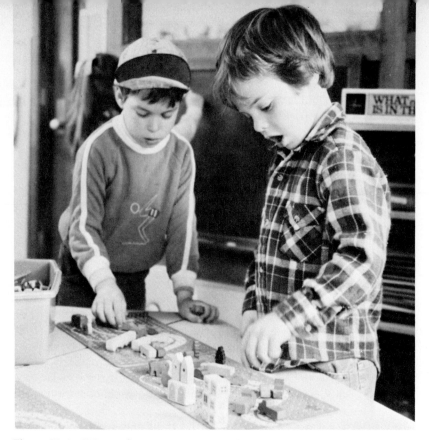

Figure 13-3. "Here's the station," says one boy. "I'm bringing in the train," says his friend as they use the small manipulatives in dramatic play. (Child Development Laboratory, Michigan State University)

Therapists such as Axline use the technique of play therapy, which includes spontaneous dramatic play, for discovering the source of a child's emotional disturbance. Axline explains, "We are seeking understanding, believing that understanding will lead us to the threshold of more effective ways of helping the person to develop and utilize his capacities more constructively."[2]

Theoretical Explanations

During play with other children, children learn morals, sex roles, and social roles. Early childhood is a period of importance for this learning. By using different theories you can gain different perspectives on play, especially dramatic play. For example, the psychoanalytic theorists like Freud and Erikson believe young children have sexual fantasies, that they have guilt feelings which result from some inner feelings and thoughts.

[2] Ibid., p. 9.

Children eventually develop a superego which contributes to the development of moral codes.

The behaviorists believe that moral codes and sex roles are learned because of the way parents and others reward children for appropriate behavior or punish them for inappropriate behavior. Social learning theorists, on the other hand, believe that these learnings come as children observe those around them. Parents are important models in early childhood. Children are imitating their parents and other significant persons, according to social learning theory. Cognitive theorists focus on the child's ability to reason. Of course, children in early education programs are too egocentric to understand another person's point of view. Most children must be in their fourth or fifth year before they understand right and wrong, and know that they can't change their sex by putting on clothes of the opposite sex.

Each of these approaches adds a dimension to understanding dramatic play. A fascinating study is to record an episode of children's play, then analyze it according to several of the theoretical approaches. None gives a complete answer; thus professionals will continue to puzzle over the meanings of children's behavior. It is wise to avoid hard-and-fast conclusions from a few samples of children's dramatic play.

Figure 13-4. "Hey, get on our train," says the engineer turning the steering wheel. The make-believe train consisted of a steering wheel and the frame of the water table. (Child Development Laboratory, Michigan State University)

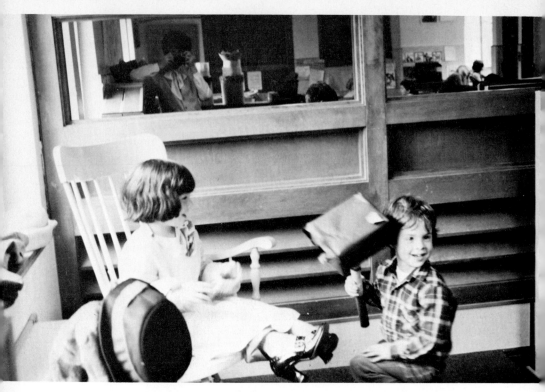

Figure 13-5. "Smile," commands the cameraman using a pretend camera following a visit of a cameraman to the school. (Child Development Laboratory, Michigan State University)

Satisfying to the Child

What are satisfactions that children derive from dramatic play? In the first place, they have a good time. Having fun is a strong motivator for young children. If they can have fun, they will willingly go along with most other goals the adult has for them.

In the second place, they make friends. They can choose companions and be chosen. Friendships grow out of a mutuality of interests and needs. When children are old enough for early childhood schools, companions their own age become increasingly important. Most children are drawn to children of their own age.

Third, each has an opportunity to learn. Children are anxious to learn. They see their friends doing something and want to try it. They imitate their actions and their speech. Imitation is a great teacher. Children don't always tackle the easy. Dramatic play encourages them to do better, climb higher, and become smarter than before. Dramatic play offers children an informal opportunity to pit themselves against new ideas and against their peers.

Fourth, by trying out various roles, the child comes to understand herself or himself better. A role repeated frequently can be considered to have special significance for the child.

Fifth, dramatic play offers the child the opportunity to release the natural abundance of energy each possesses. Children thrive on action. While awake, most are busily on the move. Freedom to keep moving and talking, which is allowed during dramatic play, permits the child to play as that energy level dictates.

* * *

Talk It Over: No. 1

Describe roles you've seen children playing out in dramatic play. Give children's ages and tell what you think the play meant for the children.

* * *

Observing Aids Understanding Children

Teachers and parents too seek ways to understand children and thus to promote their development more effectively. Dramatic play, whether it occurs at home or at school, can give insights into the behavior of

Figure 13-6. "Hey! My doll can hold its own bottle. I think that's funny!" exclaimed the kindergartner in the housekeeping corner. (Zukeran Kindergarten, Kadena Air Base, Okinawa, Japan)

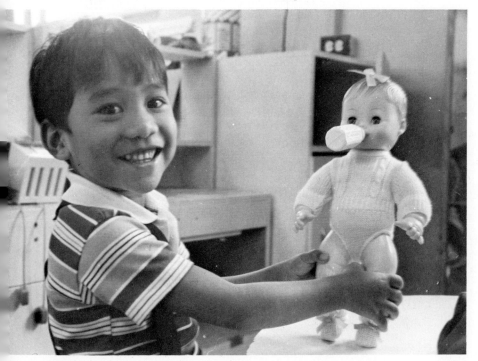

children. While the "normal" children usually enrolled in early childhood schools do not have such deep-seated problems as those requiring play therapy, they may, nevertheless, have problems that could make them candidates for therapy should those problems continue unresolved. Teachers may have occasion to recommend therapy for a child after observing him or her for some time at school.[3]

Teachers should observe children's dramatic play carefully. Through a system of periodic observing and note taking, teachers develop evidence for decisions.

What can teachers learn from such observation? They will note the recurring themes and the roles the child plays. They will know if a certain child seldom participates in dramatic play. Notes will show what he or she does instead. If a child is thought of as typically happy, or cross, or hostile, the teacher notes whether one type of incident or a particular group situation invites this typical behavior.

In a typical classroom certain children will require more adult guidance than others. Observing helps the teacher determine at what point guidance is called for with such children. For example, a child may strike out each time the teacher asks him or her to wait for attention. By observing this pattern in operation, the adults can make a concerted effort to satisfy needs for attention in some satisfactory way before the child acts out. Observation will show certain children who never cause trouble. What are they doing? Notes often point out children who seem hungry or ill or who lack physical stamina.

The teacher seeking answers will observe and listen. What questions do the children ask? What concepts are they using? What misconceptions do they have? Who are the leaders? What characteristics do the leaders have in common? Do some children enter groups easily? What techniques do they use? The answer to these questions may give the teacher a clue as to how to help a child who has difficulty entering groups.

The teacher looks at all behavior, not just negative or troublesome behavior. The positive relationships observed will build confidence that all children can learn to relate to their friends and use their blossoming intellects creatively.

Helping a Child Solve Personal Problems

The teacher's focus will be on recurring themes in a child's relationships instead of on isolated incidents. A few examples of teachers' action follow.

The teacher helps build up the child's feelings of self-confidence—a positive self-concept. If children reveal that they feel little and helpless,

[3] Ibid., Chapter 1.

the teacher seeks ways to help them feel bigger and stronger. If they reveal that they feel left out, ways are sought to help them feel included and wanted. If one reveals that big brothers are bossing him or her around, the teacher can accept his or her bossing in school, protecting only those children who can't protect themselves. If a child teases, the teacher notes whom and when the child teases and searches to understand why teasing seems satisfying.

A child may reveal certain fears through dramatic play or that family relationships are difficult. The teacher helps get feelings out in the open. The child can talk to the teacher and play out feelings with puppets or small figures. The teacher may read a story that initiates a discussion of the problem. Or, an endeavor to help the child through the parents is made.

It is not uncommon to observe a young child playing the role of the opposite sex during dramatic play. That is, a boy selects women's clothing or a girl selects men's clothing for dramatic roles. Much of this play is natural curiosity about the roles of the opposite sex. The teacher, through close observation, can attempt to determine the significance of the behavior. Is the child merely trying out a role? How frequently does the play occur? Why does the child seem to prefer the role? What is the child's place in the total group? Does the role reversal give him or her unusual attention from adults and children? What is the home situation? Do the parents accept the child's real sex role?

The teacher's role when dealing with children who frequently play the role of the opposite sex is first to be certain that the dress-up closet contains many interesting men's as well as women's clothing. Helpers are advised to avoid giving undue attention to a child who dresses in this manner and to seek to show attention at other times. One can talk to individual children and the group about their various "pretend" roles to help them differentiate real from pretend.

Consulting Parents

Teachers have an obligation to alert parents to a child's problems. Teachers are not doctors or therapists and should avoid giving the impression they are. Observations should be made carefully, then thought given as to how to present the observation to parents. Naturally parents are very protective of their child and also very sensitive about their own parenting. If blamed, they can be expected to react negatively and defensively. Thus teachers need to learn how to state observations of problem behavior in a tentative manner as "this is what we've seen at school." Parents can be encouraged to do their own observations or to discuss behavior they may have noticed already. Things to try can be suggested.

If a child has difficulty relating to others, the teacher may encourage the parents to provide a companion for her or him. Children who ride together in car pools often have their plans made when they get to school, so teachers may suggest a car pool to parents whose child is on the outside of the social groups. The teacher may suggest that they regularly invite one of the classmates home for a visit. The teacher may carefully pair this child with a child whose similar interests make her or him a prospective friend.

The teacher, who observes that a child seems consistently tired or listless, confers with the parents and may suggest a medical examination. If the child appears hungry, the teacher offers snack early and checks with the parents to learn about mealtimes at home.

Teachers can watch for physical complications. For example, if children breathe through the mouth and are unusually loud in their eating, they may have enlarged tonsils and adenoids. Need for corrective shoes may be revealed as children are observed running across a wide expanse. The teacher encourages the parents to consult a specialist when such problems are observed.

Referrals to Outside Professionals

After doing some careful observations over time, the teacher will have consulted the school's internal professional sources for advice on a child's problem. Teachers should be frank to admit when problems are beyond their training and experience, or when they lack time for dealing with a child with special problems. When referring parents to outside professionals, the teacher should check the agency or clinic to be certain that the service parents might be seeking is available. It is difficult for parents to go from agency to agency and tell their child's problem. Then the teacher and parents should meet in a private conference where each can understand the other's concern and where a plan of action for the benefit of the child can be developed. The teacher can offer to follow through with a plan a therapist helps design that can appropriately be carried out in an early childhood program.

* * *

Talk It Over: No. 2

Discuss concerns you have regarding talking to parents about a child's problem behavior. How do you think parents feel?

* * *

Planning for Dramatic Play

In planning for dramatic play, the teacher takes into consideration the group of children and the developmental tasks confronting each one. The teacher considers their age and their previous experiences at home, at school, and in the community. First plans are tentative. The plans are firmed up as the teacher gets better acquainted with the group. He or she encourages spontaneous themes to develop, and willingly discards ideas that seem insignificant at a given time or for a given group. Plans include introducing numerous concepts and reinforcing learning through dramatic play. Frequently the teacher selects the specific ideas from the questions the children initiate, realizing that children will only be able to represent roles that they have observed. For example, children who have never been to a restaurant won't know how a waiter acts. Most could play McDonald's hamburger stand, however.

A rich, coordinated program is planned to open new vistas that children can incorporate into their dramatic play. Special visitors, trips, movies, pictures, books, and science discoveries are included in the curriculum plan. The plan, however, is more of a housecoat than a straitjacket.

Teacher's Role

The teacher must be a friendly, open, spontaneous, and creative person with many strengths that keep his or her personality on an even keel, even when emergencies arise. Deep personal regard for each child, which is conveyed openly and often, helps the children feel at ease in the teacher's presence.

Teachers must support dramatic play continuously if its values are to be realized. Just because the children are playing happily is no reason for the teacher to complete office tasks or make a trip to the principal's office. Measures that prevent problems are more effective than mopping-up procedures. When the class is operating smoothly is the best time to record the positive examples that will sustain the teacher in moments of discouragement. Moreover, activities should be enriched and extended at every opportunity. The teacher who keeps close to the children, observing and listening to them, can more meaningfully plan the highly motivating, worthwhile program that each child deserves.

Atmosphere

The teacher establishes an atmosphere conducive to meaningful creative dramatic play. There is an air of freedom that the children sense. They seem to be like the old slave who got his freedom after the Civil War. Someone asked him if he wasn't as well off under slavery. He was reminded that he had the same master, the same food, and the same bed. He replied, "Yes, except there is a looseness about this freedom that I like."

There is a "looseness" in the early childhood school that allows for spontaneous, impromptu, original, and different things to take place. There is a steady hum of talking, laughing, and learning as the children work individually and in small groups.

Time

Time is required for dramatic play to develop and for themes to be carried to satisfying conclusions. If the daily schedule is interspersed with many teacher-instigated activities, the children may find little opportunity to develop an idea before the teacher calls them to another circle. In such classrooms dramatic play soon withers.

In most schools dramatic play takes place during indoor and outdoor self-selected activity periods. If such play is to flourish, a minimum of 30 minutes, but preferably about 50 minutes, will be needed for the self-selected activity period. The teacher keeps the schedule flexible. For example, if the children have worked hard on getting a "train" ready for an imaginary trip, the teacher allows them to take at least one ride before announcing that it is cleanup time. On the other hand, if the train trip if over and the children seem at loose ends for a new activity, the teacher may decide that it is a good time to clean up even though the clock doesn't quite say so. The teacher warns the children when a transition is approaching, thus encouraging them to bring their activities to a close.

Space

Space is a requirement for dramatic play. Children need space to move around. Several areas of the room and yard can contain opportunities for dramatic play. Such areas are the work tables, the housekeeping area, the block area, the music area, the literature area, the woodworking area, and the outdoor area, which includes climbing areas, digging, wheel toys, and perhaps materials typically kept indoors. Having several areas provides alternative activities should congestion occur in one area.

Limits

Limits are defined, discussed, and maintained without punishment or harshness. Only those limits necessary to protect children, the learning environment, and property are set. Limits help children feel secure. Dramatic play should not become a free-for-all.

Talk It Over: No. 3

Observe several children in dramatic play. Record what is said and done, what roles are played. What props were used? Did children improvise or make props? What theory can you use to understand these roles?

Suggested Props for Dramatic Play Themes

The following materials and equipment are suggested for enriching and extending the roles children play. Props are placed where they will be noticed by the children. They are stored so that the children can find them readily and are kept orderly to suggest constructive creative play and not disorganized destruction.

Dress-Up

Both men's and women's clothing should be available. Castoff clothing makes good "dress-ups." Rummage sales are good sources of these materials. Children seem to be attracted to texture. Things of velveteen, satin, or fur are favorites. The crinoline petticoats of a bygone era are considered extremely elegant, especially when worn as "wedding dresses." Hats, purses, shoes, boots, and costume jewelry are popular items.

Big brother's shirts, sport coats, Scout uniforms, vests, boots, and shoes are a better size for young children than are dad's. Hats for some community helpers—firefighters, police officers, bus drivers—can be purchased from school supply catalogs. Farmers' and cowboys' hats are available in variety stores. The metal hat of the lineman is popular and can be purchased in hardware stores. Painters' hats are often free at paint stores.

Long circle skirts encourage role-playing and creative dancing. A group would like a number of these, which can be made by a seamstress. She can use a simple waist pattern that fits the largest child, then cut an ankle-length circle skirt to fit the waist. A zipper should be placed in the front to make self-dressing easier. You can alter women's old skirts for self-dressing by putting elastic in the waistband or sewing velcro on the opening.

Other popular costumes that can be made by a seamstress are clown, drum major, bunny, doctor, and nurse outfits. Children like bright colors in their dress-up clothes. They should be made of lightweight material because children wear them over clothing and easily get over-heated.

"Dress-ups" should be stored so that they present a suggestive array from which children can choose and so that clothes stay in good condition. If clothes are stuffed into a trunk or a box, a chaotic disorder results that is not part of constructive learning. An open cupboard built at the children's level using regular coat hangers is one type of storage. Pegs may also be used. In most cases, some adult help will be necessary at cleanup time. Dress-up clothing should be laundered regularly. A good-quality, full-length mirror is indispensable in the dress-up area.

Housekeeping

The housekeeping area or playhouse is perhaps the most common dramatic play area. This seems logical because the first roles the child assumes are family roles. Household routines and relationships affect young children very directly. They become alert to the people and the activities of the home. In the following example, roles are carefully assigned and played.

Five-year-olds are playing in the housekeeping area. They begin building another room along the playroom wall outside the housekeeping area. They use chairs to enclose their room. They move a number of toys into the "new house." The three girls wear dress-up clothing. Susie is Mother, Ruth the baby, and Cindy a small child. Mark is the father. Baby says to Mother, "Pretend you came in and saw a baby." Mother pats Baby on the head and then says, "Now, Baby, you can get up. Your daddy is coming home." Father enters. Mother says, "Honey, will you put this toy in the box over there?" Father does as requested. The small child enters and starts to go out again. Mother commands, "Come back. Come back. Here, take this," giving the small child a toy. She then says, "Now you sit there and play until time to eat."

Furnishing the housekeeping area can be quite simple or very elegant, depending on ideas and financing. Staff and parents who have ingenuity and skill with tools can furnish the area at little cost. Old tables can be cut down, cupboards can be made with wood and cardboard boxes. Stove grills can be painted on one end of a box. The cushion from a car's back seat can be purchased at a salvage yard and used as an upholstered sofa or a child-size bed.

Durable dolls of various sizes and colors should be available. Dolls with molded hair are more durable and withstand the countless baths better than those with fabric hair. Doll clothes should be made so that children can manage the buttons and zippers. Slip-on pants and skirts can be made with elastic belts and are good for those children who are interested in undressing and dressing dolls.

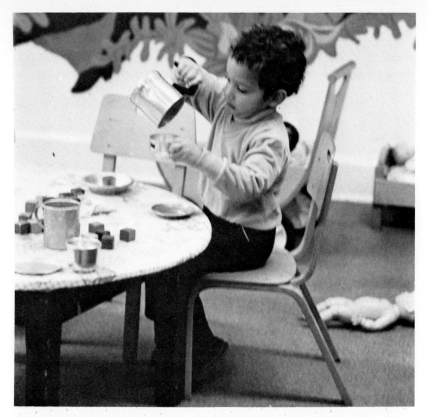

Figure 13-7. "I'm pouring some tea. I already have some cake," explains the child who uses blocks for cake. (Early Childhood Laboratory, Kansas State University)

Other furnishings are small dishes, pots and pans, silverware, several telephones, mop, broom, and carpet sweeper. A doll carriage, a bed, and a small rocker are popular. A small chest of drawers for the doll clothes is important. A few food tins, cereal boxes, and a milk carton or two can be added.

The children can be very helpful in putting the materials away each day. However, the teacher should check before their arrival to be sure the area is clean and tidy. Materials should be washed as needed and dangerous broken pieces disposed of or repaired. To make the area inviting or to stimulate its use, the teacher may place a doll in the high chair and set out the baby food. Little parents take over from there.

If children want to use water or play dough in the housekeeping area, the teacher must establish limits. These materials do add to the realism. However, if the teacher finds the mess excessive, the children can be asked to use water and play dough elsewhere and to "just pretend" in the playhouse.

The housekeeping area should be rearranged occasionally to stimulate the play. Changing the location in the room may bring it to the attention of a child who hasn't played there before. For example, when the housekeeping area is close to the large block area, the two areas may supplement each other, and the children will move back and forth between a block structure and the housekeeping area. Some of the housekeeping equipment may be moved to equip a block house or may be moved outdoors to help extend the role-playing to the yard.

In a study where the block and housekeeping areas were joined, researchers found an enhancement of social and play experiences, particularly of girls and younger children.[4]

Beauty Shop and Barbershop

The following materials invite beauty shop and barbershop play: A long mirror or several smaller ones, curlers, combs, a safety razor without the blade, whipped soap flakes for "shaving cream," and an old electric shaver. "Hairdryers" can be made of round commercial ice cream cartons obtained at an ice cream parlor or supermarket. The carton is taped to a yardstick, then taped to the back of a small chair and set against the wall for support. Don't forget a stack of magazines or books nearby!

After beauty–barber shop play, dip the tools in disinfectant. Avoid this play altogether if the children have infections on the scalp.

Restaurant

During various cooking projects—making pancakes, hamburgers, or pizzas—the housekeeping area can become a restaurant or a drive-in. Menus can be posted. Tablecloths can be made out of bright cloth. A cash register operator handles the money. Boys like Jim may like the play. He announced that he was the "cook" and this was his "restaurant." He methodically took orders. He indicated several times that a cook's role was acceptable for a boy in a restaurant but not in a house. The teacher took the opportunity during this role-playing to discuss with Jim that some men cook at home. This was an effort to broaden his view of sex roles.

Store

With a few shelves built of planks and blocks, a cash register, paper sacks, pencils, and note pads, children will enter into store play. A collection of grocery cartons and cans suggests a grocery store. The hats

[4] Cheryl A. Kinsman and Laura E. Berk, "Joining the Block and Housekeeping Areas: Changes in Play and Social Behavior," *Young Children*, 35:1 (November 1979), p. 74.

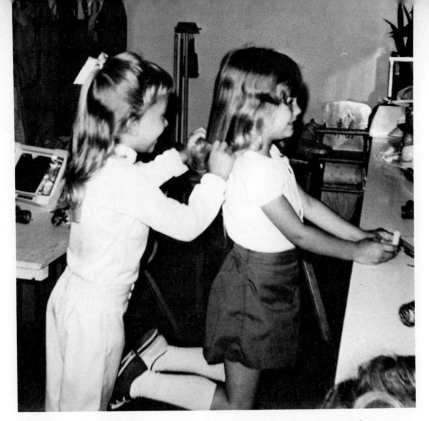

Figure 13-8. "I'm putting the curler in your hair," says one young beautician to a customer in the ever-popular beauty shop play. (Child Development Laboratory, Louisiana State University)

from the dress-up area change it to a hat store. Shoes make it a shoe store. Play is enriched by trips to a supermarket or a department store.

Office

An old typewriter (provided free by some business machine companies), telephones, tables, and chairs will be sufficient furniture for the office. It is interesting to note children's concept of an office. In one group where even a number of the children's mothers had offices, the children first used such equipment for a "doctor's office." They altered the teacher's initial arrangement by bringing in a bed from the housekeeping area. They searched for the stethoscopes. After several days of playing "doctor," they thought of using the space as the parent's office. However, the roles they played were themselves. They indicated that the crayons and paper had to be available. Drawing seems to be the child's pastime when he or she visits a parent's office.

The typewriter is a very popular piece of equipment and probably should have a permanent place in the classroom because of its impor-

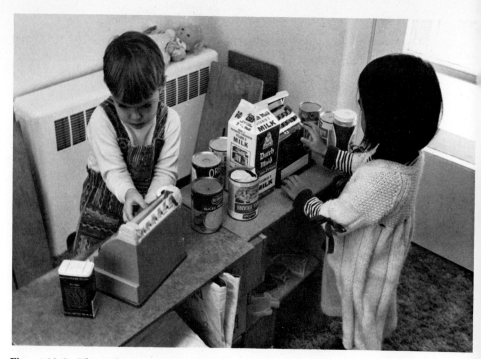

Figure 13-9. The cash register is an important attraction in the make-believe grocery. At other times they sell items such as shoes, hats, purses, books, or jewelry. (Early Childhood Laboratory, Kansas State University)

tance to modern living. A microcomputer in the classroom may offer a similar opportunity for role-playing.

Post Office

Post-office play naturally follows the mailing of a letter to a friend or the posting of valentines. A schoolbag can be the mail carrier's satchel. A cardboard box can be painted to resemble the mailboxes the children see along the street. A collection of old holiday cards or inexpensive envelopes for the children to address provides mail.

A letter can be mailed to each child to prove that the postal system works. But if you give children stamps to put on their letters, many will lick off the glue, so be prepared with the glue bottle to help finish the job. A visit to the post office and a talk with the postal clerk will add realism to the play.

Miniatures

Small figures of people, animals, cars, and trucks also contribute to dramatic play. Children are the manipulators of the scene, moving the figures around and speaking for them. Small blocks and construction toys may supplement the play. A model house of a size suitable for the people figures prompts domestic dramas.

Block Area

Both boys and girls will develop a variety of dramatic play themes in the block area. Using the large hollow blocks, children design space in which they function as actors. After one group built a room using these blocks, they all got inside and completely closed themselves in by placing a wheeled cart with a wire mesh side in front of the door. One boy said, "We are all in jail." His friends replied, "I knew we shouldn't have robbed."

During a period of reruns of "The Lone Ranger" on television, five-year-olds began building "horses" out of the large blocks. They stood three blocks upright, then stacked three lengthwise on top of the first three. They made a "neck" and a "head" with smaller blocks and finished their "Hi Ho Silver" with a tail of colored plastic scribble-sticks tucked into a crevice of the blocks in the appropriate place. They mounted

Figure 13-10. The large hollow blocks which enclose a pretend sleeper are very versatile for dramatic play. (Child Care Center, San Antonio College)

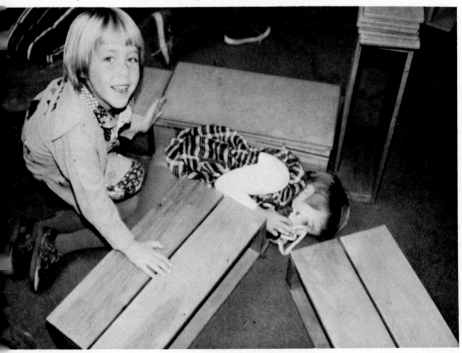

their horses and called, "I'll meet you at Ransom Canyon." (Ransom Canyon was a local picnic spot.)

The large hollow blocks and packing boxes are free of detail and therefore allow the imagination free reign. They are very strong and will hold numerous children at play. See Chapter 10 for other details regarding block play.

Auxiliary toys add to block play. A mounted steering wheel suggests the building of a car, a bus, a train, or an airplane. Models of domestic animals suggest a farm and wild animals a zoo. Cars, trucks, and trains encourage road building. Housekeeping toys, especially telephones, are popular in the block area.

In the following example economic information is combined with building, the child with the broader experience leading the way. Later on during a discussion the teacher could let Bill explain more about his ideas.

Four boys finished building a tunnel through which they could drive their cars, trains, and trucks. Everyone was lined up to make the grand entrance into the tunnel. Bill said, "We forgot one thing." Jack said, "What's that?" Bill replied, "We forgot to put someone at the start to collect money from everyone." Jeff responded, "What?" Bill explained, "Yes, to help pay for building the tunnel." Jack hurried to the art table to get paper to make money.

Firefighters

A trip to the fire station, a fire in the neighborhood, or even a fire engine screaming past the school will often stimulate firefighter play.

With a little help children can make their own firefighter's hat. Using two sheets of a double-paged newspaper (30″ × 23″), fold it along its original lengthwise fold. Bring the upper right and upper left corners together at the center line to make the usual three-cornered hat. (See Figure 13-11.) About 3 inches remain to turn up for the brim. Staple the brim to the hat body. Turn in one corner to the center peak and staple it in place. This leaves the other long corner to go down the back. These hats may be painted.

The newspaper hats or commercial plastic firefighter's hats team up with hoses, ladders, and red wagons when the children play out their helping roles, complete with sound effects.

Gas Station

Wheel toy "cars," of course, need gasoline. A large hollow block can become the gas pump if a piece of garden hose is attached to it. A plastic nozzle that comes with cleaning liquid can be attached to the hose.

Direction: Use a double
sheet of 30" x 23" news-
paper.
Step 1. Fold corners to
center.

Step 2. Fold up brim making a three-cornered
hat. Staple brim and folds in place.

Step 3. Fold one corner
under toward the peak.
Hats may be painted.

Figure 13-11. Making paper firefighter's hats.

During warm weather the children can carry out a car-wash idea by washing the wheel toys. A few pairs of pliers and screwdrivers will foster mechanics play. Visits to a gas station, a garage, or a car wash will interest the young drivers.

Television

A window cut in a large cardboard box can serve as a TV screen. A few cereal boxes will encourage TV commercials. Puppets and musical instruments may invite performances. A few chairs or cushions can be arranged for the audience. A trip to a television studio will foster this play.

Camping

Camping has become a popular family experience. A small tent erected in the yard will provide the children many opportunities for camp-related play. A sheet can be draped over equipment when no tent is available. Suitcases and fishing poles might be added.

Fishing

The children can simulate fishing by tying string to a stick. Magnets can be added to the string. If paper clips are attached to paper or plastic fish or to the creepy crawlers made with liquid plastic kits, the children will enjoy their fishing. With this same setup, the children can "fish" numbers, colors, or the lotto cards out of a box. The paper clips should be securely attached to avoid a safety problem with very young children.

Farm

Farm play is popular in rural neighborhoods. For city children, concepts learned on a trip to the farm can be reinforced through dramatic play. Models of domestic animals and farm machinery are available. Barns can be constructed out of boxes. Hay bales can be added to the yard to roll around, to walk on, and to hide behind.

For young cowboys an old saddle mounted on a wooden sawhorse makes exciting riding. Because guns do not contribute positively to the goals for the child's development, the school usually does not provide such accessories. In fact, teachers usually have rules against using any toy as a gun, and guns that are brought to school are kept in the teacher's office for safekeeping.

Construction

Construction play is fostered when road graders, bulldozers, trucks, and shovels are provided. Digging can take place in the sandbox or other digging area. Construction and road building are particularly popular when children can see construction taking place in their neighborhood. Children like to get inside large cardboard boxes that have been opened at both ends. They roll around the yard and may be called "bulldozers" by young workers.

Transportation

Youngsters' imaginations can transform ordinary packing boxes into a train. One plank across another becomes an airplane. A boat or the skeleton of an old car can be placed in the yard for the little drivers. These should be kept well painted to avoid a junk-yard appearance in the yard. Traffic signs can be added to extend the play.

Space Exploration

Space exploration intrigues even the youngest. A large refrigerator carton can become the rocket that blasts off after the countdown. With the teacher's help, opaque plastic milk jugs can be cut to resemble space helmets and large grocery bags can be made into temporary space suits by cutting out holes for the head and arms.

Conclusion

Dramatic play is the spontaneous, imaginative role-playing taking place in schools for young children during the self-selected activity period.

Dramatic play is a valuable activity because it contributes to the child's growth in all developmental areas; it affords adults an opportunity to gain insight into children's inner thoughts and feelings; and it affords teachers the opportunity to help children with some of the problems they might be having.

Children find dramatic play satisfying because they can have fun with their friends in meaningful, energy-releasing activities. Creativity is encouraged, and children enjoy learning about themselves by playing out numerous roles.

Planning is required to reap the benefits possible from dramatic play. An atmosphere of freedom is established by a teacher who is alert, warm, and responsive. Time and space are required and necessary limits must be set. An interesting array of materials and equipment will stimulate a variety of dramatic play themes.

Applications

1. Discuss the "Talk It Over" items found in the chapter.
2. Complete Lesson 13 in *A Laboratory Workbook for Introduction to Early Childhood Education*. Hand in as scheduled.
3. Write an activity plan for a dramatic play activity for a few children using information and the sample plan (Figure 6-1) in Chapter 6. Secure approval, carry out the plan, and evaluate the results from the children's point of view and your viewpoint. Prepare a report and hand it in along with your approved plan.
4. Evaluate your total participation performance on your evaluation form developed in Chapter 1.
5. Add ideas and plans for dramatic play activities to your Resource File.

Study Questions

1. Define dramatic play.
2. Explain how dramatic play contributes to children's development.
3. Explain why children find dramatic play satisfying.
4. Explain how observation of dramatic play can help teachers understand children. What theories are helpful? Does any theory tell the whole story?
5. Describe ways teachers can go about helping children with personal problems which are revealed through dramatic play.
6. State some precautions to be taken when preparing to discuss a child's problems with his or her parents.
7. Describe planning for dramatic play, especially the teacher's role, time and space allocation, and setting limits on behavior.
8. Describe typical dramatic play themes and the appropriate props for each.

Film

Dramatic Play . . . An Integrative Process for Learning   Color 32 minutes   1973

Focuses on the intellectual, social, and emotional learning in dramatic play and the strategies used by the children in dealing with individuals and materials. Campus Film Distributors, Corp., P.O. Box 206, 14 Madison Ave., Valhalla, N.Y. 10595.

Additional Readings

ANKER, DOROTHY, et al. "Teaching Children as They Play." *Young Children*, Vol. 29, No. 4, May 1974, pp. 203–213.

AXLINE, VIRGINIA M. *Dibs: In Search of Self*. New York: Ballantine, 1976.

COHEN, DOROTHY H., and VIRGINIA STERN. *Observing and Recording the Behavior of Young Children*. New York: Teachers College Press, Columbia University, 1978.

ENGSTROM, GEORGIANNA (ed.). *Play: The Child Strives Toward Self Realization*. Washington, D.C.: The National Association for the Education of Young Children, 1971.

HIRSCH, ELIZABETH S. *The Block Book*. Washington, D.C.: National Association for the Education of Young Children, 1984.

LEEPER, SARAH H., et al. *Good Schools for Young Children*. New York: Macmillan Publishing Co., Inc., 1984.

SCARFE, N. V. "Play Is Education," in *Early Childhood: Crucial Years of Learning*, Margaret Rasmussen (ed.). Washington, D.C.: Association for Childhood Education International, 1966.

SCHULMAN, ANN SHAAKER. *Absorbed in Living Children Learn*. Washington, D.C.: National Association for the Education of Young Children, 1967.

SMILANSKY, SARA. *The Effects of Sociodramatic Play on Disadvantaged Preschool Children*. New York: John Wiley & Sons, 1968.

SPONSELLER, DORIS (ed.). *Play as a Learning Medium*. Washington, D.C.: National Association for the Education of Young Children, 1974.

Creative
Music
Activities

- To explain why children enjoy music activities in the early childhood school.
- To relate creative music activities to developmental tasks.
- To identify teachers' resources for increasing their abilities for planning and carrying out music activities with young children.
- To identify, describe, and evaluate musical and movement activities for early childhood schools.

JENNIE JENKINS

Will you wear red,
O my dear, o my dear?
O will you wear red,
Jennie Jenkins?
I won't wear red,
It's the color of my head,
I'll buy me a fol-de-rol-dy
Til-dy-tol-dy seek-a-double roll
Jennie Jenkins roll. (1)[1]

Thus sang the kindergarten teacher introducing a new song. As the chorus ended, the children clapped and called, "Sing it again, teacher, sing it again." The teacher knew then that they liked the song and continued with other verses, using black, brown, blue, and green in place of red. The children picked up the rhythm and began clapping. They caught the repeat and chimed in on "roll Jennie Jenkins roll." The teacher

[1] Each song is given a number the first time it is mentioned. By referring to the end of the chapter, the reader can locate a book containing the music for that song.

Figure 14-1. "Put your finger on your nose, on your nose," sing the children and teacher. Small groups make responding to individual children easier. (Child Development Laboratory, University of Idaho)

sang a verse using "pink," they rhymed it with "stink" and laughed hilariously!

"Jennie Jenkins" became a favorite. The song would go on and on for as many verses as there were children present. They felt each must have a chance to choose a color before the teacher was permitted to terminate the song. Children liked to stump the teacher by choosing such variations as "aqua" and "striped" that were hard to rhyme.

Enjoying Music

Why was "Jennie Jenkins" a children's favorite? In the first place it has a catchy rhythm—a toe-tapping tempo that stays with you for a long time. It has a familiar element—colors—which each got a turn to name. "Jennie Jenkins" also has freshness—a surprise of nonsense words that especially tickle the funny bones of five-year-olds. But most of all, the

387

children simply enjoyed the song—the most important reason for singing it in the kindergarten.

Children are natural musicians. Their feeling for music begins early. Baby's first movements are rhythmical—two feet kicking, two hands waving. The infant experiments with different tones while crying and babbling—long before the ability to speak develops.

Singing and dancing are creative arts. The emphasis in the school for young children is on the child's enjoyment of musical expression rather than on any particular outcome. Though the teacher may start with words or a tune that is well known, creativity is encouraged by permitting the children to interpret the music in their own way, responding with new rhythms and words. This same emphasis on the process rather than on the product is suggested for all areas of learning.

Children can be musically creative, and teachers and parents should get as much fun out of their original tunes and dances as they do out of their original sayings. No one says a child lacks talent when sentences aren't adultlike, so is it fair to say the child lacks talent when tunes aren't the same as those of adults? Children do make many original composi-

Figure 14-2. "Yes, it's a string. This is a bow. The cello sounds like this," says the musician demonstrating the instrument. Such first hand experience makes the activity more interesting and more informative. (Hoeflin Stone House Child Care Center, Kansas State University)

tions that are a result of experimenting with sounds, rhythm, and singing.

Music can occur at any time of day. It happens at work time, cleanup time, outdoor time, and at dressing and undressing time. Children compose songs, chants, and dances. In an atmosphere of freedom and trust the child will express moods in spontaneous music.

The goal is to introduce music to children so that their lives will be richer. Music gives them another medium through which they can express their thoughts and feelings. Enjoyment is the first requirement. Any demand for perfection has no place at this young age. Care must be taken so music is not subverted, that is, used to upgrade deficiencies or learn concepts in a way that robs the child of an enjoyment of music.

Of course, there were some secondary values offered by "Jennie Jenkins" and other songs. By practicing the feel of words on the speech and hearing organs, children had a chance to say and hear words, rhymes, and sounds. They learned by rote, challenging their memory. Color concepts were introduced. Taking turns was required and practiced. Each of these values is important, but none is important enough for the teacher to sing the song if it does not bring joy to the children.

Planning Music Experiences

Goals

Planning is required if children are to enjoy music, have a medium for expressing their thoughts and feelings, and lead richer lives because of their introduction to music. Just as is true of other areas of the curriculum, achieving the above goals requires meaningful music experiences that will not result from haphazard teaching. Music for these years is an action art—as opposed to a spectator art or a performing art. The young child should have an opportunity to become personally involved in music, moving, trying various expressions, using no patterns, and receiving neither coercion nor criticism.

Supporting Developmental Tasks

Most of the developmental tasks of early childhood (see Chapter 2) are supported through creative music activities—independence, motor and language practice, social relations, following directions, and learning concepts including self-concept and body awareness.

Planning musical activities logically focuses on the children's developmental level and their prior experiences. Even the youngest infants are delighted with music. Singing to them readily gets their attention and often stops them from crying. Toddlers readily respond to rhythm records and like to march around a table and fall down at the end of the song.

Resources

The teacher must discover what the children know and how they feel about music. The resources can be surveyed—the teacher's personal musical skills and knowledge; also, those of the school, the families, and the community. The teacher remains open to ideas that encourage creativity in the children. Planning requires sitting down regularly to evaluate what is being done and to decide on new experiences to provide in the future.

Search for Ideas

Teachers must search constantly for ideas for music experiences. Those teachers with a music background have many advantages, of course, because they can play or sing a new song or play an accompaniment for dancing without much effort. But a teacher without formal music training can also "have music wherever she goes." To these latter teachers much of the following will be most relevant, for there are ways for teachers to compensate for lack of formal music training. Some of the best musical experiences for children are provided in groups in which the teacher's formal training in music is almost nonexistent. The secret lies in opening up the teacher's creativity and overcoming a lack of self-confidence.

Most adults know many songs that can be used with young children. The way to find out whether this statement is true of you is to make a list of songs you know. Start humming to yourself right now. Remember those old nursery songs your parents or grandparents sang? Or the camp songs for Scouts? How about hymns? Folk tunes? School songs? Popular songs? There you have six categories for your list. Add to it daily. Turn through songbooks, listen to records. You'll find a tape recorder useful for learning new song material from parents or other teachers. Before you know it, you'll have a much longer repertoire than you might believe was possible.

* * *

Talk It Over: No. 1

Before reading further, write down the titles of songs you've sung since childhood. Add others as you read on. Share your list with your class-

Figure 14-3. Popular songs with children are those that encourage the child to move the body or its parts. (Kuwae Preschool, Kadena Air Force Base, Okinawa, Japan)

mates and add to your own list as you recognize songs they know that you also know.

* * *

Get used to singing out on those songs on your list. Work at remembering tunes. Try picking up the tune in the middle of a song. Share a song that you know but have never seen in print with members of your class. Or maybe you remember a tune to which classmates can supply words.

You have songs on your list that you think aren't appropriate for young children. But wait. If you've remembered the tune for many years, it must have special holding power. Could you use the tune and adapt words to it?

An example of an adapted song is the old hymn, "Jacob's Ladder" (2). Using that tune and part of the words you can sing:

> John is climbing up the ladder,
> John is climbing up the ladder,
> John is climbing up the ladder,
> Reaching up so high.

Of course, once you start this, several children may want you to sing them up the jungle gym. You can also give John advice—musically, such as:

> John is holding very tight,
> John is holding very tight,
> John is holding very tight,
> As he climbs a way up high.

Have you heard the song, "Goodnight, Irene" (3) that the Weavers sang years ago? You could sing it at rest time merely by inserting each child's name where "Irene" appears in the song. Or you could use it outdoors when you want to help a child.

> Come here, Millicent,
> Come here, Millicent,
> Come here, Millicent,
> Come here, Millicent,
> I want to tie your bow.

Teachers should feel at complete liberty to adapt any song to their needs. Creativity is the word. It's fun for the teacher. The children will love it too. For example, here's the way "Old Roger Is Dead" (4) was adapted:

We Came to Our School

> We came to our school and we painted with paints,
> Painted with paints, painted with paints,
> We came to our school and we painted with paints,
> It was so much fun!

The teacher points to a child as the last phrase is sung, and the child comes up with the next activity phrase, i.e., we climbed on the jungle gym, we played in the dollhouse, we built with the blocks, etc.

* * *

Talk It Over: No. 2

Hum a tune that comes to mind. Think of a task at school. Now, put the tune and phrases common to the task together. Try it several times to your own work, then try it with children. Is it fun?

* * *

Use Records to Learn Songs

Children's records can be used to help teachers learn new material to teach. By listening to the record and writing down the words, you can learn quickly. You might like to take the record home and sing as you get supper ready or do your homework. Of course, you could simply use the record, having the children sing along with it. However a record often interferes with adapting songs to individual children or with adapting a song to the special needs of a group—such as giving them time to stand up, or to laugh about the words. You might not like the pitch or the tempo of the record. Having to operate the record player may also interfere with spontaneity. But the biggest drawback yet may be that the record is a crutch that teachers rely on when they could very well go it alone. Records can interfere with creativity—both yours and the children's.

Of course, records have an important place. After you've learned a song from one, put it out on the listening shelf; you'll get a response like this one from Johnny, who heard "Do-Re-Mi" (5) from *The Sound of Music*. He was overjoyed. He ran to Susie, his teacher, and pulled her to the music corner, "That's the song you taught us! We know that song. Teacher, I found our song. Listen!"

Children like to hear their favorite over and over. A familiar song is like an old friend that it's nice to run into. Therefore, teachers need not worry about using song material that some other teacher might use later on. Children will enjoy the song later if they like it now.

Trust Your Ability

Also teachers should apply the principle of enjoyment to themselves as well as to the children. They should never try to teach a song or use a record they don't enjoy. In the first place, there is such an abundance of good material, why do it? Second, the children will sense a teacher's lukewarm attitude, so they won't enjoy it either.

Many adults lack faith in their musical ability. Perhaps this is because the modern world is flooded with music via recordings, concerts, and television. It's probably because they have never been encouraged to think of themselves as musical. But even when you think you can't carry a tune you can still help children find joy in music. Children are uncritical and readily respond to a teacher's effort. Their response will be rewarding and encouraging. With repeated successes the teacher's confidence grows.

A common concern for students is, "But I have to sing in front of my supervising teacher." What they may not realize is that the teacher went through the same conflicts when in training and is likely to be the least critical of all. The demonstration teacher knows that children will respond with joy to music if adequate opportunities are being planned for them—even when the leader has stage fright.

Some nonmusician teachers feel embarrassed because they don't play an instrument. However, most songs that are suitable for young children can be sung without the piano. Rhythms too are possible without the piano.

Talk It Over: No. 3

Discuss among your classmates and with your supervising teacher your feelings regarding singing with children. Make suggestions for having trust in your ability to sing with children and enjoy it.

Using Instruments

When the piano is used for children's singing, it often overshadows the children's voices, so that neither they nor the teacher can hear them. Children may get lazy or become distracted by watching the pianist. Unskilled pianists are often slaves to the printed music and become flustered over deviations. Often they cannot watch the children and play; therefore a barrier exists between the teacher and the children. However, a mirror attached to the piano enables the teacher partially to overcome this barrier. Also, unless the pianist can transpose, the song may be played in a key that is suitable to neither the teacher nor the children.

On the other hand, an accompanist who can play by ear or one who follows the children rather than leads can be a great help at music time. Unfortunately, this talent is rare. Therefore teachers can plan to sing unaccompanied or try the chording instruments that will be discussed.

The guitar makes a delightful accompaniment for children's songs. Its simple chords need not overshadow the children's voices. Even though it is large, the children will want to have a chance to strum and test the tones resulting from changing the finger position on the strings. Many books of children's songs have chords marked that are suitable for piano, guitar, or autoharp. The teacher needs only to play a few chords because it is best to keep the harmonies simple. In some songs only one chord is required for the entire song. See Figure 14-4 for the chords commonly used in children's songs.

A baritone ukulele is a melodious instrument that teachers find relatively easy to learn to play. Children call it a "guitar" because its size is about the same proportion to them that a guitar is to an adult. In areas where western and folk music are popular this instrument will contribute to role-playing as well as to music. Because the baritone uke strings are tuned the same as the highest four strings of the guitar, any music showing guitar chords can be played. See Figure 14-4 for chord diagrams.

An autoharp is a popular instrument for schoolrooms. It is held on the lap or in the arms; therefore it easily goes to singing time either indoors or out. The autoharp has preset chords, so the player has only to push the lever to play the desired chord. A fifteen-chord autoharp offers

Figure 14-4. Chord chart.

the teacher the most variations. When the teacher wishes to use the autoharp during singing time, it is well to have it out during self-selected activity periods. Children will get their turn for experimenting. If they feel satisfied, the teacher can say at singing time, "It is my turn now to use the autoharp." The autoharp, like any instrument, should be kept tuned. If necessary, the teacher may ask a music store or a musician to tune the autoharp. Guitar and piano chords can be played on the autoharp.

Singing

Singing can occur spontaneously in both children and teachers. Singing also occurs through the systematic introduction of songs at a regular group time.

New Songs

Though repetition is necessary for learning, variety is the spice of life in schools for young children as elsewhere. Because every song the teacher presents will not appeal equally to all children, the teacher provides va-

Figure 14-5. "Teacher, I played Jingle Bells," exclaims a young musician while experimenting with the autoharp. (Hoeflin Stone House Child Care Center, Kansas State University)

riety in hopes of touching every child. It's important to bring new material to them every week; then no one song gets overworked until someone cries, "Not that again!" Because it takes several hearings before children will be able to sing a song, they should have a number of songs in various stages of learning.

The teacher keeps up a constant search for new songs. Some songs can relate to concepts being developed with the children. For example, as each season is studied, a number of songs are found that reinforce those concepts, let children practice the new vocabulary, and encourage them to express their feelings about the season. At the same time, songs related to their other interests are included, as well as nonsense songs and old favorite nursery songs.

One place to discover song material is to listen to the children. They often sing a song from home, television, or records that would be fun for the group. Children's records and songbooks will offer many suggestions. The nonmusician who needs help learning new songs can find songs in books and then locate them on records. Students and teachers often teach each other songs. Teachers make notes of songs they hear. Simply writing the words down helps them remember songs. The words help locate the song in a book or on a record.

New songs may be introduced as a story, or they may first be sung at the art or science table in the presence of only a few children. Because songs can accurately describe concepts, they may be used in this way. Having sung the song in a small group, children may want to hear it again during singing time.

If you are a student teacher, you will want to learn to manage the singing time without your teacher's help. Managing the children and handling discipline will be up to you. If the teacher feels required to step in to help you, it will be difficult for you to regain the children's attention. Therefore you must go to singing time with the confidence that your planning has been sufficient to carry you through.

Planning is very significant. It may look so easy and natural when your teacher leads singing—but she or he plans too. Your control of the group begins as you plan, long before you sit before the group. Make a list of songs that the children might request—those the teacher has taught them. Do you know all the words? If not, write them down and learn them. Make a list of the songs you expect to teach. On index cards type the words to new songs and note the tune if the words are adapted from something familiar. Notes will help you keep from forgetting. They will offer suggestions when you feel "blank." Forgetting is easy when you have had many things to consider, watch for, and remember, as teachers do at singing time.

Sit with the children on the floor or on a small chair. The piano stool is too far away for an intimate singing time to develop.

Look at each child as you sing. Smile so they know you enjoy singing with them. Shift quickly from a familiar song to a finger play, to a new song. Pick up cues from the children so that you move with the group instead of pushing against what they want to do. More than anything, have fun singing with the group and you'll find the children listening, singing, and responding. Discipline will be no problem.

Teaching a New Song

Sing a new song straight through at normal speed—just as you hope the children will learn to sing it. Let them catch the song's flavor. Don't exaggerate any part. If the song is short, sing it several times so the children get familiar with the ideas and the repeats. Don't ask them if they want to hear it again, for someone will surely say "No." Just sing. By the time it has been sung this way several times, the children will be chiming in. Don't wear it out though, and don't dissect it—singing it a line at a time. This destroys the whole effect of the song. The next day repeat the same procedure. This time you can specifically invite the children to help you sing. By the third day many of your group will be beginning to sing. You will be able to tell whether they are going to like the song. If they fail to respond after three or four days, this indicates that the song apparently isn't for them at this time. Save that song until later. A song worth singing doesn't need to be pushed onto children.

Choice of Songs

Children are attracted by action songs. Such songs give them a way to participate with their hands and sometimes their whole bodies. The actions will attract some children who may do the actions long before they sing many of the words. Clapping can accompany some songs that don't suggest other actions.

Content of Songs

Elements of familiarity are important in songs. The teacher searches for songs about things the children know, i.e., children, animals, bugs, snow, wind, space flight, etc. However, the teacher does not explain a song word for word but lets most of the song's meaning come to the children as they sing and as they experience their world. If a song has a catchy melody in a suitable range, children will sing it with gusto even if they do not understand it entirely. Their renditions of hymns and patriotic songs offer humorous examples of this fact. The range from middle C to D, a ninth above, is appropriate for kindergarten, with middle C to A being better for young children who are learning to sing.

Concepts the children are learning can be the subjects of songs, but teachers should keep in mind that children must also enjoy these songs. By singing a new word, children receive a kinesthetic or sensory experience in the speech and hearing organs from which other understandings can grow. Of course, a counting song combined with pointing to objects—fingers or children—will help a child learn numbers. The teacher sings "Mary Wore a Red Dress" (10); Mary stands up, and John sees her red dress and his color concepts are improved. If the children enjoy singing the ABC's to the tune of "Twinkle Twinkle Little Star" (11), there's no harm done and they get the kinesthetic experience necessary

---

ACTION SONGS

EENCY WEENCY SPIDER (6)

Eency weency spider went up the water spout,
Down came the rain and washed the spider out,
Out came the sun and dried up all the rain,
And the eency weency spider went up the spout again.

(Actions: Use fingers to imitate spider going up. Wiggle fingers to give rain effect, encircle face with hands for the sun, and make the spider climb again.)

Where Is Thumbkin?

(Tune "Frère Jacques," or "Are You Sleeping?") (7)

	ACTIONS
Where is Thumbkin?	(Hands behind back.)
Where is Thumbkin?	
Here I am.	(Bring hands out, thumbs
Here I am.	extended.)
Howdy-do dy day sir?	(One thumb bows to other.)
Very well I thank you,	(Other thumb bows in return.)
Run away, run away.	(Return behind child.)

Other verses: Pointer, middle, ring finger, and little finger. (The last two are difficult for small children to extend but they like to try.)

The Wheels of the Bus

(Tune: "Mulberry Bush") (8)

	ACTIONS
The wheels on the bus (car)	(Children roll hands around each
Go round and round,	other.)
Round and round,	
Round and round,	
The wheels on the bus	
Go round and round	
All over town.	

Other verses:	Money goes clink	(Short claps.)
	Wipers go swish	(Fingers go back and forth.)
	Horn goes beep	(Pretend to honk.)
	Babies go waa	(Pretend to cry.)

If You're Happy and You Know It (9)

If you're happy and you know it,
Clap your hands (clap clap).
If you're happy and you know it,
Clap your hands (clap clap).
If you're happy and you know it,
Then your smile will surely show it.
If you're happy and you know it,
Clap your hands (clap clap).

Other verses: Pat your head (pat pat); Toot your horn (toot toot); Touch your nose (tap tap).

SONGS ADAPTED TO TEACH CONCEPTS

COLOR SONG

(Tune: "Pawpaw Patch") (12)

Children wearing red, please stand up.
Children wearing red, please stand up.
Children wearing red, please stand up.
So we can see your colors.

Note: The song continues designating the colors the children know, introducing new colors, and at the same time letting each child stand at least once.

DO YOU KNOW?

(Tune: "Muffin Man") (13)

Do you know the firefighters,
   the firefighters,
   the firefighters?
Do you know the firefighters
   who drive a big red truck?

Oh, yes we know the firefighters,
   the firefighters,
   the firefighters.
Oh, yes we know the firefighters
   who drive the big red truck.

Other verses:

Police officers—police car
Mail carriers—red, white, and blue jeep
Garbage collector—gray truck

COUNTING

TEN LITTLE INDIANS (14)

(Tune: Traditional)

One little, two little, three little Indians,
Four little, five little, six little Indians,

Seven little, eight little, nine little Indians,
Ten little Indian boys.

Actions: Point to fingers as each number is sung. Verse can be changed to cowboys, astronauts, firefighters.

OLD MacDONALD's FARM (15)

(Tune: Traditional)

Old MacDonald had a farm,
E-I-E-I-O
And on this farm he had a duck,
E-I-E-I-O
With a quack quack here,
And a quack quack there,
Here a quack, there a quack,
Everywhere a quack quack,
Old MacDonald had a farm
E-I-E-I-O

Other verses: Let the children select the other farm animals to sing about.

UP IN A SPACE CAPSULE

(Tune: "Up in a Balloon") (16)

Up in a capsule, boys,
Up in a capsule,
Flying 'round the little stars
And way out to the moon.
Up in a capsule, boys,
Up in a capsule,
Won't we have a jolly time,
Up in a capsule!

PARTS OF MY FACE

(Tune: "Ten Little Indians") (14)

Eyes, ears, nose, and mouth;
Eyes, ears, nose, and mouth;
Eyes, ears, nose, and mouth;
Belong to my face.

Note: The children touch each part as they sing.

Ojos, Orejas, Nariz, Boca

(Tune: "Ten Little Indians") (14)

Ojos, orejas, nariz, boca;
Ojos, orejas, nariz, boca;
Ojos, orejas, nariz, boca;
Son parte de mi cara.

Diez Inditos

(Tune: "Ten Little Indians") (14)

Uno, dos, tres inditos,
Cuatro, cinco, seis inditos,
Siete, ocho, nueve inditos,
Diez inditos son.

Note: The Spanish "Ten Little Indians" can be adapted to say *ninitos*—children, *pollitos*—chicks, *perritos*—puppies, etc.

¿Dónde Está Juanito?

(Tune: "Pawpaw Patch") (12)

¿Dónde, dónde está Juanito?
¿Dónde, dónde está Juanito?
¿Dónde, dónde está Juanito?
¿El está alli?

¿Dónde, dónde está Maria?
¿Dónde, dónde está Maria?
¿Dónde, dónde está Maria?
¿Ella está alli?

Note: Insert each child's name. Use *el* for boys and *ella* for girls.

Vamos a la Escuela

(Tune: "Pawpaw Patch") (12)

Vamos, vamos a la escuela,
Vamos, vamos a la escuela,
Vamos, vamos a la escuela,
A la escuela hoy.

Note: Add verses with activities such as

a pintar—to paint
a jugar—to play
a leer—to read
a cortar—to cut
a dormir—to sleep

Spanish versions of songs are given above. You can use them when teaching Spanish or working with Spanish speaking children.[2]

for beginning to know the alphabet. Teachers dealing with children of all languages can use songs to help build vocabulary and provide ear training.

Songs that call for children's individual participation have strong appeal. Teachers will need as many of this type of song as they can find. They should feel perfectly comfortable adapting songs to the needs of their groups. Sometimes the child's name is used, sometimes she or he gets to select the animal or activity that goes into the verse. In the following song, the child's name and shirt color are designated:

WHERE OH WHERE?

(Tune: "Pawpaw Patch") (12)

Where oh where is dear little *Jimmy?*
Where oh where is dear little Jimmy?
Where oh where is dear little Jimmy?
Way over there with the *blue shirt* on.

Note: When the teacher must sing everybody's name, try putting several together—Where oh where are Peter, James, and John?

"What Shall We Do When We All Go Out?" (17) can be sung with each child suggesting a different outdoor activity. After a few days this song can become a cue song—like a closing hymn in a house of worship—that tells the children that outdoor time has come.

When "The Farmer in the Dell" (18) is altered to say "The Farmer Has a _____," each child can select a different animal or machine for the farmer. The children may eventually become quite imaginative, selecting such animals as deer, dolphins, or "dodo" birds. Their sugges-

---

[2] Other songs in Spanish are suggested in *Fun Learning Elementary Spanish* by Margaret Anne Carlson and others (Albuquerque: University of New Mexico, 1961).

tions are usually indications of their imaginations, not their lack of concepts. Such jokes are signs of their increasing maturity.

Other songs calling for individual contributions are "When I Was a Young Maid" (19), which calls for occupations and tools, and "Monkey See Monkey Do" (20), in which the child suggests a motion for others to make.

Teachers should know lullabies as well as rousing songs. A quiet song is worth a thousand "Shhh's," just as are the quiet finger plays suggested in Chapter 12. A quiet song can help restore order out of chaos. The teacher can start a song like "My Pigeon's House" (35) in a I'm-

---

SOOTHING SONGS

KUMBAYA (21)

Mary's listening, Kumbaya,
Mary's listening, Kumbaya,
Mary's listening, Kumbaya,
Oh, Oh, Kumbaya.

HUSH, LITTLE BABY (22)

(Tune: Traditional)

Hush, little baby, don't say a word,
Mommy's going to buy you a mocking bird.
If that mocking bird won't sing,
Mommy's going to buy you a diamond ring.

If that diamond ring turns to brass,
Mommy's going to buy you a looking glass.
If that looking glass gets broke,
Mommy's going to buy you a billy goat.

If that billy goat won't pull,
Mommy's going to buy you a cart and bull.
If that cart and bull turn over,
Mommy's going to buy you a dog named Rover.

If that dog named Rover won't bark,
Mommy's going to buy you a mule and cart.
If that mule and cart fall down,
You're still the sweetest little boy in town.

telling-a-secret voice, singing to two or three children who are sitting near, then scan the group with active eyes, encouraging others to listen and join the singing. The teacher nods and smiles to children who begin listening. The songs work their miracle as one child after another relaxes and begins to listen and sing.

Guidance can be sung instead of spoken and is often more effective as a result. Each teacher will have favorite tunes that readily come to mind and can be used with guidance phrases such as "Barry, walk around the puddle," or "Time to go indoors." Cleanup time can be lots more fun if everyone bursts into song as materials are put away. They can sing "Pickin' up blocks, put them on the shelf," instead of "Pickin' up pawpaws" (12). "Here We Go Round the Mulberry Bush" (8) readily becomes the following at cleanup time:

CLEANUP TIME

(Tune: "Here We Go Round the Mulberry Bush") (8)

> This is the way we stack the blocks,
> Stack the blocks, stack the blocks,
> This is the way we stack the blocks,
> When it's time for cleanup time.

Other verses: Wash the easel, wash the paint brushes, or wipe the tables.

The late four-year-olds and five-year-olds will enjoy songs with cumulative verses. "The Twelve Days of Christmas" (23) is a familiar example. For such long songs the teacher can prepare drawings to illustrate each verse so the children can "read" as they sing. Drawings help them learn more quickly and help the teacher too. The following are songs of this type: "Had a Little Rooster" (24), "I Bought Me a Cat" (25), and "I Know an Old Lady" (26).

The use of sad songs is often discussed by teachers. Some believe that sadness should never be a part of a song for young children. Others believe that a sad song may help the child learn about feelings. They feel that a child may use a sad song to express inner sadness. The song may help bring concerns out where they can be dealt with. "Old Roger Is Dead" (4) and "Go Tell Aunt Rhodie" (27) are considered sad by some teachers.

Of course, a child's reaction to a song will depend on the way it is sung. Songs that seem sad to adults may not seem sad to children. Whether a teacher uses sad songs should be up to the teacher because one of the requirements in choosing songs is that the teacher enjoy the music presented to children. If a sad song has special meaning for a teacher, he or she should be free to try it with the children. They may sense that feeling and appreciate the song too.

Allowing children to select songs during singing time is important because it makes the period more their own. No harm can come from singing "Jingle Bells" (28) in June, so a seasonal choice should be honored as would any other. A teacher must, however, decide from moment to moment how much to lead and how much to follow the children. If the entire music period is regularly left in the children's hands, stagnation will set in very soon. The teacher's skill and tact are required to balance the offering of a new song with the familiar songs the children enjoy. Good balance results from planning and from being sensitive to children's moods. The teacher can learn to sense the children's moods and follow the leads they give. The length of the music period will vary from day to day depending on the children's response.

The following are examples of leads that a teacher might follow: If a child kicks his or her heels, perhaps the teacher can think of a song in which kicking might be an appropriate sound effect. If the children lie down as though sleeping, try to think of a sleeping song. If a child should pretend to play the guitar, can the teacher think of a song that could work this in? If the children have been sitting for quite a while, can the choice be a song that would get them up for a stretch, then get them to sit back down so that a story could follow? By following the children's leads, the teacher can make the singing experience fun, relaxing, and creative, yet organized enough so that it is pleasant for everyone.

When teachers establish an atmosphere of freedom and use music creatively throughout their teaching, it won't be long before the children will be bursting out in song wherever they play. Both their tunes and their words may be original. If the teacher can capture some of these compositions in notes and sing them back to the child, they will show that the accomplishments are appreciated.

Carl was heard responding to the question, "Do you need a push?" He sang:

> I can push myself so high
> I can just fly
> Into the sky.

Another sang:

> Hooray for today!
> I can play all day!

Exuberance for life showed when yet another sang:

> I love these snowy days!
> It's fun today!

Young children's spontaneity and zest for living are pleasurable to behold.

*   *   *

Talk It Over: No. 4

Describe creative movement activities you've seen children do. State children's ages, the music used, and outcomes.

*   *   *

Creative Movement

Children are naturally rhythmical in their movements. Swinging, jumping, swaying, whirling, tapping, and running are rhythmic movements familiar to any teacher of young children. Movement is important to children. From the smallest wiggling finger to the largest leaps, the child loves to be in motion. The teacher's role is to establish the atmosphere of freedom that lets the children express their feelings, and there will be rhythm.

Many interesting rhythms are noted during activities that may not be thought of as rhythmical, e.g., cutting, painting, or rocking in the rocking chair or the rocking boat. Teachers may help children recognize these rhythms. They might develop a chant to go with one of them, like:

> Pound, pound, pound, pound, pound on the clay,
> Pound, pound, pound, pound, pound it down.

Spontaneous dancing often results when classical music is played on the record player. The children will enjoy wearing long skirts for whirling and twirling to the music. Long streamers of colored material or paper, or colored scarves will prompt a gentle flowing rhythmic expression.

Movement can also be accompanied by a piano, a tom-tom, a tambourine, or clapping.

Children need space so their movement doesn't interfere with that of others. However, once children are spread out in the room or the yard, they have difficulty hearing the teacher's suggestions and comments. Teachers know that shouted guidance is ineffective. The teacher can solve the problem by developing a signal so children will know when it's time for them to come together. The signal could be one loud "bang" on the tom-tom or three taps. The teacher can call them to a "secret huddle" to talk over the plans for the next activity. The huddle will help keep the children's attention.

Children can be encouraged to use their imagination to suggest movements to make. They can name birds or animals to imitate. They can imitate machines—large like a bulldozer and small like the mixer at home. Sound effects go with rhythms, of course. This is rarely a quiet time of day.

Children can be encouraged to use their space by jumping their highest or crawling their lowest. They can experiment with different ways to move through space—walk, run, hop, jog, leap, twirl, skate, slide, creep, glide, gallop, skip, and BLAST OFF! The teacher can pick up the rhythm of a particular child and tap it out on the tom-tom. "John, your rhythm pattern is—tap, tap—tap tap tap." The teacher may say, "That was a HIGH leap, Jennifer." "What a smooth glide you have, Dennis!" A child who wouldn't participate in dancing may happily jump on a jumping board or a mattress. The teacher can recognize movement by tapping out the rhythm or singing a song to its beat.

A teacher may crumple a plastic film bag in the children's presence. They watch it unfold, then they pretend to be a crumpled-up plastic bag. Many get lovely, unusual movement. With older children, who won't mind if balloons break, setting several balloons loose in the room may stimulate skipping, leaping, and running to keep the balloons floating through the air.

If the children seem overactive during planned rhythm experiences, they may need to be more active or they may already be overtired. Children can be rested by doing small movements with eye, tongue, finger, head, and nose as they relax on the floor.

There should be no desire to get every child doing the same thing. Care should be taken to recognize each child's unique contribution. Children will be freer without their shoes.

Teachers can use children's creative imitations to help at transition time. "Hop like bunnies to get your coats" or "Now on quiet feet like a mouse, let's go to the film room."

Listening

The opportunity to listen is important for growth in music appreciation. Listening is also important for language development. Many of the opportunities offered through music make important contributions to language. Acuity is tested. Memory is developed through listening activities.

Records

An area of the room can be furnished with records and a record player that the children are allowed to operate. A simple player without an automatic changer is best. If there is room near the record player, the chil-

Figure 14-6. Listening to records individually and in small groups is a pleasant music experience for children. (Child Development Laboratory, University of Hawaii)

dren will respond to their records physically—through dancing, marching, and the playing of instruments. They should also be able to listen uninterruptedly to a musical selection or a story record. Attention spans are often quite long when children are listening to music voluntarily during the self-selected activity period.

Records of good quality should be provided. The records that have only one selection are easier for the children to manage alone. Long-playing records make the selection of a particular piece difficult for a small child. Also, teachers are understandably reluctant to give children the more expensive long-playing records. Children can be taught rules for caring for the records and the record player. A rack should be available for holding records so the children can learn to place records in the rack rather than on chairs and tables. A small selection should be available and changed frequently. Other records may be available on request. Many teachers have success with tape recordings of songs they wish to teach children. Some children can handle the tape player themselves.

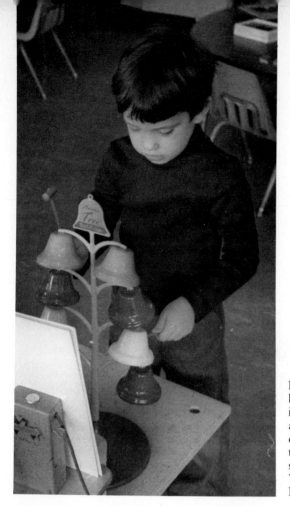

Figure 14-7. Tuned bells and other small instruments are available to give children opportunities to explore musical sounds. (Texas Woman's University Nursery School)

Sound

Many experiments with sound are related to music. Apple juice bottles can be tuned. Colored water in different amounts is added to eight bottles until the scale can be played, with a wooden mallet used for tapping. The advantage of tuning bottles instead of glasses is that lids can be placed on the bottles to prevent evaporation when not in use. Experiments also result from putting on and taking off the lids.

Vibrations cause sound. Children can feel instruments vibrate simply by placing a hand on the instrument. A shoe box can be strung with rubberbands of different widths and tautness and plucked, creating various effects. Children can relate the experiment to the guitar, the autoharp, and the piano. During such a study children will enjoy a trip to hear a harpist. Other stringed instruments may be brought into the school for listening and experimenting. Piano tuning is interesting for children to watch. Also, many listening experiences will be carried on by children as they play the piano. Rules should be established so that the piano is treated with the respect due a musical instrument.

Vibrations can be felt in one's own throat, and some children discover this themselves.

Special Events

A trip to a school music room can help children learn about the sounds made by various instruments. They will like a close-up view. They like to go to band practices and watch the players up close.

Frequently delightful music experiences can be provided by the parents and siblings of the children in a class. For example, a father who was an evangelist singer came to sing. He made up songs, using each child's name. Another father brought his banjo. After a number or two he had each child use a hollow block for a drum—what rhythm resulted!

One child's brother played the trombone, another a steel guitar. A sister twirled. Another sister came with her friend. Wearing a striking Spanish dress, the sister danced the exotic Spanish flamenco. The friend made a striking contrast with a slow, graceful dance in a pastel ballet dress and slippers.

A mother who played the lead in the community production of *The Sound of Music* taught children to sing "Do-Re-Mi" (5).

By singing songs from their countries, foreign students can help children learn about peoples of other lands. At the same time foreign students learn about American children.

Many opportunities such as those suggested will develop children's listening skills. Children also practice appropriate behavior as a member of an audience. However, each guest was advised ahead of time about ways to include the children in the presentation. The children thus became part of each experience. The involvement of family members is especially important to a child.

Rhythm Instruments

Rhythm instruments can be used creatively. They are placed in the music center so that the children will use them alone, accompany themselves in singing, or tap out a rhythm as a record plays. The children may organize their own band. When they do, the teacher will notice that they keep excellent time to the marching rhythm. A few records of good marches such as those of college marching bands will be sufficient stimulation.

Gone are the days of sitting everyone in a row to hold an instrument until time comes to tap just so. Rigid adult structure curtails creativity. When children organize a marching band, the teacher's role need only be to place a table or a collection of chairs in the center of the room to guide the direction of the march. Children think of a march tempo as "parade" music, so marching is important. If there is an insufficient number of the favorite instruments, the teacher may get agreement on a signal that tells the children when to exchange instruments. If the teacher plays the piano for the marchers, the rhythm should be clear and strong. Then the children can keep time.

Children have a number of opportunities to see marching bands on television. Attending a parade or visiting a marching band practice will create interest. If a child's sibling plays a band instrument, she or he can be invited to play. A twirler will interest children, too.

Several good-quality tom-toms, bongo drums, and maracas invite individual and small-group experimentation with primitive rhythms.

Musical Guessing Games

The teacher asks, "What tune is this?" after humming or playing a tune on the piano. The children guess. The children, too, can have turns humming tunes for others to guess.

Using the tom-tom, the teacher can tap out the children's names. First, start by choosing two children to stand up, then say, "Whose name am I tapping?" The teacher can plan ahead, selecting children whose names have contrasting beats.

By recording each child as he or she sings or talks, then bringing the tape for the children to hear, the teacher gives the children another guessing game requiring listening.

Singing Games

Some of the group games used with older children must be adapted if they are to be used with kindergarten children. Many are totally unsuited to prekindergarten children. Too many rules, too many specific directions, and competition make them too complicated. Even the traditional manner of playing "The Farmer in the Dell" (18) is too complicated. Young children don't understand not being chosen. Some teachers improvise verses until each child is in the circle. Another alternative is to divide the group into several circles with an adult in each, then the game can be played in more or less traditional manner. If all the groups are in the same room, they can still sing together.

The game of musical chairs is popular with elementary school children but is not recommended for younger children because a child cannot understand being left out. In this game sufficient chairs are available minus one. The group marches around until the music stops, then everyone runs for a chair. However, if at this point the child who is left out gets to choose a rhythm instrument and becomes part of the band, the child's concern about not having a chair is somewhat removed. Better yet, just do the game with enough chairs for everyone. Children will still enjoy the game.

Games requiring children to hold hands and move in a circle are also too structured. Often, however, it is just as well to let children stand where they will and move in their own circle. Late four- and five-year-olds will enjoy "Did You Ever See a Lassie?" (29), "Monkey See Monkey Do" (20), "Mulberry Bush" (8), "Round and Round the Village" (30), and "Punchinello" (31). Younger children may like "Ring Around the Rosy" (32), "Sally Go Round the Moon" (33), and "London Bridge" (34) if the teacher lets them move where they want to.

Singing games may be used to substitute in part for outdoor exercise when a sudden storm prevents going out. Children much prefer going outdoors; therefore singing games should be used for this purpose only occasionally. Tumbling and rhythms offer energy release in a similar manner.

Role of Parents in a Child's Musical Education

Numerous times in the previous sections suggestions have been made for involving families directly in the music program of the school. Not only does a richer program result when families are involved, but each child whose parent participates gets a special boost. Parents make a significant contribution and feel more comfortable at school when they are invited to demonstrate some special skill to the children. By coming they gain a better understanding of their child and the school.

Teachers can keep parents informed about what their children are doing in music at school. As experiences are planned with the children's developmental level in mind, the teacher should be able to provide helpful suggestions for parents. Parents may seek guidance as to the appropriateness of piano, dancing, or voice lessons. The teacher should become familiar with the music programs offered in the community in order to guide parents.

Teachers can watch for musical events in the community that families can attend to add to their enjoyment of music. Examples are a children's theater musical or a symphony concert planned especially for children. The teacher can see that parents have this information, including information on admission charges.

Music at Home

Teachers may also encourage parents' enjoyment of music with their own children. Words to children's songs can be sent home. Then when the child is singing, the parents can refer to the song sheet and grasp more clearly just what the child is singing about. Perhaps they can even sing along. In some parents' meeting they may wish to sing some of the songs. Teachers can explain their purposes and demonstrate techniques for working with children.

Parents may seek guidance as to the type of record player and recordings to buy. Teachers can be more helpful if they visit record shops and have an idea of what is available locally. Sometimes a teacher can guide the choice that is offered by conferring with the owner of the record shop. Public libraries have recordings to lend, just as they have books. Parents may need this information, as many will not be aware that records are available for children's listening.

It is important for children to have their own songbooks. This is true even though no one in the family plays an instrument. Because children's songbooks are often beautifully illustrated, children can "read" their favorite songs by recognizing the pictures. Children will turn through the book and sing to themselves. Teachers can provide parents with names of appropriate songbooks. Some are available in libraries. Many families report having songfests with their children. Others say that bedtime singing sometimes takes the place of bedtime stories.

Giving Programs

In some schools one traditional way of communicating with the home is to have the children present a program for the parents. However, caution is advised! If the tradition seems harmful to the children, the teacher has a professional obligation to ask for changes in the format. The preparation for and the performance of the program should not be harmful in any way to even one child. No child should feel that he or she is being exhibited, left out, or embarrassed. The program should have educational benefit to children.

The children and the teacher can plan a simple program. They can decide together what things they would like to share with the parents. The program should be short, only 10 to 15 minutes. It should never be rehearsed until no fun remains in the numbers. (Sadly enough, overrehearsed programs are common at Christmas time.) No child should be allowed to star. This keeps competition from developing among children and parents. Memorized lines should be avoided.

An acceptable program would be "a day in school," for example, the singing and rhythm time as customarily carried on in the classroom.

By seeing such a program, parents learn about the school's goals and techniques. There is room for the children's natural spontaneity to occur. The children will be at ease because the format is familiar.

Conclusion

Music in the early childhood school takes specific planning, just as is required by other parts of the curriculum. Planning is required if the children are to enjoy music, have another medium for expressing their thoughts and feelings, and lead richer lives because of their introduction to music.

The children's developmental levels and their previous experience are taken into consideration in the planning of music activities.

Teachers without formal music training can provide a good music program if they make a special effort to overcome feelings of inadequacy. They will seek variety in the materials they present. They will watch the children for cues and leads in order to appreciate their creativity and adapt the program to their needs. Teachers will freely adapt material to suit the children. They will plan music for quiet and active moods. They will plan music to support the concepts that the children are developing, but the enjoyment of music will have priority. Teachers will involve the parents in the children's music experiences whenever possible.

Sources of Songs Mentioned

Note: Each song was given a number in the text. It is listed below according to that number.

1. Jennie Jenkins in *Exploring Music: Kindergarten*. E. Boardman and B. Landis, pp. 66–67.
2. Jacob's Ladder, in *Sing and Strum*, Alice M. Snyder, p. 20.
3. Goodnight, Irene, in *The Weaver's Song Book*, Ronnie Gilbert (ed.), p. 34.
4. Old Roger Is Dead, in *Songs to Grow On*, Beatrice Landeck, p. 112.
5. Do-Re-Mi, in *The Sound of Music Vocal Selections*, Richard Rodgers and Oscar Hammerstein, pp. 16–21.
6. Eency Weency Spider, in *American Folk Songs for Children*, Ruth Crawford Seeger, p. 126.
7. Frère Jacques, in *The New Golden Song Book*, Norman Lloyd, p. 83.
8. Mulberry Bush, in *The New Golden Song Book*, Norman Lloyd, p. 44.
9. If You're Happy and You Know It, in *This Is Music, Book I*, William Sur, Adeline McCall, William R. Fischer, and Mary R. Tolbert, p. 16.
10. Mary Wore a Red Dress, in *Songs to Grow On*, Beatrice Landeck, p. 12.

11. Twinkle Twinkle Little Star, in *The New Golden Song Book,* Norman Lloyd, p. 16.
12. Paw Paw Patch, in *Songs to Grow On,* Beatrice Landeck, p. 116.
13. Muffin Man, in *The New Golden Song Book,* Norman Lloyd, p. 35.
14. Ten Little Indians, in *American Singer: No. 1,* John W. Beattie, p. 94.
15. Old MacDonald's Farm, in *The New Golden Song Book,* Norman Lloyd, p. 20.
16. Up in a Balloon, in *More Songs to Grow On,* Beatrice Landeck, p. 12.
17. What Shall We Do When We All Go Out? In *American Folk Songs for Children,* Ruth Crawford Seeger, p. 59.
18. The Farmer in the Dell, *The New Golden Song Book,* Norman Lloyd, p. 36.
19. When I Was a Young Maid, in *American Folk Songs for Children,* Ruth Crawford Seeger, p. 168.
20. Monkey See Monkey Do, in *Train to the Zoo,* Children's Record Guild Recording No. 1001.
21. Kumbaya, in *The Weaver's Song Book,* Ronnie Gilbert (ed.), p. 156.
22. Hush, Little Baby, in *The Weaver's Song Book,* Ronnie Gilbert (ed.), p. 24.
23. Twelve Days of Christmas, in *This Is Music, Book 4,* William R. Sur et al., pp. 174–175.
24. Had a Little Rooster, in *More Songs to Grow On,* Beatrice Landeck, p. 34.
25. I Bought Me a Cat, in *Songs to Grow On,* Beatrice Landeck, p. 76.
26. I Know an Old Lady, in *I Know an Old Lady,* Rose Bonne and Allan Mills, p. 1.
27. Go Tell Aunt Rhodie, in *The Weaver's Song Book,* Ronnie Gilbert (ed.), p. 99.
28. Jingle Bells, in *The New Golden Song Book,* Norman Lloyd, p. 56.
29. Did You Ever See a Lassie? in *The New Golden Song Book,* Norman Lloyd, p. 38.
30. Round and Round the Village, in *The New Golden Song Book,* Norman Lloyd, p. 37.
31. Punchinello, in *More Songs to Grow On,* Beatrice Landeck, p. 96.
32. Ring Around the Rosy, in *The New Golden Song Book,* Norman Lloyd, p. 39.
33. Sally Go Round the Moon, in *American Singer: No. 1,* John W. Beattie, p. 184.
34. London Bridge, in *Fifty Songs for Children,* Mary Nancy Graham, p. 2.
35. My Pigeon's House, in *Sleepy Family,* People's Record (611), 78 rpm, The Franson Corp., New York.

Record Suggestions

The following are examples of records suitable for young children. Children should be allowed a range of responses. They may listen quietly or respond actively to the suggestions on the record. Individuality can be encouraged and children challenged to think of new movements. The following titles can be located in a number of catalogs. They are available in single records and also appear in varying combinations on long-playing records. Single presentations are considered more satisfactory when children use records at the record player. Long-playing records require more adult help.

Music participation records:

Circus Comes to Town
Jingle Bells and Other Songs for Winter Fun
Little Gray Ponies
My Playful Scarf
My Playmate the Wind
Rainy Day
Sunday in the Park
Train to the Zoo
What the Lighthouse Sees

Music interpretation records:

Hungarian Dance No. 1 by Brahms
March of Toreadors by Bizet
Sousa Marches
Waltz of the Flowers and Dance of the Sugar Plum Fairy by Tchaikovsky

Applications

1. Do the "Talk It Over" items found in the chapter.
2. Complete Lesson 14 in *A Laboratory Workbook for Introduction to Early Childhood Education*. Hand in as scheduled.
3. Write an activity plan for a music or movement activity for a few children using information and the sample plan (Figure 6-1) in Chapter 6. Secure approval, carry out the plan, and evaluate the results from the children's point of view and your viewpoint. Prepare a report and hand it in along with your approved plan.
4. Evaluate your total participation performance on your evaluation form developed in Chapter 1.
5. Add ideas and plans for music and movement activities to your Resource File.

Study Questions

1. State and explain the major goal for providing music for young children.
2. Describe places for teachers to look for ideas to use as musical experiences for children.
3. Explain how to teach children a new song.
4. Give examples of ways the teacher's creativity can be used during musical activities.

5. Give examples of ways children's creativity can be encouraged during musical activities.

6. According to studies, the best place to pitch a song for young children is between ＿＿＿and ＿＿＿.

7. List and describe ways parents can become involved in musical activities for their children.

Additional Readings

*Indicates books that have coordinated records available

ANDREWS, GLADYS. *Creative Rhythmic Movement for Children.* Englewood Cliffs, N.J.: Prentice-Hall, Inc., 1954.

ANDREWS, PALMYRA. "Music and Motion: The Rhythmic Language of Children" *Young Children,* Vol. 32, No. 1, November 1976, pp. 14–19.

BAYLESS, KATHLEEN M., and MARJORIE E. RAMSEY. *Music: A Way of Life for the Young Child.* Saint Louis: The C. V. Mosby Company, 1982.

BEATTIE, JOHN W. (ed.). *The American Singer: No. 1.* New York: American Book Company, 1954.

*BOARDMAN, E., and B. LANDIS. *Exploring Music: Kindergarten* New York: Holt, Rinehart and Winston, 1969.

CHERRY, CLARE. *Creative Movement for the Developing Child.* Palo Alto, Calif.: Fearon Publishers, Inc., 1968.

GILBERT, RONNIE (ed.) *The Weaver's Song Book.* New York: Harper & Brothers, 1960.

GRAHAM, MARY NANCY. *Fifty Songs for Children.* Racine, Wis.: Whitman Publishing Company, 1964.

GUTTOLPH, EDNA G. *Music Without the Piano.* New York: Early Childhood Education Council of New York, 1966.

JAYE, MARY TINNIN. *Making Music Your Own.* Parkridge, Ill.: Silver Burdette Co., 1971.

JENKINS, ELLA. *This Is Rhythm.* Elkhart, Ind.: Lyons Band, Division of Magnavox, 1974.

*LANDECK, BEATRICE. *Songs to Grow On.* New York: William Sloane Associates, 1950.

*LANDECK, BEATRICE. *More Songs to Grow On.* New York: William Sloane Associates, 1954.

*LANDECK, BEATRICE, HAROLD C. YOUNGBERG, and ELIZABETH CROOK. *Making Music Your Own: No. 1.* Morristown, N.J.: Silver Burdette Company, 1967.

LLOYD, NORMAN. *The New Golden Song Book.* New York: Golden Press, 1966.

McDONALD, DOROTHY T., *Music in Our Lives: The Early Years.* Washington, D.C.: National Association for the Education of Young Children, 1979.

*SEEGER, RUTH CRAWFORD. *American Folk Songs for Children.* New York: Doubleday, Inc., 1948.

*SMITH, ROBERT, *Discovering Music Together: Early Childhood.* Chicago: Follett Educational Corporation, 1969.

SNYDER, ALICE M. *Sing and Strum*. New York: Mills Music, Inc., 1957.

STINSON, SUSAN W., "Movement as Creative Interaction with the Child." *Young Children*, Vol. 32, No. 6, September 1977, pp. 49–53.

SULLIVAN, MOLLY. *Feeling Strong, Feeling Free: Movement Exploration for Young Children*. Washington, D.C.: National Association for the Education of Young Children, 1982.

*SUR, WILLIAM, et al. *This Is Music: No. 1*. Boston: Allyn & Bacon, 1963.

WOLFE, IRVING, BEATRICE P. KRONE, and MARGARET FULLERTON. *Music Round the Clock*. Chicago: Follett Publishing Company, 1963.

Field Trips and Special Visitors

- *To explain how field trips and visitors are part of the cumulative curricular plan of the school for young children.*
- *To identify the values to children that come from taking field trips or having special visitors.*
- *To identify and explain the steps required in adequate planning for field trips and special visitors.*
- *To identify and describe a variety of field trips and special visitors appropriate for the early childhood school.*

OUR FALL TRIP

Once upon a time nineteen children went to the woods. It is called the Arboretum Park. We took the Sugar Bush Trail, or path, or road. We saw a squirrel. He was eating bread.

We saw cows with long horns. We saw prairie dogs and deer—reindeer.

We fed the racoon. They eat with their claws. They have a face that looks like a mask.

We found two caterpillars.

We jumped in a big pile of leaves under a tree. We made the pile. That was fun.

We saw the ducks. We fed them bread. Did you see three swans? Except one of them was a white duck.

We saw buffalo—two buffaloes.

We ate some bread, peanut butter, and Koolaid.

We came back to our school. We had fun.

The four-year-old children dictated this story to the teacher following a fall field trip to a wooded wildlife park. Such field trips take the

Figure 15-1. Children love to see themselves in photos. A visiting cameraman arranged a camera so children could shoot their own photo with a bulb operated shutter. He also arranged to video tape the children. The resulting photos were viewed with pleasure the remainder of the year. (Child Development Laboratory, Michigan State University)

child to an observation that cannot readily be brought into the classroom. Field trips and special visitors are educational methods used to provide children firsthand information, observation, and study. As children discuss and dictate stories about their new experience, opportunities are presented for clarifying misconceptions and expanding knowledge.

"Because a young child is a laboratory rather than a lecture student, teaching him is largely a matter of providing him with materials and activities in such a way that he can learn from his own experience and generalize in his own words," writes Catherine Landreth, a noted specialist in child development and in early childhood education.[1] She means that children learn most by having opportunities to see for themselves, to touch, to taste, to smell, to hear, and then to talk about their experiences. Their concepts are broadened through firsthand experience. Field trips and the special visitors invited to the school offer the children experiences that help them understand more fully the life going on around them, the books that are read to them, and the books they will later learn to read. Pictures, films, recordings, poems, and songs will also have more meaning following firsthand experiences.

Planning Field Trips[2]

Five considerations are weighed by the teacher in the decision to use the field trip method for a group of young children. These considerations are (1) the educational goals for the group, (2) the suitability of the available field trips, (3) the time required, (4) the costs involved, and (5) the dangers involved.

Cumulative planning, as described in Chapter 9, utilizes a number of basic themes which run through the entire curriculum. Learning activities are offered for each theme in varying amounts in an effort to help children link new information with that previously known. Field trips and special visitors help children receive more authentic educational experiences than if only classroom activities are used. Frequently field trips are a capstone experience following a buildup of information and exploration within the classroom. Many field trips can also be a springboard to other learning activities in the days and weeks following which is part of the spiraling effect of cumulative planning.

*　　*　　*

[1] Catherine Landreth, *Preschool Learning and Teaching* (New York: Harper & Row, 1972), p. 161.
[2] Acknowledgement is due *Childhood Education* for permission to reprint portions of my article "Trips for Preschoolers," *Childhood Education* 43:9, (May 1967), pp. 524–527.

Talk It Over: No. 1

Give an example of how a field trip can contribute to the curriculum in a school where you are acquainted. How does it contribute to the cumulative planning?

*   *   *

Educational Goals

Before the field trip educational goals should be well established. A field trip can be used to stimulate interest in a subject as well as to extend information. It can also be fun and add variety to the school program. Although the latter purposes are valued, most teachers would agree that the first two are the more important purposes of field trips.

The teacher will have some tentative goals based upon knowledge of and experience with children of the age of those in the class. However, the teacher's decision on specific field trips must be made after a period of assessing the needs of a particular group of children. The teacher will want to know: What experiences have they had previously at home and school? What questions are they asking? What interests them? What do they talk about? What books do they select? From such study the teacher can decide what information needs extending and what interests should be stimulated.

Suitability of Available Field Trips

Teachers will continuously survey their community for ideas for worthwhile field trips and special events. The interest and cooperation of the parents of the children should be enlisted in order to provide a rich curriculum. For example, one group visits the television studio because a child's mother works there and helps arrange the visit. Another group goes to the police station because a child's father works there. Parents can assist on buses, drive cars, and act as guides.

There will be differences among groups, so there is a fallacy in saying, "Kindergarteners always go to the fire station." In some schools every child goes on every trip regardless of age or previous experience. Can this practice be justified?

Attending school may be a sufficiently new, strange, and stimulating adventure for three-year-olds. Teachers must determine whether it is best to delay field trips until the children are at ease in the school setting. A trip may undermine security just when the children are beginning to feel comfortable away from home. Tammy is an example. Usually a confident, happy three-year-old, she wondered, "Will my Daddy find me here?"

during a walk less than a block from the school. She verbalized a concern that many of the others may have felt.

Field trips for the youngest children should be simple and close to school. Teachers may explore the possibility of taking only a few of the children, leaving behind those who aren't ready for field trip experiences. Such a plan, of course, requires activities, helpers, and perhaps some explanations for those who remain.

* * *

Talk It Over: No. 2

Discuss the pros and cons of taking all children from a group on a field trip.

* * *

Field trips usually serve their purposes best for those late four-year-olds and kindergarten children who are confident with the teacher and in the school situation and are fully ready for broadening adventures.

Figure 15-2. Collecting turkey feathers is a bonus experience for a class that visited a turkey farm just before Thanksgiving. (Texas Tech University Kindergarten)

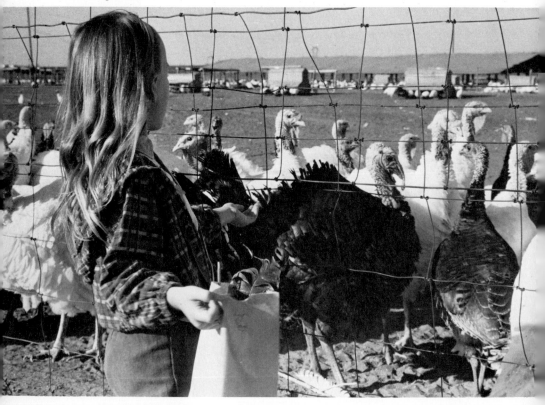

This age is ready for more things to look at, to talk about, to think about, and to use creatively in their schoolwork.

Communities offer many more resources for field trips than teachers sometimes recognize. The following are listed because they are known to have been successful for some groups. The list is not exhaustive, and teachers should use it to help them find resources in their communities. There is no set list of experiences every child should have. Therefore the teacher should develop the curriculum that makes sense for a particular group at this time.

Costs Involved

Many field trips are free. Some may require admission fees. Transportation is a cost even though it may be borne by a school district or by a number of parents who drive their private cars. A total cost should be calculated if there are numerous fees. Careful determination should be made as to whether the trip is the best use of the resources. For example, if a train trip is calculated to cost $100 for fifteen children, would this be the best use of $100?

Time Required

The time required to plan and carry through the field trip should be considered from the standpoint of the children, the teachers, and other adults who may be requested to assist. Time is a valuable resource and should be used wisely. The teacher must ask, "Is the time required for this field trip the best use of everybody's time?"

Dangers Involved

There are added dangers associated with taking children away from school, whether by bus, by car, or on foot. No concerned teacher assumes the responsibility for a group of children without giving some thought to possible accidents. The school's legal liability in case of accident is one consideration. Another is the need to provide seatbelts for each person in the car, according to regulations. Liability insurance for private automobiles is another. However, insurance is a hollow consolation to a teacher if an accident does occur. Parents should feel that utmost care for children's safety is planned. Trips that are planned haphazardly often do not give safety sufficient attention.

*   *   *

Talk It Over: No. 3

Discuss the dangers involved in taking children on field trips. Summarize precautions to take to avoid these dangers.

*   *   *

Field Trip Suggestions

Animals

Farm—sheep, cattle, horses, pigs, turkeys, chickens
County fair—animal exhibits
Dairy at milking time
Rodeo horses
Ducks in pond
Zoo

Hatchery
Wildlife exhibit
Bird sanctuary
Aquarium
Pets—in pet shop or in child's home
Museum—animal and bird exhibits

Growing Things

Botanical garden
Christmas tree farm
Flower garden
Nature walks—four seasons
Pumpkin farm

Orchard
Park
Woods
Farm

People and Places

Artist's studio
Bakery
Barbershop
Beauty shop
Bowling alley
Musicians—band, orchestra, individual instrumentalists, singers
Health clinic
Lunchroom kitchen
Museum—old fashioned house, doll collection, Indian houses, historical exhibits
Science classroom
School—kindergarten for four-year-olds, first grade for kindergarten children
Office
Post office
Potter's studio
Puppet show
Ice cream parlor

Car wash
Children's houses
County-fair-style show
Dairy bottling
Department store windows
Print shop
Restaurant
Dormitory room
Fire station
Foreign student or family
Garage mechanic
Home economics classroom
Ice skating rink
Library
Police station
Swimming pool
Teacher's house
Television studio
Grocery
Mother and baby

Transportation and Machines

Airport
Train ride
Train station
Exhibited train
Model train
Construction site
Street repair
Farm machinery show

Elevator
Escalator
Streetcar ride
Car dealer's showroom
Bus ride
Museum—machine exhibit
Museum—space exhibit
Boat ride

Other

Museum—geology exhibit, Christmas trees, children's art
Science classroom—skeleton, insect collections, botanical collections

Planetarium
Seashore
Ecology walk—litter pickup

Preparation for Field Trips

Five stages of field trip planning are outlined below which, if considered carefully, should assure the enrichment of the children's experience that the teacher seeks. These are

1. The teacher's preparation
2. The children's preparation
3. The field trip
4. Follow-up activities
5. Posttrip activities

These stages can be applied with modifications to special events brought into the school by a visitor or the teacher.

Teacher's Preparation

The teacher becomes fully informed about the subject of the trip that has been chosen. The teacher makes a trip there ahead of time to see specifically what there is for the children to learn and what things may have to be pointed out to the children. As inexperienced observers, they may miss important points unless helped in their observation. The teacher will plan for parking, note any hazards that might endanger the children's safety, and recruit additional adult helpers if needed.

The teacher talks with the guide helping the person to appreciate the level of learning of the children. Many adults have little idea what will interest children. For example, at a bus station, when children were anxious to get aboard a bus, the guide tried to inform them how to get a refund on a ticket. Needless to say, the children's attention wandered! A teacher can decide how to help the guide if he or she fails to show the things that are important, or if the talk is above the children's level. Having developed rapport prior to the actual event, it is easy to say, "Mr. Arthur, could we see those baby calves? I know the children would enjoy those." Or after a complicated explanation, one might say, "What Mr. Arthur means is that those calves get some special food to see how they will grow."

Choosing the right day of the week for the trip is an important decision. Several things must be considered. First, what immediate preparation will the teacher give the children and how many days will that take? What kinds of follow-up activities are expected to result, e.g., dramatic play, art activities, rhythm responses, and science experiments? The teacher knows that through reliving the experience, the children work out some of their concepts, roles, and feelings. If plans call for a great deal of this type of follow-up, it is best to schedule the trip early in the week so that there will be maximum carry-over into the school activity. The amount of carry-over will be greatly reduced if a weekend intervenes, and will be almost nonexistent if a vacation follows the trip. For example, children play firefighters for days after a trip to the fire station. They wear their self-made firefighters' hats and carry ladders on little red wagons, and put out fires in their "houses" made of packing boxes and wooden planks.

Where in the daily schedule is the best place for the trip? This is an important consideration. The date and time must be convenient for the host or owner of the place to be visited. The teacher considers the energy demands of the trip on the children. An active trip such as a walk on the seashore or on a farm would logically follow a quiet interlude at school rather than a period of outdoor play. A trip to hear a harpist play and accompany the children's singing logically follows a period of active play. Children's bodies will then be ready for the behavior that the situation demands. Active and quiet play have good balance in a program that meets children's needs. Some readjustment in the routine activities will be necessary to fit the trip into the schedule.

The teacher plans for sufficient time for the total trip, including leeway for any emergency. In addition, a bonus experience may occur on any trip. For example, on a walk to the museum a cement mixer was observed dumping its load of cement. What a tragedy if the schedule would not permit even a little peek!

An important part of the teacher's preparation is to think through rules for walking and riding during field trips. Walking trips will come first, while the teacher is still learning about the group. One way is to appoint a pair of leaders and call them "engines" and "cabooses." They should all practice certain signals so that the leaders will know when to stop and when to go. Learning that "red light" means stop is more fun than just having the teacher call "stop." "Green light" permits them to proceed. The meaning of traffic lights should be understood and practice sessions held in the classroom to help the children learn their meaning.

When crossing streets, the teacher may ask the child who has been designated the "engine" to stop the "train" at some landmark they see on the other side. The teacher then remains in the middle of the street until all children have crossed.

Transportation is often essential for field trips. In public schools teachers can usually depend on buses with qualified drivers. This is a real advantage. In other schools parents may be asked to drive several children. Care must be taken not to overload a car, thereby interfering with safe driving. Every passenger must have a seatbelt. Only insured cars should be taken on trips.

Thought should be given to deciding which children ride together. Two children who are noted for being hard to handle should be separated. When a parent is driving, his or her child should be allowed to ride in that car. It is essential to have an extra adult accompany each driver. The drivers should be given a list of the children who ride in their car and their phone numbers to use in any emergency. Also, the address and phone number of the destination, and detailed instructions for getting there should be written out for each driver. To depend on one car following another in city traffic with a car full of children is hazardous. Drivers can lose each other and may end up not knowing where to go.

Some schools require a signed permission slip from parents for each trip. These slips are often difficult for teachers to get returned because they are easily misplaced or forgotten. Other schools have parents sign a permission slip that covers all trips throughout the year. Such slips can be taken care of during the child's enrollment. Teachers should also clarify with the school's legal adviser the problem of liability in case of accident.

Teachers should inform parents of planned trips. Not only will parents then be able to dress the child appropriately, but they can more intelligently supplement the teacher's goals if they don't have to guess what is taking place. That is, parents can ask questions to draw out the child's information and reactions to the trip, answer questions asked, and arrange family trips that further supplement the school's efforts.

Children's Preparation

Preparing the children for the field trip is essential for maximum learning. Preparation for a field trip may cover several months, with the trip serving as a capstone, or in some cases the trip may appropriately be initiated after a few days' discussion, with most of the learning to come after the event.

Through pictures, stories, records, roleplaying, and discussions, the children can become aware of the details they can expect to find on field trips. A firefighter expressed amazement at the vocabulary of a group of kindergarteners. If they didn't readily find a tool they asked the firefighters where it was. They used the correct name. These children had learned about the firefighters' tools during the week prior to the trip. Sometimes there are exceptions or differences in what the child sees in a picture book and what will be found on the trip. The teacher can warn the children of these exceptions ahead of time and help avoid disappointment. For example, new fire stations may not have the traditional firehouse pole. This is a source of disappointment to children who are expecting it.

Stories, songs, and poems may be used to help children learn about a subject they will be seeing on a field tirp. The books by Ramona Emmons and Billy N. Pope in the *Your World* series make excellent resource material for both preparation and follow-up activities.[3]

Role-playing helps children learn more about the trip. It will help them feel self-assured in a strange place. Prior to a train trip one group arranged chairs as they expected their train seats to be arranged. Young artists designed tickets and took turns being the conductor who punched their tickets. They talked about the difference between their trip of 15 miles and one they might take with their parents—luggage, sleeping on the train, costing more, and not returning for several days. Reassurance was necessary for a child or two who wondered when they were going to return. The children pretended to see the parents' cars waiting at the station as the train pulled in. Their make-believe ride included what they were seeing from their train window. It made them better watchers as the real train rolled along a few days later.

The Field Trip

The day of the field trip finally arrives. All should be in readiness, including the enthusiasm of the children. Keep talk in a low key to avoid overstimulation. The teacher gathers the group around for a brief review of what they are going to see. Next, talk turns to how they are expected to behave—"quiet in the museum" or "quiet in the egg-laying barn." Perhaps they have to think about how quiet quiet is and why it is necessary.

Toileting cannot be forgotten when one is dealing with young chil-

[3] Ramona W. Emmons and Billy N. Pope, *Your World*, Series I through VII (Dallas: Taylor Publishing Co., 1966–1969).

dren. After specifically reminding the children to go to the bathroom before leaving the building, the teacher will check on children who are known to have difficulties. Also, it is helpful if adults carry small packages of tissues. Drinks, too, are another consideration. On warm days a picnic jug of water and some paper cups are essential. A sack of cookies will add a festive air to the excursion.

On walking trips the teacher makes assignments for "engines and cabooses" according to the practiced routine. When the children clamor for this responsibility, the teacher may keep a list to be sure to pass the favor around.

For trips by car the teacher makes car assignments by giving each driver a list of the children who will ride in his or her car. One must make it clear that the same children should always ride in the same car throughout the trip. The teacher discusses with the children the need to sit down in the car, and tells the children in the presence of the drivers that if they stand up, the driver will stop the car beside the road until all are sitting down again. Seatbelts must be used. The children's safety has high priority.

The teacher checks last-minute details. Drivers are advised where to park and what to do until all arrive. Drivers are asked to act as guides for the children in their car, to ask questions of children that will help

Figure 15-3. Feeding the goat, listening to it bleat, and petting it all give children first hand experiences—a special value of field trips. (Child Development Laboratory, Michigan State University)

the children notice details, to listen to the children's comments, and to answer their questions. Each adult should be encouraged to be alert to children's safety. Unless the teacher specifically requests it, outsiders may be hesitant to assume this helpful role. Occasionally the teacher may hold a briefing for the guides in order to better coordinate the trip.

When the group arrives, they wait for the guide who will show them the things they came to see. The children are given lots of time to look, find details, and relate what they are seeing to what they have studied. After a while the adults can point out things they feel the children have missed. A relaxed, nonrushing atmosphere is important. If unexpected learning opportunities arise, the teacher should be happy to take time to observe these, too.

The children should wear their name tags. Name tags aid assistants who do not know all of the children's names. They could help police should a child get lost. They help the host of the field trip relate to individual children by calling them by name.

The Follow-up

The follow-up occurs during the ensuing days and helps the children develop further in their learning. The children may use new concepts in the self-selected activity period. Science materials, blocks, books, pictures, dress-up clothes, records, and art materials may all be used. Sometimes the teacher brings out a new or stored piece of equipment to stimulate dramatic play. A steering wheel, for example, contributes to transportation themes.

Creative art activities may result from the trip. After visiting the prairie dog town, Cindy drew her version of what she had seen. The mounds were as big as mountains, each topped with a family of the animals, just as they were seen. Between the mounds were trees—of the same height as the mounds, giving the observer an idea that Cindy found the mounds more important than the trees as she viewed the scene. Making a fire-fighter's hat, stringing an Indian necklace, or modeling a caveman's house from clay may result, depending on the stimulus from the trip. Freedom to use crayons, chalk, clay, and paints for interpreting the trip in the children's own way is important.

The stimulation of language expressed is a prime value of a field trip. Generalizing in one's words from one's own experience promotes the child's learning. Every opportunity should be taken to encourage the children to talk about what they saw. Discussing what they saw, how they felt, and how it sounded and smelled is thoroughly enjoyed by the children and helps them remember. Frequently teachers are afraid of open discussion because they fear it will get too loud and out of hand. Having a few pet finger plays, songs, or poems in mind to use as attention-

Figure 15-4. A piñata fiesta is a special cultural event. Children use a plastic bat and typically no blindfold when hitting the piñata. (Manzanita Day Care Center, University of New Mexico)

getters helps draw young talkers back to the fold. Verbal self-expression is very important for all children, but especially for those children who haven't had much to talk about before. Thus teachers should hesitate before squelching children's language expressions.

Written expression can result too. A dictated letter to the individual who so kindly permitted the visit is one type of expression. Making a poem and dictating a story are others. The opening story in this chapter is an example of a story dictated by the children. Other examples are offered in Chapter 12.

* * *

Talk It Over: No. 4

Using the example of a field trip or special visitor within your own experience, suggest suitable follow-up activities.

* * *

Posttrip Activities

Posttrip activities provide for the children's continued learning after the original emphasis passes and the class goes on to other subjects. This step can continue from the time of the trip to the end of the year. The teacher can place a book on the library shelf or read a story that will cause the children to recall their trip. Or, a record may be played which reminds them. They like to reread their own story or letter of thanks. When these stories are sent home, the parents too can carry on posttrip activities. Communication with parents enables them to add family experiences that build on the foundation the school initiates.

Special Visitors Invited to the School

Because of the complications surrounding field trips, it is often more desirable to bring special visitors to the children. The visitor should be one who can help extend the children's information and stimulate their interest. The children should be carefully prepared for these events. Many of the steps suggested for field trips are applicable here.

Following is a list of some suggested special visitors who might be invited to the school:

Mail carrier	Clown	Rock collector
Police officer	Artist	Insect collector
Highway trooper	Santa Claus	Mother and baby
Musicians	Storyteller	Custodian
Twirlers	Magician	Rope twirler
Dancer	Nurse	Foreign visitor

Figure 15-5. A Japanese teacher visited the four-year-olds, displayed objects of interest and allowed children to dress up in authentic kimonos. (Child Development Laboratory, Michigan State University)

The daily schedule may have to be adjusted so that the children will be ready for the type of behavior the event requires. Some visitors can function well during the self-selected activity period. They can talk to small groups of children, letting them come and go from their discussion or exhibit. This works for visitors with musical instruments and for those with various collections. The children who are most interested will stay a long time; those with less interest will spend their time elsewhere.

If the visitor will be working with the group as a whole, then special plans should be made so that the children are ready for the listening behavior usually required. The teacher might want a period of vigorous outdoor play to precede the event, for example. Transition times should be given special thought. A visitor may cause overstimulation of the children. At the same time the teacher will be distracted by playing hostess to the guest. The situation is just right for chaos to develop.

An assistant might be designated to meet the guest, special songs can be prepared to use in case of delay, and activities can be planned that relax the children rather than add to their excitement.

When the visitor is a child's parent, the child too should get to be in the limelight, introducing the parent, sitting close by, and helping in any way. The parent should know that giving his or her child this bit of recognition is part of the plan. Otherwise the parent may be embarrassed at what seems to be quite possessive behavior on the child's part. Children definitely enjoy having their parent to show off and to show around.

Visitors from various countries of the world enjoy the opportunity to talk with children in an early childhood center. Perhaps they have a native garment to wear or show, or songs, dances, food, or stories to share with children. Occasionally a foreign student participates over a period of time until children realize how much like everyone else that person is. The bridge to the world community has been opened for children in such a group. A world globe is very helpful to aid in the discussion with a foreign visitor. Teachers must study to become knowledgeable about the visitor's culture.

Visitors should be helped to understand the interests of the children. For example, musicians welcome suggestions of songs the children know. Visitors like to know how much the teacher expects the children to become involved. For example, a ballet dancer can simply perform a dance, or lead the children in their own ballet, which, of course, makes the event much more meaningful for the children. The teacher should be alert to help, where needed, to be sure that the visitor has a pleasant experience too.

Special visitors also deserve children's thank-you's. The following is how one group said thanks to a young mother who brought her baby for them to see.

Dear Mrs. Smith,

Thank you for letting us see the baby. Thank you for telling us how he eats the cereal. Thank you for letting us see him eat his apple juice. Thank you for putting on the bib.

Thank you for letting us see his toes. Thank you for letting us see his hair—his little black fur. Thank you for letting us see his shoes or his slippers—his bootsies! Thank you for coming.

Please come again. Thank you. Thank you. Thank you.

Love,
The Kindergarten Kids

Conclusion

Field trips and special visitors are appropriate methods to use with young children. In some instances children are better off remaining at school than being taken on field trips prematurely.

For these methods to give maximum educational benefit, these considerations should be weighed: the educational goals for the group, the suitability of available field trips, the time required, the costs, and the dangers involved. Teachers should make adquate preparation, prepare the children, and consider details of the special event, the follow-up and the posttrip activities.

The parent can make significant contributions to this aspect of the school program, through participating directly as a visitor with a special talent or exhibit or through helping as a guide during a field trip.

Applications

1. Discuss the "Talk It Over" items found in the chapter.
2. Complete Lesson 15 in *A Laboratory Workbook for Introduction to Early Childhood Education*. Hand in as scheduled.
3. Write an activity plan for a field trip or a special visitor using information in the chapter. Secure approval and carry out the plan. Evaluate the results from children's point of view and your viewpoint. Prepare a report and hand it in along with your approved plan.
4. Evaluate your total participation performance on your evaluation form developed in Chapter 1.
5. Add ideas and plans for field trips and special visitors to your Resource File.

Study Questions

1. Using an example from your experience, show how a field trip or special visitor is part of a cumulative plan.

2. State and discuss factors determining whether the teacher should consider using the field trip method of teaching.

3. State and discuss the steps for planning high-quality field trips or planning for special visitors in the school.

4. Identify dangers in taking field trips and list the steps teachers should take to minimize dangers.

5. Discuss the advantages and disadvantages of inviting a visitor to school rather than taking a field trip to that person's place of work.

Additional Readings

COHEN, DOROTHY H., and MARGARITA RUDOLPH, *Kindergarten and Early Schooling*. Englewood Cliffs, N.J.; Prentice Hall, Inc., 1979.

EMMONS, RAMONA W., and BILLY N. POPE. *Your World*, Series I through VII. Dallas: Taylor Publishing Co., 1966–1969.

LEEPER, SARAH H., et al. *Good Schools for Young Children*. New York: Macmillan Publishing Co., Inc., 1984.

WANN, KENNETH D., MIRIAM S. DORI, and ELIZABETH LIDDLE. *Fostering Intellectual Development in Young Children*. New York: Teachers College Press, Columbia University, 1962.

Food
Activities,
Meals,
and Snacks

- To *identify nutrition information that young children can appropriately learn.*
- To *describe guides for presenting nutrition and food information to young children.*
- To *state the goals for mealtimes in early childhood schools and explain ways to fulfill each goal.*
- To *state procedures for providing snacks in early childhood schools.*
- To *describe and evaluate food activities for early childhood schools.*

"We're having jelly today," sang the teacher while passing out the food for snack. Robert, a sturdily built five-year-old, matched the song with his, "Oh, good, I'm having jelly in my belly." Robert was sitting next to Betty, his regular snacktime friend. The menu didn't please Betty so much. "I don't want any bread," she said. The teacher said perhaps someone else would like it then. Betty repeated, "I don't want any bread."

Robert's hearing acuity is good, and his reaction time was evident in the haste and skill he displayed in slipping a napkin over both of her pieces of bread and jelly and pulling them toward his place.

His snacktime friend asked him if he wanted her glass of milk as well. He replied as he pointed to his own and rhymed his answer, "Never fear. I've got some right here." He drank three glasses of milk and ate his own sandwich and the sandwich of his snacktime friend. He left one scraggly crust after inspecting it carefully to be sure there was no hint of jelly still adhering to it.

Robert was a well-nourished and peppy five-year-old who thoroughly enjoyed food. Betty was thin and listless, rejecting many foods that other children enjoyed. How can their early childhood teacher help

Figure 16-1. Preparing rolled cookies is one of many food activities that interests young children. (Hoeflin Stone House Child Care Center, Kansas State University)

them establish habits that will guide their eating and nutrition in the years to come?

A Child's Nutrition: Whose Responsibility?

A child's body is his or her closest environment. Adequate nutrition is basic to life, growth, and learning. According to Myron Winick, a nutrition researcher, malnutrition and undernutrition can irreversibly affect a child's brain development.[1]

Parents have the primary responsibility for the kind and quantity of food available to their children. When children are placed in a full-day or part-day early childhood center, the staff assumes a portion of the parents' responsibility. (Quality of food is written into regulations of child care facilities.) Homes and child care facilities keep a given supply of

[1] For information on the effects of malnutrition on brain development read, *Malnutrition and Brain Development,* by Myron Winick (New York: Oxford University Press, 1976), p. 137.

food on hand, and young children cannot secure more or other foods except those supplied. Children at the preprimary age are not responsible for their food supply and are not able to be responsible for the quality of their nutrition.

As children mature, they begin to exercise some autonomy in the choices they make within the existing food supply. They may refuse certain foods and request others. Children reach this stage just when their growth rate is slowing down. Parents may worry and often make serious efforts to get children to eat. Food advertisers, particularly on television, capitalize on parents' insecurity. For example, young children are believed by advertisers to be influential in getting their parents to buy certain foods. Certainly the firms believe advertising pays off. At the same time, there are no equally high-prestige or action-packed ads extolling the virtues of milk, meat, eggs, fruits, or vegetables. Perhaps teachers and parents need to mount a "hard sell" campaign for nutritious foods. It would pay off handsomely if the outcome is healthier human beings.

One important avenue for influencing children's nutritional status is to work with their parents. Some suggestions are found in Chapter 18. The present chapter focuses on ways that teachers of young children can initiate learning regarding food and nutrition, and work toward the long-range goal of having children *select nutritionally balanced diets independently*. Note the goal statement carefully. In the early years, if parents and teachers are doing their jobs adequately, the child has only nutritious foods from which to choose. The child begins to have opportunities to make food selections from among all sorts of choices during the school-age years and beyond. If habits of choosing nutritious foods are developed early, the chances of sustaining those habits later are greater. Teachers and parents need to realize that choice of food often depends on social or peer pressure and practice as well as on rational nutritional information, especially during school-age years.

Opportunities for Food and Nutrition Education

Full-day schools serve meals and snacks, part-day programs serve snacks, and both have ample opportunity to plan food-related experiences as part of their daily educational program. Mealtimes are expected to conform to nutritional requirements as specified in regulations. Food should be well balanced, clean, colorful, and served in a pleasant atmosphere which encourages children to eat and to look forward to mealtime. Meals and snacks are essential for refueling and maintaining children's bodies. Children also rest as they eat, which is important.

Food and cooking experiences provided within the curriculum have been encouraged because of the children's high interest level. They enjoy helping with food preparation, eating foods, and talking about food. Children's curiosity and interest in school may be stimulated through food experiences when other activities fail. Parents report hearing more about the food and cooking projects than about many other school activities. The cognitive or mental learning that occurs during food activities has been emphasized, especially contribution to vocabulary and concept building. Such concepts as classification by color, size, texture, or source—whether animal or plant—are developed, and information such as whether it is the seed, root, stem, or flower that is eaten is acquired.

In most food experiences nutritional information is overlooked. Perhaps most teachers assume that if food experiences are provided, children will automatically learn a few nutrition concepts. It seems likely that this assumption is in error.

The intent of this chapter is to encourage teachers to exploit every food experience for its contribution to nutrition education. Teachers, with prestige among children and parents, can state their high regard for the nutritional qualities of milk, meat, cereals, vegetables, and fruits and get their message across to children as effectively as TV ad writers—if they try.

* * *

Talk It Over: No. 1

Discuss your own experience in learning nutrition information and applying it. What do you think about attempting to include a few facts about nutrition as other food concepts are presented?

* * *

Guides for Food and Nutrition Program Planning

Five major guides for planning food and nutrition experiences for young children in early childhood centers are to personalize, simplify, dramatize, regularize, and mobilize. Details of these guides will now be discussed.

Personalize

The teacher makes the subjects of food and nutrition come alive for each child personally. Remember it is individual nutrition that counts.

1. Through questioning and observation, the teacher finds out how advanced children are in their knowledge of foods and nutrition. What are the sources of foods that the children know? Meal or snacktime is a good time for informal discussion. The consequences of eating or not eating certain foods can also be discussed. For example, one child, Cindy, reported to her kindergarten teacher that, "My dentist told me to never never drink any more pop or my teeth would all drop out."

2. The teacher, through observing, and talking with parents, learns the typical foods eaten by each child. Any ethnic groups with differing food patterns should be noted. Capitalizing on these food variations while planning specific projects may be a useful approach.

3. The teacher should find out if any families make their livings in fishing, farming, food processing, or the grocery or restaurant business. With this information, those families' children can be recognized as "authorities" or resource persons. The teacher may also be able to involve the parents as hosts for a field trip or in some school activity.

4. The teacher should weigh and measure the children and record the figures. A chart can be made for recording their growth during the year. With data from parents, the chart could begin with birth. When adding to the chart from time to time, the teacher could tell the children that nutritious food helps them grow and stay healthy.

5. The children may bring pictures of favorite foods from home or find them in the school's magazine collection. The teacher could help them make a poster illustrating the basic food groups.

6. The teacher could have children play a game called "I tasted something new, its name was————, it tasted like————."

7. Parents can be invited to a meal or snack or to help with a cooking project. Having one's parents at school is very important to children.

8. Each child is given an opportunity daily to have a hands-on experience with food and to relate that food to nutrition information.

Food experiences and nutrition information can form the basis for a sound science education. All the sciences can be emphasized—biological, physical, and social sciences.

Children need numerous firsthand experiences with real food. These experiences will teach more about food and nutrition than numerous pictures or lectures. It is better to have fewer experiences and have them with real food than it is to have many experiences with pictures, models, or mimeographed pages to color in. The opportunity to see, touch, taste, smell—yes, and even to hear some foods—makes lasting impressions on children. Remember that young children are here-and-now learners. (Review Chapter 9 for learning stages.) In the course of planned and incidental experiences the teacher can ask

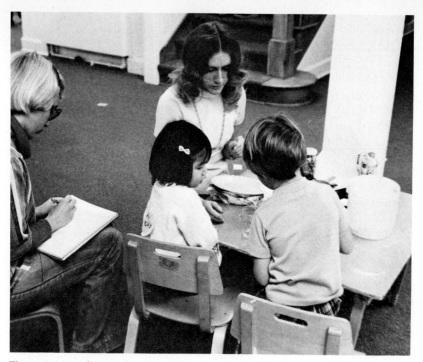

Figure 16-2. After working together to make a special dish called quiche children will pronounce it "good" when later they get to sample it. (Early Childhood Laboratory, Kansas State University)

What do you see? (color, shape, size, kind)

How does it smell? (strong, spicy, fragrant, repulsive)

How does it feel? (rough, smooth, slimy, hot, cold)

How does it sound? (loud, soft, crackly, crunchy)

How does it taste? (sweet, sour, salty, spicy, bitter)

Children should never be asked to taste food while blindfolded. In the first place, young children dislike blindfolds and many refuse to participate when they see blindfolds are called for. More importantly, parents and society want children instinctively and rationally to refuse to taste or eat any item unless they think about it and their senses tell them that the item is harmless, or good for them. For this reason a blind tasting of items that are not known or seen to come out of an appropriate container is poor educational strategy. Caution is always the way of the wise. Most adults would refuse to play some of the food-guessing games children are asked to play. Many children have been harmed fatally by tasting a substance out of curiosity. Precautionary instincts should be encouraged in early childhood programs.

Simplify

Simplifying food and nutrition concepts to meet the cognitive level of young children is essential and challenging. Young children have been eating all their lives so they are quite well acquainted with some foods. However they may not yet know or eat a variety of foods. Thinking about how food relates to their health, energy, growth, and general well-being will probably be quite new to them. Teachers can check on children's ability to generalize by asking, "Why is milk good for you?"

Nutrition information is very complex and abstract. Nutrients are not something children can see, hold, or weigh, for example. Recalling Piaget's stages of cognitive development from Chapter 9 reminds one how simplified nutrition information must be if we are to hope that children can grasp and use it. The Basic Four food groups were designated by nutritionists to help unspecialized adults with choosing their food. By eating selections daily from each group the expectation is that necessary and sufficient nutrients will be obtained. The Basic Four food groups are

Fruit-Vegetable Group

4 or more servings.
Include: A citrus fruit or other fruit or vegetable important for vitamin C. A dark-green or deep-yellow vegetable for vitamin A at least every other day. Other vegetables and fruits including potatoes.

Meat Group

2 or more servings.
Beef, veal, pork, lamb, poultry, fish, eggs. As alternates: dry beans, dry peas, nuts.

Bread-Cereal Group

4 or more servings.
Whole grain, enriched, or restored.

Milk Group

Some milk for everyone.
4 or more cups for teenagers.
2 or more cups for adults.
3 or more cups for children.
Other dairy products.

Other Foods

As needed to complete meals and to provide additional food energy and other food values.

Excellent and reliable information is available from your state's Cooperative Extension Service or from the local National Dairy Council office. Consult the phone book for the nearest office. Both have materials for school-agers which will be useful if simplified for younger children.[2]

---

[2] A useful booklet, *Fun with Good Foods* was developed by the U.S. Department of Agriculture's Food and Nutrition Service. It is available from the Government Printing Office, Washington, D.C. 20402. For an in-depth look at integrating nutrition education in classrooms see *Nutrition: A Teacher Sourcebook of Integrated Activities* by Shirley Oliver and Katherine Musgrave (Boston: Allyn & Bacon, 1984).

After labeling the chalk board with the four food groups by taping representative pictures above four columns, the cook, dietitian, or teacher, with the cooperation of the children, can plan a week's menus for meals or snacks in the center. Children can help classify the foods and help make a "balanced" menu. A picture menu poster can be arranged for the classroom using cutout foods. The foods may be discussed as they are eaten the following week.

As children eat the foods the teachers can help them verbalize statements as they eat; for example, "Meat is good for me, it helps me grow blood and muscle." "Apples are good for me, they are nice and crunchy for my teeth." "Eggs help my muscles and blood grow." "Vegetables give me energy to run and play." "Carrots are good for me, they make my eyes bright."

Children can feel their own muscles and bones to help in understanding those concepts. They can generalize that it will take lots of food to grow taller. Usually children like to talk about when they've seen blood, and how it looked on that occasion. They can be told that "Eating meat helps us grow more blood." After a mirror has been set up and the children have been given apple slices, they can talk about their teeth and jaws and how they move when they chew firm foods like apples. Of course, good chewing is essential to good nutrition. After such tasting it is interesting to see the pictures children draw of themselves.

Dramatize

The enthusiasm and involvement of the teachers and parents will inspire interest in food and nutrition among children. Teachers can brainstorm among themselves searching for creative ways to increase the appeal of nutritious food and to increase nutrition information and its meaningfulness to children. The various food and cooking projects which will be outlined later in the chapter will help dramatize the learning. Field trips, suggested in Chapter 15, may serve either to stimulate some area of study or become capstone experiences; for example, perhaps after months of intermittent projects related to the milk food group, the children can go to a dairy processing plant to see milk bottling or ice cream and cheese making.

To dramatize, the teacher and children can decorate the classroom with pictures of foods, gardens, farms, restaurants, or supermarkets, depending on the current focus. Books can be made available for individual and group reading. Songs, finger plays, and poems can be taught.

Children can play supermarket if supplied with cartons or cans from foods. They can sort out the "good-for-you-foods" and the "not-good-for-you-foods." Food-related dramatic play concerning farming, fishing, gardening, restaurant and housekeeping can be carried on in either the classroom or playyard.

For older children puppets or flannel-board figures can be made and used to develop a play focusing on foods. If desirable, the play or puppet show could be given to younger siblings or parents, perhaps at a covered-dish dinner sometime during the term.

A large supermarket picture is available in school supply houses. Children can study such a picture and talk about the places they've been while shopping with parents. Or, after a trip to a supermarket to buy groceries for a food project at school, children could all help draw or paint their own supermarket mural.

Dramatic nutrition experiments, such as the following, can be carried out with kindergarten groups. Two white rats were brought into the classroom and housed in separate cages. One rat received the food from the children's lunchroom—vegetables, fruit, bread, meat, and milk while the other received a coke and candy diet. After three weeks the children could readily see that "Whitey," who had been fed the coke and candy diet was smaller, had rough hair, and was quarrelsome. The rats were weighed each week and a chart was made to show their gains in weight. These kindergarteners perceived the effects of feeding only coke and candy to a rat. "Poor Whitey, he needs some good food," they concluded. How well did they relate the experiment to themselves? Though they were often told that if they ate only coke and candy they'd stay small, the children's ability to relate the nutrition of rats to themselves was disappointing at the close of the experiment. Later on they recalled having had the rats at school, but their ability to relate well the outcome of the experiment to themselves was still lacking. Perhaps additional effort could overcome this difficulty.

* * *

Talk It Over: No. 2

Expand on the ideas suggested for dramatizing the effects of good foods on the body.

* * *

Regularize

Food and cooking projects can become a regular part of the curriculum, occurring once or twice a week in some groups. Every day the children have a nutrition break (snack), and that may be the only emphasis on food on certain days. On some days the emphasis may be extensive, with one or more food-related activities being planned.

When planning a food experience for children, the teacher thinks first of the goals stated earlier. Which ones can be achieved through the

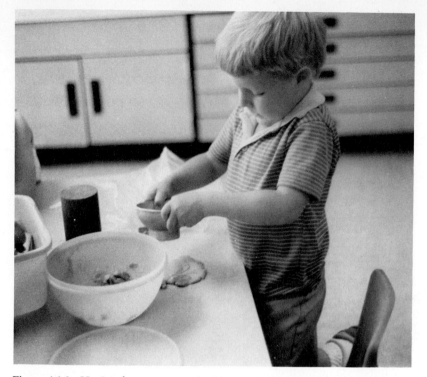

Figure 16-3. Having frequent opportunities to work on food projects helps children improve skills handling tools as well as to go over learnings from previous experiences. (Child Development Center, Metropolitan State College, Denver)

project? Experiences may be selected on the basis of the Basic Four food groups, giving children firsthand information on a food or two from each group. Foods with high sugar and fat content are avoided. Most American children eat excessive amounts of sweets. Deep-fat fried foods are extremely dangerous to make with young children due to the very high temperature of the oil. Fried foods are difficult for children to digest and, therefore, are to be avoided.

All needed ingredients and utensils should be organized. A picture recipe can be posted for children to "read." When doing a new project the teacher is wise who tries it out first at home and notes possible problems that may occur as the children do it.

Allow children to eat their food products as soon after preparing them as possible for most effective learning. In serving foods to children, one should remember that children like mild-flavored and mild-temperature foods best. They typically let their soup get cool and their ice cream get mushy.

As the children eat their food products, the teacher should remember to discuss the food. Naming, labeling, and restating the procedures

448

used will help children remember. Helping them think of adjectives to describe the appearance and the taste of the foods adds to their vocabulary. Review the food group the food belongs to. Reminding them to tell their parents about the project further strengthens their learning and helps tie the home and the school together.

Food activities can seldom constitute the whole program. Like any good thing they can be overdone. In one group one child demanded on the fifth day of a study about apples, "Do we *have* to talk about apples again today?" Apparently the study of apples was interfering with the child's other strong interests. Such reactions may occur when teachers talk too much rather than begin an action project. The cumulative plan which was described in Chapter 9 is very effective in planning for food and nutrition education. Advocating emphasis throughout the year, the cumulative plan helps children build their concepts and experiences little by little.

Mobilize

The teacher will mobilize available resources—human and nonhuman—to get food and nutrition concepts across to children. Actually, the first resource is the teacher who becomes informed and serves as a model with the kind of food habits she or he wishes children to develop. The teacher has tremendous influence on the children in the class because children want to be like the teacher. If a positive approach is used when talking about nutritious food, children will be enthusiastic about these foods. If the teacher enjoys and is willing to taste a wide variety of foods, children will be more inclined to do so.

Parents are a fine resource. They can help by trying out at home foods that are prepared at school. A class newsletter with recipes aids in getting this home activity underway. Parents may also be invited to school to make a dish for the class to try; for instance, Danish pastry from a family whose origins are in Denmark, tortillas from a parent whose roots are Mexican, or a rice dish made by a family with Asian roots. Parents are willing to contribute to the class if teachers invite them and give them personal support and guidance while they make their contributions.

Various other visitors can be helpful. Perhaps a 4-H or Scout boy or girl could give a cooking demonstration in class. A home economics student could also give a demonstration. A dental hygienist can be invited to discuss how food helps children have good teeth. A National Dairy Council spokesperson may speak or send films, booklets, or pictures.

There are many books, pictures, movies, and filmstrips that might be utilized. The teacher should be sure to preview these to see if they can be easily explained to young children. Field trips mentioned earlier may be arranged through parents, interested friends, or local businesses.

The kitchen might be considered the chemical laboratory of the school for young children. It may be the regular school kitchen, with a small table in one corner where an adult and a few children prepare their foods. Some schools have elaborately furnished child-size kitchens. Or a table or two in the classroom can become the cooking center. A hot plate and utensils can be brought in on a tray and removed when the cooking project is completed. The latter arrangement is probably the most common. Teachers often bring equipment from home. In public schools having lunchrooms or home economics classrooms, teachers often can use school equipment. Lacking cooking facilities, children's parents can be enlisted to take food home to bake after it is mixed by the children. Numerous possibilities exist. Each teacher explores the options and makes the arrangements to provide opportunities for the children to explore the world of food.

The teacher and the assistants discuss their roles during the cooking project. For example, will the assistants help with the food? Or will they carry on other activities? If so, which ones? If it is necessary to take food or children outside the room, who is to go? Will each child's product be labeled, or will it be placed in a common pan? What if a child wants to put the product in the locker or take it home? Who cleans up after the project?

Long-Range Goals for Children's Experiences with Food

By providing experiences with food the teacher helps young children build on the following long-range goals little by little. Children learn:

1. Children need foods from the Basic Four food groups in order to grow, run, and learn.
2. It is fun and interesting to try new foods.
3. Foods have names, physical characteristics, and flavors.
4. Plants and animals grown on farms or living in the water are primary sources of food.
5. The supermarket supplies some food products that are ready to eat and others that are ready to prepare.
6. Preparation of food includes such processes as heating, cooling, freezing, beating, and grinding.
7. Cooking tools, equipment, and processes have names.
8. The scientific method of observing, relating, interpreting and generalizing can be related to food.
9. Safety and cleanliness are important in the kitchen.
10. Both men and women like to cook and eat.

As specific food projects are now described, the above goals will serve as general guides. More specific short-range goals will be needed as each food project is developed.

Learning the Sources of Foods

As far as most children know, the grocery store is the source of food. The children may help the teacher buy food there occasionally. Money concepts develop as they discuss the cost and the number of coins required to pay for a purchase.

Teachers can use visual aids, field trips, or a garden to help the children further their understanding of the primary sources of most foods.

Interest is guaranteed if the children have picked the apples for apple sauce or the pumpkin for pumpkin custard, or if they have watched the cows being milked for the milk in ice cream. Garden products, too, will be pronounced "delicious" after they have been cared for by the children. The teacher can discuss the subject of primary sources by asking, "Where is this food grown?" or "What happens to it before the grocer gets it?"

Because families today buy so many foods already prepared, even adults almost forget how a food is grown or how it appears in its primary state. The chance to plant, care for, pick, clean, cook, and then eat a food crop is experienced by fewer and fewer people as the society becomes more and more urban. A garden helps children understand that some food is first a growing plant. Occasionally a window box can be used for growing plants.

If it is not feasible to grow the plants (and teachers could never grow all of them), it may be possible to visit gardens and farms to see plants growing. Teachers can ask local citizens or at a farmer's market for suggestions of local primary sources. The children might go to see such crops as wheat, corn, potatoes, fruit, pumpkins, or beans. Sometimes they may be allowed to pick a sample to take back to school.

A trip to the milking parlor of a dairy will help the children learn the source of their most common food—milk. A trip to the bottling and ice cream plant will add further to their information.

Because commercial egg producers generally won't admit visitors to egg-laying pens (because they excite the hens, so that they may stop laying), children may never see a hen lay an egg. A student teacher was telling the children that hens lay eggs, when one inquisitive child wanted to know, "How does the egg get out?" The student hadn't anticipated this question and was searching for a way to explain it when a knowledgeable five-year-old saved the day. The boy squatted henlike, then jumped around and squawked! It was real enough for everybody, and the discussion continued.

Pictures may be the only resource for teaching the primary source of many foods. Care should be taken to secure accurate information. One teacher was heard talking about pineapples growing on trees—certainly incorrect information for children to learn.

It is not easy for a child to understand how a cute little squealy pig relates to the breakfast bacon. Some children like animals so much that they really don't want to think about killing them to eat. Even a college student said, "How could you kill a chicken that you had known personally?" The children can be told the sources of meat, but the teacher need not speak of the butchering process unless the children ask. If asked, give a factual answer.

Many interesting food-related experiences can develop around the ocean and lakes with regard to the fish we eat. Children often like to talk about and play at going fishing.

Learning to Taste Fresh Foods

Many foods children eat are canned, bottled, or frozen. Teachers can look for ways to show children food in its fresh state.

Trays of fresh food can be arranged so that the children will taste

Figure 16-4. Self help is encouraged by small pitchers that enable children to pour their own beverage. (Child Development Laboratory, Michigan State University)

various foods. Vegetables or fruits can be diced, and the children can serve themselves with toothpicks. An example of the whole food should be reserved so that the children can relate physical qualities—color, shape, size, and weight—to flavor and internal characteristics as they eat. Avoid introducing too many new items in one project. It confuses children. Repeat the project with new foods to taste.

Orange juice is a familiar food. However, many families buy it frozen or canned. Squeezing their own oranges and drinking the juice will delight children. Allow 1 orange per child. Have several squeezers. Allow children to drink the juice as soon as it is squeezed. Have them talk about the taste, color, and consistency. Tell the children "Juice is good for your skin and gums." Lemons can be squeezed for lemonade. Fruits such as apple, grape, and cherry are sometimes heated to extract the juice. The children can help with this process too if reasonable precautions are taken with the hot liquids.

Children will enjoy cutting apples, bananas, celery, carrots, tomatoes, peppers, and cucumbers for their snack. To prevent discoloration, the teacher should remember to dip apples, bananas, pears, and peaches in citrus juices or in a solution made of ascorbic acid (available in the freezer supply section of the grocery store) mixed in a little water or syrup. Fruits can be served alone or in a fruit cup. Celery stuffed with cream cheese or peanut butter is popular.

Learning How the Consistency of Food Changes

The children learn that through various processes in the kitchen—heating, cooling, freezing, grinding, beating—the food is made ready to eat. Children can observe some of the changes that take place. They can talk about the machines used.

Peanut Butter

Peanut butter, a longtime favorite, can be made from peanuts ground in a blender. The children can shell the peanuts and place them in the blender. After the peanuts are ground, add jelly or honey to give a consistency that will spread. Serve a spoonful to each child and pass the crackers. Watch them spread the peanut butter and eat!

Gelatin

When making gelatin dessert, the children can see the effect of the hot water on the granules. Then they note the change to a solid after chilling. If gelatin is started at the beginning of the day, cooled with ice water or ice cubes, and poured into individual paper cups, it is possible to have it ready to serve for snack the same day. For variation, set the gelatin outdoors on a cold day. The children will conclude that "it's cold as a refrigerator outdoors."

Ice Cream

Making homemade ice cream teaches children that ice cream really does contain all the good foods that their parents say it does. They can actually see the milk, eggs, sugar and flavoring go into the ice cream as it is being made. Either an electric or a hand-turned freezer can be used— and the children will help! The proof is in the eating. M-m-m-! Good! For a variation, one group brought in snow to use in place of the ice.

Butter

Making butter gives the children yet another chance to see a change take place before their eyes. Use a pint of whipping cream for fifteen to eighteen children. Pour one cup of whipping cream into each of two quart jars and tighten the lids. The children pass the jars around the table, shaking and counting off five shakes per child. The cream first whips, then begins to separate, giving buttermilk and globules of butter. When sufficiently churned, the butter collects ("gathers") together. The buttermilk can be poured into small paper cups so that everyone can have a taste. The butter can be served on individual serving plates. Give the child a small plastic knife and watch as the butter goes on the crackers. Even children who say they hate butter will like both butter and buttermilk if it is presented to them with "Let's see how it tastes," instead of "Who wants some buttermilk?" or "Would you like some buttermilk?" Because whipping cream is sweet, the buttermilk tastes only slightly different from other milk.

Apples

Apples can be cooked into apple sauce. The children will observe the changing of the hard apples into the mushy sauce and the effect of sugar on the tart apple. Leaving the skin on the apple makes it easier for the children to do more of the project. Allow one apple per child. It is convenient to use the special apple cutter that cuts the apple in eight sections and cores it all in one operation. The children can accomplish this operation with a minimum of help. If cooking takes place in the room, the tantalizing aroma will attract other cooks. Stir the cooked apples, and add sugar and a bit of cinnamon. Serve for snack. The children will surely go home and ask to repeat this project!

Popcorn

Popcorn is a favorite of children. The addition of heat to corn makes such an aromatic odor that people in other parts of the building will drop into the classroom. An electric popper or skillet is handy for this project. Follow the usual safety precautions. Some teachers avoid pop-corn because children may choke on it. Infants and toddlers should not be given popcorn, and other children should sit quietly while eating it.

Eggs

Eggs change consistency with heat. They can be boiled or scrambled. If shells are needed for dyeing, the inside of the egg can be blown out and scrambled. To blow: first use a paring knife to tap a hole about one-quarter inch in diameter in each end, then BLOW. Let each child blow an egg into a single cup. If bits of shell break off, the shell can more easily be retrieved. The children can help beat the eggs, adding seasoning and one tablespoon of milk per egg. The children can take turns stirring the egg in the electric skillet and watching the coagulation occur as the cooking process progresses. Serve for snack or lunch. Arrange timing to serve warm.

Breads

Breads of many varieties can be made in the classroom. The children learn more if they are made from "scratch" than when they are made from mixes. Actually breads have few ingredients. Recipes can be posted near the cooking table. What could be more fun than mixing, cooking, then eating your very own pancake? Pancakes can be served with jelly or powdered sugar. Biscuits, muffins, tortillas, and banana bread are other suggestions. Yeast bread can be made, but the project may require two days.

Baked Goods

Cookies, cakes, and gingerbread can be made with various mixes. However, mixes simplify the process so much that understanding of the total ingredients required is reduced. Cookies and cakes may be made for a special day. Sometimes at the close of school a group makes a birthday cake for all the children who have summer birthdays. The group sings "Happy Birthday" to each child!

Directions follow for making special sugar cookies in the classroom. By noting the concern for details in this outline, the teacher may be helped with planning other projects.

Main Dishes

Main dishes for the lunch menu or a more substantial snack can also be made by children. Try canned soups, cheese sandwiches, tuna sandwiches or cinnamon toast.

No child will pass up a vegetable soup after helping cook the soup bone one day, chopping the vegetables the next, and watching "our soup" simmer to completion the next. By that time everyone will literally have

MAKING SUGAR COOKIES WITH YOUNG CHILDREN[3]

1. Use a sugar cookie recipe suitable for rolled cookies. Add a little more flour than is needed if an adult were going to roll them. A recipe will make fewer cookies than the recipe states because the children will not roll them very thin.

2. The children can help put the ingredients together. Mixing may be done the day before the cookies are baked, or the teacher can have the cookie dough ready when the children arrive. The time element will be the deciding factor. The rolling, cutting, and baking are usually enough for a half-day group to do.

3. Divide the dough into balls—enough for each child to make three or four cookies. Make a few extras in case of an accident.

4. Have the supplies on a tray—several rolling pins, flour, sifter, spatulas, cookie cutters, colored sugars, raisins, and plenty of cookie sheets.

5. Use a low table so that the children can stand to work. Cover the table with clean tea towels. Pull them tight and tack the edges or secure them with masking tape. Sift flour on the area where each child will roll the dough.

6. Be sure the child washes his or her hands just before coming to help. Supervise the hand washing, or hands may not be clean enough for food handling.

7. The children will be inclined to push down hard on the rolling pin, so tell them, "Let the rolling pin do the work." You may have to stand behind each child, helping each barely press the rolling pin down.

8. When the dough is rolled enough to cut, be ready with this statement, "Let me tell you a cook's secret." Then show each how to fit several cookie cutters on the dough before cutting any. Children are inclined to cut one cookie out of the middle, and then have to reroll the dough. Help the child place the cookies on a greased cookie sheet.

9. The cookie decorator's table is set up nearby. It is another low table and should be covered with paper or a cloth for catching the sugar. The children can sit to decorate cookies. Colored sugar is provided in shakers. Raisins and red hots are also popular. The children spend a long time here getting just the right effect. When a child adds so much sugar that it might burn and stick to the pan, the cookies may need to be transferred to a fresh baking sheet.

10. One adult is required to supervise the oven as soon as a pan of cookies is ready. Set a timer because cookies bake quickly. Children enjoy peeking in the oven, so let them take turns as cookie watchers.

11. It is generally best to avoid keeping track of which cookie is whose. Some get broken, or burned, so if they are mixed up no one is disappointed with the finished product.

12. Of course, the proof of a cookie is in the eating. As soon as the children are through rolling their cookies and sufficient cookies are out of the oven, it is time to bring out the milk for the pleasurable moment of eating their own cookies.

[3] Acknowledgment is due *The Progressive Farmer* for permission to reprint parts of an article by the author, "A Cookie Making Party" (February 1964), p. 106.

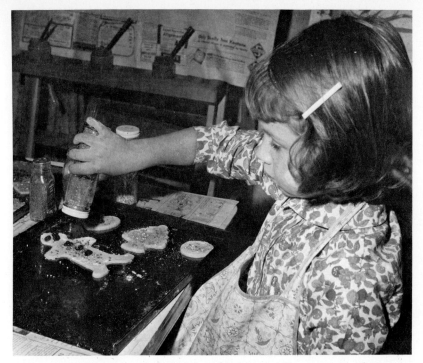

Figure 16-5. Decorating that special cookie is a creative experience that children enjoy. (Texas Tech University Kindergarten)

had a finger in the soup and surely will pronounce it "good." Some teachers like to call the soup "stone soup" and relate the old children's story to this experience.

Hamburgers, broiled hot dog bits, or pizza can be made. An electric skillet with temperature control is safest for hamburgers. The children can cut the hot dogs and watch with the teacher as they broil. The children can make pizzas by patting out canned biscuits and covering them with mildly seasoned pizza sauce and cheese. The pizzas are then baked.

Jelly

Children can help make jellies using the noncooked method. The recipe for "freezer jelly" is found on the pectin box. Sugar is stirred into fresh, canned, or reconstituted frozen juice. The pectin is boiled for one minute with three-fourths cup of water and then added to the juice and sugar. The jelly sets in a day or so. Children delight in using their "own" jelly and in spreading their own sandwiches with plastic picnic knives. It is a messy job, so teachers should prepare the table with a clean sheet of wrapping paper. Children will get jelly from ear to ear too, so a wash-up must follow the snack period. The recipe makes enough jelly for several sandwiches for a class of fifteen.

Learning About Safety and Cleanliness

Children learn safety concepts along with other concepts during cooking projects. It is best to choose cooking projects that offer a minimum of danger to the children. Nearly any project requiring heat or the use of knives requires adult supervision at all times. Locate electric cords out of traffic lanes so that the children won't trip over them. Foods just out of the oven or just off the stove are extremely hot. Care must be taken that the children are not burned. Provide a cutting board for each child and reasonably sharp knives. Take time to show the children safety measures in cutting and handing tools to each other.

Cleanliness of children's hands and of utensils can both be taught during food activities. Planning is required to get a child's hands washed just before he or she is ready to handle the food. If the child washes before the activity is ready and turns to play with toys, it is obvious that the hands are no longer clean and should be washed again. All this washing will confuse the children who, of course, can't see the germs on their hands.

Learning About Sex Roles

All activities are available to all children without regard to sex. Food activities are of great interest to boys. Teachers may have to dispel the notion that preparing food is only for girls.

* * *

Talk It Over: No. 3

Discuss safety and cleanliness procedures in relation to food activities in groups where you have participated. How would you explain precautions to children?

* * *

Mealtime in the School for Young Children

A visit to a school lunchroom is often a revelation to parents, especially if they can observe out of sight of their child. Parents make comments like the following: "He eats so well!" "I didn't know he could pour milk!" "Doesn't J.D. ask you to feed him?" The child may eat quite differently in a group of children and when guided by a skilled teacher.

When children are old enough for school, they may have recently entered an eating stage that frustrates their parents. The infant grows rapidly, so food consumption is high. At age three the growth curve has

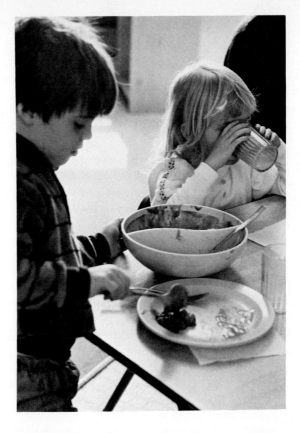

Figure 16-6. Serving themselves during meals gives children an opportunity to make decisions. (Hoeflin Stone House Child Care Center, Kansas State University)

leveled out and food needs are reduced.[4] About this same time children reach a stage where they want to assert their independence. They say "No" frequently and may refuse to eat foods they have been eating all along. Parents with a child of this age may get into the habit of bribing, cajoling, threatening, then finally feeding the child, just to get some food eaten. When entering an early childhood school, a child brings along home experience with food.

Goals for Mealtime

During mealtime the teacher wants the child:

1. To eat a well-balanced diet.
2. To enjoy mealtime.
3. To taste and ultimately enjoy eating a wide variety of food.
4. To learn to eat independently.
5. To sit at the table and develop acceptable table manners.

[4] Thelma Waylor and Rose S. Klein, *Applied Nutrition* (New York: Macmillan Publishing Co., Inc., 1965), p. 257.

A balanced diet will be planned by the nutritionist. Each food, including the dessert, is calculated to make a contribution to the child's essential nutrients. For this reason, dessert is not used as a reward for a clean plate. When school meals differ from home meals in both type of food and type of service, there is considerable adjustment for the child to make. The teacher understands that the children will need time to become accustomed to school food.

Food can be pretty as well as tasty. Plan variety in the color, texture, and shape of food. Tables and service should be orderly and attractive. Family style is the usual method of serving, with each table of five or six children having the dishes of food served by an adult at the table.

Children enjoy assuming some responsibility for meal service. Even three-year-olds can help set the table. Four- and five-year-olds will vie for the honor, and the teacher may need to keep a list of the helpers to be sure they all get turns. The children can also assist in cleaning up the tables following the meal. This training is good for all children but may be especially beneficial to children whose home routines appear inadequate.

Every effort should be made to arrange the setting so that it is pleasant, satisfying, and relaxing for both children and adults. The children should be seated on comfortable-height chairs that enable their feet to touch the floor. The youngest may need bibs. You can make self-help bibs by attaching a piece of elastic to a washcloth for the child to slip over the head.

Each child should have a special seat. Sometimes a teacher fosters a friendship by pairing a child who needs a friend with a potential friend during lunch. Although socializing is permitted at mealtime, the primary goal is to eat. The teacher may also wisely plan to seat the children who need special help near an adult, to disperse children who tend to be behavior problems, and to place independent eaters where they can be imitated by more dependent children. A seating arrangement that allows teachers to relax and get some nourishment too is important, because they may be required to spend several more hours that day being responsive to children's needs.

Breakfast is served to children who arrive early in full-day schools, in Head Start groups, and in many kindergartens since the new federal nutrition program has been instituted.

Some children may want to eat immediately on arrival, whereas others may prefer to play awhile and then have their breakfast. Breakfast is usually more informal than lunch. One teacher takes care of the eaters, and another supervises those who are playing.

Most teachers feel that when children have a quiet time just prior to lunch, they eat better. Children can do their toileting and washing and then gather around the teacher for quiet stories and songs. The period should not be rushed. It is not the best time to demand the most responsible behavior, because the children who are tired and hungry are more prone to anger.[5] When conflicts are common, teachers may wish to schedule lunch somewhat earlier, provide a more substantial mid-morning snack, or plan a less taxing morning program.

An orderly transition to the lunch tables from the story circle helps retain the quiet atmosphere. The teacher can say, "Children who sit with Mrs. D., creep like little hungry mice to your lunch table."

The teacher serves the food, adjusting the amount to an estimation of each child's appetite for a certain food. Many foods will be served in teaspoon-sized servings, especially foods that are new or less popular. The teacher assumes that each child will taste the food. When the teacher knows the child well, it is possible to gauge more accurately the portions, and a "clean plate" will occur more often. Enjoyment of food is more important than a clean plate. "There are three peak periods for the development of obesity in children: late infancy, early childhood, around six, and adolescence," according to nutrition researchers. "Obesity interferes with both health and psychological functioning."[6] Teachers and parents are cautioned by nutritionists about requiring a clean plate, as that may mean urging the child to overeat.

The teacher's small servings permit the child to ask for seconds and to serve her- or himself. Children enjoy this measure of independence. When they want more milk, the teacher will pour the amount appropriate for the glass in a small pitcher and permit the child to pour her or his own milk. If the small pitcher contains more than a glassful, the child may run it over. Children will drink numerous servings when they get to do the replenishing.

The teacher realizes that children generally like foods lukewarm. They may let soups cool and ice cream melt before eating.

*   *   *

Talk It Over: No. 4

Discuss the effect on the child of having parents and teachers understand that children prefer foods lukewarm—neither hot nor cold.

*   *   *

A typical serving arrangement allows children to take their dirty plates and silverware to a serving cart and return with their desserts when they have finished the main course. This gives them a chance to move a bit when they have been sitting for a time. They like this measure of confidence that they can walk without spilling their dessert.

---

[5] Catherine Landreth, *Early Childhood: Beahvior and Learning* (New York: Alfred A. Knopf, Inc., 1967), p. 142.

[6] Myron Winick, "Childhood Obesity," *Nutrition Today,* 9:3 (May/June 1974), pp. 9–10.

Guidance During Mealtime[7]

If the child is actively participating in the school program and is in good health physically and emotionally, he or she will eat what is needed to restore energy and to grow. Guidance during the meal will be related to the goals stated earlier. Every effort is made to help the child grow in independence. Teachers should not fall into a pattern of bribing, cajoling, or feeding children.

Even a three-year-old senses that the teacher can't spoon-feed five or six children (the number generally served at one table). The child simply imitates the others and goes about the business of eating. The teacher quietly praises the child and smiles. The child pours milk, cuts beans, and goes to the serving cart for dessert.

Children's meals at home may be come-and-go affairs, so they may think they can eat a little now and a little later even at school. The teacher can simply say, "If you are finished eating, put your plate on the cart. If you are hungry, sit at the table and eat." The teacher will give the child the choice, and after the decision, both teacher and pupil will live by it. A few days of finding food served at a regular time will help the child realize the necessity of eating at the designated time and place.

The teacher guides the child quietly in brief, positive statements, letting the child know what should be done. The teacher makes statements like: "Use your toast stick," to the child using fingers to get food on a fork; "A spoon will work better," to a child eating apple sauce with a fork; "Hold your glass up straight," to a child whose milk is about to spill; "Swallow before you talk," to the child who is talking with a mouth full; or "Keep your food on your plate," to the child who litters the tablecloth.

The teacher uses demonstrations, perhaps showing the child how to grip the fork for eating or cutting. He or she guides the child's hand to help. For example, while saying "Point the spoon toward you," the teacher may guide the child's hand to make the tip turn toward the child's mouth.

Children generally feel upset about spills. Children are sometimes scolded harshly at home and may expect the same treatment at school. When the teacher occasionally spills something, the children may feel a new sense of comradeship. Spills do occur. They are taken in stride. Extra silverware and napkins are kept close by to replace dropped items. A sponge, dust pan, and broom are available in the serving area. When accidents are frequent, a slight change in arrangement might help avoid them. For example, if the table is cluttered, it may help to place serving dishes on a side table within reach. Teachers will prevent some spills if

---

[7] For more information see Chapter 7, "Guiding Children's Eating Behavior," in *Guiding Young Children* by Verna Hildebrand (New York: Macmillan Publishing Co., Inc., 1985).

Figure 16-7. Family size groupings at lunch give children restful individualized attention. (Child Development Laboratory, University of Illinois)

they are alert to remind a child to place the glass back away from the edge of the table.

When the child has finished eating, she or he takes the plate and glass to the serving cart and leaves the dining area. A designated adult takes over for the next steps. It is important that children who remain at the lunch tables are not neglected because of all the adults becoming involved with the children who have finished eating. A routine should be established so that children know what to do next. Generally they go to the bathroom to wash and urinate, then either prepare for going home or for taking a nap, depending on the type of school.

In full-day programs, the nap room is generally prepared while the children eat; then, as children finish lunch, they prepare immediately for naps, to take advantage of the quieting effect of eating.

Snack Time

Midmorning and midafternoon snacks serve several purposes for young children. A snack provides time to rest and food to restore energy. It provides an informal, social conversation time good for summing up the day's activities. Snack may be a fairly organized time of day or it may be informal. In groups that remain at school for lunch, the teacher may plan an early snack to avoid interfering with lunch appetites. Some children are slow starters. They eat very light breakfasts but then are famished by snack time. They eat so much snack that they aren't hungry for an early lunch. If snack is served in an informal come-when-you're-hungry arrangement during the first hour of school, it meets the need of such children. In groups that take a midday nap at school, it may be customary to let a few children at a time eat their midafternoon snack as soon as they wake up. This plan offers the teacher time to talk with small groups while others are still napping.

In other groups teachers may like to hold a quiet time immediately following the self-selected activity period, then follow this with a group snack time when everyone eats together. In this way the half-day group accomplishes some of the goals that are achieved with a lunch program. No one plan is "best." The important rule is to make a good plan for a particular group of children.

The numerous suggestions for cooking projects and experiences with food offered in the first part of this chapter will contribute most if the children work together preparing the food, eat it together, and talk about it, thereby reinforcing the learning.

Of course, the children do not prepare every snack. The fare offered should be varied. There surely is no need for children to say, "Not that again!" in disparaging voices when they see the snack tray. Interesting food, attractively arranged and enthusiastically presented, will encourage the children to enjoy eating. They will be not only feeding themselves but learning about food as well.

Children can be designated "helpers" with snack. Perhaps one can serve the beverage, another place the napkins, another take the responsibility for helping serve the food. A poster showing a paper cup, a plate, and a napkin can be used to designate helpers—the names being removable and rotated during the weeks.

It is helpful to arrange in advance individual servings of food and drink at each child's place to eliminate prolonged waiting for the refreshments. For example, a glass of juice, a napkin holding three cookies, a dish of fruit, or a cupcake liner holding a serving of raisins can be set out on a tray from which the helpers can distribute the servings around the table before the children arrive at their places.

Imagine the impatience felt by the children who waited for one frustrated little girl to count out three cookies to each child in a class of twenty-five youngsters. Not only did they want three cookies, but they didn't want any broken ones. Several children could have been designated to help. The broken cookies should have been made into crumbs and used for some special dessert, as they were undesirable in the broken form.

Guidance suggestions made for serving lunch apply to snack. The children remove their glasses and napkins when they are finished, placing them on a tray for removal to the kitchen.

Communicating with Parents

Close coordination of the school and the home feeding programs may avoid unnecessary confusion for the child.[8] Parents can be invited to observe snack or lunchtime occasionally so that they will understand the experience their child is having. They should understand the goals the teacher has for a child of this age and the techniques used to foster those goals. Lunch menus can be sent home regularly.

Informing the parent when there have been special projects that the children may ask them to duplicate helps the parents carry through the learning begun in the school. Metheny et al. found that 34 percent of the children in their study requested their mothers to prepare food they had eaten at school.[9] Recipes can be exchanged. Occasionally the teacher may visit the home to demonstrate how to prepare a food that the child has liked at school. When the teacher and the parent develop rapport on such domestic interests as recipes, it may strengthen the communication between the family and the school.

Parents may enjoy contributing an item for snack or lunch. Some local sanitary codes forbid it. However, the school policy will be stated by the teacher. Parents are asked to inform the teacher ahead of time so that school food projects won't overshadow the parents' contribution. Duplications can then be avoided and parents' choice of a contribution can be guided so that it is appropriate in kind and amount. A typical occasion is a birthday or a holiday. A simple celebration at school is far easier on child and parent than giving a party at home. Teachers typically plan something festive for each child's birthday.

In one kindergarten the teacher left the snack completely up to the parents. If they wanted their child to have a snack, they had to send it to school. What happened in practice was that a group of disadvantaged children regularly sat through the snack period and watched their more well-to-do classmates sip from cans of juice and eat cookies. It is hard to understand how a thinking, feeling teacher could permit such a cruel situation in a class.

[8] Reva T. Frankle, Miriam F. Senhouse, and Catherine Cowell, "Project Head Start: A Challenge in Creativity in Community Nutrition," *Journal of Home Economics,* 59:1 (January 1967), pp. 24–27. The authors give numerous practical suggestions for helping children learn to eat nutritious foods and make suggestions for working with parents to improve nutrition in the home.

[9] Norma Y. Metheny, Fern E. Hunt, Mary B. Patton, and Helene Heye, "The Diets of Preschool Children," *Journal of Home Economics,* 54:4 (April 1962), p. 306.

If the advantaged parents had realized what was happening, they surely would have been willing to pool their funds to purchase a snack for all the children. It seems that, in fairness, what is available for one should be available to all.

Conclusion

Adequate nutrition is essential to life and learning. While the parents and teachers are responsible for the young child's nutrition, the early childhood center is a good place for that child to learn food habits which will help assure optimal nutritional status in the years ahead. There are numerous opportunities for early childhood teachers to provide food and nutrition education. Efforts must be personalized, simplified, dramatized, regularized and mobilized. The teacher mobilizes and utilizes various community resources in order to provide the needed experiences. Numerous food experiences were suggested along with some pointers on mealtime and snack time.

Applications

1. Discuss the "Talk It Over" items found in the chapter.
2. Complete Lesson 16 in *A Laboratory Workbook for Introduction to Early Childhood Education*. Hand in as scheduled.
3. Write an activity plan for a food activity for a few children using information and the sample plan (Figure 6-1) in Chapter 6. Secure approval, carry out the plan, and evaluate the results from the children's point of view and your viewpoint. Prepare a report and hand it in along with your approved plan.
4. Evaluate your total participation performance on your evaluation form developed in Chapter 1.
5. Add ideas and plans for food experiences to your Resource File.

Study Questions

1. Give an explanation of why nutrition education is more parent education than child education.
2. Identify and explain each of the five guides for planning food and nutrition activities for young children.
3. State and give examples of each of the ten long-range goals for children's experiences with food.
4. Explain in what ways experiences with food are science experiences.

5. State and discuss the goals for mealtime in full-day schools.

6. State and discuss the goals for providing snacks in part-day schools.

7. State several ways teachers can involve parents in the food activities of the school.

Film

Jenny Is a Good Thing   Color   20 minutes   1969

A film about Head Start children with a focus on food and nutrition. Shows warm feeling among staff and children. Available in Spanish. Modern Talking Pictures Services, 5000 Park St. N., St. Petersburg, Fla. 33709. Free from any Head Start Office.

Additional Readings

CHURCH, MARILYN, "Nutrition: A Vital Part of the Curriculum." *Young Children,* Vol. 35, No. 1, November 1979, pp. 61–65.

DEUTSCH, RONALD M. *The Family Guide to Better Food and Better Health.* Des Moines, Iowa: Meredith Corporation, 1974.

ENDRES, JEANNETTE B., and ROBERT E. ROCKWELL. *Food, Nutrition, and the Young Child.* St. Louis: The C. V. Mosby Company, 1980.

FERREIRA, NANCY J. *The Mother-Child Cook Book: An Introduction to Educational Cooking.* Menlo Park, Calif.: Pacific Coast Publishers, 1969.

HATFIELD, ANTOINETTE, and PEGGY STANTON. *How to Help Your Child Eat Right: The 'Fun to Eat' Cookbook and Guide to Nutrition.* Washington, D.C.: Acropolis, 1978.

HERR, JUDITH, and WINIFRED MORSE, "Food for Thought: Nutrition Education for Young Children." *Young Children,* Vol. 38, No. 1, November 1982, pp. 3–11.

McWILLIAMS, MARGARET. *Nutrition for the Growing Years.* New York: John Wiley & Sons, 1980.

OLIVER, SHIRLEY D., and KATHERINE O. MUSGRAVE. *Nutrition: A Sourcebook of Integrated Activities.* Boston: Allyn & Bacon, 1984.

Recommended Dietary Allowances, Eighth Revised Edition. Washington, D.C.: Food and Nutrition Board, National Academy of Sciences—National Research Council, 1975.

SCHLICK, MARY. "Kim, The Child Approved Nutrition Teacher." *Journal of Home Economics,* Vol. 68, No. 3, May 1976, pp. 21–23.

WAGNER, DOROTHY. *Nine Week Menu Cook Book.* Portageville, Mo.: Extension Division of University of Missouri, 1973.

WANAMAKER, NANCY, K. HEARN, and S. RICHARZ. *More than Graham Crackers: Nutrition Education and Food Preparation with Young Children.* Washington, D.C.: The National Association for the Education of Young Children, 1979.

Managing an Early Childhood Group

- To *identify and define the managerial tasks of teachers.*
- To *explain the need for setting aside planning and preparation time.*
- To *define and explain a cumulative plan for the curriculum.*
- To *differentiate between technical and social decisions.*

"I have the planning book," said Marietta to LaWanda as she and Juan entered the conference room. They accepted the glass of juice they were offered and settled down to work. LaWanda, the lead teacher, was surrounded by books and papers. Juan and Marietta, the assistants, each carried tablets and a file. The three were meeting to plan the program for their group of eighteen children for the next several weeks.

Teachers as Managers

You will perform many managerial functions as an early childhood teacher. Decisions are part of managing. There are *technical* decisions, such as "Which paper is the best buy for the money?" And *social* decisions—"Is it good to allow Jamie to play alone?" Technical decisions typically are about things, while social decisions are about people. It is easier to get hard evidence for technical decisions. Social decisions occur in unique circumstances with people, requiring the application of wisdom, experience, and technical information.

You will arrive at the point of taking charge of a group of children after successfully completing several steps in your early childhood teacher education program. Your practice teaching assignment may be your first

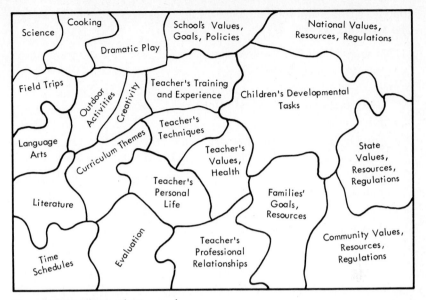

Figure 17-1. The teacher's puzzle.

experience in assuming leadership of others and being "in charge." Before long, there you are a full-fledged teacher and really in charge!

As a teacher you will be the manager of the group and classroom to which you are assigned. The mountain of decisions will be yours. Administrators like to hire well-qualified teachers and to assume you are ready to take charge. The more capably you handle your assignment, the less the principal or school administrator is likely to become involved. You'll be more autonomous. However, it is essential that you not carry autonomy too far. Early childhood teachers frequently find themselves one of a few, or sometimes even the only early childhood teacher. Thus for professional stimulation they must make friends and develop links with teachers of older children. An experienced teacher can be a great help to a new teacher just learning the ropes.

You will be isolated

Management Tasks

Management requires five major tasks. In this book the primary focus is on the managerial tasks of teachers who are in charge of groups of children. In another book this author has discussed the managerial tasks of managers, directors, and principals.[1] The five managerial tasks

---

[1] Verna Hildebrand, *Management of Child Development Centers* (New York: Macmillan Publishing Co., Inc., 1984).

apply to schools and to many types of agencies that you might manage. The tasks follow:

Planning is defined as a systematic formulation of a program of action for achieving goals.

Organizing is defined as systematically assembling and utilizing temporal, material, and spatial resources for carrying out a plan of action.

Staffing is defined as selecting, assigning, utilizing, and evaluating the human resources needed for carrying out a plan of action.

Leading is defined as setting the pace toward present goals and formulating future goals.

Monitoring and controlling are defined as being alert to performance of self and others in relation to established standards and making decisions and carrying out adjustments needed for meeting standards.

* * *

Talk It Over: No. 1

Review each of the managerial tasks and relate each to the many tasks of teachers. Discuss with your classmates.

* * *

Planning Programs for Young Children

Planning the early childhood program requires orchestrating all the distinct components as discussed throughout this book. *Planning is a systematic formulation of a program of action for achieving goals.* Planning requires giving attention to the various relationships and proportions, and achieving a program that can be expected to meet the needs of each child optimally. Just as an artist creates a unique painting by balancing component ideas, feelings, colors, and textures harmoniously, teachers likewise integrate all components. Teachers plan in depth and in detail in order to use human and nonhuman resources advantageously and to carry out a unique program in unique ways for a unique group of unique children. Teaching is a cluster of creative tasks.

Planning is the behind-the-scenes work that assures a humanistic, person-centered, developmental program responsive to children's needs and interests. Many details of plans appear on written charts, while other details are in the teachers' heads and ready for use at a moment's notice. The less experience the teachers have, the more written planning is essential to be sure that it is adequately done. Shared planning is essen-

Figure 17-2. With adequate planning children will find well prepared worthwhile activities during their hours in school. (Hoeflin Stone House Child Care Center, Kansas State University)

tial for full cooperation when working with several adults. Evaluating goes hand in hand with planning and will be discussed later.

Factors That Influence Planning

If a teacher were asked, "What is your major consideration when planning the program for your group of children?" the probable reply would be, "The children." This is, of course, as it should be. However, there are a number of other factors that teachers must also take into consideration. Some forces are national in scope, some are statewide, some are professional, and others originate in the community, the school, and the particular families of children. The planning task is somewhat like a puzzle.

Impact of the Federal Government

The democratic form of government of the United States influences teachers as they educate children to live in a democracy. In an authoritarian country the child is educated to function in that system. An example of national influence is the Supreme Court decision forbidding racial segregation in public schools. Also, the program of federal aid to education has stimulated communities to initiate Head Start and other programs. Many research projects and child care centers were assisted through federal funds.

Private schools are indirectly affected by federal action. For example, the standards established in federal Head Start guidelines regarding the teacher-pupil ratio give parents, teachers, and administrators in for-profit and nonprofit schools a standard they did not have previously.

Impact of State Governments

State governments have an impact on the teacher who plans for a group of children. States generally hold the power to set and enforce minimum standards, grant licenses to schools, and grant certificates to teachers. Most states provide state aid to public schools providing kindergartens. To receive financial aid, the schools are required to meet certain standards for curriculum, qualifications of teachers, and minimum number of days in a school year. State legislation may set some standards concerning facilities, children's medical examinations, or the number and ages of children admitted to classes. Check with the licensing agency in your state.

Influence of the Community

The community influences the program planning. In a public school, authority is vested in an elected board of community citizens that acts through a school administrator. Also, a city commission may hire the director of a community child care center or the director of the community action program. Nonprofit agencies, churches, or universities have special objectives that affect the teacher's planning. Local government agencies may also be responsible for enforcing certain fire and health regulations. Teachers must be aware of regulations as they plan.

Influence of the School Administration

The school itself establishes policies for all the classrooms in a system. School administrations control the funds that are spent for supplies, new equipment, janitorial help, and paid assistants. School traditions, such as admission policies or parent participation, will influence planning. Some coordination of programs is required when several classes use the same equipment and playyard. Ideally, the teacher will be called upon to take part in decisions affecting her or his area of specialization.

Influence of the Parents

Early childhood schools are considered a vital part of the country's family support system. Leadership is needed to build this link with the parents of children in early childhood schools.

Parents of children in a group can influence a teacher's planning. They know something of the impact the teaching is having on their child. When open communication exists between the teacher and the parents, the school gets valuable feedback regarding the positive and negative aspects of a program. The teacher's attitude toward parents can make the difference in parents' vital concern for or apathy toward school matters. If teachers listen to parents and actively involve them in school, parents can have a positive influence. Parents can also be a source of relentless pressure if their interests are consistently ignored. Head Start parents have been effective advocates for their children, saving the program from politicians several times.

In a study completed by the author on "Value Orientations for Nursery School Programs,"[2] parents rated "individuality" and "socialization" as their two most preferred value orientations for nursery school programs, when given a choice of nine orientations depicted through nine short stories. The nine value orientations were socialization, intellect, morality, aesthetics, authority, health, freedom, individuality, and economics. The economic value story was generally rated last.

A teacher must be aware of and attempt to open discussion with parents regarding their value orientations. If parents expect a type of program that is completely unacceptable to the teacher, then the two parties will have to work out some accommodation, or the teacher may decide to teach in another environment. No one value is "right," nor is it entirely unrelated to the other values, but there must be some meeting of minds between teachers and parents or the children's early education experience may suffer.

Influence of the Teacher and the Profession

Classrooms have unique characteristics because teachers are different. Teachers have different professional education and experience. Each teacher associates with other teachers to a different extent. Programs bear the mark of a teacher's philosophy, education, personality, creativity, health, and values. The teacher's personal life away from the school will have an impact on the class, just as the satisfactions gained from teaching will affect personal life.

The standards of the early childhood profession will influence the teacher throughout his or her educational experience and as a practitioner. The more the teachers are involved professionally, the more they are likely to be aware of current developments in the profession. Thus they will be able to choose from the best of current thinking and research regarding child development and early childhood education and incorporate this information into their programs for children and their parents.

The National Association for the Education of Young Children (NAEYC) is currently influential in setting and improving standards for

[2] For a summary of the study see Chapter 22 of *Guiding Young Children* by Verna Hildebrand (New York: Macmillan Publishing Co., Inc., 1985), and *Reading Improvement*, 12:3 (Fall 1975), pp. 168–173.

programs. Through NAEYC's National Academy of Early Childhood Programs, an early childhood school can become accredited. Accreditation means that the school meets standards for high quality. The standards were derived by consensus of a large group of professional early childhood educators from across the United States. For a center to become accredited means that the school meets high standards. Accreditation is a coveted designation that parents and the public are beginning to recognize as symbolic of high quality.[3]

Influence of Children

Last, but not least, the children influence the program. The school is there for them. Goals for children and characteristics of children in various age groups are discussed in Chapters 2 and 3. Teachers will spend a career searching for ways to help children reach their potentials. Knowing them and their families will be a significant part of the task. Each experienced teacher has become aware of the unique characteristics of each group before the school year is many weeks old.

*   *   *

Talk It Over: No. 2

Discuss the community conditions and the local, state and federal requirements that are influencing your planning for children.

*   *   *

Adequate Planning Requires Time

Time is required for planning. A program that meets accreditation standards happens by design, not by chance. There is a common fallacy that to teach young children, one has only to drop into the classroom and set out a few toys. Planning time is so important that the NAEYC accreditation standards require that the staff be allowed paid time for planning.[4] Not only must the teacher and staff take time to read, study, generate ideas, and make plans, but they must also prepare materials before the children arrive at school. Obviously the full-day teacher who plans for fifty-two weeks each year has a more extensive planning task than the teacher of a part-day program that meets only three days per week during the winter months. However, both teachers must have plans.

---

[3] Information about accreditation can be secured by writing the National Association for the Education of Young Children, 1843 Connecticut Avenue, N.W., Washington, D.C. 20009 or calling 1-800-424-2460. The National Academy of Early Childhood Programs can be reached at the same address. The standards are presented in the publication, *Accreditation Criteria and Procedures of the National Academy of Early Childhood Programs.* (Washington, D.C.: National Association for the Education of Young Children, 1984).

[4] Ibid., Criterion E10, p. 22.

Figure 17-3. Joy shows on young faces when the early childhood program meets their needs. (Child Development Laboratory, College of Human Development, Pennsylvania State University)

When teachers interview for new positions they should inquire about paid planning time. Many schools make no provision in the teacher's schedule for planning or evaluating. Not infrequently, teachers are paid only for the hours they spend in actual contact with children. They are not paid for time in planning and evaluation conferences. Teachers are even scheduled for as many as ten contact hours daily, with no time away from children that could be used for planning. This is a short-sighted view on the part of administrations. If teachers are to do the creative job that should be expected, they should be compensated for the planning that is basic to that job. If one cause could be singled out as the root of current criticism regarding the lack of significant learning in schools for young children, the absence of planning would surely be that cause.

Student teachers, too, may unrealistically assume that their "required hours" are merely the children's class hours. However, for students to make the most of their opportunity to learn with an experienced teacher at their side, they must be willing to attend the necessary planning conferences as well as to search for and prepare resource materials outside the children's class hours. Because the dual role of teaching and studying is heavy, students are well advised to lighten their other obligations during student-teaching assignments.

An outgrowth of conferring is the *esprit de corps* that can develop when the teachers, aides, students, volunteers, and parent-helpers meet to plan for the children. The group has a common interest—young children. They have a particular interest—a particular group of children. Their commitment to their teaching roles will be strengthened if they can participate and share their thinking with colleagues. Discussions of values shared and not shared are properly aired with some workable agreement being reached. Part of each person's job satisfaction is derived from friendships and from appreciation for each other. Such appreciation can grow through conferring.

Agenda for Planning Conferences

An agenda is helpful for any productive meeting. Using the five managerial tasks mentioned earlier, one can make an agenda form or check sheet, leaving room for additions. Some items will be more time consuming at one time than at another. When staff members have agendas early, they can come prepared with appropriate information.

Agenda for Conference
  I. Planning Tasks:
     a. Set goals
     b. Decide on themes
     c. Decide on specific activities
 II. Organizing Tasks:
     a. Setting schedules
     b. Preparing resources
     c. Arranging facility
III. Staffing Tasks:
     a. Assigning staff
     b. Communication
     c. Personal concerns
 IV. Leading Tasks:
     a. Innovations
     b. Professional opportunities
  V. Monitoring and Controlling
     a. What's happening
     b. Each child's needs, etc.
     c. Parental needs
     d. Adjustments needed

Setting Goals

Goals have been emphasized throughout the book. It is believed that without a goal or destination it is impossible to chart the best route to any place. The 15-point Program Guidelines shown in Table 17-1 provide general goals. The developmental tasks upon which those guidelines are based may be reviewed in Chapter 2. From these come *developmental goals* for individual children.

Developmental goals are based on research telling parents and professionals how children grow and develop. Using these goals the teacher plans experiences that will enhance one or more areas of the child's or children's development. The integration of development has been pointed out throughout this text along with ways that specific areas of the curriculum can be expected to enhance development. As teachers get better acquainted with children, their plans can be tailored to specific needs and interests of particular children. For example, seeing Louie's interest in airplanes, the teacher initiates a study of flying which culminates in a trip to the airport. Or, noting several children with articulation problems, the teacher plans some language games that are fun for all the children and particularly helpful to those few children.

Remember to use the Bloom *Taxonomy of Educational Objectives* as a guide for developing levels of difficulty in goals and objectives. These levels were presented in Chapter 6.

In particular cases it may be helpful to make individual plans for a child and write specific *behavioral objectives*. Behavioral objectives are carefully worded statements which describe the behavior expected and the criterion or degree of performance expected. Behavioral objectives were discussed in Chapter 6 along with details for planning specific activities for children.

All educators do not recommend behavioral objectives, some believing they lead to rigidities that are unnecessary. It has been observed that a serious problem arises when students are preparing to be teachers and are still learning the range of behaviors to expect from young children as they become involved with a particular activity or medium. Students may write objectives that sound logical on paper, but the children behave in other ways—often more interesting, unusual, and sometimes more advanced than the student anticipated in the objective. While a planned activity was a resounding success for the child or children, the student-in-training may feel that he or she has failed and certainly, on an evaluation, must check "did not accomplish objectives." It is not a failure, however, because early childhood students and teachers need a wealth of experience observing children using materials and learning before they are ready to write prescriptive behavioral objectives. Also needed is very specific information about a child or group of children which most students do not have. A therapist might write detailed objectives for a child

Table 17-1. 15-Point Program Guidelines

A fifteen-point guide for planning an effective program for children is outlined below. Teachers may also use the guides as a checklist for evaluating their programs.

1. *A good program is planned from the point of view of the whole child in the immediate environment.* Whether the child is from a small or a large family, from the city or the country, from an advantaged or a disadvantaged home, ongoing experiences are the basis for all planning. The child is observed then guided through sequential steps to new heights of accomplishment.

2. *A good program values the child's healthy, happy, responding, secure approach to living.* The teacher expects the children to respond fully and learn appropriately for their age. An important goal is for them to learn to love school and learning, teachers, and other children. Developing a self-confidence that says, "Whatever there is to do, I can do it," is very important.

3. *A good program provides for the emotional growth of the child.* It accepts the child as he or she moves from the protected, individualized home experience to a group experience. Every effort is made to give a feeling of security in the new setting—this goal being paramount for some time, depending on the child's need. Parents are helped and guided during this transition period.

4. *A good program balances active and quiet activities.* Within large time blocks the child has freedom to select the type of activity preferred. The teacher's schedule balances routines and learning experiences in logical sequences of events. Both extremes of prolonged sitting and prolonged physical exertion are avoided. Tensions build up during enforced sitting, and fatigue contributes to lack of inner control that interferes with maximum learning.

5. *A good program provides appropriate opportunities for children to grow in self direction and independence.* It provides an opportunity for them to learn to make choices through experience. Each child gains in self-understanding.

6. *A good program establishes and maintains limits on behavior for the protection of individuals, the group, and the learning environment.* By helping a child learn the reasons for various rules, the teacher encourages self-discipline.

7. *A good program is challenging to children's intellectual powers.* They are encouraged to think, reason, remember, experiment, and generalize. The laboratory rather than the lecture method is used almost exclusively.

8. *A good program provides media of self-expression.* Creativity is valued, fostered, and recognized in every learning center. Art, literature, and music are part of everyday's activity.

CK list
for
evaluating
Program

?'s for
end of
day

9. *A good program encourages children's verbal expressions.* To learn words and sentence structure, children must have an opportunity to talk. Being quiet is not necessarily valued.

10. *A good program provides opportunities for social development.* The child learns through experience to share, take turns, and interact with individuals and groups. He or she learns to choose friends and to be chosen. Yet the program also allows time to be alone if desired.

11. *A good program encourages children to learn about and care for their bodies.* A routine of washing, eating, resting, and eliminating is established. Safety training has priority, both to protect children and to teach them to protect themselves.

12. *A good program provides opportunities for each child to use the whole body in a daily period of outdoor activity.* When bad weather prevents going outdoors, adequate provision is made for gross motor activities in semisheltered or indoor areas.

13. *A good program is action packed.* It is frequently noisy compared to traditional upper-age classes. The reasons action, noise, and talking are permitted may have to be explained to administrators and others so that programs for children are not curtailed unnecessarily. Carpeting, draping, or other soundproofing should be provided in classrooms to cut down the noise level.

14. *A good program is fun for children.* Learning themes and materials are selected that especially attract young children. Their needs and interests determine the choice of learning experiences in most cases. When a theme or a concept lacks appeal, others replace it.

15. *A good program considers the interests and needs of the parents as well as the children.* The parents are helped to feel and be important to their child's growth and development. They are counseled directly and indirectly so that they will make significant contributions to the child's growth and development. Positive help is provided to individuals and groups to foster this principle. Referrals are made to appropriate agencies when the teacher recognizes a need for help she or he cannot provide.

with some developmental difficulty. For that child behavioral objectives may be warranted.

There are also *group goals.* As a social group the children and teachers expect to be living together for several hours daily over a considerable period of months. There is rarely sufficient adult help for every child to be treated as though the group does not matter. Goals for developing this group cooperation are important from the beginning. You are soon rewarded when you hear children saying, "This is MY nursery school." They are gaining their first sense of community outside their family.

✳ Deciding on Themes and Activities

Using a *cumulative plan* as discussed in Chapter 9 is the recommended approach. This approach utilizes a trusted principle of learning—that *one learns by relating new information with previously learned information*. You recognize this principle because you use it when you explain something new to someone by relating the new thing to something familiar.

Six basic themes were suggested and are given again here.

1. The child—his or her name, sex, health, safety, and relationship to the family, the school, the community, and the world.
2. The community—its people, its workers, its institutions, and its traditions, including festivals.
3. The world of plants—especially those the child sees every day and those that provide food.
4. The world of animals—especially those the child sees every day and those that provide food.
5. The world of machines—including vehicles and other large and small machines.
6. The physical forces in the world.

The teacher begins introducing basic concepts from each of these themes at the beginning of the school year, then touches and retouches the concepts throughout the year, increasing the complexity as the children grow in their understanding. It may be noticed that the first important theme concerns *the child*. The child learns about himself or herself and about the care and safety of the body. In some systems this learning is largely ignored, yet what could be more basic to a child's self-understanding? Other themes may be added.

The themes relate to the child in his or her everyday life. They can be interrelated and coordinated. Themes may run concurrently. The cumulative plan enables the teacher to adapt teaching to children's interests and leaves flexibility for covering fascinating current events.

A brief example of the use of a cumulative plan using the "World of Animals" theme follows. The teacher asks children, "Do you remember what animal we visited last week? What was it called?"

The children tell the teacher, "An elephant," and several minutes of conversation follow as children tell what they recall about the trip to see the elephant.

"Yes, an elephant," says the teacher. "Is this animal that is visiting us today an elephant?"

"No!" laugh the children. They spend several lively minutes guessing and naming. They talk about the animal's characteristics and how they differ from the elephant's. The teacher agrees with one child who says the animal is a guinea pig, and further information is given about that animal. The children are very interested in the conversation, and they do most of the talking. In future weeks other animals will be discussed in a similar manner. Memory will be stimulated as the children become personally involved.

Another planning approach is the *resource unit plan,* wherein one concept may be presented for a number of days or weeks, then dropped, and another concept selected. Such plans create programs that often seem choppy and unrelated. Also, the spontaneous interests of the children are often ignored. Frost and Rowland indicate that unit plans have a reputation "of being broad and shallow."[5]

A unit is apt to become too long for small children, as illustrated in the following example. A four-year-old asked her mother, "Why does Mrs. T. talk about food every day?" A study of the Basic Four food groups had been carried on in great detail. Although the children probably had some interest in food, the unit had become too much lecture and not enough laboratory to hold the four-year-olds' interest.

With a resource unit plan, a unit on "community helpers" might be taught in a single week. Thus children of varied interests aren't given enough opportunity to explore their interests before some topics are terminated for the year and new topics started.

In a cumulative plan, "community helpers" is a concept that is discussed from time to time. For example, throughout the year many people, including the parents of the children, are recognized for their contribution to the community.

Holidays, too, are one aspect of the child's community. However, with a cumulative plan, the temptation to hop from one holiday to another for major themes is avoided. It must be quite boring for children to hop from Halloween to Thanksgiving to Christmas and so on for all the years of their elementary school. Surely more child-oriented themes, with incidental activities related to holidays where they are appropriate, would be more interesting and educational over the years. Teachers should build their curriculum around a broad concept of what the children want and need to know—which goes far beyond the few holidays of the school year.

Activities

Specific learning activities have been detailed throughout Part Two of this book. The choices can be noted on a Daily Plan Form such as Figure 17-4. See Chapter 6 for suggestions about planning specific activities. A form such as Figure 17-5 can show the week at a glance. When interesting learning opportunities arise unexpectedly, the plans are flexible enough to incorporate them. However, advanced planning helps assure a program with educational goals for children.

[5] Joe L. Frost and G. Thomas Rowland, *Curricula for the Seventies* (Boston: Houghton Mifflin, 1969), p. 383.

Daily Plan of Activities

Date_____

Activity   Who Is Responsible?

Things to remember:

Art projects:

Science projects:

Dramatic play:

Literature-language area:

Music area:

Group time:

Outdoor activity:

Transition:

Snack menu:

Diary:

Figure 17-4. Daily plan of activities.

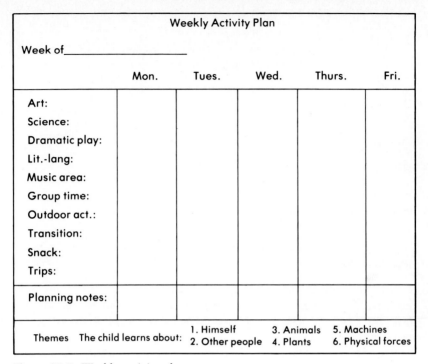

Figure 17-5. Weekly activity plan.

Commercially printed or computerized kits of teaching materials that encourage each child in every class to join in lock-step education should be avoided. Both the children's and the teacher's creativity are seriously jeopardized when the plan becomes more important than the children. Packaged materials can help teachers, but teachers should feel a definite responsibility for screening materials and adapting them to each group of children. Constance Kamii, who has spent many years researching how children learn to understand concepts of number, writes critically of workbook exercises. "These workbook exercises are undesirable because they preclude any possibility for the child to move the objects to make a set. Besides, such an exercise easily elicits the kind of thinking that yields the right answer for the wrong reason. Such children may or may not have the slightest idea about which set has *more*. If they do, this is usually because they already know how to tell which set has more. If they do not know how to tell this difference, the exercise is useless because children do not learn to make quantitative judgments by drawing lines on paper."[6]

[6] Constance Kamii, *Number in Preschool and Kindergarten* (Washington, D.C.: National Association for the Education of Young Children, 1982), p. 38.

*　　*　　*

Talk It Over: No. 3

Discuss the planning function in a school or business with which you are familiar. What rating would you give it?

*　　*　　*

Organizing Time, Materials, and Space

Organizing means systematically assembling and utilizing temporal, material, and spatial resources for carrying out a plan of action.

Setting Schedules

Scheduling means designating events for a fixed future time. Both long-term and short-term scheduling are needed. In scheduling, the teacher looks ahead to the whole year, to a convenient period of weeks, to the week, and to the day.

The *daily schedule* or sequence of events is established in the first planning session. If it fits the group well, this routine may remain in effect for a number of months with only minor variations. Scheduling was discussed in Chapter 4. Changing the schedule often creates uncertainty for young children which teachers must anticipate.

Three to six large time blocks are suggested for the schedule or sequence of events. Chapter 4 discusses the number of time blocks and the amount of time contained in each. Briefly, decisions depend upon:

1. The goals for the group.
2. The special needs of the group.
3. The time of day the children arrive.
4. How long the children stay at school.
5. What happens at home before the children come to school each day.
6. The season of the year.

To schedule long-range plans it is helpful to arrange a calendar of the entire school year in such a way that the total year can be seen. Some suitable commercial calendars are available, but a teacher can make one with a large sheet of wrapping paper. A space for notes with each date provides a ready reference for checking progress toward goals.

On the calendar, the teacher blocks out the number of school days. From the administration calendar mark holidays and other days that have significance for planning. Teachers usually write in children's birthdays. Many entries can be indicated in pencil so that they can be shifted as events dictate. Events that are regular occurrences can be placed on the calendar. For example, an end-of-school picnic or the kindergarten visit to the first grade can be noted tentatively at the beginning of school. Community events, such as a Lion's Club parade that typically occurs when the children can watch, are set months in advance and can be placed on the planning calendar. The teacher's diary can provide other tentative dates, such as when to plan a spring nature walk.

Periodic planning may mean a month, six weeks, a quarter, or a semester—whatever is a convenient administrative time unit in a particular school. For example, in a university laboratory school where plans involve the schedule of university students, the students' schedule also becomes the period for planning for the children. If student teachers typically assume certain levels of responsibility at different points during the term, these dates are marked on the planning calendar.

Preparing Resources

Resource materials are necessary for teaching each theme. The teacher will develop files of materials and ideas for teaching numerous concepts. By developing many materials, a teacher will have sufficient ideas to use in developing teaching plans to fit a particular group of children. The file will offer a collection from which to choose just the right poem or song for a group. One need never panic because of a shortage of material.

A resource file is assembled over time. If the teacher has a good filing system, newly discovered material is easily preserved. When needed, the material will be easily located. The file is suggested as a project for this course.

One filing system uses manila folders with a different color tab for each of the six themes. The colored tabs are bought where office supplies are sold. For example, all animal folders are labeled with a pink label. The file may have only two folders at first: (1) domestic birds and animals, and (2) wild birds and animals. However, as the file grows, the teacher will divide the material until there is a file for each animal of interest. Figure 17-6 is the suggested cover page for each folder; it can serve as the teacher's summary of the materials the file contains. Each folder can contain:

1. A statement of concepts to be developed.
2. Vocabulary to develop.
3. Science experiments that teach concepts.
4. Art ideas.
5. Dramatic play ideas.
6. Stories, poems, and finger plays.
7. Songs, rhythms, and records.

Resource File Cover Page

Subject_____

1. Statement of concepts to be learned:

2. Vocabulary to develop:

3. Science activities:

4. Art activities:

5. Dramatic play themes:

6. Stories, poems, finger plays:

7. Songs, rhythms, records:

8. Outdoor activities:

9. Field trips and special visitors:

10. Pictures:

Figure 17-6. Resource file cover page.

8. Outdoor activities.
9. Field trips or special visitors.
10. Pictures.

Throughout this textbook there are suggested resources for teaching ideas. As you read the chapters you are invited to use your creativity to invent new activities as you read about those invented by other teachers. Consult the section of additional readings for worthwhile resources.

Arranging the Facility

Another task of the teachers' planning conference is to consider the effectiveness of, and needed changes in, the facility. The effective use of space, its cleanliness and attractiveness, should be given attention. Details regarding room arrangement were discussed in Chapter 4 under "Setting the Stage." As teachers start a new group of young children, they find it important to keep the room arrangement the same for a while to give the children security in their new environment. However, after they are comfortable in school they will enjoy variety. Some weeks the housekeeping area and music areas can change places. A little shifting may create interest for a child who seems not to have noticed an area before.

New objects on shelves and on bulletin boards can give the children plenty to look for and talk about as they arrive each day. Children's art, neatly and colorfully arranged, should be changed regularly. Many teachers display a few of their own artifacts to brighten the room.

Beauty should be part of the environment. A tacky, unpainted look can change overnight if a civic group with do-good bent lends a hand. Parents can be enlisted to help. Student groups may enjoy assisting the teacher to improve the attractiveness of a classroom. Teachers should seek such sources of assistance when maintenance funds are inadequate.

Cleanliness and order should be important to the teacher. The children can help with getting materials back in their proper places each day. However, a continuous effort is required of the housekeeping staff to be sure that finger marks are washed off furnishings and walls, that wilted flowers are tossed out, that broken equipment is sent out for repair, and that general order is maintained in room, yard, and storage areas.

Staffing

Staffing is defined as selecting, assigning, utilizing, and evaluating the human resources needed for carrying out a plan of action. The teacher or co-teachers in an early childhood classroom may not hire the individuals, but they will be responsible for orienting them and at times training them for working with children. Wisely utilizing human resources helps both the children and the teachers. It is also very satisfying to see adults learn to be highly qualified teachers of young children.

A teaching team of a minimum of two adults per group has been the rule in nursery school classes for decades. Unfortunately kindergarten teachers have often been expected to manage alone. However, Head Start recommends two adults per fifteen children. Today most teachers are able to involve others in their programs. Many have paid aides; others have community volunteers, high school and university students who assist in various capacities, and parents who volunteer or serve as part of a cooperative plan. It is up to both the teacher and the assistants to make most meaningful use of all the available help.

The teacher will want the best learning situation for the children. Assistants extend in numerous ways the efforts the teacher can make for the children. It is desirable for each assistant to make a contribution to the children's learning and to have a satisfying experience with the children.

Conferences before each day of school are essential for those adults who work directly with the children. Such conferences are more important than ever when individuals have missed the weekly planning sessions. All will feel much more comfortable knowing the goals for the day—for the group and for individuals. Helpers must be advised of unusual circumstances that confront certain children, such as Debbie's mother going to the hospital or John's father leaving for a trip.

Safety requirements dictate that all areas of the room or yard where children are playing be staffed by adults. It seems more effective from the point of children's learning that each adult be assigned responsibility for a specific area of the room or yard. For example, if the adult's assignment is in the language arts area, such a plan makes it acceptable for that adult to remain in the language arts area with a child even though it appears that chaos is reigning in the block room. One can assume that a competent adult is in charge in the block room and will send out an SOS if assistance is needed.

An alternative plan is to let everyone move where "needed." In such a plan, however, teachers may never sit down and take time to extend the learning of children. They feel responsible for other parts of the school—particularly the trouble spots. When they hear chaos in the block room, they are likely to flock there. As a result, less troublesome children who remain absorbed in some task may be slighted, or some area needing the watchful eye of an adult may be left unattended.

Of course, when no children are at work in a learning center, the adult should feel free to observe or assist in other areas until children again show interest in that center. However, it is possible to take advantage of the lull to reorganize the center, to bring out some fresh materials, or even to clean it up if a transition time is approaching.

Space is provided in the Daily Plan sheet (Figure 17-4) for noting the assignment of assistants. Some teachers also write the daily plan on a blackboard so that all helpers can see at a glance who is taking responsibility for a given area. Such posting avoids duplication of effort or concern that no one has an area covered.

If at all possible, the assistants should be involved in the weekly planning. They need to feel they know what is going on. It is a very uncomfortable feeling when a youngster says, or implies, "I've been here longer than you have, I know the rules," as one child was heard to say.

In planning sessions, assignments should be discussed to ensure that all members of the teaching team, male and female, share equally all tasks such as affection-giving, disciplining, housekeeping, toileting, and playground teaching. Remember, all members of a team are serving as models for the children they teach.

Assignments may be agreed upon in weekly planning conferences. Each individual may assume the responsibility for bringing in the materials needed to enhance the learning in a particular area of responsibility. Regular teachers can assume responsibility in areas offering new learning situations, whereas others take the areas that offer experiences more familiar to the children and for which guidance is more predictable.

In some centers teachers divide activities into categories, agree to assume responsibility for a given category for a two-week period, then rotate to another category of activities for the next two weeks. Under such an agreement meetings to coordinate plans can be shorter.

Of course, in all groups teachers and assistants should be learning along with the children. It is often necessary for teachers or assistants to participate in an activity even though he or she lacks experience. For example, a person with little confidence in music should be encouraged to volunteer to work in the music area. Other adults can give support until that person gains the confidence needed to carry on as leader. All assistants should make their preferences and talents known so that their capabilities can be utilized in the best possible way for the good of the children.

As the teacher in charge in a group, you will become the person responsible for directing and evaluating a number of employees and, in some instances, students. This task will be discussed under the heading of Monitoring and Controlling.

*　　*　　*

Talk It Over: No. 4

Discuss the points of view of assistants and lead teachers in assigning tasks in a school. How have you felt as you've played or observed each role? What conclusions can help you in your future role as lead teacher?

*　　*　　*

Leading the Team

Leading means setting the pace toward present goals and formulating future goals. It requires a clear view of present goals and a vision of future goals. Teachers must think of themselves as leaders. You have an opportunity to lead within your group, school, community, nation, and world. There have been many innovations in early childhood education in recent history. Foresighted people envisioned Head Start and the newer Center Accreditation Project. There will always be room for new ideas.

Communicating with other early childhood professionals will stimulate new ideas. Knowing the needs of children everywhere will stimulate others. A challenging professional life will be the best medicine for preventing "burn-out," the condition that is said to occur in early childhood workers quite frequently.

There are thousands of ways to innovate in your group of children and with your adult assistants. You can ask, "Is there a part of the program, the yard, or our personal relationships that could stand improving?" Work on one of those. Value your co-workers and learn to encourage and enjoy their growth in working with children. Bring in some elementary-age children or some elderly folks and find out what happens. Your creativity will be contagious as you try new things and encourage others to innovate, too.

Early childhood educators as a group seem cautious about money. However, don't dampen an idea just because it costs money. If the idea is a good one, think of how funding might be achieved. No one will remember you for the pennies saved, but they will remember you if you spearheaded the playyard renovation or a concert series to benefit children who need scholarships. Ideas are the hallmark of leaders. Be sure to value your own and those of others.

Encourage parents and your staff to participate in community programs that are fun for children. Encourage professional participation—program appearances and professional writing—of your staff and colleagues. Through a wide professional participation you let people know about your high-quality work, and you may be able to influence positively the lives of many other children in the community through your efforts.

Monitoring and Controlling

Monitoring and controlling are defined as being alert to the performance of self and others in relation to established standards, and making decisions and carrying out adjustments needed for meeting stan-

dards. These terms are used because they seem more dynamic than the typically used word—evaluation.

The early childhood education profession is particularly concerned about high quality, therefore, it is of critical importance that teachers perform these functions well. Continuous monitoring should take place from moment to moment and from day to day. If something is unsafe or unsanitary, it must be corrected immediately; that's where control comes in. If something is being taught poorly and more preparation would help, then preparation must be undertaken. If learning activities are too easy or too hard, adjustments must be readily forthcoming. If teachers and their assistants are doing the on-the-spot monitoring that is essential, then any outside evaluator will not be frightening to the staff.

Children tell teachers and parents by their actions when things are going fine. Adults should listen to children if they are unhappy, rejecting, or refuse to participate. An experienced teacher can tell by the hum of the classroom if things are going well, much as an experienced mechanic knows if a motor is having problems. Parents' reports regarding their child's feelings about school should be listened to seriously and investigated for accuracy.

Overall Program Evaluation

Overall program evaluation must be based on program goals. The 15-Point Program Guidelines (Table 17-1) used to establish goals can be used to develop a program evaluation sheet. A one-to-five rating scale is suggested with five as highly satisfactory. Besides teachers doing an internal evaluation, parents can be very helpful. They can receive the same evaluation sheet and return it with their comments. Or, it can be presented in a parent meeting with ample opportunity provided for parents to make comments and ask questions. It is particularly imperative that teachers evaluate and seek evaluation of their programs, rather than do nothing or leave the impression that they believe that perfection has been achieved. Programs can always be improved. By taking the initiative in evaluation, teachers are less likely to be pushed into an uncomfortable defensive position by parents or others.[7]

Checking Curricular Offerings

General evaluation can begin by a checking of the daily plans against the diary of actual events. This provides a picture of what there was available to learn. Even a short diary written at the bottom or on the

[7] A form for evaluation has been prepared in Verna Hildebrand, *A Laboratory Workbook for Introduction to Early Childhood Education* (New York: Macmillan Publishing Co., Inc., 1986).

Figure 17-7. "We're ready to go," announces the student teacher as the children start their mini-field trip to a nearby museum on campus. Adequate planning and preparation will assure maximum learning from the adventure. (Child Development Laboratory, Michigan State University)

back of a daily plan sheet will provide information for evaluation. To be realistic, a diary generally must be brief, otherwise teachers won't have time to keep it.

A regular check of daily and weekly plans and diaries against the fifteen-point guides discussed earlier in this chapter will provide information on where a program is adequate and inadequate. By summarizing the daily plans the teacher can see at a glance how much variety has been offered the group. For example, if the diary shows that a few art projects were repeated frequently, efforts to bring in some new ones or add something new to the old ones can be made.

Knowing what has been offered does not tell the teacher what individual children have learned. Teachers also must make an effort to know how individual children are progressing. It is like knowing the menu at the cafeteria; one must watch the diners to see what they choose and what they actually eat to judge how well nourished they might be.

Observing Each Child

Teachers must consciously observe each child. It helps to use an attendance checklist and watch a child briefly at least once a week. Without a checklist it is easy to overlook a child or two—perhaps a quiet

492

child. Monitoring children's skills, for example in motor or language skills, helps teachers know children better. Keeping a folder on each child makes filing a sample of work or an anecdote easy.

Chapter 13 gives numerous suggestions regarding the teacher's observation notes and their value. Through routinely observing each child and recording evidence of progress toward educational goals, teachers can begin to assess a child's progress. Notes will help teachers in conferences with staff and parents. Recommendations should be made on the basis of sufficient evidence collected over time.

Staff Conferences

It is helpful for teachers to get together to discuss individual children to gain the benefit of the thinking of others regarding each child. An outsider may be asked to observe and take notes on certain children to add more objective insight into the handling of behavior and learning problems. University student observers can contribute to such conferences. Students gain from learning to relate theory to practice. Planning and evaluating go hand in hand, as we discussed under planning in this chapter.

Testing Children

A serious problem with nearly any evaluation is its subjective nature. For that reason those desiring more objective measures turn to tests. Tests taken at the beginning of a term are compared to those taken at the end. This is called pre- and posttesting. It would be helpful if there were more reliable testing materials to measure the growth that takes place in young children during the years they are in prekindergarten and kindergarten. Regardless of numerous inadequacies, pre- and posttesting is being done increasingly in schools across the country. Perhaps eventually, with improvements, more confidence can be placed in the results of such measures.

There are some problems encountered in the testing of young children. In the first place, the children are too young for the more easily administered pencil and paper tests that are common in upper-age groups. When paper and pencil tests are used with kindergarteners, the teacher cannot be sure that the children completely understand the directions. The children may copy from their neighbor, making their test an inaccurate measure.

Individual testing is time consuming and rarely done on any scale. Individual testing, too, has its drawbacks. A teacher rarely has time to test all the children. Outside testers must know tests, they must have considerable knowledge of children generally and be willing to take time to get acquainted with individuals before starting to test. Testers may play with some children several hours before the children are ready to be tested. Even removing a child from the classroom to a testing room may cause anxiety and reduce motivation because the child would rather be back in the room with friends.

Tests generally tend to be oriented toward white middle-class society and therefore may be seriously unfair to others. Even so, the I.Q. score obtained from tests given at a young age has very low predictive value, according to data from the longitudinal study by Bayley.[8] Frost and Rowland predict that "The I.Q. will be abandoned as false and unworthy—especially as educators realize that it is a sample of behavior taken at a specific time under limiting conditions. Educators will cease to attribute to the I.Q. the power to predict or determine the progress of a child; actually, the I.Q. never had such power, but it was used in a perverted way."[9]

The I.Q. tests have been criticized because they were developed with a white middle-class bias that makes them grossly unfair to children from the other cultural orientations. Adrian Dove, a black sociologist, attempted to point this up with what has become known as the "Chitling Test."[10] This is a test for whites that uses black English. In a humorous fashion, Dove has shown how the cultural bias influences one's score on a test. Therefore, until testing can eliminate such bias, one should not take its results too seriously.

If teachers expect to use test results, they should be aware of the shortcomings of the tests. They should know how to interpret the results. Psychologists generally agree that it is unwise to give parents number scores from tests because they use them incorrectly, remember them inaccurately, and may use them for their own aggrandizement.

Two examples illustrate even teachers' confusion with test scores. A parent was told, "Betty didn't do well on her math test." The mother thought of the "S" mark (satisfactory) the teacher had put on the report grade and asked, "What did she make on her test?" The teacher replied, "Only fifty percent." On further investigation, the mother, who was more knowledgeable than most, found that the teacher meant that the child ranked at "the 50th percentile" on math, as compared to ranking at the "76th percentile" on her reading. The meaning of the percentile score was that Betty, when compared to all other children taking that test,

[8] Nancy Bayley, "On the Growth of Intelligence," *American Psychologist*, 10:12 (December 1955), pp. 805–818.

[9] Joe L. Frost and G. Thomas Rowland, *Curricula for the Seventies* (Boston: Houghton Mifflin, 1969), p. 435.

[10] "Taking the Chitling Test," *Annual Editions Readings in Human Development '73–'74* (Guilford, Conn.: Dushkin Publishing Group, Inc., 1973), p. 298.

scored in the middle of the group on mathematical reasoning and in the top one fourth in reading.

Another teacher interpreted a score of 56 on a reading-readiness test to mean that the child had an I.Q. of 56. The mother naturally reacted with considerable alarm to this report. She had worked as an aide in a school for retarded children and had heard I.Q. scores bandied about. She had a vague notion of how scores were applied. When, after many worry-filled days, she talked to someone more informed, she learned that the teacher had confused percentile rank with I.Q. score.

Certainly, if tests are to be used, they should be administered expertly, interpreted correctly, and used in conjunction with other information, especially when recommendations regarding a child's future are being made.

Teachers must feel an obligation to report to parents on their child's progress. Several methods of doing this are discussed in Chapter 18.

Monitoring Self and Other Adults

As the lead teacher, you will likely be responsible for monitoring the staff and volunteers within your classroom. Each employee should have a job description that states quite precisely what the employee is to do and the standards expected. Students, likewise, should have a description in hand as to what their performance should be. These descriptions can then be used when monitoring their job performance. It is best to meet with the staff individually and communicate to them about the level of their performance. In individual conferences you can suggest things they do well and ways improvements can be made. You probably will report to a higher level of administration your findings and your suggestions. It is important to write down observations and evaluations. People working with children are given a special trust. If they break that trust, then they must be removed from working with the children. You, also, will be evaluated by your administrator. Your staff may be called on to assist with your evaluation.

Monitoring and controlling are required to assure parents and the community that the early childhood education programs are serving children and families in positive ways. Further, they are needed to assure everyone that only persons with integrity and good will are working with children. In recent years there has been considerable discussion regarding various levels of child abuse that have been discovered in a few centers. The allegations are frightening enough to everyone of good will that from now on they will be doubly alert to any undesirable behavior on any employee's part. Society expects this vigilance from anyone who plays any role in a young child's education.

Conclusion

Early childhood education teachers perform many managerial functions as they work with children and staff members in their classrooms and playyards. These functions are planning, organizing, staffing, leading, and monitoring and controlling.

Planning and the other managerial functions require lots of time and should not be slighted if high-quality programs are the goal. The NAEYC accreditation criteria require that staff be given paid planning time. Staff members must meet periodically to set goals, decide on themes, plan specific activities, set schedules, prepare resources, arrange the facility, assess children's progress, communicate as a staff, monitor the quality, and change the performance if it isn't high in quality.

Outcomes for children and parents should be analyzed. The total curricular offerings should be analyzed for quality. The task of monitoring the staff is partially a responsibility of the lead teacher and of the school's administrator. The latter should be quickly informed of serious deviations by staff in performance standards.

Applications

1. Discuss the "Talk It Over" items found in the chapter.
2. Complete Lesson 17 in *A Laboratory Workbook for Introduction to Early Childhood Education*. Hand in as scheduled.
3. Make a weekly curriculum plan for the group where you have been participating. Use the same number of children and staff. Plan assignments for staff, assuming the same skills as the present staff. Write a narrative explaining how you went about your decision making. Tell how your program is a cumulative plan, building on what children have been learning.
4. Evaluate your own performance on the evaluation form designed in Chapter 1.
5. Add your weekly curriculum plan to your Resource File.

Study Questions

1. Identify, define, and explain each of the five managerial tasks when applied to early childhood schools and teachers.
2. Identify the various influences on curricular planning.
3. Explain the need for paid planning time.
4. Explain the difference between social and technical decisions.
5. Explain a cumulative plan and a resource unit plan.
6. Explain Constance Kamii's criticism of workbook exercises for learning about numbers.

Additional Readings

COHEN, MONROE (ed). *Selecting Educational Equipment and Materials for Home and School.* Washington, D.C.: Association for Childhood Education International, 1976.

GROTBERG, EDITH H., and WILLA CHOPER. *Research: Translating Findings Into Action.* Washington, D.C.: Department of Health, Education, and Welfare, 1978.

HARTRUP, WILLARD W. (ed.). *The Young Child: Reviews of Research, Vol. II.* Washington, D.C.: National Association for the Education of Young Children, 1972.

HARTRUP, WILLARD W., and NANCY L. SMOTHERGILL (eds.). *The Young Child: Reviews of Research, Vol. I.* Washington D.C.: National Association for the Education of Young Children, 1967.

HILDEBRAND, VERNA. *Management of Child Development Centers.* New York: Macmillan Publishing Co., Inc., 1984.

HUBBELL, RUTH. *A Review of Head Start Research since 1970.* Washington, D.C.: U.S. Government Printing Office, 1983.

HYMES, JAMES L., JR. *Teaching the Child Under Six.* Columbus, Ohio: Charles E. Merrill Publishing Co., 1981.

LEEPER, SARAH H., RALPH L. WITHERSPOON, and BARBARA DAY. *Good Schools for Young Children.* New York: Macmillan Publishing Co., Inc., 1984.

SCHICKERDANZ, JUDITH A., MARY E. YORK, IDA SANTOS STEWART, DORIS A. WHITE. *Strategies for Teaching Young Children.* Englewood Cliffs, N.J.: Prentice-Hall, Inc., 1983.

SEEFELDT, CAROL. *Curriculum for Preschools.* Columbus, Ohio: Charles E. Merrill Publishing Co., 1980.

TAYLOR, BARBARA J. *A Child Goes Forth.* Provo, Utah: Brigham Young University Press, 1980.

Professional
Considerations

PART III

Teacher-Parent Relations

- *To explain in what ways all early childhood schools are part of a family support system.*
- *To explain the place of strong, positive, and personal teacher-parent relationships in high-quality early childhood programs.*
- *To identify and describe ways teachers and parents can be in contact throughout the child's early education.*
- *To describe steps to take in planning for conferences with parents.*

"Should the teacher be the one who initiates the parent-teacher relationship?" "How do I learn to relate to parents?" "How can teachers encourage parents to help a child?" "What do I do if parents don't seem interested in their child's school experience?"

These and many other questions may come to mind as you enter the final phase of a teacher preparation program. Practicum experience will be providing good preparation for communicating with parents. Perhaps you are a parent with some feelings and experience concerning communications with teachers. You may already be convinced with noted early childhood educator, James L. Hymes, Jr., that "We have to end the separation of home and school. Too much is at stake to let the foolish lack of communication persist. The left hand must know what the right is doing; the two hands must work together."[1]

[1] James L. Hymes, Jr., *Teaching the Child Under Six* (Columbus, Ohio: Charles E. Merrill Publishing Co., 1974), p. 80.

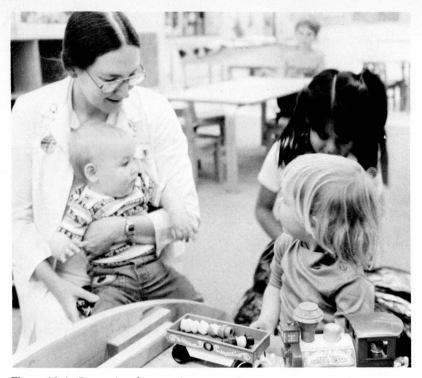

Figure 18-1. Parent involvement in a center is as easy as encouraging a parent to take a minute to watch while her daughter finishes a game. (Manzanita Day Care Center, University of New Mexico)

A Support System for Families

A high-quality early childhood school can be a tremendous support system for today's families. The school can supplement the time, energy, skills, and ideas that parents have, enabling parents to manage their children more effectively. An attitude of service must be part of the total early childhood program. Children cannot be educated apart from their families and have a high-quality program. Teachers and every early childhood staff member must realize how significant their service is to the well-being of both children and families.

High-quality early childhood schools can make it possible for dedicated parents to survive the hectic pace they lead in today's world—especially including a mother or father who plays the parenting role alone. Virtually all parents have great hopes for their children and are eager to work with the school in any way that will benefit their children. A few parents may need help in learning to relate to the school and teachers; thus teachers must devise strategies for getting them actively involved.

Parents too have their concerns about relating to teachers. They hope the teacher and child will like each other. They hope that the teacher

Figure 18-2. The needs of parents as well as children must be of primary importance in operating a high quality early childhood program. (Joe Kertesz, photographer)

knows subject matter and how to get it across to children. Parents worry when problems come up. Will the teacher react to a discussion of a child's failure by taking offense? Will the teacher blame the parents? Will they appear to be asking for special favors for their child if they seek help?

Teachers find that some parents have a very accepting leave-it-to-the-experts attitude. Such parents believe, and teach their children, that "the teacher knows best." They rarely criticize the school. Should the child have trouble, such parents usually feel it is deserved.

Parents who have had little formal education are more likely to be tolerant, or accepting, of the school. They hesitate to go to school even to enroll a child. They have experienced many rebuffs in their lives and may have failed in school. By avoiding school, they protect themselves from being hurt further. They have real and imagined reasons for not taking advantage of a teacher's overtures toward them.

On the other hand, some parents expect to be involved in educational matters. They are concerned lest their child be unprepared for the future. If they disagree with the goals or the methods of the school, they say so. Highly educated parents will make more demands for their children. Yet they may be so busy in their business or professional lives that very little time is given to school matters. For instance, some parents say that their days are filled with meetings and that they would rather stay at home with their family in the evening than hire a baby-sitter in order to go out to a parents' meeting.

Plans for relating to children's parents, like plans for educating children, must be based on knowledge of the families concerned. This chapter will focus on relations between parents and teacher more than on parent education because of the belief that the teacher's first task is to relate to parents. Education may follow. However, the teacher may derive more education than the parent. Ideally, a meaningful two-way dialogue will develop and be of substantial benefit to the teacher, the parents, and the child.

* * *

Talk It Over: No. 1

Recall your own school years, or your child's if you are now a parent. What were your parents' and teachers' attitudes toward each other? Can you learn anything from them?

* * *

Values of Teacher-Parent Relationships

Each teacher wishes to build the most relevant program for each child. By getting to know each child's parents and home situation, the teacher can more accurately assess the experiences the child has had before coming to school. Using this background the teacher builds stepping-stones to new experiences.

Reporting to parents on a child's school experience initiates exchanges with parents from which teachers gain valuable feedback regarding programs.

By knowing parents, the teachers can better encourage parental efforts on behalf of a child's education. Through various techniques teachers can help parents use the hours at home with the child to further education.

As teachers and parents get acquainted, they will learn of each other's educational goals and values. Ideally, less conflict will arise between the two to cause confusion in the child's mind.

Even some highly educated parents have little knowledge of or appreciation for little children. Teachers can help all parents develop the understanding necessary for enjoying their children more fully.

The parent-cooperative nursery schools and kindergartens have a long and positive influence on parents. In addition to the objectives for the growth and development of the children, the cooperatives have objectives for both parents' growth. Parents often mention the changes in themselves that have occurred as a result of having their child in the cooperative nursery school or kindergarten. For example, you hear parents commenting, "I didn't know anything about little kids, I had never been around any but my own, until I came to the coop." "I was scared. I was afraid I'd do something that would harm the children!" "I got a lot out of talking with the other parents." "My husband and I made friends in the coop that have been our best friends for years."

Parents in cooperatives learn about child development, about teaching children, about curriculum, about supplies and equipment, and about financing the operation. Such ideas usually elude parents who choose other types of schools for their children. For many, the financial savings offered by the coop make the difference between school and no school for their children. Cooperatives encourage a heavy dose of self-education for parents by offering them books to browse in and discussion groups and workshops in which they can share their most recent thoughts concerning their child's development.

From its beginning, Project Head Start encouraged teachers to know and work with parents. Many community resources have been coordinated through the school to improve the living situation of the Head Start children and their families.[2] Today's full-day schools are making creative efforts to communicate with the parents of the children they serve.

Teachers add to their own understanding of children, parents, and families by making the effort to develop good relationships. Even though each family is unique, like the individuals in them, each experience improves the teacher's ability to relate to other families in the future.

Parents' Presence During Beginning Days

Early childhood schools have differing procedures for introducing new children to a group. Most prefer to introduce only a few children at a time. This procedure gives the teacher time to relate to each child and leaves plenty of space for a parent to stay with a child until both the teacher and the parent feel the child is confident enough to remain for a period of time without support. Parents without jobs or without other children at home may prolong this introductory period longer than the child needs, unless the teacher is able to help parents in the separation

[2] *Project Head Start Points for Parents*, Booklet No. 10 (Washington, D.C.: Office of Economic Opportunity, 1967); *Project Head Start Parents Are Needed*, Booklet No. 6 (Washington, D.C.: Office of Economic Opportunity, 1967).

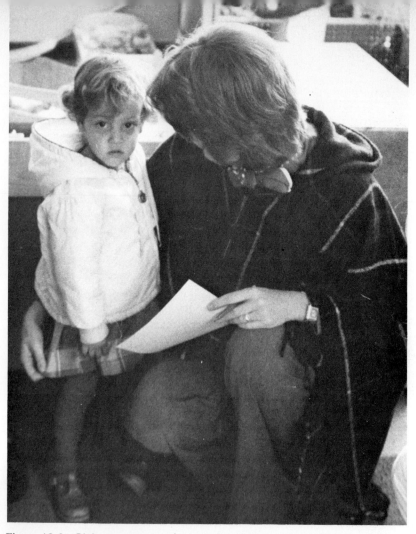

Figure 18-3. Giving parents ample time to introduce their child to the school and to say goodbye each day are part of high-quality programs. (Early Childhood Laboratory, Kansas State University)

process. Some feel guilty, thinking that "good" parents take care of children at home when they can. Or a parent may be reluctant to leave the child with a stranger. Therefore it is essential for the teachers to communicate a regard for the parent and the child and reassure them that they can handle the situation. Teachers can, of course, assure a parent that they will call if any need arises.

Debbie was an example of a three-year-old who was reluctant to enter a three-year-old group. A number of weeks were needed before she felt secure in the school. Her previous social experience had always included her mother. In fact, the parents had taken her many places but had never left her alone, even to stay with her grandmother. Intellectually, Debbie's mother wanted Debbie to go to school, but psychologically she hesitated to leave her. The process was not rushed. Some days the mother stayed all morning. Sometimes she left for an hour, then returned to take Debbie home. Debbie could easily have become a nursery school dropout if the teachers had displayed less confidence in themselves, in the child, or in the mother. Eventually they were rewarded for their patience when Debbie stood at the school door shouting, "Let me in," with a smile of confidence lighting her face.

Teachers in full-day centers will seldom have the time to let a child adjust as Debbie was able to do. They must use every technique available to help the child feel secure. Part of the problem is an outgrowth of the hurry-scurry felt in households when families are getting ready to go to work. Parents have mixed feelings as they rush their child off to the child care center and themselves off to work. Employed parents leave many undone tasks which may lead to guilt feelings.

Sometimes the teacher's role is to help the parents make parting easier for the child. If the parent has time to stay during the introductory phase, he or she should do so. If one is required to leave because of a job, one should go. If the parent says "It is time to leave," and then lingers if the child cries, this teaches the child that crying will keep a parent longer. Parting may be difficult for both child and parent; but an off-again-on-again leave-taking only complicates the matter for all.

Some parents may want to sneak out and leave the child at school. However, it is far better for the long-run adjustment if the child waves a tearful good-bye as he or she is held in the teacher's arms than for the child to discover suddenly that the parent is gone.

Kindergarten children often need a gradual introduction to school. If this is their first school experience, they may experience anxiety, but usually not of the duration felt by a younger child. Short days, staggered schedules, or many assistants may help the kindergarten teacher as a new group is introduced to the new environment.

* * *

Talk It Over: No. 2

Discuss the procedures used for introducing a child in the school where you are participating.

* * *

Types of Contacts Between Parents and Teachers

Initial Meeting

Parents may base their first opinions concerning the teacher on very little information. Perhaps they notice the teacher at a PTA meeting. They may ask other parents about personal qualities, teaching ability, and whether their child liked the teacher. They gain some idea of the teacher's patience as their questions are answered during a telephone call. Because teachers have a professional obligation to the public, they should be consistently patient, fair, and friendly with parents wherever they meet them.

Home Visit

The teacher may arrange to meet the family at home. The teacher calls in advance and asks when it is convenient to come to "say hello" and get acquainted with the new pupil. A home visit has many lasting values for helping the child make an adjustment to the school situation with a minimum of difficulty. Both child and parents will feel more at ease in their home than elsewhere. The home is more congenial for a discussion focused on the child. Before the teacher has any information to give, parents are given an opportunity to inform the teacher.

The home visit can help the teacher assess the child's psychological position in the home. Sibling competition or favoritism may be noticed as interaction is observed between family members. If the child appears to be overprotected, this may become apparent. Parents may volunteer information on a problem area as the child wanders out of the room.

Parents and child also learn from the visit. The next time they see the teacher, they will be acquainted. Children will often say, "You came to my house, didn't you, teacher?" They can tell that she or he likes children. They can ask questions they might hesitate to ask in a strange setting or when others seem to be waiting for their turn to speak to the teacher. If the teacher can put parents at ease during the initial home visit, they will look forward to other contacts. Additional home visits are planned as needed. For further details regarding home visits, see Chapter 3.

School Visit

Some teachers arrange their first meeting with a child and parent in the school setting. This plan brings the focus more quickly to the school, its equipment, and its procedures. The meeting should be private, with an effort made to learn about the child and the family. Both parents and children will feel more at ease if they have had a chance to look over the school setting when no other children are there.

Parents should always feel welcome at school. They should be invited to attend for a moment or an entire period, at their convenience. They should be able to arrive unannounced. The school program can continue on a routine basis with no alteration because of the visitor.

When parents are told that they should call before visiting, they may feel unwelcome or worry that children are mistreated when visitors aren't present. Many valuable mini-visits that working parents make would be eliminated if prior arrangements were required.

The parent's presence during a visit, or on the day a parent-cooperator participates, may cause some difficulties in the handling of that parent's child. Children sometimes exhibit dependent behavior that is not characteristic of them. It is natural for a child to want to be near his or her parent. It may be difficult for a child to share a parent, as is necessary in parent-cooperatives. If the parent reacts by admonishing the child to "run and play," the child may feel rejected. It is best to work *with* this feeling of possessiveness rather than *against* it. During a parent's visit, for example, the teacher can encourage the child to give the parent a guided tour. The parent is encouraged to follow and sit near the child until the excitement wears off.[3]

If other children do not seem to understand why the visitor's child gets special attention, a simple explanation such as the following may be all that is necessary: "You know how you like to be near your mother when she comes? That's how John feels today."

Parents' Contribution to Program

When teachers become well acquainted with parents, they may learn that certain parents have talents that would interest the children if shared at school. Many parents are musicians or have some musical talents that are delightful when shared with children. For example, a guitar-playing parent singing school songs really brightens the children's day. Some talents may be unusual, like the harpist mother who plays with the city symphony and who gave the children a musical treat that the teachers could never have provided themselves. Other suggestions have been made in various chapters.

In addition, parents may work where children could visit. A father, for example, helped arrange a visit to a TV studio where he worked. A police officer parent may enjoy stopping by the school to give children a lesson in safety on the streets. Such contributions are very valuable and help bridge the gap between home and school.

Parents from various ethnic groups can make worthwhile contributions by sharing music, stories, or costumes. Or they might be invited to help supervise a cooking project teaching about a traditional food. Thus, a Chicano mother might help with tamales or a German parent might help with German potato salad.

[3] For a touching account of a mother whose child felt hurt when she had to share her mother with others, read "But You're MY Mommy," *Early Years*, 4:6 (February 1974), pp. 52, 62–63.

Figure 18-4. Encouraging parents to drop in for a moment or longer at anytime of the day is basic in high-quality programs. (Child Development Laboratory, Utah State University)

When a parent brings a special exhibit, or in other ways helps with the program, that parent's child should be involved in the plans for the day. The child can help his or her parent get materials ready or share the "secret" of a special event that will surprise the other children. Parents should be aware that one of the values of their participating in special events is the recognition their child receives. Plans should be made for the child to be a helper or to get a front-row seat. The child's pride in the parent's participation should be recognized as a legitimate feeling on the child's part.

Casual Visits

Many casual visits between teacher and parents take place as children are delivered and picked up at school. Teachers should develop a system for sharing information when the child is picked up. Some schools have a note-pocket under each child's name which is attached to the door. Then it is handy for the teacher to slip a brief note in the pocket, which the parent remembers to look for each day.

Other visits may occur in the supermarket or at social events. At such times the teacher can report pleasurable moments the child has had in school. Parents may report an unusual family event that aids the teacher when working with the child during the day. The teacher must focus attention on the children and the other parents who are coming and going, leaving little time for discussing difficulties a child might be having. However, an appointment for a conference can be arranged, or the teacher may ask the parent to call when it is convenient to talk.

Telephone Conversations

It is a rare parent that would abuse the teacher's invitation to "Call me whenever there is any problem that concerns your child and school. If I can be of help I want to be." The "on-call" attitude of professional teachers separates them from nine-to-five workers. Teachers know that children sometimes go home confused or with real or imagined slights. They may leave a dearest treasure at school. A call to the teacher can straighten things out so that the family's evening goes smoother. Parents should feel it is all right to call the teacher at home.

Some parents in our mobile society live far away from family or friends with whom they might discuss their children. A call to the teacher may help that parent think through some difficulty. Teachers can encourage friendships between parents, which will help alleviate the loneliness of a parent in a strange city.

Regular Conferences

When parent conferences are the rule rather than the exception, parents will approach teachers with less anxiety. With this procedure all children—not just those with adjustment problems—receive the benefit of thinking and help from those two very important influences in their lives.

Purpose

The teacher's purpose for arranging the private conference is to learn the parent's impressions of the program, to gain a better understanding of the effect of the program on the child, to get more information about a child, and to encourage parents' understanding and support of the program.

Parents will feel some obligation to attend conferences. The conferences should not be threatening to the parent. Discussion is kept to the stated purposes unless parents indicate other things they wish to discuss.

Parents will be anxious to know how the child does in school and how he or she relates to other children and the teachers. They may want some indication and reassurance that the child is a good learner. They may be concerned with reading or writing.

The following letter is an example of the invitation to a conference that parents receive:

Dear Parents,

Now that we have had two months of school, I'd like us to get together so we can talk about how your child has been getting along since school started. Private conferences are being arranged with each child's parents. This conference and others will be used in place of formal report cards.

Your conference is scheduled for next week <u>Nov. 2 at 2:30 p.m.</u> in my office—106 Wilson School. If this hour is inconvenient, you may trade with another family or call me (345–9996) for a better time.

Volunteers will supervise your children in the classroom during our conference. As you recall, to enable teachers to hold conferences, there is no school during the afternoons next week.

Please do not alarm your child about this conference. You can say, "Your teacher and I are going to talk about what you like at school. What shall I say?"

Of course, both parents are invited to the conference when it is possible for you both to attend.

Sincerely,
Mrs. Verna Hildebrand
Teacher

Note the content of the letter. The date, hour, and place of conference are stated clearly. The letter suggests some flexibility by letting parents exchange times or call for a change in schedule. The purpose of the conference is stated, as is the fact that all parents are involved. Babysitting has been arranged that will help parents solve one problem they always have when the child is not in school and when they may have several younger children. Also of importance is the advice regarding interpreting the conference to the child. Having worked to develop rapport with a child, the teacher would hope that the parents would not say, "Your teacher is going to tell me how bad you've been."

A face-to-face conference is much more satisfactory for reporting a child's progress to parents than is a written form. Many schools are allowing released time for such conferences today. By meeting parents in a conference, the teacher can help them think through possible alternative solutions to problems. In a written report the parents' reaction to information could cause negative instead of the desired positive result for the child.

For example, one kindergarten teacher checked "lacks social skills" on the report card of Charley, a quiet, withdrawn child. Had the teacher mentioned this problem to his parents, their defensive reaction might have been noticed and remedies suggested that would have helped the child improve his social skills. However, the report card merely went home to the parents, who reacted by punishing the child. They kept him in the house every night after school instead of allowing Charley to play in the courtyard with his friends of the neighborhood. Surely the parents reacted in the worst possible way to the teacher's good intention. For the child's best interests it would have been better to have discussed the problem with his parents along with suggestions for helping the child.

Preparation

Teachers should make thoughtful preparations for conferences. They should collect some samples of a child's work and make notes on participation in school. When there are problems that must be discussed, the teacher should think about possible solutions ahead of time in order to be able to make suggestions for discussion. Without suggestions for alleviating a difficulty, some problems may better remain undisclosed. The teacher may find the conference more helpful for learning from the parent about the child and the impact of the program than it is for reporting. Conferring with parents requires different skills than teaching children, and teachers should spend some time developing those skills.

Procedure

When the teacher has called the conference, the discussion starts something like, "Now that we've had a few weeks of school, I thought it would be helpful for us to talk together. How do you feel things are going for Jack?" This question is usually easy for parents. They talk about things the child likes. The teacher can then ask, "How about things that have bothered Jack—things he didn't like? Do you think he's getting too tired?" By inviting negative reactions, the teacher lets the parents know that suggestions as well as praise are in order.

Nearly all parents enjoy talking about their child to someone who wants to listen. During the first conference the teacher would hope to convince parents of deep interest in the child, an awareness of what the child has been doing at school, also sincere respect for the child and parents.

Facing Problems

Most parents are grateful to teachers who bring their child's problems to their attention. Problems can develop without being noticed by parents. Parents often praise a teacher for helping them work through a problem. Common, too, is criticism of teachers who wait until difficulties are full-blown before mentioning them. The teacher's solution is usually not to ignore the child's problems but to think through possible meanings, causes, and solutions before calling parents in for a conference. If parents and teacher know each other through many pleasant instances, and mutual trust has developed, each can weather discussion of a child's problem without personal threat unless one of them has deep-seated problems.

Teachers should avoid making a premature diagnosis of the cause of a child's behavior. One mother was completely surprised when her child's teacher telephoned and asked whether she and her husband were having marital difficulty. The mother replied, "No. Why?" Then the teacher explained that their daughter was acting strangely, so she "just wondered." Months later the mother was still wondering what the child did or said that prompted the teacher to ask. Certainly, if the couple had been having problems, this was hardly an appropriate approach.

*　　*　　*

Talk It Over: No. 3

How would you feel if a parent called you, the teacher, and suggested that your marital problems were causing their child's difficulties? Discuss.

*　　*　　*

Avoid Blaming Parents

While talking with parents, it is of greatest importance to avoid arousing their defensive feelings. Such feelings are aroused if the child is criticized. There are ways of stating a concern regarding a child's behavior without fixing blame or being angry or annoyed. When too forcefully confronted with a child's problem behavior, the defensive parent may deny that the child behaves that way at home and suggest that the behavior must be the product of the school situation. Then comes the teacher's turn to be defensive. Sometimes the teacher may better say, after citing examples, "These are the things we see. Do you have any indication as to why John feels this way at school?" Not having to defend themselves, parents may volunteer the information that they are having similar problems at home.

Parents may say, "I know I'm to blame." To which the teacher can say, "Rather than fix a blame, let's think together about how we might remedy the situation. Now, here at school we've tried [enumerate a few examples]. Is there something like that you might try at home?" Such a discussion suggests possible solutions for examination. Parents can realize that problems have various solutions, and they can try one that fits their situation.

Parents often have the feeling that teachers just couldn't know how it is to be in parental shoes. As teachers grow in experience and draw on the experience of others, they may help parents realize that other parents before them have solved similar problems. Of course, teachers avoid using names or current classes for examples.

Teachers should be humble; it is extremely difficult really to know the family situation. There is very little that is clear-cut. An outsider should recognize uncertainties when giving advice. Parents' self-confidence must be protected and bolstered. If the conference is to be of any help to the child, the parents must have hope for succeeding as parents.

When parents request a conference, they are often ready to deal with some problem they face with the child. Again the teacher's role is more that of a listener and a suggester of alternatives than a giver of answers. The teacher should be willing to refer parents to other professionals whose training, experience, and available time leave them better equipped to cope with people who have problems.

A file of referral agencies should be on every teacher's desk. When teachers decide to make a referral, they should make some preliminary contacts with the agency in order to be able to give precise information to parents. Parents need to know where to go, when to go, what it will cost, and something about the personnel and procedure used. If the teacher knows the professionals in the agency by name and can personally endorse their qualifications, parents are more likely to follow through with the referral. Parents are understandably reluctant to face new people with their personal problems.

The teacher has the professional obligation to protect the confidentiality of personal information the parent reveals. Any notes the teacher makes should be kept private. Therefore information that is available to students and parent volunteers necessarily omits certain personal facts. Of course, parents should be able to see their child's file.

Occasionally in conferences and casual visits one parent seeks information about or is critical of other parents. The teacher must use diplomacy while turning the discussion back to that parent's own situation. Parents occasionally ask university student helpers about other children; students, too, must learn to handle such comments and avoid discussions that might be construed as gossip. Any information about the children should be discussed in a professional manner and in a professional setting.

Group Meetings for Parents

Getting parents together at meetings is one method of communicating with them. Meetings early in the year may help parents get acquainted with each other. The teacher may use the meeting to discuss goals for the children and outline the ways the school expects to meet these goals.

The needs and interests of parents will determine how many organized meetings are planned. The teacher may leave this decision up to the group. The teacher may encourage them to organize their own group, elect a chairperson, or appoint a committee to plan future programs. The more the parents are part of the planning process, the more interest they will have in attending meetings. Involvement of both fathers and mothers is important. An effort must be made to adjust meeting hours so as *not* to exclude working fathers or working mothers.

Some schools plan workshop programs that involve the parents in learning about school activities. For example, the parents may meet, mix finger paints and play dough, then use the materials to further their understandings of the creative experiences their child is having at school. Some groups plan programs using films or speakers to stimulate their exchange of ideas. They may prefer small-group discussions in which the focus is on their specific child-rearing problems.

Occasionally the topics parents suggest for meetings seem far removed from the child in the school. For example, parents may suggest meetings on meal planning, sewing, fashion, hairdressing, or even jewelry making. In the long run, these meetings may be helpful in developing rapport between home and school. Even when the teacher is unable to be a resource person for such topics, the group can be helped to locate someone who can. Through meeting the personal needs of parents, the child's needs are often served. If the parents are given a positive experience in the school, there will be a good chance that their interest will eventually focus more directly on the child.

Once a meeting has been planned, the teacher can help advertise it. Several notices can be sent home encouraging parents' attendance. First notices will encourage parents in advance to reserve that date on their calendars. On the day of the meeting another notice can remind them. Through personal contacts interest and enthusiasm can be aroused for the meeting. A committee of parents can contact others to encourage participation and offer transportation. Through such personal contacts parents will feel that they are wanted in the group.

Name tags help parents get acquainted and can help to break down formality because people can more readily use each other's names. It may help to put "Estelle Jones—John's Mother" on the name tag so that other parents can associate the mother with a name they may have heard their child mention from day to day. It is a common joke among parents that they lose their identity once their child goes to school. Because young children rarely know each other's last names, they refer to adults as John's mother or Bettie's daddy.

Better attendance results when baby-sitting is arranged. Transportation may also be a problem for some parents. Some schools hold meetings during the child's school hours. Extra volunteers supervise a children's program while the teacher and parents meet in another part of the building. A space may be arranged for infants and toddlers, or little ones may accompany parents to the meeting. This latter practice may cause some distractions because of the needs of the child. Proper toys for the babies should be available.

Evening meetings may not be well attended because of baby-sitting problems. When children must be brought to meetings, their bedtimes are delayed. Some teachers hold potluck suppers and early evening meetings so that parents can return home for their children's usual bedtime.

Some groups use gimmicks to attract parents to meetings. Gimmicks may be door prizes, recognition for the child's classroom, or performances by the children. Although gimmicks might be used occasionally to attract parents who cannot seem to be interested in other ways, their long-range value is questionable. Likewise, the threat that the child will be deprived of a place in the school if the parents do not participate is also questionable. A better way of attracting parents to meetings is through the personal interest of the teacher and other parents. When personal contacts are adequately made, a friendly atmosphere prevails, and if parents feel the program meets their needs, they are likely to make an effort to participate. The teacher's first meetings and first contacts set the stage for parents' participation. Well-planned, relevant programs are essential for good attendance.

Parent Effectiveness Training (P.E.T.) is a course or set of experiences designed by Thomas Gordon[4] to help parents with their interactions with their children. Sometimes these courses are offered to parents by a parent-educator or a mental health consultant. Courses and counseling for parents are available through family life educators in most religious institutions. Aside from learning some fruitful ways to deal with their youngsters of various ages, the participants gain from sharing their problems with parents having similar concerns. The techniques also have relevant applications to teaching children in the classroom.

Each chapter of Part Two of this book has suggested ways of involving parents in that particular area of the curriculum. Each curriculum area offers numerous possibilities for parents' meetings.

Printed Communication for Parents

Teachers usually rely on duplicated letters to inform parents of school affairs. A brief letter written in an interesting, warm style will encourage parents to read it and to feel that it was written especially for them. Underline dates that are to be remembered.

[4] Thomas Gordon, *P.E.T.: Parent Effectiveness Training* (New York: Peter H. Wyden, Inc., 1970).

Through letters the teacher can support other community agencies and their programs for families. The exact hours of a public health clinic might be important to some parents. Information on the hours the public library is open and when the children's story hour is held is helpful to parents and encourages library use. Parents can be reminded about musical events, art shows, exhibits, and lectures that are relevant to the many facets of the educational development of parents or children.

To emphasize to the child and to the parents that these letters are important, the teacher gives them special care. They are sealed in envelopes containing each child's name. The name helps the teacher keep track of undelivered letters. The letter can be attached to the child's coat with a safety pin. Children enjoy the responsibility of serving as "mail carriers" between their teacher and their homes.

Booklets and Newsletters

One form of written communication parents really appreciate is a newsletter or a booklet of class-related materials prepared by the teacher, duplicated, and sent home to parents. Some teachers prepare communications once a month, and others prepare them two or three times a year.

The content varies. The following materials have proved popular with parents:

1. The names, phone numbers, and addresses of the children in the group.
2. Recipes for finger paint, play dough, and paste.
3. Recipes for food projects enjoyed by the children.
4. Words to songs and finger plays the children are learning.
5. Stories and letters the children have dictated at school.
6. Toy-buying guides, including suggestions for appropriate gift items.
7. Suggested activities for the children's winter or summer vacation.
8. Examples of correct ways to learn manuscript writing.
9. Suggested books for children.
10. Suggestions for parent reading on the various school activities, family life, or sex education.

Pretty covers can be made for booklets from construction paper. One teacher helps the children place their hand prints in white paint on the colored paper. Older children can make a drawing or cut out a magazine picture for their booklet. Collage designs can be made by the children to cover their parents' booklet.

A booklet like this makes a nice gift for the children to give to their parents. The children feel the materials are theirs. They like to take the booklets home to share with the whole family. Such an educational device stimulates additional learning and often involves the whole family.

Experiences for Students and Beginning Teachers

Students often wonder how they can go about gaining the experience that enables them to feel comfortable in situations with parents. There are, of course, numerous counseling, family relations, and parent education courses that will help the student. One practical suggestion is for students to use every opportunity just to talk to people who have children. Knowing families from many walks of life also contributes to understanding. A good opportunity for the student is to volunteer for baby-sitting to get acquainted with parents and to observe how they relate to their children. As students go home for vacations, they can listen to their relatives and encourage both the eldest and the youngest parent to talk about the concerns and pleasures of child rearing. Every parent the student has the opportunity to know will provide experience that will help in developing better teacher-parent relations when the student becomes the teacher.

Explaining the Need for Parent Work

The process of accreditation of early childhood schools by the National Association for the Education of Young Children includes criteria on staff-parent interaction. The information and activities contained in this chapter would prepare a school for accreditation on this item.[5]

Very often the steps that have been outlined here for parent-teacher relations are carried on by teachers in addition to a full day of working with children. If a teacher has fifty or sixty children in two kindergarten classes, it is easy to see why she or he might be unable to carry through all the suggestions made here. However, the situation will never improve unless the teacher discusses the problem with the administrator, who can lighten the class load, give released time, or hire an assistant so that the teacher can have some time for parent work. Teachers must take a nothing-ventured-nothing-gained attitude while continuing to do the best they can for the children in their groups.

[5] *Accreditation Criteria and Procedures of the National Academy of Early Childhood Programs* (Washington, D.C.: National Association for the Education of Young Children, 1984), pp. 15–17.

A better plan is for the teacher to work half days with children, using the other half day for planning and for work with parents. This arrangement strengthens the program on two important fronts.

Special parent-educators are hired in some schools to coordinate programs for several teachers. They can readily organize parent meetings, meet with committees, and support leadership training that can be the outgrowth of a good program. However, even with a specialist in parent education the teacher will still need to maintain the relationships that have been discussed in this chapter. The work of any specialist should be incorporated into the planning for the class; therefore communication between the teacher and the parent-educator is essential.

Conclusion

Teacher-parent relationships are of utmost importance in the education of the young child. When the school and home are closely united, the child will more likely be able to reach fullest potential.

Teachers will take the leadership in initiating contacts with parents. They will maintain an open, friendly approach to parents, yet remain professional at all times.

The teacher will value relationships with parents as a teaching experience and, perhaps even more important, as a learning experience with respect to the child and parents.

Plans for the parents, like plans for the children, will be made after their needs and interests have been determined. The teacher may initiate some meetings while leaving others up to the leaders of the group.

Teachers should be prepared to explain to the administrators of their schools the importance of developing relationships with parents. Teachers should seek recognition that their work with parents on a one-to-one basis as well as on a group basis makes an important contribution to each child's education.

Communication with parents in a number of ways is stipulated in the criteria for accreditation for high-quality early childhood programs by the National Association for the Education of Young Children.

Applications

1. Discuss the "Talk It Over" items found in the chapter.
2. Complete Lesson 18 in *A Laboratory Workbook for Introduction to Early Childhood Education*. Hand in as scheduled.
3. Write a plan for a parent activity. Secure approval, carry out the plan if feasible, and evaluate the results from the parents' viewpoints and your viewpoint. Prepare a report and hand it in along with your approved plan.

4. Evaluate your total participation performance on your evaluation form developed in Chapter 1.

5. Add ideas and plans for parent activities to your Resource File.

Study Questions

1. Discuss the ways early childhood schools are part of a family support system.

2. State concerns parents may have as they begin relating to a school and teachers.

3. Discuss the value of good teacher-parent relationships in terms of the child.

4. Discuss the procedure for introducing a child gradually to the school.

5. List and discuss the various types of contacts teachers and parents could have.

6. Discuss details of planning a conference with a child's parents.

Additional Readings

AUERBACH, ALINE B., and SANDRA ROCHE. *Creating a Preschool Center: Parent Development in an Integrated Neighborhood Project.* New York: John Wiley & Sons, 1971.

AXLINE, VIRGINIA M. *Dibs: In Search of Self.* Boston: Houghton Mifflin Company, 1964.

BERGER, EUGENIA HEPWORTH. *Parents as Partners in Education.* St. Louis: The C. V. Mosby Company, 1981.

BIGNER, JERRY. *Parent-Child Relations.* New York: Macmillan Publishing Co., Inc., 1979.

DREIKURS, R., and V. SOLTZ *Children: The Challenge.* New York: Hawthorn, 1976.

DUVALL, EVELYN. *Marriage and Family Development.* New York: Harper & Row, 1977.

GINOTT, HAIM. *Between Parent and Child.* New York: Macmillan Publishing Co., Inc., 1973.

GORDON, THOMAS. *P.E.T.: Parent Effectiveness Training.* New York: David McKay Company, Inc., 1975.

GORDON, THOMAS, and JUDITH S. SANDS. *P.E.T. in Action.* New York: Bantam, 1978.

HONIG, ALICE. *Parent Involvement in Early Childhood Education.* Washington, D.C.: National Association for the Education of Young Children, 1979.

LEEPER, SARAH H., RALPH L. WITHERSPOON, and BARBARA DAY. *Good Schools for Young Children.* New York: Macmillan Publishing Co., Inc., 1984.

MARKUN, PATRICIA MALONEY (ed.). *Parenting.* Washington, D.C.: Association for Childhood Education International, 1973.

One-Parent Families. Washington, D.C.: Department of Health, Education and Welfare, 1977.

Parent Involvement: A Workbook of Training Tips for Head Start Staff. Washington, D.C.: Office of Economic Opportunity, 1969.

ROSENTHAL, ROBERT, and LENORE JACOBSON. *Pygmalion in the Classroom.* New York: Holt, Rinehart and Winston, 1983.

SEARS, R. R., E. MACCOBY, and H. LEVIN. *Patterns of Child-Rearing.* Evanston, Ill.: Row and Co., 1957.

STEVENS, J. H., and M. MATHEWS (eds.). *Mother/Child, Father/Child Relationships.* Washington, D.C.: National Association for the Education of Young Children, 1978.

SWICK, KEVIN. *Parent Involvement: Strategies for Early Childhood Educators.* Champaign, Ill.: Stipes, 1981.

SWICK, K. J., and R. ELEANOR DUFF. *The Parent-Teacher Bond: Relating-Responding-Rewarding.* Dubuque, Iowa: Kendall-Hunt Publishing Co., 1978.
The following journals will be helpful to teachers as they work with parents:

Adult Leadership. Published by the Adult Education Association of the U.S.A., 1225 19th St. N.W., Washington, D.C.

Journal of Marriage and the Family. Published by the National Council on Family Relations, 1219 University Avenue Southeast, Minneapolis, Minn.

Parent Cooperative Preschools International Journal. Published by Parent Cooperative Preschools International, 911 Alton Parkway, Silver Spring, Md.

The World's Children

- *To identify the common characteristics and needs of children around the world.*
- *To identify the mutual concerns of the world's early childhood educators.*
- *To relate international observations of children and early childhood programs to multicultural education of teachers.*

The Right:

1. To affection, love, and understanding.
2. To adequate nutrition and medical care.
3. To free education.
4. To full opportunity for play and recreation.
5. To a name and nationality.
6. To special care, if handicapped.
7. To be among the first to receive relief in times of disaster.
8. To learn to be a useful member of society and to develop individual abilities.
9. To be brought up in a spirit of peace and universal brotherhood.
10. To enjoy these rights, regardless of race, color, sex, religion, national, or social origin.

UN Declaration of the Rights of the Child

In 1979 these ten Rights of the Child were reaffirmed worldwide during the celebration of the International Year of the Child. These rights were adopted unanimously by the General Assembly of the United Nations in 1959. During 1979 citizens around the world made assessments of the problems and concerns related to children's health, education, and

Figure 19-1. A child care center in London, England provides full-day care for children of working parents.

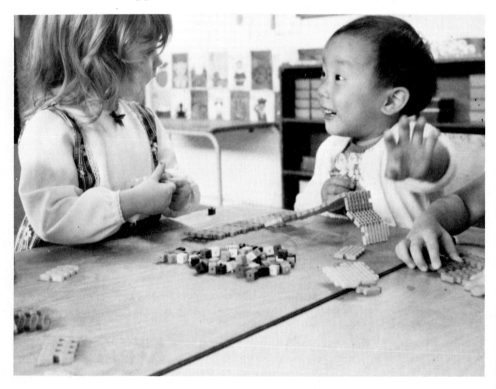

status relative to these ten rights. As is noted in Chapter 20, the United States adopted the Children's Charter in 1930. Many of the same concerns appear in both the Children's Charter and the United Nation's declaration. By the year 2000, with the help of dedicated teachers and parents around the world, great progress can be made on many of these problems crucial to the well-being of children wherever they may reside on our spaceship known as the planet Earth.

Global Interdependence

World problems in the news today are now about as close to home as local problems were a century ago. There is a rapidly growing recognition of the interdependence of the welfare of the children of the world, and that basic human rights extend to children regardless of the region of the world in which they are born. The spherical spaceship, Earth, inhabited by children and parents, is like an apartment house. What happens on one side of the global house affects children on the other side and vice versa. There is no place to hide from repercussions. This is true whether we speak of problems concerning environmental contamination, economics, conservation of resources, or the health and well-being of people. For example

1. With respect to environmental contamination, radioactivity from atomic explosions in one area spreads rapidly and contaminates the atmosphere of the entire planet.
2. With respect to economics, inflation or depression in one area soon extends damaging effects around the world.
3. With respect to conservation of resources, the world shortage of petroleum requires global conservation so all areas of the world and future generations may enjoy some of this scarce natural resource. Even population growth must now be studied concerning its impact on scarce natural resources and on environmental pollution.
4. With respect to health and well-being, contagious diseases, if unchecked, will spread around the world to the detriment of all.

Multicultural Understanding

Many of today's early childhood teachers are attempting to gain greater knowledge of the world's families and of world affairs in order to teach children more effectively for the century ahead. A current trend attracting the attention and support of many educators is the development and introduction of multicultural information, global perspectives, and aspects of global interdependence into the curriculum for each age group.

Within most countries of the world educators are recognizing and beginning to value cultural pluralism—the richness and diversity of their populations. Children and their cultures can properly remain unique with basic human rights extended to all individuals. While previous policies and socialization may have pressed for almost complete denial of ancestral roots, families now are increasingly free to choose to retain and cherish their roots. There is a growing belief that families can be free to maintain links with their ancestral culture and still prepare to function well in modern society. (Of course, over many thousands of years each family probably experienced many ancestral cultures.) A modern progressive society does not need identical human beings—only a recognition of a common humanity is needed to promote the general welfare, i.e., unity can coexist harmoniously with diversity. Intelligent application can make the world safe for differences and enrich society at the same time. One can simultaneously be a citizen of a local, state, national, and international community and enjoy to a still greater extent the benefits of diversity, unity, and progressive change for the improved welfare of all.

To be able to teach more intelligently about cultures other than one's own, teachers are making efforts to expand their horizons by study and travel, and by cultivating friendships with families from various cultural groups. For instance, opportunities are increasing for educational travel for students and teachers. Some scholarships are available. Many students spend a term or two in overseas programs operated by their own or foreign universities. Some early childhood students have taken the opportunity to do their student teaching in overseas locations. Students participate in activities abroad, such as the American Friend's Service Committee's volunteer work, various student exchange programs, and the Peace Corps; thus gaining valuable educational experience with families in cultures different from their own.

Students from countries around the world are enrolled on most university campuses and are delighted to share their cultural heritage and insights with students of their host country. These foreign students are often pleased to visit early childhood programs and to help provide cross-cultural experiences for young children—a significant educational contribution to world understanding. On some campuses international centers or organizations facilitate the interaction between American students and those students from other countries. These centers may also collect and disseminate information to teachers and to teachers-in-training regarding various cultures—perhaps through a library, an organized lecture series, films, cultural nights, and the like. On some campuses International Houses provide a multicultural meeting and living environment

Figure 19-2. Many Chinese children go to child care centers near their parents' workplace. Singing and dancing are significant parts of the children's programs.

and sponsor sessions for learning about various cultures, including excellent opportunities to learn and practice many languages.

Teachers will find that as their sensitivity and understanding of other cultures increases, so does their effectiveness in communicating with others and teaching others about various cultures. Cultural sensitivity is also gained and practiced as one interacts with minority groups at home and not need be thought of as dealing only with overseas cultures.

* * *

Talk It Over: No. 1

Discuss the opportunities you have had to know someone from another culture. Share with your class what you learned from each other.

* * *

Child Growth and Development Across Cultures

Children the world around have a common biological heritage. They develop in the same sequences, going through the same life cycle. With minor variations, children walk and talk about the same time and follow the same stages of logical reasoning. Children are all playful, though

Figure 19-3. Many Soviet children attend child care centers. Their program calls for lots of exercise and outdoor play.

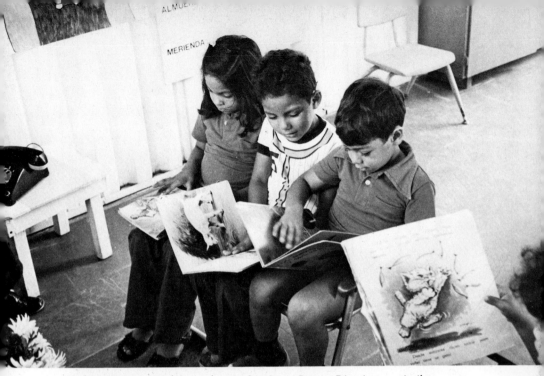

Figure 19-4. A Head Start class in San Juan, Puerto Rico is very similar to a stateside program.

what they play with depends on their culture. Children are all born into families where they receive primary care, are taught skills, and are socialized and educated in the ways of the culture.[1]

According to Werner, who analyzed many studies of physical growth done on five continents, "When we compare the physical growth curves of middle- or upper-class children from developing countries with those from U.S. and European longitudinal studies, we cannot help but be impressed with the similarity of growth patterns of normal children from different parts of the world. Longitudinal comparisons among economically favored children of different ethnic backgrounds indicate that differences in height and weight are relatively small—at best about 3 percent for height and about 6 percent for weight . . . In contrast, differences between these well-off children and those from the same ethnic stock who live in the poorest urban and rural regions of the developing world approximate 12 percent in height and 30 percent in weight. Differences in physical growth of preschool children associated with social class are much greater than those that can be attributed to ethnic factors . . ."[2] Thus, the Werner analysis indicates children grow in much the same way

[1] Kurt Fischer and Arlyne Lazerson, *Human Development* (New York: W. H. Freeman and Company, 1984), pp. 12–16.

[2] Emmy Elizabeth Werner, *Cross-Cultural Child Development* (Monterey, Calif.: Brooks/Cole Publishing Company, 1979), p. 34.

529

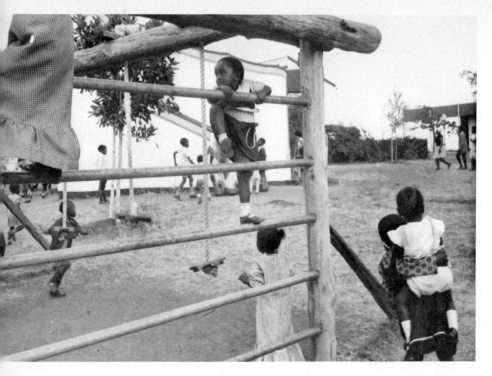

Figure 19-5. These Kenyan children in East Africa attend resident schools.

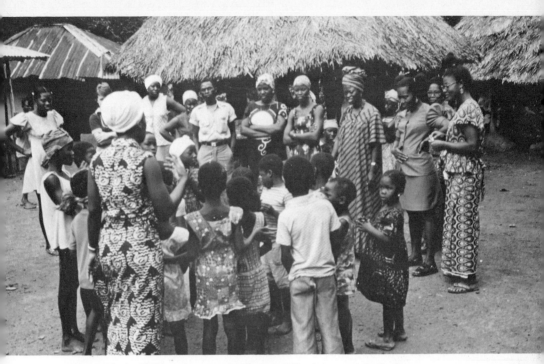

Figure 19-6. Children in a rural village in Liberia are taught by home economics students from a nearby college.

around the world if malnutrition and disease are not present as pre- or postnatal factors affecting development.

In studying languages among children in many different language groups, Dan Slobin says, "Children in all nations seem to learn their native languages in much the same way. Despite the diversity of tongues, there are linguistic universals that seem to rest upon the developmental universals of the human mind. Every language is learnable by children of preschool age, and it is becoming apparent that little children have some definite ideas about how a language is structured and what it can be used for . . ."[3]

Children have individual differences, too. These derive from their genetic makeup, their family, culture, and social class.

Early Childhood Education Around the World

Early childhood educators around the world share a common concern for young children. Many professionals are united through the *Organisation Mondiale Pour L'Education Prescolaire* (OMEP). In English it is the World Organization for Early Childhood Education. Linked to the United Nations as a nongovernmental organization, OMEP frequently lends its expertise on international issues affecting children and families. OMEP meets every three years in a study session for international early childhood scholars. It publishes a journal, *The International Journal of Early Childhood*.

*   *   *

Talk It Over: No. 2

What advantages do you see in early childhood educators from around the world communicating through meetings and publications?

*   *   *

Some programs for young children's care and education began in Europe in the 1800s, as is indicated in Chapter 20. Prominent leaders were Robert Owen in England, Frederich Froebel in Germany, the McMillan sisters in England, and Maria Montessori in Italy. Today one finds evidence of those early roots as one visits in early childhood programs in various countries. For example, some teachers will indicate that they follow the philosophy of Montessori or Froebel.

Austin, reviewing early education in eight countries—Belgium, Canada, France, Germany (F.R.), Italy, the Netherlands, Sweden, England, and Wales—writes that in all except France and Belgium, "Early child-

---

[3] Dan I. Slobin, "They Learn the Same Way All Around the World," *Psychology Today*, July 1972, reprinted in *Readings in Human Development 76–77*, Anne Kilbride (ed.) (Guilford, Conn.: Duskin Publishing Group, Inc., 1976), p. 272.

hood education tended to be adopted by the middle class who could afford it while the provision for the poor was reduced." Austin indicates that in Belgium and France most of the funding comes from the national government, guidelines are set at the national levels, and a large portion of all children above age three receive early education.[4]

Austin also reports that the regional governments of Canada and Germany (F.R.) control education and have laid down the guidelines. In the Netherlands, while the national government pays the cost of running the schools, the control is more localized. In Sweden and Italy the great majority of preschool education is financed at the local level and is controlled locally.[5]

In England, "Facilities for informal education and play for children aged two to five are provided free in public sector nursery schools and nursery classes in public sector primary schools. Classes for young children are also available in a few independent schools and a large number of 'preschool play groups' organized by voluntary organisations or by groups of parents. Apart from children only just under five, the proportion of children aged two to four who attend public sector schools remains low (the supply of places being inadequate to meet the demand for them) though attendance, and particularly part-time attendance has been increasing very rapidly in recent years. Compulsory education begins at five when children in England and Wales go to infant schools or departments. . . ."[6]

Asia

Japan's educational system is extremely competitive beginning in the early childhood years, according to several educational authorities. Families compete for places in the best schools which then track the children into lifetime jobs and connections upon graduation. A common practice is that boys and girls attend nursery school and kindergarten together, then are segregated in elementary and secondary schools. Japanese teachers report that children especially enjoy art materials in brilliant colors. Creative drawings are commonly seen in the schools.

Visiting in a kindergarten in the city of Kyoto, Japan, I was immediately impressed by the extensive display of children's creative drawings and paintings. The lively children made many efforts to communicate though the language barriers were formidable. They sang "Happy Birthday" in English and several English advertising jingles they'd learned from television. Though they were not able to speak English and I could

---

[4] Gilbert R. Austin, "A Review of Early Education in Eight Countries," *International Journal of Early Childhood*, 5:2 (1973), pp. 167–168.

[5] Ibid., p. 168.

[6] *Education in Britain*, British Information Services, London, 1976, p. 5.

not speak Japanese, communication did take place through singing and body language. I watched them use puzzles, blocks, and picture books. The class moved outdoors and demonstrated their routines of marching in various formations on the playground. In a Tokyo kindergarten children were observed doing creative movement in response to music and children listened attentively to a story. Classrooms were attractive and well equipped.

The Chinese government has taken considerable responsibility for providing nurseries and child care centers for infants and young children. Many of these facilities are attached to the factories where members of a child's family work. It is easy for the mother to drop by the nursery to nurse the infant, for instance. Most mothers do work outside the home; however, some infants remain in the care of their grandparents rather than attending a child care center. This work gives grandparents a useful occupation which is important in the Chinese culture.

There is lots of singing in the schools. In one center where this author visited, upon walking through the various rooms occupied by two or three adults with a group of children, the children could be observed standing by their seats and singing while the teacher played on an electric organ. Well-organized programs were presented by the school, complete with costumes and well-choreographed dance routines. The words to songs and the dances depicted political themes and current concerns. For example, one depicted the barefoot doctors, while another dance showed children "carrying fodder to the pigsty." Kessen characterized the Chinese nursery children as "docile and conforming, displaying little of the restlessness, rough and tumble, grabbing of property, or pushing and striking peers that are common in American homes or nursery schools."[7]

My observations fitted with Kessen's descriptions. The healthy appearance of the children was also impressive. A woman colleague who spent three months in China and who had opportunities to visit many homes mentioned that small children were handled a great deal, being passed around a room of adults, jostled on numerous knees, and spoken to frequently. It should be remembered that the press of population is ever present in China, on the streets, in child care centers, and in homes where many people occupy a small space. Sharing limited space is a part of socialization from the beginning.

Upon visiting schools in India one is continuously reminded that India has many many children to educate. A very high birth rate exists, despite efforts to encourage spacing children to reduce family size in order to have healthier children with more opportunity for well-being throughout their lives. The high birth rate swells the number needing

[7] William Kessen (ed.), *Childhood in China* (New Haven, Conn.: Yale University Press, 1976), p. 56.

Figure 19-7. Tokyo kindergarteners are painting pictures. In a Kyoto kindergarten the children sing in front of a display of their paintings.

Figure 19-8. In India early education has a long tradition. In Calcutta (Top) the school is operated by the Sisters of Loretto. In Delhi (Bottom) the school is part of Lady Erwin College.

schooling, and classroom spaces are scarce. Consequently, competition is keen for available spaces in schools. Wealthy people's children attend tuition-based schools. Few poor children receive the benefits of early education. However, it was heartening to see one group of small children, who literally lived on the Bombay streets, being taught by a religious group after each child was given a cup of milk and a banana for breakfast.

Testing is common in India at every educational level and is used as a means for excluding children. As a result, parents pressure teachers to push children to undertake formal school activities that help them pass test items, regardless of the child's motivation, readiness, or interest. One teacher reported screening two-year-olds to determine which children could pass a test to qualify for a toddler school.

Africa

In parts of Africa, for example, in Liberia and Kenya where I visited, many children from upper-income families are enrolled in private prekindergarten and kindergarten programs in the major cities. Social agency personnel expressed to me the need for more child care centers for children of low-income families. Some observers pointed out that the use of child labor is so prevalent in some poorer families that compulsory school attendance laws are unpopular. When children are required to attend school, parents lose needed labor on the farms or in vending operations.

In Kenya in East Africa the separation between preprimary education and child care was pointed out by educators—child care being primarily a caretaker function in the domain of a welfare or social agency, while preprimary education becomes primarily an educational function in the domain of an educational agency. This separation is common in many parts of the world, including the United States. In visiting a residential school for orphaned children in Nairobi, I learned the children lived in family groups with a house parent. Siblings stayed together and helped each other. In another school, care was being provided for handicapped children. Young children suffering with the effects of polio were observed here—a startling reminder of a generation or so ago when epidemics of this dread disease were common in all countries. With internationally coordinated public health and immunization programs many feared diseases threatening children and families can probably be eliminated worldwide.

The director of the home economics program at the Liberian agricultural college arranged for me to visit a village where several of her students were helping with family and child care programs. Upon arrival the college students and the group of young children they had organized and worked with proceeded to sing a variety of delightful songs they had learned.

In the Liberian capital city of Monrovia a child care center for children of working mothers was visited. The need for more child care centers providing good child care for the children of working mothers was evident from the discussion—a need often expressed the world around.

A similar conclusion was reached by Professor Eleanor R. Fapohunda of the University of Lagos in Nigeria. In a 1975 survey of 824 working mothers she found that, as a result of difficulty finding relatives or domestic help to care for children, "working women of Lagos are turning to commercial businesses, largely unregulated by government agencies to take care of their children."[8]

Another alternative Fapohunda suggested was voluntary association with other women to provide child care. This could be the beginning of a cooperative child care movement. As an economist, one of Fapohunda's concerns was more equitable economic development benefiting women and the country as a whole.

In South Africa a European-style early childhood education program is provided to white children whose standard of living is said to be among the highest in the world. Black children, on the other hand, because of the apartheid policies, are given few educational opportunities. Black people must live in separate townships away from white people. Black fathers are typically housed away from their families in workers' housing, and black working mothers who serve the white households as domestics may also be separated from their children, leaving them in care of others.

Latin America

Visiting early childhood centers in Central America, Panama, and Puerto Rico I noticed a number of similarities that developing areas face. The large population of infants and schoolage children is immediately evident. One learns that, though not many middle- and upper-class mothers are employed outside the home, some are sending their children to private preprimary schools. Others leave children at home in the care of maids. There are only a few child care centers organized especially for children of typical working mothers. These child care centers require some public financial support.

A variety of private schools is available. In the capital cities where embassy personnel and business people from a variety of countries live, one may find excellent private schools teaching in one or more lan-

[8] Eleanor R. Fapohunda, "The Child-Care Dilemma of Working Mothers in African Cities: The Case of Lagos, Nigeria," unpublished paper presented at the conference on "Women and Work in Africa," May 1, 1979, at the University of Illinois, Urbana, Ill.

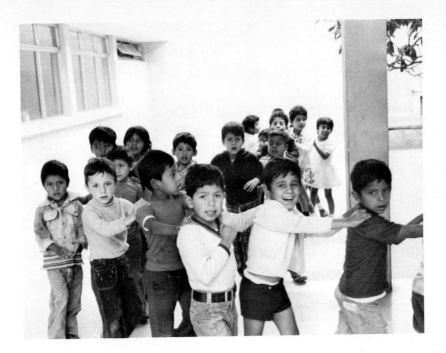

Figure 19-9. A center in Guatemala City cares for young children of working mothers.

Figure 19-10. These children of San Salvador were waiting to start their first day of a new term of school.

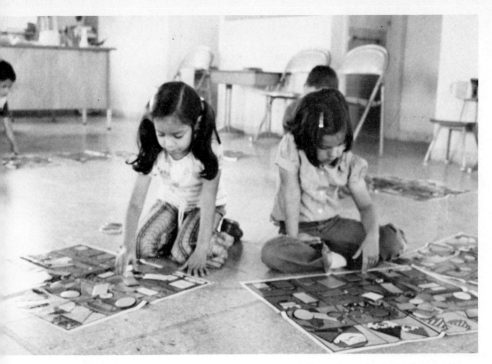

Figure 19-11. These kindergarteners in Honduras learn both English and Spanish.

Figure 19-12. A Panamanian center admitted both young children and an after school group.

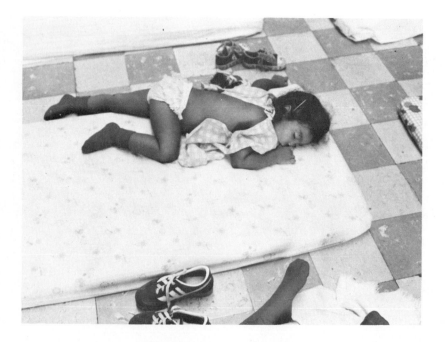

guages in addition to Spanish. The upper-class local children and children from the international community often attend these schools, benefiting from the multilanguage approach used. About half of the program is taught in the local language and the other half in another language.

In Puerto Rico many children have benefited from Project Head Start according to teachers, directors, and involved faculty from the University of Puerto Rico with whom I visited. Head Start teachers throughout the island receive training similar to the training and support that stateside Head Start teachers receive.

Upon visiting a Head Start center one notes typical early childhood educational experiences led by dedicated teachers. The children were involved with books, blocks, and dramatic play, for example.

In South America large numbers of young children put pressure on educational resources, just as they do in Central America. The wealthier people's children attend private early childhood schools. The public schools do not offer kindergarten. Child care centers are available only in larger cities and, according to administrators, demand far exceeds supply of spaces. One attractive child care center in Santiago, Chile was located in the middle of a municipal park, affording wonderful shade and a swimming pool nearby. Santiago requires companies and agencies hiring more than nineteen women to provide child care for the women's young children. The children were bussed between the center of the city where their mothers worked and the child care center in the park each morning and evening.

Soviet Union

The Soviet Union is one of four countries often cited as examples of major governmental commitment to support and extend child care to children. These countries are the People's Republic of China, the Soviet Union, Israel, and Cuba. Each of these countries places early childhood education in high regard and believes that the child care programs they provide for young children are important for the health and education of these youngest citizens and for developing national strengths. However, even in these countries many children do not attend child care programs. Though mothers typically work outside the home in these countries, much child care comes from grandparents if they are nearby.

Bronfenbrenner, an American child development authority, was a visiting scholar in the Soviet Union in the 1960–1967 period. He wrote that the Russian child care program at that time served over 10 percent of all Soviet children under two years and about 20 percent of three- to

Figure 19-13. In Halifax, Nova Scotia, Canada, children play in a protected play area of Mount St. Vincent's College Child Study Center.

Figure 19-14. Children in an early childhood school in Guaymas, Mexico invent a lively game using old tires.

six-year-olds. The enrollment was limited chiefly by the shortage of places available.[9]

Henry Chauncey had translated the Russian program of instruction into English, providing a detailed look at the volumes that are read throughout Russia by early childhood "upbringers" and teachers. Bronfenbrenner indicates that he saw the books in use in several localities and that they provided the base for numerous other publications related to providing care and education for young children. Upon reading the books one is impressed with the similarity of activities recommended to those commonly used in the United States and elsewhere. There is an emphasis on nature, fresh air, physical activity, and working for the common good. The emphasis on chores or work comes through in this portion. "Training in self-control, courtesy, and respect for adults acquires greater and greater significance at this age level. The chores assigned to the children become more involved."[10]

As an observer in a number of Russian nursery schools in several cities, on collective farms, and state farms, I was impressed with the health and liveliness of the children and the cleanliness of the environment. In many instances teachers did not know visitors were coming, but the child care facilities were always orderly and clean with good programs and teachers. Outdoor activities were emphasized in the centers visited. A protective roof (similar to an open carport) provided a nice outdoor place for storytime and other activities, thus keeping the children out in the fresh air for longer periods.

Israel

In the Israeli kibbutz, according to Marcbls and Robinson, the communal care of children has been customary even to the extent that caregivers care for children at night. The infant enters the infant house at about four to nine months of age. The infant house accommodates fifteen to twenty children. Babies are placed in groups of five or six. When the child reaches the toddler age, he or she is transferred to a toddler house. At about three years of age the child begins cooperative group activities. The activities provided are similar to those of many United States child care centers.[11]

Israel also has part-day and full-day early childhood schools. These

[9] Urie Bronfenbrenner, *Two Worlds of Childhood: US and USSR* (New York: Russell Sage Foundation, 1970), p. 15.

[10] Henry Chauncey (ed.), *Soviet Preschool Education. Volume I: Program of Instruction* (New York: Holt Rinehart and Winston, 1969), p. 101. The second volume is *Soviet Preschool Education. Volume II: Teacher's Commentary* (New York: Holt, Rinehart and Winston, 1969).

[11] Joseph Marcbls and Halbert B. Robinson, *Growing Up In Groups* (New York: Gordon and Breach, 1972), p. 218.

a

Figure 19-15. Early childhood programs in South American countries.
(a) Orphanage in Cusco, Peru. (b) Municipal child care center, Santiago, Chile.
(c) Child care center in La Paz, Bolivia. (d) YMCA school in Quito, Ecuador.

b

c

d

are in the cities and typically follow a European model of early education.

Conclusion

The numerous similarities among children around the world are indeed the most striking discovery of study and travel with related observing. By comparison the differences among the world's children are
few. Children grow, learn, laugh, love, and cry much the same the world
around. Differences in income levels of parents apparently account for
more differences among the world's children than does culture or nationality. The basic needs of the children are universal.

The children of today will become the world's leaders of tomorrow.
Throughout the world *all* of these precious human resources must be
nurtured and activated to solve serious world problems. May the children's bright lights of love, laughter, and learning shine more brightly
around the world throughout the years ahead and light the way to a
more just, peaceful, and happy planetary home.

Applications

1. Discuss the "Talk It Over" items in the chapter.
2. Complete Lesson 19 in *A Laboratory Workbook for Introduction to Early Childhood Education*. Hand in as scheduled.
3. Do some library reading on early childhood education in the international arena. See Additional Readings section for suggestions, or, use the encyclopedia or the *Reader's Guide*. Follow up a reference to a country of interest to you. (Key words are Child Care, Education: preschool.)
4. Add ideas on multicultural activities to your Resource File.
5. Evaluate your participation on your evaluation form and discuss your performance with your teacher. Secure a written evaluation for your final record.

Study Questions

1. What is the *UN Declaration of the Rights of the Child?* What does it say? When was it written? When was it used for the International Year of the Child?
2. What happened during the International Year of the Child?
3. Discuss global interdependence and its relationship to children and families.

4. Identify ways to increase your multicultural understanding.

5. In what ways do all children have a common heritage?

6. What is the name of an international organization for early childhood educators? What does it do?

7. Write some generalizations regarding the state of early childhood education after reading the descriptions of early education in the various countries.

Film

What Rights Has the Child?   Color   15 minutes   1979

Pictorially depicts each of the United Nation's Ten Rights of the Child. Children's voices partly narrate. Children's drawings from UNICEF and photographs are used to show the status of children during the International Year of the Child, 1979. Instructional Media Center, Michigan State University, East Lansing, Mich. 48824.

Additional Readings

AUSTIN, GILBERT. *Early Childhood Education: An International Perspective.* New York: Academic Press, 1976.

BRONFENBRENNER, URIE. *Two Worlds of Childhood: U.S. and U.S.S.R.* New York: Russell Sage Foundation, 1970.

CHAUNCEY, HENRY (ed.). *Soviet Preschool Education. Volume I: Program of Instruction.* New York: Holt, Rinehart and Winston, 1969.

CHAUNCEY, HENRY (ed.). *Soviet Preschool Education. Volume II: Teacher's Commentary.* New York: Holt, Rinehart and Winston, 1969.

Children and Youth in National Development in Latin America. New York: United Nations Children's Fund, 1965.

HILDEBRAND, VERNA. "Families and Child Care: A Global Ecosystem Perspective," chapter in *Child Nurturance, Vol. II.* Marjorie Kostelnik et al. (eds.). New York: Plenum Publishing Corporation, 1982.

HILDEBRAND, VERNA, and JOHN R. HILDEBRAND. *China's Families: Experiment in Societal Change.* Minneapolis, Minn. Burgess Publishing Co., 1981.

KESSEN, WILLIAM (ed.). *Childhood in China.* New Haven, Conn.: Yale University Press, 1976.

MCHALE, M. C., and JOHN MCHALE. *Population Bulletin: World of Children.* Washington, D.C.: Population Reference Bureau, 1979.

WALD, KAREN. *Children of Che: Childcare and Education in Cuba.* Palo Alto, Calif.: Ramparts Press, 1978.

WEISER, MARGARET G. "Public Policy: For or Against Children and Families? An International Perspective." *Childhood Education,* Vol. 59: No. 2. March/April 1982, pp. 227–234.

WERNER, EMMY E. *Cross-Cultural Child Development.* Monterey, Calif.: Brooks/Cole Publishing Company, 1979.

The Profession— Past, Present, and Future

- *To identify significant periods in the history of early childhood education.*
- *To identify individuals who were leaders of the early childhood education movement.*
- *To identify historical and current trends and issues in the early childhood education movement.*

"Why were the standards for nursery schools set higher than the standards for child care?" asked an early childhood teacher who was helping with revising the state's rules for licensing child care.

"Why is Montessori teacher education different than other teacher education?" asked a student about to graduate from a teacher education program.

"Is it true that this state doesn't support kindergartens?" asked a sixty-year-old newcomer incredulously. He went on to say that he had attended a publicly funded kindergarten in his hometown fifty-five years earlier.

After one has an opportunity to become acquainted with current ideas, issues, and practices in a professional field, one's curiosity may be aroused about the history of that profession. In early childhood education a number of historical eras are significant and numerous individuals have made contributions. The reader is encouraged to pursue additional sources on topics of particular interest.

European Roots

For those who might be inclined to think that early childhood education has only recently been discovered, it is well to note that the early Greeks—Socrates (469–399 B.C.), Plato (425–347 B.C.), and Aristotle

550

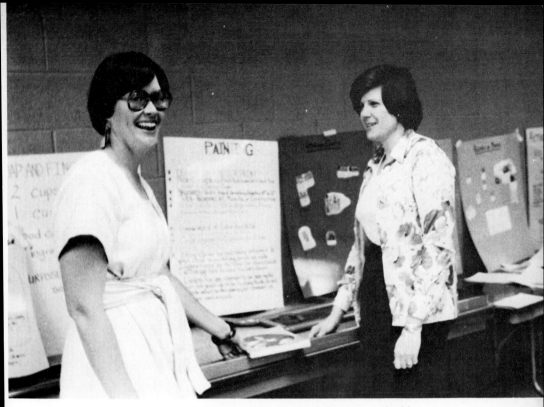

Figure 20-1. Both attending and presenting workshops are valuable experiences for teachers. It is a pleasure to exchange ideas and become acquainted with other teachers. (Southern Association for Children Under Six)

(384–322 B.C.)—spoke out regarding the education of the child.

During the Industrial Revolution of the eighteenth and nineteenth centuries, European philosophers wrote about educating the young child. In Rousseau's mind (1712–1778) the best education for the child in the later part of the eighteenth century was the education that least hampered the development of the pupil's natural ways.[1] Pestalozzi, a Swiss (1746–1827), was influenced by Rousseau. Especially concerned with education of the poor, he developed a home for paupers and a school for refugees. He felt that schooling should directly involve the child and suggested methods appealing to the senses.[2] Many ideas from the eighteenth-century philosophers are still in practice today.

The era of nursery school-kindergarten education that heavily influenced the American movement occurred in early nineteenth-century Europe. Mothers and older siblings were going off to work, leaving small

[1] Jean Jacques Rousseau, *Emile*, trans. Barbara Foxley (London: J. M. Dent & Sons Ltd., 1911), p. 50.
[2] Johann Heinrich Pestalozzi, *How Gertrude Teaches Her Children*, trans. Lucy E. Holland and Francis C. Turner (London: George Allen and Unwin Ltd. 1894), pp. 200–201.

Figure 20-2. Arranging exhibits at conferences is a typical professional activity. This booth promoted an organization of community college child development educators at the Southern Association for Children Under Six.

children uncared for. The first institution for the children of working mothers was founded in Germany in 1802.[3]

Friedrich Froebel (1782–1852), a German philosopher, believed that educating children was similar to cultivating plants, and so he coined the term *kindergarten* meaning "garden of children." He founded the first kindergarten in 1837.[4] Froebel's philosophy was naturalistic. He felt that children should be allowed to play, but that teachers could arrange play for them that developed their minds, bodies, and senses. Froebel had become convinced through work with older boys that their problems were really rooted in their earlier experience. In 1817 he admitted boys just three years old to his school. Froebel's writings later provided the philosophy for the kindergarten movement in America and other countries. Teachers went to Germany for special training.[5]

Another historic early childhood education movement occurred in

[3] "Nursery Schools," *The Encyclopedia Americana,* Vol. 20 (New York: American Corporation, 1967), pp. 554–557.

[4] Ilse Forest, *Preschool Education: A Historical and Critical Study* (New York: Macmillan Publishing Co., Inc., 1927), pp. 154–183; Friedrich Froebel, *Pedagogics of the Kindergarten* (New York: D. Appleton and Co., 1917), pp. 1–33. See also, Friedrich Froebel, *Mother Play and Nursery Songs,* trans. Elizabeth Peabody (Boston: Lothrop, and Shepard, 1878).

[5] "Nursery Schools," op. cit.

Figure 20-3. Montessori materials are invitingly arranged. Children select one and take it to a work place. (Montessori School of East Lansing, Michigan)

Scotland in 1816, when Robert Owen, a socialist, established an infant school. In France in 1833 Jean Frederic Oberlin founded a nursery school. *Crèches* were organized in Vienna, Austria, in 1847; in Spain in 1855; and in Russia in 1864.[6]

The McMillan sisters, Rachel and Margaret, organized the first English nursery school in London between 1908 and 1910. The McMillans' school and writings were inspirations for American schools.[7]

Dr. Maria Montessori, founder of schools bearing her name, was born in Italy in 1870 and died in 1952. She was trained before the turn of the century as a medical doctor and psychologist. Her major work centered around training feebleminded children in an Italian slum housing project. Her teaching stressed cleanliness and self-help. She designed numerous tasks and felt that children should learn these tasks in a designated sequence. She appears to have been quite successful in getting children to learn.

Montessori schools using Montessori methods and materials have continued to be formed throughout the world. Some of these schools seem to hold a semimystic faith in Montessori's ideas. Surely Dr. Montessori would make some changes if she were alive today. She was a woman ahead of her times. Probably such a creative woman would use any scientific knowledge and experience available and update her methods accordingly.[8]

Nearly all nursery schools and kindergartens today emphasize the idea of self-help and the development of independence—both stressed in Montessori schools. Children generally help care for their room. "Self-correcting" materials similar to Montessori's have been adapted for general use. In most schools children are allowed to use learning materials in as many creative ways as the mind can suggest. However, in a strict Montessori school, there is only one correct way to use a learning material.[9] To be an authentic Montessori teacher one must complete training in a Montessori teacher education program, which probably will be in addition to the education required for licensing in a given state. Unfortunately, some Montessori schools are not authentic, but only using the name which is not considered protected by copyright laws. Thus, the trademark of high quality, which being a Montessori school usually signifies, could not be guaranteed.

---

[6] "Nursery Schools," op. cit.

[7] Margaret McMillan, *The Nursery School* (New York: Dutton, 1921), p. 22.

[8] *Montessori in Perspective*, publication No. 406 (Washington, D.C.: National Association for the Education of Young Children, 1966).

[9] Lois Barklay Murphy, "Multiple Factors in Learning in the Day Care Center," *Childhood Education*, 45:6 (February 1969), p. 317.

Early American Roots

"Nursery for the Children of Poor Women in the City of New York" was the lengthy title given the first child care program in the United States in 1854. There wage-earning women left their children (ages six weeks to six years) for as long as twelve hours.[10]

Thus child care centers began for the children of poor, destitute, often immigrant mothers. The center took "custody" of the child while the mother worked in the factory or elsewhere. The term "custodial child care" has over the years become associated with low quality. Placing one's child in child care was also considered a last resort. Social workers are said to have encouraged women to stay at home to care for their children, even in cases when their husband's job did not pay enough to sustain the family.

In the meantime, nursery schools and kindergartens were being organized for the more elite and affluent people's children. Thus evolved a two-level standard of quality, one for poor children, another for the elite. Problems with this dichotomy are still with the profession today, as are arguments about whether mothers should leave their children in a center while they go out to work.

The first American kindergarten was founded in Wisconsin in 1856 by Mrs. Carl Schurz, who had been a student of Froebel. The kindergarten was taught in German. Mrs. Schurz's husband, an editor and later a senator, was a leader of the German element against slavery. The first kindergarten for English-speaking children was organized in Massachusetts by Elizabeth Peabody in 1860. These kindergartens were organized under private auspices. In 1873 the first public-supported kindergarten was established in Saint Louis. Patty Hill of Teachers College, Columbia University, and Alice Temple of the University of Chicago were early American leaders in nursery-kindergarten education.[11]

Lizzie Merrill-Palmer, in her will of 1916, provided funds for establishing a center in Detroit to train girls for motherhood.[12] Today the Merrill-Palmer Institute enrolls both men and women and contributes outstanding leadership to studies of children and families. It is now operating under the auspices of Wayne State University of Detroit.

The Laura Spelman Rockefeller Memorial provided for increased emphasis in child-centered research when in the 1920s it was used to sponsor child study centers at a number of major universities. The University of California, the University of Minnesota, Columbia University,

---

[10] "Nursery Schools," op. cit.

[11] Forest, op. cit., pp. 170–182. For additional insight on early leaders see *Dauntless Women in Early Childhood Education: 1856–1931* by Agnes Snyder (Washington, D.C.: Association for Childhood Education International, 1972).

[12] Forest, op. cit., p. 297.

and Yale University were four involved.[13] Early research supported the idea that nursery schools contribute to the child's physical progress as well as to his ability to respond to intelligence tests. Children who had behavior problems seemed to be helped when attending nursery school. Nursery schools were looked upon as a supplement to the home and not a replacement of it.

In the years between 1920 and 1930 the number of nursery schools in the United States grew from 3 to 262.[14]

The first White House Conference concerning children was called by President Theodore Roosevelt in 1909. Since then, conferences have been called by each President at the beginning of each decade. Out of the first conference came the recommendation for and subsequent organization of the Children's Bureau, which was first housed in the Department of Commerce and Labor. It is now housed in the Department of Health and Human Services.

The final meeting of the 1930 White House Conference was reported in *The New York Times*, November 20, 1930: "Dr. F. J. Kelly of University of Chicago summarized the needs of the child in a machine age, expressed opposition to lock-step education and supported the statement that the cardinal principle in education should be the development of each child to his or her highest level of attainment because 'the danger of a dead level of mediocrity is more grave in a democracy than in any other form of government.' "[15]

Also reported in *The New York Times* was a classic document that came out of the 1930 Conference. It was *The Children's Charter*, reproduced here so that the reader can see that many of the 1930 problems are with us today—especially when one thinks of the world as the community and of our increasing concern for the world's children.

The Great Depression Era

The Great Depression of the 1930s was felt by children, families, and teachers. The federal Emergency Relief Administration organized schools for young children. In 1934–1935 there were 75,000 children benefiting from a program designed more to put teachers to work than to educate children. The number decreased when conditions improved, but in 1942 there were still 944 nursery schools operating for 38,735 chil-

---

[13] Mary Dabney Davis, *Nursery Schools: Their Development and Current Practices in the United States*, U.S. Office of Education Bulletin No. 9, 1932 (Washington, D.C.: Government Printing Office, 1933), pp. 1–10.

[14] Gertrude E. Chittenden, Margaret Nesbitt, and Betsy Williams, "The Nursery School in American Education Today," *Education Digest* (January 1949), pp. 46–51.

[15] "19 Point Program of Child Aid Carried," *The New York Times*, November 23, 1930, p. 20. (© 1930 by The New York Times Company, Reprinted by permission.)

CHILDREN'S CHARTER [16]

1. Every Child is entitled to be understood, and all dealings with him should be based on the fullest understanding of the child.

2. Every prospective mother should have suitable information, medical supervision during the prenatal period, competent care at confinement. Every mother should have post-natal medical supervision for herself and child.

3. Every child should receive periodical health examinations before and during the school period, including adolescence, by the family physician or the school or other public physicians and such examinations by specialists and such hospital care as its special needs may require.

4. Every child should have regular dental examination and care.

MEASURES FOR PROTECTION

5. Every child should have instruction in the schools in health and in safety from accidents, and every teacher should be trained in health programs.

6. Every child should be protected from communicable diseases to which it might be exposed at home or at play, and protected from impure milk and food.

7. Every child should have proper sleeping rooms, diet, hours of sleep and play, and parents should receive expert information as to the needs of children of various ages as to these questions.

8. Every child should attend a school which has proper seating, lighting, ventilation, and sanitation. For younger children, kindergartens and nursery schools should be provided to supplement home care.

9. The school should be so organized as to discover and develop the special abilities of each child, and should assist in vocational guidance, for children, like men, succeed by the use of their strongest qualities and special interests.

10. Every child should have some form of religious, moral, and character training.

11. Every child has a right to play with adequate facilities therefor.

12. With the expanding domain of the community's responsibilities for children, there should be proper provision for and supervision of recreation and entertainment.

PROVISION FOR THE HANDICAPPED

13. Every child should be protected against labor that stunts growth, either physical or mental, that limits education, that deprives children of the rights of comradeship, of joy and play.

14. Every child who is blind, deaf, crippled or otherwise physically

[16] Ibid.

handicapped should be given expert study and corrective treatment where there is the possibility of relief, and appropriate development or training. Children with subnormal or abnormal mental conditions should receive adequate study, protection, training and care. Where the child does not have these services, due to inadequate income of the family, then such services must be provided to him by the community. Obviously, the primary necessity in protection and development of children where poverty is an element in the problem is an adequate standard of living and security for the family within such groups.

15. Every waif and orphan in need must be supported.

16. Every child is entitled to the feeling that he has a home. The extension of services in the community should supplement and not supplant parents.

17. Children who habitually fail to meet normal standards of human behavior should be provided special care under the guidance of the school, the community health, or welfare centre or other agency for continued supervision, or, if necessary, control.

18. The rural child should have satisfactory schooling, health, protection and welfare facilities.

COORDINATED ORGANIZATION

19. In order that these minimum protections of the health and welfare of children may be everywhere available, there should be a district, county or community organization for health education and welfare, with full-time officials, coordinating with a statewide program which will be responsible to a nationwide service of general information, statistics and scientific research. This should include:

   a. Trained full-time public health officials and public health nurses, sanitary inspection and laboratory workers.
   b. Available hospital beds.
   c. Full-time public welfare services for the relief and aid of children in special need from poverty or misfortune, for the protection of children from abuse, neglect, exploitation or moral hazard.
   d. The development of voluntary organization of children for purposes of instruction, health, and recreation through private effort and benefaction. When possible, existing agencies should be coordinated.

dren. Kindergartens slowed their pace of growth soon after 1930, after sixty years of progress toward acceptance as a public school service. From an enrollment of 15,000 in 1888, to 725,000 in 1930, enrollment dropped to 600,000 in 1934.[17]

[17] Bess Goodykoontz, Mary Dabney Davis, and Hazel F. Gabbard, "Recent History and Present Status of Education for Young Children," *Early Childhood Education (46th Yearbook), Part II, National Society for the Study of Education* (Chicago: University of Chicago Press, 1947), pp. 45–46.

World War II Era

Child care facilities received a major boost during World War II. They were essential to free women who were needed in production plants. The Lanham Act of 1942 provided funds for the day care of young children and for the extended day care of school-age children. These schools were held in quickly built "temporary" buildings. The facilities were in many cases a vast improvement in design and convenience over the renovated buildings that commonly housed nursery schools. The direct relationship with the public school system was also a step forward. The U.S. Office of Education and the U.S. Children's Bureau were designated to assume responsibility for the program. Children were the secondary concern of the planners of Lanham Act nursery schools—the war effort's need for women workers being their first concern.

In 1945, at the close of the era, there were over 50,000 children enrolled in almost 1,500 child care centers, and there were 18,000 receiving extended day care. Kindergartens enrolled 700,877 in 1944.[18]

Sigmund Freud's (1856–1939) theory of human motivation[19] began having an impact on early childhood education. For example, play therapy and dramatic play in the prekindergarten and kindergarten contributed to the understanding of a child's inner feelings. The importance of the parent-child relationship and the significance of the early years, much emphasized by Freud and others, began to guide the early childhood programs.

The Early Post-World War II Era

The post-World War II era witnessed a return to normality as far as the nation's young children were concerned; that is, federal funds for operating child care centers were no longer available. States were allowed to continue operation of their Lanham Act child care centers, but most permitted them to close. However, women did not all go back to the cookstove after World War II. They either needed or wanted to remain in the labor force. The need for child care facilities continued and continues today.

It is of interest to note that the 1950 White House Conference dealt with the components of a healthy personality for children and youth. Mental health was finally receiving attention after being neglected so long.

---

[18] Ibid., p. 45.
[19] Sigmund Freud, *The Basic Writings of Sigmund Freud,* trans. and ed. A. S. Brill (New York: Random House, 1938).

In the 1960 Conference there was a recommendation for public kindergartens and day-care facilities.[20]

In 1959 the Office of Education reported that 70 percent of the public elementary schools maintained kindergartens and 5 percent maintained nursery schools.[21] Private and cooperative schools increased during this time. The shift to the suburbs, improved standards of living, smaller families, smaller housing, increased mobility, and the increased level of parental education are frequently cited sociological factors contributing to the interest of parents in early education for their children.

Research at Yale by Dr. Arnold Gesell provided normative data to which parents and teachers could compare a child's growth.[22] During the 1930s and 1940s Gesell utilized the new moving-picture techniques to record young children's behavior. He published ages and stages of development which he saw as flexible, but parents often took as rigid. Gesell's work is still used today with adaptations based on later information.

During the postwar decades Dr. Benjamin Spock's book *Baby and Child Care* sold millions of copies in a pocket edition.[23] Parents of young children needed the reassurance of a more experienced hand, and Spock substituted for the older generation's Grandma next door.

The United Nations, which was organized in 1945, contributed to better communication between the peoples of the world. Several specialized agencies dealt with the health and well-being of children and families. These were the World Health Organization (WHO), the Food and Agriculture Organization (FAO), the United Nations Educational Scientific and Cultural Organization (UNESCO), and the United Children's Emergency Fund (UNICEF).[24] In 1948 the *Organisation Mondiale Pour L'Education Prescolaire* (OMEP) or World Organization for Early Childhood Education was founded for the purpose of uniting those who care about children the world around.

The War on Poverty Era: 1960s

The "War on Poverty" was begun in the 1960s. The accelerated migration of rural America to the cities to work, the need for more technically trained workers, the rising school dropout rate, and the growing

[20] Kathryn Close, "Impressions of the White House Conference," *Children* (May–June 1960).

[21] S. E. Dean, *Elementary School Administration and Organization,* U.S. Office of Education, Bulletin No. 11 (Washington, D.C.: U.S. Government Printing Office, 1960), p. 19.

[22] Arnold Gesell and F. L. Ilg, *Infant and the Child in the Culture of Today* (New York: Harper & Row, 1943).

[23] Benjamin Spock, *Baby and Child Care* (New York: Pocket Books, Simon & Schuster, 1953).

[24] *United Nation's Visitor's Guide* (New York: United Nations).

unrest among minorities woke the nation to some festering ills in its midst. The war in Vietnam contributed to inflation and required resources that might have been used domestically.

The Economic Opportunity Act was passed in March 1964 and, on April 11, 1965, the Elementary and Secondary School Act became law.[25] Finally, after long years of debate, federal aid to education was granted. Federal aid was expected to equalize the educational opportunities between the country's rich and poor states, just as state aid helped to equalize opportunities within a state. For decades district financing has helped to equalize educational opportunities among families of a district.

Head Start programs for disadvantaged children under six became one of the more popular programs in President Lyndon Johnson's War on Poverty. The program was heralded with great expectation in many quarters. Education for young children was given professional leadership and funds. Leaders were saying that Head Start is a program for educating children, not an employment program for the poor. If this attitude did, in fact, guide the leadership, it represents the first time that the needs of children were given top priority in an emergency program. However, the Head Start program maintains a strong commitment to involve local parents and school dropouts.

Margaret Rasmussen, editor of *Childhood Education,* reported in September 1965 that the first summer of Head Start had involved 536,108 children, 39,463 professionals, 44,589 paid neighborhood residents, 54,996 neighborhood volunteers, and 40,187 other volunteers throughout the nation.[26] By the end of 1979 over 6 million children had been enrolled in the Head Start program since its beginning.[27]

Early Head Start planners held out for a trained, qualified teacher and a low pupil-teacher ratio—two paid teachers for fifteen disadvantaged children, plus volunteer helpers. Short courses were established by universities across the country to train teachers, assistant teachers, and aides for the programs. In 1969, 3,600 paraprofessionals were trained in 150 colleges.[28]

The Head Start program also includes the Parent and Child Center, which "represents the drawing together of all those resources—family, community, and professional—which can contribute to the child's total

[25] J. William Rioux, "New Opportunities Economic Opportunity Act and Elementary and Secondary Education Act of 1965," *Childhood Education,* **42:**1 (September 1965), pp. 9–11.

[26] Margaret Rasmussen, "Over the Editor's Desk," *Childhood Education,* **42:**1 (September 1965), p. 65.

[27] Office of Children, Youth, and Families (Washington, D.C.: Department of Health, Education, and Welfare, 1979).

[28] Harriette Merhill, "Highlighting the National Conference on the Paraprofessional, Career Advancement, and Pupil Learning," *Childhood Education,* **45:**7 (March 1969), p. 369k.

development. It draws heavily on the professional skills of persons in nutrition, health, education, psychology, social work, and recreation. It recognizes that both paid and volunteer nonprofessionals can make important contributions. Finally the concept emphasizes that the family is fundamental to the child's development. Parents should play an important role in developing policies; they should work in the Centers and participate in the programs."[29]

Early Childhood Education in the 1970s and 1980s

Increasing enrollments occurred during the 1970s in early childhood programs even as birth rates dropped. More people enrolled their children in programs, especially full-day child care programs. The full-day programs increased in number, while the number of part-day nursery schools appeared to decline. This decline reflected several factors. First, the number of families in which both parents work, or that are headed by one parent, increased, and the parents tended to choose full-day child care centers or family day care over two- or three-hour programs. Second, in some states the designation "nursery school" required a certified teacher, while the child care designation did not; therefore, in an effort to economize, some centers hired less qualified persons and relabeled and relicensed their center as a child care center. Third, during the 1970s a number of states increased their commitment to support kindergartens in the public schools, thereby increasing the total number of five-year-olds enrolled. Some states instituted prekindergarten programs within the public schools. In addition, though the numbers of children are relatively small, the provision of programs for handicapped young children added to the increase in total numbers. The number of franchise or private child-care-for-profit schools increased in the 1970s.

Teacher preparation programs increased rapidly in the late 1960s and early 1970s. Head Start and increased numbers of child care centers required more personnel. Four-year colleges, community colleges and vocational technical schools all experienced an increase in enrollment in child care-early childhood education curricula. The Child Development Associate program (CDA) was proposed by Dr. Edward Zigler in the 1970s when he was head of the Office of Child Development in the Department of Health, Education, and Welfare. The CDA was designed to enhance the skills of child care workers outside the formal education system and provide a career ladder for them. The program met with nu-

---

[29] *Project Head Start Points for Parents*, Booklet 10 (Washington, D.C.: Office of Economic Opportunity, 1967), p. 1.

Figure 20-4. Conferring with students is a common practice of teachers when students are working with young children. (Edna, Texas High School)

Figure 20-5. These researchers were presenting findings from their research. Teachers get updated by attending such meetings and meet others who share their interests. (Southern Association for Children Under Six)

Figure 20-6. A workshop for sharing successful ideas about language activities is one way a teacher helps other teachers. Here, finger puppets surprise listeners when they come out of the versatile apron pockets. (Family Life Center, Georgia Southern University, Statesboro)

merous setbacks but finally published the list of competencies candidates were to achieve and by 1975 the first candidate was certified. The program faced uncertainties in funding. By September 1984, 28 states and the District of Columbia accept CDA in state child care licensing requirements.[30]

Governmental responsibility increased in the 1970s. Hopes were high in the early 1970s for passage at the federal level of a comprehensive child development program—including funding for child care and work with parents. The White House Conference on Children and Youth had endorsed the measure in 1970. These hopes were doused by President Richard Nixon's veto of the bill in 1971. Each time the bill was introduced, opposition surfaced until it was finally decided to set it aside. Some federal funding for child care came about through the Social Security Act as amended in 1975 which, through Title XX funds, gave three federal dollars for each state dollar raised. The use of these dollars for child care varied among states.

[30] *Competence: News of the CDA Community.* **2:**1 (Fall 1984), p. 7.

Standards for Child Care

Custodial care for children is thought by some to be a relic of the past. However, at nearly every meeting of social service personnel and others who are in daily contact with child care services, horror stories are heard concerning children who are being poorly and unsafely housed in centers, poorly fed, inadequately educated, and even mistreated. The minimal standards imposed by most states do not protect all children. In fact, the licensing regulations that control child care centers are so minimal that children sometimes suffer.

Recognizing the need for improved standards for child care licensing, the U.S. Office of Child Development held forums on licensing. With the help of representatives from licensing agencies of the fifty states and some cities, and from national and state organizations with interest in child care, a model for state licensing was prepared. The outcome was an excellent publication, *Guides for Day Care Licensing,* which was designed for use by states and cities to improve their regulatory functions.

In 1974 when it was proposed that the Federal Interagency Day Care Requirements be attached to some federal child care legislation, a storm of controversy arose—particularly over the staff-child ratio. Congress suspended implementation of the ratio requirements because the mandated ratios exceeded the ratio requirements in most states and were believed to be too costly. The recommended ratio was one adult to ten children of nursery school age.

In 1974 a large-scale research project was launched under the auspices of the Department of Health, Education, and Welfare to study child care. Recommendations for government policies were to come from the study. An important finding showed that "Across all study sites, smaller groups are consistently associated with better care, more socially active children, and higher gains on developmental tests." The study concluded that a group enrolling a maximum of sixteen children with two caregivers was the most desirable size and ratio. As a result of the study it was also recommended that caregivers should be required to have child-related education/training and that states should make such training available.[31] When the Department of Health, Education, and Welfare published the final rules, eighteen three- to six-year-olds were allowed to be enrolled in each group, or sixteen average daily attendance, with two caregivers. Training requirements for caregivers were also set. The rules were published in the *Federal Register* in March 1980 and were to take effect in September 1980.[32] Alas! It was not to be. To the dismay

[31] Richard Ruopp et al., *Children at the Center: Final Report of the National Day Care Study, Vol. I.* (Washington, D.C.: Department of Health, Education, and Welfare, 1979), pp. XXXVI–XXXIX.

[32] "HEW Day Care Regulations," *Federal Register,* March 19, 1980, Vol. 45, No. 55, pp. 17870–17885 (Washington, D.C.: U.S. Department of Health, Education, and Welfare).

of many in the child care community, the rules were shelved and were not expected to be unshelved anytime soon. The country was experiencing severe inflation and an economic depression. The staff-child ratios were considered too costly.

With the federal government apparently out of the picture of helping to set standards, the National Association for the Education of Young Children and others looked for alternative routes to assure higher quality in child care. The Center Accreditation Project was initiated by NAEYC. The criteria for high-quality were arrived at by consensus of a large number of professionals. The staff-child ratios were the same as those of the HEW rules. The resulting criteria were field-tested in four sites across the country. By November 1984 the project was ready to start.

Accreditation was described in Chapter 1 of this book. In brief, a center is expected to work for accreditation and, when it is granted, will be able to advertise that it meets the standards of excellence.[33] A campaign of public information regarding the values to children of having a center that is of high quality was to accompany the accreditation project. Professionals will want to watch as these events unfold in the years ahead.

Monitoring education is considered by many to be as important as monitoring restaurants—a practice that has been accepted for years. As services previously carried on in the home are moved out of the home into the commercial arena, governments must move to protect consumers. Early childhood services are consumer services as surely as food, health, or dry cleaning services and, therefore, should be monitored by local, state, and national governments.

* * *

Talk It Over: No. 1

Discuss the procedure for having a school accredited. Report on schools that are accredited.

* * *

The Women's Movement

The women's movement increased its momentum throughout the country during these years, and women pressed for increased and improved child care services. No women's meeting was complete without at least one workshop on the need for child care, and the need was usually dramatized by provision of child care for the children of the women in attendance. Through such organizations as the National Organiza-

[33] *Accreditation Criteria and Procedures of the National Academy of Early Childhood Programs* (Washington, D.C.: National Association for the Education of Young Children, 1984).

tion for Women (NOW), the National Women's Political Caucus, and the Women's Equity Action League (WEAL), women were raising their voices for equal access to education, jobs, and the political arena. Full-day early childhood education would enable many women to pursue their goals and to provide their children more than custodial care.

During the 1970s and 1980s society became aware of many fathers who, for various reasons, were rearing children alone. They too needed child care. Therefore, child care is a family issue rather than just a women's issue. Many persons who care about children continue to hope that someday high-quality, full-day early education will be provided by communities because children need it, rather than simply because adults need their children cared for.

Contrasted with the poor women who first used child care centers in 1854, many of the mothers and fathers today are very well educated. Most want their children to be in a high-quality school that gives them an education, along with food, shelter, and nurturing, while the parents work. These are the parents who in an earlier era probably would have enrolled their children in a nursery school because of its educational component.

However, the part-day early childhood education programs simply do not adequately meet the needs of modern parents. Some are single without backup support to cover the hours when part-day schools are not in session. Others are career women who must work a full day and need full-day care for their children. If they drop to part-time work or stay home altogether, their careers and income to support family needs would have a decided setback.

Well-educated parents are pressing teachers in early childhood schools to raise the standards of full-day programs. They want stability of staff so constant shifts in assignments and staff shortages do not interfere with the quality of the program. Most are willing to pay what is required during their child's early childhood years. These parents want assurances that their child is in a good school; then they can concentrate on their careers.

*　　*　　*

Talk It Over: No. 2

Discuss the standards you'd expect in an early childhood school where you would be willing to send your own child.

*　　*　　*

Research Findings

Research findings focused on children's learning, on the outcome of early childhood education experiences, and on parent involvement. Some research was initiated in the 1960s during the early days of Head Start.

At Age 19	Preschool	No Preschool
1. Graduated from high school	67%	49%
2. Enrolled in postsecondary education	38%	21%
3. Employed at age 19	50%	32%
4. Receiving welfare assistance	18%	32%
5. Teenage pregnancy rate	64 per 100	117 per 100
6. Detention/arrest rate	31%	51%
7. Classified at some time as mentally retarded	15%	35%

An example of long-term outcomes is given in a report of the Ypsilanti Perry Preschool Project directed by David Weikart and Lawrence Schweinhart. This longitudinal study followed 123 low-income children for 22 years. The group was divided into those who had a high-quality preschool experience plus visits in the home with the child's mother each week, and a second group who had no preschool experience but entered the same Ypsilanti, Michigan schools.

According to the researchers, "The return on initial investment was equal to three-and-a-half times the cost of two years of preschool and seven times the cost of one year of preschool. The economic benefits obtained by the end of high school were sufficient to justify public investment in one year of preschool education for disadvantaged children." [34]

A Review of Head Start Research Since 1970 was published in 1983. Ten selected quotations from the research conclusions follow:

1. Head Start has significant short-term effects on measures of intelligence.
2. Head Start children usually perform better than non-Head Starters on measures of school success.
3. No single Head Start curriculum appears to be superior to other curricula on cognitive measures.
4. Head Start usually improves language development, especially for bilingual children.
5. Achievement motivation in Head Start children does not appear to be increased by experimental interventions.
6. Head Start children are usually rated as performing as well as the general school population in the elementary school years in social development.
7. Head Start children improve in hemoglobin levels, motor control, and physical development over the program year.
8. Dental status of children is poor initially. Large percentages receive dental treatment.
9. Head Start programs provide many opportunities for parental involvement.

---

[34] For more detailed information see David P. Weikart et al., *Changed Lives: The Effects of the Perry Preschool Program on Youths Through Age 19.* (Ypsilanti, Mich.: High/Scope Educational Research Foundation, 1984).

10. Large numbers of parents participate in these programs, but a core of parents provide most of the volunteer hours.

(For more details and conclusions see the entire report.)[35]

*   *   *

Talk It Over: No. 3

Discuss the research findings and suggest ways such information could be helpful to a teacher explaining or defending a high-quality early childhood program.

*   *   *

Handicapped Young Children

The Education for the Handicapped Act (Public Law 94–142) was passed in 1975. This act facilitated the placement of young handicapped children into appropriate services and programs, and provides for free public education for all handicapped children from age three. In some states programs for the handicapped started at birth, while others started at age three. Teachers with knowledge and skills in child development and early childhood education are in demand and are especially helpful in mainstreaming children into the regular classroom, as they gain understanding of particular handicaps.

Head Start mandated inclusion of some handicapped children in the program. In 1983, 11 percent of the children in Head Start were mildly or moderately handicapped.[36] All early childhood educators made efforts to adapt their programs to enable young handicappers to participate.[37]

Public Concern

The White House Conference on Families was held in July 1980 and extended the concept of the White House Conference on Children and Youth to include families. There was an emphasis on the place of the family in the life of the child and of the child in the life of the family. Besides concern for child care and early education, the subjects of child abuse and children of teenaged parents were of major concern. A coa-

---

[35] Ruth Hubbell, *A Review of Head Start Research since 1970.* Washington, D.C.: U.S. Government Printing Office, 1983), pp. 1–71.

[36] Hubbell, ibid, p. 71.

[37] For a useful guide to adapting ideas for use with young handicappers, see *Mainstreaming: Ideas for Teaching Young Children* by Judith Souweine, Sheila Crimmins, and Carolyn Mazel (Washington, D.C.: National Association for the Education of Young Children, 1981).

lition of several organizations concerned with children and families spearheaded the planning of the White House Conference on Families.[38]

The National Association for the Education of Young Children is the early childhood field's most inclusive organization inviting all teachers, researchers, parents, and paraprofessionals interested in children to join. During the 1970s and 1980s the organization had a meteoric rise in memberships. Its annual conference attracts 10–15,000 participants with workshops for every member. Other organizations of interest to professionals may be found at the close of Chapter 1 in connection with the list of professional journals.

The Future of Early Childhood Education

The early childhood education profession has come of age! We've agreed to call ourselves the early childhood education profession. That's a start. We've also agreed on terminology for a career ladder of four levels. Starting with the highest level they are:

Early Childhood Specialist

Early Childhood Teacher

Early Childhood Associate Teacher

Early Childhood Teacher Assistant

Also spelled out are the differences in education, experience, and salary for these levels.[39]

These decisions and the system of center accreditation which were all decided by the National Association for the Education of Young Children should help give the profession the drive to thrive during the remainder of the twentieth century.

Trends and predictions are all pointing upward for increases in the numbers of children to be enrolled in groups of infants through four-year-olds. The five-year-olds are now practically all in school, but an important change for them is already taking place—a change to a full-day program. A full day means a day equal in length to the elementary school day. Having one group of children for a full day instead of two groups for a half day each will reduce by 50 percent the number of people the kindergarten teacher will have to relate to and should make it possible for him or her to increase work with parents and with individual children.

[38] *A Summary: Listening to America's Families, Action for the 80's* (Washington, D.C.: U.S. Government Printing Office, 1980).

[39] "NAEYC Position Statement on Nomenclature, Salaries, Benefits, and the Status of the Early Childhood Profession," *Young Children,* 40:1 (November 1984), pp. 52-55.

Children under age five are attending early childhood schools in buildings or classrooms which once were filled with elementary school children. These early childhood programs are expected to increase, in part, because of decreasing total numbers of school-age children and shifts in school-age populations which cause districts to have additional empty classrooms that could be available for needed community services. Empty classrooms and school buildings are being used increasingly for both latch-key school-agers and other groups of younger children. School districts presently operate some of these programs, while others are operated by various community groups.

Professional early childhood educators must promote high-quality early childhood education services. Each professional must start by being conscientious about meeting high standards. Professionals must improve programs to eliminate real differences in quality between and among child care centers and nursery schools. Child care centers and nursery schools should be renamed as *early childhood schools* or *child development centers* to help get away from old practices and connotations such as custodial care or mere baby-sitting which do not signify a high-quality educational setting under professional guidance and standards conforming to the current state of the art.

Each early childhood educator should accept responsibility for helping parents and the general public to understand the significance of high-quality programs to children, families, communities, nations, and the world. Each educator should become an advocate for center accreditation and the new professionalization. Advocating can be done through professional associations or personal conversations, through talks on radio, television, or to civic clubs, and by writing articles for local papers and for magazines.

Finally, the future will depend to a great extent upon the activity of early childhood education associations at the local, state, national, and international levels. At the various levels these associations generally can be active not only in developing programs but in generating community and political support for the high-quality education needed for all young children. In many cases, an effective action is the passage of resolutions by associations and the transmittal of these resolutions to the communications media and to the appropriate political bodies, or making visits to appropriate decisionmakers.

Actions by organizations are often the most effective way to bring matters to the attention of elected officials and political bodies. Political bodies generally welcome and respect the views of organized constituents. The future quality and availability of early childhood education depend upon the maintenance of a continual community dialogue in which significant issues are presented, discussed, and evaluated. Don't hesitate to fulfill your responsibility to your profession and to children by making your thoughtful contributions to the dialogue concerning the future course of early childhood education. As many will testify, you and your organization can make a difference!

Conclusion

Between Socrates and Head Start are over two thousand years of ideas and experience contributing to the education of young children today. Yet, in a sense, early childhood education is still a young profession, with many ideas to be tested and evaluated.

Growth in early childhood education has resulted from recognized crises. The plight of women workers who needed a safe place to leave their children stimulated initial programs as the Industrial Revolution proceeded to gain momentum. The economic depression of the 1930s and World War II led to a major expansion of early childhood education in the United States. In the first instance, the need was for jobs for numerous unemployed people; in the second, the need was for child care for the children of women working in war industries. However, in the United States no period equals the 1960s and 1970s for interest in the education of young children. Since 1965 large numbers of children have been enrolled in Head Start, and many professionals, volunteers, and parents have become involved.

Head Start programs were initiated to help overcome our recognized national failure to support in word *and* action the American ideal of equality of opportunity for numerous disadvantaged children. The growth of the 1960s continued into the 1970s as programs and services were extended to more young children, including the handicapped.

The first half of the 1980s has been a period of consolidating professional strengths and for proposing and agreeing on standards for teacher education and for early childhood education services. As professionals work in concert, the real winners are young children and their parents.

In a real sense, whether people will survive and thrive on this planet depends upon the development of the full constructive potential of *all* children—children who will be capable of building a harmonious world community. Thus early childhood education becomes a relevant and vital movement with which to be associated if one wishes to help solve significant interrelated local, national, and global problems.

Applications

1. Discuss the "Talk It Over" items found in the chapter.
2. Complete Lesson 20 in *A Laboratory Workbook for Introduction to Early Childhood Education*. Hand in as scheduled.

3. Use the library to learn more about the development of the early childhood education profession. Select one or more references from the Additional Readings section or from citations in the footnotes. Summarize your findings and discuss with your class.

4. Add ideas or information about the past, present, and future of the early childhood profession to your Resource File.

Study Questions

1. Identify significant periods in early childhood education history.

2. Identify significant individuals and their contributions to early childhood education over the years.

3. Discuss advances in early childhood education in the United States since 1965.

4. State conclusions from cited research on early education concerning children's cognitive development, personal relations, language development, and parental involvement.

5. Explain how the women's movement for economic and political participation and for equality has affected early childhood education.

6. Explain how the people involved in early childhood education have become increasingly professional during the 1970s and 1980s.

7. State ways that increased professionalization of early childhood education helps children and families.

Additional Readings

America's Children 1976. Washington, D.C.: National Council of Organizations of Children and Youth, 1976.

BALDWIN, WENDY H., and CHRISTINE WINQUIST NORD. *Delayed Childbearing in the U.S.: Facts and Fictions*. Washington, D.C.: Population Reference Bureau, Inc., 1984.

BRONFENBRENNER, URIE. *Vol. II: Is Early Intervention Effective?*. Washington, D.C.: Department of Health, Education, and Welfare, 1974.

DAVIS, MARY DABNEY. *Nursery Schools: Their Development and Current Practices in the United States*. Washington, D.C.: U.S. Government Printing Office, 1933.

FEIN, GRETA G., and ALISON CLARKE-STEWART. *Day Care in Context*. New York: John Wiley & Sons, 1973.

FISHER, DOROTHY C. *The Montessori Manual*. Cambridge, Mass.: Robert-Bentley, Inc., 1964.

FOREST, ILSE. *Preschool Education: A Historical and Critical Study*. New York: Macmillan Publishing Co., Inc., 1927.

GROTBERG, EDITH (ed.). *200 Years of Children*. Washington, D.C.: Department of Health, Education, and Welfare, 1977.

GROTBERG, EDITH H., and WILLA CHOPER. *Research: Translating Findings into Action*. Washington, D.C.: Department of Health, Education, and Welfare, 1978.

HUBBELL, RUTH. *A Review of Head Start Research Since 1970*. Washington, D.C.: U.S. Government Printing Office, 1983.

McFADDEN, DENNIS N. (ed.). *Early Childhood Development Programs and Services: Planning for Action*. Washington, D.C.: National Association for the Education of Young Children, 1972.

McHALE, M. C., and JOHN McHALE. *Population Bulletin: World of Children*. Washington, D.C.: Population Reference Bureau, 1979.

McMILLAN, MARGARET. *The Nursery School*. New York: E. P. Dutton and Co., Inc., 1921.

MONTESSORI, MARIA. *The Montessori Elementary Material*. Cambridge, Mass.: Robert Bentley, Inc., 1965.

MONTESSORI, MARIA. *The Montessori Method*. Cambridge, Mass.: Robert Bentley, Inc., 1965.

Montessori in Perspective. Washington D.C.: The National Association for the Education of Young Children, 1966.

OSBORN, D. KEITH. *Early Childhood Education in Historical Perspective*. Athens, Ga.: Education Associates, 1980.

A Review of Head Start Research Since 1969 and An Annotated Bibliography. Washington, D.C.: U.S. Government Printing Office, 1977.

ROUPP, RICHARD, et al. *Children at the Center, Vol. I. Final Report of the National Day Care Study*. Washington, D.C.: Department of Health, Education, and Welfare, 1979.

RYAN, SALLY. *Volume I: Longitudinal Evaluations of Preschool Programs*. Washington, D.C.: Department of Health, Education, and Welfare, 1974.

SNAPPER, KURT J., and JoANNE S. OHMS. *The Status of Children 1977*. Washington, D.C.: Department of Health, Education, and Welfare, 1978.

SNYDER, AGNES. *Dauntless Women in Early Childhood Education 1856–1931*. Washington, D.C.: Association Childhood Education International, 1972.

Summary: The Persistence of Preschool Effects. Washington, D.C.: Department of Health, Education, and Welfare, 1977.

Summary Report: Lasting Effects After Preschool. Washington, D.C.: Department of Health, Education, and Welfare, 1979.

Index
of Authors

Subject Index